Minor Poets of the Period, Vol. III

CW00498764

Contributor

John Cleveland, Thomas Flatman, Henry King,

Thomas Stanley, Nathaneel Whiting

(Editor: George Saintsbury)

Alpha Editions

This edition published in 2023

ISBN : 9789357391177

Design and Setting By
Alpha Editions
www.alphaedis.com
Email - info@alphaedis.com

PREFATORY NOTE

I am afraid that this third and last volume of *Caroline Poets* must reverse the famous apology of the second of the monarchs from whom it derives its title. It has been an unconscionable time in being born; though I do not, to speak in character with my authors, know what hostile divinity bribed Lucina. I cannot blame any one else: and—though for the first ten years after the appearance of Vol. II I was certainly very busy, professionally and with other literary work—I do not think I omitted any opportunity of getting on with the book. I think I may say that if the time I have actually spent thereon at spare moments could be put together it would represent a full year's solid labour, if not more. I make neither complaint nor boast of this; for it has always been my opinion that a person who holds such a position as I then held should, if he possibly can, do something, in unremunerative and unpopular ways, to make the treasure of English literature more easily accessible. I have thoroughly enjoyed the work; and I owe the greatest thanks to the authorities of the Clarendon Press for making it possible.

But no efforts of mine, unless I had been able to reside in Oxford or London, would have much hastened the completion of the task: for the materials were hard to select, and, when selected, harder to find in copies that could be used for printing. Some of them we could not get hold of in any reasonable time: and the Delegates of the Press were good enough to have bromide rotographs of the Bodleian copies made for me. I worked on these as long as I could: but I found at last that the white print on black ground, crammed and crowded together as it is in the little books of the time, was not merely troublesome and painful, but was getting really dangerous, to my extremely weak eyesight.

This necessitated, or almost necessitated, some alterations in the scheme. One concerned the modernization of spelling, which accordingly will be found disused in a few later pieces of the volume; another, and more important one, the revision of the text. This latter was most kindly undertaken principally by Mr. Percy Simpson, who has had the benefit of Mr. G. Thorn-Drury's unrivalled knowledge of these minors. I could not think of cramping the hands of scholars so well versed as these were in seventeenth-century work: and they have accordingly bestowed rather more attention than had originally formed part of my own plan on *apparatus criticus* and comparison of MSS. The reader of course gains considerably in yet other respects. I owe these gentlemen, who may almost be called part-editors of this volume as far as text is concerned, very sincere thanks; and I have endeavoured as far as possible to specify their contributions.

When the war came the fortunes of the book inevitably received another check. The Clarendon Press conducted its operations in many other places besides Walton Street, and with many other instruments besides types and paper. Nor had its Home Department much time for such mere *belles lettres* as these. Moreover the loss of my own library, and the difficulties of compensating for that loss in towns less rich in books than Edinburgh, put further drags on the wheel. So I and my Carolines had to bide our time still: and even now it has been thought best to jettison a part of the promised cargo of the ship rather than keep it longer on the stocks.

The poets whom I had intended to include, and upon whom I had bestowed more or less labour, but who now suffer exclusion, were Heath, Flecknoe, Hawkins, Beedome, Prestwich, Lawrence, Pick, Jenkyn, and a certain 'Philander'. Of these I chiefly regret Heath—the pretty title of whose *Clarastella* is not ill-supported by the text, and who would have 'taken out the taste' of Whiting satisfactorily for some people—Hawkins, Lawrence, and Jenkyn. Henry Hawkins in *Partheneia Sacra* has attained a sort of mystical unction which puts him not so very far below Crashaw, and perhaps entitles him to rank with that poet, Southwell, and Chideock Tichborne earlier as the representative quartette of English Roman Catholic poetry in the major Elizabethan age. Lawrence's *Arnalte and Lucetida*, not a brilliant thing in itself, has real literary interest of the historical-comparative kind as representing a Spanish romance by Diego de San Pedro (best known as the author of the *Carcel de Amor*) and its French translation by Herberay, the translator of *Amadis*. But such things remain to be taken up by some general historian of the 'Heroic' Romance. As for 'Patheryke' [*sic*] Jenkyn he attracted me many years ago by the agreeable heterography of his name (so far preferable to more recent sham-Celticizings thereof) and held me by less fantastic merits. Flecknoe pleaded for a chance against the tyranny of 'glorious John'. But when it was a question between keeping these and the others with further delay and letting them go, there could not be much doubt in which way England expected this man to do his infinitesimal duty.

One instance, not of subtraction but of addition to the original contents, seems to require slight notice. The eye-weakness just mentioned having always prevented me from making any regular study of palaeography, I had originally proposed only to include work already printed. I was tempted to break my rule in the case of Godolphin: and made rather a mess of it. An errata list in the present volume (p. 552) will, I believe, repair the blunder. The single censurer of this (I further believe) single serious lapse of mine was, I remember, troubled about it as a discredit to the University of Oxford. I sincerely trust that he was mistaken. None of us can possibly do credit to our University; we can only derive it from her. To throw any discredit on her is equally impossible: though of course any member may achieve such discredit for himself. Let me hope that the balance against me for indiscreet dealing with perhaps one per cent. of my fifteen hundred or two thousand pages is not too heavy.

Little need be said of the actual constituents of the volume, which has however perhaps lost something of its intended 'composition', in the artistic sense, by losing its tail. A good English edition of Cleveland has long been wanted: and I think—the thought being stripped of presumption by the number and valiancy of my helpers—that we have at last given one. Stanley and King—truer poets than Cleveland, if less interesting to the general public—also called for fresh presentation. If anybody demurs to Flatman and still more to Whiting he must be left to his own opinion. I shall only note here that on Cleveland I was guilty of injustice to the Library of the University of Edinburgh (to which I owe much) by saying that it contained no edition of this reviler of Caledonia. None was discoverable in my time, the process of overhauling and re-cataloguing being then incomplete. But my friend and successor, Professor Grierson, tells me that one has since been found. As to King, I have recently seen doubts cast on his authorship of 'Tell me no more'. But I have seen no valid reasons alleged for them, and I do not know of any one else who has the slightest claim to it.

Of the whole three volumes it is still less necessary to say much. I have owed special thanks in succession to Mr. Doble, Mr. Milford, and Mr. Chapman (now Secretary) of the Clarendon Press; to Professors Firth and Case (indeed, but for the former's generous imparting of his treasures the whole thing could hardly have been done) for loan of books as well as answering of questions; and to not a few others, among whom I may specially mention my friend of many years, the Rev. William Hunt, D.Litt., Honorary Fellow of Trinity College, Oxford. I wish the work had done greater credit to all this assistance and to the generous expenditure of the University and its Press. But such as it is I can say (speaking no doubt as a fool) that I should myself have been exceedingly grateful if somebody had done it fifty years ago: and that I shall be satisfied if only a few people are grateful for it between now and fifty or five hundred years hence. For there is stuff in it, though not mine, which will keep as long as the longest of these periods and longer.[1]

GEORGE SAINTSBURY.

1 *Royal Crescent, Bath.*
  Oak-Apple Day, 1921.

[1] The tolerably gentle reader will easily understand that, in a book written, and even printed, at considerable intervals of time, Time itself will sometimes have affected statements. There may be a few such cases here. But it seems unnecessary to burden the thing with possible Corrigenda, as to the post-war price of the Cross-bath (p. 360), &c.

INTRODUCTION TO JOHN CLEVELAND.

Almost everybody—an everybody not including many bodies—who has dealt with Cleveland since the revival of interest in seventeenth-century writers has of necessity dwelt more or less on the moral that he points, and the tale that he illustrates, if he does not exactly adorn it. Moral and tale have been also generally summarized by referring to the undoubted fact that Cleveland had twenty editions while Milton's *Minor Poems* had two. I do not propose myself to dwell long on this part of the matter. The moral diatribe is not my trade: and while almost any one who wants such a thing can deduce it from the facts which will be given, those who are unable to effect the deduction may as well go without it. What I wish to provide is what it is not easy for any one to provide, and impossible for any one to provide 'out of his own head'—that is to say an edition, sufficient for reading and for all literary purposes, of the most probably authentic of the heterogeneous poems which have clustered round Cleveland's name. Such an edition did not exist when this collection of Caroline poets was planned, nor when it was announced: nor has it been supplied since in this country. One did appear very shortly afterwards in America,[1] and it has been of use to me: but it certainly does not make Cleveland's appearance here superfluous. Had not Professor Case of Liverpool, who had long made Cleveland a special study, insisted on my giving him in this collection, and most kindly provided me with stores of his own material, I should not have attempted the task: and I still hope that Mr. Case will execute a more extensive edition with the prose, with the doubtful or even certainly spurious poems duly annotated, and with apparatus which would be out of place here. It cannot, however, be out of place to include—in what is almost a corpus of 'metaphysical' poetry of the less easily accessible class—one who has been regarded from different, but not very distant, points of view as at once the metaphysical 'furthest' and as the metaphysical *reductio ad absurdum.*

Cleveland (the name was also very commonly spelt in his own day 'Cleiveland'[2] and 'Cleaveland', as well as otherwise still) was born at Loughborough, and christened on June 20, 1613. His father, Thomas, was curate of the parish and assistant master at the Grammar School. Eight years later the father was made vicar of Hinckley, also provided with a grammar school, at which John appears to have been educated till in 1627 he went to Christ's College, Cambridge—where, of course, the everlasting comparison with his elder contemporary Milton comes in again for those who like it. He remained at Christ's for seven years as usual, performing divers college exercises on public occasions, occasionally of some importance; took his bachelor's degree (also as usual) in 1631; and in 1634 was elected to a fellowship at St. John's, proceeding to his M.A. next year. At the end of his probationary period he did not take orders, but was admitted as *legista*—perhaps also, though the statement is uncorroborated officially, to the third learned faculty of Physic. There is also doubt about his incorporation at Oxford. He served as Tutor and as Rhetoric Praelector: nor are we destitute of Orations and Epistles of an official character from his pen. Like the majority of university men at the time—and indeed like the majority of men of letters and education—he was a strong Royalist: and was unlikely to stay in Cambridge when the Roundhead mob of the town was assisted by a Parliamentary garrison in rabbling the University. It was natural that he should 'retire to Oxon.', and it is probable that Oxford was his head-quarters from 1642 to 1645. But he does not seem to have been actually deprived of his fellowship at St. John's till the last-named year, when the Earl of Manchester, whom (especially as Lord Kimbolton) Cleveland had bitterly satirized, had his opportunity of revenge and took it.

For Cleveland had already been active with his pen in the Royalist cause, and was now appointed to a post of some importance as 'Judge Advocate' of Newark. The Governor was Sir Richard Willis, for whom Cleveland replied to Leven's summons to surrender. They held the town for the King from November to May, when it was given up on Charles's own order. Then comes the anecdote—more than a hundred years after date—of Leven's dismissing him with contemptuous lenity. 'Let the poor fellow go about his business and sell his ballads.' This, though accepted by Carlyle, and a smart enough invention, has no contemporary authority, and is made extremely suspicious by its own addition that Cleveland was so vexed that he took to strong liquors which hastened his death. Now Newark fell in 1646 and Cleveland lived till 1658. It would make an interesting examination question, 'How much must a man drink in a day in order to hasten his death thereby twelve years afterwards?' And it must be admitted, if true, to be a strong argument on the side of the good fellow who pleaded that alcohol was a very *slow* poison.

He escaped somehow, however: and we hear nothing of his life for another decade. Then he is again in trouble, being informed against, to the Council of State, by some Norwich Roundheads who have, however, nothing to urge against him but his antecedents, his forgathering with 'papists and delinquents', his 'genteel garb' with 'small and scant means', and (which is important) his 'great abilitie whence he is able to do the greater disservice', this last a handsome testimonial to Cleveland, and a remarkable premium upon imbecility. He was imprisoned at Yarmouth and wrote a very creditable letter to Cromwell, maintaining his principles, but asking for release, which seems to have been granted. Cromwell—to do him justice and to alter a line of his greatest panegyrist save one in verse on another person—

Never *persecuted* but for gain,

and he probably did not agree with the officious persons at Norwich that there was much to be gained by incarcerating a poor Royalist poet. But Cleveland had been at least three months in prison, and it is alleged, with something more like *vera causa* in the allegation, that he there contracted 'such a weakness and disorder as soon after brought him to the grave'. A seventeenth-century prison was much more likely to kill a man in two years than 'strong waters' which had already been vigorously applied and successfully resisted for ten. He died in Gray's Inn, of an intermittent fever, on April 29, 1658.

Something will be said presently of the almost hopeless tangle of the so-called editions of Cleveland's *Poems*. It seems at least probable that no single one of the twenty—or whatever the number is—can be justly called authoritative. That he was an extremely popular poet or rather journalist in verse as well as prose, is absolutely beyond dispute—the very tangle just referred to proves it—and, though it may be excessive to call him the most popular poet of his time, he may fairly be bracketed with Cowley as joint holder of that position. Nor did his popularity cease as quickly as Cowley's did—the Restoration indeed was likely to increase rather than diminish it; and the editions went on till close upon the Revolution itself, while there were at least two after it, one just on the eve of the eighteenth century in 1699 and one near its middle in 1742.[3] Considerably before this, however, the critics had turned against him. 'Grave men', to quote Edward Phillips and the *Theatrum Poetarum*, 'affirmed him the best of English poets', but not for long. Fuller, who actually admired him, admitted that 'Clevelandizing' was dangerous; and Dryden, who must have admired him at one time, and shows constant traces of his influence, talks in the *Essay of Dramatic Poesy* of a 'Catachresis or Clevelandism'. In the eighteenth century he passed almost out of sight till Johnson brought him up for 'awful exampling' in the famous Life of Cowley: and he has had few advocates since. Let us, without borrowing from these advocates or attempting tediously to confute his enemies, deal with the facts, so far as they are known, of his life, and with the characteristics of the carefully sifted, but in no sense 'selected', poetry which will follow.

As for his character as a man, the evidence is entirely in his favour. He was an honest and consistent politician on his own side, and if some people think it the wrong side, others are equally positive that it was the right. If (rather unfairly) we dismiss the encomia on his character as partisan, there remains the important fact that no one on the other side says anything definite against it. If he was abusive, it certainly does not lie with anybody who admires Milton to reproach him with that. But the fact is, once more, that except in so far as there is a vague idea that a cavalier, and especially a cavalier poet, must have been a 'deboshed' person, there is absolutely no evidence against

Cleveland and much in his favour. Also, this is not our business, which is with him as a poet.

As such he has been subjected to very little really critical examination.[4] The result of such as I myself have been able to give him was arrived at somewhat slowly: or rather it flashed upon me, after reading the poems several times over in different arrangements, that which gives the serious and satiric pieces higgledy-piggledy as in the older editions, and that which separates them, as in 1677 and in Mr. Berdan's American reprint. This result is that I entertain a very serious doubt whether Cleveland *ever* wrote 'serious' poetry, in one sense—he was of course serious enough in his satires—at all. That, on the other hand, he deliberately set himself to burlesque the 'metaphysical' manner I do not think: or at least (for rather minute definition is necessary here) I do not think that he executed this burlesque with any reforming intention or any particular contempt for the style. Like Butler, whom he in so many ways resembles—who pretty certainly owed him not a little, and of whom he was, as has often been pointed out, a sort of rough copy or spoiled draft—he was what he satirized in the literary way, and he caricatured himself. Of course if anybody thinks, as the *Retrospective* Reviewer thought, that 'Fuscara' and 'To the State of Love' are actually and intrinsically 'beautiful specimens of poetic conception', he will scout my notion. But I do not think that any one who has done me the honour even to look into these volumes will think me an 'antimetaphysical', and I must confess that I can see only occasional poetry here—only a caricature of such methods as may be suggested by Donne's 'Bracelet' piece, and the best things in Crashaw. It is, for instance, a very tell-tale thing that there is not, in Cleveland's work, a single one of the lovely lyrics that enshrine and ennoble the conceits in almost every one else of the school, from Donne himself to Sherburne. An American critic, defending Cleveland with the delightful indiscreetness of most defenders, maintains that these lyrics were failures—that they were *not* characteristic of the time. Well, let us be thankful that almost everybody down to Kynaston and John Hall 'failed' in this way not seldom.

But Cleveland never failed in it: and unfortunately it wants a failure or two at least of this kind to make a poet. To illustrate what I mean, let me refer readers to Benlowes—comparison of Cleveland with whom would not long ago have been impossible except in a large library. Benlowes is as extravagant as Cleveland, whom (I rather think) he sometimes copied.[5] But he cannot help this kind of poetic 'failure' from breaking in. Cleveland can, or rather I should say that he does not try—or has no need to try—to keep it out. In 'Fuscara', eminently; in 'To the State of Love', perhaps most prettily; in the 'Antiplatonic', most vigorously—in all his poems more or less, he sets himself to work to accumulate and elaborate conceits for their own sake. They are not directly suggested by the subject and still less by each other; they are no spray or froth of passion; they never suggest (as all the best examples and many not so good in others do) that indomitable reaching after the infinite which results at least in an infinite unexpectedness. They are merely card-castles of 'wit' in its worst sense; mechanical games of extravagant idea-twisting which simply aim at 'making records'. It is true that people admired them for being this. It is still truer that similar literary exercises may be found, and found popular, at the present day. It is even true, as will be shown later, that it is possible positively to enjoy them still. But these are different questions.

If Cleveland had little or nothing of the poetry of enthusiastic thought and feeling, he had not much more of the poetry of accomplished form, though here also he is exceptionally interesting. His 'Mark Antony'[6] has been indicated as an early example of 'dactylic' metre. It certainly connects interestingly with some songs of Dryden's, and has an historical position of its own, but I am by no means sure (*v. inf.*) that it was meant to be dactylic or even anapaestic.

Cleveland, therefore, was not a great poet, nor even a failure of one: but he was but just a failure of a very great satirist. Even here, of course, the Devil's Advocate will find only too much to say against him. Every one of the pieces requires the editing, polishing, and criticizing which (we know pretty well) the author never gave to anything of his. Every one suffers from Cleveland's adoption of the same method which he used in his purely metaphysical poems, that of stringing together and heaping up images and observations, instead of organizing and incorporating them. Every one is a tangled tissue of temporary allusion, needing endless scholiastry to unravel and elucidate it. It has been said, and it is true, that we find not a few reminiscences of Cleveland in Dryden. There is even in the couplet of the older and smaller poet something of the weight, the impetus, the *animosity* of that of the younger and greater. But of Dryden's *ordonnance*, his generalship, his power of coupling up his couplets into irresistible column, Cleveland has practically nothing. He has something of his own 'Rupertismus': but nothing more.

But, for all that, the Satires give us ample reason for understanding why the Roundheads persecuted Cleveland, and justify their fear of his 'abilities'. He has, though an unequal, an occasional command of the 'slap-in-the-face' couplet which—as has just been said—not impossibly taught something to Dryden, or at least awoke something in him. 'The Rebel Scot', his best thing, does not come so very far short of the opportunity which the Scots had given: and its most famous distich

Had Cain been Scot, God would have changed his doom,

Not forced him wander, but confined him home,

was again and again revived till the unpopularity of North with South Britain flamed out last in Bute's time, a hundred years and more after Cleveland's. Of course it is only ignorance which thinks that this form of the couplet was invented by Cleveland, or even in his time. It may be found in Elizabeth's, and in Cleveland's own day was sporadic; nor did he himself ever approach such continuous and triumphant use of it as Dryden achieved only two years after Cleveland's own death. But there is, so to speak, the 'atmosphere' of it, and that atmosphere occasionally condenses into very concrete thunderbolts. Unfortunately he knew no mood but abuse, and such an opportunity as that of the 'Elegy on Laud' is almost entirely lost.

However, such as he is—in measure as full as can with any confidence be imparted; and omitting of course prose work—he is now before the reader, who will thus be able at last to form his own judgement on a writer who, perhaps of all English writers, combines the greatest popularity in his own time with the greatest inaccessibility in modern editions.

Nor should any reader be deterred from making the examination by the strictures which have been given above on Cleveland's purely poetical methods and merits. These strictures were made as cautions, and as a kind of antidote to the writer's own undisguised partiality for the 'metaphysical' style. It is true that Cleveland, like Benlowes, has something of a helot of that style about him: and that his want of purely lyrical power deprives his readers of much of the solace of his (if not of their) sin. But those natures must be very morose, very prosaic, or at best steeled against everything else by abhorrence of 'False Wit' who can withstand a certain tickling of amused enjoyment at the enormous yet sometimes pretty quaintnesses of 'Fuscara' itself; and still more at those of the 'To the State of Love', which is his happiest non-satirical thing. From the preliminary wish to be a 'Shaker' to the final description of Chanticleer as

That Baron Tell-Clock of the night,

the thing is a kind of a carnival of conceit, a fairy-tale of the fantastic. 'To Julia to expedite her Promise' is somewhat more laboured and so less happy: and the loss of the lyric form in 'The Hecatomb to his Mistress' is considerable. The heroic couplet squares ill with this sort of thing: but the octasyllabic admits it fairly, and so 'The Antiplatonic' with its greater part, and 'Upon Phillis walking' with the whole in this metre, are preferable. Yet it must be acknowledged that one heroic couplet in the former—

Like an ambassador that beds a queen

With the nice caution of a sword between,

is worthy of Dryden. Most of the other *seria* are but *nugae*: and the chief interest of the 'Edward King' epicede, besides its contrast with *Lycidas*, is its pretty certain position as model to Dryden's 'Lord Hastings'. But the two 'Mark Antony' pieces and 'Square-Cap' demand, both from the point of view of tone and from that of metre, more attention than was given to them above.

If any one not previously acquainted with the piece or the discussions about it will turn to the text of 'Mark Antony' and read it either aloud or to himself, I should say that, in the common phrase, it is a toss-up what scansion his voice will adopt supposing that he 'commences with the commencement'. The first stanza can run quite agreeably to the usual metrical arrangements of the time, thus:

When as | the night | ingale | chanted | her vespers

And the | wild for | ester | couched on | the ground,

Venus | invi | ted me | in th' eve | ning whispers

Unto | a fra | grant field | with ros | es crowned,

Where she | before | had sent

My wish | es' com | pliment;

Unto | my heart's | content

Played with | me on | the green.

Never | Mark Ant | ony

Dallied | more wan | tonly

With the fair | Egypt | ian Queen.

or, in technical language, a decasyllabic quatrain, like *Annus Mirabilis* or Gray's *Elegy*, but with hypercatalexis or redundance in the first and third lines and occasional trochees for iambics; followed by a batch, rhymed *a a a b c c b*, of seven three-foot lines also iambic. This, which as far as the first quatrain is concerned is very nearly the exact metre of Emily Brontë's *Remembrance* and of Myers's *St. Paul*, suits the second and third stanzas as well as the first.

When the reader comes to the fourth stanza, or if, like some irregular spirits, he takes the last first and begins with it, the most obvious scansion, though the lines are syllabically the same, will be different.

Mys | tical | gram | mar of | am | orous | glan | ces;

Feel | ing of | pul | ses, the | phy | sic of | love;

Rhetor | ical | cour | tings and | mu | sical | dan | ces;

Num | bering of | kiss | es a | rith | metic | prove;

Eyes ¦ like a | stron ¦ omy;

Straight- ¦ limbed ge | om ¦ etry;

In ¦ her art's | in ¦ geny

Our wits ¦ were | sharp ¦ and keen.

Ne ¦ ver Mark | An ¦ tony

Dal ¦ lied more | wan ¦ tonly

With the fair ¦ | Egypt ¦ ian | Queen.

(Trisyllabic rhythm either dactylic[7] or anapaestic[8] as may be on general principles preferred.) And this may have occurred to him even with the first as thus:

When ¦ as the | night ¦ ingale | chan ¦ ted her | ves ¦ pers.

Now which of these is to be preferred? and which did the author mean? (two questions which are not so identical as they may seem). My own answer, which I have already given elsewhere,[9] is that both are uncertain, and that he probably had each of the rhythms in his head, but confusedly.[10]

'Square Cap' is much less doubtful, or not doubtful at all, and it may be thought to prove the anapaestic-dactylic scansion, especially the anapaestic of 'Mark Antony'. For it will be observed that, even from the first two verses, you can get no iambic run, except of the most tumbling character, on the line *here*.

Come hith | er, Apoll | o's bounc | ing girl,

And in | a whole hip | pocrene | of sherry

Let 's drink | a round | till our brains | do whirl,

Tu | ning our pipes | to make | ourselves merry.

A Cam | bridge lass, Ve | nus-like born | of the froth

Of an old | half-filled jug | of bar | ley broth,

She, she | is my mis | tress, her sui | tors are many,

But she'll | have a Square | -cap if e'er | she have any.

The problem is scarcely one for dogmatic decision, but it is one of some interest, and of itself entitles Cleveland to attention of the prosodic kind. For these pieces are quite early—before 1645—and a third, 'How the

Commencement grows new' (q.v.), is undeniably trisyllabic and meant for some such a tune as the 'Sellenger's Round' which it mentions.

With such a combination of interests, political, historical, poetical (as regards school and period), and prosodic, it will hardly be denied that Cleveland deserves his place here. But I must repeat that I am here endeavouring to deal with him strictly on the general principles of this Collection, and am in no way trying to occupy the ground so as to keep out a more elaborate edition. I have had help from my friends Professors Firth and Case in information and correction of contemporary facts; but full comment on Cleveland, from the historical side, would nearly fill this volume: and the problems of the work attributed to him would suffice for a very substantial bibliographical monograph. Neither of these, nor any exhaustive apparatus, even of the textual kind, do I pretend to supply. I simply endeavour—and have spent not a little time and trouble in endeavouring—to provide the student and lover of English literature with an accessible copy, sufficient in amount and fairly trustworthy in substance, of a curious and memorable figure in English verse.[11]

[1] *Poems of John Cleveland*, by John M. Berdan, New York, 1903.

[2] It has been said that we ought to adopt this spelling because of its connexion with a district of Yorkshire, which, before it was ransacked for iron ore, was both wild and beautiful. But as everybody now spells *this* 'Cleveland', and as the title derived from it has always been so spelt, the argument seems an odd one.

[3] I am not certain that I have seen a copy of this, and its existence has been denied: but I have certainly seen it catalogued somewhere. It should perhaps be added that *1699* is only *1687* with a fresh title.

[4] The most important treatments besides Johnson's, treatments usefully separated in date, are contained in the *Retrospective Review* (vol. xii), Mr. Gosse's remarks in *From Shakespeare to Pope*, and Mr. Berdan's in the edition above mentioned.

[5] They were both St. John's men; and Benlowes must have been a benefactor of the College (see Evelyn's *Diary*) while Cleveland was Fellow. Also Cleveland's Poems had been published, and again and again republished, years before *Theophila* appeared.

[6] The *Retrospective* eulogist was deeply hurt by Cleveland's parodying this, and of course drags in Milton once more. 'Could one fancy Milton parodying *Lycidas*?' Now there is considerable difference between 'Mark Antony' and *Lycidas*: nor did Cleveland, so far as we know, dream of

parodying his own poem on King. If Milton had had the humour to parody some of his own work, it would have been much the better for him and for us. No doubt Cleveland's actual parody is rather coarse and not extraordinarily witty: but there is no more objection to it in principle than to Thackeray's two forms of the 'Willow Song' in *Ottilia.*

7   Marked by straight bars.

8   Marked by dotted bars.

9   *History of English Prosody* (London, 1906-10), vol. iii, app. iii.

10   *Very* confusedly on the trisyllabic side or ear: for 'In th' ĕvenĭng' is a very awkward dactyl, and 'th' ĕvenīng whīsp' not a much cleverer anapaest, while the same remark applies to 'frāgrănt fĭeld' and 'wīth rōsĕs' and their anapaestic counterparts.

11   The extraordinary complexity of the editions of Cleveland has been glanced at above. The following summary will at least give the reader some idea of the facts, and the two original Prefaces will extra-illustrate these facts with some views of causes. It need only be added here that the principle of the collection now given is, of course, to exclude everything that is certainly *not* Cleveland's: and, in giving what certainly and probably is his, to arrange the items as far as possible in the order of their publication in the author's lifetime, though the impossibility of working with an actually complete collection of all the issues before one may have occasioned some error here. In the following abstract only the *Poems* are referred to, as they alone concern us.

The original collection is contained in *The Character of a London Diurnal* [prose] with several select *Poems*, London, 1647. This was reprinted in the same year and the next so often that some admit *thirteen* different issues (of course, as was usual at the time, sometimes only 'stop-press' batches with slight changes made in what is practically the same edition), while no one I think has allowed less than *five.* There are substantive additions in several of these, but the singular characteristic of the whole, and indeed of Cleveland's published *Poems* generally, is that part of the matter, even in the very earliest issue, is certainly not his: and that in very early forms these pieces were coolly headed 'Uncertain Authors'. The extent to which this jumbling and misattributing went on in the seventeenth century is generally if not very precisely known from the famous cases of *Sic Vita* (*v. inf.,* on Bishop King, &c.), and of the epitaph sometimes assigned to Browne, more usually to Jonson. Another almost equally strange, though perhaps not so commonly known, is the assignment of some of the poems of a writer of position like the dramatist James Shirley to Carew. But Cleveland must have been rather exceptionally careless of his work during his life, and he was treated with exceptional impudence (see Williamson's *Preface*) after his death. The process went on in 1651, to which two issues are assigned, with three or four pretty certainly spurious additions, while 1653 and 1654 each saw two more, the last being printed again in 1656 and 1657. This last was also the last printed in Cleveland's lifetime.

But he was hardly dead when in 1659 two different issues, each of them many times reprinted, took the most astounding liberties with his name. The first foisted in more than thirty pieces by Robert Fletcher, the translator of Martial. The other, calling itself *Cleveland Revived*, contains the remarkable and perfectly frank explanation, given below, of the principles on which the work of Mr. Williamson was conducted, and the critical notions which directed his 'virtuous endeavours'.

From the disaster of this singular fashion of building a poet's monument out of the fragments of other people's work, Cleveland may be said to have never been entirely relieved. For though twenty years later, in 1677 *Clievelandi Vindiciae* (Preface and full title again subjoined) undertook the task and provided a sort of standard (which may, however, be over-valued), ten years later still, in 1687, the purged collection was reissued with all the spurious matter from previous ones heaped again on it, and this, with a fresh reissue (new title-paged and with a pasted-on finis*) in 1699, appear to be the commonest copies that occur.

In such a tangle it is not easy to know how to proceed, and I had made and discarded several plans before I fixed upon that actually adopted. I have taken the edition of 1653, which, with its reprints almost unaltered to 1657, represents the latest text current during the author's life and during a full lustrum of that. The contents of this I have printed, putting its few *spuria* in italic, in the order in which they there appear. Next, I have given a few additions from 1677 (the only one of the later accessible editions which even pretends to give Cleveland, the whole Cleveland, and nothing but Cleveland) and other sources. As was notified above, complete *apparatus criticus* is not attempted in a text with such a history, for this would only suit a complete edition of Cleveland's whole works: but variants of apparent importance are supplied. I should add that while I myself have for many years possessed the *textus quasi-receptus* of 1677, the exceeding kindness of Mr. Case left on my shelves—for a time disgracefully long as far as I am concerned—copies of 1653 itself, 1654, 1659, 1662 (with the 'exquisite remains' of Dick, Tom, and Harry), 1665, 1668, 1669 (with the letters added), and the *omnium gatherums* of 1687 and 1699. The Bodleian copies of the *Poems* of 1647, 1651, 1653, 1654, 1657, 1659, 1662, 1668, 1669, 1677, 1687 have also been used to check the collations; and the stitched quartos of *The King's Disguise* (undated, but known to be 1647) and the *News from Newcastle*, 1651. The British Museum broadside of *The Scots' Apostasy* has also been collated. Mr. Berdan's edition I have already mentioned. I have treated the text, as far as modernization of spelling goes, on the same principles as in preceding volumes.†

* This is apparently peculiar to some, perhaps to one, copy. The British Museum, Bodleian, &c. copies have it not.

† Since the above Introduction was first written an additional revision of the texts has been made by Mr. Percy Simpson with assistance from Mr. Thorn-Drury, as referred to in the General Preface of this volume. There can be no doubt that their labours, superadded to those of Professor Case, have enabled me to put forth in this edition a text infinitely superior to any previous one, though my part of the credit is the least. Yet, after all, I dare say Cleveland remains, as he has been impartially described, 'a terrible tangle'.

Preface of Cleaveland Revived

To the Discerning Reader.

⟨Prefixed to *Cleaveland Revived*, 1659[1]⟩

Worthy Friend, there is a saying, *Once well done, and ever done;* the wisest men have so considerately acted in their times, as by their learned works to build their own monuments, such as might eternize them to future ages: our Jonson named his, Works, when others were called Plays, though they cost him much of the lamp and oil; yet he so writ, as to oblige posterity to admire them. Our deceased Hero, Mr. Cleveland, knew how to difference legitimate births from abortives, his mighty genius anvilled out what he sent abroad, as his informed mind knew how to distinguish betwixt writing much and well; a few of our deceased poet's pages being worth cartloads of the scribblers of these times. It was my fortune to be in Newark, when it was besieged, where I saw a few [some] manuscripts of Mr. Cleveland's. Amongst others I have heard that he writ of the Treaty at Uxbridge, as I have been informed since by a person I intrusted to speak with one of Mr. Cleveland's noble friends, who received him courteously, and satisfied his inquiries; as concerning the papers that were left in his custody, more particularly of the Treaty at Uxbridge, that it was not finished, nor any of his other papers fit for the press. They were offered to the judicious consideration of one of the most accomplished persons of our age, he refusing to have them in any further examination, as he did not conceive that they could be published without some injury to Mr. Cleveland; from which time they have remained sealed and locked up: neither can I wonder at this obstruction, when I consider the disturbances our author met with in the time of the siege, how scarce and bad the paper was, the ink hardly to be discerned on it. The intimacy I had with Mr. Cleveland before and since these civil wars, gained most of these papers from him, it being not the least of his misfortunes, out of the love he had to pleasure his friends, to be unfurnished with his own manuscripts, as I have heard him say often. He was not so happy as to have any considerable collection of his own papers, they being dispersed amongst his friends; some whereof when he writ for them, he had no other answer, but that they were lost, or through the often reading, transcribing, or folding of them, worn to pieces. So that though he knew where he formerly bestowed some of them, yet they were not to be regained. For which reason, the poems he had left in his hands being so few, [and] of so inconsiderable [small] a volume, he could not (though he was often solicited) with honour to himself give his consent to the publishing of them, though indeed most of his former printed poems were truly his own, except such as have been lately added, to make up the volume. At the first some few of his verses were printed with the[2] character of the London Diurnal, a stitched pamphlet in quarto. Afterwards, as I have heard Mr. Cleveland say, the copies of verses that he communicated to his friends, the book-seller by chance meeting with them, being added to his book, they sold him another impression; in like manner such small additions (though but a paper or two of his incomparable verses or prose) posted off other editions, [whereas this edition hath the happiness to flourish with the remainder of Mr. Cleveland's last never before printed pieces.] I acknowledge some few of these papers I received [many of these last new printed papers] from one of Mr. Cleveland's near acquaintance, which when I sent to his ever to be honoured friend of Grays-Inn, he had not at that time the leisure to peruse them; but for what he had read of them, he told the person I intrusted, that he did believe them to be Mr. Cleveland's, he having formerly spoken of such papers of his, that were abroad in the hands of his friends, whom he could not remember. My intention was to reserve the collection of these manuscripts for my own private use; but finding many of these I had in my hands already published in the former poems, not knowing what further proceedings might attend the forwardness of the press, I thought myself concerned, not out of any worldly [unworthy] ends of profit, but out of a true affection to my deceased friend, to publish these his never [other] before extant pieces in Latin and English and to make this to be somewhat [like] a volume for the study. Some other poems are intermixed, such as the reader shall find to be of such persons as were for the most part Mr. Cleveland's contemporaries; some of them no less eminently known to the three nations. I hope the world cannot be so far mistaken in his genuine muse, as not to discern his pieces from any of the other poems; neither can I believe there are any persons so unkind, as not candidly to entertain the heroic fancies of the other gentlemen that are worthily placed to live in this volume. Some of their poems, contrary to my expectation—I being at such a distance—I have since heard[3] were before in print, but as they are excellently good and so few, the [but in this second edition I have crossed them out, only reserving those that were excellently good, and never before extant. The] reader (I hope) will the more freely accept them. Thus having ingenuously satisfied thee in these particulars, I shall not need to insert more; but that I have, to prevent surreptitious editions, published this collection; that by erecting this Pyramid of Honour, I might oblige posterity to perpetuate their memories, which is the highest ambition of him, who is,

Newark. Nov. 21, 1658.

Yours in all virtuous endeavours,

E. WILLIAMSON.

[1] This singular production is, in the original, punctuated after a fashion very suitable, in its entire irrationality, to the sentiments of its writer; but I have

taken the liberty (and no other) of relieving the reader of an additional burden by at least separating the sentences. The second edition of 1660 shows some alterations which are given above in brackets.

Whether Mr. Williamson was one of the most impudent persons in the world, or merely (which seems more probable) an abject fool, may be left to the reader to determine. The thing does not seem to require much, if any, annotation. The author, I think, is not otherwise known, and the name is common enough. The well-known Secretary Williamson must have been his contemporary, and may have had some connexion with our paragon besides that of Cavalier principles. But *he* was Joseph.

2   'a character' 1662 (third edition).

3   'I have since heard' omitted in 1662.

The Stationer to the Reader.

⟨Prefixed to *Cleaveland Revived*, 1660⟩

Courteous Reader, thy free Acceptance of the former edition, encouraged me so far as to use my best diligence to gain what still remained in the hands of the Author's friends. I acknowledge myself to be obliged to Mr. Williamson, whose worthy example Mr. Cleveland's other honourers have since pursued. I shall not trouble thee, Reader, with any further Apologies, but only subscribe Mr. W. W. his last Verses in his following Elegy on Mr. Cleveland.

That Plagiary that can filch but one

Conceit from Him, and keep the Theft unknown,

At Noon from Phoebus, may by the same sleight,

Steal Beams, and make 'em pass for his own light.

⟨Prefixed to *Clievelandi Vindiciae*, 1677[1]⟩

To the Right Worshipful and Reverend Francis Turner, D.D., Master of St. John's College in Cambridge, and to the Worthy Fellows of the same College.

GENTLEMEN,

That we interrupt your more serious studies with the offer of this piece, the injury that hath been and is done to the deceased author's ashes not only pleadeth our excuse, but engageth you (whose once he was, and within whose walls this standard of wit was first set up) in the same quarrel with us.

Whilst Randolph and Cowley lie embalmed in their own native wax, how is the name and memory of Cleveland equally profaned by those that usurp, and those that blaspheme it?—by those that are ambitious to lay their cuckoo's eggs in his nest, and those that think to raise up Phœnixes of wit by firing his spicy bed about him?

We know you have, not without passionate resentments, beheld the prostitution of his name in some late editions vended under it, wherein his orations are murthered over and over in barbarous Latin, and a more barbarous translation: and wherein is scarce one or other poem of his own to commute for all the rest. At least every Cuirassier of his hath a fulsome dragooner behind him, and Venus is again unequally yoked with a sooty anvil-beater. Cleveland thus revived dieth another death.

You cannot but have beheld with like zealous indignation how enviously our late mushroom-wits look up at him because he overdroppeth them, and snarl at his brightness as dogs at the Moon.

Some of these grand Sophys will not allow him the reputation of wit at all: yet how many such authors must be creamed and spirited to make up his Fuscara?[2] And how many of their slight productions may be gigged[3] out of one of his pregnant words? There perhaps you may find some leaf-gold, here massy wedges; there some scattered rays, here a galaxy; there some loose fancy frisking in the air, here Wit's Zodiac.

The quarrel in all this is upbraiding merit, and eminence his crime. His towering[4] fancy scareth so high a pitch that they fly like shades below him. The torrent thereof (which riseth far above their high water mark) drowneth their levels. Usurping upon the State Poetic of the time, he hath brought in such insolent measures of Wit and Language that, despairing to imitate, they must study to understand. That alone is Wit with them to which they are commensurate, and what exceedeth their scantling[5] is monstrous.

Thus they deifie[6] his Wit and Fancy as the clown the plump oyster when he could not crack it. And now instead of that strenuous masculine style which breatheth in this author, we have only an enervous effeminate froth offered, as if they had taken the salivating pill before they set pen to paper. You must hold your breath in the perusal lest the jest vanish by blowing on.

Another blemish in this monster of perfection is the exuberance of his fancy. His manna lieth so thick upon the ground they loathe it. When he should only fan, he with hurricanos of wit stormeth the sense, and doth not so much delight his reader, as oppress and overwhelm him.

To cure this excess, their frugal wit hath reduced the world to a Lessian Diet.[7] If perhaps they entertain their reader with one good thought (as these new Dictators affect to speak) he may sit down and say Grace over it: the rest is words and nothing else.

We will leave them therefore to the most proper vengeance, to humour themselves with the perusal of their own poems: and leave the barber to rub their thick skulls with bran[8] until they are fit for musk. Only we will leave this friendly advice with them; that they have one eye upon John Tradescant's executor,[9] lest among his other Minims of Art and Nature he expose their slight conceits: and another upon the Royal Society, lest they make their poems the counterbalance when they intend to weigh air.

From these unequal censures we appeal to such competent judges as yourselves, in whose just value of him Cleveland shall live the wonder of his own, and the pattern of succeeding ages. And although we might (upon several accompts) bespeak your affections, yet (abstracting from these) we submit him to your severer judgements, and doubt not but he will find that patronage from you which is desired and expected by

Your humble Servants.

J. L.   S. D.[10]

[1] Here we get into *terra cognita* as regards authorship. The editors had been, both of them, Cleveland's pupils at St. John's. 'J. L.' was John Lake (1624-1689), a man of great distinction—at this time Vicar of Leeds and Prebendary of York, later Bishop, first of Sodor and Man and then of Chichester, who while he held the last-named see had the double glory of withstanding James II as one of 'the Seven', and of refusing the Oath to William. 'S. D.' was also a Yorkshire clergyman—Samuel Drake—who had not only studied under Cleveland at Cambridge, but fought under him at Newark. He became Vicar of Pontefract; but (if the *D.N.B.* is right in assigning his death to the year

1673) his work on the great vindication of his tutor must have been done some time before publication. Francis Turner (1638-1700), of a much younger generation and an Oxford man, though admitted *ad eundem* at Cambridge in 1662, had been Master of St. John's College since 1670, and was therefore properly selected as chief dedicatee. He was destined to be connected with Lake again in the great actions above noted as Bishop of Ely, and for the last ten years of his life was an active Jacobite agent.

[2]   The description of *Cleaveland Revived* in the third paragraph is perfectly just, and 'anvil-beater' is an obvious echo-gibe at Williamson's own phraseology. It is less certain what 'grand Sophys' are specially referred to further on—but Dryden *might* be one.

[3]   A Clevelandish word; *v. infra*, p. 65 (*Rupertismus*, l. 120).

[4]   In orig., as often, 'touring', but to print this nowadays would invite misconception.

[5]   'Scantling' is used in various senses. Either that of 'rough draft' or, as in Taylor, 'small piece' would do; but it is at least possible that it is not a noun at all, but a direct participle from the verb to 'scantle', found in Drayton, and meaning 'to be deficient', 'come short'. Some, however, prefer the sense 'dimension' or 'measurement', which would make it a sort of varied repetition of 'commensurate'.

[6]   'Deifie' is of course wrong. 'Defy' is likeliest, and in a certain sense (frequent in Elizabethan writers) would do; but 'decry' seems wanted.

[7]   A common phrase for an earlier 'Banting' regime derived from the *Hygiasticon* (Antwerp, 1623) of Leonard Lessius (1554-1624). I owe this information to the kindness of Dr. Comrie, Lecturer on the History of Medicine in the University of Edinburgh. The next sentence may, or rather must, be a reference to (in fact, a fling at) Dryden, *Essay of Dramatic Poesy* (vol. i, p. 52, ed. Ker, Oxford, 1900), who censures Cleveland for not giving 'a *great* thought' in 'words ... commonly received'. I owe the reminder of this to Mr. Thorn-Drury.

[8]   The use of bran for shampooing is not perhaps so well known as that for poultices, foot-baths, &c. It is always a *softener* as well as a detergent.

[9]   Ashmole.

[10]   Perhaps I should add a very few words explaining why I have not made this 'authenticated' edition the base of mine. I have not done so because the editors, excellent as was evidently their intention, have after all given us no reasons for their exclusions and inclusions; because, though they have corrected some obvious errors, their readings by no means always intrinsically commend themselves to me; and especially because the distance

between 1647 and 1677 reflects itself, to no small degree, in a certain definite *modernisation* of form, grammatical and prosodic. 1653 has much more *contemporariness*.

POEMS.

To the State of Love. Or the Senses' Festival.

I saw a vision yesternight,

Enough to sate a Seeker's sight;

I wished myself a Shaker there,

And her quick pants my trembling sphere.

It was a she so glittering bright,

You'd think her soul an Adamite;

A person of so rare a frame,

Her body might be lined with' same.

Beauty's chiefest maid of honour,

10You may break Lent with looking on her.

Not the fair Abbess of the skies,

With all her nunnery of eyes,

Can show me such a glorious prize!

And yet, because 'tis more renown

To make a shadow shine, she's brown;

A brown for which Heaven would disband

The galaxy, and stars be tanned;

Brown by reflection as her eye

Deals out the summer's livery.

20Old dormant windows must confess

Her beams; their glimmering spectacles,

Struck with the splendour of her face,

Do th' office of a burning-glass.

Now where such radiant lights have shown,

No wonder if her cheeks be grown

Sunburned, with lustre of her own.

My sight took pay, but (thank my charms!)

I now impale her in mine arms;

(Love's compasses confining you,

30Good angels, to a circle too.)

Is not the universe strait-laced

When I can clasp it in the waist?

My amorous folds about thee hurled,

With Drake I girdle in the world;

I hoop the firmament, and make

This, my embrace, the zodiac.

How would thy centre take my sense

When admiration doth commence

At the extreme circumference?

40Now to the melting kiss that sips

The jellied philtre of her lips;

So sweet there is no tongue can praise 't

Till transubstantiate with a taste.

Inspired like Mahomet from above

By th' billing of my heavenly dove,

Love prints his signets in her smacks,

Those ruddy drops of squeezing wax,

Which, wheresoever she imparts,

They're privy seals to take up hearts.

50Our mouths encountering at the sport,

My slippery soul had quit the fort,

But that she stopped the sally-port.

Next to these sweets, her lips dispense

(As twin conserves of eloquence)

The sweet perfume her breath affords,

Incorporating with her words.

No rosary this vot'ress needs—

Her very syllables are beads;

No sooner 'twixt those rubies born,

60But jewels are in ear-rings worn.

With what delight her speech doth enter;

It is a kiss o' th' second venter.

And I dissolve at what I hear,

As if another Rosamond were

Couched in the labyrinth of my ear.

Yet that 's but a preludious bliss,

Two souls pickeering in a kiss.

Embraces do but draw the line,

'Tis storming that must take her in.

70When bodies join and victory hovers

'Twixt the equal fluttering lovers,

This is the game; make stakes, my dear!

Hark, how the sprightly chanticleer

(That Baron Tell-clock of the night)

Sounds boutesel to Cupid's knight.

Then have at all, the pass is got,

For coming off, oh, name it not!

Who would not die upon the spot?

To the State of Love, &c. appeared first *1651*. The stanzas are not divided in the early editions, but are so in *1677*. Carew's *Rapture* may have given some suggestions, Apuleius and Lucretius also; but not much is required. The substance is shocking to pure prudery, no doubt; but, as observed in the introduction, there is perhaps more gusto in the execution than in *Fuscara*.

A copy of this poem, with many minor variants, is in Bodleian MS. Tanner 306, fol. 424: it has one noteworthy reading, 'took sey', i.e. 'say' or 'assay'—the hunting term—in l. 27.

2, 3 The use of capitals in the seventeenth century is so erratic that it is dangerous to base much on it. But both 'Seekers' and 'Shakers' (a variant of 'Quakers') were actually among the countless sects of the time, as well of course as 'Adamites'. *1651. 1653, 1654,* and *1657* have 'tempt' for *1677* 'sate'.

4 pants *1677*: 'pulse' *1651, 1653, 1654, 1657.*

10 'You'd break a Lent' *1651, 1653.*

11-13 Benlowes's lines (*v. sup.* i. 356)—

The lady prioress of the cloistered sky, &c.—

are more poetic than these, but may be less original. Even that, however, is uncertain. Both poets, though Benlowes was a good deal the elder, were of St. John's, and must, even in other ways, have known each other: *Theophila* appeared a year after the edition in which this poem was first included. But the indebtedness may be the other way, or common to an earlier original, or non-existent.

19 Deals out] The earlier texts have 'Dazzle's', but *1677* seems here to have introduced the true reading found also in the *MS.* 'Deals out' is far more poetical: the eye clothes with its own reflection sky and stars, and earth.

20-3 The punctuation of all editions, including Mr. Berdan's, makes these lines either totally unintelligible, or very confused, by putting a stop at 'spectacles' and none at 'beams'. That adopted in the text makes it quite clear.

30 circle] 'compass' *1651, 1653,* evidently wrong.

33 It is not impossible that Aphra Behn had these lines unconsciously in her head when she wrote her own finest passage. Unconsciously, for the drift is quite different; but 'hurled', 'amorous', and 'world' come close together in both.

34 *1651, 1653* again 'compass' for 'girdle'.

37 'would', the reading of *1651, 1653,* infinitely better than 'could', that of *1677.*

45 In this pyramidally metaphysical passage Cleveland does not quite play the game. Mahomet's pigeon did not *kiss* him. But 'privy seals to take up hearts' is very dear to fancy, most delicate, and of liberal conceit. So also 'jewels are in ear-rings worn' below; where the game is played to its rigour, though the reader may not at first see it.

46 his] 'her' *1651, 1653*; but it clearly should be 'his', which is in *1677*.

53 *1651, 1653* read 'Next to those sweets her lips dispense', *nescio an melius.*

61 her] 'our,' a variant of one edition (*1665*) is all wrong.

62 Mr. Berdan has strangely misinterpreted 'venter'. The phrase is quite a common one—'of the second *marriage.*' The first kiss comes of lip and lip, the second of lip and love.

67 pickeering] 'marauding', 'skirmishing in front of an army'.

70 For 'join' [jine] *1651, 1653* and others have 'whine'—suggesting the Latin *gannitus* frequent in such contexts. But 'join' must be right. Professor Gordon points out that the passage is a reminiscence of Donne, in his *Extasie*:

As 'twixt two equall Armies, Fate

Suspends uncertaine victorie,

Our soules (which to advance their state

Were gone out,) hung 'twixt her, and mee.(13-16.)

This is contrasted with the bodily 'entergrafting' of l. 9, &c.

74 When 'prose and sense' came in they were very contemptuous of this Baron Tell-clock. But the image is complete, congruous, and capable of being championed.

75 'Boutesel' of course = 'boot and saddle', albeit 'boute' does not mean 'boot'.

The Hecatomb to his Mistress.

Be dumb, you beggars of the rhyming trade,

Geld your loose wits and let your Muse be spayed.

Charge not the parish with the bastard phrase

Of balm, elixir, both the Indias,

Of shrine, saint, sacrilege, and such as these

Expressions common as your mistresses.

Hence, you fantastic postillers in song.

My text defeats your art, ties Nature's tongue,

Scorns all her tinselled metaphors of pelf,

10Illustrated by nothing but herself.

As spiders travel by their bowels spun

Into a thread, and, when the race is run,

Wind up their journey in a living clew,

So is it with my poetry and you.

From your own essence must I first untwine,

Then twist again each panegyric line.

Reach then a soaring quill that I may write,

As with a Jacob's staff, to take her height.

Suppose an angel, darting through the air,

20Should there encounter a religious prayer

Mounting to Heaven, that Intelligence

Should for a Sunday-suit thy breath condense

Into a body.—Let me crack a string

In venturing higher; were the note I sing

Above Heaven's Ela, should I then decline,

And with a deep-mouthed gamut sound the line

From pole to pole, I could not reach her worth,

Nor find an epithet to set it forth.

Metals may blazon common beauties; she

30Makes pearls and planets humble heraldry.

As, then, a purer substance is defined

But by a heap of negatives combined,

Ask what a spirit is, you'll hear them cry

It hath no matter, no mortality:

So can I not define how sweet, how fair;

Only I say she 's not as others are.

For what perfections we to others grant,

It is her sole perfection to want.

All other forms seem in respect of thee

40The almanac's misshaped anatomy,

Where Aries head and face, Bull neck and throat,

The Scorpion gives the secrets, knees the Goat;

A brief of limbs foul as those beasts, or are

Their namesake signs in their strange character.

As the philosophers to every sense

Marry its object, yet with some dispense,

And grant them a polygamy with all,

And these their common sensibles they call:

So is 't with her who, stinted unto none,

50Unites all senses in each action.

The same beam heats and lights; to see her well

Is both to hear and feel, to taste and smell.

For, can you want a palate in your eyes,

When each of hers contains a double prize,

Venus's apple? Can your eyes want nose

When from each cheek buds forth a fragrant rose?

Or can your sight be deaf to such a quick

And well-tuned face, such moving rhetoric?

Doth not each look a flash of lightning feel

60Which spares the body's sheath, and melts the steel?

Thy soul must needs confess, or grant thy sense

Corrupted with the object's excellence.

Sweet magic, which can make five senses lie

Conjured within the circle of an eye!

In whom, since all the five are intermixed,

Oh now that Scaliger would prove his sixt!

Thou man of mouth, that canst not name a she

Unless all Nature pay a subsidy,

Whose language is a tax, whose musk-cat verse

70Voids nought but flowers, for thy Muse's hearse

Fitter than Celia's looks, who in a trice

Canst state the long disputed Paradise,

And (what Divines hunt with so cold a scent)

Canst in her bosom find it resident;

Now come aloft, come now, and breathe a vein,

And give some vent unto thy daring strain.

Say the astrologer who spells the stars,

In that fair alphabet reads peace and wars,

Mistakes his globe and in her brighter eye

80Interprets Heaven's physiognomy.

Call her the Metaphysics of her sex,

And say she tortures wits as quartans vex

Physicians; call her the square circle; say

She is the very rule of Algebra.

What e'er thou understand'st not, say 't of her,

For that 's the way to write her character.

Say this and more, and when thou hopest to raise

Thy fancy so as to inclose her praise—

Alas poor Gotham, with thy cuckoo-hedge!

90Hyperboles are here but sacrilege.

Then roll up, Muse, what thou hast ravelled out,

Some comments clear not, but increase the doubt.

She that affords poor mortals not a glance

Of knowledge, but is known by ignorance;

She that commits a rape on every sense,

Whose breath can countermand a pestilence;

She that can strike the best invention dead

Till baffled poetry hangs down the head—

She, she it is that doth contain all bliss,

100And makes the world but her periphrasis.

The Hecatomb to his Mistress.] (*1651.*) This poem is perhaps the best text to prove (or endeavour to prove) that Cleveland's object was really burlesque.

1 you] 'ye' *1651, 1653.*

2 *1651, 1653* read 'the' for 'your', and 'splaid': 'spade' *1677.* 'Spay' or 'splay' to destroy the reproductive powers of a female.

3 the bastard] *1677* again alters 'the' to 'your', which does not seem good.

5 sacrilege] sacrifice *1677.*

6 your] their *1653,* &c.

7 postillers] The word means glossers or commentators on Scripture, and has acquired in several languages a contemptuous meaning from the frequently commonplace and trivial character of such things. 'ye fantastic' *1653.*

9 *1651, 1653* have 'his' for 'her', and in the next line 'his self' for 'herself'. The poem is particularly badly printed in this group, and I think the *1677* editors, in trying to mend it, have mistaken some places. Thus in ...

22 They print 'Would' for 'Should'. This may look better at first; but I at least can make no real sense of it. With 'Should' I can make some. The poet starts an extravagant comparison in 19-21; continues it in '[suppose] that Intelligence should', &c.; finds it will not do, and breaks it off with the parenthetical 'Let me' &c. To bring this out I have inserted the —.

24 *1677* 'And venture', with a full-stop at 'higher', not so well; but in ...

'*un*decline' *1651, 1653,* &c. is nonsense; while in the next line 'sound *agen*' either points to a complete breakdown or indicates that, on the most recent Cockney principles, 'again' could be pronounced '*agine*' and rhymes *à la* Mrs. Browning. The text is *1677.*

28 set] shadow *1677.*

35 define] describe *1677.*

37 perfections *1651, 1653*: perfection *1677*.

43 brief = 'list'.

44 name-sak'd *1651, 1653*.

45 the] your *1677*.

52 *1677*, not nearly so well, 'see and' for 'feel, to'. You want the list of senses completed and summed up by such a palate in 'see', which, repeated, spoils all.

54 *1651, 1653* have 'his' for 'hers'; but 'a double prize' is more vivid if less strictly defensible than 'the beauteous' of *1677*. So in 56 *1677* opens with 'Seeing each' instead of 'When from'—much feebler. But in 57-8 The text, which is *1677*, is better than *1653*:

Or can the sight be deaf *if she but speak*,

A well-tuned face, such moving rhetoric?

which indeed is, if not nonsense, most clumsily expressed, even if comma at 'face' be deleted.

60 and melts] yet melts *1677*.

66 'sixt' *1651, 1653, 1677*.

70-1 The punctuation of the old texts—no comma at 'flowers' and one at 'hearse'—makes the passage hard to understand. As I have altered this punctuation, it is clear.

73 what Divines] *1651, 1653*, &c. 'with Divines'.

75 come now *1677*: come, come *1651, 1653*.

83 square] squared *1677*. If all this is not burlesque it is very odd.

85 you undertake not *1651, 1653*.

91 roll] rouse *1651, 1653*. ravelled] revealed *1651, 1653*.

98 the] her *1651, 1653*.

100 The hundred lines making the *heca*tomb—and the metaphysical matter the subject of sacrifice.

Upon Sir Thomas Martin,

Who subscribed a Warrant thus: 'We the
Knights and Gentlemen of the Committee,' &c.
when there was no Knight but himself.

Hang out a flag and gather pence—A piece

Which Afric never bred nor swelling Greece

With stories' tympany, a beast so rare

No lecturer's wrought cap, nor Bartholomew Fair

Can match him; nature's whimsey, that outvies

Tradescant and his ark of novelties;

The Gog and Magog of prodigious sights,

With reverence to your eyes, Sir Thomas Knights.

But is this bigamy of titles due?

10Are you Sir Thomas and Sir Martin too?

Issachar couchant 'twixt a brace of sirs,

Thou knighthood in a pair of panniers;

Thou, that look'st, wrapped up in thy warlike leather,

Like Valentine and Orson bound together;

Spurs' representative! thou, that art able

To be a voider to King Arthur's table;

Who, in this sacrilegious mass of all,

It seems has swallowed Windsor's Hospital;

Pair-royal-headed Cerberus's cousin.

20Hercules' labours were a baker's dozen,

Had he but trumped on thee, whose forked neck

Might well have answered at the font for Smec.

But can a knighthood on a knighthood lie?

Metal on metal is ill armory;

And yet the known Godfrey of Bouillon's coat

Shines in exception to the herald's vote.

Great spirits move not by pedantic laws;

Their actions, though eccentric, state the cause,

And Priscian bleeds with honour. Caesar thus

30Subscribed two consuls with one Julius.

Tom, never oaded squire, scarce yeoman-high,

Is Tom twice dipped, knight of a double dye!

Fond man, whose fate is in his name betrayed!

It is the setting sun doubles his shade.

But it 's no matter, for amphibious he

May have a knight hanged, yet Sir Tom go free!

Upon Sir Thomas Martin.] (*1651*.) We here turn to the other side of Cleveland's work, where jest and earnest are combined in a very different fashion. Martin was a member of the Committee of Sequestration appointed under the Act of April 1, 1643, which, in a more fearless and thoroughgoing fashion than that of some later legislation, confiscated in a lump the property of certain bishops and of political opponents generally. The sequestrators for Cambridge were this man and two other knights—Sir Dudley North and Sir John Cutts; with two esquires—a Captain Symonds and Dudley Pope.

1 'pence apiece' *1651*, which makes doubtful sense. *1653, 1677*, and all others before me, have 'pence a piece', which I believe to be careless printing for the text above. The 'piece' is the same as the 'beast', and the brackets which follow in the originals are a printer's error. 'Piece', in this sense of 'rare object', is not uncommon. Cf. Prospero's 'Thy mother was a *piece* of *virtue*.' 'Pence apiece' (about the same as the Scotch fishwife's 'pennies each'), if not, as Mr. Berdan says, 'proverbial', is certainly a perfectly common expression, still I think existing, but it is difficult to see how what follows can thus suit it. 'Which' must have an antecedent.

4 'Bartlemew' *1651, 1653*: 'Bartholmew' *1654*. The word was, of course, pronounced 'Bartlemy,' and almost dissyllabically.

5 that outvies] *1651, 1653* 'one that outvies', perhaps rightly.

6 Tredeskin *1651, 1653*: Tredescant *1677*.

11 The reference to the animal between two burdens to whom Issachar is biblically compared (Gen. xlix. 14) is perhaps meant to be additionally pointed by 'Sir *Martin*', the latter being one of the story-names of the much-enduring beast.

16 voider] The servant who clears the table; also, but here less probably, the tray or basket used for the purpose.

18 The 'Poor Knights of Windsor' having fallen, like other institutions, into the maw of plebeian and Puritan plunder.

19 The hyphen at 'Pair-royal', which Mr. Berdan has dropped, is important, the term being technical in certain card-games and meaning *three* cards of the same value—kings, &c.

21 trumped on thee = turned thee up like a trump.

22 'Smec'—of course—'tymnuus', and used both for the sake of contempt and as denoting a plurality of person.

24 The principle of this line is of course part of the A B C of the more modern and dogmatic heraldry: the application will lie either on sword or spur, the two characteristic insignia of knighthood and both metallic. *1677* changed 'ill armory' to 'false heraldry', and Scott was probably thinking of this line when he made Prince John and Wamba between them use the phrase in *Ivanhoe*.

25 Godfrey's arms as King of Jerusalem—five golden crosses on a silver shield—were commonly quoted, as Cleveland quotes them, in special exception to the rule. But my friend Mr. F. P. Barnard, Professor of Mediaeval Archaeology in the University of Liverpool, to whom I owe the materials of this note, tells me that he has collected many other cases, English and foreign. The objection, however, was originally a practical one, metal on metal and colour on colour being difficult to distinguish *in the field*. It passed into a technical rule later.

29 Priscian's head may not have bled here before it was broken by Butler; but the dates of the *writing* of *Hudibras* are quite uncertain.

31 oaded] This singular word is in all the editions I have seen. *1699* makes it 'loaded', with no sense that I can see in this passage. Can it be 'oathèd'—be sworn either to the commission of the peace or something else that gave the title 'Esquire'? 'Oad', however, = woad; cf. Minsheu, *Guide into Tongues*, 1617 'Oade, *an hearbe*. Vide *Woade*'. This would certainly suit the next line.

On the memory of Mr. Edward King, drowned in the Irish Seas.

I like not tears in tune, nor do I prize

His artificial grief who scans his eyes.

Mine weep down pious beads, but why should I

Confine them to the Muse's rosary?

I am no poet here; my pen 's the spout

Where the rain-water of mine eyes run out

In pity of that name, whose fate we see

Thus copied out in grief's hydrography.

The Muses are not mermaids, though upon

10His death the ocean might turn Helicon.

The sea's too rough for verse; who rhymes upon 't

With Xerxes strives to fetter th' Hellespont.

My tears will keep no channel, know no laws

To guide their streams, but (like the waves, their cause)

Run with disturbance, till they swallow me

As a description of his misery.

But can his spacious virtue find a grave

Within th' imposthumed bubble of a wave?

Whose learning if we sound, we must confess

20The sea but shallow, and him bottomless.

Could not the winds to countermand thy death

With their whole card of lungs redeem thy breath?

Or some new island in thy rescue peep

To heave thy resurrection from the deep,

That so the world might see thy safety wrought

With no less wonder than thyself was thought?

The famous Stagirite (who in his life

Had Nature as familiar as his wife)

Bequeathed his widow to survive with thee,

30Queen Dowager of all philosophy.

An ominous legacy, that did portend

Thy fate and predecessor's second end.

Some have affirmed that what on earth we find,

The sea can parallel in shape and kind.

Books, arts, and tongues were wanting, but in thee

Neptune hath got an university.

We'll dive no more for pearls; the hope to see

Thy sacred reliques of mortality

Shall welcome storms, and make the seamen prize

40His shipwreck now more than his merchandise.

He shall embrace the waves, and to thy tomb

As to a Royaller Exchange shall come.

What can we now expect? Water and fire,

Both elements our ruin do conspire.

And that dissolves us which doth us compound:

One Vatican was burnt, another drowned.

We of the gown our libraries must toss

To understand the greatness of our loss;

Be pupils to our grief, and so much grow

50In learning, as our sorrows overflow.

When we have filled the rundlets of our eyes

We'll issue 't forth and vent such elegies

As that our tears shall seem the Irish Seas,

We floating islands, living Hebrides.

On the Memory of Mr. Edward King.] First printed in the memorial volume of Cambridge verse to King, *1638*; included in the *Poems* of *1651*. It is of course easy (and it may be feared that it has too often been done) to contrast this disadvantageously with *Lycidas*. A specific or generic comparison, bringing out the difference of ephemeral and eternal style in verse, will not be found unprofitable and is almost as easy to make. No reader of Milton—and any one who has not read Milton is very unlikely to read this—can need information on King or on the circumstances of his death. *1651* and *1653* add a spurious duplicate, the last fourteen lines of W. More's elegy which followed Cleveland's in the Cambridge volume.

* On the Same.

Tell me no more of Stoics: canst thou tell

Who 'twas that when the waves began to swell,

The ship to sink, sad passengers to call

'Master, we perish'—slept secure of all?

Remember this, and him that waking kept

A mind as constant as he did that slept.

Canst thou give credit to his zeal and love

That went to Heaven, and to those flames above,

Wrapt in a fiery chariot? Since I heard

Who 'twas, that on his knees the vessel steered

With hands bolt up to Heaven, since I see

As yet no signs of his mortality,—

Pardon me, Reader, if I say he's gone

The self-same journey in a wat'ry one.

1 do] will *1638*.

2 who] that *1638*.

6 *1651* 'runs': all other editions (including *1638*) 'run'. The attraction to 'eyes' is one of the commonest of things.

10 The everlasting confusion of 'mount' and 'fount' occurs in 'Helicon.'

26 wonder] miracle *1638*.

34 *1638*, *1677*, and later editions read, harmlessly but needlessly, '*for* shape'.

46 'Vatican' used (as Mr. Berdan justly notes) as = 'library'.

Cleveland's warmest defenders must admit that this epicede is a triumph of 'frigidity'. And the personal note which *Lycidas* itself has been unfairly accused of wanting is here non-existent to my eyes, though some have discovered it.

Upon an Hermaphrodite.

Sir, or Madam, choose you whether!

Nature twists you both together

And makes thy soul two garbs confess,

Both petticoat and breeches dress.

Thus we chastise the God of Wine

With water that is feminine,

Until the cooler nymph abate

His wrath, and so concorporate.

Adam, till his rib was lost,

10Had both sexes thus engrossed.

When Providence our Sire did cleave,

And out of Adam carved Eve,

Then did man 'bout wedlock treat,

To make his body up complete.

Thus matrimony speaks but thee

In a grave solemnity.

For man and wife make but one right

Canonical hermaphrodite.

Ravel thy body, and I find

20In every limb a double kind.

Who would not think that head a pair

That breeds such factions in the hair?

One half so churlish in the touch

That, rather than endure so much

I would my tender limbs apparel

In Regulus's nailèd barrel:

But the other half so small,

And so amorous withal,

That Cupid thinks each hair doth grow

30A string for his invis'ble bow.

When I look babies in thine eyes

Here Venus, there Adonis, lies.

And though thy beauty be high noon

Thy orb contains both sun and moon.

How many melting kisses skip

'Twixt thy male and female lip—

Twixt thy upper brush of hair

And thy nether beard's despair?

When thou speak'st (I would not wrong

40Thy sweetness with a double tongue)

But in every single sound

A perfect dialogue is found.

Thy breasts distinguish one another,

This the sister, that the brother.

When thou join'st hands my ear still fancies

The nuptial sound, 'I, John, take Frances.'

Feel but the difference soft and rough;

This is a gauntlet, that a muff.

Had sly Ulysses, at the sack

50Of Troy, brought thee his pedlar's pack,

And weapons too, to know Achilles

From King Lycomedes' Phillis,

His plot had failed; this hand would feel

The needle, that the warlike steel.

When music doth thy pace advance,

Thy right leg takes the left to dance.

Nor is 't a galliard danced by one,

But a mixed dance, though alone.

Thus every heteroclite part

60Changes gender but thy heart.

Nay those, which modesty can mean

But dare not speak, are epicene.

That gamester needs must overcome

That can play both Tib and Tom.

Thus did Nature's mintage vary,

Coining thee a Philip and Mary.

Upon an Hermaphrodite.] (*1647.*) This poem appeared in the 1640 and all subsequent editions of Randolph's poems and in the 1653 edition of Beaumont's. Beaumont had preceded Cleveland as a 'dumping-ground' for odds and ends of all kinds. But see the following poem.

1 *1647* and *1651* 'Madame', which is not English, and which spoils the run of the verse.

2 twists] *1647, 1651, 1653,* and others 'twist'd', which is very like the time.

10 both sexes] *1677* and later '*the* sexes'.

13 I do not know whether it is worth while to point out that catalectic or seven-syllabled lines with trochaic effect (cf. 9. this, 16, and others), as well as complete trochaic dimeters (1, 2, &c.), occur more frequently here than in *The Senses' Festival, Fuscara,* &c. This, though of course Milton has it, was rather more frequent in Randolph's generation than in Cleveland's.

22 *1647, 1651, 1677,* and later 'faction', but 'factions' *1653.*

25 *1651, 1653* &c. '*It* would', which can hardly be right. On the other hand *1677* and its follower have '*With* Regulus his' (l. 26).

31 It can hardly be necessary to interpret this famous and charming phrase.

48 Line shortened to the trochaic run in *1677,* &c. by dropping 'is'.

52 'Lycomedes' puzzled the earlier printers, who in *1647* and *1651* make it 'Nicomedes' (corrupted by *1653* to 'Nichomedes')—a curiously awkward blunder, as it happens.

56 the left *1647, 1653*: thy left *1651.*

58 The late edition of *1687,* when 'regularity' was becoming a fetish, inserted 'all' before 'alone', though *1677*—its standard for the genuine poems—has not got it, and it is not wanted.

59 heteroclite part] *1677* and its followers, puzzled by this, the original, reading, read 'apart' (apostrophating 'Het'roclite'), the sense of which is not clear; while Mr. Berdan would emend to 'heteroclitic', which is unnecessary. Cleveland may well have scanned 'heterōclite', which is by no means an extravagant licence, and has been paralleled by Longfellow in 'Eurōclydon'. Indeed, since I wrote this note Mr. Simpson has furnished me with a parallel of 'heterōclite' itself from Harl. MS. 4126, f. 102.

60 but thy heart *1649*: not the heart *1651, 1653*.

62 'But' *1677*: 'And' in earlier texts.

The Author's Hermaphrodite.

(Made after Mr. Randolph's death, yet inserted into his Poems.)

Problem of sexes! Must thou likewise be

As disputable in thy pedigree?

Thou twins in one, in whom Dame Nature tries

To throw less than aums ace upon two dice.

Wert thou served up two in one dish, the rather

To split thy sire into a double father?

True, the world's scales are even; what the main

In one place gets, another quits again.

Nature lost one by thee, and therefore must

10Slice one in two to keep her number just.

Plurality of livings is thy state,

And therefore mine must be impropriate.

For, since the child is mine and yet the claim

Is intercepted by another's name,

Never did steeple carry double truer;

His is the donative and mine the cure.

Then say, my Muse (and without more dispute),

Who 'tis that fame doth superinstitute.

The Theban wittol, when he once descries
20Jove is his rival, falls to sacrifice.
That name hath tipped his horns; see, on his knees!
A health to Hans-in-kelder Hercules!
Nay, sublunary cuckolds are content
To entertain their fate with compliment;
And shall not he be proud whom Randolph deigns
To quarter with his Muse both arms and brains?
Gramercy Gossip, I rejoice to see
She'th got a leap of such a barbary.
Talk not of horns, horns are the poet's crest;
30For, since the Muses left their former nest
To found a nunnery in Randolph's quill,
Cuckold Parnassus is a forked hill.
But stay, I've waked his dust, his marble stirs
And brings the worms for his compurgators.

Can ghost have natural sons? Say, Og, is't meet
Penance bear date after the winding sheet?
Were it a Phœnix (as the double kind
May seem to prove, being there's two combined)
I would disclaim my right, and that it were
40The lawful issue of his ashes swear.
But was he dead? Did not his soul translate
Herself into a shop of lesser rate;
Or break up house, like an expensive lord
That gives his purse a sob and lives at board?
Let old Pythagoras but play the pimp
And still there's hopes 't may prove his bastard imp.

But I'm profane; for, grant the world had one

With whom he might contract an union,

They two were one, yet like an eagle spread,

50I' th' body joined, but parted in the head.

For you, my brat, that pose the Porph'ry Chair,

Pope John, or Joan, or whatsoe'er you are,

You are a nephew; grieve not at your state,

For all the world is illegitimate.

Man cannot get a man, unless the sun

Club to the act of generation.

The sun and man get man, thus Tom and I

Are the joint fathers of my poetry.

For since, blest shade, thy verse is male, but mine

60O' th' weaker sex, a fancy feminine,

We'll part the child, and yet commit no slaughter;

So shall it be thy son, and yet my daughter.

The Author's Hermaphrodite.] (*1647*.) The note, which appears in all editions, seems evidently conclusive as to this poem. Moreover the quibbles are right Clevelandish.

7 'main' is a little ambiguous, or may appear so from the recent mention of dice. But that sense will hardly come in, and Cleveland was probably thinking of the famous passage in Spenser (Artegall's dispute with the giant, *F. Q.* v. ii) as to the washing away and washing up of the *sea*. Yet 'main' *might* mean 'stock'. The reading of 'gets place' in one edition (*1662*), rather notable for blunders, cannot be listened to.

15 steeple] By synecdoche for 'church' or 'parish'.

16 donative] A play on words, as also in 'cure'.

19 Theban wittol] Amphitryon.

22 Hans-in-kelder] = 'unborn'.

28 She'th] *1667* changes to 'Th'hast'. barbary] 'Barbs' or Spanish horses were imported for the stud as early as Anglo-Saxon times; but before Cleveland's day actual Arabs had been tried.

34 compurgators] persons who swear in a court of law to the innocence or the veracity of some other person.

35 I was unable to say why the King of Bashan comes in here, except that the comparison of the *Dialogue on the &c.*, 'Og the great *commissary*', and the put case about 'penance', suggest some church lawyer of portly presence. But Mr. Simpson and Mr. Thorn-Drury have traced the thing from this point as follows:

Cf. *A Dialogue upon the &c.*, l. 47 'Og the great commissary', where the copy in Rawlinson MS. Poet. 26, fol. 94 *b*, has a marginal note 'Roan'. This was Dr. William Roan, of whom an account is given in the *Catalogue of Prints and Drawings in the British Museum*, Division 1, 'Political and Personal Satires', p. 156: 'Dr. Roane was one of the most eminent doctors who acted in Laud's Ecclesiastical Courts; he fled from the indignation of the House of Commons, and is frequently alluded to in pamphlets and broadsides of the time (see *Times Alteration*, Jan. 8, 1641,... *Old News newly Revived*, Dec. 21, 1640,...and *The Spirituall Courts Epitomised*, June 26, 1641).' The pamphlet illustrated in this note is *A Letter front Rhoan in France Written by Doctor Roane one of the Doctors of the late Sicke Commons, to his Fellow Doctor of the Civill Law. Dated 28, of Iune last past. With an Ellegy written by his oune hand upon the death and buriall of the said Doctors Commons. Printed in this happy yeare, 1641.* (Thomason's copy dated June 28.)

Mr. Thorn-Drury supplies the following references bearing directly on the nickname, and not noticed in the B.M. Catalogue: *Foure fugitives meeting Or, The Discourse amongst my Lord Finch, Sir Frances Windebank, Sir John Sucklin, and Doctor Roane, as they accidentally met in France, with a detection of their severall pranks in England. Printed In the Yeare, 1641.* 4°.

Suckling says to Roane, 'Hold there good Doctor *Roane*, and take me with you, you are to be blamed too, for not bidding farewell to Sir *Paul Pinder*, (at whose beauteous house, you have devoured the carkasse of many a cram'd Capon) before you fled, but I wonder more, why you came hither so unprovided; methinks some English dyet would have bin good for a weake stomack: the Church-Wardens of Northhamptonshire promised to give you a good fee, if you will goe to 'em, and resolve 'em whether they may lawfully take the oath &c. or no.

'*Wind.* That may very well be, for they have given him a great Addition, they stile him, Og the great Commissary, they say he was as briske in discharging the new Canons, as he that made them.'

Suckling addresses Roane as 'Immense Doctor Roane': so it is possible that it was his personal appearance which suggested the name of Og.

Cf. also *Canidia. The Third Part*, p. 150 (1683):

Are you a Smock-Sinner, or so,

Commute soundly, and you shall be let go.

Fee *Ogg* the great *Commissary* before and behind,

Then sin on, you know my mind.

39 *1647, 1651, 1653*, &c. '*It* would', which can hardly be right.

44 'sob' *1647, 1651: 1653* clearly '*fob*': 'Sob' 1677. Cf. *Comedy of Errors* (iv. iii. 22) 'gives a sob'. 'Sob' is literally 'an act on the part of a horse of recovering its wind after exertion'—hence 'respite' (*N.E.D.*).

51 Porph'ry Chair] The Pope's throne, the myths of which, as well as of Pope Joan herself, are vulgate. 'Nephew' carries out the allusion: Popes' sons being called so

Better to preserve the peace.

59 thy] this *1651, 1653*.

62 The merit of the style for burlesque use could hardly be better brought out.

To the Hectors, upon the unfortunate death of H. Compton.

You Hectors! tame professors of the sword,

Who in the chair state duels, whose black word

Bewitches courage, and like Devils too,

Leaves the bewitch'd when 't comes to fight and do.

Who on your errand our best spirits send,

Not to kill swine or cows, but man and friend;

Who are a whole court-martial in your drink,

And dispute honour, when you cannot think,

Not orderly, but prate out valour as

10You grow inspired by th' oracle of the glass;

Then, like our zeal-drunk presbyters, cry down

All law of Kings and God, but what's their own.

Then y' have the gift of fighting, can discern

Spirits, who 's fit to act, and who to learn,

Who shall be baffled next, who must be beat,

Who killed—that you may drink, and swear, and eat.

Whilst you applaud those murders which you teach

And live upon the wounds your riots preach.

Mere booty-souls! Who bid us fight a prize

20To feast the laughter of our enemies,

Who shout and clap at wounds, count it pure gain,

Mere Providence to hear a Compton 's slain.

A name they dearly hate, and justly; should

They love 't 'twere worse, their love would taint the blood.

Blood always true, true as their swords and cause,

And never vainly lost, till your wild laws

Scandalled their actions in this person, who

Truly durst more than you dare think to do.

A man made up of graces—every move

30Had entertainment in it, and drew love

From all but him who killed him, who seeks a grave

And fears a death more shameful than he gave.

Now you dread Hectors! you whom tyrant drink

Drags thrice about the town, what do you think?

(If you be sober) Is it valour, say,

To overcome, and then to run away?

Fie! Fie! your lusts and duels both are one;

Both are repented of as soon as done.

To the Hectors (*1653*) is struck out in *1677* and Mr. Berdan does not give it. I asterisk it in text; but as it might be Cleveland's (though I do not think it is)

I do not exclude it. The Comptons were a good Royalist family in those days. This Henry (not the Bishop) was killed in 1652 in a duel by George Brydges, Lord Chandos, who died three years later (see Professor Firth's *House of Lords during the Civil War*, p. 223). The fame of the Hectors as predecessors of the Mohocks and possible objects of Milton's objurgation 'flown with insolence and wine', &c., is sufficient. But they seem to have been more methodical maniacs and ruffians than their successors, and even to have had something of the superior quality of Sir Lucius O'Trigger and Captain McTurk about them, as professors and painful preachers of the necessity and etiquette of the duel.

2 state duels] Arrange them like the said Captain McTurk in *St. Ronan's Well*?
word] *1653* (wrongly for rhyme, though not necessarily for concord) 'words'.

19 booty-souls] Apparently 'souls interested in nothing but booty'. The piece would seem to have been addressed to Hectors in the actual Cavalier camp, or at least party. The 'enemies' are of course the Roundheads, and it will soon be noticed that there is no apodosis or consequence to all these 'who's', &c. It is literally an 'Address' and no more.

25 their] = 'the Comptons'—nothing to do with 'their' and 'they' in the preceding lines.

31 Does not run very smoothly: the second 'him' may be a foist.

Square-Cap.

Come hither, Apollo's bouncing girl,

And in a whole Hippocrene of sherry

Let 's drink a round till our brains do whirl,

Tuning our pipes to make ourselves merry.

A Cambridge lass, Venus-like, born of the froth

Of an old half-filled jug of barley-broth,

She, she is my mistress, her suitors are many,

But she'll have a Square-cap if e'er she have any.

And first, for the plush-sake, the Monmouth-cap comes,

10Shaking his head like an empty bottle;

With his new-fangled oath by Jupiter's thumbs,

That to her health he'll begin a pottle.

He tells her that, after the death of his grannam,

He shall have God knows what per annum.

But still she replied, 'Good Sir, la-bee;

If ever I have a man, Square-cap for me!'

Then Calot Leather-cap strongly pleads,

And fain would derive the pedigree of fashion.

The antipodes wear their shoes on their heads,

20And why may not we in their imitation?

Oh, how this football noddle would please,

If it were but well tossed on S. Thomas his leas!

But still she replied, 'Good sir, la-bee;

If ever I have a man, Square-cap for me!'

Next comes the Puritan in a wrought-cap,

With a long-waisted conscience towards a sister.

And, making a chapel of ease of her lap,

First he said grace and then he kissed her.

'Beloved,' quoth he, 'thou art my text.'

30Then falls he to use and application next;

But then she replied, 'Your text, sir, I'll be;

For then I'm sure you'll ne'er handle me.'

But see where Satin-cap scouts about,

And fain would this wench in his fellowship marry.

He told her how such a man was not put out

Because his wedding he closely did carry.

He'll purchase induction by simony,

And offers her money her incumbent to be;

But still she replied, 'Good sir, la-bee;

40If ever I have a man, Square-cap for me!'

The lawyer's a sophister by his round-cap,

Nor in their fallacies are they divided,

The one milks the pocket, the other the tap;

And yet this wench he fain would have brided.

'Come, leave these thread-bare scholars,' quoth he,

'And give me livery and seisin of thee.'

'But peace, John-a-Nokes, and leave your oration,

For I never will be your impropriation;

I pray you therefore, good sir, la-bee;

50For if ever I have a man, Square-cap for me!'

Square-Cap (*1647*) is one of the pleasantest of all Cleveland's poems. Its prosodic puzzle and profit have been indicated in the Introduction, and it might sometimes run more easily. But the thorough good-fellowship and *esprit de corps* carry it off more than sufficiently. It would be pleasant to think that Mr. Samuel Pepys sang it on the famous occasion when he was 'scandalously over-served with drink' as an undergraduate. It had been printed only three years when he went up, though no doubt written earlier.

2 Cleveland has got the fount right here.

7 she is] she's *1653*.

9 Monmouth-cap] A soldier.

13, 14 A most singular blunder in *1677* (and the editions that follow it) shows that Cleveland's 'Vindicators' were by no means always attentive to his sense. It reads '*her* grannam' and '*She* shall have'—the exact effect of which, as an inducement to marry him, one would like to hear.

15 la-bee] = 'let-a-be', 'let me alone'.

17 One or two editions (but not very good ones) '*Thin* Calot'. Calot of course = 'calotte', the lawyer's cap or coif.

18 This is a signal instance of the way in which these early anapaestic lines break down into heroics. *1677* and others read '*his* pedigree'—not so well.

22 S. Thomas his leas] A decree of Oct. 29, 1632, ordains that scholars and students of Corpus and Pembroke shall play football only 'upon St. Thomas Layes', the site of Downing College later. This decree and the 'S.' of *1651*, *1653*, would seem to show that *1677* is wrong in expanding to 'Sir',

though two Cambridge editors ought to have known the right name. It was also called 'Swinecroft'. (Information obtained from the late Mr. J. W. Clark's *Memories and Customs*, Cambridge, 1909, through the kindness of Mr. A. J. Bartholomew.)

33 Satin-cap] Clerical: cf. Strode's poem on *The Caps* (*Works*, ed. Dobell, p. 106):

The Sattin and the Velvet hive

Unto a Bishopric doth drive.

36 closely ... carry] = 'disguise', 'conceal'.

Upon Phillis walking in a morning before sun-rising.

The sluggish morn as yet undressed,

My Phillis brake from out her East,

As if she'd made a match to run

With Venus, usher to the sun.

The trees, like yeomen of her guard,

Serving more for pomp than ward,

Ranked on each side, with loyal duty

Weave branches to enclose her beauty.

The plants, whose luxury was lopped,

10Or age with crutches underpropped,

Whose wooden carcasses are grown

To be but coffins of their own,

Revive, and at her general dole

Each receives his ancient soul.

The winged choristers began

To chirp their mattins, and the fan

Of whistling winds like organs played,

Until their voluntaries made

The wakened Earth in odours rise

20To be her morning sacrifice.

The flowers, called out of their beds,

Start and raise up their drowsy heads;

And he that for their colour seeks

May find it vaulting in her cheeks,

Where roses mix—no civil war

Between her York and Lancaster.

The marigold (whose courtier's face

Echoes the sun and doth unlace

Her at his rise—at his full stop

30Packs and shuts up her gaudy shop)

Mistakes her cue and doth display:

Thus Phillis antedates the day.

These miracles had cramped the sun,

Who, thinking that his kingdom 's won,

Powders with light his frizzled locks

To see what saint his lustre mocks.

The trembling leaves through which he played,

Dappling the walk with light and shade

Like lattice-windows, give the spy

40Room but to peep with half an eye;

Lest her full orb his sight should dim

And bid us all good-night in him,

Till she should spend a gentle ray

To force us a new-fashioned day.

But what religious palsy 's this

Which makes the boughs divest their bliss,

And, that they might her footsteps straw,

Drop their leaves with shivering awe?

Phillis perceived and (lest her stay

50Should wed October unto May,

And, as her beauty caused a Spring,

Devotion might an Autumn bring)

Withdrew her beams, yet made no night,

But left the sun her curate-light.

Upon Phillis, &c. (1647.) This is perhaps the prettiest, as *The Senses' Festival* is the most vigorous and *Fuscara* the most laboured, of Cleveland's Clevelandisms.

6 *1677* &c. insert 'her' between 'serving' and 'more'—doubtless on the principle, noticed before, of patching lines to supposed 'regularity'.

7 'Ranked' *1647, 1677*: 'Banked' *1651, 1653*. As it happens either will do; and at the same time either, if original, is likely to have been mistaken for the other.

8 'Weave' *1647*: 'Wave' *1651, 1653*: 'Weav'd' *1677* (the printer unconsciously assimilating it to the 'Ranked' of l. 8). The same remark applies as to the preceding line.

11 are] were *1677, 1687*.

18 *1654* 'Un*to*'.

19 *1677* &c. 'weaken'd': *putide*.

20 A meeting-point of many pious poems.

24 *1677* 'vaulting *to*'—hardly an improvement.

26 Dryden may have had Cleveland in mind (as he pretty often, and most naturally had, seeing that the poems must have 'spent their youth with him') when he wrote some of the latest and most beautiful of his own lines to the Duchess of Ormond (Lady Mary Somerset):

O daughter of the Rose whose cheeks unite

The differing titles of the Red and White.

1677 '*Divides* her York and Lancaster'—pretty palpable emendation to supply the apparent lack of a verb.

27-30 It has been suggested to me that the sense wants mechanical aid to clear it up; and I have therefore made a visible parenthesis of 'whose ... shop', following *1677*.

34 thinking] fearing *1677*.

36 *1653* &c. 'saints'—a misprint, as *1647*, *1651* have the singular.

38 Here, for once, Cleveland achieves the really poetical conceit.

42 *1647*, *1651*, *1653*, &c. 'bids'—again a mere misprint.

43 *1647*, *1651*, *1653* 'would'.

47 straw] For 'strew', as in the A. V.

49 *1649*, *1651*, *1653*, 'perceives' (an unconscious echo of 'leaves' in l. 48).

Upon a Miser that made a great feast, and the next day died for grief.

Nor 'scapes he so; our dinner was so good

My liquorish Muse cannot but chew the cud,

And what delight she took in th' invitation

Strives to taste o'er again in this relation.

After a tedious grace in Hopkins' rhyme,

Not for devotion but to take up time,

Marched the trained-band of dishes, ushered there

To show their postures and then as they were.

For he invites no teeth; perchance the eye

10He will afford the lover's gluttony.

Thus is our feast a muster, not a fight,

Our weapons not for service, but for sight.

But are we tantalized? Is all this meat

Cooked by a limner for to view, not eat?

Th' astrologers keep such houses when they sup

On joints of Taurus or their heavenly Tup.

Whatever feasts be made are summed up here,

His table vies not standing with his cheer.

His churchings, christenings, in this meal are all,

20And not transcribed but in th' original.

Christmas is no feast movable; for lo,

The self-same dinner was ten years ago!

'Twill be immortal if it longer stay,

The gods will eat it for ambrosia.

But stay a while; unless my whinyard fail

Or is enchanted, I'll cut off th' entail.

Saint George for England then! have at the mutton

When the first cut calls me bloodthirsty glutton.

Stout Ajax, with his anger-coddled brain,

30Killing a sheep thought Agamemnon slain;

The fiction's now proved true; wounding his roast

I lamentably butcher up mine host.

Such sympathy is with his meat, my weapon

Makes him an eunuch when it carves his capon.

Cut a goose leg and the poor soul for moan

Turns cripple too, and after stands on one.

Have you not heard the abominable sport

A Lancaster grand-jury will report?

The soldier with his Morglay watched the mill;

40The cats they came to feast, when lusty Will

Whips off great puss's leg which (by some charm)

Proves the next day such an old woman's arm.

'Tis so with him whose carcass never 'scapes,

But still we slash him in a thousand shapes.

Our serving-men (like spaniels) range to spring

The fowl which he had clucked under his wing.

Should he on widgeon or on woodcock feed

It were, Thyestes like, on his own breed.

To pork he pleads a superstition due,

50But we subscribe neither to Scot nor Jew.

[No liquor stirs; call for a cup of wine.

'Tis blood we drink; we pledge thee, Catiline.]

Sauces we should have none, had he his wish.

The oranges i' th' margent of the dish

He with such huckster's care tells o'er and o'er,

The Hesperian dragon never watched them more.

But being eaten now into despair

(Having nought else to do) he falls to prayer.

'As thou didst once put on the form of bull

60And turned thine Io to a lovely mull,

Defend my rump, great Jove, grant this poor beef

May live to comfort me in all this grief.'

But no Amen was said: see, see it comes!

Draw, boys, let trumpets sound, and strike up drums.

See how his blood doth with the gravy swim,

And every trencher hath a limb of him.

The venison's now in view, our hounds spend deeper.

Strange deer, which in the pasty hath a keeper

Stricter than in the park, making his guest,

70(As he had stoln't alive) to steal it drest!

The scent was hot, and we, pursuing faster

Than Ovid's pack of dogs e'er chased their master,

A double prey at once may seize upon,

Acteon, and his case of venison.

Thus was he torn alive; to vex him worse

Death serves him up now as a second course.

Should we, like Thracians, our dead bodies eat,

He would have lived only to save his meat.

[Lastly; we did devour that corpse of his

80Throughout all Ovid's Metamorphoses.]

Upon a Miser, &c. (1647.) This juxtaposition of the serious-sentimental-fanciful with the burlesque-satiric may not please some readers. But the older editions which give it seem to me better to represent the ideas of the time than the later siftings and reclassifications of the age of prose and sense. And this is one reason why I follow the order of *1653* rather than that of *1677.*

2 'Cud' is spelt in *1647* here and elsewhere in Cleveland 'cood'.

3 In some copies '*imi*tation', of course wrongly.

4 taste] cast *1653.*

5 Cleveland gibed at Sternhold and Hopkins in prose (*The Character of a London Diurnall*) as well as verse. *1647, 1651* misprint 'rhythm'.

11 The text, from *1677*, is a clear improvement at first sight on the earlier '*This* is *a* feast': though I would not be too sure that Cleveland did not write it thus.

16 *1677* '*the* heavenly'.

17 *1677* 'he made'.

18 Meaning, apparently, that, as was the custom, the table between these sham feast-days was moved off its trestles and cleared away; but the feast was a 'standing' one, kept to reappear.

20 in th'] i' th' *1647, 1651.*

26 is] it *1647, 1651.*

28 *1677* 'Wher*e*'.

29 Stout] What *1651, 1653.*

31 *1677* '*the* roast'.

34 carves] One edition, of no value (*1665*), '*serves*'.

35 soul] fool *1677*.

38 Lancaster, because of the Lancashire witches. See Heywood, *Lancashire Witches*, Act V.

39 Morglay] The sword of Bevis.

43 'Tis] It's *1677*.

44 'him' *1647*: 'them' *1651*, *1653*.

46 These lines appear with some variants and are not clear in any text: 'which he had cluck'd under his wing' *1677*, for the earlier 'when he hath clock't under her wing' *1647*, *1651*, *1653*. Professor Case suggests 'cloakt' (i.e. 'hidden') for 'clock't'.

50 Mr. Berdan says, '*Englishmen supposed* that the Scotch did not eat pork'. But, until quite recently, it was a fact; and even now there is much less eaten north than south of the Tweed. As for Cleveland's day, James the First's aversion to it was well known and had been celebrated by Ben Jonson. In *1647*, *1651*, *1653* 'But not a mouth is muzzled by the Jew'.

51-2 Not in earlier editions. Added in *1677*.

54 *1677* 'margin of *his* dish'.

55 *1647*, *1651*, *1653*, &c. omit 'care' and read 'tells them'.

59 *1677* 'Thou that didst'.

60 'turned thine' *1677*, *1687*: 'turn'st thy' *1647*, *1651*, *1653*, &c. mull] Dialectic for 'cow', especially as a call-name. It seems to be connected with the sense of the word for 'lips', especially large loose ones.

61 *1677*

allay my grief,

O spare me this, this monumental beef.

66 'hath' *1677*, *1687*: 'has' *1651*, *1653* and its group.

73 'may' *1651*, *1653*, &c.: 'we' *1677*.

79, 80 Added in *1677* &c., with very doubtful advantage.

A Young Man to an Old Woman courting him.

Peace, Beldam Eve, surcease thy suit;

There 's no temptation in such fruit;

No rotten medlars, whilst there be
Whole orchards in virginity.
Thy stock is too much out of date
For tender plants t' inoculate.
A match with thee thy bridegroom fears
Would be thought interest in his years,
Which, when compared to thine, become
10Odd money to thy grandam sum.
Can wedlock know so great a curse
As putting husbands out to nurse?
How Pond and Rivers would mistake
And cry new almanacs for our sake.
Time sure hath wheeled about his year,
December meeting Janiveer.
The Egyptian serpent figures Time,
And stripped, returns unto his prime.
If my affection thou wouldst win,
20First cast thy hieroglyphic skin.
My modern lips know not, alack!
The old religion of thy smack.
I count that primitive embrace
As out of fashion as thy face.
And yet, so long 'tis since thy fall,
Thy fornication 's classical.
Our sports will differ; thou mayst play
Lero, and I Alphonso way.

I'm no translator, have no vein
30To turn a woman young again,

Unless you'll grant the tailor's due,

To see the fore-bodies be new.

I love to wear clothes that are flush,

Not prefacing old rags with plush,

Like aldermen, or under-shrieves

With canvass backs and velvet sleeves:

And just such discord there would be

Betwixt thy skeleton and me.

Go study salve and treacle, ply

40Your tenant's leg or his sore eye.

Thus matrons purchase credit, thank

Six pennyworth of mountebank;

Or chew thy cud on some delight

That thou didst taste in 'eighty-eight;

Or be but bed-rid once, and then

Thou'lt dream thy youthful sins again.

But if thou needs wilt be my spouse,

First hearken and attend my vows.

When Aetna's fires shall undergo

50*The penance of the Alps in snow;*

When Sol at one blast of his horn

Posts from the Crab to Capricorn;

When th' heavens shuffle all in one

The Torrid with the Frozen Zone;

When all these contradictions meet,

Then, Sibyl, thou and I will greet.

For all these similes do hold

In my young heat and thy dull cold.

Then, if a fever be so good

60A pimp as to inflame thy blood,

Hymen shall twist thee and thy page,

The distinct tropics of man's age.

Well, Madam Time, be ever bald.

I'll not thy periwig be called.

I'll never be 'stead of a lover,

An aged chronicle's new cover.

A Young Man, &c. (1647.)

8 *1677*, &c. have 'incest', which is rather tempting, but considering the 'odd money' which follows, not, I think, absolutely certain.

13 Edward Pond died in 1629; but the almanac, published by him first in 1601, lasted till 1709. Rivers was probably Peregrine Rivers, 'Student in Mathematics', writer of one of the numerous almanacs of the period. There are in the Bodleian copies of his almanacs for 1629, 1630, 1638, all printed at Cambridge. (Information supplied to me from Oxford.)

15 Some copies 'this'.

22 Rather a good line.

27 *1651, 1653*, &c. 'mayst': *1647, 1677*, &c. 'must'.

35 *1647* 'Monster Shrieves', *1653* 'Monster-Sheriffs', which can hardly be right.

44 'eighty-eight] The Armada year, often taken as a standard of remoteness not too remote. This, which is the later reading, of 1677 *sqq.*, seems better than '*Thou takest in thy* Eighty Eight' (*1647, 1651, 1653*, &c.).

49-62 The italics of *1653*, though discarded in *1677*, seem worth keeping, because of the solemn call of attention to the particulars of the 'Vow'; they extend in the *1653* text to l. 60. But *1647* and *1651*, prefix inverted commas to ll. 49-56, which seems a more effective ending to the 'Vow'.

53 Some inferior editions put in 'shall'. *1647, 1651, 1653*, and *1677* exclude it.

61 twist] In the sense of 'twine', 'unite'. 'page' = 'boy'.

62 *1647, 1651* 'Tropicks': *1653* 'Tropick'; but both Cancer and Capricorn are wanted.

To Mrs. K. T.

(Who asked him why he was dumb.)

Stay, should I answer, Lady, then

In vain would be your question:

Should I be dumb, why then again

Your asking me would be in vain.

Silence nor speech, on neither hand,

Can satisfy this strange demand.

Yet, since your will throws me upon

This wished contradiction,

I'll tell you how I did become

10So strangely, as you hear me, dumb.

Ask but the chap-fallen Puritan;

'Tis zeal that tongue-ties that good man.

(For heat of conscience all men hold

Is th' only way to catch their cold.)

How should Love's zealot then forbear

To be your silenced minister?

Nay, your Religion which doth grant

A worship due to you, my Saint,

Yet counts it that devotion wrong

20That does it in the Vulgar Tongue.

My ruder words would give offence

To such an hallowed excellence,

As th' English dialect would vary

The goodness of an Ave Mary.

How can I speak that twice am checked

By this and that religious sect?

Still dumb, and in your face I spy
Still cause and still divinity.
As soon as blest with your salute,
30My manners taught me to be mute.
For, lest they cancel all the bliss
You signed with so divine a kiss,
The lips you seal must needs consent
Unto the tongue's imprisonment.
My tongue in hold, my voice doth rise
With a strange E-la to my eyes,
Where it gets bail, and in that sense
Begins a new-found eloquence.

Oh listen with attentive sight
40To what my pratling eyes indite!
Or, lady, since 'tis in your choice
To give or to suspend my voice,
With the same key set ope the door
Wherewith you locked it fast before.
Kiss once again, and when you thus
Have doubly been miraculous,
My Muse shall write with handmaid's duty
The Golden Legend of your beauty.
He whom his dumbness now confines
50But means to speak the rest by signs.
I. C.

To Mrs. K. T., &c. (1647). To this title *1677* and its followers add
'Written *calente calamo*'. The variant on *currente* is of some interest, and the
statement may have been made to excuse the bad opening rhyme.

5 neither] either *1677*.

14 'their cold' *1651, 1653*: 'that cold' *1647, 1677*.

16 silenced] As some Puritans were before Cleveland wrote, and all, or almost all, Churchmen afterwards.

31 *1677* 'Lest I should cancel all the bliss'.

37 bail] *1653* &c. '*h*ail', which is doubtless a misprint.

40 'prating' *1677*.

47 'handmaid' *1677*.

50 *1677* '*Intends* to speak'—an obvious correction of the 'red-hot pen'. But whether Cleveland's or his vindicators' who shall say?

51 So *1647, 1651, 1653*. The couplet is meaningless without them.

A Fair Nymph scorning a Black Boy courting her.

Nymph. Stand off, and let me take the air;

Why should the smoke pursue the fair?

Boy. My face is smoke, thence may be guessed

What flames within have scorched my breast.

Nymph. The flame of love I cannot view

For the dark lantern of thy hue.

Boy. And yet this lantern keeps Love's taper

Surer than yours, that's of white paper.

Whatever midnight hath been here,

10The moonshine of your light can clear.

Nymph. My moon of an eclipse is 'fraid,

If thou shouldst interpose thy shade.

Boy. Yet one thing, Sweetheart, I will ask;

Take me for a new-fashioned mask.

Nymph. Yes, but my bargain shall be this,

I'll throw my mask off when I kiss.

Boy. Our curled embraces shall delight

To checker limbs with black and white.

Nymph. Thy ink, my paper, make me guess

20Our nuptial bed will prove a press,

And in our sports, if any came,

They'll read a wanton epigram.

Boy. Why should my black thy love impair?

Let the dark shop commend the ware;

Or, if thy love from black forbears,

I'll strive to wash it off with tears.

Nymph. Spare fruitless tears, since thou must needs

Still wear about thee mourning weeds.

Tears can no more affection win

30Than wash thy Ethiopian skin.

A Fair Nymph, &c. (1647.)

2 An odd fancy included by Browne among the *Vulgar Errors.*

5 'Thy flaming love' *1677* &c.

10 'face will clear' *1677* &c.

14 *1677* 'Take me for a new-fashioned mask': *1647, 1651* 'Buy me for a new false mask', varied in *1653* 'Buy for me'—apparently a misprint, as the boy does not seem to wish to disguise himself.

15 Yes] Done *1677.*

20 *1647, 1651, 1653*, 'make a press', ill repeated from above.

24 'the ware' *1677*: *1647, 1651, 1653*, not so well, '*thy* ware'.

28 *1677* changed 'thee' to 'thy'.

30 Some inferior copies '*the* Ethiopian'.

A Dialogue between two Zealots upon the &c. in the Oath.

Sir Roger, from a zealous piece of frieze

Raised to a vicar of the children's threes;

Whose yearly audit may by strict account

To twenty nobles and his vails amount;

Fed on the common of the female charity

Until the Scots can bring about their parity;

So shotten that his soul, like to himself,

Walks but in cuerpo; this same clergy-elf,

Encountering with a brother of the cloth,

10 Fell presently to cudgels with the Oath.

The quarrel was a strange misshapen monster,

&c., (God bless us) which they conster

The brand upon the buttock of the Beast,

The Dragon's tail tied on a knot, a nest

Of young Apocryphas, the fashion

Of a new mental Reservation.

While Roger thus divides the text, the other

Winks and expounds, saying, 'My pious brother,

Hearken with reverence, for the point is nice.

20 I never read on 't, but I fasted twice,

And so by revelation know it better

Than all the learn'd idolaters o'th' letter.'

With that he swelled, and fell upon the theme

Like great Goliah with his weaver's beam.

'I say to thee, &c., thou li'st!

Thou art the curléd lock of Antichrist;

Rubbish of Babel; for who will not say

Tongues were confounded in &c.?

Who swears &c., swears more oaths at once

30 Than Cerberus out of his triple sconce.

Who views it well, with the same eye beholds

The old half Serpent in his numerous folds.
Accurst &c. thou, for now I scent
What lately the prodigious oysters meant!
Oh Booker! Booker! How camest thou to lack
This sign in thy prophetic almanac?
It 's the dark vault wherein th' infernal plot
Of powder 'gainst the State was first begot.
Peruse the Oath and you shall soon descry it
40By all the Father Garnets that stand by it;

'Gainst whom the Church, (whereof I am a member,)
Shall keep another Fifth Day of November.
Yet here's not all; I cannot half untruss
&c.—it's so abhominous!
The Trojan nag was not so fully lined;
Unrip &c., and you shall find
Og the great commissary, and (which is worse)
The apparitor upon his skew-bald horse.
Then finally, my babe of grace, forbear,
50&c. will be too far to swear,
For 'tis (to speak in a familiar style)
A Yorkshire wee bit longer than a mile.'
Here Roger was inspired, and by God's diggers
He'll swear in words at large but not in figures.
Now by this drink, which he takes off, as loath
To leave &c. in his liquid oath.
His brother pledged him, and that bloody wine
He swears shall seal the Synod's Catiline.
So they drunk on, not offering to part

60'Till they had quite sworn out th' eleventh quart,

While all that saw and heard them jointly pray

They and their tribe were all &c.

A Dialogue, &c. (1647.) This occurs also in the *Rump* (1662, reprinted London, N. D.). A MS. copy is found in Rawlinson MS. Poet. 26 of the Bodleian, at fol. 94, with the title '*A Dialogue between 2. Zelots concerning &c. in the new Oath.*' 'The Oath' is the famous one formulated in 1640 by Convocation. Fuller, who was proctor for the diocese of Bristol (and who would have been fined heavily for his part, 'moderate' as he was, if the Puritan Ultras of the Commons could have had their way), has left much about it. This oath, to be taken by all the clergy, imported approval of the doctrine, discipline, and government of the Church, and disclaimed, twice over, 'Popish' doctrine and the usurpations of the see of Rome. Unluckily the government of the Church was defined as 'by archbishops, bishops, deans, and archdeacons, *&c.*', which last was, in the absence of any other handle, seized by the Puritan party as possibly implying all sorts of horrors. Cleveland banters them well enough, but hardly with the force and directness which he was to show later. The Royalists were then under the fatal error of underrating the strength of their opponents, and the gullibility of the people of England.

2 'vicar', *1647, 1651, 1653, MS.:* 'vicarage' *1677.* 'children' *1651, 1653*: I have been waiting a long time to know what 'children's threes' means. It occurs elsewhere, but to my thinking as an obvious reminiscence of Cleveland.

7 shotten] 'like a herring that has spawned', 'thin'.

8 in cuerpo] 'in body-clothes',
'cloakless'. *1647, 1651, 1653* 'Querpo': *MS.* 'Quirpo', with 'cuerpo' written above it.

12 *1677* extends '&c.' to 'et caetera'. This is a mistake, as the actual ampersand occurred in the oath and gave some slight assistance to the cavillers. Cleveland's expressions—'tail tied on a knot' (l. 14), 'curled lock' (l. 26), 'numerous folds' (l. 32)—lose their point without the ampersand. *1677* also has '*may* conster', which though possible enough, seems to me neither necessary nor even much of an improvement.

17 *1677*, less euphoniously, 'Whil*st*'.

22 A reading of the *Rump* version, 'Than all the Idolaters of the letter', though almost certainly a mere mistaken correction, has some interest.

23 fell] sett *MS.*

24 Goliah] This form occurs in all the texts.

25 In this and other lines that follow much of the quaintness is lost by 'extending' the '&c.' of the older editions.

28 were] are *1677, MS.*

32 All editions, I think, before *1677* (which substitutes 'false') have 'half'. 'False' is very feeble; 'half' refers picturesquely to the delineation of the Serpent tempting Eve with a human head, being coiled below like the curves of the *&c.* 'False' *MS.*

33 *1677, MS.* 'Accurst Et Caetera! now, now I scent'.

34 I do not know whether these very Livyish oysters have been traced. *1677* and *MS.* omit 'lately' and read 'prodigious bloody oysters'.

35 John Booker (1603-1677), Manchester man, haberdasher, writing-master, and astrologer, gained a great deal of credit by interpreting an eclipse after the usual fashion as portending disaster to kings and princes, the great Gustavus Adolphus and the unfortunate Frederick, 'Winter'-King of Bohemia, being complaisant enough to die in accordance.

36 This sign] *1677, MS.* 'This *fiend*—more energetically.

37 "Tis the dark vault where the' *MS.*

40 The sting of 'the *Father Garnets* that *stand by* it' lies in the words immediately preceding the obnoxious '&c.'—'archbishops, bishops, &c.'— whom the Puritan divine stigmatizes as Jesuits and traitors to Church and State. As has been stated, the oath distinctly, in set terms and twice over, abjured Rome and all things Roman; but the Puritans of those days, like their descendants, paid no attention to trifles of this kind. For 'stand' *MS.* reads 'stood'.

43 Yet] Nay *MS.*

44 *1647, 1651* 'abominous'; *1653* 'abhominous'. The 'h' must be kept in 'ab*h*ominous', though not unusual for 'ab*om*-', because it helps to explain, and perhaps to justify, *1677* and *MS.* in reading 'ab*d*ominous'. This, though something suggestive of a famous Oxford story, derives some colour from 'untruss' and may be right, especially as I do not know another example of 'abominous' for 'abominable'.

47 Og] *v. sup.*, p. 31. *MS.* has marginal note 'Roan'.

48 'Skew-bald' is not = 'piebald', though most horses commonly called piebald are skewbalds. 'Pie[magpie]bald' is *black* and white; skewbald *brown* (or some other colour not black) and white. The Church-courts were much more unpopular, in these as in mediaeval times, than the

Church, and High Commissioners and commissaries and apparitors were alleged to lurk under the guileful and dreadful '&c.'

49 'babes' *1677*.

52 Blount's *Glossographia* (1656), a useful book, shows the ignorance of Northern English then prevailing by supposing 'we*a*-bit' (the form found in Cleveland originally) to be '*way*-bit'. It is, of course, 'little bit', the Scotch 'mile and a bittock'.

53 Here] Then *1647, 1651, 1653*. God's diggers] = nails or fingers. Commoner in the corruption 'Ods niggers'.

54 'in words at large' *1647* ('at length', one issue of *1647*): 'at words in large' *1651, 1653*: 'in words at length, and not in figures' *MS.*

58 Edd. 'Cat*a*line', as usual, but *1677* 'Catiline'. 'He swears he'll be the Synod's' *MS.*

59 'Thus they drink on, not offering to depart' *MS.*

60 *1677* omits 'quite'—no doubt for the old syllabic reason. *MS.* substitutes 'fully'.

62 Perhaps nowhere is the comic surprise of the symbol more wanted than here, and more of a loss when that symbol is extended.

Smectymnuus, or the Club-Divines.

Smectymnuus! The goblin makes me start!

I' th' name of Rabbi Abraham, what art?

Syriac? or Arabic? or Welsh? what skill't?

Ap all the bricklayers that Babel built,

Some conjurer translate and let me know it;

Till then 'tis fit for a West Saxon poet.

But do the brotherhood then play their prizes

Like mummers in religion with disguises,

Out-brave us with a name in rank and file?

10 A name, which, if 'twere trained, would spread a mile!

The saints' monopoly, the zealous cluster

Which like a porcupine presents a muster
And shoots his quills at bishops and their sees,
A devout litter of young Maccabees!
Thus Jack-of-all-trades hath devoutly shown
The Twelve Apostles on a cherry-stone;
Thus faction 's *à la mode* in treason's fashion,
Now we have heresy by complication.
Like to Don Quixote's rosary of slaves
20Strung on a chain; a murnival of knaves
Packed in a trick, like gipsies when they ride,
Or like colleagues which sit all of a side.
So the vain satyrists stand all a row
As hollow teeth upon a lute-string show.
Th' Italian monster pregnant with his brother,
Nature's diæresis, half one another,
He, with his little sides-man Lazarus,
Must both give way unto Smectymnuus.
Next Sturbridge Fair is Smec's; for, lo! his side
30Into a five-fold lazar's multiplied.

Under each arm there 's tucked a double gizzard;
Five faces lurk under one single vizard.
The Whore of Babylon left these brats behind,
Heirs of confusion by gavelkind.
I think Pythagoras' soul is rambled hither
With all the change of raiment on together.
Smec is her general wardrobe; she'll not dare
To think of him as of a thoroughfare.
He stops the gossiping dame; alone he is

40The purlieu of a metempsychosis;

Like a Scotch mark, where the more modest sense

Checks the loud phrase, and shrinks to thirteen pence:

Like to an ignis fatuus whose flame,

Though sometimes tripartite, joins in the same;

Like to nine tailors, who, if rightly spelled,

Into one man are monosyllabled.

Short-handed zeal in one hath cramped many

Like to the Decalogue in a single penny.

See, see how close the curs hunt under sheet

50As if they spent in quire and scanned their feet.

One cure and five incumbents leap a truss;

The title sure must be litigious.

The Sadducees would raise a question

Who must be Smec at th' Resurrection.

Who cooped them up together were to blame.

Had they but wire-drawn and spun out their name,

'Twould make another Prentices' Petition

Against the bishops and their superstition.

Robson and French (that count from five to five,

60As far as nature fingers did contrive—

She saw they would be 'sessors, that 's the cause

She cleft their hoof into so many claws)

May tire their carrot-bunch, yet ne'er agree

To rate Smectymnuus for poll-money.

Caligula—whose pride was mankind's bail,

As who disdained to murder by retail,

Wishing the world had but one general neck,—

His glutton blade might have found game in Smec.

No echo can improve the author more

70Whose lungs pay use on use to half a score.

No felon is more lettered, though the brand

Both superscribes his shoulder and his hand.

Some Welshman was his godfather, for he

Wears in his name his genealogy.

The banns are asked, would but the times give way,

Betwixt Smectymnuus and Et Caetera.

The guests, invited by a friendly summons,

Should be the Convocation and the Commons.

The priest to tie the foxes' tails together

80Mosely, or Sancta Clara, choose you whether.

See what an offspring every one expects,

What strange pluralities of men and sects!

One says he'll get a vestry, but another

Is for a synod; Bet upon the mother.

Faith, cry St. George! Let them go to 't and stickle

Whether a conclave or a conventicle.

Thus might religions caterwaul, and spite

Which uses to divorce, might once unite.

But their cross fortunes interdict their trade;

90The groom is rampant but the bride displayed.

My task is done, all my he goats are milked.

So many cards i' th' stock, and yet be bilked?

I could by letters now untwist the rabble,

Whip Smec from constable to constable;

But there I leave you to another dressing;

Only kneel down and take your father's blessing.

May the Queen Mother justify your fears

And stretch her patent to your leather ears!

Smectymnuus, &c. (1647.) Whether this lively skit on the five 'reverend men whose friend' Milton was (as far as he could be proud of being anything but himself) proud of being was in Milton's own mind when he wrote his *Apology* for the acrostically named treatise, one cannot say. It is a lively 'mime' enough, and he seems to throw back that word with some special meaning. Cleveland's poem may have appeared in the summer of 1641. Naturally, it is in the *Rump* poems.

3 All editions 'skilt'. It apparently must be as in text: 'skill't' for 'skill'st' = 'dost thou [or 'does it'] signify?'

4 *1677*, &c. 'Ape', but 'Ap' in the Welsh sense (Welsh having just been mentioned) does well enough. It would go, not too roughly for Cleveland's syntax, with 'conjurer'. Let some wizard, descended from all these, *and therefore knowing all tongues*, translate.

6 This is rather interesting. Does it refer to Wessex or Devonshire dialect of the day, or to old West Saxon? Junius did not edit Cædmon till fourteen years later, but there was study of Anglo-Saxon from Parker's time at Cambridge.

7 the brotherhood] 'Brother' and 'sister' being constant sneers at the Puritan.

play their prizes] = 'fight'.

10 Perhaps another sneer at the 'train-bands' of the City.

15 'distinctly' *1677*.

16 '*in* a' *1677*.

18 I suppose *à la mode*, which is in *1677*, is right; but the '*all*-a-mode' of *1647, 1651, 1653* is tempting.

20 'murnival' or 'mournival'. Four aces, kings, &c., especially at gleek.

22 *1677*, &c. 'Or like *the College*'.

24 'hallow' *1653*.

25 I knew not this monster, and suspected that he would not be a delicate monster to know. But Mr. Thorn-Drury has found him in the *Gentleman's Magazine*, 1777, p. 482. Lazarus Collondo, a Genoese, had a small brother growing out of his side, with one leg, two arms, &c., &c.

29 'Smec' will now be an even greater attraction at the Sturbridge fair at Cambridge. All fairs rejoiced in monsters.

36 *'The* change', as in *1647, 1651, 1653* and its group, including the *Rump* version, is not so good as 'her', which *1677* reads.

38 i.e. 'to go on to any *other* body'.

40 'Purlieu' seems to be used in the sense of 'precinct' or 'province'.

41-2 These lines are in all the seventeenth-century editions I have seen, but not in Mr. Berdan's. The Scots pound was of course only twenty English pence, and so the mark (two thirds) 'shrank' accordingly.

49 *1647, 1651, 1677* insert 'a' before 'sheet'. The metaphor is probably as old as hunting. 'Spend', as Professor Case reminds me, has had already in *The Miser*, l. 67, the sense of 'give tongue'. 'Scanned their feet' for 'kept pace' is good enough; but why the five should leap a truss, and why this should be litigious, I again frankly confess myself to have been ignorant. Mr. Simpson, however, quotes R. Fletcher in *Ex Otio Negotium*, 1656, p. 202, 'The model of the new Religion':

How many Queere-religions? clear your throat,

May a man have a penyworth? four a groat?

Or do the *Iuncto* leap at truss a fayle?

Three tenents clap while five hang on the tayle?

Cleveland seems to have tried in this piece to equal the mystery of the title of 'Smec' by his own matter, and to have succeeded very fairly.

54 *1677*, &c. '*shall* be'. 'at th'' *1647, 1677*: 'at the' *1651, 1653*.

55 cooped] cooked *1647, 1651*.

56 *1677*, &c. '*the* name'.

57 An absurd, but doubtless in the circumstances dangerous, document of the kind was actually disseminated, in which the prentices bold engaged 'to defend his Sacred Majesty against Popish innovations such as archbishops and bishops appear to be'.

63 carrot-bunch] Cant for 'fingers'.

70 'pay' *1653, 1677*: 'pays' *1647, 1651. 1677* '*and* use'.

75 'Banns' *1677*: 'Banes' in earlier texts. *1653* 'time'.

78 The Convocation which had been guilty of '&c.', and the Commons who mostly sympathized with 'Smec'.

79 foxes' tails] As at Samson's marriage (Judges xv. 4-7.)

80 Mosel[e]y, Milton's printer; and Sancta Clara, the Jesuit?

82 *1677* 'plurality'.

83 'Vestry, but' *1677*: 'Vestery' *1647, 1651, 1653*.

84 *1677* 'Bets'.

90 The heraldic terms are pretty plain, but *1677* reads 'is spade' i.e. 'spayed', as in *The Hecatomb to his Mistress*, l. 2.

94 Rhyme here really badly managed.

95 *1677* 'another's'.

97 The fear and dislike of Henrietta Maria (whom Mr. Berdan supposes to be meant) among the disaffected is only too certain: and the fate of Prynne's ears for his scandal of her is notorious. But why *at this time* she should be called a Queen Mother (it was her proper title afterwards, and she was one of the very few to whom it was actually given), and what the last line means, I know not. Nor does Professor Firth, unless Marie de Médicis (who *was* Queen Mother in France and had visited England) had, as he suggests, a share in some leather patent, and is meant here. Smec's ears are 'vellum' in *Rupertismus*, 169 (*v. inf.*, p. 67).

The Mixed Assembly.

Flea-Bitten synod, an assembly brewed

Of clerks and elders *ana*, like the rude

Chaos of Presbyt'ry, where laymen guide

With the tame woolpack clergy by their side.

Who asked the banns 'twixt these discoloured mates?

A strange grotesco this; the Church and states,

Most divine tick-tack, in a piebald crew,

To serve as table-men of divers hue!

She, that conceived an Ethiopian heir

10By picture, when the parents both were fair,

At sight of you had born a dappled son,

You checkering her imagination.

Had Jacob's flock but seen you sit, the dams

Had brought forth speckled and ring-streakéd lambs.

Like an impropriator's motley kind

Whose scarlet coat is with a cassock lined;

Like the lay-thief in a canonic weed,

Sure of his clergy ere he did the deed;

Like Royston crows, who are (as I may say)

20Friars of both the Orders, Black and Gray;

So mixed they are, one knows not whether 's thicker,

A layer of burgess, or a layer of vicar.

Have they usurped what Royal Judah had,

And now must Levi too part stakes with Gad?

The sceptre and the crosier are the crutches,

Which, if not trusted in their pious clutches,

Will fail the cripple State. And were 't not pity

But both should serve the yardwand of the City?

That Isaac might stroke his beard and sit

30Judge of εἰς Ἅιδον and *elegerit*?

Oh that they were in chalk and charcoal drawn!

The miscellany-satyr and the faun

And all th' adulteries of twisted nature

But faintly represent this riddling feature;

Whose members being not tallies, they'll not own

Their fellows at the Resurrection.

Strange scarlet doctors these! They'll pass in story

For sinners half refined in Purgatory,

Or parboiled lobsters, where there jointly rules

40The fading sables and the coming gules.

The flea that Falstaff damned thus lewdly shows

Tormented in the flames of Bardolph's nose.

Like him that wore the dialogue of cloaks

This shoulder John-a-Stiles, that John-a-Nokes;

Like Jews and Christians in a ship together

With an old neck-verse to distinguish either;

Like their intended discipline to boot,

Or whatsoe'er hath neither head nor foot;

Such may their stript-stuff-hangings seem to be,

50Sacrilege matched with codpiece simony.

Be sick and dream a little, you may then

Fancy these linsey-woolsey vestry-men.

Forbear, good Pembroke, be not over-daring.

Such company may chance to spoil thy swearing,

And thy drum-major oaths, of bulk unruly,

May dwindle to a feeble 'By my truly'!

He that the noble Percy's blood inherits,

Will he strike up a Hotspur of the spirits?

He'll fright the Obadiahs out of tune

60With his uncircumciséd Algernoon;

A name so stubborn, 'tis not to be scanned

By him in Gath with the six-fingered hand.

See, they obey the magic of my words!

Presto! they're gone, and now the House of Lords

Looks like the withered face of an old hag,

But with three teeth like to a triple gag.

A jig! a jig! and in this antic dance

Fielding and Doxie Marshall first advance.

Twisse blows the Scotch-pipes, and the loving brace

70Puts on the traces and treads cinque-a-pace.

Then Saye and Sele must his old hamstrings supple,

And he and rumpled Palmer make a couple.

Palmer 's a fruitful girl if he'll unfold her;

The midwife may find work about her shoulder.

Kimbolton, that rebellious Boanerges,

Must be content to saddle Dr. Burges.

If Burges get a clap, 'tis ne'er the worse,

But the fifth time of his compurgators.

Noll Bowles is coy; good sadness, cannot dance

80But in obedience to the ordinance.

Here Wharton wheels about till mumping Lidy,

Like the full moon, hath made his lordship giddy.

Pym and the members must their giblets levy

T' encounter Madam Smec, that single bevy.

If they two truck together, 'twill not be

A child-birth, but a gaol-delivery.

Thus every Ghibelline hath got his Guelph

But Selden,—he 's a galliard by himself;

And well may be; there 's more divines in him

90Than in all this, their Jewish Sanhedrim:

Whose canons in the forge shall then bear date

When mules their cousin-germans generate.

Thus Moses' law is violated now;

The ox and ass go yoked in the same plough.

Resign thy coach-box, Twisse; Brooke's preacher he

Would sort the beasts with more conformity.

Water and earth make but one globe; a Roundhead

Is clergy-lay, party-per-pale compounded.

The Mixed Assembly (1647.) This was the famous 'Westminster' Assembly which met in July, 1643—a hodge-podge of half a score peers, a score of commoners, and about four times as many divines as laymen. Tanner MS. 465, of the Bodleian, has a poor copy of this poem; but some transpositions and omissions suggest that it preserves an earlier draft. Lines 63-6 follow 52; 71-8, 81-2, are omitted.

1 Flea-bitten] As of a horse—the laymen appearing like specks on the body of clergy.

2 *ana*] Usually interpreted in the apothecary's sense, 'in equal quantities', written so in prescriptions and said to be from the Greek—ἀνά being thus used.

6, 7 'Church and State's, Most divine' *MS.*

19 In a fable a Royston crow (the town being on the way to Cambridge had probably a bad reputation for fleecing the guileless undergraduate) advised an innocent of his kind to drop a shellfish from a height on rocks where the Royston bird was waiting and secured the meat.

28 *1677* changes 'But' to 'That'.

29 *1677* inserts '*go*' before 'stroke'. But Cleveland probably scanned 'I-sa-ac'. The reference is to Isaac Pennington: cf. *The Rebel Scot*, l. 79.

30 The phrase is of course Homeric (*sc.* δόμους) and with its companion combines the idea of an ecclesiastical condemnation ('delivering over to Satan') and a civil execution, a writ of *elegit*.

32 faun] All old editions, I think, and Mr. Berdan, 'fawn'. But the *animal* (always now indicated by that spelling) is not of a 'twisted nature', the half-god is.

40 One of those that taught Dryden something.

41 Cleveland, like most Royalists and their master, was evidently sound on Shakespeare. A copy of *1677* in my possession has a manuscript list of references on the fly-leaf.

46 'neck-verse'] = for benefit of clergy.

49 'Stript', *1647, 1651, 1653*, is evidently 'striped', and is printed 'strip'd' in *1677*.

53 Philip Herbert, fourth Earl of Pembroke, though a patron of literature and the arts, was a man of bad character and a virulent Roundhead.

55   'thy' *1677*:   'these' *1647, 1651, 1653.*
of bulk unruly] if Vulcan rule you *MS*.

59 *1647, 1651* 'Obadiahs': *1653* and its group 'Obadiah': *1677* 'Obadiah's'.

60 Algernon Percy, tenth Earl of Northumberland—who repented too late of his rebellion and tried to prevent the consequences—seems to have joined the Roundheads out of pique (his pride was notorious) at neglect of his suggestions and interference with his powers as Lord High Admiral). By putting the fleet into the hands of the Parliament he did the King perhaps more hurt than any other single person at the beginning of the war. 'Algernoon' *1647, 1651*: later texts spoil the point of the next line by using the conventional form.

68 Fielding] Basil, the degenerate son of the first Earl of Denbigh. He actually served in the Parliamentary Army, but like Northumberland, who did not go that length, repented too late.

Doxie Marshall] The Stephen Marshall of *Smectymnuus* and the 'Geneva Bull' of *The Rebel Scot*, l. 21; exactly why 'Doxie' I do not know. Possibly 'prostitute' from his eager Presbyterianism. It is odd that Anne and Rebecca Marshall, two famous actresses of the Restoration to whom the term might be applied with some direct justification, used to be counted his daughters, though this is now denied.

69 Twisse] William (1578-1646), the Prolocutor of the Assembly.

71 Saye and Sele] William Fiennes, first Viscount (1582-1662). Of very bad reputation as a slippery customer.

72 rumpled] Mr. Berdan 'rumbled', on what authority and with what meaning I do not know. 'Rumpled', which is in *1647, 1651, 1653*, and *1677*, no doubt refers to the untidy bands, &c. of a slovenly priest. Herbert Palmer (1604-1647) was a man of good family but a bitter Puritan. He was first Fellow and then President of Queens' College, Cambridge, where Cleveland doubtless knew him. The odd description reads like that of a sort of deformed dwarf.

75 Kimbolton] Edward, Lord (1602-1671), just about to become the well-known Earl of Manchester of the Rebellion. Like Northumberland and Denbigh, he repented, but only after he had been not too politely shelved for Fairfax and Cromwell.

76 Cleveland would have been delighted had he known the fate of Cornelius Burges (1589?-1665), of whom he evidently had a pretty bad idea. Burges, a Wadham and Lincoln man, was one of the leaders of the Puritans among the London clergy, and a great favourite with the House of Commons in the Long Parliament. He wanted to suppress cathedrals; and, being a practical man and preacher at Wells during the Commonwealth, did his best by buying

the deanery and part of the estates. Wherefore he was promptly and properly ruined by the Restoration, and died in well-deserved poverty. He was vice-president of the Westminster Assembly.

79 Oliver Bowles, a Puritan divine. *1653* omits the comma after 'sadness' found in *1651*,—a neat punctuation, meaning 'in good sadness, he cannot dance'. Phrases like 'in good truth', 'in good sadnesse' were the utmost licence of speech which the Puritans permitted themselves.

81 Philip, fourth Lord Wharton (1613-1696) took the anti-Royalist side very early, but cut a very poor figure at Edgehill and abandoned active service. He did not figure under the Commonwealth, but was a zealous Whig after the Restoration, and a prominent Williamite in the last years of his long life. Who 'Lidy' (*1653*) or 'Lidie' (*1677*) was seems unknown. Professor Firth suggests a misprint for 'Sidie,' i.e. Sidrach Simpson (1600?-1655), a busy London Puritan and member of the Assembly. Another ingenious suggestion made to me is that 'mumping Lid[d]y' may be one of the queer dance-names of the period, or actually a woman, Wharton being no enemy to the sex. But I do not know that there was such a dance, and as all the other pairs are males, being members of the Assembly, it would be odd if there were an exception here. For 'Here' *1647, 1651* read 'Her'.

88 The exceptional position of Selden is well hit off here. His character and his earning were just able to neutralize, though not to overcome, the curse of Laodicea.

95 'Brooke' is Robert Brooke, second Lord Brooke, cousin and successor of Fulke Greville—the 'fanatic Brooke' who had his 'guerdon meet' by being shot in his attack on Lichfield Cathedral. *Mercurius Anti-Britannicus*, 1645, p. 23, has:

Like my Lord Brooke's *Coachman*

Preaching out of a tub.

(I owe this citation to Mr. Simpson.)

The King's Disguise.

And why a tenant to this vile disguise

Which who but sees, blasphemes thee with his eyes?

My twins of light within their penthouse shrink,

And hold it their allegiance now to wink.

O, for a state-distinction to arraign

Charles of high treason 'gainst my Sovereign!

What an usurper to his prince is wont,
Cloister and shave him, he himself hath don' 't.
His muffled feature speaks him a recluse—
10His ruins prove him a religious house!
The sun hath mewed his beams from off his lamp
And majesty defaced the royal stamp.
Is 't not enough thy dignity 's in thrall,
But thou'lt transmute it in thy shape and all,
As if thy blacks were of too faint a dye
Without the tincture of tautology?
Flay an Egyptian for his cassock skin,
Spun of his country's darkness, line 't within
With Presbyterian budge, that drowsy trance,
20The Synod's sable, foggy Ignorance;
Nor bodily nor ghostly negro could
Roughcast thy figure in a sadder mould.
This privy-chamber of thy shape would be
But the close mourner of thy Royalty.
Then, break the circle of thy tailor's spell,
A pearl within a rugged oyster's shell.
Heaven, which the minster of thy person owns,
Will fine thee for dilapidations.
Like to a martyred abbey's coarser doom,
30Devoutly altered to a pigeon-room;
Or like a college by the changeling rabble,
Manchester's elves, transformed into a stable;
Or if there be a profanation higher;

Such is the sacrilege of thine attire,
By which thou'rt half deposed.—Thou look'st like one
Whose looks are under sequestration;
Whose renegado form at the first glance
Shows like the Self-denying Ordinance;

Angel of light, and darkness too, (I doubt)
40Inspired within and yet possessed without;
Majestic twilight in the state of grace,
Yet with an excommunicated face.
Charles and his mask are of a different mint;
A psalm of mercy in a miscreant print.
The sun wears midnight, day is beetle-browed,
And lightning is in kelder of a cloud.
O the accursed stenography of fate!
The princely eagle shrunk into a bat!
What charm, what magic vapour can it be
50That checks his rays to this apostasy?
It is no subtile film of tiffany air,
No cobweb vizard such as ladies wear,
When they are veiled on purpose to be seen,
Doubling their lustre by their vanquished screen.
No, the false scabbard of a prince is tough
And three-piled darkness, like the smoky slough
Of an imprisoned flame; 'tis Faux in grain;
Dark lantern to our bright meridian.
Hell belched the damp; the Warwick Castle vote
60Rang Britain's curfew, so our light went out.
[A black offender, should he wear his sin

For penance, could not have a darker skin.]
His visage is not legible; the letters
Like a lord's name writ in fantastic fetters;
Clothes where a Switzer might be buried quick;
Sure they would fit the body politic;

False beard enough to fit a stage's plot
(For that 's the ambush of their wit, God wot),
Nay, all his properties so strange appear,
70Y' are not i' th' presence though the King be there.
A libel is his dress, a garb uncouth,
Such as the *Hue and Cry* once purged at mouth.
Scribbling assassinate! Thy lines attest
An earmark due, Cub of the Blatant Beast;
Whose breath, before 'tis syllabled for worse,
Is blasphemy unfledged, a callow curse.
The Laplanders, when they would sell a wind
Wafting to hell, bag up thy phrase and bind
It to the bark, which at the voyage end
80Shifts poop and breeds the colic in the Fiend.
But I'll not dub thee with a glorious scar
Nor sink thy sculler with a man-of-war.
The black-mouthed *Si quis* and this slandering suit
Both do alike in picture execute.
But since w' are all called Papists, why not date
Devotion to the rags thus consecrate?
As temples use to have their porches wrought
With sphinxes, creatures of an antic draught,
And puzzling portraitures to show that there

90Riddles inhabited; the like is here.
But pardon, Sir, since I presume to be
Clerk of this closet to your Majesty.
Methinks in this your dark mysterious dress
I see the Gospel couched in parables.
At my next view my purblind fancy ripes
And shows Religion in its dusky types;
Such a text royal, so obscure a shade
Was Solomon in Proverbs all arrayed.
Come, all the brats of this expounding age
100To whom the spirit is in pupilage,
You that damn more than ever Samson slew,
And with his engine, the same jaw-bone too!

How is 't he 'scapes your inquisition free
Since bound up in the Bible's livery?
Hence, Cabinet-intruders! Pick-locks, hence!
You, that dim jewels with your Bristol sense:
And characters, like witches, so torment
Till they confess a guilt though innocent!
Keys for this coffer you can never get;
110None but St. Peter's opes this cabinet,
This cabinet, whose aspect would benight
Critic spectators with redundant light.
A Prince most seen is least. What Scriptures call
The Revelation, is most mystical.
Mount then, thou Shadow Royal, and with haste
Advance thy morning-star, Charles, overcast.
May thy strange journey contradictions twist

And force fair weather from a Scottish mist.

Heaven's confessors are posed, those star-eyed sages,

120T' interpret an eclipse thus riding stages.

Thus Israel-like he travels with a cloud,

Both as a conduct to him and a shroud.

But oh, he goes to Gibeon and renews

A league with mouldy bread and clouted shoes!

The Kings Disguise.] That assumed on the fatal journey from Oxford to the camp of the Scots. (First printed as a quarto pamphlet of four leaves; Thomason bought his copy on 21 January, 1647; reprinted in the 1647 *Poems*. Vaughan wrote a poem on the same subject about the same time.)

1 a tenant to] so coffin'd in *1677*.

2 Which] That *1677*.

4: *1677* omits 'now', rather to one's surprise, as the value 'allegi-ance' is of the first rather than of the second half of the century. It is therefore probably right.

14 transmute] transcribe *1677*. The two readings obviously pertain to two different senses of 'blacks'—'clothes' and 'ink'.

17 for] from *1647* (pamphlet).

18 line 't] lin'de *1647* (pamphlet).

19 The *1677* 'Vindicators' had forgotten 'budge' in the sense of 'fur' (perhaps they were too loyal to read Milton) and made it 'b*a*dge'.

20 *1651, 1653* 'Synod', with no hyphen but perhaps meant for a compound. The genitive is perhaps better. The comma at 'sable', which Mr. Berdan omits, is important.

21-2 The error of those who say that such a rhyme points to the pronunciation of the *l* in words like 'could' is sufficiently shown by the fact that 'coud' is frequent. It is, of course, a mere eye-rhyme, like many of Spenser's earlier. 'No bodily' *1647* (pamphlet).

23 shape] garb *1677*.

24 of] to *1677*.

25 'Twill break' *1647, 1653*. tailor's] jailor's *1647, 1651, 1653*.

29 *1653*, but obviously by a mere misprint, 'co*u*rser'.

31 *1647, 1651, 1653 'the* college'. It is said that the definite article usually at this time designates 'the College *of Physicians*'. But, as Mr. Berdan well observes, 'the case was unfortunately too common to admit of identification'. Cleveland's restless wit was not idle in calling 'Manchester's elves'—the Parliamentary troops—'changelings'. The soldier ought to be a King's man: and indeed pretended to be.

32 *1647* (pamphlet) 'reformed'.

40 This and l. 47 are examples of the Drydenian line before Dryden, so frequent in Cleveland.

46 = 'The unborn child of a cloud'.

47 Alliteration, and some plausibility of verse, seduced *1677* into 'of State', but I think 'fate' is better.

50 checks] shrinks *1647, 1651, 1653*.

55-6 *1647, 1651, 1653* read

Nor the false scabbard of a Princ*e's* tough

Metal and three-piled darkness like the slough.

Some fight might be made for 'Metal', but 'Nor' is indefensible. I am half inclined to transfer it above to l. 52 and take 'No' thence. The text, which is *1677*, is I suppose a correction. Both *1647* texts mark 'slough' with an asterisk, and have a marginal note 'A damp in coal-pits usual'.

57 I cannot understand what Mr. Berdan—who prints 'Fawkes'—means by saying it is not authorized by any edition, whereas his own apparatus gives 'Faux' in every one. It is a mere question of spelling. 'Three-piled darkness' equally surrounds to me his further remark that he 'adopted it as the only reading approximating sense; *treason in grain*'. The metaphor of the dark lantern cloaked is surely clear enough; and this 'in grain' is one of the innumerable passages showing the rashness of invariably interpreting 'in grain' as = 'with the grain of the cochineal insect'. Beyond all doubt it has the simple sense of *penitus*, 'inward'.

58 bright] high *1647, 1653*.

59 the Warwick Castle vote] The Resolution of the Commons on May 6, 1646, that the King, after the Scots sold him, should be lodged in Warwick Castle.

61-2 Not in *1647, 1651, 1653* and its group, but added in *1677*.

63 *1647, 1651, 1653 'Thy* visage'.

67 *1677* has the very considerable and not at once acceptable alteration of 'thatch a poet's plot'. But it may have been Cleveland.

72 *1647*, *1651*, again give an asterisked note, 'Britanicus', showing the definite, not general, reference of 'Hue and Cry'. It seems that *Mercurius Britannicus* did issue a 'Hue and Cry' after the King, for which the editor, Captain Audley, was put in the Gate-house till he apologized.

75 *1651* 'wreath', corrupted into 'wrath' in *1653*.

76 Blount stupidly thought 'callow' to mean 'lewd or wicked', as if 'unfledged' did not ratify the usual sense.

80 breeds] brings *1647*, *1651*.

83 *Si quis*] The first words of a formal inquiry as to disqualifications in a candidate for orders, &c. It would apply to the Hue and Cry itself.

85 It being a favourite Puritan trick to identify 'Royalist' with 'Papist'. 'Date' apparently in the sense of 'begin', which it usually has only as neuter.

89 puzzling] *1677* and its followers 'purling', with no sense.

95 *1677* 'The second view' and 'wipes'.

106 Bristol] as of diamonds.

109 coffer] cipher *1677*, &c.

110 opes] ope *1677*.

116 'Charles' *1677*: *1647*, *1651*, *1653*, by a clear error 'Charles's'.

120 'T' interpret an' *1647* (pamphlet): 'To interpret an' *1647* (Poems) *1653*, *1677*. *1651* omits 'To' and reads the 'an' which seems bad in metre and meaning alike.

The Rebel Scot.

How, Providence? and yet a Scottish crew?

Then Madam Nature wears black patches too!

What? shall our nation be in bondage thus

Unto a land that truckles under us?

Ring the bells backward! I am all on fire.

Not all the buckets in a country quire

Shall quench my rage. A poet should be feared,

When angry, like a comet's flaming beard.

And where 's the stoic can his wrath appease,

10To see his country sick of Pym's disease?

By Scotch invasion to be made a prey

To such pigwiggin myrmidons as they?

But that there 's charm in verse, I would not quote

The name of Scot without an antidote;

Unless my head were red, that I might brew

Invention there that might be poison too.

Were I a drowsy judge whose dismal note

Disgorgeth halters as a juggler's throat

Doth ribbons; could I in Sir Emp'ric's tone

20Speak pills in phrase and quack destruction;

Or roar like Marshall, that Geneva bull,

Hell and damnation a pulpit full;

Yet to express a Scot, to play that prize,

Not all those mouth-grenadoes can suffice.

Before a Scot can properly be curst,

I must like Hocus swallow daggers first.

Come, keen iambics, with your badger's feet

And badger-like bite till your teeth do meet.

Help, ye tart satirists, to imp my rage

30With all the scorpions that should whip this age.

Scots are like witches; do but whet your pen,

Scratch till the blood come, they'll not hurt you then.

Now, as the martyrs were enforced to take

The shapes of beasts, like hypocrites, at stake,

I'll bait my Scot so, yet not cheat your eyes;

A Scot within a beast is no disguise.

No more let Ireland brag her harmless nation

Fosters no venom since the Scot's plantation:

Nor can ours feigned antiquity maintain;

40Since they came in, England hath wolves again.

The Scot that kept the Tower might have shown,

Within the grate of his own breast alone,

The leopard and the panther, and engrossed

What all those wild collegiates had cost

The honest high-shoes in their termly fees;

First to the salvage lawyer, next to these.

Nature herself doth Scotchmen beasts confess,

Making their country such a wilderness:

A land that brings in question and suspense

50God's omnipresence, but that Charles came thence,

But that Montrose and Crawford's loyal band

Atoned their sins and christ'ned half the land.

Nor is it all the nation hath these spots;

There is a Church as well as Kirk of Scots.

As in a picture where the squinting paint

Shows fiend on this side, and on that side saint.

He, that saw Hell in 's melancholy dream

And in the twilight of his fancy's theme,

Scared from his sins, repented in a fright,

60Had he viewed Scotland, had turned proselyte.

A land where one may pray with cursed intent,

'Oh may they never suffer banishment!'

Had Cain been Scot, God would have changed his doom;

Not forced him wander but confined him home!
Like Jews they spread and as infection fly,
As if the Devil had ubiquity.
Hence 'tis they live at rovers and defy
This or that place, rags of geography.
They're citizens o' th' world; they're all in all;
70Scotland's a nation epidemical.
And yet they ramble not to learn the mode,
How to be dressed, or how to lisp abroad;
To return knowing in the Spanish shrug,
Or which of the Dutch States a double jug
Resembles most in belly or in beard,
(The card by which the mariners are steered).
No, the Scots-errant fight and fight to eat,
Their Ostrich stomachs make their swords their meat.

Nature with Scots as tooth-drawers hath dealt
80Who use to hang their teeth upon their belt.
Yet wonder not at this their happy choice,
The serpent 's fatal still to Paradise.
Sure, England hath the hemorrhoids, and these
On the north postern of the patient seize
Like leeches; thus they physically thirst
After our blood, but in the cure shall burst!
Let them not think to make us run o' th' score
To purchase villenage, as once before
When an act passed to stroke them on the head,
90Call them good subjects, buy them gingerbread.
Not gold, nor acts of grace, 'tis steel must tame

The stubborn Scot; a Prince that would reclaim

Rebels by yielding, doth like him, or worse,

Who saddled his own back to shame his horse.

Was it for this you left your leaner soil,

Thus to lard Israel with Egypt's spoil?

They are the Gospel's life-guard; but for them,

The garrison of New Jerusalem,

What would the brethren do? The Cause! The Cause!

100Sack-possets and the fundamental laws!

Lord! what a godly thing is want of shirts!

How a Scotch stomach and no meat converts!

They wanted food and raiment, so they took

Religion for their seamstress and their cook.

Unmask them well; their honours and estate,

As well as conscience, are sophisticate.

Shrive but their titles and their money poise,

A laird and twenty pence pronounced with noise,

When construed, but for a plain yeoman go,

110And a good sober two-pence; and well so.

Hence then, you proud impostors; get you gone,

You Picts in gentry and devotion;

You scandal to the stock of verse, a race

Able to bring the gibbet in disgrace.

Hyperbolus by suffering did traduce

The ostracism and shamed it out of use.

The Indian, that Heaven did forswear

Because he heard some Spaniards were there,

Had he but known what Scots in Hell had been,

120He would Erasmus-like have hung between.

My Muse hath done. A voider for the nonce!

I wrong the Devil should I pick their bones;

That dish is his; for, when the Scots decease,

Hell, like their nation, feeds on barnacles.

A Scot, when from the gallow-tree got loose,

Drops into Styx and turns a Solan goose.

The Rebel Scot.] This famous piece is said to be the only one of Cleveland's poems which is in every edition. In *1677* it is accompanied by a Latin version (of very little merit, and probably if not certainly by 'another hand') which I do not give. A poor copy is in Tanner MS. 465 of the Bodleian, at fol. 92, with the title 'A curse on the Scots'. The piece is hot enough, and no wonder; but it would no doubt have been hotter if it had been written later, when Cleveland was actually gagged by Leven's dismissal of him. It is not unnoteworthy that the library of the University of Edinburgh contains not a single one of the numerous seventeenth-century editions of Cleveland. Years afterwards, when a Douglas had chequered the disgrace of 'the Dutch in the Medway' by a brave death, Marvell, who probably knew our poet, composed for 'Cleveland's Ghost' a half palinode, half continuation, entitled 'The *Loyal* Scot'.

10 It would seem that Pym had not yet gone to his account, as he died on December 6, 1643, after getting Parliament to accept the Covenant and the Scots to invade England.

12 The early texts have Drayton's name correctly: *1677* makes it 'Pigwidgin'.

15 It seems hardly necessary to remind the reader of the well-known habit of painting Judas's hair red.

19 could ... tone] or in the Empiric's misty tone *MS.*

21 Stephen Marshall, the 'Smec.' man and a mighty cushion-thumper (who denounced the 'Curse of Meroz' on all who came not to destroy those in any degree opposed to the Parliament), actually preached Pym's funeral sermon.

22 'Damnati-on'. But *MS.* reads 'a whole pulpit full'.

28 *1653* has the obvious blunder of 'feet' repeated for 'teeth'. The first 'feet' is itself less obvious, but I suppose the strong claw and grip of the badger's are meant. Some, however, refer it to the supposed lop-sidedness or inequality of badgers' feet, answering to the □ — of the iamb. I never knew

but one badger, who lived in St. Clement's, Oxford, and belonged (surreptitiously) to Merton College. I did not notice his feet.

32 The more usual reproach was the other way—that 'the Scot would not fight *till* he saw his own blood'.

38 *1677*, less well, '*that* Scot'.

39 'ours ... maintain' *1647, 1651, 1653*: 'our ... obtain' *1677*.

41 The Scot] Sir William Balfour, a favoured servant of the King, who deserted to the other side.

44 A difficulty has been made about 'collegiate', but there is surely none. The word (or 'colle*gian*') is old slang, and hardly slang for 'jail-bird'. The double use of the Tower as a prison and a menagerie should of course be remembered.

45 high-shoes] Country folk in boots.

termly] = 'when they came up to business'.

51 Crawford] Ludovic, sixteenth Earl, who fought bravely all through the Rebellion, served after the downfall in France and Spain, and died, it is not accurately known when or where, but about 1652.

52 A fine line. *1677* does not improve it by reading '*their* land'.

63-4 The central and most often quoted couplet.

65-6 follow 70 in the *MS*.

67 at rovers] Common for shooting not at a definite mark, but at large.

70 epidemical] In the proper sense of 'travelling from country to country', not doubtless without the transferred one of a 'travelling *plague*'.

74 States] not the Provinces; but the representative Hogan Mogans themselves.

78 'Ostrich' in *1677*: *1647, 1651,* and *1653* the older 'estrich'.

80 hang] string *1677*.

81 'But why should we be made your frantic choice?' *MS*.

82 'England too hath emerods' *MS*.

83 *1651, 1653* have a middle form between 'emerod' and 'hemorrhoid'— 'Hemeroids'. *1647* 'Hemerods'.

84 *1647, 1651, 1653* and its group, oddly, 'posture'.

89 The Parliamentary bribe or Danegelt of 1641.

95 'left' *1653*, &c., *1677*: 'gave' *1647, 1651*. The *MS.* reads 'But they may justly quit their leaner soil. 'Tis to lard ...'

101 *1651, 1653* 'goodly', but here, I think, the old is not the better.

107 'money' *1647, 1651, 1653*: 'moneys' *1677*.

108 *1647, 1653*, &c. 'pound', wrongly. Twenty Scots pence = not quite two-pence English. Therefore 'well so'.

118 *1641, 1651*, and *1653* 'the Spaniards', but 'some' (*1677*) is more pointed.

120 Erasmus] Regarded as neither Papist nor Protestant?

Cleveland never wrote anything else of this force and fire: and it, or parts of it, were constantly revived when the occasion presented itself.

The Scots' Apostasy.

Is 't come to this? What? shall the cheeks of Fame,

Stretched with the breath of learned Loudoun's name,

Be flagged again? And that great piece of sense,

As rich in loyalty as eloquence,

Brought to the test, be found a trick of state?

Like chemists' tinctures, proved adulterate?

The Devil sure such language did achieve

To cheat our unforewarned Grandam Eve,

As this impostor found out to besot

10Th' experienced English to believe a Scot!

Who reconciled the Covenant's doubtful sense,

The Commons' argument, or the City's pence?

Or did you doubt persistence in one good

Would spoil the fabric of your brotherhood,

Projected first in such a forge of sin,

Was fit for the grand Devil's hammering?

Or was 't ambition that this damned fact

Should tell the world you know the sins you act?

The infamy this super-treason brings

20Blasts more than murders of your sixty kings;

A crime so black, as being advis'dly done,

Those hold with this no competition.

Kings only suffered then; in this doth lie

Th' assassination of Monarchy.

Beyond this sin no one step can be trod,

If not t' attempt deposing of your God.

Oh, were you so engaged that we might see

Heaven's angry lightning 'bout your ears to flee

Till you were shrivelled to dust, and your cold Land

30Parched to a drought beyond the Lybian sand!

But 'tis reserved! Till Heaven plague you worse,

Be objects of an epidemic curse.

First, may your brethren, to whose viler ends

Your power hath bawded, cease to count you friends,

And, prompted by the dictate of their reason,

Reproach the traitors though they hug the treason:

And may their jealousies increase and breed

Till they confine your steps beyond the Tweed:

In foreign nations may your loath'd name be

40A stigmatizing brand of infamy,

Till forced by general hate you cease to roam

The world, and for a plague go live at home;

Till you resume your poverty and be

Reduced to beg where none can be so free

To grant: and may your scabby Land be all

Translated to a general hospital:

Let not the sun afford one gentle ray

To give you comfort of a summer's day;

But, as a guerdon for your traitorous war,

50Live cherished only by the Northern Star:

No stranger deign to visit your rude coast,

And be to all but banished men as lost:

And such, in heightening of the infliction due,

Let provoked princes send them all to you:

Your State a chaos be where not the Law,

But power, your lives and liberties may awe:

No subject 'mongst you keep a quiet breast,

But each man strive through blood to be the best;

Till, for those miseries on us you've brought,

60By your own sword our just revenge be wrought.

To sum up all—let your religion be,

As your allegiance, masked hypocrisy,

Until, when Charles shall be composed in dust,

Perfumed with epithets of good and just,

HE saved, incenséd Heaven may have forgot

T' afford one act of mercy to a Scot,

Unless that Scot deny himself and do

(What's easier far) renounce his Nation too.

The Scots' Apostasy was first printed as a broadside in *1646*, and assigned at the time to Cleveland by Thomas Old. It was included in *1651*, but not admitted by the 'Vindicators' in *1677*. But it is in all the central group of editions except *Cleaveland Revived*, where absence is usually a strong proof of genuineness; and it is extremely like him. Mr. Berdan has admitted it, and so do I. Professor Case has noted a catalogue entry of *The Scot's Constancy, an answer to J. C's.* [*al.* Or an Answer to Cleveland's] *Scots' Apostasy* (G. R. Bastick) [*al.* Robin Bostock], London April 1647. The 'J. C's' is of course pertinent.

2 John Campbell (1598-1633), from 1620 Baron Loudoun in his wife's right, was, after taking a violent part on the Covenant side in the earlier Scotch-English war, instrumental in concluding peace; and was made in 1641 Chancellor of Scotland and Earl of Loudoun.

4 as] 'and' *1653*.

9 'imposture' *1651, 1653*.

20 The celebrated and grisly collection of Scottish monarchs in Holyrood was not yet in existence; for its imaginative creator only painted it in 1684, and there are 106, not sixty. But the remoteness of Scottish pedigrees was popularly known: and if it be not true that all Scottish kings were murdered, not a few had been.

24 'Assassination' is valued at six syllables.

28 'to' *1651*, &c.: 'into' *1646*.

31 Till] and tell *1646, 1651*.

34 'count you' *1646, 1651, 1653*, &c.: 'be your' *1687*. This prayer, at any rate, was heard pretty soon.

38 'steps' *1651*, &c.: 'ships' *1646*.

42 'go', misprinted 'to' in *1653*, &c.

67-8 Not in *1646*.

Rupertismus.

O that I could but vote myself a poet,

Or had the legislative knack to do it!

Or, like the doctors militant, could get

Dubbed at adventure Verser Banneret!

Or had I Cacus' trick to make my rhymes

Their own antipodes, and track the times!

'Faces about,' says the remonstrant spirit,

'Allegiance is malignant, treason merit.'

Huntingdon colt, that posed the sage recorder,

10Might be a sturgeon now and pass by order.

Had I but Elsing's gift (that splay-mouthed brother

That declares one way and yet means another),
Could I thus write asquint, then, Sir, long since
You had been sung a great and glorious Prince!
I had observed the language of these days,
Blasphemed you, and then periwigged the phrase
With humble service and such other fustian,
Bells which ring backward in this great combustion.
I had reviled you, and without offence;
20The literal and equitable sense

Would make it good. When all fails, that will do 't;
Sure that distinction cleft the Devil's foot!
This were my dialect, would your Highness please
To read me but with Hebrew spectacles;
Interpret counter what is cross rehearsed;
Libels are commendations when reversed.
Just as an optic glass contracts the sight
At one end, but when turned doth multiply 't.
But you're enchanted, Sir, you're doubly free
30From the great guns and squibbing poetry,
Whom neither bilbo nor invention pierces,
Proof even 'gainst th' artillery of verses.
Strange that the Muses cannot wound your mail!
If not their art, yet let their sex prevail.
At that known leaguer, where the bonny Besses
Supplied the bow-strings with their twisted tresses,
Your spells could ne'er have fenced you, every arrow
Had lanced your noble breast and drunk the marrow.
For beauty, like white powder, makes no noise

40And yet the silent hypocrite destroys.

Then use the Nuns of Helicon with pity

Lest Wharton tell his gossips of the City

That you kill women too, nay maids, and such

Their general wants militia to touch.

Impotent Essex! Is it not a shame

Our Commonwealth, like to a Turkish dame,

Should have an eunuch guardian? May she be

Ravished by Charles, rather than saved by thee!

But why, my Muse, like a green-sickness girl,

50Feed'st thou on coals and dirt? A gelding earl

Gives no more relish to thy female palate

Than to that ass did once the thistle sallet.

Then quit the barren theme and all at once,

Thou and thy sisters like bright Amazons,

Give Rupert an alarum. Rupert! one

Whose name is wit's superfetation,

Makes fancy, like eternity's round womb,

Unite all valour, present, past, to come!

He who the old philosophy controls

60That voted down plurality of souls!

He breathes a Grand Committee; all that were

The wonders of their age constellate here.

And as the elder sisters, Growth and Sense,

Souls paramount themselves, in man commence

But faculties of reasons queen; no more

Are they to him (who was complete before),

Ingredients of his virtue. Thread the beads

Of Caesar's acts, great Pompey's and the Swede's,

And 'tis a bracelet fit for Rupert's hand,

70By which that vast triumvirate is spanned.

Here, here is palmistry; here you may read

How long the world shall live and when 't shall bleed.

What every man winds up, that Rupert hath,

For Nature raised him of the Public Faith;

Pandora's brother, to make up whose store

The gods were fain to run upon the score.

Such was the painter's brief for Venus' face;

Item, an eye from Jane; a lip from Grace.

Let Isaac and his cits flay off the plate

80That tips their antlers, for the calf of state;

Let the zeal-twanging nose, that wants a ridge,

Snuffling devoutly, drop his silver bridge;

Yes, and the gossip spoon augment the sum

Although poor Caleb lose his christendom;

Rupert outweighs that in his sterling self

Which their self-want pays in commuting pelf.

Pardon, great Sir, for that ignoble crew

Gains when made bankrupt in the scales with you.

As he, who in his character of Light

90Styled it God's shadow, made it far more bright

By an eclipse so glorious (light is dim

And a black nothing when compared to Him),

So 'tis illustrious to be Rupert's foil

And a just trophy to be made his spoil.

I'll pin my faith on the Diurnal's sleeve

Hereafter, and the Guildhall creed believe;

The conquests which the Common Council hears

With their wide listening mouth from the great Peers

That ran away in triumph. Such a foe

100Can make them victors in their overthrow;

Where providence and valour meet in one,

Courage so poised with circumspection

That he revives the quarrel once again

Of the soul's throne; whether in heart, or brain,

And leaves it a drawn match; whose fervour can

Hatch him whom Nature poached but half a man;

His trumpet, like the angel's at the last,

Makes the soul rise by a miraculous blast.

Was the Mount Athos carved in shape of man

110As 'twas designed by th' Macedonian

(Whose right hand should a populous land contain,

The left should be a channel to the main),

His spirit would inform th' amphibious figure

And, strait-laced, sweat for a dominion bigger.

The terror of whose name can out of seven,

Like Falstaff's buckram men, make fly eleven.

Thus some grow rich by breaking. Vipers thus,

By being slain, are made more numerous.

No wonder they'll confess no loss of men,

120For Rupert knocks 'em till they gig again.

They fear the giblets of his train, they fear

Even his dog, that four-legged cavalier;

He that devours the scraps that Lunsford makes;

Whose picture feeds upon a child in steaks;

Who, name but Charles, he comes aloft for him,

But holds up his malignant leg at Pym.

'Gainst whom they have these articles in souse:

First, that he barks against the sense o' th' House;

Resolved delinquent, to the Tower straight,

130Either to th' Lions' or the Bishop's Grate:

Next, for his ceremonious wag o' th' tail.

(But there the sisterhood will be his bail,

At least the Countess will, Lust's Amsterdam,

That lets in all religions of the game.)

Thirdly, he smells intelligence; that 's better

And cheaper too than Pym's from his own letter,

Who 's doubly paid (Fortune or we the blinder!)

For making plots and then for fox the finder:

Lastly, he is a devil without doubt,

140For, when he would lie down, he wheels about,

Makes circles, and is couchant in a ring;

And therefore score up one for conjuring.

'What canst thou say, thou wretch!' 'O quarter, quarter!

I'm but an instrument, a mere Sir Arthur.

If I must hang, O let not our fates vary,

Whose office 'tis alike to fetch and carry!'

No hopes of a reprieve; the mutinous stir

That strung the Jesuit will dispatch a cur.

'Were I a devil as the rabble fears,

150I see the House would try me by my peers!'

There, Jowler, there! Ah, Jowler! 'st, 'tis nought!

Whate'er the accusers cry, they're at a fault:

And Glyn and Maynard have no more to say

Than when the glorious Strafford stood at bay.

Thus libels but annexed to him, we see,

Enjoy a copyhold of victory.

Saint Peter's shadow healed; Rupert's is such

'Twould find Saint Peter's work and wound as much.

He gags their guns, defeats their dire intent;

160The cannons do but lisp and compliment.

Sure, Jove descended in a leaden shower

To get this Perseus; hence the fatal power

Of shot is strangled. Bullets thus allied

Fear to commit an act of parricide.

Go on, brave Prince, and make the world confess

Thou art the greater world and that the less.

Scatter th' accumulative king; untruss

That five-fold fiend, the State's Smectymnuus,

Who place religion in their vellum ears

170As in their phylacters the Jews did theirs.

England's a paradise (and a modest word)

Since guarded by a cherub's flaming sword.

Your name can scare an atheist to his prayers,

And cure the chincough better than the bears.

Old Sibyl charms the toothache with you; Nurse

Makes you still children; and the ponderous curse

The clowns salute with is derived from you,

'Now, Rupert take thee, rogue, how dost thou do?'

In fine the name of Rupert thunders so,

180Kimbolton's but a rumbling wheelbarrow.

Rupertismus] '*To P. Rupert*' in the *1647* texts (Bodley and Case copies). The odd title *Rupertismus* was first given in *1651*. This poem expresses the earlier and more sanguine Cavalier temper, when things on the whole went well. Rupert's admirable quality as an officer naturally made him a sort of Cavalier cynosure and (with his being half a foreigner) a bugbear to the Roundheads; while neither party had yet found out his fatal defects as a general. Hence 'Rupertismus' not ill described the humour of both sides. The dog who figures so largely was a real dog (said of course to be a familiar spirit), and Professor Firth tells me that he has a pamphlet (1642) entitled *Observations upon P. R.'s white dog called Boy, carefully taken by T. B.*, with a picture of the animal. It was replied to by *The Parliament's Unspotted Bitch* next year.

1, 2 The 'legislative knack' to vote oneself everything good and perfect has always been a gift of Houses of Commons. It was rather shrewd of Cleveland to formulate it so early and so well.

4 Bannerets being properly dubbed on the field of battle. 'Adventure' *1677*: 'Adventures' *1647, 1651, 1687*: 'adventurers' *1653* and its group.

5 Cacus' trick] of dragging his cattle by the tails.

7 spirit] A word their abuse of which was constantly thrown in the face of the Puritans till Swift's thrice rectified vitriol almost destroyed the abuse itself.

8 malignant] in the technical Roundhead sense.

9 The gibe at Huntingdon, clear enough from the passage, is one of many old local insults. I can remember when it was a little unsafe, in one of the Channel islands, to speak of a donkey. This particular jest recurs in Pepys (May 22, 1677), who was in a way a Huntingdon man.

11 Elsing] Clerk to the House of Commons.

13 'thus' *1677*: 'but' *1647* and the earlier texts. write] *1653*, 'right'—evidently one of the numerous mistakes due to dictating copy.

14 '*The* Prince' was a title which Rupert monopolized early and kept till his death.

15 'these' *1677*: 'the' *1647, 1651, 1653, 1687*.

20 *1677* 'th' equitable'.

24 The rhyme of '-cles' to an *ee* syllable occurs in Dryden.

31 'Who' *1653* and its group.

35 Carthage. Rupert's devotion to ladies was lifelong.

39 'White' or noiseless powder was a constant object of research.

45 Essex was *twice* divorced on the ground mentioned, and his efficiency in the field was not to be much greater than that in the chamber.

53 *1677*, &c., '*his* barren theme'.

65 *1654* 'faculty'. *1677* 'Reason Queen'. I am not sure which is right.

66-7 So punctuated in *1677*. Earlier texts and *1687* 'who were to him complete before. Ingredients of his virtue thread' ... *1677* reads 'virtues'.

68 '*the* Swede': of course Gustavus Adolphus.

73 *1647*, *1651*, *1653* 'Whatever'.

74 *1677*, apparently alone, 'o*n* the'].

78 *1653*, evidently by slip, '*for* Jane'.

79 *1647*, *1651*, *1653* 'Cit'z' (not quite bad for '*citiz*ens) and 'flea of the place'. 'Flea' for 'flay' is not uncommon: the rest is absurd. 'Isaac' was Isaac Pennington, father of that Judith whose obliging disposition Mr. Pepys has commemorated.

80 'Antl*ets*', which occurs in all, is not impossible for 'antl*ers*' (the everlastingly ridiculed citizen 'horns'). But *1647*, *1651*, *1653* forgot the Golden Calf altogether in their endeavour to provide a rhyme for their own misprint (l. 79) by reading 'Stace'.

83 'Gossip's' (*1651*, *1677*) is not wanted and hisses unnecessarily.

86 'self-wants' *1647*, *1651*, *1653*, *1687*. *1677*, most improbably, 'committee'. The whole passage refers to the subscriptions of plate and money in lieu of personal service which Pennington, as Lord Mayor, promised 'on the Public Faith'. Rupert's self outweighs all this vicarious performance.

89 'whom' *1653*, *1654*.

92 to] with *1677*.

95 Diurnal] Which Cleveland satirized in his first published (prose) work.

98 As Wharton at Edgehill. 'Mouths' *1647*, *1687*.

100 them] men *1677*.

109 Was the] 'Twas the *1647*, *1651*, *1653*: Was that *1677*. 'Was' = 'if it were'.

110 designed] *1647*, *1651*, *1653* 'defin'd', with a clear *f*, not long *s*.

113 would] *1647*, *1651*, *1653* might.

114 The text is *1677*, which, however, reads (with the usual want of strait-lacedness) 'straight'. *1651, 1653*, have 'Yet' for 'And', which is corrected in some of their own group, and 'sweats'.

117 some] Like Mr. Badman a little later.

120 gig] = 'spin like a top'. Dryden uses the word in the same sense and almost in the same phrase in the Prologue to *Amphitryon*, l. 21: *v. sup.*, p. 17.

121 giblets] Apparently in the sense of 'offal', 'refuse'.

123 Lunsford] Sir Thomas, 1610?-1653. The absurd legends about this Cavalier's 'child-eating' are referred to in, originally, *Hudibras* and in Lacy's *Old Troop*, and at second-hand (probably from the text also, though it is not quoted) in the notes to Scott's *Woodstock*. *1651* and *1653* have 'which' for second 'that'.

124 steaks] All old editions 'stakes'—a very common spelling, which Mr. Berdan keeps. As he modernizes the rest, his readers may be under the impression that the ogre impaled the infants before devouring them, which was not, I think, alleged by the most savoury professor on the Roundhead side.

127 souse] = 'pickle'. 'they have these' *1677*: 'they've several' *1647, 1651*: 'they have several' *1653*.

130 Bishop's] *1677, 1687* editions have the apostrophe. Laud is probably referred to in 'Bishop's'. The force of all this, and its application to other times, are admirable.

133 The Countess—pretty clearly Lucy Hay, Countess of Carlisle (1599-1660)—beauty, wit, harlot, and traitress (though, too late, she repented). Amsterdam] The religious indifference of the Dutch being a common reproach. *1677* and its followers read 'with' for 'will', which would alter the sense completely.

134 *1647, 1651, 1653* have 'religious' in the well-known noun sense, and it is possibly better.

144 Sir Arthur Haselrig (died 1661)—a very busy person throughout the troubles, but not considered as exactly a prime mover.

148 *1677* '*the* cur'.

149 'rabble' is *1677* and seems good, though the earlier 'rebel' might do.

152 a fault] *1677* default—not so technical.

153 Serjeants John Glyn[ne] (1607-66) and John Maynard (1602-90) were well-known legal bandogs on the Roundhead side in the earlier stages; but

both trimmed cleverly during the later, and sold themselves promptly to the Crown at the Restoration. Glynne died soon. Maynard lived to prosecute the victims of the Popish Plot, and to turn his coat once more, at nearly ninety, for William of Orange.

155 *1647, 1651, 1653* 'labels': *1677* 'Thus libels but amount to him we see T' enjoy'.

158 *1677* 'St. Peter', which looks plausible, though I am not sure that it is better than the genitive. *1647, 1651, 1653* have 'yet' for 'and' as in other cases.

167 the accumulative king] Pym? who was nicknamed 'king' Pym, and if not exactly 'accumulative' (for his debts were paid by Parliament) must have been expensive and was probably rapacious. Others think it means 'the Committee', 'accumulative' being = 'cumulative' (or rather 'plural'). They quote, not without force, our poet's prose *Character of a Country Committee man*, 'a Committee man is a name of multitude', the phrase 'accumulative treason' occurring in the context.

175 *1677* transfers 'the' to before 'Nurse'—a great loss, the unarticled and familiar 'Nurse' being far better—and reads 'Sibils charm'.

176 'and' *1653*, 1677: 'nay and' *1647, 1651, 1687*.

177 *1677* 'Clown salutes'.

Epitaph on the Earl of Strafford.

Here lies wise and valiant dust

Huddled up 'twixt fit and just;

Strafford, who was hurried hence

'Twixt treason and convenience.

He spent his time here in a mist;

A Papist, yet a Calvinist;

His Prince's nearest joy and grief

He had, yet wanted all relief;

The prop and ruin of the State;

10The People's violent love and hate;

One in extremes loved and abhorred.

Riddles lie here, or in a word,

Here lies blood; and let it lie

Speechless still and never cry.

Epitaph, &c. In the Bodleian copy of *1647* and in Professor Case's (3rd issue) and in all others except *Cleaveland Revived* (*1659*) and *1677*; but in some of the earliest classed with the work of 'Uncertain Authors'. Winstanley (no very strong authority, it is true) calls it Cleveland's and 'excellent'. It is perhaps too much to say with Mr. Berdan, that it is 'unlike his manner'. There is certainly in it a manner which he does not often display, but the pity and the terror of that great tragedy might account for part of this, and the difficulty (for any Royalist) of speaking freely of it for more. It is rather fine, I think.

4 The pitiful truth could hardly be better put.

6 Obscure, but not un-Clevelandish.

7-8 Punctuation altered to get what seems the necessary sense. A comma which *1653* has at 'grief' (not to mention a full stop in the *1647* texts) obscures this, and a comma at 'wanted', which Mr. Berdan puts, does so even more. The phrase is once more fatally just and true. He enjoyed all his master's affection and received all his grief, but 'wanted' his support and relief. Professor Case, however, would cling to the stop, at least the comma, at 'grief'.

12 or] Other editions 'and'. For 'Riddles' cf. *The King's Disguise*, ll. 89-90.

13-14 For the third time 'he says it', and there is no more to say.— In *1653* there follows a Latin Epitaph on Strafford which has nothing to do with this. It is in some phrases enigmatic enough to be Cleveland's, but it is not certainly his, and as it is neither English nor verse we need hardly give it.

An Elegy upon the Archbishop of Canterbury.

I need no Muse to give my passion vent,

He brews his tears that studies to lament.

Verse chemically weeps; that pious rain

Distilled with art is but the sweat o' th' brain

Whoever sobbed in numbers? Can a groan

Be quavered out by soft division?

'Tis true for common formal elegies

Not Bushel's Wells can match a poet's eyes
In wanton water-works; he'll tune his tears
10From a Geneva jig up to the spheres.
But then he mourns at distance, weeps aloof.
Now that the conduit head is our own roof,
Now that the fate is public, we may call
It Britain's vespers, England's funeral.
Who hath a pencil to express the Saint
But he hath eyes too, washing off the paint?
There is no learning but what tears surround,
Like to Seth's pillars in the Deluge drowned.

There is no Church; Religion is grown
20So much of late that she 's increased to none,
Like an hydropic body, full of rheums,
First swells into a bubble, then consumes.
The Law is dead or cast into a trance,—
And by a law dough-baked, an Ordinance!
The Liturgy, whose doom was voted next,
Died as a comment upon him the text.
There's nothing lives; life is, since he is gone,
But a nocturnal lucubration.
Thus you have seen death's inventory read
30In the sum total,—Canterbury's dead;
A sight would make a Pagan to baptize
Himself a convert in his bleeding eyes;
Would thaw the rabble, that fierce beast of ours,
(That which hyena-like weeps and devours)
Tears that flow brackish from their souls within,

Not to repent, but pickle up their sin.

Meantime no squalid grief his look defiles.

He gilds his sadder fate with nobler smiles.

Thus the world's eye, with reconciléd streams,

40Shines in his showers as if he wept his beams.

How could success such villanies applaud?

The State in Strafford fell, the Church in Laud;

The twins of public rage, adjudged to die

For treasons they should act, by prophecy;

The facts were done before the laws were made;

The trump turned up after the game was played.

Be dull, great spirits, and forbear to climb,

For worth is sin and eminence a crime.

No churchman can be innocent and high.

50'Tis height makes Grantham steeple stand awry.

An Elegy, &c. (1647.) If the Strafford epitaph seemed too serious, as well as too concentrated and passionate, for Cleveland, this on Strafford's fellow worker and fellow victim may seem almost a caricature of our author's more wayward and more fantastic manner. Yet there are fine lines in it, and perhaps nowhere else do we see the Dryden fashion of verse (though not of thought) more clearly foreshadowed. It appears to come under 'Uncertain Authors' in some *1647* texts, but *1677* gives it. Title in *1647, 1651, 1653* 'On the Archbishop of Canterbury' only.

4 *1677* '*by* art'.

6 *1677* '*in* soft'.

8 Thomas Bushel[l] or Bushnell (1594-1674) was a page of Bacon's and afterwards a great 'projector' in mining and mechanical matters generally. He dabbled largely in fancy fountains and waterworks—a queer taste of the seventeenth century in which even the sober Evelyn records his own participation.

9-10 Cf. the opening of the elegy on King, 'I like not tears in tune'.

11 *1647, 1651, 1653*, &c. '*when* he mourns', which is hardly so good.

18 Seth's pillars] A tradition, preserved in Josephus, that the race of Seth engraved antediluvian wisdom on two pillars, one of brick, the other of stone, the latter of which outlasted the Deluge.

20 *1647, 1651, 1653*, &c. '*From* much'.

34 *1647, 1651* misprint '*Agena*-like.

35 *1653* misprints 'blackish'.

38 *1647, 1651, 1653* 'noble'.

44 *1677*, omitting the comma at 'act', makes something like nonsense; 'by prophecy' goes, I think, with 'adjudged to die'.

50 One would expect 'Chesterfield', for Grantham nowadays does not look very crooked—at least from the railway. But Fuller in the *Worthies* quotes this as a proverb. Some take it as referring to the height and slenderness of the steeple and an optical illusion. They might quote 'The high masts *flickered* as they lay afloat'. But few travellers had the excuse of Iphigenia.

---

*On I. W. A. B. of York.

Say, my young sophister, what think'st of this?

Chimera's real, *Ergo falleris.*

The lamb and tiger, fox and goose agree

And here concorp'rate in one prodigy.

Call an Haruspex quickly: let him get

Sulphur and torches, and a laurel wet,

To purify the place: for sure the harms

This monster will produce transcend his charms.—

'Tis Nature's masterpiece of Error, this,

10And redeems whatever she did amiss

Before, from wonder and reproach, this last

Legitimateth all her by-blows past.

Lo! here a general Metropolitan,

And arch-prelatic Presbyterian!

Behold his pious garbs, canonic face,

A zealous *Episcopo-mastix* Grace—

A fair blue-apron'd priest, a Lawn-sleeved brother,

One leg a pulpit holds, a tub the other.

Let 's give him a fit name now if we can,

20And make th' Apostate once more Christian.

'Proteus' we cannot call him: *he* put on

His change of shapes by a succession,

Nor 'the Welsh weather-cock', for that we find

At once doth only wait upon the wind.

These speak him not: but if you'll name him right,

Call him Religion's Hermaphrodite.

His head i' the sanctified mould is cast,

Yet sticks th'abominable mitre fast.

He still retains the 'Lordship' and the 'Grace',

30And yet hath got a reverend elder's place.

Such acts must needs be his, who did devise

By crying altars down to sacrifice

To private malice; where you might have seen

His conscience holocausted to his spleen.

Unhappy Church! the viper that did share

Thy greatest honours, helps to make thee bare,

And void of all thy dignities and store.

Alas! thine own son proves the forest boar,

And, like the dam-destroying cuckoo, he,

40When the thick shell of his Welsh pedigree

By thy warm fostering bounty did divide

And open—straight thence sprung forth parricide:

As if 'twas just revenge should be dispatched

In thee, by th' monster which thyself hadst hatched.

Despair not though, in Wales there may be got,

As well as Lincolnshire, an antidote

'Gainst the foul'st venom he can spit, though 's head

Were changed from subtle grey to pois'nous red.

Heaven with propitious eyes will look upon

50 Our party, now the curséd thing is gone;

And chastise Rebels who nought else did miss

To fill the measure of their sins, but his—

Whose foul imparalleled apostasy,

Like to his sacred character, shall be

Indelible. When ages, then of late

More happy grown, with most impartial fate

A period to his days and time shall give,

He by such Epitaphs as this shall live.

Here York's great Metropolitan is laid,

60 *Who God's Anointed, and His Church, betrayed.*

On I. W. A. B. of York. (*1647.*) This vigorous onslaught on the trimmer John Williams, Archbishop of York, who began public life as a tool of Buckingham's and ended it as a kind of tolerated half-deserter to the Parliament, was turned out by the 'Vindicators' in *1677.* There may, however, have been reasons for this, other than certain spuriousness. Williams, though driven to doubtful conduct by his enmity with Laud, never called himself anything but a Royalist, was imprisoned as such, and is said to have died of grief (perhaps of compunction) at the King's execution. Also both Lake and Drake were Yorkshire men. The piece is vigorous, if not quite Clevelandish in the presence of some enjambment, and the absence of extravagant conceit.

2 *falleris*] In advancing the general observation that 'twy-natured is no nature'.

10 whatever] Perhaps we should read 'whatsoe'er'.

15 'garb' *1653.*

16 A parody of course on Prynne's *Histrio-mastix.*

21 'he' = Proteus. Williams went right over.

23 Williams was very popular with his fellow provincials. He took refuge in Wales when the war broke out, and was made a sort of mediator by the Welsh after Naseby.

26 'Religion's' *1647*; 'Religious' *1651, 1653*.

27 *1651, 1653*, 'I' th'': but here, as often, the apostrophation ruins the verse.

30 'hath' *1653*: 'has' *1647, 1651*.

32 Williams had been chairman of the Committee 'to consider innovations' in 1641. His private malice was to Laud.

46 I am not certain of the meaning. But Lincolnshire (at least Lindsey) was strongly Royalist early in the war till Cromwell's successes at Grantham, Lea Moor, and Winceby in 1643.

53 *1647, 1651* 'unparalleled'.

Mark Antony.

When as the nightingale chanted her vespers,

And the wild forester couched on the ground,

Venus invited me in th' evening whispers

Unto a fragrant field with roses crowned,

Where she before had sent

My wishes' compliment;

Unto my heart's content

Played with me on the green.

Never Mark Antony

10Dallied more wantonly

With the fair Egyptian Queen.

First on her cherry cheeks I mine eyes feasted,

Thence fear of surfeiting made me retire;

Next on her warmer lips, which, when I tasted,

My duller spirits made active as fire.

Then we began to dart,

Each at another's heart,

Arrows that knew no smart,

Sweet lips and smiles between.

20Never Mark, &c.

Wanting a glass to plait her amber tresses

Which like a bracelet rich deckéd mine arm,

Gaudier than Juno wears when as she graces

Jove with embraces more stately than warm,

Then did she peep in mine

Eyes' humour crystalline;

I in her eyes was seen

As if we one had been.

Never Mark, &c.

30Mystical grammar of amorous glances;

Feeling of pulses, the physic of love;

Rhetorical courtings and musical dances;

Numbering of kisses arithmetic prove;

Eyes like astronomy;

Straight-limbed geometry;

In her art's ingeny

Our wits were sharp and keen.

Never Mark Antony

Dallied more wantonly

With the fair Egyptian Queen.

Mark Antony. The unusual prosodic interest of this piece, and its companion, has been explained in the Introduction. The pair appeared first in 1647 (3rd), where they follow *The Character of a London Diurnal* and precede the *Poems*.

14 'warmer' some copies of *1653*: *1647*, *1651* 'warm'. Cf. 'bluer' in the 'Mock Song', l. 14 (below).

15 *1677*, &c. 'made *me* active'—a bad blunder.

35 'Straight limb' *1647*.

36 'art's' is *1677* for 'heart's' in *1647, 1651, 1653*. I rather prefer it, but with some doubts.

37 *1677*, &c. emends by substituting 'were' for *1647, 1651, 1653* 'are'.

The Author's Mock Song to Mark Antony.

When as the night-raven sung Pluto's matins

And Cerberus cried three amens at a howl,

When night-wandering witches put on their pattens,

Midnight as dark as their faces are foul;

Then did the furies doom

That the nightmare was come.

Such a misshapen groom

Puts down Su. Pomfret clean.

Never did incubus

10Touch such a filthy sus

As this foul gypsy quean.

First on her gooseberry cheeks I mine eyes blasted,

Thence fear of vomiting made me retire

Unto her bluer lips, which when I tasted,

My spirits were duller than Dun in the mire.

But then her breath took place

Which went an usher's pace

And made way for her face!

You may guess what I mean.

20Never did, &c.

Like snakes engendering were platted her tresses,

Or like the slimy streaks of ropy ale;

Uglier than Envy wears, when she confesses

Her head is periwigged with adder's tail.

But as soon as she spake

I heard a harsh mandrake.

Laugh not at my mistake,

Her head is epicene.

Never did, &c.

30Mystical magic of conjuring wrinkles;

Feeling of pulses, the palmistry of hags;

Scolding out belches for rhetoric twinkles;

With three teeth in her head like to three gags;

Rainbows about her eyes

And her nose, weather-wise;

From them the almanac lies,

Frost, Pond, and Rivers clean.

Never did incubus

Touch such a filthy sus

40As this foul gypsy quean.

The Author's Mock Song. In *1647* this runs on as a continuation of 'Mark Anthony'.

1 *1677 putidissime* 'nightingale', as in the preceding poem. 'Night-raven' *1647, 1651, 1653* is certainly right. Mr. Berdan's copy seems to have '*But* as', which I rather like; but mine has 'When'.

2 howl] hole *1647.*

16 *1677* 'when', not impossibly.

21 platted] placed *1647.*

22 *1647, 1651* 'the': omitted in *1653*: 'to' inserted in *1677.*

37 Cf. *A Young Man, &c.,* l. 13.

How the Commencement grows new.

It is no coranto-news I undertake;

New teacher of the town I mean not to make;

No New England voyage my Muse does intend;
No new fleet, no bold fleet, nor bonny fleet send.
But, if you'll be pleased to hear out this ditty,
I'll tell you some news as true and as witty,
And how the Commencement grows new.
See how the simony doctors abound,
All crowding to throw away forty pound.
10They'll now in their wives' stammel petticoats vapour
Without any need of an argument draper.
Beholding to none, he neither beseeches
This friend for venison nor t'other for speeches,
And so the Commencement grows new.
Every twice a day teaching gaffer
Brings up his Easter-book to chaffer;
Nay, some take degrees who never had steeple,—
Whose means, like degrees, comes from placets of people.
They come to the fair and, at the first pluck,
20The toll-man Barnaby strikes 'um good luck,
And so the Commencement grows new.
The country parsons come not up
On Tuesday night in their old College to sup;
Their bellies and table-books equally full,
The next lecture-dinner their notes forth to pull;
How bravely the Margaret Professor disputed,
The homilies urged, and the school-men confuted;
And so the Commencement grows new.

The inceptor brings not his father the clown

30To look with his mouth at his grogoram gown;

With like admiration to eat roasted beef,

Which invention posed his beyond-Trent belief;

Who should he but hear our organs once sound,

Could scarce keep his hoof from Sellenger's round,

And so the Commencement grows new.

The gentleman comes not to show us his satin,

To look with some judgment at him that speaks Latin,

To be angry with him that marks not his clothes,

To answer 'O Lord, Sir' and talk play-book oaths,

40And at the next bear-baiting (full of his sack)

To tell his comrades our discipline's slack;

And so the Commencement grows new.

We have no prevaricator's wit.

Ay, marry sir, when have you had any yet?

Besides no serious Oxford man comes

To cry down the use of jesting and hums.

Our ballad (believe 't) is no stranger than true;

Mum Salter is sober, and Jack Martin too,

And so the Commencement grows new.

How the Commencement, &c., belongs to the same group as the *Mark Antony* poems and *Square-Cap*, and there is the same ambiguity between four anapaests and five iambs. You would certainly take line 1 as it stands in *1677* with "Tis' for 'It is', and probably as it stands here, for a heroic if line 2 did not come to undeceive you. And this line 2 is bad as either.

First printed in *1653*. MS. copies are found in Rawlinson MS. Poet. 147, pp. 48-9, and Tanner MS. 465, fol. 83, of the Bodleian. Neither copy is good, but each helps to restore the text (see ll. 18 and 38). The Tanner MS. also has on fol. 44 an indignant poem 'Upon Mr. Cl. who made a Song against the DD^{rs}', beginning

Leave off, vain Satirist, and do not think,

To stain our reverend purple with thy ink.

It adds the interesting evidence that the poem became a popular song at Cambridge:

Must gitterns now and fiddles be made fit,

Be tuned and keyed to sweake [?squeak] a Johnian wit?

Must now thy poems be made fidlers' notes,

Puffed with Tobacco through their sooty throats?

.   .   .   .

Are thy strong lines and mighty cart-rope things

Now spun so small, they'll twist on fiddle strings?

Canst thou prove Ballad-poet of the times?

Can thy proud fancy stoop to penny rimes?

(This latter information, as to MSS., is Mr. Simpson's.)

5 out] but *1653*.

9 forty pound] Still the regular doctorate fee, though relatively three or four times heavier then than now.

10 stammel] Properly a stuff; but, as generally or often red in colour, the colour itself.

11 I am not certain of the meaning of this line though I could conjecture.

13 nor t'other for speeches] *MS.* 'that for his breeches'.

15 *1677* inserts 'the' before 'teaching', but the absence of the article is much more characteristic.

18 The 'Vindicators', in the new bondage of grammar, 'come'.

Placets] both *MSS.*: places *1653*: placers *1677*. 'Placets', evidently right, would baffle a non-university printer; probably the editors of *1677* attempted to correct it, but were again baffled by the printer.

22 *1677* 'they do not come up'—a natural but unnecessary patching of the line.

23 old] *1677* own—less well, I think.

Both *MSS.* read in ll. 22-3:

The country parson cometh not up,

Till Tuesday night in his old College to sup.

26 'Marg*e*ret' *1653*: Marg'ret' *1677*.

29 inceptor] = 'M.A. to be'.

30 'o' of 'grog[o]ram' usually omitted, but both *1653* and *1677* have it here.

32 The North usually salting and boiling its beef?

38 Tanner MS. has the metrical punctuation 'To be'angry' found occasionally in texts of the time: 'marks' Tanner MS., all the texts have 'makes'.

40 at the next bear-baiting] in his next company *MSS.*

44 *1653* 'we' for 'you', less pointedly, I think.

45 Cleveland lived to think better of Oxford—at least to take refuge and be warmly welcomed there. There has probably been no time at which either University was not convinced that the other, whatever its merits, could not see a joke.

48 *1665* (not a very good edition) and the *MSS.* read 'Mu*n*', which was of course the usual short for Edmund. But 'Mu*m*' in the context is appropriate enough and generally read.

The intense Cambridge flavour of this seems to require special comment by a Cambridge man. For the duties of the 'Prevaricator' refer to Peacock's *Observations on the Statutes of the University of Cambridge*, 1841 (information kindly furnished by Mr. A. J. Bartholomew).

The Hue and Cry after Sir John Presbyter.

With hair in characters and lugs in text;

With a splay mouth and a nose circumflexed;

With a set ruff of musket-bore that wears

Like cartridges or linen bandoleers

Exhausted of their sulphurous contents

In pulpit fire-works, which that bomball vents;

The Negative and Covenanting Oath,

Like two mustachoes issuing from his mouth;

The bush upon his chin like a carved story,

10In a box-knot cut by the Directory:

Madam's confession hanging at his ear,

Wire-drawn through all the questions, how and where;

Each circumstance so in the hearing felt

That when his ears are cropped he'll count them gelt;

The weeping cassock scared into a jump,

A sign the presbyter's worn to the stump,—

The presbyter, though charmed against mischance

With the divine right of an Ordinance!

If you meet any that do thus attire 'em,

20*Stop them, they are the tribe of Adoniram.*

What zealous frenzy did the Senate seize,

That tare the Rochet to such rags as these?

Episcopacy minced, reforming Tweed

Hath sent us runts even of her Church's breed,

Lay-interlining clergy, a device

That 's nickname to the stuff called lops and lice.

The beast at wrong end branded, you may trace

The Devil's footsteps in his cloven face;

A face of several parishes and sorts,

30Like to a sergeant shaved at Inns of Courts.

What mean the elders else, those Kirk dragoons,

Made up of ears and ruffs like ducatoons;

That hierarchy of handicrafts begun;

Those New Exchange men of religion?

Sure, they're the antick heads, which placed without

The church, do gape and disembogue a spout.

Like them above the Commons' House, have been

So long without; now both are gotten in.

Then what imperious in the bishop sounds,

40The same the Scotch executor rebounds;

This stating prelacy the classic rout

That spake it often, ere it spake it out.

(So by an abbey's skeleton of late

I heard an echo supererogate

Through imperfection, and the voice restore,

As if she had the hiccough o'er and o'er.)

'Since they our mixed diocesans combine

Thus to ride double in their discipline,

That Paul's shall to the Consistory call

50A Dean and Chapter out of Weavers' Hall,

Each at the ordinance for to assist

With the five thumbs of his groat-changing fist.

Down, Dagon-synod, with thy motley ware,

Whilst we do swagger for the Common Prayer

(That dove-like embassy that wings our sense

To Heaven's gate in shape of innocence)

Pray for the mitred authors, and defy

These demicastors of divinity!

For, when Sir John with Jack-of-all-trades joins,

60His finger 's thicker than the prelates' loins.'

The Hue and Cry. (*1653.*) 1 'in characters' = in shorthand: *1677* has 'character', wrongly. 'lugs' = ears. 'in text' = in capitals.

Cf. *Clievelandi Vindiciae*, 1677, p. 122 (Cleveland's letter on a Puritan who had deserted to the Royalists. His officer complained that he had absconded with official money): 'I doubt not, but you will pardon your Man. He hath but transcribed Rebellion, and copied out that Disloyalty in Shorthand, which you have committed in Text.'

6 bomball] A compound of 'bomb' and 'ball'.

20 Adoniram] Byfield, a clerk of the Westminster Assembly whose minutes have been published in modern times. A great ejector of the clergy, who unfortunately did not live long enough to be ejected himself.

26 This stuff does not by any means sound nice.

32 ducatoons] One would take it that the ducatoon had a back view of some one's head; but a passage of *Hudibras*, and Grey's note on it, have complicated the matter with a story about the Archduke Albert of Austria, which seems to have little if any relevance *here*.

35 antick heads] = 'gargoyles'.

41 classic] As in Milton. Nor is this the only point in which the two old Christ's men, now on such opposite sides, agree in the 'New Forcers of Conscience' and this piece.

52 *1653* great-changing—a mere misprint.

54 do swagger for] *1677* most suspiciously improves to '*are champions* for'.

From l. 43 onwards *1653* has the whole in italics, and it is pretty clear that after the first four lines the Echo speaks to the end. The 'Vindicators' do not seem to have seen this, though the absence of the quotes above would not prove it. Professor Case, however, thinks that 'So' refers to what precedes, and that in l. 47 and onwards the author and Echo speaks. It is possible.

The Antiplatonic.

For shame, thou everlasting wooer,

Still saying grace and never falling to her!

Love that 's in contemplation placed

Is Venus drawn but to the waist.

Unless your flame confess its gender,

And your parley cause surrender,

Y' are salamanders of a cold desire

That live untouched amidst the hottest fire.

What though she be a dame of stone,

10The widow of Pygmalion,

As hard and unrelenting she

As the new-crusted Niobe,

Or (what doth more of statue carry)
A nun of the Platonic quarry?
Love melts the rigour which the rocks have bred—
A flint will break upon a feather-bed.

For shame, you pretty female elves,
Cease for to candy up your selves;
No more, you sectaries of the game,
20No more of your calcining flame!
Women commence by Cupid's dart
As a king hunting dubs a hart.
Love's votaries enthral each other's soul,
Till both of them live but upon parole.
Virtue's no more in womankind
But the green-sickness of the mind;
Philosophy (their new delight)
A kind of charcoal appetite.
There 's no sophistry prevails
30Where all-convincing love assails,
But the disputing petticoat will warp,
As skilful gamesters are to seek at sharp.
The soldier, that man of iron,
Whom ribs of horror all environ,
That's strung with wire instead of veins,
In whose embraces you're in chains,
Let a magnetic girl appear,
Straight he turns Cupid's cuirassier.
Love storms his lips, and takes the fortress in,
40For all the bristled turnpikes of his chin.

Since love's artillery then checks

The breastworks of the firmest sex,

Come, let us in affections riot;

Th' are sickly pleasures keep a diet.

Give me a lover bold and free,

Not eunuched with formality,

Like an ambassador that beds a queen

With the nice caution of a sword between.

The Antiplatonic. (*1653.*) This is a sort of half-way house between Cleveland's burlesques and his serious or semi-serious poems like *Fuscara*. It is also nearer to Suckling and the graceful-graceless school than most of his things. It is good.

2 The alteration of *1677* 'and ne'er fall to her' may be only an example of the tendency to 'regularize' (in this case by the omission of an extra foot). But I confess it seems to me better: for the slight irregularity of the construction replaces that of the line to advantage.

10 I don't know whether the conceit of 'Pygmalion's *widow*' returning to marble (or ivory) when her husband-lover's embraces ceased is original with Cleveland. If it is, I make him my compliment. There is at any rate no hint of it in Ovid.

18 *1677* changed the good old '*for*' to 'thus'.

19 sectaries of] = 'heretics in'.

20 This is good: 'calcining flame' is good.

22 'dubs' is said to mean 'stabs', as it certainly means 'strikes'; but this seems to have little or no appropriateness here and to ignore the quaint conceit of 'commence' in its academic meaning. 'Women *take their degrees* by Cupid's dart: as the fact of being hunted by a king *ennobles* a hart.' Cupid = the King of Love.

24 'parole' too has a very delectable double meaning. This poem is really full of most excellent differences.

25-9 The lesson of the unregenerate Donne and the never-regenerate Carew.

32 gamesters] = 'fencers'. to seek at sharp] = 'not good at sword-play'.

33 'The sol-di-er'. By the way, did Butler borrow this 'iron' and 'environ' rhyme from Cleveland?

43 The apostrophating mania made *1653* contract to 'let's' and spoil the verse.

44 Th'] here of course = 'they'.

Fuscara, or the Bee Errant.

Nature's confectioner, the bee

(Whose suckets are moist alchemy,

The still of his refining mould

Minting the garden into gold),

Having rifled all the fields

Of what dainties Flora yields,

Ambitious now to take excise

Of a more fragrant paradise,

At my Fuscara's sleeve arrived

10Where all delicious sweets are hived.

The airy freebooter distrains

First on the violets of her veins,

Whose tincture, could it be more pure,

His ravenous kiss had made it bluer.

Here did he sit and essence quaff

Till her coy pulse had beat him off;

That pulse which he that feels may know

Whether the world 's long-lived or no.

The next he preys on is her palm,

20That alm'ner of transpiring balm;

So soft, 'tis air but once removed;

Tender as 'twere a jelly gloved.

Here, while his canting drone-pipe scanned

The mystic figures of her hand,

He tipples palmistry and dines
On all her fortune-telling lines.
He bathes in bliss and finds no odds
Betwixt her nectar and the gods',

He perches now upon her wrist,
30A proper hawk for such a fist,
Making that flesh his bill of fare
Which hungry cannibals would spare;
Where lilies in a lovely brown
Inoculate carnation.
He *argent* skin with *or* so streamed
As if the milky way were creamed.
From hence he to the woodbine bends
That quivers at her fingers' ends,
That runs division on the tree
40Like a thick-branching pedigree.
So 'tis not her the bee devours,
It is a pretty maze of flowers;
It is the rose that bleeds, when he
Nibbles his nice phlebotomy.
About her finger he doth cling
I' th' fashion of a wedding-ring,
And bids his comrades of the swarm
Crawl as a bracelet 'bout her arm.
Thus when the hovering publican
50Had sucked the toll of all her span,
Tuning his draughts with drowsy hums
As Danes carouse by kettle-drums,

It was decreed, that posie gleaned,

The small familiar should be weaned.

At this the errant's courage quails;

Yet aided by his native sails

The bold Columbus still designs

To find her undiscovered mines.

To th' Indies of her arm he flies,

60Fraught both with east and western prize;

Which when he had in vain essayed,

Armed like a dapper lancepresade

With Spanish pike, he broached a pore

And so both made and healed the sore:

For as in gummy trees there 's found

A salve to issue at the wound,

Of this her breach the like was true:

Hence trickled out a balsam, too.

But oh, what wasp was 't that could prove

70Ravaillac to my Queen of Love!

The King of Bees now 's jealous grown

Lest her beams should melt his throne,

And finding that his tribute slacks,

His burgesses and state of wax

Turned to a hospital, the combs

Built rank-and-file like beadsmen's rooms,

And what they bleed but tart and sour

Matched with my Danae's golden shower,

Live-honey all,—the envious elf

80Stung her, 'cause sweeter than himself.

Sweetness and she are so allied

The bee committed parricide.

Fuscara. (*1651.*) Cleveland's most famous poem of the amatory, as *The Rebel Scot* is of the political, kind. In *1677* and since it has been set in the forefront of his *Poems*, and Johnson draws specially on it for his famous diatribe against the metaphysicals in the 'Life of Cowley'. It seems to me inferior both to *The Muses' Festival* and to *The Antiplatonic*, and, as was said in the Introduction, it betrays, to me, something of an intention to fool the lovers of a fashionable style to the top of their bent. But it has extremely pretty things in it; and Mr. Addison, who denounced and scorned 'false wit', never 'fair-sexed it' in half so poetical a manner.

2 'Suckets' or 'succades' should need interpretation to no reader of *Robinson Crusoe*: and no one who has not read *Robinson Crusoe* deserves to be taken into consideration.

13 tincture] Said to be used here in an alchemical sense for 'gold'. But the plain meaning is much better.

18 Although the sense is not quite the same as, it is much akin to, that of Browning's question—

'Who knows but the world may end to night?'

20 Cleveland of course uses the correct and not the modern and blundering sense of 'transpire'.

22 This 'jelly gloved' is *not* like 'mobled queen' or 'calcining flame'.

25-6 *1653* and its group have a queer misprint (carried out so as to rhyme, but hardly possible as a true reading) of 'dives' and 'lives'. If they had had 'In' instead of 'On' it would have been on the (metaphysical) cards, especially with 'bathes' following.

28 *1653*, less well, '*the* nectar'.

30 Neat, i' faith!

33 'a lovely *brown*' as being *Fuscara*.

35 Here Cleveland dares his 'ill armoury again'; *v. sup.*, p. 25. 'He' *1651, 1653*: 'Her' *1677*.

48 as] *1677*, unnecessarily, 'like'. Some (baddish) editions '*on* a bracelet'.

52 Hardly necessary to notice as another of Cleveland's Shakespearian touches.

62 The correcter form is 'lancepesade'.

70 *'Ratillias'* *1651*: *'Ratilias'* *1653*: corrected in *1677*.

71 *1677*, dropping the verb from 'now's', improves the sense very much.

---

*An Elegy upon Doctor Chad[d]erton, the first Master of Emanuel College in Cambridge, being above an hundred years old when he died.

(Occasioned by his long-deferred funeral.)

Pardon, dear Saint, that we so late

With lazy sighs bemoan thy fate,

And with an after-shower of verse

And tears, we thus bedew thy hearse.

Till now, alas! we did not weep,

Because we thought thou didst but sleep.

Thou liv'dst so long we did not know

Whether thou couldst now die or no.

We looked still when thou shouldst arise

10And ope the casements of thine eyes.

Thy feet, which have been used so long

To walk, we thought, must still go on.

Thine ears, after a hundred year,

Might now plead custom for to hear.

Upon thy head that reverend snow

Did dwell some fifty years ago:

And then thy cheeks did seem to have

The sad resemblance of a grave.

Wert thou e'er young? For truth I hold

20And do believe thou wert born old.

There 's none alive, I'm sure, can say

They knew thee young, but always grey.

And dost thou now, venerable oak,

Decline at Death's unhappy stroke?

Tell me, dear son, why didst thou die

And leave 's to write an elegy?

We're young, alas! and know thee not.

Send up old Abram and grave Lot.

Let them write thy Epitaph and tell

30The world thy worth; they kenned thee well.

When they were boys, they heard thee preach

And thought an angel did them teach.

Awake them then: and let them come

And score thy virtues on thy tomb,

That we at those may wonder more

Than at thy many years before.

An Elegy, &c. This and the following piece are among the disputed poems, but as they occur in *1653* I give them, with warning and asterisked. The *D.N.B.* allows (with a ?) 104 years (1536?-1640) to Chadderton. As the first Master of the House of pure Emmanuel he might be supposed unlikely to extract a tear from Cleveland. But he had resigned his Mastership nearly twenty years before his death, and that death occurred before the troubles became *insanabile vulnus.* There is nothing to require special annotation in it, or indeed in either, though in *Doctor Chadderton,* l. 23, one may safely guess that either 'thou' or 'now' is an intrusion; in l. 25 of the same that 'son' should be 'sir', 'sire', 'saint', &c.; and in l. 29 that 'th' Epitaph' is likelier.

---

*Mary's Spikenard.

Shall I presume,

Without perfume,

My Christ to meet

That is all sweet?

No! I'll make most pleasant posies,

Catch the breath of new-blown roses,

Top the pretty merry flowers,

Which laugh in the fairest bowers,

Whose sweetness Heaven likes so well,

10It stoops each morn to take a smell.

Then I'll fetch from the Phœnix' nest

The richest spices and the best,

Precious ointments I will make;

Holy Myrrh and aloes take,

Yea, costly Spikenard in whose smell

The sweetness of all odours dwell.

I'll get a box to keep it in,

Pure as his alabaster skin:

And then to him I'll nimbly fly

20Before one sickly minute die.

This box I'll break, and on his head

This precious ointment will I spread,

Till ev'ry lock and ev'ry hair

For sweetness with his breath compare:

But sure the odour of his skin

Smells sweeter than the spice I bring.

Then with bended knee I'll greet

His holy and belovéd feet;

I'll wash them with a weeping eye,

30And then my lips shall kiss them dry;

Or for a towel he shall have

My hair—such flax as nature gave.

But if my wanton locks be bold,

And on Thy sacred feet take hold,

And curl themselves about, as though

They were loath to let thee go,

O chide them not, and bid away,

For then for grief they will grow grey.

Mary's Spikenard (*1652*) of course suggests Crashaw; and yet when one reads it the thought must surely occur, 'How differently Crashaw would have done it!' I do not think either is Cleveland's, though the odd string of unrelated conceits in the Chadderton piece is not unlike him. In the other there is nothing like his usual style; but it is very pretty, and I will not say he could not have done it as an exception. But in that case it is a pity he did not make it a rule.

To Julia to expedite her Promise.

Since 'tis my doom, Love's undershrieve,

Why this reprieve?

Why doth my she-advowson fly

Incumbency?

Panting expectance makes us prove

The antics of benighted love,

And withered mates when wedlock joins,

They're Hymen's monkeys, which he ties by th' loins

To play, alas! but at rebated foins.

10To sell thyself dost thou intend

By candle end,

And hold the contract thus in doubt,

Life's taper out?

Think but how soon the market fails;

Your sex lives faster than the males;

As if, to measure age's span,

The sober Julian were th' account of man,

Whilst you live by the fleet Gregorian.

Now since you bear a date so short,

20Live double for 't.

How can thy fortress ever stand

If 't be not manned?

The siege so gains upon the place

Thou'lt find the trenches in thy face.

Pity thyself then if not me,

And hold not out, lest like Ostend thou be

Nothing but rubbish at delivery.

The candidates of Peter's chair

Must plead grey hair,

30And use the simony of a cough

To help them off.

But when I woo, thus old and spent,

I'll wed by will and testament.

No, let us love while crisped and curled;

The greatest honours, on the agéd hurled,

Are but gay furloughs for another world.

To-morrow what thou tenderest me

Is legacy.

Not one of all those ravenous hours

40But thee devours.

And though thou still recruited be,

Like Pelops, with soft ivory,

Though thou consume but to renew,

Yet Love as lord doth claim a heriot due;

That 's the best quick thing I can find of you.

I feel thou art consenting ripe

By that soft gripe,

And those regealing crystal spheres.

I hold thy tears

50Pledges of more distilling sweets,

The bath that ushers in the sheets.

Else pious Julia, angel-wise,

Moves the Bethesda of her trickling eyes

To cure the spital world of maladies.

To Julia, &c. Johnson singled out the opening verse of this as a special example of 'bringing remote ideas together'.

1 'Shrieve' of course = 'Sheriff'.

3-4 'advowson' (again of course, but these things get curiously mistaken nowadays) = '*right* of presenting to or enjoying a benefice'. 'Incumbency' = 'the actual *occupation* or enjoyment'. Cf. *Square-Cap*, ll. 37-8.

9 rebated] The opposite of '*un*bated' in *Hamlet*—with the button *on*.

11 Mr. Pepys on November 6, 1660, watched this process (which was specially used in ship-selling) for the first time and with interest. 'candle' *1653*: 'candle's' *1677*.

17-18 Not a very happy 'conceiting' of the fact that in a millennium and a half the Julian reckoning had got ten days behindhand.

27 The siege of Ostend (1601-4) lasted three years and seventy-seven days.

34 Did a far greater Cambridge poet think of this in writing

'When the locks are crisp and curl'd?'

(*The Vision of Sin.*)

48 regealing] Cleveland seems to use this unusual word in the sense of '*un*freezing'.

51 *1677* spoils sense and verse alike by beginning the line with 'Than'. The 'tears' *are* the 'bath'.

Poems in 1677 but not in 1653.

Upon Princess Elizabeth, born the night before New Year's Day.

Astrologers say Venus, the self-same star,

Is both our Hesperus and Lucifer;

The antitype, this Venus, makes it true;

She shuts the old year and begins the new.

Her brother with a star at noon was born;

She, like a star both of the eve and morn.

Count o'er the stars, fair Queen, in babes, and vie

With every year a new Epiphany.

Upon Princess Elizabeth. Not before *1677*. This slight thing is inaccurately entitled, for the Princess was born on December 26, 1638.

1 The rhyme of 'star' and 'Lucif*er*', which occurs (with 'travell*er*') in Dryden, is—like all Cleveland's rhymes, I think without exception—perfectly sound on the general principle then observed, and observed partly at all times, that *a vowel may, for rhyming purposes, take the sound that it has in a similar connexion but in another word.*

5 brother] Charles II.

The General Eclipse.

Ladies that gild the glittering noon,

And by reflection mend his ray,

Whose beauty makes the sprightly sun

To dance as upon Easter-day,

What are you now the Queen 's away?

Courageous Eagles, who have whet

Your eyes upon majestic light,

And thence derived such martial heat

That still your looks maintain the fight,

10What are you since the King's good-night?

Cavalier-buds, whom Nature teems
As a reserve for England's throne,
Spirits whose double edge redeems
The last Age and adorns your own,
What are you now the Prince is gone?
As an obstructed fountain's head
Cuts the entail off from the streams,
And brooks are disinherited,
Honour and Beauty are mere dreams
20Since Charles and Mary lost their beams!

Criminal Valours, who commit
Your gallantry, whose paean brings
A psalm of mercy after it,
In this sad solstice of the King's,
Your victory hath mewed her wings!
See, how your soldier wears his cage
Of iron like the captive Turk,
And as the guerdon of his rage!
See, how your glimmering Peers do lurk,
30Or at the best, work journey-work!
Thus 'tis a general eclipse,
And the whole world is al-a-mort;
Only the House of Commons trips
The stage in a triumphant sort.
Now e'en John Lilburn take 'em for't!

The General Eclipse. The poem is of course a sort of variation or *scherzo* on
'You meaner beauties of the night'.

20 We are so accustomed to the double name 'Henrietta Maria' that the simple 'Queen Mary' may seem strange. But it was the Cavalier word at Naseby.

32 al-a-mort] Formerly quite naturalized, especially in the form all-amort. See *N.E.D.*, s.v. 'Alamort'.

Upon the King's Return from Scotland.

Returned, I'll ne'er believe 't; first prove him hence;

Kings travel by their beams and influence.

Who says the soul gives out her gests, or goes

A flitting progress 'twixt the head and toes?

She rules by omnipresence, and shall we

Deny a prince the same ubiquity?

Or grant he went, and, 'cause the knot was slack,

Girt both the nations with his zodiac,

Yet as the tree at once both upward shoots,

10And just as much grows downward to the roots,

So at the same time that he posted thither

By counter-stages he rebounded hither.

Hither and hence at once; thus every sphere

Doth by a double motion interfere;

And when his native form inclines him east,

By the first mover he is ravished west.

Have you not seen how the divided dam

Runs to the summons of her hungry lamb;

But when the twin cries halves, she quits the first?

20Nature's commendam must be likewise nursed.

So were his journeys like the spider spun

Out of his bowels of compassion.

Two realms, like Cacus, so his steps transpose,

His feet still contradict him as he goes.

England 's returned that was a banished soil.

The bullet flying makes the gun recoil.

Death 's but a separation, though endorsed

With spade and javelin; we were thus divorced.

Our soul hath taken wing while we express

30The corpse, returning to our principles.

But the Crab-tropic must not now prevail;

Islands go back but when you're under sail.

So his retreat hath rectified that wrong;

Backward is forward in the Hebrew tongue.

Now the Church Militant in plenty rests,

Nor fears, like th' Amazon, to lose her breasts.

Her means are safe; not squeezed until the blood

Mix with the milk and choke the tender brood.

She, that hath been the floating ark, is that

40She that 's now seated on Mount Ararat.

Quits Charles; our souls did guard him northward thus

Now he the counterpart comes south to us.

Upon the King's Return, &c. In 1641—an ill-omened and unsuccessful journey, which lasted from August to November. The piece is one of the very few of those in *Cleaveland Revived* acknowledged and admitted by *Clievelandi Vindiciae*.

3 *1659* 'ghests'; *1662, 1668* 'guests'; *1677* 'gests'. See *N.E.D.*, s.v. 'gest' *sb.*[4]. which defines it as 'the various stages of a journey, especially of a royal progress; the route followed or planned'.

20 commendam] (misprinted '-dum' from *1659* to *1677*). A benefice held with another; something additional.

21: 'spider' *1677*; 'spider's' *1659, 1662, 1668*.

25 'banished' *1677*: 'barren' *1659, 1662, 1668*.

30 In this very obscure and ultra-Clevelandian line *1677* reads 'their'. I think 'our'—the reading of *Cleaveland Revived*, followed by *1662* and *1668*—is better. But the whole poem (one of Cleveland's earliest political attempts) is weak and pithless.

33 'that' *1687*: 'the' *1659, 1662, 1668*.

42 'counterpart' *1677*: 'counterpane' *1659, 1662, 1668*.

Poems certainly or almost certainly Cleveland's but not included in 1653 or 1677.

Poems, &c. I have been exceedingly chary of admission under this head, for there seems to me to be no reasonable *via media* between such severity and the complete reprinting of *1687*—with perhaps the *known* larcenies in that and its originals left out. Thus, of eleven poems given—but as 'not in *1677*'— by Mr. Berdan I have kept but three, besides one or two which, though not in *1677*, are in *1653*, and so appear above. Of these the Jonson Elegy from *Jonsonus Virbius* is signed, and as well authenticated as anything can be; *News from Newcastle* is quoted by Johnson and therefore of importance to students of the *Lives.* The *Elegy upon Charles I* is in *1654* among the poems which that collection adds to *1653*, is very like him, and relieves Cleveland partly, if not wholly, from the charge of being wanting to the greatest occasion of his life and calling.

Poems certainly or almost certainly Cleveland's but not included in 1653 or 1677.

An Elegy on Ben Jonson.

Who first reformed our stage with justest laws,

And was the first best judge in his own cause;

Who, when his actors trembled for applause,

Could (with a noble confidence) prefer

His own, by right, to a whole theatre;

From principles which he knew could not err:

Who to his fable did his persons fit,

With all the properties of art and wit,

And above all that could be acted, writ:

10Who public follies did to covert drive,

Which he again could cunningly retrive,

Leaving them no ground to rest on and thrive:

Here JONSON lies, whom, had I named before,

In that one word alone I had paid more

Than can be now, when plenty makes me poor.

J. CL.

An Elegy, &c. Although this appears neither in *1653* nor in *1677*, it is included, with some corruptions not worth noting, in some editions both before and after the latter. Gifford ascribed to Cleveland another unsigned Elegy in *Jonsonus Virbius* and one of the Odes to Ben Jonson on his own Ode to himself, 'Come, quit the loathèd stage'. There is no authority for the ascription in either case, and the styles of both pieces are as unlike as possible to Cleveland's.

2 Orig., by a slip, '*your* own cause'. Cleveland may have meant to address the poet throughout, or till the last verse; but, if so, he evidently changed his mind.

News from Newcastle:
Upon the Coal-pits about Newcastle-upon-Tyne.

England 's a perfect world, has Indies too;

Correct your maps, Newcastle is Peru!

Let th' haughty Spaniard triumph till 'tis told

Our sooty min'rals purify his gold.

This will sublime and hatch the abortive ore,

When the sun tires and stars can do no more.

No! mines are current, unrefined, and gross;

Coals make the sterling, Nature but the dross.

For metals, Bacchus-like, two births approve;

10Heaven's heat 's the Semele, and ours the Jove.

Thus Art doth polish Nature; 'tis her trade:

So every madam has her chambermaid.

Who'd dote on gold? A thing so strange and odd,

'Tis most contemptible when made a god!

All sins and mischiefs thence have rise and swell;

One Indies more would make another Hell.

Our mines are innocent, nor will the North

Tempt poor mortality with too much worth.

Th' are not so precious; rich enough to fire

20A lover, yet make none idolater.

The moderate value of our guiltless ore

Makes no man atheist, nor no woman whore.

Yet why should hallowed Vesta's glowing shrine

Deserve more honour than a flaming mine?

These pregnant wombs of heat would fitter be,

Than a few embers, for a deity.

Had he our pits, the Persian would admire

No sun, but warm 's devotion at our fire.

He'd leave the trotting Whipster, and prefer

30This profound Vulcan 'bove that Wagoner.

For wants he heat, or light? would he have store

Of both? 'Tis here. And what can suns give more?

Nay, what 's that sun but, in a different name,

A coal-pit rampant, or a mine on flame?

Then let this truth reciprocally run,

The sun 's Heaven's coalery, and coals our sun;

A sun that scorches not, locked up i' th' deep;

The bandog 's chained, the lion is asleep.

That tyrant fire, which uncontrolled doth rage,

40Here 's calm and hushed, like Bajazet i' th' cage.

For in each coal-pit there doth couchant dwell

A muzzled Etna, or an innocent Hell.

Kindle the cloud, you'll lightning then descry;

Then will a day break from the gloomy sky;

Then you'll unbutton though December blow,

And sweat i' th' midst of icicles and snow;

The dog-days then at Christmas. Thus is all

The year made June and equinoctial.

If heat offend, our pits afford us shade,

50Thus summer 's winter, winter 's summer made.

What need we baths, what need we bower or grove?

A coal-pit's both a ventiduct and stove.

Such pits and caves were palaces of old;

Poor inns, God wot, yet in an age of gold;

And what would now be thought a strange design,

To build a house was then to undermine.

People lived under ground, and happy dwellers

Whose jovial habitations were all cellars!

These primitive times were innocent, for then

60Man, who turned after fox, but made his den.

But see a fleet of rivals trim and fine,

To court the rich infanta of our mine;

Hundreds of grim Leanders dare confront,

For this loved Hero, the loud Hellespont.

'Tis an armado royal doth engage

For some new Helen with this equipage;

Prepared too, should we their addresses bar,

To force their mistress with a ten years' war,

But that our mine 's a common good, a joy

70Made not to ruin but enrich our Troy.

Thus went those gallant heroes of old Greece,

The Argonauts, in quest o' th' Golden Fleece.

But oh! these bring it with 'em and conspire

To pawn that idol for our smoke and fire.

Silver 's but ballast; this they bring ashore

That they may treasure up our better ore.

For this they venter rocks and storms, defy

All the extremities of sea and sky.

For the glad purchase of this precious mould,

80Cowards dare pirates, misers part with gold.

Hence 'tis that when the doubtful ship sets forth

The knowing needle still directs it north,

And Nature's secret wonder, to attest

Our Indies' worth, discards both east and west.
For 'tis not only fire commends this spring,
A coal-pit is a mine of everything.
We sink a jack-of-all-trades shop, and sound
An inversed Burse, an Exchange under ground.
This Proteus earth converts to what you'd ha' 't:
90Now you may weave 't to silk, then coin 't to plate,

And, what 's a metamorphosis more dear,
Dissolve it and 'twill melt to London beer.
For whatsoe'er that gaudy city boasts,
Each month derives to these attractive coasts.
We shall exhaust their chamber and devour
Their treasures of Guildhall, the Mint, the Tower.
Our staiths their mortgaged streets will soon divide,
Blathon owe Cornhill, Stella share Cheapside.
Thus will our coal-pits' charity and pity
100At distance undermine and fire the City.
Should we exact, they'd pawn their wives and treat
To swap those coolers for our sovereign heat.
'Bove kisses and embraces fire controls;
No Venus heightens like a peck of coals.
Medea was the drudge of some old sire
And Aeson's bath a lusty sea-coal fire.
Chimneys are old men's mistresses, their inns,
A modern dalliance with their measled shins.
To all defects the coal-heap brings a cure,
110Gives life to age and raiment to the poor.
Pride first wore clothes; Nature disdains attire;

She made us naked 'cause she gave us fire.

Full wharfs are wardrobes, and the tailor's charm

Belongs to th' collier; he must keep us warm.

The quilted alderman with all 's array

Finds but cold comfort on a frosty day;

Girt, wrapped, and muffled, yet with all that stir

Scarce warm when smoth'red in his drowsy fur;

Not proof against keen Winter's batteries

120Should he himself wear all 's own liveries,

But chilblains under silver spurs bewails

And in embroid'red buckskins blows his nails.

Rich meadows and full crops are elsewhere found:

We can reap harvest from our barren ground.

The bald parched hills that circumscribe our Tyne

Are no less fruitful in their hungry mine.

Their unfledged tops so well content our palates,

We envy none their nosegays and their sallets.

A gay rank soil like a young gallant grows

130And spends itself that it may wear fine clothes,

Whilst all its worth is to its back confined.

Our wear 's plain outside, but is richly lined;

Winter 's above, 'tis summer underneath,

A trusty morglay in a rusty sheath.

As precious sables sometimes interlace

A wretched serge or grogram cassock case.

Rocks own no spring, are pregnant with no showers,

Crystals and gems grow there instead of flowers;

Instead of roses, beds of rubies sweat

140And emeralds recompense the violet.

Dame Nature not, like other madams, wears,

Where she is bare, pearls on her breasts or ears.

What though our fields present a naked sight?

A paradise should be an adamite.

The northern lad his bonny lass throws down

And gives her a black bag for a green gown.

News from Newcastle, if not Cleveland's, is infinitely more of a Clevelandism than any other attributed piece, either in the untrustworthy (or rather upside-down-trustworthy) *Cleaveland Revived* or elsewhere. It first appeared as a quarto pamphlet, 'London. Printed in the year 1651. By William Ellis', and with a headline to the poem 'Upon the Coalpits about Newcastle-upon-Tyne'. This quarto furnishes the only sound text. It was reprinted very corruptly in *Cleaveland Revived*, *1660*, and thence in the editions of *1662*, *1668*, *1687*, and later. A collation of *1660* is given. Title in *1660* 'News from Newcastle, Or, Newcastle Coal-pits'. MS. Rawlinson Poet, 65 of the Bodleian has a version agreeing in the main with *1660*.

1 has] hath *1660, MS.*

5 'obortive' *1668.*

7 *1651*, later texts, and *MS.* 'No mines', which has no meaning without a stop or interjection.

8 'nature's' *MS.*

10 'Heaven heats' *1660*. The mine is the womb of Semele warmed by the sun: the furnace the thigh of Jove heated by coal.

11 her] the *1660*: its *MS.*

12 has] hath *1660, MS.*

15 'sin and mischief hence' *1660*: 'sin and mischief thence' *MS.*

16 Indies] India *1660.*

17 mines] times *MS.*

19 *1660* 'so': *1651* 'too', unconsciously repeating the 'too much' of l. 18.

20 none] no *MS.*

22 Simply an adaptation of the earlier conclusion—

'Should make men atheists and not women whores'.

23 Vesta's glowing] Vestals' sacred *1660*. shrine] shine *MS*.

29 trotting Whipster] Phoebus, of course.

30 This] Our *1660, MS*.

31 light? would he] light, or would *1660*. store] Misprinted 'more' in *1651*.

32 suns] Sun *MS*.

33 that] the *1660*.

34 on flame] or flame *1660*.

36 coalery] Original and pleasing. 'Collier' is used below.

37 scorches] scorcheth *1660, MS*.

38 bandog's] lion's *1660*. lion] bandog *1660*.

42 or] and *MS*.

43 the] this *MS*.

45 'Un*bottom*,' by evident error, in *1668*.

47 Thus] Then *MS*.

49 'offends' *1660*. 'affords' *1660*.

60 but made] made but *1660, MS*.

61 rivals] vitals *1660*.

63 dare] do *1660*.

68 their] this *1660, MS*.

71-2 Omitted in *1660* and all later texts. *1651* misprints 'Argeuauts'.

73 'em] them *1660, MS*.

75 ashore] on shore *1660, MS*.

76 better] richer *MS*.

78 extremities] extremity *1660*.

81 'tis that] is it *1660, MS*.

82 knowing] naving *1660*: knavish *MS*.

83 wonder] wonders *1660*.

84 both] with *MS*.

85 For 'tis not] For Tyne. Not *1660* (without the period at l. 84), *MS*.

86 of] for *1660*.

87 *1651* mispunctuates with a comma at 'sink'; *1660* adds comma at 'jack-of-all-trades' and 'sound': *MS*. punctuates correctly.

88 inversed] inverse *1660*.

89 you'd] you'l *1660*.

90 weave 't] wear't *1660*. then] now *1660*. coin 't] com't *1660*.

91 And] Or *MS*.

92 melt] turn *1660*, *MS*.

93 boasts] boast *1660*.

94 derives] doth drive *1660*, *MS*. these] our *1660*, *MS*. coasts] coast *1660*.

96 treasures] treasure *1660*, *MS*. the Mint, the] and mint o' th' *1660*, *MS*.

97 staiths] Wooden erections projecting into the river, which were used to store the coal and fitted with spouts for shooting it into the ships. divide] deride *1660*.

98 'Blathon their Cornhill, Stella' *MS*: 'Blazon their Cornhill-stella,' *1660*.] Blathon, now Blaydon, the mining district. 'owe' = own. 'Stella' Hall, near Blaydon, was a nunnery before the Dissolution, when it passed into the hands of the Tempests. (Mr. Nichol Smith kindly supplied this information.)

102 swap] swop *1660*.

105 drudge] drugge *1660*, *MS*.

109 the] a *1659*. brings] gives *1660*, *MS*.

110 life] youth *1660*.

113 tailor's] sailor's *MS*.

115 with] in *1660*.

116 on] in *1660*, *MS*.

117 that] this *1660*.

119 Not] Nor'st *MS*. 'proof enough' *1651*: 'enough' is omitted in *1660*, and deleted by a seventeenth-century corrector in the Bodleian copy of *1651*.

121 chilblains] chilblain *1660*.

126 fruitful] pregnant *1660*.

128 and] or *MS*.

134 Cleveland has used 'morglay', Bevis's sword, as a common noun elsewhere; but of course an imitator might seize on this.

138 grow] are *1660*.

139 sweat] sweet *1668, 1687, MS.*

142 on] in *1660*. or] and *1660*. 'breasts, not ears' *MS.*

145-6 Or as a modern Newcastle song, more decently but less picturesquely, puts it in the lass's own mouth—

'He sits in his hole,

As black as a coal,

And brings the white money to me—O!'

An Elegy upon King Charles the First, murdered publicly by his Subjects.

Were not my faith buoyed up by sacred blood,

It might be drowned in this prodigious flood;

Which reason's highest ground doth so exceed,

It leaves my soul no anch'rage but my creed;

Where my faith, resting on th' original,

Supports itself in this, the copy's fall.

So while my faith floats on that bloody wood,

My reason 's cast away in this red flood

Which near o'erflows us all. Those showers past

10Made but land-floods, which did some valleys waste.

This stroke hath cut the only neck of land

Which between us and this red sea did stand,

That covers now our world which curséd lies

At once with two of Egypt's prodigies

(O'ercast with darkness and with blood o'errun),

And justly since our hearts have theirs outdone.

Th' enchanter led them to a less known ill
To act his sin, than 'twas their king to kill;
Which crime hath widowed our whole nation,
20Voided all forms, left but privation
In Church and State; inverting every right;
Brought in Hell's state of fire without light.
No wonder then if all good eyes look red,
Washing their loyal hearts from blood so shed;
The which deserves each pore should turn an eye
To weep out even a bloody agony.
Let nought then pass for music but sad cries,
For beauty bloodless cheeks and blood-shot eyes.
All colours soil but black; all odours have
30Ill scent but myrrh, incens'd upon this grave.
It notes a Jew not to believe us much
The cleaner made by a religious touch
Of this dead body, whom to judge to die
Seems the Judaical impiety.
To kill the King, the Spirit Legion paints
His rage with law, the Temple and the saints.
But the truth is, he feared and did repine
To be cast out and back into the swine.
And the case holds, in that the Spirit bends
40His malice in this act against his ends;
For it is like the sooner he'll be sent
Out of that body he would still torment.
Let Christians then use otherwise this blood;
Detest the act, yet turn it to their good;
Thinking how like a King of Death he dies

We easily may the world and death despise.

Death had no sting for him and its sharp arm,

Only of all the troop, meant him no harm.

And so he looked upon the axe as one

50Weapon yet left to guard him to his throne.

In his great name then may his subjects cry,

'Death, thou art swallowed up in victory.'

If this, our loss, a comfort can admit,

'Tis that his narrowed crown is grown unfit

For his enlargéd head, since his distress

Had greatened this, as it made that the less.

His crown was fallen unto too low a thing

For him who was become so great a king.

So the same hands enthroned him in that crown

60They had exalted from him, not pulled down.

And thus God's truth by them hath rendered more

Than e'er man's falsehood promised to restore;

Which, since by death alone he could attain,

Was yet exempt from weakness and from pain.

Death was enjoined by God to touch a part,

Might make his passage quick, ne'er move his heart,

Which even expiring was so far from death

It seemed but to command away his breath.

And thus his soul, of this her triumph proud,

70Broke like a flash of lightning through the cloud

Of flesh and blood; and from the highest line

Of human virtue, passed to be divine.

Nor is 't much less his virtues to relate

Than the high glories of his present state.

Since both, then, pass all acts but of belief,

Silence may praise the one, the other grief.

And since upon the diamond no less

Than diamonds will serve us to impress,

I'll only wish that for his elegy

80This our Josias had a Jeremy.

An Elegy, &c. See above. First printed in *Monumentum Regale, 1649,* p. 49; then in the *1654* edition of Cleveland.

3 *1654, 1657, 1669* 'doth'. Other (it is true inferior) texts, such as *1659, 1665,* and the successors of *1677,* 'do': which any one who has ever read his Pepys must know to be possible in the singular.

33 'this' *1649*: 'their' *1653* and later editions.

35: paints = 'tries to disguise'.

Since these sheets were last revised, and when they were ready for press, Mr. Simpson discovered and communicated to me some variants (from Bodley MSS.) of Cleveland's pieces on Chadderton (*v. sup.* p. 81) and Williams (p. 69). His note is as follows:

"There is a version of the *Elegy upon Doctor Chadderton* (page 81) in Ashmole MS. 36-7, fol. 263. After l. 14 four lines are inserted:

We thought, for so we would it have,

Thou hadst outlived death and the grave,

Hadst been past dying, and by thine own

Brave virtue been immortal grown.

Not very brilliant, but no one would have any motive for interpolating such lines. Further, ll. 17-18 are omitted.

25 'dear S^{nt}.' i.e. as conjectured in the note, 'Saint.'

30 'Kend' written in a larger hand, with a view to emphasis. Query, a favourite word of Chadderton?

In the same MS. is a version of the poem on Archbishop Williams (p. 69). Most readings are bad, but the following are noteworthy:

4 concorporate one.

11 And vindicate whate'er.

55 when happier ages (which of late

The viper cherish'd) with unpartial fate."

---

* *
*

POEMS,

BY

THOMAS STANLEY

Esquire.

Quæ mea culpa tamen, nisi si lusisse vocari
Culpa potest: nisi culpa potest & amasse, vocari?

INTRODUCTION TO THOMAS STANLEY

Thomas Stanley, poet, scholar, translator, and historian of philosophy, occupies a position in literary history, and in the general knowledge of fairly instructed people, which is less unenviable than that of Cleveland, almost equally curious, but more distinctly accidental. In a way—in more ways than one—he cannot be said to be exactly unknown. Everybody who has received the once usual 'liberal education', if not directly acquainted with his work on classical literature, has seen his *History of Philosophy* referred to in later histories; and his notes on Aeschylus quoted, and sometimes fought over, in later editions. His translations have attained a place in that private-adventure Valhalla of English translations—Bohn's Library. A few at least of his poems are in all or most of the anthologies. Not many writers have such an anchor with four flukes, lodged in the general memory, as this. And yet there are probably few people who have any very distinct knowledge or idea of his work as a whole; his *Poems* (until a time subsequent to the original promise of them in this Collection) had never been issued since his own day save in one of the few-copied reprints of the indefatigable Sir Egerton Brydges; and he makes small figure in most literary histories.

The reasons of this, however, are not very far to seek. For a very considerable time during the later seventeenth and the whole of the eighteenth century, if not later, Stanley was a recognized authority on history and scholarship: but during this time a philosopher and a scholar would have been usually thought to derogate, strangely and not quite pardonably, by writing and translating love poetry in a style of 'false wit' the most contrary to the precepts of Mr. Addison. We cannot even be sure that Stanley himself would not have been short-sighted enough to feel a certain shame at his harmless *fredaines* in verse, for he certainly never published or fully collected them at all after he was six and twenty, though he lived to double that age. He seems, moreover, though most forward to help other men of letters, to have been in all other ways a decidedly retiring person—a man of books rather than of affairs. Though an unquestioned Royalist, and not accused of any dishonourable compliance, he seems to have been quite undisturbed during the Civil War, no doubt because of his observation of the precept λάθε βιώσας. In short, he took no trouble to keep himself before any public except the public of letters, and the public of letters chose to keep him only in his capacity as scholar.

If, however, he put himself not forward it was not for want of means and opportunity to do so. After some mistakes about his genealogy, it has been made certain that he was descended, though with the bend sinister, from the great house that bears the same name, and through a branch which enriched itself by commerce and settled in Hertfordshire and Essex. His mother was a Hammond of the family which has been referred to in dealing with his uncle the poet (vol. ii), and he was also connected with Sandys, Lovelace, and Sherburne, all of whom were his intimate friends, as were John Hall and Shirley the dramatist. He seems always to have been a man of means: and used them liberally, though less thoughtlessly than Benlowes, in assisting brother men of letters. He is not said to have been at any of the great schools, but his private tutor William Fairfax (son of Edward of Tasso fame) appears to have grounded him thoroughly in scholarship. At thirteen he went to Pembroke College (then Hall), Cambridge, entering in June 1639 and matriculating in December. He is said to have entered at Oxford next year. He was co-opted at Cambridge in 1642 as (apparently) a gentleman pensioner or commoner. He married early, his wife's name being Dorothy Enyon, and they had several children, of whom four survived him when he died, in 1678, at Suffolk Street, St. Martin's-in-the-Fields.

There is a tendency—which is perhaps rather slightly unfair than positively unjust—to suspect a poet who is specially given to translation: and not exactly to discard the suspicion in the ratio of his excellence as a translator. The reason behind this is sufficient, as has been said, to free it from the charge of positive injustice as a general rule, for it may be plausibly contended that a true poet, with nature and his own soul to draw upon, will not experience any great necessity to go to some one else for matter. But these general rules are always dangerous in particular application, and therefore it has been said that the notion is not quite fair. In fact, if it is examined as it does apply to individuals, it becomes clear that it will not do as a general rule at all—that like some other general rules it is practically useless. That Chaucer was *grant translateur* may be said to be neither here nor there in the circumstances. But Spenser did not disdain translation; Dryden evidently did it for love as well as for money, though the latter may have been its chief attraction for Pope; and a poet such as Shelley, who was very nearly *the* poet, by no means despised it.

When, however, we come to examine Stanley's work we may perhaps discover something in the very excellence of his translations which connects itself usefully with his original poems. These translations are excellent because he has almost unerringly selected writers who are suitable to the poetical style of his own day, and has transposed them into English verse of that style. But in his original poems there is perhaps a little too much suggestion of something not wholly dissimilar. They are (pretty as they almost always are, and beautiful as they sometimes are) a little devoid of the spontaneity and *élan* which distinguish the best things of the time from Carew and Crashaw down to Kynaston and John Hall. There is a very little of the *exercise* about them. Moreover, not quite as a necessary consequence of this, there is a want of decided character. Stanley is much more a typical minor Caroline poet than he is Stanley, and so much must needs be said critically in these volumes on the type that it seems unnecessary to repeat it on an individual who gives that type with little idiosyncrasy, even while giving it in some abundance and with real charm. Only let it be added that we could not have a better foil to Cleveland, who, though unpolished, is always 'Manly, Sir, manly!' than this scholarly and graceful but somewhat epicene poet.

There are, however, some peculiarities about his work which made me slow to make up my mind about the fashion of presenting it. His translations are numerous: but this collection was not originally intended to include translations unless they were inextricably connected with issues of original work, or where, as in Godolphin's case, there was a special reason. Further, the translations, which are from a large number of authors, ancient and modern, sometimes include prose as well as verse. Thirdly, even the original poems were cross-issued in widely different arrangements. In short, the thing was rather a muddle, and though no one has occupied me in my various visits to the British Museum and the Bodleian during the past ten or twelve years oftener than Stanley, I postponed him from volume to volume. At last, and very recently a feasible plan suggested itself—to give the edition of 1651 as Brydges had done, this being after all the only one which at once represents revision and definite literary purpose, and to let the translations in this represent—as the poet seems himself to have selected them to do—his translating habits and studies. Before these I have printed the original poems of the first or 1647 edition, and after them the few which he seems to have allowed to be added to the set versions in Gamble's *Airs and Dialogues* ten years later. I think this will put Stanley on a fair level with the rest of our flock. Those who want his classical translations from Anacreon, Ausonius, the Idylls, and the *Pervigilium*, as well as from Johannes Secundus, will not have much difficulty in finding them; and I did not see my way to load this volume with Preti's *Oronta*, Montalvan's *Aurora*, &c. The bibliography of these things is rather complicated, and I do not pretend to have followed it out exhaustively. In fact this is certainly the case as far as my own collations of 1647, made at the British Museum, and those furnished me from the Bodleian copy are concerned.[1] But the differences are rarely of importance. 1647, a private issue, was reprinted in 1650 and 1651: while Gamble's *Airs and Dialogues* appeared in 1656 and was reissued with a fresh title-page in 1657. In the latter year Stanley furnished another composer— John Wilson, Professor of Music at Oxford—with the letterpress of *Psalterium Carolinum*, the King's devotions from the *Eikon* versified. His *History of Philosophy* appeared in 1655: his *Aeschylus* in 1663.

Some years ago (London, 1893) a beautiful illustrated edition of his *Anacreon* appeared, and more recently—but, as I have noted, after the announcement of this collection—a carefully arranged and collated edition of the original *Lyrics* with a few selected translations (Tutin, Hull, 1907), edited by Miss L. Imogen Guiney. I have not found Miss Guiney's work useless, and if I have occasionally had to question her emendations that is only a matter of course.

1 I am informed by three subsequent collators more experienced in such work than myself—Mr. Percy Simpson, Mr. Thorn-Drury, and a Clarendon Press reader—that they have not found some differences which my own comparison-notes of some years ago seemed to show between the British Museum and the Bodleian copies of 1647. No doubt they are right. Some of the dates given above have also been corrected by them.

POEMS NOT PRINTED AFTER 1647

Despair.

No, no, poor blasted Hope!

Since I (with thee) have lost the scope

Of all my joys, I will no more

Vainly implore

The unrelenting Destinies:

He that can equally sustain

The strong assaults of joy or pain,

May safely laugh at their decrees.

Despair, to thee I bow,

10Whose constancy disdains t' allow

Those childish passions that destroy

Our fickle joy;

How cruel Fates so e'er appear,

Their harmless anger I despise,

And fix'd, can neither fall nor rise,

Thrown below hope, but rais'd 'bove fear.

Despair.] Note here the skill and success of the use of the short—almost 'bob'—lines, and the *In Memoriam* arrangement of rhyme in the last half of each stanza.

The Picture.

Thou that both feel'st and dost admire

The flames shot from a painted fire,

Know Celia's image thou dost see:

Not to herself more like is she.

He that should both together view

Would judge both pictures, or both true.

But thus they differ: the best part

Of Nature this is; that of Art.

The Picture.] The conceit wraps up the point of the epigram.

Opinion.

Whence took the diamond worth? the borrow'd rays

That crystal wears, whence had they first their praise?

Why should rude feet contemn the snow's chaste white,

Which from the sun receives a sparkling light,

Brighter than diamonds far, and by its birth

Decks the green garment of the richer earth?

Rivers than crystal clearer, when to ice

Congeal'd, why do weak judgements so despise?

Which, melting, show that to impartial sight

10Weeping than smiling crystal is more bright.

But Fancy those first priz'd, and these did scorn,

Taking their praise the other to adorn.

Thus blind is human sight: opinion gave

To their esteem a birth, to theirs a grave;

Nor can our judgements with these clouds dispense,

Since reason sees but with the eyes of sense.

Opinion.] As in *The Dream*, distinctly nervous stopped couplet.

POEMS PRINTED IN 1647 AND REPRINTED IN 1656 BUT NOT IN 1651

The Dream.

That I might ever dream thus! that some power

To my eternal sleep would join this hour!

So, willingly deceiv'd, I might possess

In seeming joys a real happiness.

Haste not away: oh do not dissipate

A pleasure thou so lately didst create!

Stay, welcome Sleep; be ever here confin'd;

Or if thou wilt away, leave her behind.

The Dream.] Closed couplets, already of considerable accomplishment. Reprinted in *1656* in an enlarged form; after ll. 1-4 the poem continued:—

Death, I would gladly bow beneath thy charms,

If thou couldst bring my Doris to my arms,

That thus at last made happy I might prove

In life the hell, in death the heaven of love.

Haste not away so soon, mock not my joy,

With the delusive sight or empty noise

Of happiness; oh do not dissipate

A pleasure thou so lately didst create!

Shadows of life or death do such bliss give,

That 'tis an equal curse to wake or live.

Stay then, kind Sleep; be ever here confin'd;

Or if thou wilt away, leave her behind.

To Chariessa, beholding herself in a Glass.

Cast, Chariessa, cast that glass away,

Nor in its crystal face thine own survey.

What can be free from Love's imperious laws

When painted shadows real flames can cause?

The fires may burn thee from this mirror rise

By the reflected beams of thine own eyes;

And thus at last, fallen with thyself in love,

Thou wilt my rival, thine own martyr prove.

But if thou dost desire thy form to view,

10Look in my heart where Love thy picture drew;

And then, if pleased with thine own shape thou be,

Learn how to love thyself in loving me.

To Chariessa &c.]   12 *1656* 'by loving'.

The Blush.

So fair Aurora doth herself discover

(Asham'd o' th' aged bed of her cold lover)

In modest blushes, whilst the treacherous light

Betrays her early shame to the world's sight.

Such a bright colour doth the morning rose

Diffuse, when she her soft self doth disclose

Half drown'd in dew, whilst on each leaf a tear

Of night doth like a dissolv'd pearl appear;

Yet 'twere in vain a colour out to seek

10To parallel my Chariessa's cheek;

Less are conferr'd with greater, and these seem

To blush like her, not she to blush like them.

But whence, fair soul, this passion? what pretence

Had guilt to stain thy spotless innocence?

Those only this feel who have guilty been,

Not any blushes know, but who know sin.

Then blush no more; but let thy chaster flame,

That knows no cause, know no effects of shame.

The Blush.] Interesting to compare prosodically with *The Dream* and *Opinion.* A much older fashion of couplet, here and there overlapped and breathless, but pointing towards the newer. In l. 11 Miss Guiney has unfortunately altered 'conferr'd' (*confero* = 'to set side by side') to 'compar'd'. In l. 15, *1647* has the common 'bin' and l. 16 'knows' for the second 'know'.

The Cold Kiss.

Such icy kisses, anchorites that live

Secluded from the world, to dead skulls give;

And those cold maids on whom Love never spent

His flame, nor know what by desire is meant,

To their expiring fathers such bequeath,

Snatching their fleeting spirits in that breath:

The timorous priest doth with such fear and nice

Devotion touch the Holy Sacrifice.

Fie, Chariessa! whence so chang'd of late,

10As to become in love a reprobate?

Quit, quit this dullness, Fairest, and make known

A flame unto me equal with mine own.

Shake off this frost, for shame, that dwells upon

Thy lips; or if it will not so be gone,

Let 's once more join our lips, and thou shalt see

That by the flame of mine 'twill melted be.

The Cold Kiss.] There are some very trifling alterations, all for the worse, in *1656* (Gamble).

The Idolater.

Think not, pale lover, he who dies,

Burnt in the flames of Celia's eyes,

Is unto Love a sacrifice;

Or, by the merit of this pain,

Thou shalt the crown of martyrs gain!

Those hopes are, as thy passion, vain.

For when, by death, from these flames free,

To greater thou condemn'd shalt be,

And punish'd for idolatry,

10Since thou (Love's votary before

Whilst He was kind) dost him no more,

But, in his shrine, Disdain adore.

Nor will this fire (the gods prepare

To punish scorn) that cruel Fair,

(Though now from flames exempted) spare;

But as together both shall die,

Both burnt alike in flames shall lie,

She in thy breast, thou in her eye.

The Idolater.]   11 'He' altered in *1656* to 'she', which Miss Guiney adopts. But of course 'He' is Love.

18 breast *1647*: later, much worse, 'heart'.

The Magnet.

Ask the empress of the night

How the Hand which guides her sphere,

Constant in unconstant light,

Taught the waves her yoke to bear,

And did thus by loving force

Curb or tame the rude sea's course.

Ask the female palm how she

First did woo her husband's love;

And the magnet, ask how he

10Doth th' obsequious iron move;

Waters, plants, and stones know this:

That they love; not what Love is.

Be not then less kind than these,

Or from Love exempt alone!

Let us twine like amorous trees,

And like rivers melt in one.

Or, if thou more cruel prove,

Learn of steel and stones to love.

The Magnet.]   9 'he' *1647*, altered to 'she' in *1656*. One would expect 'he' to avoid identical rhyme, but Stanley was a scholar and the Greek is ἡ Μαγνῆτις λίθος, and the other things to be 'asked' are feminine.

In l. 13 'then' became 'thou', neither for better nor for worse.

On a Violet in her Breast.

See how this violet, which before

Hung sullenly her drooping head,

As angry at the ground that bore

The purple treasure which she spread,

Doth smilingly erected grow,

Transplanted to those hills of snow.

And whilst the pillows of thy breast

Do her reclining head sustain,

She swells with pride to be so blest,

10And doth all other flowers disdain;

Yet weeps that dew which kissed her last,

To see her odours so surpass'd.

Poor flower! how far deceiv'd thou wert,

To think the riches of the morn,

Or all the sweets she can impart,

Could these or sweeten or adorn,

Since thou from them dost borrow scent,

And they to thee lend ornament!

On a Violet in her Breast.]   6 'hills of snow' is probably as old as the Garden of Eden (if there was snow there). But Stanley must have known the exquisite second verse of 'Take, oh take those lips away' in *The Bloody Brother.* I would ask any one who despises this as a mere commonplace love-poem to note— if he can—the splendid swell of the verse to the fourth line, and then the 'turn' of the final couplet. With Stanley and his generation that swell and turn passed—never to reappear till William Blake revived it nearly a century and a half afterwards.

Song.

Foolish Lover, go and seek

For the damask of the rose,

And the lilies white dispose

To adorn thy mistress' cheek;

Steal some star out of the sky,

Rob the phoenix, and the east

Of her wealthy sweets divest,

To enrich her breath or eye!

We thy borrow'd pride despise:

10For this wine, to which we are

Votaries, is richer far

Than her cheek, or breath, or eyes.

And should that coy fair one view

These diviner beauties, she

In this flame would rival thee,

And be taught to love thee too.

Come, then, break thy wanton chain,

That when this brisk wine hath spread

On thy paler cheek a red,

30Thou, like us, mayst Love disdain.

Love, thy power must yield to wine!

And whilst thus ourselves we arm,

Boldly we defy thy charm:

For these flames extinguish thine.

Song.] A Donne-inspired one, doubtless, but not ill justified. 'Distinguish' in the last line is one of the numerous misprints of *1656*.

The Parting.

I go, dear Saint, away,

Snatch'd from thy arms

By far less pleasing charms,

Than those I did obey;

But when hereafter thou shall know

That grief hath slain me, come,

And on my tomb

Drop, drop a tear or two;

Break with thy sighs the silence of my sleep,

10And I shall smile in death to see thee weep.

Thy tears may have the power

To reinspire

My ashes with new fire,

Or change me to some flower,

Which, planted 'twixt thy breasts, shall grow:

Veil'd in this shape, I will

Dwell with thee still,

Court, kiss, enjoy thee too:

Securely we'll contemn all envious force,

20And thus united be by death's divorce.

The Parting.]   19 contemn *1647*: contain *1656*.

Counsel.

When deceitful lovers lay

At thy feet their suppliant hearts,

And their snares spread to betray

Thy best treasure with their arts,

Credit not their flatt'ring vows:

Love such perjury allows.

When they with the choicest wealth

Nature boasts of, have possess'd thee;

When with flowers (their verses' stealth),

10Stars, or jewels they invest thee,

Trust not to their borrow'd store:

'Tis but lent to make thee poor.

When with poems they invade thee,

Sing thy praises or disdain;

When they weep, and would persuade thee

That their flames beget that rain;

Let thy breast no baits let in:

Mercy 's only here a sin!

Let no tears or offerings move thee,

20All those cunning charms avoid;

For that wealth for which they love thee,

They would slight if once enjoy'd.

Who would keep another's heart

With her own must never part.

Counsel.]   7 'the' altered in *1656* to 'their', which is clearly wrong. But the untrustworthiness of Gamble's text is still better illustrated by l. 10, which he twists into—

Stars *to* jewels they *di*vest thee.

The copy was probably dictated to a very careless, ignorant, or stupid workman.

23-4. This pointed if cynical conclusion was changed in *1657* to the much feebler

Guard thy unrelenting mind;

None are cruel but the kind.

Expostulation with Love in Despair.

Love, with what strange tyrannic laws must they

Comply, which are subjected to thy sway!

How far all justice thy commands decline,

Which though they hope forbid, yet love enjoin!

Must all are to thy hell condemn'd sustain

A double torture of despair and pain?

Is 't not enough vainly to hope and woo,

That thou shouldst thus deny that vain hope too?

It were some joy, Ixion-like, to fold

10The empty air, or feed on hopes as cold;

But if thou to my passion this deny,

Thou mayst be starv'd to death as well as I;

For how can thy pale sickly flame burn clear

When death and cold despair inhabit near?

Rule in my breast alone, or thence retire;

Dissolve this frost, or let that quench thy fire.

Or let me not desire, or else possess!

Neither, or both, are equal happiness.

Expostulation, &c.] The texts of *1647* and *1656* differ considerably here, and Miss Guiney has attempted a 'composite text'—a thing for which I have small fancy. That given above is from *1647*: *1656* runs as follows in the first quatrain:

Love, what tyrannic laws must they obey

Who bow beneath thy uncontrolled sway;

Or how unjust will that harsh empire prove

Forbids to hope, and yet commands to love.

and reads in l. 9 'hope' for 'joy'; l. 10 'thought that's cold'; l. 14 'old' and 'here' for 'cold' and 'near'; l. 15 (entirely different)

Then let thy dim heat warm, or else expire.

l. 16 'the' for 'thy'; and in the closing distich '*Thus* let me not' and '*Either* or both'. The interest of this piece is almost wholly centred on the penultimate line, which, being an evident and intended contradiction to

Amare liceat si potiri non licet,

gives us at once the connexion, in Stanley's mind, with that strange, Mrs. Grundy-shocking, but 'insolent and passionate' piece which is attributed, credibly enough, to Apuleius, but rather less credibly as a latinizing of Menander's Ἀνεχόμενος. The contrast of the sensuous fire of this with Stanley's rather vapid and languid metaphysicalities is a notable one.

Song.

Faith, 'tis not worth thy pains and care

To seek t' ensnare

A heart so poor as mine:

Some fools there be

Hate liberty,

Whom with more ease thou mayst confine.

Alas! when with much charge thou hast

Brought it at last

Beneath thy power to bow,

10It will adore

Some twenty more,

And that, perhaps, you'll not allow.

No, Chloris, I no more will prove

The curse of love,

And now can boast a heart

Hath learn'd of thee

Inconstancy,

And cozen'd women of their art.

Song.]   2, 3. The quality and value of *1656* are again well illustrated by its readings of 'inspire' for 'ensnare' and 'pure' for 'poor'.

Expectation.

Chide, chide no more away

The fleeting daughters of the day,

Nor with impatient thoughts outrun

The lazy sun,

Or think the hours do move too slow;

Delay is kind,

And we too soon shall find

That which we seek, yet fear to know.

The mystic dark decrees

10Unfold not of the Destinies,

Nor boldly seek to antedate

The laws of Fate;

Thy anxious search awhile forbear,

Suppress thy haste,

And know that Time at last

Will crown thy hope or fix thy fear.

Expectation.] There is a suggestion here of John Hall's beautiful *Call* ('Romira, stay'), and the two pieces appeared so close together that it is difficult to say which may have been the first. Perhaps the resemblance was what made Stanley omit it in *1651*. In l. 5 *1656* reads 'Nor'.

1651 POEMS

THE DEDICATION

To Love.

Thou, whose sole name all passions doth comprise,

Youngest and oldest of the Deities;

Born without parents, whose unbounded reign

Moves the firm earth, fixeth the floating main,

Inverts the course of heaven; and from the deep

Awakes those souls that in dark Lethe sleep,

By thy mysterious chains seeking t' unite,

Once more, the long-since torn Hermaphrodite.

He, who thy willing pris'ner long was vow'd,

10And uncompell'd beneath thy sceptre bow'd,

Returns at last in thy soft fetters bound,

With victory, though not with freedom crown'd:

And, of his dangers pass'd a grateful sign,

Suspends this tablet at thy numerous shrine.

The Dedication. In 1647 printed at p. 49 with the title 'Conclusion, to Love', and obviously intended to end that collection, but a number of unpaged leaves were subsequently added containing the complimentary verses addressed to Fletcher and others. The following variants occur: 11 'by thy kind power unbound'. 12 'At least with freedom, though not conquest crown'd'. 14 'Suspends these papers'. Stanley also appended a list of Greek quotations justifying the cento. There is an intrinsic interest attaching to them in that they *may* have suggested a similar process to Gray. A further comparison-contrast may also interest some as to the lines themselves—that of the famous and magnificent opening of Mr. Swinburne's *Tristram of Lyonesse*.

The notes annotate the following phrases:—1 '(*a*) all passions', 2 '(*b*) Youngest and (*c*) oldest', 3 '(*d*) Born', 4 '(*e*) Moves', 7 '(*f*) By thy mysterious ...' The Greek has been slightly corrected in spelling and accents.

(*a*) Alexis apud Athenaeum:

συνενηνεγμένος

Πανταχόθεν ἐν ἑνὶ τόπῳ πόλλ' εἴδη φέρων,

Ἡ τόλμα μὲν γὰρ ἀνδρός, ἡ δὲ δειλία

Γυναικός, &c.

Sophocles:

Κύπρις οὐ Κύπρις μόνον,

Ἀλλ' ἔστι πάντων ὀνομάτων ἐπώνυμος.

(*b*) Plato, *Sympos.*: Φημὶ νεώτατον αὐτὸν εἶναι θεῶν, καὶ ἀεὶ νέον.

(*c. d*) Plato: Τὸ γὰρ ἐν τοῖς πρεσβυτάτοις εἶναι τῶν θεῶν τίμιον. Τεκμήριον δὲ τούτου·
γονεῖς γὰρ ἔρωτος οὔτ' εἰσὶν, οὔτε λέγονται ὑπ' οὐδενὸς οὔτε ἰδιώτου οὔτε ποιητοῦ.

(*e*) Oppian. *Cyneg.* 2:

Γαῖα πέλει σταθερὴ, βελέεσσι δὲ σοῖσι δονεῖται·

Ἄστατος ἔπλετο πόντος, ἀτὰρ σύ γε καὶ τὸν ἔπηξας·

Ἤλυθες εἰς αἰθῆρ', οἶδεν δέ σε μακρὸς Ὄλυμπος.

Δειμαίνει δέ σε πάντα, καὶ οὐρανὸς εὐρὺς ὕπερθε

Γαίης ὅσσα τ' ἔνερθε καὶ ἔθνεα λυγρὰ καμόντων

Οἵ λήθης μὲν ἄφυσσαν ὑπὸ στόμα νηπαθὲς ὕδωρ.

(*f*) Plato: Πρῶτον μὲν γὰρ τρία ἦν τὰ γένη τὰ τῶν ἀνθρώπων (sc. ἄρρεν, θῆλυ, καὶ ἀνδρόγυνον). Mox addit, Ἔστι δὴ οὖν ἐκ τόσου ὁ ἔρως ἔμφυτος ἀλλήλων τοῖς ἀνθρώποις καὶ τῆς ἀρχαίας φύσεως συναγωγεὺς καὶ ἐπιχειρῶν ποιῆσαι ἕν ἐκ δυοῖν, ⟨καὶ⟩ ἰάσασθαι τὴν φύσιν τὴν ἀνθρωπίνην. Phil. Jud. περὶ τῆς κοσμοποιίας. Ἐπεὶ δὲ ἐπλάσθη ἡ γυνὴ θεασάμενος ἀδελφὸν εἶδος καὶ συγγενῆ μορφὴν ἠσμένισε τῇ θέᾳ ἔρως δὲ ἐπιγινόμενος καθάπερ ἑνὸς ζώον διττὰ τμήματα διεστηκότα συναγωγῶν εἰς ταὐτὸν ἁρμόττεται.

POEMS

The Glow-worm.

Stay, fairest Chariessa, stay and mark

This animated gem, whose fainter spark

Of fading light its birth had from the dark.

A Star thought by the erring passenger,

Which falling from its native orb dropt here,

And makes the earth (its centre) now its sphere.

Should many of these sparks together be,

He that the unknown light far off should see,

Would think it a terrestrial Galaxy.

10Take 't up, fair Saint; see how it mocks thy fright!

The paler flame doth not yield heat, though light,

Which thus deceives thy reason, through thy sight.

But see how quickly it (ta'en up) doth fade,

To shine in darkness only being made,

By th' brightness of thy light turn'd to a shade;

And burnt to ashes by thy flaming eyes,

On the chaste altar of thy hand it dies,

As to thy greater light a sacrifice.

The Glow-worm.] Sir Egerton Brydges thought that 'A stile of poetry so full of quaint and far-fetched conceits cannot be commended as the most chaste and classical'; but that, 'among trifles of this kind, *The Glow-worm* is singularly elegant and happy'. Perhaps a later judgement, while waiving the indispensableness, or even pre-eminence, of chastity and classicality in verse, may doubt whether *The Glow-worm* itself is not rather too 'elegant' to be as 'happy' as some other things even of its author's. The last verse redeems it, though, to some extent.

2 *1647* 'This living star of earth'. I suppose Stanley did not like the recurrence of 'star', or he may have thought that the same sound (*-ar*) recurred still more excessively in the rhymes. In itself the earlier reading is certainly the better.

4 erring] deceiv'd *1647.*

12 'Which doth deceive' *1647*.

15 thy] the *1647*.

The Breath.

Favonius the milder breath o' th' Spring,

When proudly bearing on his softer wing

Rich odours, which from the Panchean groves

He steals, as by the Phoenix' pyre he moves,

Profusely doth his sweeter theft dispense

To the next rose's blushing innocence,

But from the grateful flower, a richer scent

He back receives than he unto it lent.

Then laden with his odours' richest store,

10He to thy breath hastes; to which these are poor!

Which whilst the amorous wind to steal essays,

He like a wanton Lover 'bout thee plays,

And sometimes cooling thy soft cheek doth lie,

And sometimes burning at thy flaming eye:

Drawn in at last by that breath we implore,

He now returns far sweeter than before,

And rich by being robb'd, in thee he finds

The burning sweets of Pyres, the cool of Winds.

The Breath.] This appears in all three editions, *1656* following *1647* in the following variants: l. 8 'He doth receive'; l. 11 'while he sportively'; l. 16 'back' for 'now'.

Desiring her to burn his Verses.

These papers, Chariessa, let thy breath

Condemn; thy hand unto the flames bequeath;

'Tis fit, who gave them life, should give them death.

And whilst in curled flames to Heaven they rise,

Each trembling sheet shall as it upwards flies,

Present itself to thee a sacrifice.

Then when about its native orb it came,

And reach'd the lesser lights o' th' sky, this flame

Contracted to a star should wear thy name.

10Or falling down on earth from its bright sphere,

Shall in a diamond's shape its lustre bear,

And trouble (as it did before) thine ear.

But thou wilt cruel even in mercy be,

Unequal in thy justice, who dost free

Things without sense from flames, and yet not Me.

Desiring her to burn his Verses.] *Title, 1647* 'To Chariessa, desiring', &c.

4 whilst] as *1647.*

7 about] above *1647.*

14 who] that *1647.*

The Night.
A DIALOGUE.

Chariessa.

What if Night

Should betray us, and reveal

To the light

All the pleasures that we steal?

Philocharis.

Fairest, we

Safely may this fear despise;

How can She

See our actions who wants eyes?

Chariessa.

Each dim star

10And the clearer lights, we know,

Night's eyes are;

They were blind that thought her so!

Philocharis.

Those pale fires

Only burn to yield a light

T' our desires,

And though blind, to give us sight.

Chariessa.

By this shade

That surrounds us might our flame

Be betray'd,

20And the day disclose its name.

Philocharis.

Dearest Fair,

These dark witnesses we find

Silent are;

Night is dumb as well as blind.

Chorus.

Then whilst these black shades conceal us,

We will scorn

Th' envious Morn,

And the Sun that would reveal us.

Our flames shall thus their mutual light betray,

30And night, with these joys crown'd, outshine the day.

The Night.] Entitled in *1647* 'Amori Notturni. A Dialogue between Philocharis and Chariessa'.

2 and] or *1647*.

8 who] that *1647*.

18 surrounds] conceals *1647*.

The metrical arrangement here is very delightful, and the Chorus-adjustment particularly happy.

Excuse for wishing her less Fair.

Why thy passion should it move

That I wish'd thy beauty less?

Fools desire what is above

Power of nature to express;

And to wish it had been more.

Had been to outwish her store!

If the flames within thine eye

Did not too great heat inspire,

Men might languish yet not die,

10At thy less ungentle fire;

And might on thy weaker light

Gaze, and yet not lose their sight.

Nor wouldst thou less fair appear,

For detraction adds to thee;

If some parts less beauteous were,

Others would much fairer be:

Nor can any part we know

Best be styl'd, when all are so.

Thus this great excess of light,

20Which now dazzles our weak eyes,

Would, eclips'd, appear more bright;

And the only way to rise,

Or to be more fair, for thee,

Celia, is less fair to be.

Excuse for wishing her less Fair.] *1647* prefixes 'To Celia'.

7 the] thy *1647*.

9 yet] and *1647*.

10 less ungentle] then less scorching *1647*.

23 for] *1656* 'than', which, like much else in this edition, is pure nonsense.

Brydges thought that 'one cannot avoid admiring the ingenuity exercised in this continual play upon words'. But surely

In things like this the play of words became

A play of thought, and therefore shames all shame.

Chang'd, yet Constant.

Wrong me no more

In thy complaint,

Blam'd for inconstancy;

I vow'd t' adore

The fairest Saint,

Nor chang'd whilst thou wert she:

But if another thee outshine,

Th' inconstancy is only thine.

To be by such

10Blind fools admir'd,

Gives thee but small esteem,

By whom as much

Thou'dst be desir'd,

Didst thou less beauteous seem:

Sure why they love they know not well,

Who why they should not cannot tell.

Women are by

Themselves betray'd,

And to their short joys cruel,

20Who foolishly

Themselves persuade

Flames can outlast their fuel;

None (though Platonic their pretence)

With reason love unless by sense.

And He, by whose

Command to thee

I did my heart resign,

Now bids me choose

A Deity

30Diviner far than thine;

No power can Love from Beauty sever;

I'm still Love's subject, thine was never.

The fairest She

Whom none surpass

To love hath only right,

And such to me

Thy beauty was

Till one I found more bright;

But 'twere as impious to adore

40Thee now, as not t' have done 't before.

Nor is it just

By rules of Love

Thou shouldst deny to quit

A heart that must

Another's prove,

Ev'n in thy right to it;

Must not thy subjects captives be

To her who triumphs over Thee?

Cease then in vain

50To blot my name

With forg'd Apostasy,

Thine is that stain

Who dar'st to claim

What others ask of Thee.

Of Lovers they are only true

Who pay their hearts where they are due.

Chang'd, yet Constant.] Here, perhaps for the first time, we get the *fire* of the period communicating to the verse its own glow and flicker. It is a pity he allowed himself double rhymes in stanza 3, which break the note (those at the end of st. 4 do not). There are no variants; the poem is not in *1647*. But Miss Guiney has proposed to substitute 'hearts' for 'they' in the last line.

The Self-deceiver.

MONTALVAN.

Deceiv'd and undeceiv'd to be

At once I seek with equal care,

Wretched in the discovery,

Happy if cozen'd still I were:

Yet certain ill of ill hath less

Than the mistrust of happiness.

But if when I have reach'd my aim

(That which I seek less worthy prove),

Yet still my love remains the same,

10The subject not deserving love;

I can no longer be excus'd,

Now more in fault as less abus'd.

Then let me flatter my desires,

And doubt what I might know too sure,

He that to cheat himself conspires,

From falsehood doth his faith secure;

In love uncertain to believe

I am deceiv'd, doth undeceive.

For if my life on doubt depend,

20And in distrust inconstant steer,

If I essay the strife to end

(When Ignorance were Wisdom here),

All thy attempts how can I blame

To work my death? I seek the same.

The Self-deceiver.] (On Stanley's translations see Introduction.) Juan Perez de Montalvan (1602-1638) belonged to the best age of Spanish literature, and was, in proportion, almost as prolific in plays and *autos* as his master Lope. He was accused of 'Gongorism', and this piece is one somewhat of 'conviction'.

The Cure.

Nymph.

What busy cares too timely born

(Young Swain!) disturb thy sleep?

Thy early sighs awake the Morn,

Thy tears teach her to weep.

Shepherd.

Sorrows, fair Nymph, are full alone;

Nor counsel can endure.

Nymph.

Yet thine disclose, for until known
Sickness admits no cure.

Shepherd.

My griefs are such as but to hear
10Would poison all thy joys,
The pity which thou seem'st to bear
My health, thine own destroys.

Nymph.

How can diseaséd minds infect?
Say what thy grief doth move!

Shepherd.

Call up thy virtue to protect
Thy heart, and know 'twas love.

Nymph.

Fond Swain!

Shepherd.

By which I have been long
Destin'd to meet with hate.

Nymph.

Fy, Shepherd, fy: thou dost love wrong,
20To call thy crime thy fate.

Shepherd.

Alas what cunning could decline
What force can love repel?

Nymph.

Yet, there 's a way to unconfine
Thy heart.

Shepherd.

For pity tell.

Nymph.

Choose one whose love may be allur'd

By thine: who ever knew

Inveterate diseases cur'd

But by receiving new?

Shepherd.

All will like her my soul perplex.

Nymph.

Yet try.

Shepherd.

30Oh could there be,

But any softness in that sex,

I'd wish it were in thee.

Nymph.

Thy prayer is heard: learn now t' esteem

The kindness she hath shown,

Who thy lost freedom to redeem

Hath forfeited her own.

The Cure. As this appears only in *1651* there are no variants. The 'common measure' has little of the magic common at the time, and is sometimes banal to eighteenth-century level. But we rise in the next.

Celia Singing.

Roses in breathing forth their scent,

Or stars their borrowed ornament;

Nymphs in the wat'ry sphere that move,

Or Angels in their orbs above;

The wingéd chariot of the light,

Or the slow silent wheels of night;

The shade, which from the swifter sun

Doth in a circular motion run;

Or souls that their eternal rest do keep,

10Make far more noise than Celia's breath in sleep.

But if the Angel, which inspires

This subtile flame with active fires,

Should mould this breath to words, and those

Into a harmony dispose,

The music of this heavenly sphere

Would steal each soul out at the ear,

And into plants and stones infuse

A life that Cherubins would choose;

And with new powers invert the laws of Fate,

20Kill those that live, and dead things animate.

Celia Singing.] *1647* 'Celia sleeping or singing', and printed without stanza-break.

10 more] Some imp of the press altered 'more' to 'less' in the later 'edition'. *1647* has 'more', which has been restored in text.

12 *1647* 'frame'—tempting, but perhaps not certain.

13 *1647* 'his'—again *nescio an recte*.

19 *1647* 'power'.

A la Mesme.

Belle voix, dont les charmes desrobent mon âme,

Et au lieu d'un esprit m'animent d'une flamme,

Dont je sens la subtile et la douce chaleur

Entrer par mon oreille et glisser dans mon cœur;

Me faisant esprever par cette aimable vie,

Nos âmes ne consistent que d'une harmonie;

Que la vie m'est douce, la mort m'est sans peine,

Puisqu'on les trouve toutes deux dans ton haleine:

Ne m'espargne donc pas; satisfais tes rigueurs;

10Car si tu me souffres de vivre, je me meurs.

A la Mesme] *1647* 'A une Dame qui chantoit'. Stanley does not, like some more modern English writers of French verse, neglect his final *e*'s, but he takes remarkable liberties with the caesura. 'Esprever' (l. 5) is not wrong necessarily.

The Return.

Beauty, whose soft magnetic chains

Beauty, thy harsh imperious chains

Nor time nor absence can untie,

As a scorned weight I here untie,

Thy power the narrow bounds disdains

Since thy proud empire those disdains

Of Nature or philosophy,

Of reason or philosophy,

That canst by unconfinéd laws

That wouldst within tyrannic laws

A motion, though at distance, cause.

Confine the power of each free cause.

Drawn by the sacred influence

Forced by the potent influence

Of thy bright eyes, I back return;

Of thy disdain I back return,

And since I nowhere can dispense

Thus with those flames I do dispense,

10With flames that do in absence burn,

Which, though they would not light, did burn;

I rather choose 'midst them t' expire

And rather will through cold expire

Than languish by a hidden fire.

Than languish at a frozen fire.

But if thou the insulting pride

But whilst I the insulting pride

Of vulgar Beauties dost despise,

Of thy vain beauty do despise,

Who by vain triumphs deified,

Who gladly wouldst be deified,

Their votaries do sacrifice,

By making me thy sacrifice;

Then let those flames, whose magic charm

May love thy heart, which to his charm

At distance scorch'd, approach'd but warm.

Approached seemed cold, at distance warm.

The Return—(Palinode.)] The *1647* edition contains *two* poems, *The Return* and *Palinode*, which stand to each other in a curious relation. In *1651 Palinode* has disappeared. I have thought it best to print them together. The lines in roman type are those of *The Return*, those in italic belong to *Palinode*. The latter reappeared in *1657*, with slight alterations as below. In *Pal.* 5 Miss Guiney reads 'would' for 'wouldst', evidently not quite understanding the sense or the grammar of the time. The second person connects itself with the vocative in 'Beauty' and the 'thou' twice implied in 'thy'.

In *Palinode*, l. 7, *1657* reads 'powerful' for 'potent'; l. 12 'in' for 'at'.

In *The Return*, l. 2, *1651* 'unite'—an obvious misprint; l. 3, *1647* 'bound'; l. 5, *1647* 'That', *1651* 'Thou'; l. 10, *1657* 'which' for 'that'; l. 11, 'twixt'—not so well; l. 13, 'the' is dropped by mere accident in *1651*—'the', not 'th',' is required.

Song.

When I lie burning in thine eye.

Or freezing in thy breast,

What Martyrs, in wish'd flames that die,

Are half so pleas'd or blest?

When thy soft accents through mine ear

Into my soul do fly,

What Angel would not quit his sphere,

To hear such harmony?

Or when the kiss thou gav'st me last

10My soul stole in its breath,

What life would sooner be embrac'd

Than so desir'd a death?

[When I commanded am by thee,

Or by thine eye or hand,

What monarch would not prouder be

To serve than to command?]

Then think no freedom I desire,

Or would my fetters leave,

Since Phoenix-like I from this fire

20Both life and youth receive.

Song.] Sir Egerton thought this (which, by the way, Lovelace may have seen, or *vice versa*) 'a very elegant little song, with all the harmony of *modern* rhythm'. One might perhaps substitute 'with more of the harmony of *contemporary* rhythm than Stanley always attains'. It is certainly much better than *The Cure*. The bracketed stanza was dropped in *1651*, but it seemed better to restore it thus in text than to degrade it hither. One or two extremely unimportant misprints occur in one or other version, but are not worth noting.

The Sick Lover.

GUARINI.

My sickly breath

Wastes in a double flame;

Whilst Love and Death

To my poor life lay claim;

The fever, in whose heat I melt,

By her that causeth it not felt.

Thou who alone

Canst, yet wilt grant no ease,

Why slight'st thou one

10To feed a new disease?

Unequal fair! the heart is thine;

Ah, why then should the pain be mine?

The Sick Lover.] Not a great thing. In l. 6, Miss Guiney thinks 'it', which is in all texts, should be 'is'. But 'it' is wanted and 'is' is not. 'The fever not [*being*] felt' is no excessively 'absolute' construction.

Song.

Celinda, by what potent art

Or unresisted charm,

Dost thou thine ear and frozen heart

Against my passion arm?

Or by what hidden influence

Of powers in one combin'd,

Dost thou rob Love of either sense,

Made deaf as well as blind?

Sure thou, as friends, united hast

10Two distant Deities;

And scorn within thy heart hast plac'd,

And love within thine eyes.

Or those soft fetters of thy hair,

A bondage that disdains

All liberty, do guard thine ear

Free from all other chains.

Then my complaint how canst thou hear,

Or I this passion fly,

Since thou imprison'd hast thine ear,

20And not confin'd thine eye?

Song—Celinda, &c.] Again, mere commonplace common measure. '*Those* soft fetters of thy hair' (l. 13) is at least as good as 'mobled queen', but otherwise the phrase rather sinks to the measure. 'friends' (l. 9) is misprinted 'friend' in *1647*, and Sir Egerton has mispunctuated 'friends united'.

Song.

Fool, take up thy shaft again;

If thy store

Thou profusely spend in vain,

Who can furnish thee with more?

Throw not then away thy darts

On impenetrable hearts.

Think not thy pale flame can warm

Into tears,

Or dissolve the snowy charm

10Which her frozen bosom wears,

That expos'd, unmelted lies

To the bright suns of her eyes.

But since thou thy power hast lost,

Nor canst fire

Kindle in that breast, whose frost

Doth these flames in mine inspire,

Not to thee but her I'll sue,

That disdains both me and you.

Song—Fool, &c.] An extremely pretty measure, not ill-parted with phrase and imagery. The 'Take, oh! take' motive reappears.

Delay.

Delay! Alas, there cannot be

To Love a greater tyranny:

Those cruel beauties that have slain

Their votaries by their disdain,

Or studied torments, sharp and witty,

Will be recorded for their pity,

And after-ages be misled

To think them kind, when this is spread.

Of deaths the speediest is despair,

10Delays the slowest tortures are;

Thy cruelty at once destroys,

But Expectation starves my joys.

Time and Delay may bring me past

The power of Love to cure, at last;

And shouldst thou wish to ease my pain,

Thy pity might be lent in vain;

Or if thou hast decreed, that I

Must fall beneath thy cruelty,

O kill me soon! Thou wilt express

20More mercy, ev'n in showing less.

Commanded by his Mistress to woo for her.
MARINO.

Strange kind of love! that knows no president,

A faith so firm as passeth Faith's extent,

By a tyrannic beauty long subdu'd,

I now must sue for her to whom I su'd,

Unhappy Orator! who, though I move

For pity, pity cannot hope to prove:

Employing thus against myself my breath,

And in another's life begging my death.

But if such moving powers my accents have,

10Why first my own redress do I not crave?

What hopes that I to pity should incline

Another's breast, who can move none in thine?

Or how can the griev'd patient look for ease,

When the physician suffers the disease?

If thy sharp wounds from me expect their cure,

'Tis fit those first be heal'd that I endure.

Ungentle fair one! why dost thou dispense

Unequally thy sacred influence?

Why pining me, offer'st the precious food

20To one by whom nor priz'd, nor understood;

So some clear brook to the full main, to pay

Her needless crystal tribute hastes away,

Profusely foolish; whilst her niggard tide

Starves the poor flowers that grow along her side.

Thou who my glories art design'd to own,

Come then, and reap the joys that I have sown:

Yet in thy pride acknowledge, though thou bear

The happy prize away, the palm I wear.

Nor the obedience of my flame accuse,

30That what I sought, myself conspir'd to lose:

The hapless state where I am fix'd is such,

To love I seem not, 'cause I love too much.

Commanded by his Mistress, &c.] Marino[i]'s name is so frequent in books on literature, and his work so little known to the ordinary reader, that this example may be welcome. The rather snip-snap antithesis, and the somewhat obvious conceit, show the famous Italian really at his worst. 'President' (l. 1), though not impossible, is probably for 'pre*ce*dent'. The whole piece has a special interest as showing how this 'conceit' and 'false wit' actually encouraged the growth of the stopped antithetic couplet which was to be turned against both.

The Repulse.

Not that by this disdain

I am releas'd,

And freed from thy tyrannic chain,

Do I myself think bless'd;

Nor that thy flame shall burn

No more; for know

That I shall into ashes turn,

Before this fire doth so.

Nor yet that unconfin'd

10I now may rove,

And with new beauties please my mind,

But that thou ne'er didst love:

For since thou hast no part

Felt of this flame,

I only from thy tyrant heart

Repuls'd, not banish'd am.

To lose what once was mine

Would grieve me more

Than those inconstant sweets of thine

20Had pleas'd my soul before.

Now I have not lost the bliss

I ne'er possest;

And spite of fate am blest in this,

That I was never blest.

The Repulse.] In the third line of this rather fine poem *1656* reads 'romantic' for 'tyrannic', and Miss Guiney adopts it. To me it seems quite inappropriate, and one of the errors of dictation so common in that 'edition'.

21 *1647* reads '*that* bliss'.

The Tomb.

When, cruel fair one, I am slain

By thy disdain,

And, as a trophy of thy scorn,

To some old tomb am borne,

Thy fetters must their power bequeath

To those of Death;

Nor can thy flame immortal burn,

Like monumental fires within an urn;

Thus freed from thy proud empire, I shall prove

10There is more liberty in Death than Love.

And when forsaken Lovers come,

To see my tomb,

Take heed thou mix not with the crowd

And (as a Victor) proud

To view the spoils thy beauty made

Press near my shade,

Lest thy too cruel breath or name

Should fan my ashes back into a flame,

And thou, devour'd by this revengeful fire,

20His sacrifice, who died as thine, expire.

[Or should my dust thy pity move

That could not love,

Thy sighs might wake me, and thy tears

Renew my life and years.

Or should thy proud insulting scorn

Laugh at my urn,

Kindly deceived by thy disdain,

I might be smil'd into new life again.

Then come not near, since both thy love and hate

30Have equal power to love or animate.]

But if cold earth, or marble, must

Conceal my dust,

Whilst hid in some dark ruins, I

Dumb and forgotten lie,

The pride of all thy victory

Will sleep with me;

And they who should attest thy glory,

Will, or forget, or not believe this story.

Then to increase thy triumph, let me rest,

40Since by thine eye slain, buried in thy breast.

The Tomb.] Brydges, though thinking the end of this poem 'a feeble conceit', admits that 'there are passages in it that are more than pretty'. It is certainly one of Stanley's best, and he seems to have taken some trouble with it. In *1651* he dropped the bracketed stanza 3 and substituted the text for the last couplet of stanza 2, which reads in *1647*:

And (thou in this fire sacrificed to me)

We might each other's mutual martyr be.

In the last line of the omitted stanza 'love' is certainly wrong, and Miss Guiney's suggestion of 'kill' is almost *certissima*. But she seems to have had a different copy of *1647* before her from that which I collated, for she does not notice a variant, or set of variants, in ll. 37-9:

And they *that* should *this triumph know*

Will or forget or not believe *it so,*

Then to increase thy *glories*, &c.

In l. 5 *1647* reads 'thy power'.

The Enjoyment.

ST.-AMANT.

Far from the court's ambitious noise

Retir'd, to those more harmless joys

Which the sweet country, pleasant fields,

And my own court, a cottage, yields;

I liv'd from all disturbance free,

Though prisoner (Sylvia) unto thee;

Secur'd from fears, which others prove,

Of the inconstancy of Love;

A life, in my esteem, more blest,

10Than e'er yet stoop'd to Death's arrest.

My senses and desires agreed,

With joint delight each other feed:

A bliss, I reach'd, as far above

Words, as her beauty, or my love;

Such as compar'd with which, the joys

Of the most happy seem but toys:

Affection I receive and pay,

My pleasures knew not Grief's allay:

The more I tasted I desir'd,

20The more I quench'd my thirst was fir'd.

Now, in some place where Nature shows

Her naked beauty, we repose;

Where she allures the wand'ring eye

With colours, which faint art outvie;

Pearls scatter'd by the weeping morn,

Each where the glitt'ring flowers adorn;

The mistress of the youthful year

(To whom kind Zephyrus doth bear

His amorous vows and frequent prayer)

30Decks with these gems her neck and hair.

Hither, to quicken Time with sport,

The little sprightly Loves resort,

And dancing o'er the enamel'd mead,

Their mistresses the Graces lead;

Then to refresh themselves, repair

To the soft bosom of my fair;

Where from the kisses they bestow

Upon each other, such sweets flow

As carry in their mixéd breath

40A mutual power of life and death.

Next in an elm's dilated shade

We see a rugged Satyr laid,

Teaching his reed, in a soft strain,

Of his sweet anguish to complain;

Then to a lonely grove retreat,

Where day can no admittance get,

To visit peaceful solitude;

Whom seeing by repose pursu'd,

All busy cares, for fear to spoil

50Their calmer courtship, we exile.

There underneath a myrtle, thought

By Fairies sacred, where was wrought

By Venus' hand Love's mysteries,

And all the trophies of her eyes,

Our solemn prayers to Heaven we send,

That our firm love might know no end;

Nor time its vigour e'er impair:

Then to the wingéd God we sware,

And grav'd the oath in its smooth rind,

60Which in our hearts we deeper find.

Then to my dear (as if afraid

To try her doubted faith) I said,

'Would in thy soul my form as clear,

As in thy eyes I see it, were.'

She kindly angry saith, 'Thou art

Drawn more at large within my heart;

These figures in my eye appear

But small, because they are not near,

Thou through these glasses seest thy face,

70As pictures through their crystal case.'

Now with delight transported, I

My wreathéd arms about her tie;

The flattering Ivy never holds

Her husband Elm in stricter folds:

To cool my fervent thirst, I sip

Delicious nectar from her lip.

She pledges, and so often past

This amorous health, till Love at last

Our souls did with these pleasures sate,

80And equally inebriate.

Awhile, our senses stol'n away,

Lost in this ecstasy we lay,

Till both together rais'd to life,

We re-engage in this kind strife.

Cythaera with her Syrian boy

Could never reach our meanest joy.

The childish God of Love ne'er tried

So much of love with his cold bride,

As we in one embrace include,

90Contesting each to be subdu'd.

The Enjoyment.] *La Jouissance*, one of Saint-Amant's early lyric pieces, which is here translated, was not so famous as his *Solitude*, which will be found (Englished by the matchless Orinda a little after Stanley's time) in vol. i, p. 601, of this collection; but it was popular and much imitated. Stanley has cut it down considerably, for the original has nineteen stanzas—some of them, I suppose, too 'warm' for the translator's modest muse.

59 Brydges misprints '*k*ind'

To Celia Pleading Want of Merit.

Dear, urge no more that killing cause

Of our divorce;

Love is not fetter'd by such laws,

Nor bows to any force:

Though thou deniest I should be thine,

Yet say not thou deserv'st not to be mine.

Oh rather frown away my breath

With thy disdain,

Or flatter me with smiles to death;

10By joy or sorrow slain,

'Tis less crime to be kill'd by thee,

Than I thus cause of mine own death should be.

Thyself of beauty to divest,

And me of love,

Or from the worth of thine own breast

Thus to detract, would prove

In us a blindness, and in thee

At best a sacrilegious modesty.

But, Celia, if thou wilt despise

20What all admire,

Nor rate thyself at the just price

Of beauty or desire,

Yet meet my flames, and thou shalt see

That equal love knows no disparity.

To Celia Pleading, &c.] *1647* has in title 'To *One that Pleaded her own*', and 'Dearest' for 'Celia' in l. 19.

Love's Innocence.

See how this Ivy strives to twine

Her wanton arms about the Vine,

And her coy lover thus restrains,

Entangled in her amorous chains;

See how these neighb'ring Palms do bend

Their heads, and mutual murmurs send,

As whispering with a jealous fear

Their loves, into each other's ear.

Then blush not such a flame to own,

10As like thyself no crime hath known;

Led by these harmless guides, we may

Embrace and kiss as well as they.

And like those blessèd souls above,

Whose life is harmony and love,

Let us our mutual thoughts betray,

And in our wills our minds display;

This silent speech is swifter far

Than the ears' lazy species are;

And the expression it affords,

As our desires, 'bove reach of words.

20Thus we, my dear, of these may learn

A passion others not discern;

Nor can it shame or blushes move,

Like plants to live, like Angels love:

Since all excuse with equal innocence,

What above reason is, or beneath sense.

Love's Innocence.] In *1647* the following differences occur: Title, 'The Innocence of Love'; l. 1, '(Dear) doth twine' for 'strives to twine'; l. 7, 'To one another whispering there'; ll. 9-10, 'Then blush not, *Fair, that* flame to *show, Which* like thyself no crime *can know*'; ll. 11-12, '*Thus led by those chaste* guides, we may Embrace and kiss as *free* as they'; l. 20, 'As *are our flames*'; l. 21, 'Thus, *Doris, we*'.

The Bracelet.

TRISTAN.

Now Love be prais'd! that cruel fair,

Who my poor heart restrains

Under so many chains,

Hath weav'd a new one for it of her hair.

These threads of amber us'd to play

With every courtly wind;

And never were confin'd;

But in a thousand curls allow'd to stray.

Cruel each part of her is grown;

10Nor less unkind than she

These fetters are to me,

Which to restrain my freedom, lose their own.

The Bracelet.] Little survives, even in literary memories, of François Tristan l'Hermite (1601-1655), except the success of his *Marianne* (Mariamne), 1636, one of the most famous French tragedies of the period outside Corneille. M. Ed. Fournier gave him a niche in Crépet's *Poètes Français* (Paris, 1861), ii. 539-52, but did not include the original of this piece. The *In Memoriam* rhyme-order, though the line lengths are different, is interesting. Stanley had perhaps borrowed, before translating it, the 'soft fetters of her hair', noted above, though the fancy is of course primaeval and perennial.

The Kiss.

When on thy lip my soul I breathe,

Which there meets thine,

Freed from their fetters by this death

Our subtle forms combine;

Thus without bonds of sense they move,

And like two Cherubins converse by love.

Spirits, to chains of earth confin'd,

Discourse by sense;

But ours, that are by flames refin'd,

10With those weak ties dispense.

Let such in words their minds display;

We in a kiss our mutual thoughts convey.

But since my soul from me doth fly,

To thee retir'd,

Thou canst not both retain: for I

Must be with one inspir'd.

Then, dearest, either justly mine

Restore, or in exchange let me have thine.

Yet, if thou dost return mine own,

20Oh tak't again!

For 'tis this pleasing death alone

Gives ease unto my pain.

Kill me once more, or I shall find

Thy pity, than thy cruelty, less kind.

The Kiss.] Title in *1647* 'The *killing* Kiss', and several other variants. An answer to this poem appears in Jordan's *Claraphi and Clarinda.*

4 *1647* 'They both unite and join'. But Miss Guiney's suspicion that 'forms' may be a misprint obviously shows forgetfulness of the philosophical sense of the word = 'ideas', 'immortal parts'. Cf. Spenser, 'For soul is *form*'.

6 by] *1647* 'and'—perhaps better.

12 *1647* 'Our lips, not tongues, each other's thoughts betray'. (Miss Guiney's copy seems to have '*our* tongues', which cannot be right.)

15 for I] and I *1647.*

17 dearest] *1647* 'Doris'. This is the second time (*v. sup.*, p. 126) that poor Doris has been disestablished.

Apollo and Daphne.
GARCILASSO MARINO.

When Phoebus saw a rugged bark beguile

His love, and his embraces intercept,

The leaves, instructed by his grief to smile,

Taking fresh growth and verdure as he wept:

'How can', saith he, 'my woes expect release,

When tears the subject of my tears increase!'

His chang'd, yet scorn-retaining Fair he kiss'd,

From the lov'd trunk plucking a little bough;

And though the conquest which he sought he miss'd,

10With that triumphant spoil adorns his brow.

Thus this disdainful maid his aim deceives:

Where he expected fruit he gathers leaves.

Apollo and Daphne.] Why Garcilasso I do not know. Marini's name was Giambattista.

6 The first 'tears' certainly looks odd, and Miss Guiney conjectures 'leaves'. But the ways of Marinism are not thus. Apollo's tears *watered* the laurel and so made it grow. His tears increased their subject, the vapid vegetable substitute for Daphne's flesh and blood.

Speaking and Kissing.

The air, which thy smooth voice doth break,

Into my soul like lightning flies;

My life retires whilst thou dost speak,

And thy soft breath its room supplies.

Lost in this pleasing ecstasy,

I join my trembling lips to thine;

And back receive that life from thee,

Which I so gladly did resign.

Forbear, Platonic fools, t' inquire

What numbers do the soul compose!

No harmony can life inspire,

But that which from these accents flows.

Speaking and Kissing.] This is *smarter* than Stanley's usual style.

The Snow-ball.

Doris, I that could repel

All those darts about thee dwell,

And had wisely learn'd to fear,

'Cause I saw a foe so near;

I that my deaf ear did arm

'Gainst thy voice's powerful charm,

And the lightning of thine eye

Durst (by closing mine) defy,

Cannot this cold snow withstand

10From the whiter of thy hand.

Thy deceit hath thus done more

Than thy open force before:

For who could suspect or fear

Treason in a face so clear;

Or the hidden fires descry

Wrapt in this cold outside lie?

Flames might thus involv'd in ice

The deceiv'd world sacrifice;

Nature, ignorant of this

20Strange antiperistasis,

Would her falling frame admire,

That by snow were set on fire.

The Snow-ball.] Doris maintains here the place she lost above. The tripping seventeenth-century 'sevens' are well spent on her. In l. 10 Miss Guiney thinks that 'whiter', the sole reading, must be 'winter'. ἥκιστα: that Stanley meant 'the whiter *snow*' is, to me, certain.

20 'Antiperistasis' = 'reaction' or 'topsyturvyfication' (Thackeray).

The Deposition.

Though when I lov'd thee thou wert fair,

Thou art no longer so;

Those glories all the pride they wear

Unto opinion owe;

Beauties, like stars, in borrow'd lustre shine;

And 'twas my love that gave thee thine.

The flames that dwelt within thine eye

Do now, with mine, expire;

Thy brightest graces fade and die

10At once with my desire;

Love's fires thus mutual influence return;

Thine cease to shine, when mine to burn.

Then, proud Celinda, hope no more

To be implor'd or woo'd,

Since by thy scorn thou dost restore

The wealth my love bestow'd;

And thy despis'd disdain too late shall find

That none are fair but who are kind.

The Deposition.] In *1647* '*A* Deposition *from Beauty*'. Also l. 3, 'do' for 'all'; l. 9, 'glories' for 'graces'; l. 16, 'That' for 'The' and 'which' for 'my'.

To his Mistress in Absence.

TASSO.

Far from thy dearest self, the scope

Of all my aims,

I waste in secret flames;

And only live because I hope.

Oh, when will Fate restore

The joys, in whose bright fire

My expectation shall expire,

That I may live because I hope no more!

Love's Heretic.

He whose active thoughts disdain
To be captive to one foe,
And would break his single chain,
Or else more would undergo;
Let him learn the art of me,
By new bondage to be free!

What tyrannic mistress dare
To one beauty love confine,
Who, unbounded as the air,
10All may court but none decline?
Why should we the heart deny
As many objects as the eye?
Wheresoe'er I turn or move,
A new passion doth detain me:
Those kind beauties that do love,
Or those proud ones that disdain me;
This frown melts, and that smile burns me;
This to tears, that ashes turns me.
Soft fresh Virgins, not full blown,
20With their youthful sweetness take me;
Sober Matrons, that have known
Long since what these prove, awake me;
Here staid coldness I admire;
There the lively active fire.
She that doth by skill dispense
Every favour she bestows,

Or the harmless innocence,

Which nor court nor city knows,

Both alike my soul enflame,

30That wild Beauty, and this tame.

She that wisely can adorn

Nature with the wealth of Art,

Or whose rural sweets do scorn

Borrow'd helps to take a heart,

The vain care of that's my pleasure,

Poverty of this my treasure.

Both the wanton and the coy,

Me with equal pleasures move;

She whom I by force enjoy,

40Or who forceth me to love:

This, because she'll not confess,

That not hide, her happiness.

She whose loosely flowing hair,

Scatter'd like the beams o' th' morn,

Playing with the sportive air,

Hides the sweets it doth adorn,

Captive in that net restrains me,

In those golden fetters chains me.

Nor doth she with power less bright

50My divided heart invade,

Whose soft tresses spread like night

O'er her shoulders a black shade;

For the starlight of her eyes

Brighter shines through those dark skies.

Black, or fair, or tall, or low,

I alike with all can sport;

The bold sprightly Thais woo,

Or the frozen Vestal court;

Every Beauty takes my mind,

60Tied to all, to none confin'd.

Love's Heretic.] This, for Stanley, longish piece has few *vv. ll.* But *1647* reads in l. 34 'that' instead of 'to', and the singular 'pleasure' in l. 38. The piece is rather in the Suckling vein; but Stanley did not play the light-o'-love quite successfully.

La Belle Confidente.

You earthly souls that court a wanton flame,

Whose pale weak influence

Can rise no higher than the humble name,

And narrow laws of sense,

Learn by our friendship to create

An immaterial fire,

Whose brightness Angels may admire,

But cannot emulate.

Sickness may fright the roses from her cheek,

10Or make the lilies fade;

But all the subtile ways that Death doth seek,

Cannot my love invade.

Flames that are kindled by the eye,

Through time and age expire;

But ours, that boast a reach far higher,

Can nor decay nor die.

For when we must resign our vital breath,

Our loves by Fate benighted,

We by this friendship shall survive in death,

20Even in divorce united.

Weak Love, through fortune or distrust,

In time forgets to burn,

But this pursues us to the urn,

And marries either's dust.

La Belle Confidente.] On this Sir Egerton: 'However far-fetched these ideas may be, there is uncommon elegance and ingenuity in the expression, and polish in the versification.' There is also something more than polish— a *concerted* effect which 'elegance and ingenuity' do not often reach. In l. 16, 'Cannot' appears in *1647* for 'Can nor'; 'And' for 'For' in l. 17; and ll. 18, 20 are changed over and run:

Even in divorce delighted,

.   .   .   .   .   .

Still in the grave united.

La Belle Ennemie.

I yield, dear enemy, nor know

How to resist so fair a foe!

Who would not thy soft yoke sustain,

And bow beneath thy easy chain,

That with a bondage bless'd might be,

Which far transcends all liberty?

But since I freely have resign'd

At first assault my willing mind,

Insult not o'er my captiv'd heart

10With too much tyranny and art,

Lest by thy scorn thou lose the prize

Gain'd by the power of thy bright eyes,

And thou this conquest thus shalt prove,

Though got by Beauty, kept by Love!

The Dream.

LOPE DE VEGA.

To set my jealous soul at strife,

All things maliciously agree,

Though sleep of Death the image be,

Dreams are the portraiture of life.

I saw, when last I clos'd my eyes,

Celinda stoop t' another's will;

If specious Apprehension kill,

What would the truth without disguise?

The joys which I should call mine own,

10Methought this rival did possess:

Like dreams is all my happiness;

Yet dreams themselves allow me none.

The Dream.] The actual and full *In Memoriam* arrangement is the point of interest here. Stanley, however, is even less successful than the few other seventeenth-century practitioners in getting the full rhythmical sweep of the form into operation. He breaks the circle and so loses the charm.

To the Lady D.

MADAM,

The blushes I betray,

When at your feet I humbly lay

These papers, beg you would excuse

Th' obedience of a bashful Muse,

Who, bowing to your strict command,

Trusts her own errors to your hand,

Hasty abortives, which, laid by,

She meant, ere they were born should die:

But since the soft power of your breath

10Hath call'd them back again from Death,

To your sharp judgement now made known,

She dares for hers no longer own;

The worst she must not, these resign'd

She hath to th' fire, and where you find

Those your kind Charity admir'd,

She writ but what your eyes inspir'd.

To the Lady D.] This in *1647* is the Dedication 'To my most honour'd Aunt the Lady Dormer'. She was a daughter of Sir William Hammond and wife of Sir Robert Dormer, Knight, of Chearsley, Bucks. In *1647* Stanley added to the poem '*Madam, Your Ladyships Greatest admirer and most humble Servant,* THO. STANLEY'.

Love Deposed.

You that unto your mistress' eyes

Your hearts do sacrifice,

And offer sighs or tears at Love's rich shrine,

Renounce with me

Th' idolatry,

Nor this infernal Power esteem divine.

The brand, the quiver, and the bow,

Which we did first bestow,

And he as tribute wears from every lover,

10I back again

From him have ta'en,

And the impostor, now unveil'd, discover.

I can the feeble child disarm,

Untie his mystic charm,

Divest him of his wings, and break his arrow;

We will obey

No more his sway,

Nor live confin'd to laws or bounds so narrow.

20And you, bright Beauties, that inspire

The Boy's pale torch with fire,

We safely now your subtle power despise,

And unscorch'd may

Like atoms play,

And wanton in the sunshine of your eyes.

Nor think hereafter by new arts

You can bewitch our hearts,

Or raise this devil by your pleasing charm;

We will no more

His power implore,

30Unless, like Indians, that he do no harm.

The Divorce.

Dear, back my wounded heart restore,

And turn away thy powerful eyes;

Flatter my willing soul no more!

Love must not hope what Fate denies.

Take, take away thy smiles and kisses!

Thy love wounds deeper than disdain;

For he that sees the heaven he misses,

Sustains two hells, of loss and pain.

Shouldst thou some other's suit prefer,

10I might return thy scorn to thee,

And learn apostasy of her,

Who taught me first idolatry.

Or in thy unrelenting breast

Should I disdain or coyness move,

He by thy hate might be releas'd,

Who now is prisoner to thy love.

Since then unkind Fate will divorce

Those whom Affection long united,

Be thou as cruel as this force,

20And I in death shall be delighted.

Thus while so many suppliants woo.

And beg they may thy pity prove,

I only for thy scorn do sue:

'Tis charity here not to love.

The Divorce.] A rise from one or two preceding pieces.

12 Who] That *1647*.

14 I] cold *1647*.

15 He] I *1647*.

16 is] am *1647*.

21 while] whilst *1647*. woo] do *1647*.

22 'Implore thy pity they may prove' *1647*.

Time Recovered.

CASONE.

Come, my dear, whilst youth conspires

With the warmth of our desires;

Envious Time about thee watches,

And some grace each minute snatches;

Now a spirit, now a ray,

From thy eye he steals away;

Now he blasts some blooming rose,

Which upon thy fresh cheek grows;

Gold now plunders in a hair;

10Now the rubies doth impair

Of thy lips; and with sure haste

All thy wealth will take at last;

Only that of which thou mak'st

Use in time, from time thou tak'st.

Time Recovered.] This 'very light and good' version is from Guido Casoni (so more usually), a poet of the Trevisan March (1587-1640), and founder of the Academy of the *Incogniti* at Venice, to the Transactions of which he contributed most of his work.

The Bracelet.

Rebellious fools that scorn to bow

Beneath Love's easy sway,

Whose stubborn wills no laws allow,

Disdaining to obey,

Mark but this wreath of hair, and you shall see,

None that might wear such fetters would be free!

I once could boast a soul like you,

As unconfin'd as air;

But mine, which force could not subdue,

10Was caught within this snare;

And, by myself betray'd, I, for this gold,

A heart that many storms withstood, have sold.

No longer now wise Art inquire,

With this vain search delighted,

How souls, that human breasts inspire,

Are to their frames united;

Material chains such spirits well may bind,

When this soft braid can tie both arm and mind

Now, Beauties, I defy your charm,

20Rul'd by more powerful art:

This mystic wreath which crowns my arm,

Defends my vanquish'd heart;

And I, subdu'd by one more fair, shall be

Secur'd from Conquest by Captivity.

The Bracelet.] Almost certainly suggested by Donne. If so the suggestion was very rashly taken, but the result might have been worse.

7 soul] heart *1647*. l. 12 is an alteration—as Miss Guiney very rightly says to its detriment—of *1647*, which reads—

Have to mine enemy my freedom sold.

15 *1647* 'that do our life inspire'.

22 *1647* 'Guards and defends my heart'.

The Farewell.

Since Fate commands me hence, and I

Must leave my soul with thee, and die,

Dear, spare one sigh, or else let fall

A tear to crown my funeral,

That I may tell my grievéd heart,

Thou art unwilling we should part,

And Martyrs, that embrace the fire,

Shall with less joy than I expire.

With this last kiss I will bequeath

10My soul transfus'd into thy breath,

Whose active heat shall gently slide

Into thy breast, and there reside,

And be in spite of Fate, thus bless'd

By this sad death, of Heaven possess'd.

Then prove but kind, and thou shalt see

Love hath more power than Destiny.

The Farewell.] In lines 13 and 14 of this all editions vary slightly. *1647* has 'may' for 'be', which latter word opens the next line, turning out 'sad'. The text is *1651, 1656,* keeping l. 13 of *1647,* has for l. 14 the text of *1651.*

Claim to Love.
GUARINI.

Alas! alas! thou turn'st in vain

Thy beauteous face away,

Which, like young sorcerers, rais'd a pain

Above its power to lay.

Love moves not, as thou turn'st thy look,

But here doth firmly rest;

He long ago thy eyes forsook,

To revel in my breast.

Thy power on him why hop'st thou more

10Than his on me should be?

The claim thou lay'st to him is poor,

To that he owns from me.

His substance in my heart excels

His shadow in thy sight;

Fire, where it burns, more truly dwells,

Than where it scatters light.

To his Mistress, who dreamed he was wounded.

GUARINI.

Thine eyes, bright Saint, disclose,

And thou shalt find

Dreams have not with illusive shows

Deceiv'd thy mind:

What sleep presented to thy view,

Awake, and thou shalt find is true.

Those mortal wounds I bear,

From thee begin,

Which though they outward not appear,

10Yet bleed within.

Love's flame like active lightning flies,

Wounding the heart, but not the eyes.

But now I yield to die

Thy sacrifice,

Nor more in vain will hope to fly

From thy bright eyes:

Their killing power cannot be shunn'd,

Open or closed alike they wound.

To his Mistress, &c.] *1647* 'To Doris dreaming he was wounded'. Guarini is not there mentioned.

The Exchange.
DIALOGUE.

Phil.

That kiss, which last thou gav'st me, stole

My fainting life away,

Yet, though to thy breast fled, my soul

Still in mine own doth stay;

Char.

And with the same warm breath did mine

Into thy bosom slide;

There dwell contracted unto thine,

Yet still with me reside.

Chor.

Both souls thus in desire are one,

10And each is two in skill;

Doubled in intellect alone,

United in the will.

Weak Nature no such power doth know:

Love only can these wonders show.

The Exchange.] *1647* 'Exchange of Souls'. In editions other than *1651* there is
a refrain after each stanza-speech:

Weak Nature no such power doth know,

Love only can these wonders show.

Unaltered by Sickness.

Sickness, in vain thou dost invade

A Beauty that can never fade!

Could all thy malice but impair

One of the sweets which crown this fair,

Or steal the spirits from her eye,

Or kiss into a paler dye

The blushing roses of her cheek,

Our drooping hopes might justly seek

Redress from thee, and thou might'st save

10Thousands of lovers from the grave:

But such assaults are vain, for she

Is too divine to stoop to thee;

Blest with a form as much too high

For any change, as Destiny,

Which no attempt can violate;

For what's her Beauty, is our Fate.

Unaltered by Sickness.] Lines 1 and 2 are expanded in *1656* to:

Pale, envious Sickness, hence! no more

Possess our breast, too cold before.

In vain, alas! thou dost invade

Those beauties which can never fade.

4 'On those sweets which crown the fair' *1656.*

7 blushing] blooming *1657.*

8 drooping] dropping *1647*: suffering *1656.*

14 For any] *1656 But* any—nonsensically.

On his Mistress's Death.

PETRARCH.

Love the ripe harvest of my toils

Began to cherish with his smiles,

Preparing me to be indued

With all the joys I long pursued,

When my fresh hopes, fair and full blown,

Death blasts, ere I could call my own.

Malicious Death! why with rude force

Dost thou my Fair from me divorce?

False Life! why in this loathéd chain

10Me from my Fair dost thou detain?

In whom assistance shall I find?

Alike are Life and Death unkind.

Pardon me, Love; thy power outshines,

And laughs at their infirm designs.

She is not wedded to a tomb,

Nor I to sorrow in her room.

They, what thou join'st, can ne'er divide

She lives in me, in her I died.

The Exequies.

Draw near,

You Lovers that complain

Of Fortune or Disdain,

And to my ashes lend a tear;

Melt the hard marble with your groans,

And soften the relentless stones,

Whose cold embraces the sad subject hide,

Of all Love's cruelties, and Beauty's pride!

No verse,

10No epicedium bring,

Nor peaceful requiem sing,

To charm the terrors of my hearse;

No profane numbers must flow near

The sacred silence that dwells here.

Vast griefs are dumb; softly, oh! softly mourn,

Lest you disturb the peace attends my urn.

Yet strew

Upon my dismal grave

Such offerings as you have,

20Forsaken cypress and sad yew;

For kinder flowers can take no birth,

Or growth, from such unhappy earth.

Weep only o'er my dust, and say, Here lies

To Love and Fate an equal sacrifice.

The Exequies.] A very good stanza, the rhythm rising and swelling admirably.
In the final couplet of the first, *1647* reads—

do a victim hide,

That, paid to Beauty, on Love's altar died.

The Silkworm.

This silkworm, to long sleep retir'd,

The early year hath re-inspir'd,

Who now to pay to thee prepares

The tribute of her pleasing cares;

And hastens with industrious toil

To make thy ornament, her spoil:

See with what pains she spins for thee

The thread of her own destiny;

Then growing proud in Death, to know

10That all her curious labours thou

Wilt, as in triumph, deign to wear,

Retires to her soft sepulchre.

Such, dearest, is that hapless state,

To which I am design'd by Fate,

Who by thee, willingly, o'ercome,

Work mine own fetters and my tomb.

The Silkworm.]   1 This] The *1647*.

6 Miss Guiney insists, in the teeth of all texts, upon changing over 'thy' and
'her', saying that 'facts and the context force' the reversal. I am afraid that the
genius of seventeenth-century poetry did not care much for facts or context
at any time. But here no violence is done to either. Nine men out of ten

wishing to say 'to make out of the spoil of herself an ornament for thee' would have probably put it in the same way, especially if they wanted the rhyme 'spoil'.

10 'That *her rich work and* labours' *1647*.

14 'I destined am' *1647*.

A Lady Weeping.

MONTALVAN.

As when some brook flies from itself away,

The murmuring crystal loosely runs astray;

And as about the verdant plain it winds,

The meadows with a silver riband binds,

Printing a kiss on every flower she meets,

Losing herself to fill them with new sweets,

To scatter frost upon the lily's head,

And scarlet on the gilliflower to spread;

So melting sorrow, in the fair disguise

10Of humid stars, flow'd from bright Cloris' eyes,

Which wat'ring every flower her cheek discloses,

Melt into jasmines here, there into roses.

A Lady Weeping.] Few people, I think, will accept Miss Guiney's suggestion of 'tears' for 'stars' in l. 10, especially after 'humid'. The shooting star, which dissolved on reaching earth into dew or 'jelly', is very common with Carolines.

Ambition.

I must no longer now admire

The coldness which possess'd

Thy snowy breast,

That can by other flames be set on fire.

Poor Love, to harsh Disdain betray'd,

Is by Ambition thus out-weigh'd.

Hadst thou but known the vast extent

Of constant faith, how far

'Bove all that are

10Born slaves to Wealth, or Honour's vain ascent;

No richer treasure couldst thou find

Than hearts with mutual chains combin'd.

But Love is too despis'd a name,

And must not hope to rise

Above these ties;

Honour and Wealth outshine his paler flame;

These unite souls, whilst true desire

Unpitied dies in its own fire.

Yet, cruel fair one, I did aim

20With no less justice too,

Than those that sue

For other hopes, and thy proud fortunes claim.

Wealth honours, honours wealth approve,

But Beauty's only meant for Love.

Ambition.]   16 Miss Guiney thinks that the singular 'Honour', though in all texts, is obviously wrong. I should say that the plural would be more obviously wronger. The mistake, of course, comes from importing a modern distinction.

Song.

When, dearest beauty, thou shalt pay

Thy faith and my vain hope away

To some dull soul that cannot know

The worth of that thou dost bestow;

Lest with my sighs and tears I might

Disturb thy unconfin'd delight,

To some dark shade I will retire,

And there, forgot by all, expire.

Thus, whilst the difference thou shalt prove

10Betwixt a feign'd and real love,

Whilst he, more happy, but less true,

Shall reap those joys I did pursue,

And with those pleasures crownéd be

By Fate, which Love design'd for me,

Then thou, perhaps, thyself wilt find

Cruel too long, or too soon kind.

Song.] Not one of Stanley's worst.

The Revenge.
RONSARD.

Fair Rebel to thyself and Time,

Who laugh'st at all my tears,

When thou hast lost thy youthful prime,

And Age his trophy rears,

Weighing thy inconsiderate pride

Thou shalt in vain accuse it,

Why beauty am I now denied,

Or knew not then to use it?

Then shall I wish, ungentle fair,

10Thou in like flames mayst burn;

Venus, if just, will hear my prayer,

And I shall laugh my turn.

The Revenge.] Not one of his best, even as a translation. The suspicion of *flatness* which occurs too often in him could not be more fatal than in connexion with Ronsard's famous and beautiful sonnet. But Stanley has handicapped himself almost inconceivably. He has thrown away the half-sad, half-scornful burst of the opening 'Quand vous serez bien vieille'—the vivid picture of the crone half boasting, half regretting her love and her disdain, by the flicker of fire and candle, to the listening handmaiden, and the final touch as to the use of life. In fact I have sometimes wondered whether he really meant this masterpiece.

Song.

I will not trust thy tempting graces,

Or thy deceitful charms;

Nor pris'ner be to thy embraces,

Or fetter'd in thy arms;

No, Celia, no, not all thy art

Can wound or captivate my heart.

I will not gaze upon thy eyes,

Or wanton with thy hair,

Lest those should burn me by surprise,

10Or these my soul ensnare;

Nor with those smiling dangers play,

Or fool my liberty away.

Since then my wary heart is free,

And unconfin'd as thine,

If thou wouldst mine should captiv'd be,

Thou must thine own resign,

And gratitude may thus move more

Than Love or Beauty could before.

Song.] Another capital stanza-mould, especially in 1. The next is even better. This Song is also in *Select Airs and Dialogues, set by Mr. Jeremy Savill, 1659.*

Song.

No, I will sooner trust the wind,

When falsely kind

It courts the pregnant sails into a storm,

And when the smiling waves persuade,

Be willingly betray'd,

Than thy deceitful vows or form.

Go, and beguile some easy heart

With thy vain art;

Thy smiles and kisses on those fools bestow,

10Who only see the calms that sleep

On this smooth flatt'ring deep,

But not the hidden dangers know.

They that like me thy falsehood prove,

Will scorn thy love.

Some may, deceiv'd at first, adore thy shrine;

But he that, as thy sacrifice,

Doth willingly fall twice,

Dies his own martyr, and not thine.

Song. 12 the] thy *1647*.

To a Blind Man in Love.
MARINO.

Lover, than Love more blind, whose bold thoughts dare

Fix on a woman is both young and fair!

If Argus, with a hundred eyes, not one

Could guard, hop'st thou to keep thine, who hast none?

To a Blind Man in Love.] 2 The ellipsis of 'who' before 'is' is one of the few grammatical licences which are really awkward in poetry. In *Oronta 1647,* where this poem also appeared with two other translations from Marino, the reading is 'woman that is young'; and in 7 'Senses too'.

Answer.

I'm blind, 'tis true, but, in Love's rules, defect

Of sense is aided by the intellect;

And senses by each other are supplied:

The touch enjoys what's to the sight denied.

Song.

I Prithee let my heart alone,

Since now 'tis rais'd above thee,

Not all the beauty thou dost own,

Again can make me love thee:

He that was shipwreck'd once before

By such a Syren's call,

And yet neglects to shun that shore,

Deserves his second fall.

Each flatt'ring kiss, each tempting smile,

10Thou dost in vain bestow,

Some other lovers might beguile,

Who not thy falsehood know.

But I am proof against all art.

No vows shall e'er persuade me

Twice to present a wounded heart

To her that hath betray'd me.

Could I again be brought to love

Thy form, though more divine,

I might thy scorn as justly move,

20As now thou sufferest mine.

Song.] Pretty, and the double rhymes in stanzas 1 and 4 well brought off.
7 *1656* '*the* shore'.

The Loss.

Yet ere I go,

Disdainful Beauty, thou shall be

So wretched, as to know

What joys thou fling'st away with me.

A faith so bright,

As Time or Fortune could not rust;

So firm, that lovers might

Have read thy story in my dust,

And crown'd thy name

10With laurel verdant as thy youth,

Whilst the shrill voice of Fame

Spread wide thy beauty and my truth.

This thou hast lost;

For all true lovers, when they find

That my just aims were crost,

Will speak thee lighter than the wind.

And none will lay

Any oblation on thy shrine,

But such as would betray

20Thy faith, to faiths as false as thine.

Yet, if thou choose

On such thy freedom to bestow,

Affection may excuse,

For love from sympathy doth flow.

The Loss.] Still good. But I have once more to demur to Miss Guiney's opinion that 'Thy' in l. 20, though found in all texts, should 'almost certainly' be 'Their'. In the first place, conjectural emendations in the teeth of text-agreement are never to be made without absolute necessity. In the second, the hackneyed observation about the less obvious reading is never so true as of the Caroline poets. In the third, this particular correction, if obvious in one sense, is but specious in another, and '*Their* faith' will be found on examination to make less, not more, sense than 'Thy'. The meaning is, 'Such faith as thou mightest repose in them after being false to me', i.e. 'They would leave thee for other light-o'-loves'.

The Self-Cruel.

Cast off, for shame, ungentle Maid,

That misbecoming joy thou wear'st;

For in my death, though long delay'd,

Unwisely cruel thou appear'st.

Insult o'er captives with disdain,

Thou canst not triumph o'er the slain.

No, I am now no longer thine,

Nor canst thou take delight to see

Him whom thy love did once confine,

10Set, though by Death, at liberty;

For if my fall a smile beget,

Thou gloriest in thy own defeat.

Behold how thy unthrifty pride

Hath murder'd him that did maintain it!

And wary souls, who never tried

Thy tyrant beauty, will disdain it:

But I am softer, and that me

Thou wouldst not pity, pity thee.

The Self-Cruel.] Merely 'Song' in *1647*.

The observations in the preceding note apply to Miss Guiney's supposition that 'that' in the penultimate line is a misprint for 'though'. 'I pity thee *in* (or 'for') that thou wouldst not pity me.'

Song.

BY M. W. M.

Wert thou yet fairer than thou art,

Which lies not in the power of Art;

Or hadst thou in thine eyes more darts

Than ever Cupid shot at hearts;

Yet if they were not thrown at me,

I would not cast a thought on thee,

I'd rather marry a disease,

Than court the thing I cannot please;

She that will cherish my desires,

10Must meet my flames with equal fires.

What pleasure is there in a kiss

To him that doubts the heart's not his?

I love thee not because th' art fair,

Softer than down, smoother than air;

Nor for the Cupids that do lie

In either corner of thine eye:

Wouldst thou then know what it might be?

'Tis I love you, 'cause you love me.

Song.] In *1647* the song itself is not given, and the title of Stanley's piece is *'In Answer to a Song*, Wert thou much fairer than thou art, &c.' I do not know who Master W. M. was—possibly Walter Montagu, Abbé de Saint-Martin, whom we have met once or twice in commendatory poems, and who was of the Cavalier literary set.

Answer.

Wert thou by all affections sought,

And fairer than thou wouldst be thought;

Or had thine eyes as many darts

As thou believ'st they shoot at hearts;

Yet if thy love were paid to me,

I would not offer mine to thee.

I'd sooner court a fever's heat,

Than her that owns a flame as great;

She that my love will entertain,

10Must meet it with no less disdain;

For mutual fires themselves destroy,

And willing kisses yield no joy.

I love thee not because alone

Thou canst all beauty call thine own

Nor doth my passion fuel seek

In thy bright eye or softer cheek:

Then, fairest, if thou wouldst know why

I love thee, 'cause thou canst deny.

The Relapse.

Oh, turn away those cruel eyes,

The stars of my undoing!

Or Death, in such a bright disguise,

May tempt a second wooing.

Punish their blindly impious pride,

Who dare contemn thy glory;

It was my fall that deified

Thy name, and seal'd thy story.

Yet no new sufferings can prepare

10A higher praise to crown thee;

Though my first Death proclaim thee fair,

My second will unthrone thee.

Lovers will doubt thou canst entice

No other for thy fuel,

And if thou burn one victim twice,

Both think thee poor and cruel.

The Relapse.] One of the author's best. Double rhymes often brought him luck. It was reprinted in Lawes's *Airs and Dialogues, the Second Book*, 1655, p. 7, with the heading 'He would not be tempted'. In *1647* called 'Song' only. This edition also reads in l. 5 'blind and impious', and in l. 7 'thy name' for 'my fall'. This last, which doubtless is a slip, seems to occur in some copies of *1651*, but Brydges prints it correctly.

To the Countess of S. with the Holy Court.

MADAM,

Since every place you bless, the name

This book assumes may justlier claim,

(What more a court than where you shine?

And where your soul, what more divine?)

You may, perhaps, doubt at first sight,

That it usurps upon your right;

And praising virtues, that belong

To you, in others, doth yours wrong;

No; 'tis yourself you read, in all

10Perfections earlier ages call

Their own; all glories they e'er knew

Were but faint prophecies of you.

You then have here sole interest whom 'tis meant

As well to entertain, as represent.

To the Countess of S.] This lady has been supposed, probably enough, to be Dorothy Sidney or Spencer, Countess of Sunderland, and Waller's 'Sacharissa'. *The Holy Court* was a manual of devotion by the Jesuit Caussin, translated into English as early as 1626.

Song.

DE VOITURE.

I languish in a silent flame;

For she, to whom my vows incline,

Doth own perfections so divine,

That but to speak were to disclose her name

If I should say that she the store

Of Nature's graces doth comprise,

The love and wonder of all eyes,

Who will not guess the beauty I adore?

Or though I warily conceal

10The charms her looks and soul possess;

Should I her cruelty express,

And say she smiles at all the pains we feel;

Among such suppliants as implore

Pity, distributing her hate,

Inexorable as their fate,

Who will not guess the beauty I adore?

Song.] Stanley was less *impar congressus* with Voiture than with Ronsard, and this is well done. The stanza is well framed and is different from the French ('Je me tais et me sens brûler', Chanson LIV, *Œuvres* de Voiture, ed. Ubicini, Paris, 1855, ii. 336).

Drawn for Valentine by the L. D. S.

Though 'gainst me Love and Destiny conspire,

Though I must waste in an unpitied fire,

By the same Deity, severe as fair,

Commanded adoration and despair;

Though I am mark'd for sacrifice, to tell

The growing age what dangerous glories dwell

In this bright dawn, who, when she spreads her rays,

Will challenge every heart, and every praise;

Yet she who to all hope forbids my claim,

10By Fortune's taught indulgence to my flame.

Great Queen of Chance! unjustly we exclude

Thy power an interest in beatitude,

Who, with mysterious judgement, dost dispense

The bounties of unerring Providence,

Whilst we, to whom the causes are unknown,

Would style that blindness thine, which is our own;

As kind in justice to thyself as me,

Thou hast redeem'd thy name and votary;

Nor will I prize this less for being thine,

20Nor longer at my destiny repine:

Counsel and choice are things below thy state;

Fortune relieves the cruelties of Fate.

The Modest Wish.
BARCLAY.

Reach incense, boy! thou pious Flamen, pray!

To genial Deities these rites we pay.

Fly far from hence, such as are only taught

To fear the Gods by guilt of crime or thought!

This is my suit; grant it, Celestial Powers,

If what my will affects, oppose not yours.

First, pure before your altars may I stand,

And practise studiously what you command;

My parents' faith devoutly let me prize,

10Nor what my ancestors esteem'd, despise;

Let me not vex'd inquire (when thriving ill

Depresseth good) why thunder is so still?

No such ambitious knowledge trouble me;

Those curious thoughts advance not Piety:

Peaceful my house, in wife and children bless'd,

Nor these beyond my fortunes be increas'd:

None cozen me with Friendship's specious gloss;

None dearly buy my friendship with their loss:

To suits nor wars my quiet be betray'd;

20My quiet, to the Muses justly paid:

Want never force me court the rich with lies,

And intermix my suit with flatteries:

Let my sure friends deceive the tedious light,

And my sound sleeps, with debts not broke, the night:

Cheerful my board, my smiles shar'd by my wife,

O Gods! yet mindful still of human life,

To die nor let me wish nor fear; among

My joys mix griefs, griefs that not last too long:

My age be happy; and when Fate shall claim

30My thread of life, let me survive in fame.

Enough: the gods are pleas'd; the flames aspire,

And crackling laurel triumphs in the fire.

E Catalectis Vet[erum] Poet[arum]

A small well-gotten stock and country seat

I have, yet my content makes both seem great.

My quiet soul to fears is not inur'd,

And from the sins of Idleness secur'd.

Others may seek the camp, others the town,

And fool themselves with pleasure or renown;

Let me, unminded in the common crowd,

Live master of the time that I'm allow'd.

On the Edition of Mr. Fletcher's Works.

Fletcher (whose fame no age can ever waste;

Envy of ours, and glory of the last)

Is now alive again; and with his name

His sacred ashes wak'd into a flame;

Such as before did by a secret charm

The wildest heart subdue, the coldest warm,

And lend the ladies' eyes a power more bright,

Dispensing thus to either, heat and light.

He to a sympathy those souls betray'd,

10Whom Love or Beauty never could persuade;

And in each mov'd spectator could beget

A real passion by a counterfeit:

When first Bellario bled, what lady there

Did not for every drop let fall a tear?

And when Aspasia wept, not any eye

But seem'd to wear the same sad livery.

By him inspir'd, the feign'd Lucina drew

More streams of melting sorrow than the true;

But then the Scornful Lady did beguile

20Their easy griefs, and teach them all to smile.

Thus he affections could or raise or lay;

Love, Grief, and Mirth thus did his charms obey:

He Nature taught her passions to outdo,

How to refine the old, and create new;

Which such a happy likeness seem'd to bear,

As if that Nature Art, Art Nature were.

Yet all had nothing been, obscurely kept

In the same urn wherein his dust hath slept,

Nor had he ris' the Delphic wreath to claim,

30Had not the dying scene expir'd his name.

Oh the indulgent justice of this age,

To grant the Press, what it denies the Stage!

Despair our joy hath doubled; he is come

Twice welcome by this *post-liminium*;

His loss preserv'd him; they that silenc'd wit

Are now the authors to eternize it:

Thus poets are in spite of Fate reviv'd,

And plays, by intermission, longer liv'd.

On [the Edition of Mr.] Fletcher's Works.] The bracketed words omitted in *1647*, when, as the book itself (the first folio of Beaumont and Fletcher) had just appeared, they were unnecessary. The variants are slight: 'could' and 'did' in lines 5 and 11 are changed over; in l. 19, 'doth' (again reflecting the immediate presentation). In l. 29 'rise': the form 'ris'' is recognized by Ben Jonson. In l. 30 Miss Guiney thinks 'not' 'clearly a misprint' for 'with'. But this is clearly a misunderstanding of 'expir'd', which is used with its proper transitive force as in Latin. 'Had not the dying stage [the suppressed and decadent theatre of 1647] expired [uttered with its passing breath] his name, the book would not

have been published [and so made him rise and claim the crown].' ll. 31, 32
were omitted in the Beaumont and Fletcher Folio, 1647.

It can hardly be necessary to annotate the well-known characters of 'the
twins' that Stanley introduces. Brydges, by printing 'Scornful Lady' without
capitals, unnecessarily obscured one of them.

To Mr. W. Hammond.

Thou best of friendship, knowledge, and of art!

The charm of whose lov'd name preserves my heart

From female vanities (thy name, which there,

Till Time dissolves the fabric, I must wear),

Forgive a crime which long my soul opprest,

And crept by chance in my unwary breast,

So great, as for thy pardon were unfit,

And to forgive were worse than to commit,

But that the fault and pain were so much one,

10The very act did expiate what was done.

I, who so often sported with the flame,

Play'd with the Boy, and laugh'd at both as tame,

Betray'd by Idleness and Beauty, fell

At last in love, love, both the sin and hell:

No punishment great as my fault esteem'd,

But to be that which I so long had seem'd.

Behold me such, a face, a voice, a lute,

The sentence in a minute execute!

I yield; recant; the faith which I before

20Denied, profess; the power I scorn'd, implore.

Alas, in vain! no prayers, no vows can bow

Her stubborn heart, who neither will allow.

But see how strangely what was meant no less

Than torment, prov'd my greatest happiness:

Delay, that should have sharpen'd, starv'd Desire,

And Cruelty not fann'd, but quench'd my fire;

Love bound me: now by kind Disdain set free,

I can despise that Love as well as she.

That sin to friendship I away have thrown:

30My heart thou mayst without a rival own,

While such as willingly themselves beguile,

And sell away their freedoms for a smile,

Blush to confess our joys as far above

Their hopes, as Friendship's longer liv'd than Love.

To Mr. W. Hammond.] In *1647*, as usually, initials only. His relation (see Introduction) and the author of the poems in vol. ii. As in some other cases, this poem shows the *nisus* of the more or less stopped couplet—the way in which it was communicating energy to writers of the time even when they mainly belong to the older division.

30 *1647* 'Nor any flame, but what is thine, will own'.

On Mr. Shirley's Poems.

When, dearest friend, thy verse doth re-inspire

Love's pale decaying torch with brighter fire,

Whilst everywhere thou dost dilate thy flame,

And to the world spread thy Odelia's name,

The justice of all ages must remit

To her the prize of Beauty, thee of Wit.

Then, like some skilful artist, that to wonder

Framing a piece, displeas'd, takes it asunder,

Thou Beauty dost depose, her charms deny,

10And all the mystic chains of Love untie:

Thus thy diviner Muse a power 'bove Fate

May boast, that can both make and uncreate.

Next thou call'st back to life that love-sick boy,

To the kind-hearted nymphs less fair than coy,

Who, by reflex beams burnt with vain desire,

Did, Phoenix-like, in his own flames expire:

But should he view his shadow drawn by thee,

He with himself once more in love would be.

Echo (who though she words pursue, her haste

20Can only overtake and stop the last)

Shall her first speech and human veil obtain

To sing thy softer numbers o'er again.

Thus, into dying poetry, thy Muse

Doth full perfection and new life infuse;

Each line deserves a laurel, and thy praise

Asks not a garland, but a grove of bays;

Nor can ours raise thy lasting trophies higher,

Who only reach at merit to admire.

But I must chide thee, friend: how canst thou be

30A patron, yet a foe to poetry?

For while thou dost this age to verse restore,

Thou dost deprive the next of owning more;

And hast so far e'en future aims surpast,

That none dare write: thus being first and last,

All, their abortive Muses will suppress,

And poetry by this increase grow less.

On Mr. Shirley's Poems.] *1647* initials (I. S.), as usual. The same remark applies here as to the last piece. Shirley's *Poems* (which include a reciprocal compliment to our author's) appear at the end of the sixth volume of Dyce's standard edition of his plays, and therefore are not included in this collection. They are, however, interesting, though there is nothing in them so good as the famous 'Glories of our blood and state'. 'Odelia' (a curious and rather suspicious name) appears pretty frequently in them. Shirley was a friend not merely of Stanley, but of Hammond and Prestwich (*v. inf.*) and others of the set. Some of the poems usually attributed to Carew appear to be really his. His *Poems* were published in 1646, a year before Stanley's.—There are some quite unimportant variants between *1647* and *1651*: 'that' and 'who' in l. 7; 'a' and 'some' in l. 8; 'words' and 'speech' in l. 19; and l. 30 has the absurd reading 'A patron, yet a *friend* to poesy'. *1647* omits lines 31 and 32, and reads

Thou hast so far all future times surpassed

in l. 33. Miss Guiney suggests 'voice' for 'veil' in l. 21. But 'veil' is far more poetical as = The *body* of her disguise and humiliation after her aerial enfranchisement.

On Mr. Sherburn's Translation of Seneca's Medea, and Vindication of the Author.

That wise philosopher, who had design'd

To life the various passions of the mind,

Did wrong'd Medea's jealousy prefer

To entertain the Roman theatre;

Both to instruct the soul, and please the sight,

At once begetting horror and delight.

This cruelty thou dost once more express,

Though in a strange, no less becoming dress;

And her revenge hast robb'd of half its pride,

10To see itself thus by itself outvied,

That boldest ages past may say, our times

Can speak, as well as act their highest crimes.

Nor was 't enough to do his scene this right,

But what thou gav'st to us, with equal light

Thou wouldst bestow on him, nor wert more just

Unto the author's work, than to his dust;

Thou dost make good his title, aid his claim,

Both vindicate his poem and his name,

So shar'st a double wreath; for all that we

Unto the poet owe, he owes to thee. 20

Though change of tongues stol'n praise to some afford,

Thy version hath not borrow'd, but restor'd.

On Mr. Sherburn's Translation, &c.] Title in *1647* rather longer, but with initials, 'To Mr. E. S. on his Translation of Medea, with the other Tragedies of Seneca the Philosopher and vindicating of their Author'. Sherburn (afterwards Sir Edward) had the rather capriciously adjudged honour of appearing in Chalmers's *Poets*, which accounts for his absence here.

20 *1647* reads 'author' for 'poet', an obvious overlooking of the occurrence of the word just before.

On Mr. Hall's Essays.

Wits that matur'd by time have courted praise,

Shall see their works outdone in these Essays;

And blush to know, thy earlier years display

A dawning, clearer than their brightest day.

Yet I'll not praise thee, for thou hast outgrown

The reach of all men's praises, but thine own.

Encomiums to their objects are exact;

To praise, and not at full, is to detract.

And with most justice are the best forgot,

10For praise is bounded when the theme is not:

Since mine is thus confin'd, and far below

Thy merit, I forbear it, nor will show

How poor the autumnal pride of some appears,

To the ripe fruit thy vernal season bears.

Yet though I mean no praise, I come t'invite

Thy forward aims still to advance their flight;

Rise higher yet, what though thy spreading wreath

Lessen to their dull sight who stay beneath?

To thy full learning how can all allow

20Just praise, unless that all were learn'd as thou?

Go on in spite of such low souls, and may

Thy growing worth know age, though not decay,

Till thou pay back thy theft; and live to climb

As many years as thou hast snatch'd from Time.

On Mr. Hall's Essays.] *1647* 'To Mr. I. H. on his Essays'. These were the much-praised *Horae Vacivae* (see Introduction to Hall, vol. ii). Besides the slight difference in general title the *1647* version divides itself. The first division consists of the first four lines only. A second, to Mr. I. H., appears elsewhere, beginning:

I'll not commend thee, for thou hast outgrown—

and going on as above, except that 'full' is foisted up from l. 8 to l. 7 ('full objects'), to the destruction of sense and metre.

3 earlier] early *1647*.

13 'The pride of others' autumns poor appears' *1647*.

On S[ir] J[ohn] S[uckling], his Picture and Poems.

Suckling, whose numbers could invite

Alike to wonder and delight,

And with new spirit did inspire

The Thespian scene and Delphic lyre,

Is thus express'd in either part,

Above the humble reach of Art.

Drawn by the pencil, here you find

His form, by his own pen, his mind.

On Sir John Suckling, his Picture and Poems.] Initials only in original titles. These poems were the *Fragmenta Aurea* of 1646.

The Union.

Μία ψυχὴ δύο σώματα.

BY MR. WILLIAM FAIRFAX.

As in the crystal centre of the sight,
Two subtle beams make but one cone of light,
Or when one flame twin'd with another is,
They both ascend in one bright pyramis;
Our spirits thus into each other flow,
One in our being, one in what we know,
In what we will, desire, dislike, approve,
In what we love, and one is that pure love,
As in a burning glass th' aërial flame,
10With the producing ray, is still the same:
We to Love's purest quintessence refin'd,
Do both become one undefilèd mind.
This sacred fire into itself converts
Our yielding spirits, and our melting hearts,
Till both our souls into one spirit run,
So several lines are in their centre one.
And when thy fair idea is imprest
In the soft tablet of my easier breast,
The sweet reflection brings such sympathy,
20That I my better self behold in thee;
And all perfections that in thee combine,
By this resultance are entirely mine;
Thy rays disperse my shades, who only live
Bright in the lustre thou art pleas'd to give.

The Union]   12 undefiled] undivided *1647.*

18 tablet] table *1647*.

Answer.

If we are one, dear friend! why shouldst thou be

At once unequal to thyself and me?

By thy release thou swell'st my debt the more,

And dost but rob thyself to make me poor.

What part can I have in thy luminous cone?

What flame, since my love's thine, can call my own?

The palest star is less the son of night,

Who, but thy borrow'd, know no native light:

Was 't not enough thou freely didst bestow

10The Muse, but thou wouldst give the laurel too?

And twice my aims by thy assistance raise,

Conferring first the merit, then the praise?

But I should do thee greater injury,

Did I believe this praise were meant to me,

Or thought, though thou hast worth enough to spare,

T' enrich another soul, that mine should share.

Thy Muse, seeming to lend, calls home her fame,

And her due wreath doth in renouncing claim.

Answer.] In l. 10 of the 'Answer' *1647* has 'must'. At the end of the poem in *1647* is the couplet

Δύσμορε θηλυμανῶν γλυκὺ μὴ λέγε κέντρον ἐρώτων·

  Μοῦνος ΤΑΣ ΜΟΥΣΑΣ ὄλβιός ἐστι ΘΕΛΩΝ.

Pythagoras, his Moral Rules.

First to immortal God thy duty pay,

Observe thy vow, honour the saints: obey

Thy prince and rulers, nor their laws despise:

Thy parents reverence, and near allies:

Him that is first in virtue make thy friend;

And with observance his kind speech attend:

Nor, to thy power, for light faults cast him by;

Thy power is neighbour to necessity.

These know, and with intentive care pursue;

10But Anger, Sloth, and Luxury subdue.

In sight of others, or thyself, forbear

What 's ill; but of thyself stand most in fear.

Let Justice all thy words and actions sway,

Nor from the even course of reason stray;

For know that all men are to die ordain'd,

And riches are as quickly lost as gain'd.

Crosses that happen by divine decree,

If such thy lot, bear not impatiently.

Yet seek to remedy with all thy care,

20And think the just have not the greatest share.

'Mongst men discourses good and bad are spread,

Despise not those, nor be by these misled.

If any some notorious falsehood say,

Thou the report with equal judgement weigh.

Let not men's smoother promises invite,

Nor rougher threats from just resolves thee fright.

If ought thou wouldst attempt, first ponder it,

Fools only inconsiderate acts commit.

Nor do what afterward thou mayst repent,

30First learn to know the thing on which th'art bent.

Thus thou a life shalt lead with joy replete.

Nor must thou care of outward health forget;

Such temperance use in exercise and diet,

As may preserve thee in a settled quiet.

Meats unprohibited, not curious, choose,

Decline what any other may accuse:

The rash expense of vanity detest,

And sordidness: a mean in all is best.

Hurt not thyself; act nought thou dost not weigh;

40And every business of the following day

As soon as by the morn awak'd, dispose;

Nor suffer sleep at night thy eyes to close,

Till thrice that diary thou hast o'errun;

How slipt? what deeds, what duty left undone?

Thus thy account summ'd up from first to last,

Grieve for the ill, joy for what good hath past.

These, if thou study, practise, and affect,

To sacred Virtue will thy steps direct.

Nature's eternal fountain I attest,

50Who did the soul with fourfold power invest.

Ere thou begin, pray well thy work may end,

Then shall thy knowledge to all things extend,

Divine and human; where enlarg'd, restrain'd;

How Nature is by general likeness chain'd.

Vain Hope nor Ignorance shall dim thy sight:

Then shalt thou see that hapless men invite

Their ills; to good, though present, deaf and blind;

And few the cure of their misfortunes find:

This only is the fate that harms, and rolls,

60Through miseries successive, human souls.

Within is a continual hidden fight,

Which we to shun must study, not excite:

Good God! how little trouble should we know,

If thou to all men wouldst their genius show!

But fear not thou; men come of heav'nly race,

Taught by diviner Nature what t' embrace;

Which, if pursued, thou all I nam'd shalt gain,

And keep thy soul clear from thy body's stain:

In time of prayer and cleansing meats denied

70Abstain from; thy mind's reins let reason guide:

Then rais'd to Heaven, thou from thy body free,

A deathless saint, no more shalt mortal be.

Pythagoras, his Moral Rules.] Stanley's three vocations of poet, translator, and philosopher come well together in this closing piece, and the prose commentary completes the exposition in little.

The common received opinion that *Pythagoras* is not the author of these verses, seems to be defended by *Chrysippus* in *Agellius*, *Plutarch*, *Laertius*, and *Iamblichus*, who affirm that the rules and sense only were his, digested into verse by some of his scholars. But it is not improbable that they did no more than collect the verses, and so gave occasion to the mistake; for *Laertius* confesseth that *Pythagoras* used to deliver his precepts to his disciples in verse, one of which was

Πῆ παρέβην; τί δ' ἔρεξα; τί μοι δέον οὐκ ἐτελέσθη;

How slipt? what deeds, what duty left undone?

Of this opinion I believe *Clemens Alexandrinus*, who cites one of these lines under his name, and *Proclus*, when he calls him τῶν χρυσῶν ἐπῶν πατέρα, *the father of the golden verses.*

[*thy duty pay*]

Νόμῳ ὡς διάκειται; though *Hierocles* in another sense read διάκεινται.

[thy vow]

Ὅρκος. *Hierocles*, τήρησις τῶν θείων νόμων, *observance of religious rules.*

[honour the saints]

Ἥρωας. *Laertius* on these words explains *souls whereof the air is full. Hierocles, angels, the sons of God, &c.*

[Thy prince and rulers]

Καταχθονίους δαίμονας, *Hierocles*, Τοὺς ἐπὶ γῆς πολιτεύεσθαι δυναμένους; *capable of government.*

[nor their laws despise]

Ἔννομα ῥέζειν. *Hierocles* Πείθεσθαι οἷς ἀπολελοίπασιν ἡμῖν παραγγέλμασι; *to obey their commands.*

[with observance]

Ἔργα ἐπωφέλιμα, *that is,* εὐεργεσία, θεραπεία: *yet, Hierocles otherwise.*

[Thy power is neighbour to necessity]

Whatsoever necessity can force thee to bear, it is in thy power to bear voluntarily. If thy friend have wronged thee, how canst thou say, thou art not able to endure his company, when imprisonment might constrain thee to it? See *Hierocles.*

['Mongst men discourses good and bad are spread;

Despise not these,[1] nor be by those misled.]

So *Hierocles; Marcilius* reads ὧν (that is, οὖν) for ὧν which best agrees with this sense.

[what any other may accuse]

φθόνον. *Hierocles* interprets μέμψιν, *invidia,* so taken sometimes by *Cicero, Marcell.*

[And every business of the following day

As soon as by the morn awak'd, dispose]

These two lines I have inserted upon the authority of *Porphyrius,*

Πρὸ μὲν οὖν τοῦ ὕπνου ταῦτα ἑαυτῷ τὰ ἔπη ἐπᾴδειν ἕκαστον.

Μηδ' ὕπνον μαλακοῖσιν, &c.

Πρὸ δὲ τῆς ἐξαναστάσεως ἐκεῖνα·

Πρῶτα μὲν ἐξ ὕπνοιο μελίφρονος ἐξυπανιστὰς

Εὖ μάλα ποιπνεύειν ὅσ' ἐν ἤματι ἔργα τελέσσει.

He advised every one before he slept to repeat these verses to himself,

Nor suffer sleep at night, &c.

And before he rose these,

And every business, &c.

How much this confirms *Pythagoras* the author, and his scholars but disposers of the verses (who, as it appears, forgot these two), is evident enough. The main argument they insist upon, who labour to prove the contrary, is derived from these words,

[*Nature's eternal fountain I attest,*

Who did the soul with fourfold power invest]

Where *Marcilius* expounds παραδόντα   τετρακήν[2] *illum*   *a*   *quo scientiam* τετρακτύος, *acceperant, is autem doctor eorum Pythagoras,* as if it were

Him who the Tetrad to our souls exprest,

(*Nature's eternal fountain*) *I attest;*

And then takes pains to show that his scholars used to swear by him. But παραδιδόναι ψυχῇ μαθητῶν for διδάσκειν is not without a little violence to ἀμετέρα   ψυχᾷ (which   makes *Iamblic[h]us* read ἀμετέρας σοφίας) *Marcilius* in this being the less excusable for confessing immediately, *Animae vero nostrae dixerunt Pythagorei quoniam quaternarius animae numerus est,* an explanation inconsistent with the other, but (as I conceive) truer; *Macrobius* expressly agreeth with it; *Iuro tibi per eum qui dat animae nostrae quaternarium numerum;* or, as others,

Per qui nostrae animae numerum dedit ipse quaternum.

By him who gave us life—God. In which sense, παγὰν ἀεννάου φύσεως, much more easily will follow παραδόντα than τετρακήν. The four powers of the soul are, *mens, scientia, opinio, sensus,* which *Aristotle* calls *the four instruments of judgement, Hierocles,* κριτικὰς δυνάμεις. The *mind* is compared to a unit, in that of many singulars it makes one. *Science* to the number *two* (which amongst the Pythagoreans is *numerus infinitatis*), because it proceeds from things certain and granted to uncertain and infinite. *Opinion* to *three,* a number of indefinite variety. *Sense* to *four,* as furnishing the other three. In this exposition I am the more easily persuaded to dissent from *Plutarch, Hierocles, Iamblichus,* and other interpreters, since they differ no less amongst themselves.

[*Within is a continual hidden fight*]

Betwixt Reason and Appetite.

[*how little trouble*]

As *Marcilius* reads, Ἢ πολλῶν, &c.

[*their genius*]

Οἴῳ δαίμονι, *Hierocles* expounds οἴᾳ ψυχῇ. *Genius* includes both.

[*what t' embrace*]

Hierocles πάντα τὰ δέοντα, *all that they ought to do.*

[*from the³ body's stain*]

Hierocles from the infection of the body.

[*In times³ of prayer*]

Ἔν τε λύσει ψυχῆς, *Meditation.* See *Plato in Phaedone.*

[*and cleansing*]

Which extended (saith *Hierocles*) ἕως σιτίων καὶ ποτῶν καὶ τῆς ὅλης διαίτης τοῦ θνητοῦ ἡμῶν σώματος *to meat and drink,* &c.

[*meats denied*]

What they were is expressed by *Laertius, Suidas, Hierocles, Agellius,* &c. *Hierocles* affirms that in these words ὧν εἴπομεν, he cites his *sacred Apothegms:* τὰ δὲ ἐπὶ μέρους ἐν τοῖς ἱεροῖς ἀποφθέγμασιν, ἐν ἀπορρήτῳ παρεδίδοιτο, *Concerning meat is particularly delivered in his holy Apothegms, that which was not lawful to make known to every one.* Which is a great testimony that *Pythagoras,* and not any of his disciples, writ these verses; for if the author had cited him before in the third person (as they argue from παραδόντα τετρακήν⁴), he would have cited him now in the first.

¹ 'These' and 'those' are originally 'crossed over' in text and note.

² τετρακήν should, as indeed the context proclaims, be τετρακτύν.

³ Slight alteration of text in notes again original.

⁴ See above. The mistake is an odd one because the original oath is in hexameters and τετρακτύν is absolutely necessary as the last word.

FINIS.

POEMS APPEARING ONLY IN THE EDITION OF 1656

On this swelling bank, once proud
Of its burden, Doris lay:
Here she smil'd, and did uncloud
Those bright suns eclipse the day;
Here we sat, and with kind art
She about me twin'd her arms,
Clasp'd in hers my hand and heart,
Fetter'd in those pleasing charms.
Here my love and joys she crown'd,
10Whilst the hours stood still before me,
With a killing glance did wound,
And a melting kiss restore me.
On the down of either breast,
Whilst with joy my soul retir'd,
My reclining head did rest,
Till her lips new life inspir'd.

Thus, renewing of these sights
Doth with grief and pleasure fill me,
And the thought of these delights
20Both at once revive and kill me!
Dear, fold me once more in thine arms!
And let me know
Before I go
There is no bliss but in those charms.
By thy fair self I swear
That here, and only here,

I would for ever, ever stay:

But cruel Fate calls me away.

How swiftly the light minutes slide!

10The hours that haste

Away thus fast

By envious flight my stay do chide.

Yet, Dear, since I must go,

By this last kiss I vow,

By all that sweetness which dwells with thee,

Time shall move slow, till next I see thee.

The lazy hours move slow,

The minutes stay;

Old Time with leaden feet doth go,

And his light wings hath cast away.

The slow-pac'd spheres above

Have sure releas'd

Their guardians, and without help move,

Whilst that the very angels rest.

The number'd sands that slide

10Through this small glass,

And into minutes Time divide,

Too slow each other do displace;

The tedious wheels of light

No faster chime,

Than that dull shade which waits on night:

For Expectation outruns Time.

How long, Lord, must I stay?

How long dwell here?

O free me from this loathèd clay!

20Let me no more these fetters wear!

With far more joy

Shall I resign my breath,

For, to my griev'd soul, not to die

Is every minute a new death.

The three pieces which appear in *1656* only have no great character, and were very likely written for Gamble *to* tunes—seldom a very satisfactory process.

---

* *
*

POEMS,

ELEGIES,

PARADOXES,

and

SONNETS.

INTRODUCTION TO HENRY KING.

Among the numerous possible extensions of that practice of writing *Dialogues of the Dead* which has been, at various times, rather unusually justified of its practitioners, not the least tempting would be one which should embody the expectations and the disappointment of the pious Bishop who held the see of Chichester in Fuller's Bad and Better Times—long afterwards, between 1843 and 1888. In the former year, as most students of English poetry know, the late Archdeacon Hannah, then a young Fellow of Lincoln College, published a most admirable edition of part of King's *Poems*; and announced that the rest must be left for a separate volume 'which will be published without delay'. He lived forty-five years longer, and 'the rest' was by no means an extensive one; but, whatever may have been the reason,[1] the second volume never appeared, while, to complete the misfortune, King's one famous thing, the beautiful

Tell me no more how fair she is—

is not in the first. Nor has any one since attempted to supply the deficiency,[2] though that benefactor of the lovers of Caroline poetry, Mr. J. R. Tutin, included a fifteen-page selection of King's poems, with Donne and Walton, in one of his 'Orinda Booklets' (Hull, 1904) some little time after the plan of this collection was announced, and when its first volume was passing through the press.

There must have been many readers who, like the present writer long enough ago, have felt a sensation of mingled amazement and chagrin on buying Dr. Hannah's book and *not* finding 'Tell me no more' in it. For that poem, though in certain 'strange and high' qualities it is the inferior of the best jets of the Caroline genius, is one of the most faultless and perfect things in this or indeed in any period of English poetry, and may be said to impart the Caroline essence in a form that can be (in the medical sense) 'borne' by all who have any feeling for poetry at all, as hardly anything else does. It enlists, with unerring art, the peculiar virtue of the metre—that of expressing settled but not violent hopelessness—which Cowper afterwards utilized, more terribly but hardly more skilfully, in 'The Castaway'. It has the 'metaphysical' fancifulness of thought and diction, tempered to a reasonable but not an excessive degree 'below proof' and so fit for general consumption. No one who possesses literary 'curiosity'—in the good old sense, not the degenerate modern one—can be indifferent to seeing what else the author of this could do.

It may be frankly and at once admitted that he has nothing exactly to match it. The once even more famous—and still perhaps not much less famous—*Sic Vita*, is not certainly his; and, though a fine thing, is very distinctly open to the metaphysical reproach of *playing with* its subject too much—of that almost wilfully mechanical and factory-like conceit-mongering which reaches its extreme in Cleveland. If it is King's, 'The Dirge' is a sort of extended handling of it—less epigrammatic but more poetical, and brought down again to that *via media* of metaphysicality which is King's special path. He is, in fact, a sort of Longfellow of this particular style and school of poetry—from the other side; a sort of Donne *in usum vulgi*. 'The Exequy' and 'The Elegy', 'Silence' and 'Brave Flowers', are all in this middle way; and perhaps his treading of it may be a reason why he has been comparatively neglected—the great vulgar not being grateful for poetry which never can fully please it, and the small wanting something more concentrated and '*above* proof'. But even if he had not lacked complete presentment so long, such a collection as this would be manifestly incomplete without him. It has not, however, been thought necessary to include his verse translations of the Psalms, which form a separate volume, not much more successful than most of the attempts at that impossible task. With the admirable English of the Authorized or the Prayer-Book Versions at choice, and the admirable Latin of the Vulgate to fall back upon, nobody can want stuff like

Earth is the Lord's with her increase,

And all that there have place:

He founded it upon the Seas,

And made the floods her base.[3]

Henry King's private and public history (for he had more to do with public affairs than can have been at all comfortable to himself) had no very obvious connexion with poetry, except in so far as circumstances fed what was clearly a special taste of his for elegiac writing. He was born in 1592 at Worminghall in Bucks., for some time the abode of a family which, whether its tracing to 'the ancient Kings [by function, not name merely] of Devonshire' was fiction or fact, was, and had been for generations, highly respectable. The Kings had recently addicted themselves very specially to education at Westminster and Christ Church (there are said to have been five of the same family on the books of the House at one time) and to the clerical profession. The poet-bishop was the eldest son of John King, Prebendary of St. Paul's and Chaplain to the Queen, himself a verse-writer, and after having been Dean of Christ Church, Bishop of London from 1611 to 1621. The son—if not without some nepotism yet with results which fully justified it—became himself Prebendary of St. Paul's (as did a brother, who was still younger, in the same year) when he was only four-and-twenty; and successively received the archdeaconry of Colchester (1617); a canonry at Christ Church (1624); and the deanery of Rochester (1639). He had then the good and evil luck to be one of the large batch of Bishops made or translated by Charles on the very eve of the Rebellion. He never sat in the House of Lords before its suppression; and he had taken possession of his see but a short time when he was rabbled out of his palace at Chichester and plundered of his property, contrary to the terms of surrender of the City, by Waller's soldiers. He was also ousted from the rich living of Petworth, usually held *in commendam* with the (poor) bishopric of Chichester, by that particularly pestilent Puritan, Francis Cheynell. He seems to have passed great part of the Interregnum with the Salters of Richkings, near Langley in Bucks. (a house well famed for hospitality at different times and under different owners and names[4]), and at the Restoration he recovered his preferments, Edmund Calamy *tertius* having the extraordinary impudence to state that Cheynell was 'put out to make room for King'. And he held them for nearly a decade longer, dying in 1669. He left children and also grandchildren, one of whom, Elizabeth, seems to have married Isaac Houblon, Pepys's 'handsome man'.

Despite King's persecutions by the Puritans he was accused of a leaning to Puritanism, as his father had been before him,[5] but seemingly without much foundation. He appears to have been a sound Churchman, and a very good man in every way, though with a slight tendency (not to be too harshly judged by those who have lived in quieter times) to 'grizzle', as it is familiarly called, over his tribulations. He was also what was termed at the time 'a painful preacher' and a popular one. Pepys, it is true, did not like him when he first heard him, and afterwards thought a sermon of his 'mean'. But between these two he describes a third as 'good and eloquent'; and Samuel's judgements on such matters, always unliterary, were also much conditioned by circumstances, and by the curious remnant of Puritan leaven which always remained in that very far from pure lump.

King's poems must, from various signs, have been much handed about in manuscript; but how they came to be collected and published in 1657 is quite unknown. They were at first attributed by some to his brother Philip; and a reprint, or perhaps merely the remainder with a fresh title-page, in 1700 actually attributed them to Ben Jonson, which was going far even in a period which had seen Kirkman and was to see Curll.[6] One or two pieces besides *Sic Vita* are doubtful, and one or two more certainly not his; but on the whole the collection seems to be fairly trustworthy, from Dr. Hannah's comparison of it with MS. copies. And it rarely offers *cruces* of interpretation.

As to the origin and general character of the pieces there is nothing surprising about it either. King belonged to a time when, fortunately, churchmanship, scholarship, and literature were almost inseparably connected; and by accident or preference he seems, all his life, to have been thrown or drawn into the society of men of letters. He was a friend if not a 'son' of Ben Jonson; he was an intimate of Donne's, and one of the recipients of the famous blood-stone seals; he was for more than forty years (as he has himself recorded in a letter to Walton) a friend of 'honest Isaac' [*sic*]. And if his middle days were politically unhappy, they, and still more his earlier, were poetically fortunate. How, and in what degree, he caught the wind as it blew has been partly indicated above: the text should show the rest.[7]

[1] I have suggested below that some slight scruples of pudibundity may have had their influence; but if they had been serious the Archdeacon would hardly have promised this rest.

[2] Until quite recently, and after this present edition had been long printed, one appeared in America (Yale University Press, 1914) by Lawrence Mason, Ph.D.

[3] I think this will justify the critic (whoever he was) whose sentence—'quaint mediocrity and inappropriate metre'—offended Hannah's editorial chivalry as 'very unjust'. Indeed, I should make it stronger and say 'irritating inadequacy alike in metre and phrase'.

[4] Especially that of Percy Lodge in the eighteenth century, when it was the Dowager Duchess of Somerset's: see Shenstone, Lady Luxborough, and Southey's *Doctor*, chaps. 107 and 108. Between the times it had belonged to Bathurst, and was then also a home of men of letters.

[5] With the complementary and not unusual libel that he died a Romanist.

[6] Between the two dates there had been a fresh *issue* in 1664, with four new elegies. But it has been doubted whether even this was a new *edition*.

[7] The text of the following poems will be found, as far as Hannah's edition goes, to differ not greatly from his; but it has been collated with the originals in print and MS. by myself and, more carefully still, by Mr. Percy Simpson. The remaining poems (including the fourth or 'King Charles' Elegy added in 1664, which Hannah did not give) are adapted in the same way from direct photographic copies of the originals—collated where necessary. The variants of *Sic Vita* which the Archdeacon collected are of such interest and so characteristic of seventeenth-century poetry that it seemed desirable to reproduce them.

It may perhaps be added that the 1657 text is very carefully and well printed, requiring so little modernization as practically to justify the standard adopted in this collection. To modernize Chaucer or Chatterton has always seemed to me, though from slightly different points of view, a grievous error or worse. But to show how close, when scholarly writing met careful printing, the result even before the Restoration was to what it would have been to-day, I have printed the opening poem exactly as it originally stood, and have drawn attention in a note to the fewness of the differences. Because other typographers, not deacons in their craft, and confronted perhaps with copy as bad as, say, mine, *plus* the eccentric *ethelorthography* of the period, lavished italics and capitals and superfluous *e*'s, and strappadoed the spelling, I cannot see why the eyes of a present-day reader should be unnecessarily vexed.—Hannah's edition, as far as it goes, can hardly be too well spoken of by any one who does not think that, in order to magnify himself, it is necessary to belittle his predecessors. One cannot but regret that he did not (as he might most easily have done, even in the single volume) complete his work. As it is, I am deeply indebted to him. I have, however, restored the order of the original, which he altered partly to get chronological sequence in the Elegies, &c., and partly to make subject-heads for his groups—a proceeding which to me is rarely satisfactory. But I have borrowed his useful datings of the individual pieces under their titles.

The Publishers to the Author.

SIR,

It is the common fashion to make some address to the Readers, but we are bold to direct ours to you, who will look on this publication with anger, which others must welcome into the world with joy.

The Lord Verulam comparing ingenious authors to those who had orchards ill neighboured, advised them to publish their own labours, lest others might steal the fruit: Had you followed his example, or liked the advice, we had not thus trespassed against your consent, or been forced to an apology, which cannot but imply a fault committed. The best we can say for ourselves is, that if we have injured you, it is merely in your own defence, preventing the present attempts of others, who to their theft would (by their false copies of these Poems) have added violence, and some way have wounded your reputation.

Having been long engaged on better contemplations, you may, perhaps, look down on these *Juvenilia* (most of them the issues of your youthful Muse) with some disdain; and yet the courteous reader may tell you with thanks, that they are not to be despised, being far from abortive, nor to be disowned, because they are both modest and legitimate. And thus if we have offered you a view of your younger face, our hope is you will behold it with an unwrinkled brow, though we have presented the mirror against your will.

We confess our design hath been set forward by friends that honour you, who, lest the ill publishing might disfigure these things from whence you never expected addition to your credit (sundry times endeavoured and by them defeated) furnished us with some papers which they thought authentic; we may not turn their favour into an accusation, and therefore give no intimation of their names, but wholly take the blame of this hasty and immethodical impression upon ourselves, being persons at a distance, who are fitter to bear it than those who are nearer related. In hope of your pardon we remain,

Your most devoted servants,

RICH. MARRIOT.

HEN. HERRINGMAN.

POEMS

Printed in 1657.

Sonnet. The Double Rock.

Since thou hast view'd some Gorgon, and art grown

A solid stone:

To bring again to softness thy hard heart

Is past my art.

Ice may relent to water in a thaw;

But stone made flesh Loves Chymistry ne're saw.

Therefore by thinking on thy hardness, I

Will petrify;

And so within our double Quarryes Wombe,

10Dig our Loves Tombe.

Thus strangely will our difference agree;

And, with our selves, amaze the world, to see

How both Revenge and Sympathy consent

To make two Rocks each others Monument.

The Double Rock.] In this very typical metaphysicality of a good *second* water (see note on Introduction), it will be observed that there is nothing archaic or irregular in the spelling except the usual 'ne'*re*' for 'ne'*er*', the insertion of the three superfluous *e*'s in lines 9, 10, and at most two or three gratuitous capitals with, if anybody pleases, the omission of the apostrophe for the possessive in ll. 6, 9, 10, and 14. 'Chymistry' I should have kept, of course, even if I had altered these others.

The Vow-Breaker.

When first the magic of thine eye,

Usurp'd upon my liberty,

Triumphing in my heart's spoil, thou

Didst lock up thine in such a vow;

When I prove false, may the bright day

Be governed by the Moon's pale ray!

(As I too well remember.) This

Thou said'st, and seal'dst it with a kiss.

O Heavens! and could so soon that tie

10Relent in slack apostacy?

Could all thy oaths, and mortgag'd trust,

Vanish? like letters form'd in dust

Which the next wind scatters. Take heed,

Take heed, Revolter; know this deed

Hath wrong'd the world, which will fare worse

By thy example than thy curse.

Hide that false brow in mists. Thy shame

Ne'er see light more, but the dim flame

Of funeral lamps. Thus sit and moan,

20And learn to keep thy guilt at home.

Give it no vent; for if again

Thy Love or Vows betray more men,

At length (I fear) thy perjur'd breath

Will blow out day, and waken Death.

The Vow-Breaker. 9 Orig. 'Ty', no doubt on the Spenserian principle of eye-rhyme. This and some others of the shorter poems which follow have been found by Mr. Thorn-Drury in miscellanies of the period, not merely well-known ones like *Wits' Recreations* (1641), but more obscure collections such as *Parnassus Biceps*, 1651, and *Wits' Interpreter*, 1655. The usual variants occur; but they are seldom, if ever, *me judice* of interest. One or two I have borrowed with acknowledgement.

Upon a Table-Book presented to a Lady.

When your fair hand receives this little book

You must not there for prose or verses look.

Those empty regions which within you see,

May by yourself planted and peopled be:

And though we scarce allow your sex to prove

Writers (unless the argument be Love);

Yet without crime or envy you have room

Here, both the scribe and author to become.

Upon a Table-Book, &c.] The title in one of Hannah's MS. copies has 'Noble Lady'. The person addressed does not seem to have been identified.

To the same Lady upon Mr. Burton's Melancholy.

If in this Glass of Humours you do find

The passions or diseases of your mind,

Here without pain, you safely may endure,

Though not to suffer, yet to read your cure.

But if you nothing meet you can apply,

Then, ere you need, you have a remedy.

And I do wish you never may have cause

To be adjudg'd by these fantastic laws;

But that this book's example may be known,

10By others' Melancholy, not your own.

To the Same Lady.] 6 MS. '*before* you need'—perhaps better. The lady to whom the *Anatomy* was likely to be congenial must have been worth knowing.

The Farewell.

Splendidis longùm valedico nugis.

Farewell, fond Love, under whose childish whip,

I have serv'd out a weary prenti'ship;

Thou that hast made me thy scorn'd property,

To doat on rocks, but yielding loves to fly:

Go, bane of my dear quiet and content,
Now practise on some other patient.

Farewell, false Hope, that fann'd my warm desire
Till it had rais'd a wild unruly fire,
Which nor sighs cool, nor tears extinguish can,
10Although my eyes out-flow'd the Ocean:
Forth of my thoughts for ever, Thing of Air,
Begun in error, finish'd in despair.
Farewell, vain World, upon whose restless stage
'Twixt Love and Hope I have fool'd out my age;
Henceforth, ere sue to thee for my redress,
I'll woo the wind, or court the wilderness;
And buried from the day's discovery,
Study a slow yet certain way to die.
My woful monument shall be a cell,
20The murmur of the purling brook my knell;
My lasting epitaph the rock shall groan:
Thus when sad lovers ask the weeping stone,
What wretched thing does in that centre lie?
The hollow Echo will reply, 'twas I.
The Farewell.] The following are the variants of Malone MS. 22:
4-6
To doat on those that lov'd not and to fly
Love that woo'd me. Go, bane of my content,
And practise ...
21
And for an epitaph the rock shall groan
Eternally: if any ask the stone.

23 centre] compass.

A Blackmoor Maid wooing a fair Boy: sent to the Author by Mr. Hen. Rainolds.

Stay, lovely boy, why fly'st thou me

That languish in these flames for thee?

I'm black, 'tis true: why so is Night,

And Love doth in dark shades delight.

The whole world, do but close thine eye,

Will seem to thee as black as I;

Or ope 't, and see what a black shade

Is by thine own fair body made,

That follows thee where'er thou go;

10(O who, allow'd, would not do so?)

Let me for ever dwell so nigh,

And thou shall need no other shade than I.

Mr. Hen. Rainolds.

The Boy's Answer to the Blackmoor.

Black maid, complain not that I fly,

When Fate commands antipathy:

Prodigious might that union prove,

Where Night and Day together move,

And the conjunction of our lips

Not kisses make, but an eclipse;

In which the mixed black and white

Portends more terror than delight.

Yet if my shadow thou wilt be,

10Enjoy thy dearest wish: but see

Thou take my shadow's property,

That hastes away when I come nigh:

Else stay till death hath blinded me,

And then I will bequeath myself to thee.

A Blackmoor Maid, and *Answer.*] I do not know whether the exact connexion between these two poems and Cleveland's 'Fair Nymph scorning a Black Boy' (*v. sup.*, p. 42) has ever been discussed. But if 'Mr. Hen. Rainolds' is Drayton's friend, the verses printed above must have the priority, for nothing seems to be known of him after 1632.

In Rawlinson MS. 1092, fol. 271, there are curious versions of these poems (the first is ascribed to William Strode), inverting the parts 'A black boy in love with a fair maid', and 'The fair maid's answer'.

To a Friend upon Overbury's Wife given to her.

I know no fitter subject for your view

Than this, a meditation ripe for you,

As you for it. Which, when you read, you'll see

What kind of wife yourself will one day be:

Which happy day be near you, and may this

Remain with you as earnest of my wish;

When you so far love any, that you dare

Venture your whole affection on his care,

May he for whom you change your virgin-life

10Prove good to you, and perfect as this Wife.

To a Friend upon Overbury's Wife, &c.] King seems to have been fond of giving this popular production as a present, for the first of the three poems is certainly not addressed to the recipient of the others, and it seems probable that 2 and 3 are also independent. Hannah, without giving any reason, save the initials, suggests that 'A. R.' was Lady Anne Rich (*v. inf.*).

Upon the same.

Madam, who understands you well would swear,

That you the Life, and this your Copy were.

To A. R. upon the same.

Not that I would instruct or tutor you

What is a wife's behest, or husband's due,

Give I this Widow-Wife. Your early date

Of knowledge makes such precepts slow and late.

This book is but your glass, where you shall see

What yourself are, what other wives should be.

To A. R.] 3 Widow-] Overbury himself being dead.

An Epitaph on Niobe turned to Stone.

This pile thou seest built out of flesh, not stone,

Contains no shroud within, nor mould'ring bone.

This bloodless trunk is destitute of tomb

Which may the soul-fled mansion enwomb.

This seeming sepulchre (to tell the troth)

Is neither tomb nor body, and yet both.

Upon a Braid of Hair in a Heart sent by Mrs. E. H.

In this small character is sent

My Love's eternal monument.

Whilst we shall live, know this chain'd heart

Is our affection's counterpart.

And if we never meet, think I

Bequeath'd it as my legacy.

Upon a Braid of Hair, &c.] There is something rather out of the common way about this little piece. King married early and his wife died after a few years. How he loved her *The Exequy* and *The Anniverse* will tell in a few pages. But her initials were A. B. (Anne Berkeley) not E. H. On the other hand, his sister *Elizabeth* married Edward *Holt*, groom of the bedchamber to Charles I, who died in attendance on his master (see Elegy on him, *inf.*). The verses might be fraternal, and are certainly sincere.

Sonnet.

Tell me no more how fair she is,

I have no mind to hear

The story of that distant bliss

I never shall come near:

By sad experience I have found

That her perfection is my wound.

And tell me not how fond I am

To tempt a daring Fate,

From whence no triumph ever came,

10But to repent too late:

There is some hope ere long I may

In silence dote myself away.

I ask no pity, Love, from thee,

Nor will thy justice blame,

So that thou wilt not envy me

The glory of my flame:

Which crowns my heart whene'er it dies,

In that it falls her sacrifice.

Tell me no more, &c.] The heading of this famous thing as 'Sonnet' has, of course, nothing surprising in it: in fact, the successive attachment of the title to five poems in a batch here and to four more a little lower down—no one of which is a quatorzain, and hardly two of which agree in form—is a capital example of the looseness with which that title was used. MS. copies appear to have 'Sonnet' with *no* particular addition in some cases.

On 'Tell me no more' itself see Introduction. The last two lines are, as they should be, the finest part—with the fullness of contrasted vowel-sound in 'crowns', 'heart', 'e'er', and 'dies', and the emphasis of 'her'.

Sonnet.

Were thy heart soft as thou art fair,

Thou wer't a wonder past compare:

But frozen Love and fierce disdain

By their extremes thy graces stain.

Cold coyness quenches the still fires

Which glow in lovers' warm desires;

And scorn, like the quick lightning's blaze,

Darts death against affections gaze.

O Heavens, what prodigy is this

10When Love in Beauty buried is!

Or that dead pity thus should be

Tomb'd in a living cruelty.

Were thy heart, &c.] This is not much inferior except as concerns the metre.

Sonnet.

Go, thou that vainly dost mine eyes invite

To taste the softer comforts of the night,

And bid'st me cool the fever of my brain

In those sweet balmy dews which slumber pain;

Enjoy thine own peace in untroubled sleep,

Whilst my sad thoughts eternal vigils keep.

O couldst thou for a time change breasts with me,

Thou in that broken glass shouldst plainly see

A heart which wastes in the slow smoth'ring fire

10Blown by Despair, and fed by false Desire,

Can only reap such sleeps as sea-men have,

When fierce winds rock them on the foaming wave.

Go, thou that, &c.] What made the excellent Archdeacon-to-be select this in preference to 'Tell me no more' as a specimen of King's presumed 'juvenile productions' it is difficult to discover. But

Blown by Despair, and fed by false Desire

is certainly a fine line.

Sonnet. To Patience.

Down, stormy passions, down; no more

Let your rude waves invade the shore

Where blushing reason sits, and hides

Her from the fury of your tides.

Fit only 'tis, where you bear sway,

That fools or frantics do obey;

Since judgement, if it not resists,

Will lose itself in your blind mists.

Fall easy, Patience, fall like rest

10Whose soft spells charm a troubled breast:

And where those rebels you espy,

O in your silken cordage tie

Their malice up! so shall I raise

Altars to thank your power, and praise

The sovereign vertue of your balm,

Which cures a tempest by a calm.

To Patience.] So also he gave this very commonplace 'production' and the next, which is a little better.

Silence. A Sonnet.

Peace, my heart's blab, be ever dumb,

Sorrows speak loud without a tongue:

And, my perplexed thoughts, forbear

To breathe yourselves in any ear:

'Tis scarce a true or manly grief,

Which gads abroad to find relief.

Was ever stomach that lack'd meat

Nourish'd by what another eat?

Can I bestow it, or will woe

10Forsake me, when I bid it go?

Then I'll believe a wounded breast

May heal by shrift, and purchase rest.

But if, imparting it, I do

Not ease myself, but trouble two,

'Tis better I alone possess

My treasure of unhappiness:

Engrossing that which is my own

No longer than it is unknown.

If silence be a kind of death,

20He kindles grief who gives it breath;

But let it rak'd in embers lie,

On thine own hearth 'twill quickly die:

And spite of fate, that very womb

Which carries it, shall prove its tomb.

Love's Harvest.

Fond Lunatic forbear, why dost thou sue

For thy affection's pay ere it is due?

Love's fruits are legal use; and therefore may

Be only taken on the marriage day.

Who for this interest too early call,

By that exaction lose the principal.

Then gather not those immature delights,

Until their riper autumn thee invites.

He that abortive corn cuts off his ground,

10No husband but a ravisher is found:

So those that reap their love before they wed,

Do in effect but cuckold their own bed.

Love's Harvest.   11, 12, Malone MS. 22 has the singular: 'So he', &c.

The Forlorn Hope.

How long, vain Hope, dost thou my joys suspend?

Say! must my expectation know no end?

Thou wast more kind unto the wand'ring Greek

Who did ten years his wife and country seek:

Ten lazy winters in my glass are run,

Yet my thought's travail seems but new begun.

Smooth quicksand which the easy world beguiles,

Thou shall not bury me in thy false smiles.

They that in hunting shadows pleasure take,

10May benefit of thy illusion make.

Since thou hast banish'd me from my content

I here pronounce thy final banishment.

Farewell, thou dream of nothing! thou mere voice!

Get thee to fools that can feed fat with noise:

Bid wretches mark'd for death look for reprieve,

Or men broke on the wheel persuade to live.

Henceforth my comfort and best hope shall be,

By scorning Hope, ne'er to rely on thee.

The Forlorn Hope.]   10 *MS.* 'illusions'—perhaps better.

14 can] *MS.* 'will'.

The Retreat.

Pursue no more (my thoughts!) that false unkind,

You may as soon imprison the North-wind;

Or catch the lightning as it leaps; or reach

The leading billow first ran down the breach;

Or undertake the flying clouds to track

In the same path they yesterday did rack.

Then, like a torch turn'd downward, let the same

Desire which nourish'd it, put out your flame.

Lo! thus I do divorce thee from my breast,

10False to thy vow, and traitor to my rest!

Henceforth thy tears shall be (though thou repent)

Like pardons after execution sent.

Nor shalt thou ever my love's story read,

But as some epitaph of what is dead.

So may my hope on future blessings dwell,

As 'tis my firm resolve and last farewell.

The Retreat.]   4 'first' of course = 'that first'. One naturally asks 'beach'? but perhaps unreasonably.

6 'rack' as a verb in this sense is interesting, and certainly not common.

Sonnet.

Tell me, you stars that our affections move,

Why made ye me that cruel one to love?

Why burns my heart her scorned sacrifice,

Whose breast is hard as crystal, cold as ice?

God of Desire! if all thy votaries

Thou thus repay, succession will grow wise;

No sighs for incense at thy shrine shall smoke,

Thy rites will be despis'd, thy altars broke.

O! or give her my flame to melt that snow

10Which yet unthaw'd does on her bosom grow;

Or make me ice, and with her crystal chains

Bind up all love within my frozen veins.

Tell me, &c.] 6 succession] = 'those who come after us'.

Sonnet.

I prithee turn that face away

Whose splendour but benights my day.

Sad eyes like mine, and wounded hearts

Shun the bright rays which beauty darts.

Unwelcome is the Sun that pries

Into those shades where sorrow lies.

Go, shine on happy things. To me

That blessing is a misery:

Whom thy fierce Sun not warms, but burns,

10Like that the sooty Indian turns.

I'll serve the night, and there confin'd

Wish thee less fair, or else more kind.

I prithee, &c.] Part of this is very neat and good, but it tails off.

Sonnet.

Dry those fair, those crystal eyes,

Which like growing fountains rise

To drown their banks. Grief's sullen brooks

Would better flow in furrow'd looks.

Thy lovely face was never meant

To be the shore of discontent.

Then clear those wat'rish stars again

Which else portend a lasting rain;

Lest the clouds which settle there

10Prolong my winter all the year:

And the example others make

In love with sorrow for thy sake.

Dry those fair, &c.] This piece is also claimed for Lord Pembroke (see *Preface* to this volume). It might be his, King's, or the work of almost any lyrical poet in this collection and of many outside of it.

Sonnet.

When I entreat, either thou wilt not hear,

Or else my suit arriving at thy ear

Cools and dies there. A strange extremity!

To freeze i' th' Sun, and in the shade to fry.

Whilst all my blasted hopes decline so soon,

'Tis evening with me, though at high noon.

For pity to thyself, if not to me,

Think time will ravish, what I lose, from thee.

If my scorch'd heart wither through thy delay,

10Thy beauty withers too. And swift decay

Arrests thy youth. So thou whilst I am slighted

Wilt be too soon with age or sorrow nighted.

To a Lady who sent me a copy of verses at my going to bed.

Lady, your art or wit could ne'er devise

To shame me more than in this night's surprise.

Why, I am quite unready, and my eye

Now winking like my candle, doth deny

To guide my hand, if it had aught to write;

Nor can I make my drowsy sense indite

Which by your verses' music (as a spell

Sent from the Sybellean Oracle)

Is charm'd and bound in wonder and delight,

10Faster than all the leaden chains of night.

What pity is it then you should so ill

Employ the bounty of your flowing quill,

As to expend on him your bedward thought,

Who can acknowledge that large love in nought

But this lean wish; that fate soon send you those

Who may requite your rhymes with midnight prose?

Meantime, may all delights and pleasing themes

Like masquers revel in your maiden dreams,

Whilst dull to write, and to do more unmeet,

20I, as the night invites me, fall asleep.

To a Lady.] Malone MS. 22, at fol. 34, has a first draft of this poem, in which ll. 1-10 appear thus:

Doubtless the Thespian Spring doth overflow

His learned bank: else how should ladies grow

Such poets as to court th' unknowing time

In verse, and entertain their friends in rhyme?

Or you some Sybil are, sent to untie

The knotty riddles of all poetry,

Whilst your smooth numbers such perfections tell

As prove yourself a modern oracle.

ll. 11-20 follow as in the text.

8 'Sybellean', though an incorrect, is a rather pretty form and good to keep. It will be remembered that as a girl's name 'Sybella' or 'Sibella' is not unknown, beside 'Sybilla' and 'Sybil'.

20 This outrageous assonance may have been meant in character—the poet being too much 'in the arms of Porpus' to notice it.

There follows in the original a piece called *The Pink*, but in the Errata acknowledgement is made that King did not write it. It is therefore omitted here.

To his Friends of Christ Church upon the mislike of the Marriage of the Arts acted at Woodstock.

But is it true, the Court mislik'd the play,

That Christ Church and the Arts have lost the day;

That *Ignoramus* should so far excel,

Their hobby-horse from ours hath born the bell?

Troth! you are justly serv'd, that would present

Ought unto them, but shallow merriment;

Or to your marriage-table did admit

Guests that are stronger far in smell than wit.

Had some quaint bawdry larded ev'ry scene,

10 Some fawning sycophant, or courted quean;

Had there appear'd some sharp cross-garter'd man

Whom their loud laugh might nickname Puritan,

Cas'd up in factious breeches and small ruff,

That hates the surplice, and defies the cuff:

Then sure they would have given applause to crown

That which their ignorance did now cry down.

Let me advise, when next you do bestow

Your pains on men that do but little know,

You do no Chorus nor a comment lack,

20Which may expound and construe ev'ry Act:

That it be short and slight; for if 't be good

Tis long, and neither lik'd nor understood.

Know 'tis Court fashion still to discommend

All that which they want brain to comprehend.

To his Friends of Christ Church.] The occasion of this piece was one of those 'sorrowful chances' which befall those who endeavour to please kings, whatever their name. 'The play' was Barton Holyday's *Technogamia*, and the 'misliking' (James actually 'offered' to go away twice, though, being a good-natured person, he was persuaded to sit it out) is chronicled by Antony Wood under the author's name. It had been acted with great applause in the House itself, and two of King's younger brothers were among the performers. Also the 'frost' was made more unkind by the success at Cambridge of Ruggles's *Ignoramus*. So King's spleen, if unwise, was not quite unmotived. The date was August, 1621.

14 There is no probable reference to Malvolio, despite the association of 'cross-garter'd' and 'Puritan'; but the tone of the passage enables one to some extent to understand why the Puritan party conceived themselves to be deserted by King.

The Surrender.

My once dear Love! hapless that I no more

Must call thee so; the rich affection's store

That fed our hopes, lies now exhaust and spent,

Like sums of treasure unto bankrupts lent.

We, that did nothing study but the way

To love each other, with which thoughts the day

Rose with delight to us, and with them, set,

Must learn the hateful art, how to forget.

We, that did nothing wish that Heav'n could give,

10Beyond ourselves, nor did desire to live

Beyond that wish, all these now cancel must,

As if not writ in faith, but words and dust.

Yet witness those clear vows which lovers make,

Witness the chaste desires that never brake

Into unruly heats; witness that breast

Which in thy bosom anchor'd his whole rest,

'Tis no default in us; I dare acquite

Thy maiden faith, thy purpose fair and white,

As thy pure self. Cross planets did envy

20Us to each other, and Heaven did untie

Faster than vows could bind. O that the stars,

When lovers meet, should stand oppos'd in wars!

Since then some higher Destinies command,

Let us not strive nor labour to withstand

What is past help. The longest date of grief

Can never yield a hope of our relief;

And though we waste ourselves in moist laments,

Tears may drown us, but not our discontents.

Fold back our arms, take home our fruitless loves,

30That must new fortunes try, like turtle-doves

Dislodged from their haunts. We must in tears

Unwind a love knit up in many years.

In this last kiss I here surrender thee

Back to thyself, so thou again art free.

Thou in another, sad as that, resend

The truest heart that lover ere did lend.

Now turn from each. So fare our sever'd hearts,

As the divorc'd soul from her body parts.

The Surrender.] Title 'An Elegy' in Malone MS. 22.

13 Yet] *MS.* 'But'.

17 'acquite' may be for rhyme only; but if 'requite', why not?

34 so] *MS.* 'lo'.

This piece and the next must be interpreted as each reader chooses. They are not without touches of sincerity, but might as well be exercises in the school of King's great friend and master, Donne.

The Legacy.

My dearest Love! when thou and I must part,

And th' icy hand of death shall seize that heart

Which is all thine; within some spacious will

I'll leave no blanks for legacies to fill:

'Tis my ambition to die one of those,

Who, but himself, hath nothing to dispose.

And since that is already thine, what need

I to re-give it by some newer deed?

Yet take it once again. Free circumstance

10Does oft the value of mean things advance:

Who thus repeats what he bequeath'd before,

Proclaims his bounty richer than his store.

But let me not upon my love bestow

What is not worth the giving. I do owe

Somewhat to dust: my body's pamper'd care,

Hungry corruption and the worm will share.

That mould'ring relic which in earth must lie,

Would prove a gift of horror to thine eye.

With this cast rag of my mortality,

20Let all my faults and errors buried be.

And as my cere-cloth rots, so may kind fate

Those worst acts of my life incinerate.

He shall in story fill a glorious room,

Whose ashes and whose sins sleep in one tomb.

If now to my cold hearse thou deign to bring

Some melting sighs as thy last offering,

My peaceful exequies are crown'd. Nor shall

I ask more honour at my funeral.

Thou wilt more richly balm me with thy tears,

30Than all the nard fragrant Arabia bears.

And as the Paphian Queen by her grief's show'r

Brought up her dead Love's spirit in a flow'r:

So by those precious drops rain'd from thine eyes,

Out of my dust, O may some virtue rise!

And like thy better Genius thee attend,

Till thou in my dark period shall end.

Lastly, my constant truth let me commend

To him thou choosest next to be thy friend.

For (witness all things good) I would not have

40Thy youth and beauty married to my grave,

'T would show thou didst repent the style of wife,

Shouldst thou relapse into a single life.

They with preposterous grief the world delude,

Who mourn for their lost mates in solitude;

Since widowhood more strongly doth enforce

The much lamented lot of their divorce.

Themselves then of their losses guilty are,

Who may, yet will not, suffer a repair.

Those were barbarian wives, that did invent

50Weeping to death at th' husband's monument;

But in more civil rites she doth approve

Her first, who ventures on a second love;

For else it may be thought, if she refrain,

She sped so ill, she durst not try again.

Up then, my Love, and choose some worthier one,

Who may supply my room when I am gone;

So will the stock of our affection thrive

No less in death, than were I still alive.

And in my urn I shall rejoice, that I

60Am both testator thus and legacy.

The Legacy.] The remark made above applies especially to *The Legacy*, for there are no known or likely circumstances in King's life corresponding to it; while at the same time it might be the fancy of a young lover-husband. The first six stanzas have something of the 'yew-and-roses' charm of their great originals: the last four justify the ancients in holding that extravagance too often comports frigidity.

The Short Wooing.

Like an oblation set before a shrine,

Fair one! I offer up this heart of mine.

Whether the Saint accept my gift or no,

I'll neither fear nor doubt before I know.

For he whose faint distrust prevents reply,

Doth his own suit's denial prophesy.

Your will the sentence is; who free as Fate

Can bid my love proceed, or else retreat.

And from short views that verdict is decreed
10Which seldom doth one audience exceed.
Love asks no dull probation, but like light
Conveys his nimble influence at first sight.
I need not therefore importune or press;
This were t' extort unwilling happiness:
And much against affection might I sin:
To tire and weary what I seek to win.
Towns which by ling'ring siege enforced be
Oft make both sides repent the victory.
Be Mistress of yourself: and let me thrive
20Or suffer by your own prerogative.
Yet stay, since you are Judge, who in one breath
Bear uncontrolled power of Life and Death,
Remember (Sweet) pity doth best become
Those lips which must pronounce a suitor's doom.

If I find that, my spark of chaste desire
Shall kindle into Hymen's holy fire:
Else like sad flowers will these verses prove,
To stick the coffin of rejected Love.
The Short Wooing.] A fair average metaphysicality.

St. Valentine's Day

Now that each feather'd chorister doth sing
The glad approaches of the welcome Spring:
Now Phœbus darts forth his more early beam
And dips it later in the curled stream,
I should to custom prove a retrograde

Did I still dote upon my sullen shade.

Oft have the seasons finish'd and begun;

Days into months, those into years have run,

Since my cross stars and inauspicious fate

10Doom'd me to linger here without my mate

Whose loss ere since befrosting my desire,

Left me an Altar without gift or fire.

I therefore could have wish'd for your own sake

That Fortune had design'd a nobler stake

For you to draw, than one whose fading day

Like to a dedicated taper lay

Within a tomb, and long burnt out in vain,

Since nothing there saw better by the flame.

Yet since you like your chance, I must not try

20To mar it through my incapacity.

I here make title to it, and proclaim

How much you honour me to wear my name;

Who can no form of gratitude devise,

But offer up myself your sacrifice.

Hail, then, my worthy lot! and may each morn

Successive springs of joy to you be born:

May your content ne'er wane until my heart

Grown bankrupt, wants good wishes to impart.

Henceforth I need not make the dust my shrine,

Nor search the grave for my lost Valentine.

St. Valentine's Day.] I suppose, though I do not remember an instance, that in the good days before the prettiest of English customs succumbed—partly to the growth of Vulgarity and partly to the competition of the much less interesting Christmas Card—some one, or more than one, must have made a collection of *literary* Valentines. In that case this should have figured. It has a good deal of 'Henry King, his mark'—good taste, freedom from mawkishness, melody, and enough poetical essence to save it from the merely mediocre. The coincidence of l. 24 with the more passionate close of 'Tell me no more' should not escape notice.—I have not altered '*ere* since' to '*e'er* since' in text, because the emendation, though almost, is not quite certain.

To his unconstant Friend.

But say, thou very woman, why to me

This fit of weakness and inconstancy?

What forfeit have I made of word or vow,

That I am rack'd on thy displeasure now?

If I have done a fault, I do not shame

To cite it from thy lips, give it a name:

I ask the banes, stand forth, and tell me why

We should not in our wonted loves comply?

Did thy cloy'd appetite urge thee to try

10If any other man could love as I?

I see friends are like clothes, laid up whilst new,

But after wearing cast, though ne'er so true.

Or did thy fierce ambition long to make

Some lover turn a martyr for thy sake?

Thinking thy beauty had deserv'd no name

Unless someone do perish in that flame:

Upon whose loving dust this sentence lies,

Here 's one was murther'd by his mistress' eyes.

Or was't because my love to thee was such,

20I could not choose but blab it? swear how much

I was thy slave, and doting let thee know,

I better could myself than thee forgo.

Hearken! ye men that e'er shall love like me,

I'll give you counsel gratis: if you be

Possess'd of what you like, let your fair friend

Lodge in your bosom, but no secrets send

To seek their lodging in a female breast;

For so much is abated of your rest.

The steed that comes to understand his strength

30Grows wild, and casts his manager at length:

And that tame lover who unlocks his heart

Unto his mistress, teaches her an art

To plague himself; shows her the secret way

How she may tyrannize another day.

And now, my fair Unkindness, thus to thee;

Mark how wise Passion and I agree:

Hear and be sorry for't. I will not die

To expiate thy crime of levity:

I walk (not cross-arm'd neither), eat, and live,

40Yea live to pity thy neglect, not grieve

That thou art from thy faith and promise gone,

Nor envy him who by my loss hath won.

Thou shalt perceive thy changing Moon-like fits

Have not infected me, or turn'd my wits

To lunacy. I do not mean to weep

When I should eat, or sigh when I should sleep;

I will not fall upon my pointed quill,

Bleed ink and poems, or invention spill

To contrive ballads, or weave elegies

50For nurses' wearing when the infant cries.

Nor like th' enamour'd Tristrams of the time,

Despair in prose and hang myself in rhyme.

Nor thither run upon my verses' feet,

Where I shall none but fools or madmen meet,

Who midst the silent shades, and myrtle walks,

Pule and do penance for their mistress' faults.

I'm none of those poetic malcontents

Born to make paper dear with my laments:

Or wild Orlando that will rail and vex,

60And for thy sake fall out with all the sex.

No, I will love again, and seek a prize

That shall redeem me from thy poor despise.

I'll court my fortune now in such a shape

That will no faint dye, nor starv'd colour take.

Thus launch I off with triumph from thy shore,

To which my last farewell; for never more

Will I touch there. I put to sea again

Blown with the churlish wind of thy disdain.

Nor will I stop this course till I have found

70A coast that yields safe harbour, and firm ground.

Smile, ye Love-Stars; wing'd with desire I fly,

To make my wishes' full discovery:

Nor doubt I but for one that proves like you,

I shall find ten as fair, and yet more true.

To his unconstant Friend.] 7 I have thought it better to keep the form 'ban*e*', which was not uncommon (and, if I am not mistaken, was sometimes made to carry a pun with it), instead of the now usual, and even then authoritative, 'ban*n*'.

11 laid] Orig. 'lad'—an evident misprint.

16 had perisht *Malone MS.* 22.

57 Orig., as often, 'mal*e*contents'.

This piece is one of King's few attempts to play the 'dog'. It is, as one would expect, not very happy, but it might be worse.

Madam Gabrina, Or the Ill-favour'd Choice.

Con mala Muger el remedio
Mucha Tierra por el medio.

I have oft wond'red why thou didst elect

Thy mistress of a stuff none could affect,

That wore his eyes in the right place. A thing

Made up, when Nature's powers lay slumbering.

One, where all pregnant imperfections met

To make her sex's scandal: Teeth of jet,

Hair dy'd in orp'ment, from whose fretful hue

Canidia her highest witchcrafts drew.

A lip most thin and pale, but such a mouth

10Which like the poles is stretched North and South

A face so colour'd, and of such a form,

As might defiance bid unto a storm:

And the complexion of her sallow hide

Like a wrack'd body wash'd up by the tide:

Eyes small: a nose so to her vizard glued

As if 'twould take a Planet's altitude.

Last for her breath, 'tis somewhat like the smell

That does in Ember weeks on Fish-street dwell;

Or as a man should fasting scent the Rose

20Which in the savoury Bear-garden grows.

If a Fox cures the paralytical,

Hadst thou ten palsies, she'd outstink them all.

But I have found thy plot: sure thou didst try

To put thyself past hope of jealousy:

And whilst unlearned fools the senses please,

Thou cur'st thy appetite by a disease;

As many use, to kill an itch withal,

Quicksilver or some biting mineral.

Dote upon handsome things each common man

30With little study and less labour can;

But to make love to a deformity,

Only commends thy great ability,

Who from hard-favour'd objects draw'st content,

As estriches from iron nutriment.

Well, take her, and like mounted George, in bed

Boldly achieve thy Dragon's maiden-head:

Where (though scarce sleep) thou mayst rest confident

None dares beguile thee of thy punishment:

The sin were not more foul that he should commit,

40Than is that She with whom he acted it.

Yet take this comfort: when old age shall raze,

Or sickness ruin many a good face,

Thy choice cannot impair; no cunning curse

Can mend that night-piece, that is, make her worse.

Madam Gabrina] 7 'Orp[i]ment' = yellow arsenic—then, and to some extent still, used as a gold-dye.

39 Malone MS. 22 omits *that*.

41 It is curious that King, who has elsewhere followed Spenser in the matter of eye-rhyme pretty closely, did not spell 'raze', 'race', which was a very usual form and perhaps, as in 'race-ship', the commoner pronunciation.—The whole poem is one of his most disappointing. His Spanish distich—which (adopting Mr. Browning's use of 'fix') might be paraphrased:

If a bad woman once has fix'd you,

Put many a mile of ground betwixt you—

says nothing about mere *ugliness*; while, on the other hand, King does not utilize the prescription of absence as the only cure for ill-placed love. He has at first sight simply added (though, as one would expect, not in the most offensive form) another to the far too numerous dull and loathsome imitations of one of Horace's rare betrayals of the fact that he was not a gentleman. But see on next.

The Defence.

Piensan   los   Enamorados
Que tienen los otros los ojos quebrantados.

Why slightest thou what I approve?

Thou art no Peer to try my love,

Nor canst discern where her form lies,

Unless thou saw'st her with my eyes.

Say she were foul and blacker than

The Night, or sunburnt African,

If lik'd by me, 'tis I alone

Can make a beauty where was none;

For rated in my fancy, she

10Is so as she appears to me.

But 'tis not feature, or a face,

That does my free election grace,

Nor is my liking only led

By a well-temper'd white and red;

Could I enamour'd grow on those,

The Lily and the blushing Rose

United in one stalk might be

As dear unto my thoughts as she.

But I look farther, and do find

20A richer beauty in her mind;

Where something is so lasting fair,

As time or age cannot impair.

Hadst thou a perspective so clear,

Thou couldst behold my object there;

When thou her virtues shouldst espy,

They'd force thee to confess that I

Had cause to like her, and learn thence

To love by judgement, not by sense.

The Defence.] This is very much better, though we need not have had to wade through the other poem to get to it. It has neither the conciseness nor the finish of Ausonius's triumphant confession to Crispa, but is good enough. The Spanish heading here, which in the original has an unnecessary comma at *otros* and an unnecessary divorce of space between *quebranta* and *dos*, may be roughly rendered:

For it is still the lover's mind

That all, except himself, are blind.

The piece is also assigned to Rudyard. Mr. Thorn-Drury notes a variant at ll. 23-8 of some interest from *Parnassus Biceps*, where the title is 'A Lover to one dispraising his Mistress':

so clear

That thou couldst view my object there;

When thou her virtues didst espy,

Thou 'ldst wonder and confess that I

Had cause to like; and learn from hence

To love.

To One demanding why Wine sparkles.

So diamonds sparkle, and thy mistress' eyes;

When 'tis not fire but light in either flies.

Beauty not thaw'd by lustful flames will show

Like a fair mountain of unmelted snow:

Nor can the tasted vine more danger bring

Than water taken from the crystal spring,

Whose end is to refresh and cool that heat

Which unallay'd becomes foul vice's seat:

Unless thy boiling veins, mad with desire

10Of drink, convert the liquor into fire.

For then thou quaff'st down fevers, thy full bowls

Carouse the burning draughts of Portia's coals.

If it do leap and sparkle in the cup,

'Twill sink thy cares, and help invention up.

There never yet was Muse or Poet known

Not dipt or drenched in this Helicon.

But Tom! take heed thou use it with such care

As witches deal with their familiar.

For if thy virtue's circle not confine

20And guard thee from the Furies rais'd by wine,

'Tis ten to one this dancing spirit may

A Devil prove to bear thy wits away;

And make thy glowing nose a map of Hell

Where Bacchus' purple fumes like meteors dwell.

Now think not these sage morals thee invite

To prove Carthusian or strict Rechabite;

Let fool's be mad, wise people may be free,

Though not to license turn their liberty.

He that drinks wine for health, not for excess,

30Nor drowns his temper in a drunkenness,

Shall feel no more the grape's unruly fate,

Then if he took some chilling opiate.

To One demanding, &c.] If not exactly Poetry, this is at least sense, as was once remarked (or in words to that effect), with 'Latin' for 'Poetry', by the late Professor Nettleship, with regard to a composition not in verse.

Malone MS. 22, fol. 24, has an earlier draft of this poem, commencing:

We do not give the wine a sparkling name,

As if we meant those sparks implied a flame;

The flame lies in our blood: and 'tis desire

Fed by loose appetite sets us on fire,

and concluding with lines 29-32.

By occasion of the Young Prince his happy Birth.

[Charles II. Born May 29, 1630.]

At this glad triumph, when most poets use

Their quill, I did not bridle up my Muse

For sloth or less devotion. I am one

That can well keep my Holy-days at home;

That can the blessings of my King and State

Better in pray'r than poems gratulate;

And in their fortunes bear a loyal part,

Though I no bonfires light but in my heart.

Truth is, when I receiv'd the first report

10Of a new star risen and seen at Court;

Though I felt joy enough to give a tongue

Unto a mute, yet duty strook me dumb:

And thus surpris'd by rumour, at first sight

I held it some allegiance not to write.

For howe'er children, unto those that look

Their pedigree in God's, not the Church book,

Fair pledges are of that eternity

Which Christians possess not till they die;
Yet they appear, view'd in that perspective
20Through which we look on men long since alive,
Like succours in a Camp, sent to make good
Their place that last upon the watches stood.
So that in age, or fate, each following birth
Doth set the parent so much nearer earth:
And by this grammar we our heirs may call
The smiling Preface to our funeral.
This sadded my soft sense, to think that he
Who now makes laws, should by a bold decree
Be summon'd hence, to make another room,
30And change his royal palace for a tomb.
For none ere truly lov'd the present light,
But griev'd to see it rivall'd by the night:
And if 't be sin to wish that light extinct,
Sorrow may make it treason but to think't.
I know each malcontent or giddy man,
In his religion, with the Persian
Adores the rising Sun; and his false view
Best likes, not what is best, but what is new.
O that we could these gangrenes so prevent
40(For our own blessing, and their punishment),
That all such might, who for wild changes thirst,
Rack'd on a hopeless expectation, burst,

To see us fetter time, and by his stay
To a consistence fix the flying day;
And in a Solstice by our prayers made,

Rescue our Sun from death or envy's shade.

But here we dally with fate, and in this

Stern Destiny mocks and controls our wish;

Informing us, if fathers should remain

50For ever here, children were born in vain;

And we in vain were Christians, should we

In this world dream of perpetuity.

Decay is Nature's Kalendar; nor can

It hurt the King to think he is a man;

Nor grieve, but comfort him, to hear us say

That his own children must his sceptre sway.

Why slack I then to contribute a vote,

Large as the kingdom's joy, free as my thought?

Long live the Prince! and in that title bear

60The world long witness that the King is here:

May he grow up, till all that good he reach

Which we can wish, or his Great Father teach:

Let him shine long, a mark to land and main,

Like that bright spark plac'd nearest to Charles' Wain,

And, like him, lead succession's golden team,

Which may possess the British diadem.

But in the mean space, let his Royal Sire,

Who warms our hopes with true Promethean fire,

So long his course in time and glory run,

70Till he estate his virtue on his son.

So in his father's days this happy One

Shall crowned be, yet not usurp the Throne;

And Charles reign still, since thus himself will be

Heir to himself, through all posterity.

By occasion, &c. 8 Orig. 'bon*e*-fires', as often, the spelling being accepted by recent authorities as etymological. But bones do not make good fires: 'ba*ne*-fire', the acknowledged Northern form, which has been held to support this origin, is a very likely variant of' ba*le*-fire', and the obvious '*bon*-fire' in the holiday sense is by no means so absurd as it has been represented to be.

10 This 'new star' occurs again and again in courtly verse throughout Charles's life and at his death, but the accounts of it are uncomfortably conflicting. Some say that Venus was visible all day long—a phenomenon of obvious application; others make it Mercury—whereto also an application, at which the person concerned would have laughed very genially, is possible. But neither is a '*new* star'; and the miracle is perhaps more judiciously put as that of *a* star, no matter what, shining brightly at noonday.

22 that] *MS.* 'who'.

27 'sadded' has some interest.

47 'But here we with fate dally' *Malone MS. 22.*

50 were born] *MS.* 'would live'—not so well.

57 vote] In the sense of *votum* = 'wish'.

60 long] *MS.* 'glad'.

63 long] *MS.* 'forth'.

70 *MS.* 'virtues'.

Upon the King's happy return from Scotland.

So breaks the day, when the returning Sun

Hath newly through his winter tropic run,

As You (Great Sir!) in this regress come forth

From the remoter climate of the North.

To tell You now what cares, what fears we past,

What clouds of sorrow did the land o'er-cast,

Were lost, but unto such as have been there,

Where the absented Sun benights the year:

Or have those countries travel'd, which ne'er feel

10The warmth and virtue of his flaming wheel.

How happy yet were we! that when You went,

You left within Your Kingdom's firmament

A Partner-light, whose lustre may despise

The nightly glimm'ring tapers of the skies,

Your peerless Queen; and at each hand a Star,

Whose hopeful beams from You enkindled are.

Though (to say truth) the light, which they could bring,

Serv'd but to lengthen out our evening.

Heaven's greater lamps illumine it; each spark

20Adds only this, to make the sky less dark.

Nay, She, who is the glory of her sex,

Did sadly droop for lack of Your reflex:

Oft did She her fair brow in loneness shroud,

And dimly shone, like Venus in a cloud.

Now are those gloomy mists dry'd up by You,

As the world's eye scatters the ev'ning dew:

And You bring home that blessing to the land,

Which absence made us rightly understand.

Here may You henceforth stay! there need no charms

30To hold You, but the circle of her arms,

Whose fruitful love yields You a rich increase,

Seals of Your joy, and of the kingdom's peace.

O may those precious pledges fix You here,

And You grow old within that crystal sphere!

Pardon this bold detention. Else our love

Will merely an officious trouble prove.

Each busy minute tells us, as it flies,

That there are better objects for Your eyes.

To them let us leave You, whilst we go pray,

40Raising this triumph to a Holy-day.

And may that soul the Church's blessing want,

May his content be short, his comforts scant,

Whose bosom-altar does no incense burn,

In thankful sacrifice for Your return.

Upon the King's happy return, &c.] Hannah notes that this appears with variants, but signed, in MS. Ashm. 38, fol. 51. I have not thought it necessary to collate this version from a work described by good authorities as 'a bad MS.'. The piece itself, however, with others of King's, may well have been in Dryden's mind when he composed his own batch of Restoration welcome-poems to Charles II and Clarendon, within three or four years of the publication of these. There is no plagiarism: Heaven forbid that I should take part in plagiarism-hunting. But there is a sort of resemblance in form and tone (especially in the use of 'You' and 'Your' as pivots), and (though with great improvement) in versification.—The capital Y's here are almost complete in the original, and I have completed them.

To the Queen at Oxford.

Great Lady! that thus, quite against our use,

We speak your welcome by an English Muse,

And in a vulgar tongue our zeals contrive,

Is to confess your large prerogative,

Who have the pow'rful freedom to dispense

With our strict Rules, or Custom's difference.

'Tis fit, when such a Star deigns to appear,

And shine within the academic sphere,

That ev'ry college, grac'd by your resort,

10Should only speak the language of your Court;

As if Apollo's learned quire, but You,

No other Queen of the Ascendent knew.

Let those that list invoke the Delphian name,

To light their verse, and quench their doting flame;

In Helicon it were high treason now,

Did any to a feign'd Minerva bow;

When You are present, whose chaste virtues stain

The vaunted glories of her maiden brain.

I would not flatter. May that diet feed

20Deform'd and vicious souls; they only need

Such physic, who, grown sick of their decays,

Are only cur'd with surfeits of false praise;

Like those, who, fall'n from youth or beauty's grace,

Lay colours on, which more belie the face.

Be You still what You are; a glorious theme

For Truth to crown. So when that diadem

Which circles Your fair brow drops off, and time

Shall lift You to that pitch our prayers climb;

Posterity will plait a nobler wreath,

30To crown Your fame and memory in death.

This is sad truth and plain, which I might fear

Would scarce prove welcome to a Prince's ear;

And hardly may you think that writer wise,

Who preaches there where he should poetize;

Yet where so rich a bank of goodness is,

Triumphs and Feasts admit such thoughts as this,

Nor will your virtue from her client turn,

Although he bring his tribute in an urn.

Enough of this: who knows not when to end

40Needs must, by tedious diligence, offend.

Tis not a poet's office to advance

The precious value of allegiance.

And least of all the rest do I affect

To word my duty in this dialect.

My service lies a better way, whose tone

Is spirited by full devotion.

Thus, whilst I mention *You, Your Royal Mate*,

And *Those* which your blest line perpetuate,

I shall such votes of happiness rehearse,

50Whose softest accents will out-tongue my verse.

To the Queen at Oxford.] This poem was omitted in Hannah's MS., and it is in no way clear to what visit it refers. The absence of any reference to politics shows that it cannot have been Henrietta's residence at Merton during the Rebellion.

29 plait] Orig 'plat'.

A Salutation of His Majesty's ship The Sovereign.

Move on, thou floating trophy built to Fame!

And bid her trump spread thy majestic name;

That the blue Tritons, and those petty Gods

Which sport themselves upon the dancing floods,

May bow, as to their Neptune, when they feel

The awful pressure of thy potent keel.

Great wonder of the time! whose form unites

In one aspect two warring opposites,

Delight and horror; and in them portends

10Diff'ring events both to thy foes and friends;

To these thy radiant brow, Peace's bright shrine,

Doth like that golden constellation shine,

Which guides the seaman with auspicious beams,

Safe and unshipwrack'd through the troubled streams.

But, as a blazing meteor, to those

It doth ostents of blood and death disclose.

For thy rich decks lighten like Heaven's fires,

To usher forth the thunder of thy tires.

O never may cross wind, or swelling wave,

20Conspire to make the treach'rous sands thy grave:

Nor envious rocks, in their white foamy laugh,

Rejoice to wear thy loss's Epitaph.

But may the smoothest, most successful gales

Distend thy sheet, and wing thy flying sails:

That all designs which must on thee embark,

May be securely plac'd, as in the Ark.

May'st thou, where'er thy streamers shall display,

Enforce the bold disputers to obey:

That they, whose pens are sharper than their swords,

30May yield in fact, what they denied in words.

Thus when th' amazed world our seas shall see

Shut from usurpers, to their own Lord free,

Thou may'st, returning from the conquered main,

With thine own triumphs be crown'd *Sovereign*.

A Salutation, &c.] The *Sovereign, Sovereign of the Seas*, or *Royal Sovereign* (I am not sure what name she bore during the Rebellion) is one of the famous *literary* ships of the English Navy. She was built in 1637 at Woolwich by Phineas and Peter Pett out of a whole year's ship-money; and if the means for raising her cost (£80,000) were unpopular, a great deal of pride was taken in the ship herself. Thomas Heywood wrote an account of her which has been frequently quoted. See, for instance, Mr. David Hannay's *Short History of the Royal Navy*, i. 172, 173. She was of 1637 tons burthen; was pierced for 98 great guns with many smaller murdering-pieces and chasers; and was most elaborately decorated, with carved stern, galleries, black and gold angels, trophies and emblems of all sorts—besides a baker's dozen of allegorical, mythological, and historical statues of personages from Cupid to King Edgar on horseback, as figureheads and elsewhere. She fought all through the Dutch wars; escaped the disgraceful disaster in the Medway; distinguished herself at La Hogue, where a great part is assigned to her by some accounts in chasing Tourville's *Soleil Royal* ashore; and was burnt by accident, not long after, at Chatham in 1696—her sixtieth year.

11 The 'radiant brow' is of course the gilded figurehead group. There was no actual 'Peace' among the allegories, but the Cupid, a 'child bridling a lion', might perhaps stand for her.

18 'Tire' is of course 'tier': the *Sovereign* was a three-decker. Professor Skeat approves the spelling, which occurs in Milton and elsewhere. But some would have a special word 'tire', not for the *row* but the actual 'fire' or 'shooting' (*tir*) of the guns—which would do well enough here.

19-22 King's own age would, after the event, have instanced this as an example of Fate granting prayers to the letter yet evading them in the spirit. The *Sovereign* did escape wind and wave, sand and rock, as well as the enemy, but only to perish otherwise.

24 'Sheets' in plural in Hannah's MS. Another in the Ashmolean collection 'clo[a]th[e]s'—a good naval technicality.

27-34 Referring to the *Mare Clausum* dispute and the English insistence on the lowering of foreign flags.

An Epitaph on his most honoured friend, Richard, Earl of Dorset.

[Died March 28, 1624.]

Let no profane ignoble foot tread near

This hallow'd piece of earth: *Dorset lies here.*

A small sad relique of a noble spirit,

Free as the air, and ample as his merit;

Whose least perfection was large, and great

Enough to make a common man complete.

A soul refin'd and cull'd from many men,

That reconcil'd the sword unto the pen,

Using both well. No proud forgetting Lord,

10But mindful of mean names, and of his word.

One that did love for honour, not for ends,

And had the noblest way of making friends

By loving first. One that did know the Court,

Yet understood it better by report

Than practice, for he nothing took from thence

But the king's favour for his recompense.

One for religion, or his country's good,

That valu'd not his fortune, nor his blood.

One high in fair opinion, rich in praise,

20And full of all we could have wish'd, but days.

He that is warn'd of this, and shall forbear

To vent a sigh for him, or lend a tear;

May he live long and scorn'd, unpitied fall,

And want a mourner at his funeral.

An Epitaph.] This Dorset was the third earl, Richard. As a very young man he married the famous Lady Anne Clifford, whose ill-luck in husbands may have been partly caused, but must have been somewhat compensated, by her masterful temper. Dorset, who died young, was both a libertine and a spendthrift; but King seems to have thought well enough of him not only to write this epitaph, but to lend him, or guarantee for him, a thousand pounds (quite £3,000 to-day), which he had at any rate not got back thirty years afterwards. The present piece appears, with variants, in Corbet's *Poems*, but King seems to have the better claim. Hannah gives a considerable body of various readings from the Corbet version and one in the Ashmole MS. 38, but it hardly seems worth while to burden the page-foot with them, for the epitaph is mere 'common-form' and of no special interest.

The Exequy.

Accept, thou Shrine of my dead Saint,

Instead of dirges this complaint;

And for sweet flowers to crown thy hearse,

Receive a strew of weeping verse

From thy griev'd friend, whom thou might'st see

Quite melted into tears for thee.

Dear loss! since thy untimely fate,

My task hath been to meditate

On thee, on thee: thou art the book,

10The library, whereon I look,

Though almost blind. For thee (lov'd clay)

I languish out, not live, the day,

Using no other exercise

But what I practise with mine eyes:

By which wet glasses, I find out

How lazily time creeps about

To one that mourns; this, only this,

My exercise and bus'ness is:

So I compute the weary hours

20With sighs dissolved into showers.

Nor wonder, if my time go thus

Backward and most preposterous;

Thou hast benighted me; thy set

This eve of blackness did beget,

Who wast my day (though overcast,

Before thou hadst thy noon-tide past),

And I remember must in tears,

Thou scarce hadst seen so many years

As day tells hours. By thy clear Sun,

30My love and fortune first did run;

But thou wilt never more appear

Folded within my hemisphere,

Since both thy light and motion

Like a fled star is fall'n and gone,

And 'twixt me and my soul's dear wish

The earth now interposed is,

Which such a strange eclipse doth make,

As ne'er was read in almanac.

I could allow thee, for a time,

40To darken me and my sad clime,

Were it a month, a year, or ten,

I would thy exile live till then;

And all that space my mirth adjourn,

So thou wouldst promise to return;

And putting off thy ashy shroud,

At length disperse this sorrow's cloud.

But woe is me! the longest date

Too narrow is to calculate

These empty hopes: never shall I

50Be so much blest as to descry

A glimpse of thee, till that day come,

Which shall the earth to cinders doom,

And a fierce fever must calcine

The body of this world, like thine,

My Little World! That fit of fire

Once off, our bodies shall aspire

To our souls' bliss: then we shall rise,

And view ourselves with clearer eyes

In that calm region, where no night

60Can hide us from each other's sight.

Meantime, thou hast her, Earth; much good

May my harm do thee. Since it stood

With Heaven's will, I might not call

Her longer mine, I give thee all

My short-liv'd right and interest

In her, whom living I lov'd best:

With a most free and bounteous grief,

I give thee, what I could not keep.

Be kind to her, and prithee look

70Thou write into thy Dooms-day book

Each parcel of this rarity,

Which in thy casket shrin'd doth lie:

See that thou make thy reck'ning straight,

And yield her back again by weight;

For thou must audit on thy trust

Each grain and atom of this dust,

As thou wilt answer *Him* that lent,

Not gave thee, my dear monument.

So close the ground, and 'bout her shade

80Black curtains draw;—my Bride is laid.

Sleep on, my Love, in thy cold bed,

Never to be disquieted!

My last good night! Thou wilt not wake,

Till I thy fate shall overtake:

Till age, or grief, or sickness, must

Marry my body to that dust

It so much loves; and fill the room

My heart keeps empty in thy tomb.

Stay for me there; I will not fail

90To meet thee in that hollow vale:

And think not much of my delay;

I am already on the way,

And follow thee with all the speed

Desire can make, or sorrows breed.

Each minute is a short degree,

And ev'ry hour a step towards thee.

At night, when I betake to rest,

Next morn I rise nearer my West

Of life, almost by eight hours' sail

100Than when sleep breath'd his drowsy gale.

Thus from the Sun my bottom steers,

And my day's compass downward bears:

Nor labour I to stem the tide,

Through which to *Thee* I swiftly glide.

'Tis true, with shame and grief I yield,

Thou, like the van, first took'st the field,

And gotten hast the victory,

In thus adventuring to die

Before me, whose more years might crave

110A just precedence in the grave.

But heark! My pulse, like a soft drum,

Beats my approach, tells *Thee* I come;

And slow howe'er my marches be,

I shall at last sit down by *Thee*.

The thought of this bids me go on,

And wait my dissolution

With hope and comfort. Dear (forgive

The crime), I am content to live

Divided, with but half a heart,

120Till we shall meet and never part.

The Exequy.] This beautiful poem (which bore in Hannah's MS. the sub-title, itself not unmemorable, 'To his Matchless never-to-be forgotten Friend') makes, with 'Tell me no more', King's chief claim to poetic rank. It is not— he never is—splendid, or strange, or soul-shaking; but for simplicity, sincerity, tenderness, and grace—nay, as the time went, nature—it has, in its modest way, not many superiors.

Versions are found in Ashmole MS. 36, fol. 253, and Rawlinson Poet. MS. 160. fol. 41 verso.

36 The] All three MSS. read 'An', which, considering the obvious double meaning of 'earth', is perhaps better.

67-8 Assonance, though not elsewhere unknown, is not common in King.

81 seq. If the last paragraph has seemed to any to approach 'False Wit' this ought to make amends. And so with the conclusion.

The Anniverse. An Elegy.

So soon grown old! hast thou been six years dead?

Poor earth, once by my Love inhabited!

And must I live to calculate the time

To which thy blooming youth could never climb,

But fell in the ascent! yet have not I

Studied enough thy loss's history.

How happy were mankind, if Death's strict laws

Consum'd our lamentations like the cause!

Or that our grief, turning to dust, might end

10With the dissolved body of a friend!

But sacred Heaven! O, how just thou art

In stamping death's impression on that heart,

Which through thy favours would grow insolent,

Were it not physic'd by sharp discontent.

If, then, it stand resolv'd in thy decree,

That still I must doom'd to a desert be,

Sprung out of my lone thoughts, which know no path

But what my own misfortune beaten hath;—

If thou wilt bind me living to a corse,

20And I must slowly waste; I then of force

Stoop to thy great appointment, and obey

That will which nought avails me to gainsay.

For whilst in sorrow's maze I wander on,

I do but follow life's vocation.

Sure we were made to grieve: at our first birth,

With cries we took possession of the earth;

And though the lucky man reputed be

Fortune's adopted son, yet only he

Is Nature's true-born child, who sums his years

30(Like me) with no arithmetic but tears.

The Anniverse.] Not quite so good as *The Exequy*, but not bad. The Hannah-Pickering MS. had a few variants, not worth entering here in most cases.

19 corse] This word had odd luck in a well-printed book, and a generally well-written MS., for it shows in the one as 'coarse', in the other as 'course'—both errors not infrequent at the time.

22 avails] This is the MS. reading: the book has 'avail'.

26 took] *MS*. 'take'.

On Two Children, dying of one disease, and buried in one grave.

Brought forth in sorrow, and bred up in care,

Two tender children here entombed are:

One place, one sire, one womb their being gave,

They had one mortal sickness, and one grave.

And though they cannot number many years

In their account, yet with their parent's tears

This comfort mingles; Though their days were few,

They scarcely sin, but never sorrow knew;

So that they well might boast, they carried hence

10What riper ages lose, their innocence.

You pretty losses, that revive the fate,

Which, in your mother, death did antedate,

O let my high-swoln grief distil on you

The saddest drops of a parental dew:

You ask no other dower than what my eyes

Lay out on your untimely exequies:

When once I have discharg'd that mournful score,

Heav'n hath decreed you ne'er shall cost me more,

Since you release and quit my borrow'd trust,

20By taking this inheritance of dust.

On Two Children, &c.] The number of King's children is uncertain, but as the eldest certainly died *before* the mother, and his sons lived, one nearly as long as the Bishop, the other a little longer, Hannah seems justified in arguing from this piece that there were five.

A Letter.

I ne'er was dress'd in forms; nor can I bend

My pen to flatter any, nor commend,

Unless desert or honour do present

Unto my verse a worthy argument.

You are my friend, and in that word to me

Stand blazon'd in your noblest heraldry;

That style presents you full, and does relate

The bounty of your love, and my own fate,

Both which conspir'd to make me yours. A choice,

10Which needs must, in the giddy people's voice,

That only judge the outside, and, like apes,

Play with our names, and comment on our shapes,

Appear too light: but it lies you upon,

To justify the disproportion.

Truth be my record, I durst not presume

To seek to you, 'twas you that did assume

Me to your bosom. Wherein you subdu'd

One that can serve you, though ne'er could intrude

Upon great titles; nor knows how t' invade

20Acquaintance: Like such as are only paid

With great men's smiles; if that the passant Lord

Let fall a forc'd salute, or but afford

The nod regardant. It was test enough

For me, you ne'er did find such servile stuff

Couch'd in my temper; I can freely say,

I do not love you in that common way

For which Great Ones are lov'd in this false time:

I have no wish to gain, nor will to climb;

I cannot pawn my freedom, nor outlive

30My liberty, for all that you can give.

And sure you may retain good cheap such friends,

Who not your fortune make, but you, their ends.

I speak not this to vaunt in my own story,

All these additions are unto your glory;

Who, counter to the world, use to elect,

Not to take up on trust, what you affect.

Indeed 'tis seldom seen that such as you

Adopt a friend, or for acquaintance sue;

Yet you did this vouchsafe, you did descend

40Below yourself to raise an humble friend,

And fix him in your love: where I will stand

The constant subject of your free command.

Had I no airy thoughts, sure you would teach

Me higher than my own dull sphere to reach:

And, by reflex, instruct me to appear

Something (though coarse and plain) fit for your wear.

Know, best of friends, however wild report

May justly say, I am unapt to sort

With your opinion or society

50(Which truth would shame me, did I it deny),

There 's something in me says, I dare make good,

When honour calls me, all I want in blood.

Put off your giant titles, then I can

Stand in your judgement's blank an equal man.

Though hills advanced are above the plain,

They are but higher earth, nor must disdain

Alliance with the vale: we see a spade

Can level them, and make a mount a glade.

Howe'er we differ in the Heralds' book,

60He that mankind's extraction shall look

In Nature's rolls, must grant we all agree

In our best part's immortal pedigree:

You must by that perspective only view

My service, else 'twill ne'er show worthy you.

You see I court you bluntly, like a friend,

Not like a mistress; my Muse is not penn'd

For smooth and oily flights: and I indent

To use more honesty than compliment.

But I have done; in lieu of all you give,

70Receive his thankful tribute, who must live

Your vow'd observer, and devotes a heart

Which will in death seal the bold counterpart.

A Letter.] I do not know any clue to the object of this epistle. King, like most churchmen of distinction at the time, was on familiar terms with divers 'persons of quality'. But it *might* be a mere literary exercise—a 'copy of verses'.

23 'Nod regardant' is good. It shows, with 'passant' just before that his own reference to heraldry was still floating in King's mind.

54 Either of two of the numerous senses of 'blank' would come in here. One is *tabula rasa*, the judgement being obscured by no prepossession; the other 'bull's-eye' or 'target'.

59 Orig. as usual, 'Heralds', with no apostrophe to make case or number. If anybody prefers 'herald's' I have no objection.

67 indent] In the sense of 'contract', 'engage'.

An Acknowledgement.

My best of friends! what needs a chain to tie

One by your merit bound a votary?

Think you I have some plot upon my peace,

I would this bondage change for a release?

Since 'twas my fate your prisoner to be,

Heav'n knows I nothing fear, but liberty.

Yet you do well, that study to prevent,

After so rich a stock of favour spent

On one so worthless, lest my memory

10Should let so dear an obligation die

Without record. This made my precious Friend

Her token, as an antidote, to send,

Against forgetful poisons; That as they

Who Vespers late, and early Mattins say

Upon their beads, so on this linked score

In golden numbers I might reckon o'er

Your virtues and my debt, which does surmount

The trivial laws of popular account:

For that, within this emblematic knot,

20Your beauteous mind, and my own fate, is wrote.

The sparkling constellation which combines

The lock, is your dear self, whose worth outshines

Most of your sex; so solid and so clear

You like a perfect diamond appear;

Casting, from your example, fuller light

Than those dim sparks which glaze the brow of night,

And gladding all your friends, as doth the ray

Of that East-star which wakes the cheerful day.

But the black map of death and discontent

30Behind that adamantine firmament,

That luckless figure, which, like Calvary,

Stands strew'd and copied out in skulls, is I:

Whose life your absence clouds, and makes my time

Move blindfold in the dark ecliptic line.

Then wonder not, if my removed Sun

So low within the western tropic run;

My eyes no day in this horizon see,

Since where You are not, all is night to me.

Lastly, the anchor which enfast'ned lies

40Upon a pair of deaths, sadly applies

That Monument of Rest, which harbour must

Our ship-wrackt fortunes in a road of dust.

So then, how late soe'er my joyless life

Be tired out in this affection's strife:

Though my tempestuous fancy, like the sky,

Travail with storms, and through my wat'ry eye,

Sorrow's high-going waves spring many a leak;

Though sighs blow loud, till my heart's cordage break;

Though Faith, and all my wishes prove untrue,

50Yet Death shall fix and anchor Me with You.

'Tis some poor comfort, that this mortal scope

Will period, though never crown, my Hope.

An Acknowledgement.] This is evidently of the same class as the last poem, if not as evidently addressed to the same person. The recipient of the *Letter* might be of either sex, for 'mistress' in l. 66 (*v. sup.*) is not quite decisive in the context. This 'precious Friend' is definitely feminine. Nineteenth—I do not know about twentieth—century man would have been a little uncomfortable about receiving from a lady a gold chain with a grouped diamond pendant, welcome as the enclosed 'lock' might be. But, as Scott and others have long ago remarked, there was none of this false pride in the seventeenth, and you might even take money from the beloved. The combination of death's heads, equally of the time, is more of all time.

The Acquittance.

Not knowing who should my acquittance take,

I know as little what discharge to make.

The favour is so great, that it outgoes

All forms of thankfulness I can propose.

Those grateful levies which my pen would raise,

Are stricken dumb, or buried in amaze.

Therefore, as once in Athens there was shown

An Altar built unto the God Unknown,

My ignorant devotions must by guess

10This blind return of gratitude address,

Till you vouchsafe to show me where and how

I may to this revealed Goddess bow.

The Acquittance.] This group of poems is so obviously a group that Hannah's principles of selection in rejecting the present piece and admitting the others may seem unreasonably 'undulating and diverse'. I suppose he thought it rather profane for a bishop even *in futuro*, and perhaps rather ambiguous in other ways. But though King became a bishop there is no chance of my becoming an archdeacon, and I think the piece rather pretty.

The Forfeiture.

My Dearest, To let you or the world know

What debt of service I do truly owe

To your unpattern'd self, were to require

A language only form'd in the desire

Of him that writes. It is the common fate

Of greatest duties, to evaporate

In silent meaning, as we often see

Fires by their too much fuel smother'd be:

Small obligations may find vent, and speak,

10When greater the unable debtor break.

And such are mine to you, whose favour's store

Hath made me poorer then I was before;

For I want words and language to declare

How strict my bond, or large your bounties are.

Since nothing in my desp'rate fortune found,

Can payment make, nor yet the sum compound;

You must lose all, or else of force accept

The body of a bankrupt for your debt.

Then, Love, your bond to execution sue,

20And take myself, as forfeited to you.

The Forfeiture.] This piece, which Hannah did not find in his MS., is almost certainly connected with the preceding, and, I think, with *An Acknowledgement* and *The Departure*, if not also with *A Letter*. The suggested unreality in this *Letter* disappears to a large extent in them, which is not unnatural.

9-10 An ingenious adaptation of *Curae leves*, &c.

The Departure. An Elegy.

Were I to leave no more than a good friend,

Or but to hear the summons to my end,

(Which I have long'd for) I could then with ease

Attire my grief in words, and so appease

That passion in my bosom, which outgrows

The language of strict verse or largest prose.

But here I am quite lost; writing to you,

All that I pen or think is forc'd and new.

My faculties run cross, and prove as weak

10T' indite this melancholy task, as speak:

Indeed all words are vain; well might I spare

This rend'ring of my tortur'd thoughts in air,

Or sighing paper. My infectious grief

Strikes inward, and affords me no relief,

But still a deeper wound, to lose a sight

More lov'd than health, and dearer than the light.

But all of us were not at the same time

Brought forth, nor are we billeted in one clime.

Nature hath pitch'd mankind at several rates,

20Making our places diverse as our fates.

Unto that universal law I bow,

Though with unwilling knee, and do allow

Her cruel justice, which dispos'd us so

That we must counter to our wishes go.

'Twas part of man's first curse, which order'd well,

We should not alway with our likings dwell.

'Tis only the Triumphant Church where we

Shall in unsever'd neighbourhood agree.

Go then, best soul, and, where You must appear,

30Restore the day to that dull hemisphere.

Ne'er may the hapless night You leave behind

Darken the comforts of Your purer mind.

May all the blessings wishes can invent

Enrich your days, and crown them with content.

And though You travel down into the West,

May Your life's Sun stand fixed in the East,

Far from the weeping set; nor may my ear

Take in that killing whisper, *You once were.*

Thus kiss I Your fair hands, taking my leave,

40As prisoners at the bar their doom receive.

All joys go with You: let sweet peace attend

You on the way, and wait Your journey's end.

But let Your discontents and sourer fate

Remain with me, borne off in my retrait.

Might all your crosses, in that sheet of lead

Which folds my heavy heart, lie buried:

'Tis the last service I would do You, and the best

My wishes ever meant, or tongue profest.

Once more I take my leave. And once for all,

50Our parting shows so like a funeral,

It strikes my soul, which hath most right to be

Chief Mourner at this sad solemnity.

And think not, Dearest, 'cause this parting knell

Is rung in verses, that at Your farewell

I only mourn in poetry and ink:

No, my pen's melancholy plummets sink

So low, they dive where th' hid affections sit,

Blotting that paper where my mirth was writ.

Believe 't, that sorrow truest is, which lies

60Deep in the breast, not floating in the eyes:

And he with saddest circumstance doth part,

Who seals his farewell with a bleeding heart.

The Departure.] The special title of this poem was not in Hannah's MS.

6 largest] *MS.* 'larg*er*'.

47 An irregular line of this kind (for it is practically an Alexandrine) is so very rare in King that one suspects an error, but Hannah notes no MS. variant. Many, perhaps most, contemporary poets would not have hesitated at 'serv'ce', which with 'I'd' adjusts the thing; but our Bishop is seldom rough and still seldomer licentious.

53 this] *MS.* 'the'.

56 Orig. 'plommets'.

Paradox.

That it is best for a Young Maid to marry an Old Man.

Fair one, why cannot you an old man love?

He may as useful, and more constant prove.

Experience shows you that maturer years

Are a security against those fears

Youth will expose you to; whose wild desire
As it is hot, so 'tis as rash as fire.
Mark how the blaze extinct in ashes lies,
Leaving no brand nor embers when it dies
Which might the flame renew: thus soon consumes
10Youth's wand'ring heat, and vanishes in fumes.
When age's riper love unapt to stray
Through loose and giddy change of objects, may
In your warm bosom like a cinder lie,
Quick'ned and kindled by your sparkling eye.
'Tis not deni'd, there are extremes in both
Which may the fancy move to like or loathe:
Yet of the two you better shall endure
To marry with the cramp than calenture.
Who would in wisdom choose the Torrid Zone
20Therein to settle a plantation?
Merchants can tell you, those hot climes were made
But at the longest for a three years' trade:
And though the Indies cast the sweeter smell,
Yet health and plenty do more Northward dwell;
For where the raging sunbeams burn the earth,
Her scorched mantle withers into dearth;
Yet when that drought becomes the harvest's curse,
Snow doth the tender corn most kindly nurse:
Why now then woo you not some snowy head
30To take you in mere pity to his bed?
I doubt the harder task were to persuade

Him to love you: for if what I have said

In virgins as in vegetals holds true,

He'll prove the better nurse to cherish you.

Some men we know renown'd for wisdom grown

By old records and antique medals shown;

Why ought not women then be held most wise

Who can produce living antiquities?

Besides if care of that main happiness

40Your sex triumphs in, doth your thoughts possess,

I mean your beauty from decay to keep;

No wash nor mask is like an old man's sleep.

Young wives need never to be sunburnt fear,

Who their old husbands for umbrellas wear:

How russet looks an orchard on the hill

To one that 's water'd by some neighb'ring drill?

Are not the floated meadows ever seen

To flourish soonest, and hold longest green?

You may be sure no moist'ning lacks that bride,

50Who lies with winter thawing by her side.

She should be fruitful too as fields that join

Unto the melting waste of Apennine.

Whilst the cold morning-drops bedew the rose,

It doth nor leaf, nor smell, nor colour lose;

Then doubt not, Sweet! Age hath supplies of wet

To keep You like that flower in water set.

Dripping catarrhs and fontinells are things

Will make You think You grew betwixt two springs.

And should You not think so, You scarce allow

60The force or merit of Your marriage-vow;

Where maids a new creed learn, and must from thence

Believe against their own or others' sense.

Else love will nothing differ from neglect,

Which turns not to a virtue each defect.

I'll say no more but this; you women make

Your children's reck'ning by the almanac.

I like it well, so you contented are,

To choose their fathers by that kalendar.

Turn then, old *Erra Pater*, and there see

70According to life's posture and degree,

What age or what complexion is most fit

To make an English maid happy by it;

And You shall find, if You will choose a man,

Set justly for Your own meridian,

Though You perhaps let *One and Twenty* woo,

Your elevation is for *Fifty-Two*.

Paradox. That it is best, &c.] After Hannah's omission of *The Acquittance* it is not surprising that he did not give this or the next—though a greater excess of prudishness appears in the exclusion of *The Change*, and one begins to think that something more than accident, indolence, or business prevented the appearance of the promised second volume. But if there is some nastiness there is very little naughtiness in them.

33 Some have thought 'vegetal', which was not uncommon in the seventeenth century, a better form than 'vegetable', though this latter has prevailed. It is the French word, and though in Latin there is no 'vegetalis' and there is 'vegetabilis', yet this latter has quite a different sense.

44 Orig. has 'umbrell*aes*', not 'umbrell*os*' (or -oes), which seems to be the older form.

46 It would be pardonable to suppose 'drill' an error for 'rill'. But the word is unquestionably used in the sense by Sandys and Jeremy Taylor, and seems to be the same as the slightly older 'trill' in the sense of 'trickle'.

Paradox.

That Fruition destroys Love.

Love is our Reason's Paradox, which still

Against the judgement doth maintain the will:

And governs by such arbitrary laws,

It only makes the act our liking's cause:

We have no brave revenge, but to forgo

Our full desires, and starve the tyrant so.

They whom the rising blood tempts not to taste,

Preserve a stock of love can never waste;

When easy people who their wish enjoy,

10Like prodigals at once their wealth destroy.

Adam till now had stay'd in Paradise

Had his desires been bounded by his eyes.

When he did more than look, that made th' offence,

And forfeited his state of innocence.

Fruition therefore is the bane t' undo

Both our affection and the subject too.

'Tis Love into worse language to translate,

And make it into Lust degenerate:

'Tis to dethrone, and thrust it from the heart,

20To seat it grossly in the sensual part.

Seek for the star that 's shot upon the ground,

And nought but a dim jelly there is found.

Thus foul and dark our female stars appear,

If fall'n or loos'ned once from Virtue's Sphere.

Glow-worms shine only look'd on, and let lie,

But handled crawl into deformity:

So beauty is no longer fair and bright,

Than whilst unstained by the appetite:

And then it withers like a blasted flower,

30Some pois'nous worm or spider hath crept o'er.

Pygmalion's dotage on the carved stone,

Shows amorists their strong illusion.

Whilst he to gaze and court it was content,

He serv'd as priest at Beauty's monument:

But when by looser fires t' embraces led,

It prov'd a cold hard statue in his bed.

Irregular affects, like madmen's dreams

Presented by false lights and broken beams,

So long content us, as no near address

40Shows the weak sense our painted happiness.

But when those pleasing shadows us forsake,

Or of the substance we a trial make,

Like him, deluded by the fancy's mock,

We shipwrack 'gainst an alabaster rock.

What though thy mistress far from marble be?

Her softness will transform and harden thee.

Lust is a snake, and Guilt the Gorgon's head,

Which Conscience turns to stone, and Joys to lead.

Turtles themselves will blush, if put to name

50The act, whereby they quench their am'rous flame.

Who then that 's wise or virtuous, would not fear

To catch at pleasures which forbidden were,

When those which we count lawful, cannot be

Requir'd without some loss of modesty?

Ev'n in the marriage-bed, where soft delights

Are customary and authoriz'd rites;
What are those tributes to the wanton sense,
But toleration of Incontinence?

For properly you cannot call that Love
60Which does not from the soul, but humour move.
Thus they who worship'd Pan or Isis' Shrine,
By the fair front judg'd all within divine:
Though ent'ring, found 'twas but a goat or cow
To which before their ignorance did bow.
Such temples and such goddesses are these
Which foolish lovers and admirers please:
Who if they chance within the shrine to pry,
Find that a beast they thought a Deity.
Nor makes it only our opinion less
70Of what we lik'd before, and now possess;
But robs the fuel, and corrupts the spice
Which sweetens and inflames Love's sacrifice,
After fruition once, what is Desire
But ashes kept warm by a dying fire?
This is (if any) the Philosopher's Stone
Which still miscarries at projection.
For when the Heat *ad Octo* intermits,
It poorly takes us like Third Ague fits,
Or must on embers as dull drugs infuse,
80Which we for med'cine not for pleasure use.
Since lovers' joys then leave so sick a taste,
And soon as relish'd by the sense are past;
They are but riddles sure, lost if possest,

And therefore only in reversion best.
For bate them expectation and delay,
You take the most delightful scenes away.
These two such rule within the fancy keep,
As banquets apprehended in our sleep;
After which pleasing trance next morn we wake
90Empty and angry at the night's mistake.
Give me long dreams and visions of content,
Rather than pleasures in a minute spent.
And since I know before, the shedding rose
In that same instant doth her sweetness lose,
Upon the virgin-stock still let her dwell
For me, to feast my longings with her smell.
Those are but counterfeits of joy at best,
Which languish soon as brought unto the test.
Nor can I hold it worth his pains who tries
100To in that harvest which by reaping dies.
Resolve me now what spirit hath delight,
If by full feed you kill the appetite?
That stomach healthi'st is, that ne'er was cloy'd,
Why not that Love the best then, ne'er enjoy'd?

Since nat'rally the blood, when tam'd or sated,
Will cool so fast it leaves the object hated.
Pleasures, like wonders, quickly lose their price
When Reason or Experience makes us wise.
To close my argument then. I dare say
110(And without Paradox) as well we may
Enjoy our Love and yet preserve Desire,

As warm our hands by putting out the fire.

Paradox. That Fruition, &c.] Put less tersely but perhaps better by Dryden's most original heroine, Doralice, in *Marriage à la Mode*, 'The only way to keep us true to each other is never to enjoy'. The notion is old enough, and several other seventeenth-century poets have treated it.

22 Nobody has ever assigned a (to me, at least) plausible reason for this universal fancy of the seventeenth century about the jellification of shooting-stars. It is curious, but not inexplicable, that Browne does not touch it.

31 King has very coolly turned the Pygmalion story upside down to suit his thesis.

50 The talking and blushing turtle (i.e. dove) is another remarkable poetical licence.

77 Heat *ad Octo*] An obviously alchemical phrase which I have not interpreted.

100 in] Orig. 'inne' = 'get in'. Cf. *All's Well that Ends Well*, 1. iii, 'to in the crop'.

The Change.

El sabio muda conscio: El loco persevera.

We lov'd as friends now twenty years and more:

Is't time or reason, think you, to give o'er?

When, though two prenti'ships set Jacob free,

I have not held my Rachel dear at three.

Yet will I not your levity accuse;

Continuance sometimes is the worse abuse.

In judgement I might rather hold it strange,

If, like the fleeting world, you did not change:

Be it your wisdom therefore to retract,

10When perseverance oft is folly's act.

In pity I can think, that what you do

Hath Justice in't, and some Religion too;

For of all virtues Moral or Divine,

We know, but Love, none must in Heaven shine:

Well did you the presumption then foresee

Of counterfeiting immortality:

Since had you kept our loves too long alive,

We might invade Heaven's prerogative;

Or in our progress, like the Jews, comprise

20The Legend of an earthly Paradise.

Live happy, and more prosperous in the next.

You have discharg'd your old friend by the text.

Farewell, fair Shadow of a female faith,

And let this be our friendship's Epitaph:

Affection shares the frailty of our fate,

When (like ourselves) 'tis old and out of date:

'Tis just all human loves their period have,

When friends are frail and dropping to the grave.

The Change.] This poem is almost less of a commonplace than any of King's, and the expression is vigorous. The nearest parallel I know to it is Crabbe's 'Natural Death of Love', and like that it has a curious, if not cheerful, ring of actuality. But the case is more unusual. The Spanish motto (rather dog-Spanish in original) means: 'The wise man changes consciously: the fool [or, rather, madman] perseveres.'

22 by the text] = 'formally'? as it were, 'by the card'. Or perhaps with direct reference to the motto.

To my Sister Anne King, who chid me in verse for being angry.

Dear Nan, I would not have thy counsel lost,

Though I last night had twice so much been crost;

Well is a passion to the market brought,

When such a treasure of advice is bought

With so much dross. And couldst thou me assure,

Each vice of mine should meet with such a cure,

I would sin oft, and on my guilty brow

Wear every misperfection that I owe,

Open and visible; I should not hide

10But bring my faults abroad: to hear thee chide

In such a note, and with a quill so sage,

It passion tunes, and calms a tempest's rage.

Well, I am charm'd, and promise to redress

What, without shrift, my follies do confess

Against myself: wherefore let me entreat,

When I fly out in that distemper'd heat

Which frets me into fasts, thou wilt reprove

That froward spleen in poetry and love:

So though I lose my reason in such fits

20Thou'lt rhyme me back again into my wits.

To my Sister, &c.] Anne King, afterwards Mrs. Dutton and Lady Howe. Howell, the epistoler, admitted her (in rather execrable verse) to that Tenth Museship which has had so many fair incumbents. Izaak Walton left her a ring and called her 'a most generose and ingenious Lady'. The verses assigned to her, which may be found in Hannah's notes, are not of the worst Tenth Muse quality.

2 It has been observed, once or twice, that a placid and philosophical temper does not seem to have been one of the Bishop's gifts, and he here acknowledges the fact.

8 'Owe', as so often noted, = 'own'.

17 And seems to have done due penance for it.

An Elegy upon the immature loss of the most vertuous Lady Anne Rich.

[Died August 24, 1638.]

I envy not thy mortal triumphs, Death

(Thou enemy to Virtue, as to breath),

Nor do I wonder much, nor yet complain

The weekly numbers by thy arrow slain.

The whole world is thy factory, and we,

Like traffic, driven and retail'd by Thee:

And where the springs of life fill up so fast,

Some of the waters needs must run to waste.

It is confess'd, yet must our griefs dispute

10That which thine own conclusion doth refute,

Ere we begin. Hearken! for if thy ear

Be to thy throat proportion'd, thou canst hear.

Is there no order in the work of Fate?

Nor rule, but blindly to anticipate

Our growing seasons? or think'st thou 'tis just,

To sprinkle our fresh blossoms with thy dust,

Till by abortive funerals, thou bring

That to an Autumn, Nature meant a Spring?

Is't not enough for thee, that wither'd age

20Lies the unpitied subject of thy rage;

But like an ugly amorist, thy crest

Must be with spoils of Youth and Beauty drest?

In other camps, those which sat down to-day

March first to-morrow, and they longest stay,

Who last came to the service: but in thine,

Only confusion stands for discipline.

We fall in such promiscuous heaps, none can

Put any diff'rence 'twixt thy rear or van;

Since oft the youngest lead thy files. For this,

30The grieved world here thy accuser is,

And I a plaintiff, 'mongst those many ones,

Who wet this Lady's urn with zealous moans;

As if her ashes, quick'ning into years,

Might be again embodied by our tears.

But all in vain; the moisture we bestow

Shall make as soon her curled marble grow,

As render heat or motion to that blood,

Which through her veins branch't like an azure flood;

Whose now still current in the grave is lost,

40Lock'd up, and fetter'd by eternal frost.

Desist from hence, doting Astrology!

To search for hidden wonders in the sky;

Or from the concourse of malignant stars,

Foretell diseases, gen'ral as our wars:

What barren droughts, forerunners of lean dearth,

Threaten to starve the plenty of the earth:

What horrid forms of darkness must affright

The sickly world, hast'ning to that long night

Where it must end. If there no portents are,

50No black eclipses for the Kalendar,

Our times sad annals will rememb'red be

I' th' loss of bright Northumberland and Thee:

Two stars of Court, who in one fatal year

By most untimely set drop'd from their sphere.

She in the winter took her flight, and soon

As her perfections reach'd the point of noon,

Wrapt in a cloud, contracted her wish'd stay

Unto the measure of a short-liv'd day.

But *Thou* in Summer, like an early rose,

60By Death's cold hand nipp'd as *Thou* didst disclose,

Took'st a long day to run that narrow stage,

Which in two gasping minutes summ'd thy age.

And, as the fading rose, when the leaves shed,

Lies in its native sweetness buried,

Thou in thy virtues bedded and inhearst,

Sleep'st with those odours thy pure fame disperst,

Where till that Rising Morn thou must remain,

In which thy wither'd flowers shall spring again,

And greater beauties thy wak'd body vest,

70Than were at thy departure here possest.

So with full eyes we close thy vault. Content

(With what thy loss bequeaths us) to lament,

And make that use of thy griev'd funeral,

As of a crystal broken in the fall;

Whose pitied fractures, gather'd up, and set,

May smaller mirrors for thy sex beget;

There let them view themselves, until they see

The end of all their glories shown in *Thee*.

Whilst in the truth of this sad tribute, I

80Thus strive to canonize thy memory.

Elegy on Lady Anne Rich.] Properly Lady Rich, who had been Lady Anne Cavendish. Her brother Charles was that leader of the 'Ca'ndishers' in Lincolnshire whose defeat and death at Gainsborough, after repeated victories in the spring and summer of 1643, was one of the first and most serious blows to the Royal cause. Waller wrote epitaphs both on him and on his sister, but the best on her is Sidney Godolphin's (*v. sup.*, vol. ii, p. 248). She is one of the candidates for the personage of Waller's 'Amoret', and was not impossibly King's 'A. R.' (*v. sup.*, p. 172).

4 *MS.* 'arrows'.

38 Which] *MS.* 'Once'.

48 *MS.* 'hasting'.

52 Northumberland] Lady Anne Cecil, first wife of Algernon Percy, tenth Earl.

55 winter] December 6, 1637.

An Elegy upon Mrs. Kirk, unfortunately drowned in Thames.

For all the shipwracks, and the liquid graves

Lost men have gain'd within the furrow'd waves,

The Sea hath fin'd, and for our wrongs paid use,

When its wrought foam a Venus did produce.

But what repair wilt thou, unhappy Thames,

Afford our loss? thy dull unactive streams

Can no new beauty raise, nor yet restore

Her who by thee was ravish'd from our shore:

Whose death hath stain'd the glory of thy flood,

10And mix'd the guilty channel with her blood.

O Neptune! was thy favour only writ

In that loose element where thou dost sit?

That, after all this time, thou shouldst repent

Thy fairest blessing to the continent?

Say, what could urge this Fate? is Thetis dead,

Or Amphitrite from thy wet arms fled?

Wast thou so poor in Nymphs, that thy moist love

Must be maintain'd with pensions from above?

If none of these, but that, whilst thou didst sleep

20Upon thy sandy pillow in the deep,

This mischief stole upon us; may our grief

Waken thy just revenge on that sly thief,

Who, in thy fluid empire, without leave,

And unsuspected, durst her life bereave.

Henceforth, invert thy order, and provide

In gentlest floods a pilot for our guide.

Let rugged seas be lov'd, but the brook's smile

Shunn'd like the courtship of a crocodile;

And where the current doth most smoothly pass,

30Think for her sake, that stream Death's looking-glass,

To show us our destruction is most near,

When pleasure hath begot least sense of fear.

Else break thy forked sceptre 'gainst some rock,

If thou endure a flatt'ring calm to mock

Thy far-fam'd pow'r, and violate that law

Which keeps the angry Ocean in awe.

Thy trident will grow useless, which doth still

Wild tempests, if thou let tame rivers kill.

Meantime, we owe thee nothing. Our first debt

40Lies cancell'd in thy wat'ry cabinet.

We have for Her thou sent'st us from the main,

Return'd a Venus back to thee again.

An Elegy upon Mrs. Kirk, &c.] This and the following were not in Hannah's MS. He, perhaps not quite accurately, regards this as King's *only* indulgence in what he also regarded as 'the frigid and artificial style popular among his contemporaries'. But he thought it better than the companion piece in Heath's *Clarastella* (*v. inf.*). From this latter we learn that Mrs. Kirk was one of the numerous victims of 'shooting the bridge'. The piece is frigid enough certainly, but rather from want of 'conceit' than because of it. (Mr. Thorn-Drury has reminded me of Glapthorne's two elegies on the same subject. They form the last contents of the 1874 reprint and give more detail in their title, 'On the noble and much to be lamented Mrs. Anne Kirk, wife to Mr. Geo. Kirk, Gent. of the Robes and of his Majesty's Bed Chamber, who was unfortunately drowned passing London Bridge, July 6. 1641'.)

3 fin'd] = '*paid* fine', as often.

An Elegy upon the death of Mr. Edward Holt.

Whether thy father's, or disease's rage,

More mortal prov'd to thy unhappy age,

Our sorrow needs not question; since the first

Is known for length and sharpness much the worst.

Thy fever yet was kind; which the ninth day

For thy misfortunes made an easy way.

When th' other barbarous and hectic fit,

In nineteen winters did not intermit.

I therefore vainly now not ask thee why

10Thou didst so soon in thy youth's mid-way die:

But in my sense the greater wonder make,

Thy long oppressed heart no sooner brake.

Of force must the neglected blossom fall,

When the tough root becomes unnatural,

And to his branches doth that sap deny,

Which them with life and verdure should supply.

For parents' shame, let it forgotten be,

And may the sad example die with thee.

It is not now thy grieved friend's intent

20To render thee dull Pity's argument.

Thou hast a bolder title unto fame,

And at Edge Hill thou didst make good the claim;

When, in thy Royal Master's cause and war,

Thy ventur'd life brought off a noble scar.

Nor did thy faithful services desist,

Till death untimely strook thee from the list.

Though in that prouder vault, then, which doth tomb

Thy ancestors, thy body find not room,

Thine own deserts have purchas'd thee a place,

30Which more renowned is than all thy race;

For in this earth thou dost ennobled lie

With marks of valour and of loyalty.

Mr. Edward Holt.] Holt was King's brother-in-law, having married his sister Elizabeth (*v. sup.*, p. 173). He died at Oxford in 1643 while attending the King as Groom of the Bedchamber, and was buried in the Cathedral. His father, who outlived him, was a Baronet, and is again abused by King in his will as having been 'implacable'; but the Bishop apparently thought better of his nephew Sir Robert, who was a stout Royalist and churchman both before and after the Restoration. Walton dedicated his *Life of Donne* to this Sir Robert Holt. His much-abused grandfather had at any rate set the example of loyalty, and is said to have been plundered or extortioned by Parliamentary 'contributions' or 'compositions' to the amount of about £20,000.

To my dead friend Ben. Jonson.

[Died August 6, 1637.]

I see that wreath, which doth the wearer arm

'Gainst the quick strokes of thunder, is no charm

To keep off Death's pale dart. For, Jonson, then

Thou hadst been number'd still with living men.

Time's scythe had fear'd thy laurel to invade,

Nor thee this subject of our sorrow made.

Amongst those many votaries who come

To offer up their garlands at thy tomb;

Whilst some more lofty pens, in their bright verse

10(Like glorious tapers flaming on thy hearse),

Shall light the dull and thankless world to see,

How great a maim it suffers, wanting thee;

Let not thy learned shadow scorn, that I

Pay meaner rites unto thy memory;
And since I nought can add but in desire,
Restore some sparks which leap'd from thine own fire.
What ends soever others' quills invite,
I can protest, it was no itch to write,
Nor any vain ambition to be read,
20But merely love and justice to the dead,
Which rais'd my fameless Muse; and caus'd her bring
These drops, as tribute thrown into that spring,
To whose most rich and fruitful bead we owe
The purest streams of language which can flow.
For 'tis but truth, thou taught'st the ruder age
To speak by grammar, and reform'dst the stage:
Thy comic sock induc'd such purged sense,
A Lucrece might have heard without offence.
Amongst those soaring wits that did dilate
30Our English, and advance it to the rate
And value it now holds, thyself was one
Help'd lift it up to such proportion;
That thus refin'd and rob'd, it shall not spare
With the full Greek or Latin to compare.
For what tongue ever durst, but ours, translate
Great Tully's eloquence, or Homer's state?
Both which in their unblemish'd lustre shine,
From Chapman's pen, and from thy *Catiline*.
All I would ask for thee, in recompense
40Of thy successful toil and time's expense,
Is only this poor boon; that those who can
Perhaps read French, or talk Italian,

Or do the lofty Spaniard affect,

To show their skill in foreign dialect,

Prove not themselves so unnaturally wise,

They therefore should their mother-tongue despise

(As if her poets, both for style and wit,

Not equall'd, or not pass'd, their best that writ),

Until by studying Jonson they have known

50The height and strength and plenty of their own.

Thus in what low earth or neglected room

Soe'er thou sleep'st, thy book shall be thy tomb.

Thou wilt go down a happy corse, bestrew'd

With thine own flowers; and feel thyself renew'd,

Whilst thy immortal, never-with'ring bays

Shall yearly flourish in thy readers' praise.

And when more spreading titles are forgot,

Or spite of all their lead and cere-cloth rot,

Thou wrapp'd and shrin'd in thine own sheets wilt lie,

60A relic fam'd by all posterity.

Ben. Jonson.] In orig., as so often, 'Jo*h*nson'. A contribution to *Jonsonus Virbius*, which, printed nearly twenty years before these *Poems*, has one slight variant = 'that' for 'who' in l. 7.

5 scythe] Orig. 'sithe', which some great ones (including even the other Johnson) will have to be the proper spelling, and which is certainly usual in Middle English. But 'scythe' is consecrated by the only Sainte Ampoule of orthography—usage; 'sithe' also means 'a path' and 'a sigh', and may be mistaken for 'since', while 'scythe' is unmistakable. And for my part, if I may not have 'scythe' I stickle for 'sigðe'—the undoubted original.

38 It was a little dangerous, in Ben's lifetime, to praise others in company with him. But King here corroborates Drummond's *Conversations*, in which Ben is made to speak well of Chapman on several occasions, and (more particularly) to declare his *Iliad*, or part of it, 'well done'.

42 It is rather curious that Drummond (in one of those *Marginalia* in which he relieves his feelings somewhat subacidly) declares that his robustious guest 'neither understood French nor Italian'.

An Elegy upon Prince Henry's death

[Died Nov. 6, 1612.]

Keep station, Nature, and rest, Heaven, sure

On thy supporters' shoulders, lest, past cure,

Thou dash'd in ruin fall, by a grief's weight

Will make thy basis shrink, and lay thy height

Low as the centre. Hark! and feel it read

Through the astonish'd Kingdom, Henry's dead.

It is enough; who seeks to aggravate

One strain beyond this, prove[s] more sharp his fate

Than sad our doom. The world dares not survive

10To parallel this woe's superlative.

O killing Rhetoric of Death! two words

Breathe stronger terrors than plague, fire, or swords

Ere conquer'd. This were epitaph and verse,

Worthy to be prefix'd in Nature's hearse,

Or Earth's sad dissolution; whose fall

Will be less grievous, though more general:

For all the woe ruin e'er buried

Sounds in these fatal accents, Henry's dead.

Cease then, unable Poetry; thy phrase

20Is weak and dull to strike us with amaze

Worthy thy vaster subject. Let none dare

To copy this sad hap, but with despair

Hanging at his quill's point. For not a stream

Of ink can write, much less improve, this theme.

Invention highest wrought by grief or wit

Must sink with him, and on his tombstone split;

Who, like the dying Sun, tells us the light

And glory of our Day set in his Night.

Prince Henry.] Besides composing these English verses King contributed two Latin sets to *Justa Oxoniensium,* one of several Oxford *tombeaux* for the Prince who was taken away from the evil to come. The present poem appears to me (though, of course, the high-strung character of the mourning seems to have been both general and sincere) to be much more 'frigid and artificial' than the *Mrs. Anne Kirk.* Hannah gives several variants, not merely from his usual MS. but from Malone 21. I have taken those which seem to have some point.

5-6 For 'Hark ... dead.' the Malone reading is:

Death and horror wed

To vent their teeming mischief: Henry's dead.

The other MS., for l. 6, has:

Through the astonisht *world,* Henry *is* dead.

11 Malone MS. '*Compendious Eloquence* of Death', &c.

18 For the first half, Malone MS. 'lies in this narrow compass'; the other, 'throngs' for 'lies'.

An Elegy upon S. W. R.

[Sir W. Raleigh? Executed Oct. 29, 1618.]

I will not weep, for 'twere as great a sin

To shed a tear for thee, as to have bin

An actor in thy death. Thy life and age

Was but a various scene on fortune's stage,

With whom thou tugg'st and strov'st ev'n out of breath

In thy long toil: ne'er master'd till thy death;

And then, despite of trains and cruel wit,

Thou didst at once subdue malice and it.

I dare not then so blast thy memory

10As say I do lament or pity thee.

Were I to choose a subject to bestow

My pity on, he should be one as low

In spirit as desert;—that durst not die,

But rather were content by slavery

To purchase life: or I would pity those,

Thy most industrious and friendly foes;

Who, when they thought to make thee scandal's story,

Lent thee a swifter flight to Heav'n and glory;—

That thought, by cutting off some wither'd days

20(Which thou couldst spare them), to eclipse thy praise;

Yet gave it brighter foil, made thy ag'd fame

Appear more white and fair, than foul their shame:

And did promote an execution

Which (but for them) Nature and Age had done.

Such worthless things as these were only born

To live on Pity's alms (too mean for scorn).

Thou diedst an envious wonder, whose high fate

The world must still admire, scarce imitate.

S. W. R.] The initials are not in *MS.*, and the identification, though almost certain, is a conjecture of Hannah's. Almost every line fits Raleigh.

27 envious] Spenser has this sense, to which in some cases the original 'invidious' comes very close.

An Elegy upon the L. Bishop of London, John King.

[Died on Good Friday, 1621.]

Sad relic of a blessed soul! whose trust

We sealed up in this religious dust:

O do not thy low exequies suspect,

As the cheap arguments of our neglect.

'Twas a commanded duty, that thy grave

As little pride as thou thyself should have.

Therefore thy covering is an humble stone,

And but a word for thy inscription.

When those that in the same earth neighbour thee,

10Have each his chronicle and pedigree:

They have their waving pennons and their flags

(Of matches and alliance formal brags),

When thou (although from ancestors thou came,

Old as the Heptarchy, great as thy name,)

Sleep'st there inshrin'd in thy admired parts,

And hast no heraldry but thy deserts.

Yet let not them their prouder marbles boast,

For they rest with less honour, though more cost.

Go, search the world, and with your mattocks wound

20The groaning bosom of the patient ground:

Dig from the hidden veins of her dark womb

All that is rare and precious for a tomb;

Yet when much treasure, and more time, is spent,

You must grant his the nobler monument,

Whose Faith stands o'er him for a hearse, and hath

The Resurrection for his epitaph.

John King.] Hannah thought this piece in bad taste, and a neglect of the dead Bishop's wishes. As epitaphs go this seems rather severe.

8 but a word] *Resurgam.* Orig. note.

9 neighbour] In St. Paul's.

13 ancestors] The Kings of Devonshire referred to in Introduction.

Upon the death of my ever desired friend, Doctor Donne, Dean of Paul's.

[Died March 31, 1631.]

To have lived eminent, in a degree

Beyond our loftiest flights, that is, like thee;

Or t' have had too much merit is not safe;

For such excesses find no epitaph.

At common graves, we have poetic eyes,

Can melt themselves in easy elegies;

Each quill can drop his tributary verse,

And pin it, with the hatchments, to the hearse:

But at thine, poem or inscription

10(Rich soul of wit and language!) we have none;

Indeed a silence does that tomb befit,

Where is no herald left to blazon it.

Widow'd invention justly doth forbear

To come abroad, knowing thou art not here,

Late her great patron; whose prerogative

Maintain'd and cloth'd her so, as none alive

Must now presume to keep her at thy rate,

Though he the Indies for her dower estate:

Or else that awful fire, which once did burn

20In thy clear brain, now fall'n into thy urn,

Lives there to fright rude empirics from thence,

Which might profane thee by their ignorance.

Who ever writes of thee, and in a style

Unworthy such a theme, does but revile

Thy precious dust, and wake a learned spirit

Which may revenge his rapes upon thy merit.

For all a low-pitch'd fancy can devise,

Will prove, at best, but hallow'd injuries.

Thou, like the dying swan, didst lately sing

30Thy mournful dirge in audience of the king;

When pale looks, and faint accents of thy breath,

Presented so to life that piece of death,

That it was fear'd and prophesied by all

Thou thither cam'st to preach thy funeral.

O! hadst thou in an elegiac knell

Rung out unto the world thine own farewell;

And in thy high victorious numbers beat

The solemn measure of thy griev'd retreat,

Thou might'st the poet's service now have miss'd,

40As well as then thou didst prevent the priest:

And never to the world beholden be

So much as for an epitaph for thee.

I do not like the office. Nor is 't fit,

Thou, who didst lend our age such sums of wit,

Shouldst now reborrow from her bankrupt mine

That ore to bury thee, which once was thine.

Rather still leave us in thy debt; and know

(Exalted soul!) more glory 'tis to owe

Unto thy hearse what we can never pay,

50Than with embased coin those rites defray.

Commit we then thee to thyself: nor blame

Our drooping loves, which thus to thine own fame

Leave thee executor; since, but thy own,

No pen could do thee justice, nor bays crown

Thy vast desert; save that, we nothing can

Depute to be thy ashes' guardian.

So jewellers no art or metal trust

To form the diamond, but the diamond's dust.

Dr. Donne.] This is also found in some editions of Donne's *Poems* and in Walton's *Life*, and Hannah took repeated pains to record the variants. I have borrowed those which seemed of importance. King's friendship with Donne (whose executor he was) was peculiarly intimate, as Walton, a friend of both, elaborately testifies. But the greatest of the many great Deans of St. Paul's was certainly 'beyond' King's 'loftiest flights' (or, as Walton read, 'thoughts'), and the Bishop is here below even these.

8 pin it] This was literally done.

30 Refers to Donne's last sermon at Court, to his long illness, and to the ghastly pallor perpetuated by the famous picture of him in his shroud.

37 'High victorious numbers' is not bad, and the whole passage does bare justice to Donne's mastery of the graver epicede, which equalled Jonson's of the lighter.

41 beholden] Some versions have the common form 'behold*ing*'.

44 'Wit'—in that seventeenth-century sense of which Sir Henry Craik has so well defined the object—'not to excite laughter but to compel attention'— was regarded, and rightly, as Donne's special glory, and the best thing written on his death was Carew's

A king who ruled as he thought fit

The universal monarchy of Wit.

49 For 'Unto thy hearse' the Walton version reads 'Thy memory'.

An Elegy upon the most victorious King of Sweden, Gustavus Adolphus.

[Killed at the battle of Lützen, Nov. 6, 1632.]

Like a cold fatal sweat which ushers death,

My thoughts hang on me, and my lab'ring breath

Stopp'd up with sighs, my fancy, big with woes,

Feels two twinn'd mountains struggle in her throes,—

Of boundless sorrow one,—t' other of sin;—
For less let no one rate it, to begin
Where honour ends.—In great Gustavus' flame,
That style burnt out, and wasted to a name,
Does barely live with us. As when the stuff
10That fed it, fails, the taper turns to snuff,
With this poor snuff, this airy shadow, we
Of Fame and Honour must contented be;
Since from the vain grasp of our wishes fled
Their glorious substance is, now He is dead.
Speak it again, and louder, louder yet;
Else, whilst we hear the sound, we shall forget
What it delivers. Let hoarse rumour cry,
Till she so many echoes multiply,
Those may like num'rous witnesses confute
20Our unbelieving souls, that would dispute

And doubt this truth for ever. This one way
Is left our incredulity to sway;
To waken our deaf sense, and make our ears
As open and dilated as our fears;
That we may feel the blow, and feeling, grieve,
At what we would not fain, but must believe.
And in that horrid faith, behold the world
From her proud height of expectation hurl'd,
Stooping with him, as if she strove to have
30No lower centre now than Sweden's grave.
O could not all thy purchas'd victories
Like to thy fame thy flesh immortalize?

Were not thy virtue nor thy valour charms

To guard thy body from those outward harms

Which could not reach thy soul? could not thy spirit

Lend somewhat which thy frailty might inherit

From thy diviner part, that Death, nor Hate,

Nor Envy's bullets e'er could penetrate?

Could not thy early trophies in stern fight

40Torn from the Dane, the Pole, the Moscovite?

Which were thy triumph's seeds, as pledges sown,

That when thy honour's harvest was ripe grown,

With full-summ'd wing thou falcon-like wouldst fly,

And cuff the Eagle in the German sky:

Forcing his iron beak and feathers feel

They were not proof 'gainst thy victorious steel.

Could not all these protect thee? or prevail

To fright that coward Death, who oft grew pale

To look thee and thy battles in the face?

50Alas! they could not: Destiny gives place

To none; nor is it seen that princes' lives

Can saved be by their prerogatives.

No more was thine; who, clos'd in thy cold lead,

Dost from thyself a mournful lecture read

Of man's short-dated glory: learn, you kings,

You are, like him, but penetrable things;

Though you from demi-gods derive your birth

You are at best but honourable earth:

And howe'er sifted from that coarser bran,

60Which does compound and knead the common man,

Nothing's immortal, or from earth refin'd

About you, but your office and your mind.
Here then break your false glasses, which present
You greater than your Maker ever meant:
Make truth your mirror now, since you find all
That flatter you, confuted by his fall.
Yet, since it was decreed, thy life's bright Sun
Must be eclips'd ere thy full course was run,
Be proud thou didst, in thy black obsequies,
70With greater glory set, than others rise.

For in thy death, as life, thou heldest one
Most just and regular proportion.
Look how the circles drawn by compass meet
Indivisibly joined, head to feet,
And by continued points which them unite,
Grow at once circular and infinite:
So did thy Fate and Honour now contend
To match thy brave beginning with thy end.
Therefore thou hadst, instead of passing bells,
80The drums' and cannons' thunder for thy knells;
And in the field thou didst triumphing die,
Closing thy eyelids with a victory:
That so by thousands who there lost their breath,
King-like thou might'st be waited on in death.
Lived Plutarch now, and would of Caesar tell,
He could make none but Thee his parallel;
Whose tide of glory, swelling to the brim,
90Needs borrow no addition from him.
When did great Julius, in any clime,

Achieve so much, and in so small a time?
Or if he did, yet shalt Thou in that land
Single, for him, and unexampled stand.
When o'er the Germans first his Eagle towr'd,
What saw the legions which on them he pour'd?
But massy bodies, made their swords to try,
Subjects, not for his fight, but slavery.
In that so vast expanded piece of ground
100(Now Sweden's theatre and tomb), he found
Nothing worth Caesar's valour or his fear,
No conqu'ring army, nor a Tilly there,
Whose strength, nor wiles, nor practice in the war
Might the fierce torrent of thy triumphs bar,
But that thy winged sword twice made him yield,
Both from his trenches beat, and from the field.
Besides, the Roman thought he had done much,
Did he the bank of Rhenus only touch.
But though his march was bounded by the Rhine,
110Not Oder nor the Danube thee confine;
And, but thy frailty did thy fame prevent,
Thou hadst thy conquests stretch'd to such extent,
Thou might'st Vienna reach, and after span
From Mulda to the Baltic Ocean.
But death hath spann'd thee: nor must we divine
What heir thou leav'st to finish thy design,
Or who shall thee succeed, as champion
For liberty and for religion.

Thy task is done; as in a watch, the spring,

120Wound to the height, relaxes with the string:

So thy steel nerves of conquest, from their steep

Ascent declin'd, lie slack'd in thy last sleep.

Rest then, triumphant soul! for ever rest!

And, like the Phœnix in her spicy nest,

Embalm'd with thine own merit, upward fly,

Born in a cloud of perfume to the sky.

Whilst as in deathless urns, each noble mind

Treasures thy ashes which are left behind.

And if perhaps no Cassiopeian spark

130(Which in the North did thy first rising mark)

Shine o'er thy hearse; the breath of our just praise

Shall to the firmament thy virtues raise;

Then fix, and kindle them into a star,

Whose influence may crown thy glorious war.

——*O Famâ ingens, ingentior armis,*

Rex Gustave, quibus Coelo te laudibus aequem?

Virgil. *Aeneid. lib. 2.* [11?]

Gustavus Adolphus.] This piece had been previously printed in the *Swedish Intelligencer*, 1633, with other elegies on the subject, one of which (in Malone MS. 21) is also ascribed to King, but without any other evidence, and (as Hannah seems to be right in thinking) very improbably. He gives some variants, only two of which seem to me important enough to reproduce. There are also versions in Rawlinson Poetic MS. 26, fol. 51, and 160, fol. 39.

4 throes] Orig. 'thro*w*s'.

6-7 Hannah in his note, though in his text he had followed *1657*, as above, prefers the reading of the *Intelligencer*—a full-stop at 'it', and 'To begin', which is to a certain extent supported by a capitalized 'To' in his MS., though there is not a full-stop. He has two notes on the subject, and for a moment I was perplexed. But I feel certain that the *1657* text is right. Hannah's parallel from King's prose, 'I begin there where all must end', is specious, but not convincing. On the other hand, 'To begin, &c.' is wanted to complete 'for less' and to explain 'sin'. Honour, as the next sentence further tells us, perished with Gustavus, and it is a solecism to attempt to continue it in verse. This is, in the Archdeacon's words elsewhere, 'frigid and artificial' enough; but it is also sufficiently 'metaphysical'.

10 Orig. has full-stop at 'snuff', but this (which Hannah keeps and does not comment on) leaves nothing to complete 'as'.

11 airy] For the 'ayerie' of edition and Malone MS., the *Intelligencer*, and Rawlinson MS. 160 have 'fiery'—I think, in the context, better.

96. Orig. note. *Magis triumphati quam victi.* Tacit. *de Mor. Ger.*

135-7 The end quotation (from *Aen.* xi. 124-5) is not in MS.

To my Noble and Judicious Friend Sir Henry Blount upon his Voyage.

Sir, I must ever own myself to be

Possess'd with human curiosity

Of seeing all that might the sense invite

By those two baits of profit and delight:

And since I had the wit to understand

The terms of native or of foreign land;

I have had strong and oft desires to tread

Some of those voyages which I have read.

Yet still so fruitless have my wishes prov'd,

10That from my Country's smoke I never mov'd:

Nor ever had the fortune (though design'd)

To satisfy the wand'rings of my mind.

Therefore at last I did with some content,

Beguile myself in time, which others spent;

Whose art to provinces small lines allots,

And represents large kingdoms but in spots.

Thus by Ortelius and Mercator's aid

Through most of the discover'd world I stray'd.

I could with ease double the Southern Cape,

20And in my passage Afric's wonders take:

Then with a speed proportion'd to the scale
Northward again, as high as Zemla sail.
Oft hath the travel of my eye outrun
(Though I sat still) the journey of the Sun:
Yet made an end, ere his declining beams
Did nightly quench themselves in Thetis' streams.
Oft have I gone through Egypt in a day,
Not hinder'd by the droughts of Lybia;
In which, for lack of water, tides of sand
30By a dry deluge overflow the land.
There I the Pyramids and Cairo see,
Still famous for the wars of Tomombee,
And its own greatness; whose immured sense
Takes forty miles in the circumference.
Then without guide, or stronger caravan
Which might secure the wild Arabian,
Back through the scorched deserts pass, to seek
Once the world's Lord, now the beslaved Greek,
Made by a Turkish yoke and fortune's hate
40In language as in mind, degenerate.
And here all wrapp'd in pity and amaze
I stand, whilst I upon the Sultan gaze;
To think how he with pride and rapine fir'd
So vast a territory hath acquir'd;
And by what daring steps he did become
The Asian fear, and scourge of Christendom:
How he achiev'd, and kept, and by what arts

He did concentre those divided parts;

And how he holds that monstrous bulk in awe,

50By settled rules of tyranny, not Law:

So rivers large and rapid streams began,

Swelling from drops into an Ocean.

Sure who e'er shall the just extraction bring

Of this gigantic power from the spring;

Must there confess a higher Ordinance

Did it for terror to the earth advance.

For mark how 'mongst a lawless straggling crew,

Made up of Arab, Saracen, and Jew,

The world's disturber, faithless Mahomet

60Did by impostures an opinion get:

O'er whom he first usurps as Prince, and than

As prophet does obtrude his Alcoran.

Next, how fierce Ottoman his claim made good

From that unblest religion, by blood;

Whilst he the Eastern kingdoms did deface,

To make their ruin his proud Empire's base.

Then like a comet blazing in the skies,

How death-portending Amurath did rise,

When he his horned crescents did display

70Upon the fatal plains of Servia;

And farther still his sanguine tresses spread,

Till Croya life and conquests limited.

Lastly, how Mahomet thence styl'd the Great,

Made Constantine's his own Imperial seat;

After that he in one victorious bond

Two Empires grasp'd, of Greece and Trebizond.

This, and much more than this, I gladly read,

Where my relators it had storyed;

Besides that people's manners and their rites,

80Their warlike discipline and order'd fights;

Their desp'rate valour, hard'ned by the sense

Of unavoided Fate and Providence:

Their habit, and their houses, who confer

Less cost on them than on their sepulchre:

Their frequent washings, and the several bath

Each Meschit to itself annexed hath:

What honour they unto the Mufty give,

What to the Sovereign under whom they live:

What quarter Christians have; how just and free

90To inoffensive travellers they be:

Though I confess, like stomachs fed with news,

I took them in for wonder, not for use,

Till your experienc'd and authentic pen

Taught me to know the places and the men;

And made all those suspected truths become

Undoubted now, and clear as axiom.

Sir, for this work more than my thanks is due;

I am at once inform'd and cur'd by you.

So that, were I assur'd I should live o'er

100My periods of time run out before;

Ne'er needed my erratic wish transport

Me from my native lists to that resort,

Where many at outlandish marts unlade

Ingenuous manners, and do only trade

For vices and the language. By your eyes
I here have made my full discoveries;
And all your countries so exactly seen,
As in the voyage I had sharer been.
By this you make me so; and the whole land
110Your debtor: which can only understand
How much she owes you, when her sons shall try
The solid depths of your rare history,

Which looks above our gadders' trivial reach,
The commonplace of travellers, who teach
But table-talk; and seldomly aspire
Beyond the country's diet or attire;
Whereas your piercing judgement does relate
The policy and manage of each State.
And since she must here without envy grant
120That you have further journey'd the Levant
Than any noble spirit by her bred
Hath in your way as yet adventured;
I cannot less in justice from her look,
Than that she henceforth canonize your book
A rule to all her travellers, and you
The brave example; from whose equal view
Each knowing reader may himself direct,
How he may go abroad to some effect,
And not for form: what distance and what trust
130In those remoter parts observe he must:
How he with jealous people may converse,
Yet take no hurt himself by that commerce.

So when he shall embark'd in dangers be,

Which wit and wary caution not foresee;

If he partake your valour and your brain,

He may perhaps come safely off again,

As you have done; though not so richly fraught

As this return hath to our staple brought.

I know your modesty shuns vulgar praise,

140And I have none to bring; but only raise

This monument of Honour and of Love,

Which your long known deserts so far improve,

They leave me doubtful in what style to end,

Whether more your admirer or your friend.

Sir Henry Blount, &c.] Blount (1602-82) was of Trinity College, Oxford, published his *Voyage to the Levant* in 1636, and was knighted four years later. He was a good Royalist in the early days of the Rebellion, but something of a renegade later. His book has been variously judged, but was very popular, and was translated into more than one foreign language.

61 'Than' for 'then' as often.

76 Orig. 'Tr*a*bezond', which at any rate keeps closer than the usual form to Trapezus.

86 'Meschit' = of course 'mosque'. The form seems to be nearest to the Spanish *mezquita*.

102 lists] Here in the sense (akin to the flannelly one) of boundary, as in *Hamlet*, IV. v. 99, 'The ocean, overpeering of his *list*', and several other Shakespearian places.

124-5 canonize ... rule] A play of words.

To my honoured Friend Mr. George Sandys.

It is, Sir, a confess'd intrusion here

That I before your labours do appear,

Which no loud herald need, that may proclaim

Or seek acceptance, but the Author's fame.

Much less that should this happy work commend,

Whose subject is its licence, and doth send

It to the world to be receiv'd and read,

Far as the glorious beams of truth are spread.

Nor let it be imagin'd that I look

10Only with custom's eye upon your book;

Or in this service that 'twas my intent

T' exclude your person from your argument:

I shall profess, much of the love I owe,

Doth from the root of our extraction grow;

To which though I can little contribute,

Yet with a natural joy I must impute

To our tribe's honour, what by you is done

Worthy the title of a Prelate's son.

And scarcely have two brothers farther borne

20A father's name, or with more value worn

Their own, than two of you; whose pens and feet

Have made the distant points of Heav'n to meet;

He by exact discoveries of the West,

Yourself by painful travels in the East

Some more like you might pow'rfully confute

Th' opposers of Priests' marriage by the fruit.

And (since 'tis known for all their straight vow'd life,

They like the sex in any style but wife)

Cause them to change their cloister for that state

30Which keeps men chaste by vows legitimate:

Nor shame to father their relations,

Or under nephews' names disguise their sons.

This child of yours, born without spurious blot,

And fairly midwiv'd as it was begot,

Doth so much of the parent's goodness wear,

You may be proud to own it for your heir.

Whose choice acquits you from the common sin

Of such, who finish worse than they begin:

You mend upon yourself, and your last strain

40Does of your first the start in judgement gain;

Since what in curious travel was begun,

You here conclude in a devotion.

Where in delightful raptures we descry

As in a map, Sion's chorography

Laid out in so direct and smooth a line,

Men need not go about through Palestine:

Who seek Christ here will the straight road prefer,

As nearer much than by the Sepulchre.

For not a limb grows here, but is a path;

50Which in God's City the blest centre hath:

And doth so sweetly on each passion strike,

The most fantastic taste will somewhat like.

To the unquiet soul Job still from hence

Pleads in th' example of his patience.

The mortified may hear the wise King preach,

When his repentance made him fit to teach.

Nor shall the singing Sisters be content

To chant at home the Act of Parliament,

Turn'd out of reason into rhyme by one

60Free of his trade, though not of Helicon,

Who did in his poetic zeal contend

Others' edition by a worse to mend.

Here are choice Hymns and Carols for the glad,

With melancholy Dirges for the sad:

And David (as he could his skill transfer)

Speaks like himself by an interpreter.

Your Muse rekindled hath the Prophet's fire,

And tun'd the strings of his neglected lyre;

Making the note and ditty so agree,

70They now become a perfect harmony.

I must confess, I have long wish'd to see

The Psalms reduc'd to this conformity:

Grieving the songs of Sion should be sung

In phrase not diff'ring from a barbarous tongue.

As if, by custom warranted, we may

Sing that to God we would be loath to say.

Far be it from my purpose to upbraid

Their honest meaning, who first offer made

That book in metre to compile, which you

80Have mended in the form, and built anew:

And it was well, considering the time,

Which hardly could distinguish verse and rhyme.

But now the language, like the Church, hath won

More lustre since the Reformation;

None can condemn the wish or labour spent

Good matter in good words to represent.

Yet in this jealous age some such there be,

So without cause afraid of novelty,

They would not (were it in their pow'r to choose)

90An old ill practice for a better lose.

Men who a rustic plainness so affect,

They think God served best by their neglect.

Holding the cause would be profan'd by it,

Were they at charge of learning or of wit.

And therefore bluntly (what comes next) they bring

Coarse and unstudied stuffs for offering;

Which like th' old Tabernacle's cov'ring are,

Made up of badgers' skins, and of goat's hair.

But these are paradoxes they must use

100Their sloth and bolder ignorance t'excuse.

Who would not laugh at one will naked go,

'Cause in old hangings truth is pictur'd so?

Though plainness be reputed honour's note,

They mantles use to beautify the coat;

So that a curious (unaffected) dress

Adds much unto the body's comeliness:

And wheresoe'er the subject's best, the sense

Is better'd by the speaker's eloquence.

But, Sir, to you I shall no trophy raise

110From other men's detraction or dispraise:

That jewel never had inherent worth,

Which ask'd such foils as these to set it forth.

If any quarrel your attempt or style,

Forgive them; their own folly they revile.

Since, 'gainst themselves, their factious envy shall

Allow this work of yours canonical.

Nor may you fear the Poet's common lot,

Read, and commended, and then quite forgot:

The brazen mines and marble rocks shall waste,

120When your foundation will unshaken last.

'Tis Fame's best pay, that you your labours see

By their immortal subject crowned be.

For ne'er was writer in oblivion hid

Who firm'd his name on such a Pyramid.

Mr. George Sandys.] These verses appeared as commendatory to Sandys' well-known *Paraphrase upon the Divine Psalms*, 1648. Sandys was not only a friend of King (as of all his group), but, according to l. 14 of this piece, a relation: the exact connexion, however, was unknown to Hannah and Hooper, and is to me. Indeed, l. 18 might be taken to mean that we were not to look further for 'extraction' than to the fact that they were both sons of bishops. Hannah saw this, but drew the inference somewhat too positively.

Mr. Percy Simpson has found the following variants in Sandys' own book:

25 might] would.

27 straight vow'd] strait-vow'd.

57-62 *absent.*

64 With] And skill] Art.

89 They would by no means (had they power to choose).

90 practice] Custom.

96 stuffs] stuff.

116 Allow] Confess.

King may have retouched the piece.

23 Orig. note: [Sir Edwin Sandys' survey of Religion in the West] More properly entitled *Europae Speculum* (1559).

53 seq. In the original there are side-notes: 'Job', 'Ecclesiastes', 'The Act of Parliament for Public Thanksgiving on the fifth of November, set to a tune by H. Dod a tradesman of London, at the end of his Psalms, which stole from the Press Anno Domini 1620'; 'Hymns', 'Lamentations', 'Psalms', referring to other Paraphrases of Sandys on the various books named, and (in the third place) on certain Songs selected from other parts of the Bible. The unfortunate 'H. Dod a tradesman' may have had his Manes refreshed by a notice in the *D.N.B.*

70 It was too early for King to recognize, as has been done since, the reason of the 'perfect harmony' he relished as a fact in Sandys. That poet was one of the earliest after Fairfax, and probably before Beaumont or Waller, to master (though not always to practise) the stopped antithetic couplet which was conquering, and to conquer, public favour.

71 It were much to be desired (though Hannah did not think so) that King had allowed his wishes to be satisfied by Sandys' performance, without attempting competition.

79 The reference is, of course, to the universally heard of, but perhaps by extremely few read, 'Sternhold and Hopkins'. The actual terms of King's criticism are not very happy, but nobody then knew, or easily could know, much about literary history. It was a fifteenth- rather than a sixteenth-century fault 'hardly to distinguish *verse* and *rhyme*'. Where Sternhold and Hopkins— in common with much greater men, from Wyatt to Gascoigne—sometimes went wrong, was in their inability to attain anything but a 'butterwoman's rank to market'—a sing-song and soulless uniformity of cadence, and (a sin more specially their own) in the hopeless dullness and drabness of their diction.

The Woes of Esay.

Woe to the worldly men, whose covetous

Ambition labours to join house to house,

Lay field to field, till their enclosures edge

The plain, girdling a country with one hedge:

That leave no place unbought, no piece of earth

Which they will not engross, making a dearth

Of all inhabitants, until they stand

Unneighbour'd, as unblest, within their land.

This sin cries in God's ear, who hath decreed

10The ground they sow shall not return the seed.

They that unpeopled countries to create

Themselves sole Lords,—made many desolate

To build up their own house,—shall find at last

Ruin and fearful desolation cast

Upon themselves. Their mansion shall become

A desert, and their palace prove a tomb.

Their vines shall barren be, their land yield tares;

Their house shall have no dwellers, they no heirs.

Woe unto those, that with the morning Sun

20 Rise to drink wine, and sit till he have run

His weary course; not ceasing until night

Have quench'd their understanding with the light:

Whose raging thirst, like fire, will not be tam'd,

The more they pour, the more they are inflam'd.

Woe unto them that only mighty are

To wage with wine; in which unhappy war

They who the glory of the day have won,

Must yield them foil'd and vanquish'd by the tun.

Men that live thus, as if they liv'd in jest,

30 Fooling their time with music and a feast;

That did exile all sounds from their soft ear

But of the harp, must this sad discord hear

Compos'd in threats. The feet which measures tread

Shall in captivity be fettered:

Famine shall scourge them for their vast excess;

And Hell revenge their monstrous drunkenness;

Which hath enlarg'd itself to swallow such,

Whose throats ne'er knew enough, though still too much.

Woe unto those that countenance a sin,

40 Siding with vice, that it may credit win

By their unhallow'd vote: that do benight

The truth with error, putting dark for light,

And light for dark; that call an evil good,
And would by vice have virtue understood:
That with their frown can sour an honest cause,
Or sweeten any bad by their applause.
That justify the wicked for reward;
And, void of moral goodness or regard,
Plot with detraction to traduce the fame
50Of him whose merit hath enroll'd his name
Among the just. Therefore God's vengeful ire
Glows on his people, and becomes a fire,
Whose greedy and exalted flame shall burn,
Till they like straw or chaff to nothing turn.
Because they have rebell'd against the right,
To God and Law perversely opposite,
As plants which Sun nor showers did ever bless,
So shall their root convert to rottenness;
And their succession's bud, in which they trust,
60Shall (like Gomorrah's fruit) moulder to dust.
Woe unto those that, drunk with self-conceit,
Value their own designs at such a rate
Which human wisdom cannot reach; that sit
Enthron'd, as sole monopolists of wit;
That outlook reason, and suppose the eye
Of Nature blind to their discovery,
Whilst they a title make to understand
Whatever secret's bosom'd in the land.
But God shall imp their pride, and let them see
70They are but fools in a sublime degree:

He shall bring down and humble those proud eyes,

In which false glasses only they look'd wise;

That all the world may laugh, and learn by it,

There is no folly to pretended wit.

Woe unto those that draw iniquity

With cords, and by a vain security

Lengthen the sinful trace, till their own chain

Of many links, form'd by laborious pain,

Do pull them into Hell; that, as with lines

80And cart-ropes, drag on their unwilling crimes:

Who, rather than they will commit no sin,

Tempt all occasions to let it in.

As if there were no God, who must exact

The strict account for every vicious fact;

Nor judgement after death. If any be,

Let him make speed (say they), that we may see.

Why is his work retarded by delay?

Why doth himself thus linger on the way?

If there be any judge, or future doom,

90Let It and Him with speed together come.

Unhappy men, that challenge and defy

The coming of that dreadful Majesty!

Better by much for you, he did reverse

His purposed sentence on the Universe;

Or that the creeping minutes might adjourn

Those flames in which you, with the earth, must burn;

That time's revolting hand could lag the year,

And so put back his day which is too near.

Behold his signs advanc'd like colours fly,

100To tell the world that his approach is nigh;

And in a furious march, he's coming on

Swift as the raging inundation,

To scour the sinful world; 'gainst which is bent

Artillery that never can be spent:

Bows strung with vengeance, and flame-feather'd darts

Headed with death, to wound transgressing hearts;

His chariot wheels wrapp'd in the whirlwind's gyre,

His horses hoov'd with flint, and shod with fire:

In which amaze, where'er they fix their eye,

110Or on the melting earth, or up on high,

To seek Heaven's shrunk lights, nothing shall appear,

But night and horror in their hemisphere:

Nor shall th' affrighted sense more objects know

Than dark'ned skies above, and Hell below.

The Woes of Esay.] It may seem strange that a man of poetical velleities, with the magnificent range of choice open to him in the Book of Isaiah, should choose these 'Woes' for verse-paraphrase. But the fact is interesting as combining with others, which have been pointed out here and there already, to show that King, at one time of his life, *had* leanings to that Puritan-popular temper which, from the days of Langland downwards, had shown itself in England. The couplet verse has some vigour.

84 The original apostrophation (kept by Hannah) of 'every' is 'e'ry'— interesting to compare with the common forms of 'e're' for 'ever' and 'ne're' for 'never'. *N. E. D.* traces it to the fifteenth century, and notes an eighteenth-century extension to 'e'ery'.

An Essay on Death and a Prison.

A prison is in all things like a grave,

Where we no better privileges have

Than dead men, nor so good. The soul once fled

Lives freer now, than when she was cloistered

In walls of flesh; and though she organs want

To act her swift designs, yet all will grant

Her faculties more clear, now separate,

Than if the same conjunction, which of late

Did marry her to earth, had stood in force,

10Uncapable of death, or of divorce:

But an imprison'd mind, though living, dies,

And at one time feels two captivities;

A narrow dungeon which her body holds,

But narrower body which herself enfolds.

Whilst I in prison lie, nothing is free,

Nothing enlarg'd, but thought and misery;

Though every chink be stopp'd, the doors close barr'd,

Despite of walls and locks, through every ward

These have their issues forth; may take the air,

20Though not for health, but only to compare

How wretched those men are who freedom want,

By such as never suffer'd a restraint.

In which unquiet travel could I find

Aught that might settle my distemper'd mind,

Or of some comfort make discovery,

It were a voyage well employ'd: but I,

Like our raw travellers that cross the seas

To fetch home fashions, or some worse disease,

Instead of quiet, a new torture bring

30Home t' afflict me, malice and murmuring.

What is't I envy not? no dog nor fly

But my desires prefer, and wish were I;

For they are free, or, if they were like me,

They had no sense to know calamity.

But in the grave no sparks of envy live,

No hot comparisons that causes give

Of quarrel, or that our affections move

Any condition, save their own, to love.

There are no objects there but shades and night,

40And yet that darkness better than the light.

There lives a silent harmony; no jar

Or discord can that sweet soft consort mar.

The grave's deaf ear is clos'd against all noise

Save that which rocks must hear, the angel's voice:

Whose trump shall wake the world, and raise up men

Who in earth's bosom slept, bed-rid till then.

What man then would, who on death's pillow slumbers,

Be re-inspired with life, though golden numbers

Of bliss were pour'd into his breast; though he

50Were sure in change to gain a monarchy?

A monarch's glorious state compar'd with his,

Less safe, less free, less firm, less quiet is.

For ne'er was any Prince advanc'd so high

That he was out of reach of misery:

Never did story yet a law report

To banish fate or sorrow from his Court;

Where ere he moves, by land, or through the main,

These go along, sworn members of his train.

But he whom the kind earth hath entertain'd,

60Hath in her womb a sanctuary gain'd,

Whose charter and protection arm him so,

That he is privileg'd from future woe.

The coffin 's a safe harbour, where he rides

Land-bound, below cross winds, or churlish tides.

For grief, sprung up with life, was man's half-brother,

Fed by the taste, brought forth by sin, the mother.

And since the first seduction of the wife,

God did decree to grief a lease for life;

Which patent in full force continue must,

70Till man that disobey'd revert to dust.

So that life's sorrows, ratifi'd by God,

Cannot expire, or find their period,

Until the soul and body disunite,

And by two diff'rent ways from each take flight.

But they dissolved once, our woes disband,

Th' assurance cancell'd by one fatal hand;

Soon as the passing bell proclaims me dead,

My sorrows sink with me, lie buried

In the same heap of dust, the self-same urn

80Doth them and me alike to nothing turn.

If then of these I might election make

Whether I would refuse, and whether take,

Rather than like a sullen anchorite

I would live cas'd in stone, and learn to write

A *Prisoner's story*, which might steal some tears

From the sad eyes of him that reads or hears;

Give me a peaceful death, and let me meet

My freedom seal'd up in my winding sheet.

Death is the pledge of rest, and with one bail

90Two prisons quits, the Body and the Jail.

An Essay.] This piece stands to some work of Donne's much as others of King's do to the lyrics of the greater poet. The couplets are more enjambed than in *The Woes of Esay*, and the metaphysicality is of the satiric kind. It should not be needful, but may be well, to say that King had no actual experience of prisons. On the other side of the matter the piece might, but by no means need, belong to the series connected with his wife's death.

The Labyrinth.

Life is a crooked labyrinth, and we

Are daily lost in that obliquity.

'Tis a perplexed circle, in whose round

Nothing but sorrows and new sins abound.

How is the faint impression of each good

Drown'd in the vicious channel of our blood?

Whose ebbs and tides by their vicissitude

Both our great Maker and ourselves delude.

O wherefore is the most discerning eye

10Unapt to make its own discovery?

Why is the clearest and best judging mind

In her own ills' prevention dark and blind?

Dull to advise, to act precipitate,

We scarce think what to do, but when too late.

Or if we think, that fluid thought, like seed,

Rots there to propagate some fouler deed.

Still we repent and sin, sin and repent;

We thaw and freeze, we harden and relent.

Those fires, which cool'd to-day, the morrow's heat

20Rekindles. Thus frail nature does repeat

What she unlearnt, and still, by learning on,

Perfects her lesson of confusion.

Sick soul! what cure shall I for thee devise,

Whose leprous state corrupts all remedies?

What medicine or what cordial can be got

For thee, who poison'st thy best antidote?

Repentance is thy bane, since thou by it

Only reviv'st the fault thou didst commit.

Nor griev'st thou for the past, but art in pain,

30For fear thou mayst not act it o'er again.

So that thy tears, like water spilt on lime,

Serve not to quench, but to advance the crime.

My blessed Saviour! unto thee I fly

For help against this homebred tyranny.

Thou canst true sorrows in my soul imprint,

And draw contrition from a breast of flint.

Thou canst reverse this labyrinth of sin,

My wild affects and actions wander in.

O guide my faith! and, by thy grace's clew,

40Teach me to hunt that kingdom at the view

Where true joys reign, which like their day shall last;

Those never clouded, nor that overcast.

The Labyrinth.] 12 her] our *Malone MS. 22.*

26 Orig. 'anti*dot*', on the eye-[and ear]-system as before.

Being waked out of my sleep by a snuff of candle which offended me, I thus thought.

Perhaps 'twas but conceit. Erroneous sense!

Thou art thine own distemper and offence.

Imagine then, that sick unwholesome steam

Was thy corruption breath'd into a dream.

Nor is it strange, when we in charnels dwell,

That all our thoughts of earth and frailty smell.

Man is a Candle, whose unhappy light

Burns in the day, and smothers in the night.

10And as you see the dying taper waste,

By such degrees does he to darkness haste.

Here is the diff'rence: When our bodies' lamps

Blinded by age, or chok'd with mortal damps,

Now faint, and dim, and sickly 'gin to wink,

And in their hollow sockets lowly sink;

When all our vital fires ceasing to burn,

Leave nought but snuff and ashes in our urn:

God will restore those fallen lights again,

And kindle them to an eternal flame.

Sic Vita.

KING AND BEAUMONT.

[I.]

Like to the falling of a star;

Or as the flights of eagles are;

Or like the fresh springs gaudy hue;

Or silver drops of morning dew;

Or like a wind that chafes the flood;

Or bubbles which on water stood;

Even such is man, whose borrow'd light

Is straight call'd in, and paid to night.

The wind blows out; the bubble dies;

10The Spring entomb'd in Autumn lies;

The dew dries up; the star is shot;

The flight is past; and man forgot.

WASTELL.

[II.]

Like as the damask rose you see;

Or like the blossom on the tree;

Or like the dainty flower of May;

Or like the morning to the day;

Or like the Sun; or like the shade;

Or like the gourd which Jonas had;

Even such is man, whose thread is spun,

Drawn out, and cut, and so is done.

The rose withers; the blossom blasteth;

The flower fades; the morning hasteth;

The sun sets; the shadow flies;

The gourd consumes; and man he dies.

[III.]

Like to the Grass that's newly sprung;

Or like a tale that's new begun;

Or like the bird that's here to-day;

Or like the pearled dew of May;

Or like an hour; or like a span;

Or like the singing of a swan;

Even such is man, who lives by breath,

Is here, now there, in life, and death.

The grass withers; the tale is ended;

The bird is flown; the dew's ascended;

The hour is short; the span not long;

The swan's near death; man's life is done.

[IV.]

Like to the bubble in the brook;
Or, in a glass, much like a look;
Or like a shuttle in weaver's hand;
Or like the writing on the sand;
Or like a thought; or like a dream;
Or like the gliding of the stream;
Even such is man, who lives by breath,
Is here, now there, in life, and death.
The bubble's cut; the look's forgot;
The shuttle's flung; the writing's blot;
The thought is past; the dream is gone;
The water glides; man's life is done.

[V.]

Like to an arrow from the bow;
Or like swift course of watery flow;
Or like the time twixt flood and ebb;
Or like the spider's tender web;
Or like a race; or like a goal;
Or like the dealing of a dole;
Even such is man whose brittle state
Is always subject unto fate.
The arrow's shot; the flood soon spent;
The time no time; the web soon rent;
The race soon run; the goal soon won;
The dole soon dealt; man's life first done.

[VI.]

Like to the lightning from the sky;

Or like a post that quick doth hie;

Or like a quaver in short song;

Or like a journey three days long;

Or like the snow when summer's come;

Or like the pear; or like the plum;

Even such is man, who heaps up sorrow,

Lives but this day, and dies to-morrow,

The lightning's past; the post must go;

The song is short; the journey's so;

The pear doth rot; the plum doth fall;

The snow dissolves; and so must all.

QUARLES.

Like to the damask Rose you see, &c.

[VII.]

Like to the blaze of fond delight;

Or like a morning clear and bright;

Or like a post; or like a shower;

Or like the pride of Babel's Tower;

Or like the hour that guides the time;

Or like to beauty in her prime;

Even such is man, whose glory lends

His life a blaze or two, and ends.

Delights vanish; the morn o'er casteth;

The frost breaks; the shower hasteth;

The Tower falls; the hour spends;

The beauty fades; and man's life ends.

BROWNE.

[VIII.]

Like to a silkworm of one year;

Or like a wronged lover's tear;

Or on the waves a rudder's dint;

Or like the sparkles of a flint:

Or like to little cakes perfum'd;

Or fireworks made to be consum'd;

Even such is man, and all that trust

In weak and animated dust.

The silkworm droops; the tear's soon shed;

The ship's way lost; the sparkle dead;

The cake is burnt; the firework done;

And man as these as quickly gone.

STRODE.

[IX.]

Like to the rolling of an eye:

Or like a star shot from the sky;

Or like a hand upon a clock;

Or like a wave upon a rock;

Or like a wind; or like a flame;

Or like false news which people frame;

Even such is man, of equal stay

Whose very growth leads to decay.

The eye is turned; the star down bendeth;

The hand doth steal; the wave descendeth;

The wind is spent; the flame unfir'd;

The news disprov'd; man's life expir'd.

[X.]

Like to an eye which sleep doth chain;

Or like a star whose fall we faine [= feign];

Or like a shade on A[t]haz' watch:

Or like a wave which gulfs do snatch;

Or like a wind or flame that's past;

Or smother'd news confirm'd at last;

Even so man's life, pawn'd in the grave,

Waits for a rising it must have

The eye still sees; the star still blazeth;

The shade goes back; the wave escapeth;

The wind is turn'd, the flame reviv'd,

The news renew'd; and man new liv'd.

Sic Vita.] On this famous piece see Introduction. Only the first form is attributed to King and appears in his *Poems*; but it also appears not merely in the singular higgledy-piggledy called the poems of Francis Beaumont, 1653, but in the earlier and better edition of 1640. Simon Wastell was a schoolmaster who had been at Queen's College, Oxford; and who in 1629 appended these sets of verses to a book then entitled *Microbiblion*. The first is claimed by Quarles, who also wrote another in the form. William Browne's version was not published till 1815, and the authors of the two from the Malone MS. are unknown. The group is probably the palmary example in English of that coterie-and school-verse which distinguished the seventeenth century. The King-Beaumont form is certainly the best and probably the original. (It will be observed that X is *palinodic* to the others. It is, *with* IX, attributed as a single piece to Strode and entitled 'On Death and Resurrection' in MS. Malone 16, fol. 35, and Dobell's *Poetical Works of W. Strode*).

My Midnight Meditation.

Ill busi'd man! why shouldst thou take such care

To lengthen out thy life's short kalendar?

When every spectacle thou look'st upon

Presents and acts thy execution.

Each drooping season and each flower doth cry,

Fool! as I fade and wither, thou must die.

The beating of thy pulse (when thou art well)

Is just the tolling of thy passing bell:

Night is thy hearse, whose sable canopy

10Covers alike deceased day and thee.

And all those weeping dews which nightly fall,

Are but the tears shed for thy funeral.

My Midnight Meditation.] 11 which] *MS.* 'that'. In *Parnassus Biceps*, p. 80, with title 'On Man': ll. 9-10 are absent from this version. Mr. Thorn-Drury thinks that this is Dr. *John* King's (so ascribed in Malone MS. 21, fol. 2*b*, and Mr. Dobell's MS. of Strode).

A Penitential Hymn.

Hearken, O God, unto a wretch's cries,

Who low dejected at thy footstool lies.

Let not the clamour of my heinous sin

Drown my requests, which strive to enter in

At those bright gates, which always open stand

To such as beg remission at thy hand.

Too well I know, if thou in rigour deal,

I can nor pardon ask, nor yet appeal:

To my hoarse voice, heaven will no audience grant,

10But deaf as brass, and hard as adamant

Beat back my words; therefore I bring to thee

A gracious Advocate to plead for me.

What though my leprous soul no Jordan can

Recure, nor floods of the lav'd Ocean

Make clean? yet from my Saviour's bleeding side

Two large and medicinable rivers glide.

Lord, wash me where those streams of life abound,

And new Bethesdas flow from ev'ry wound.

If I this precious lather may obtain,

20I shall not then despair for any stain;

I need no Gilead's balm, nor oil, nor shall

I for the purifying hyssop call:

My spots will vanish in His purple flood,

And crimson there turn white, though wash'd with blood.

See, Lord! with broken heart and bended knee,

How I address my humble suit to Thee;

O give that suit admittance to Thy ears,

Which floats to Thee, not in my words, but tears:

And let my sinful soul this mercy crave,

30Before I fall into the silent grave.

A Penitential Hymn.] This piece is referred to by Anthony Wood as one of several 'anthems'. It was, he tells us, intended for Lenten use, and set by Dr. John Wilson, gentleman of the Chapel Royal. To this Dr. Wilson, Hannah thought that his collated MS. copy of King's *Poems*, which bears the name, had belonged, additional evidence being found in the curious fact that the Hymn appears in that copy out of order, and first.

An Elegy occasioned by Sickness.

Well did the Prophet ask, *Lord, what is Man?*

Implying by the question none can

But God resolve the doubt, much less define

What elements this child of dust combine.

Man is a stranger to himself, and knows

Nothing so naturally as his woes.

He loves to travel countries, and confer

The sides of Heaven's vast diameter:

Delights to sit in Nile or Bætis' lap,

10Before he hath sail'd over his own map;

By which means he returns, his travel spent,

Less knowing of himself than when he went.

Who knowledge hunt kept under foreign locks,

May bring home wit to hold a paradox,

Yet be fools still. Therefore, might I advise,

I would inform the soul before the eyes:

Make man into his proper optics look,

And so become the student and the book.

With his conception, his first leaf, begin;

20What is he there but complicated sin?

When riper time, and the approaching birth

Ranks him among the creatures of the earth,

His wailing mother sends him forth to greet

The light, wrapp'd in a bloody winding sheet;

As if he came into the world to crave

No place to dwell in, but bespeak a grave.

Thus like a red and tempest-boding morn

His dawning is: for being newly born

He hails th' ensuing storm with shrieks and cries,

30And fines for his admission with wet eyes.

How should that plant, whose leaf is bath'd in tears,

Bear but a bitter fruit in elder years?

Just such is this, and his maturer age

Teems with event more sad than the presage.

For view him higher, when his childhood's span

Is raised up to youth's meridian;

When he goes proudly laden with the fruit

Which health, or strength, or beauty contribute;

Yet,—as the mounted cannon batters down

40The towers and goodly structures of a town,—

So one short sickness will his force defeat,

And his frail citadel to rubbish beat.

How does a dropsy melt him to a flood,

Making each vein run water more than blood?

A colic wracks him like a northern gust,

And raging fevers crumble him to dust.

In which unhappy state he is made worse

By his diseases than his Maker's curse.

God said in *toil and sweat* he should earn bread,

50And without labour not be nourished:

There, though like ropes of falling dew, his sweat

Hangs on his lab'ring brow, he cannot eat.

Thus are his sins scourg'd in opposed themes,

And luxuries reveng'd by their extremes.

He who in health could never be content

With rarities fetch'd from each element,

Is now much more afflicted to delight

His tasteless palate, and lost appetite.

Besides, though God ordain'd, that with the light

60Man should begin his work, yet he made night

For his repose, in which the weary sense

Repairs itself by rest's soft recompense.

But now his watchful nights and troubled days

Confused heaps of fear and fancy raise.

His chamber seems a loose and trembling mine;

His pillow quilted with a porcupine;

Pain makes his downy couch sharp thorns appear,

And ev'ry feather prick him like a spear.
Thus, when all forms of death about him keep,
70He copies death in any form, but sleep.
Poor walking-clay! hast thou a mind to know
To what unblest beginnings thou dost owe
Thy wretched self? fall sick a while, and than
Thou wilt conceive the pedigree of Man.
Learn shalt thou from thine own anatomy,
That earth his mother, worms his sisters be.
That he's a short-liv'd vapour upward wrought,
And by corruption unto nothing brought.
A stagg'ring meteor by cross planets beat,
80Which often reels and falls before his set;

A tree which withers faster than it grows;
A torch puff'd out by ev'ry wind that blows;
A web of forty weeks spun forth in pain,
And in a moment ravell'd out again.
This is the model of frail man: then say
That his duration's only for a day:
And in that day more fits of changes pass,
Than atoms run in the turn'd hour-glass.
So that th' incessant cares which life invade
90Might for strong truth their heresy persuade,
Who did maintain that human souls are sent
Into the body for their punishment:
At least with that Greek sage still make us cry,
Not to be born, or, being born, to die.
But Faith steers up to a more glorious scope,

Which sweetens our sharp passage; and firm hope

Anchors our torn barks on a blessed shore,

Beyond the Dead Sea we here ferry o'er.

To this, Death is our pilot, and disease

100The agent which solicits our release.

Though crosses then pour on my restless head,

Or ling'ring sickness nail me to my bed:

Let this my thought's eternal comfort be,

That my clos'd eyes a better light shall see.

And when by fortune's or by nature's stroke

My body's earthen pitcher must be broke,

My soul, like Gideon's lamp, from her crack'd urn

Shall Death's black night to endless lustre turn.

An Elegy, &c.] It is always well to placate Nemesis before finding fault with a fellow-creature's complaints. But this piece, like some others, does rather illustrate that 'tendency to *grizzle*' which has been noticed in the Introduction. It was no doubt natural to King, and was probably confirmed in him by his wife's early death. It is worth noticing that—a thing rare in his time—he never remarried.

33 this] *MS.* 'his'.

73 'Than' for 'then' is much rarer than the converse, though we have it once *supra*. It is odd too here, for 'then' would have done just as well.

90 'Their' = Origen and the Priscillianists.

93 Posidippus? But the thing was a commonplace.

94 Side-note in orig.: *Non nasci, aut quam citissime mori.*

The Dirge.

What is th' existence of Man's life

But open war, or slumber'd strife?

Where sickness to his sense presents

The combat of the elements;

And never feels a perfect peace,

Till Death's cold hand signs his release.

It is a storm, where the hot blood

Outvies in rage the boiling flood;

And each loud passion of the mind

10Is like a furious gust of wind,

Which beats his bark with many a wave,

Till he casts anchor in the grave.

It is a flower, which buds and grows,

And withers as the leaves disclose;

Whose spring and fall faint seasons keep,

Like fits of waking before sleep:

Then shrinks into that fatal mould,

Where its first being was enroll'd.

It is a dream, whose seeming truth

20Is moraliz'd in age and youth:

Where all the comforts he can share

As wand'ring as his fancies are;

Till in a mist of dark decay

The dreamer vanish quite away.

It is a dial, which points out

The sun-set as it moves about:

And shadows out in lines of night

The subtile stages of Time's flight,

Till all obscuring earth hath laid

30The body in perpetual shade.

It is a weary interlude

Which doth short joys, long woes include.

The World the stage, the Prologue tears,

The Acts vain hope, and varied fears;

The Scene shuts up with loss of breath,

And leaves no Epilogue but Death.

The Dirge.] An obvious extension-variation of *Sic Vita*.

8 *MS.* 'Vies rages with'—rather well.

12 *MS.* 'cast'—perhaps better.

26 *MS.* 'His sun-set'.

27-8 These run in *MS.*:

Whilst it demonstrates Time's swift flight

In the black lines of shady night.

30 The] *MS.* 'His'.

35 *MS.* '*in* loss'.

An Elegy, occasioned by the loss of the most incomparable Lady Stanhope, daughter to the Earl of Northumberland.

[Died November 29, 1654.]

Light'ned by that dim torch our sorrow bears,

We sadly trace thy coffin with our tears;

And though the ceremonious rites are past

Since thy fair body into earth was cast,

Though all thy hatchments into rags are torn,

Thy funeral robes and ornaments outworn;

We still thy mourners, without show or art,

With solemn blacks hung round about our heart,

Thus constantly the obsequies renew,

10Which to thy precious memory are due.

Yet think not that we rudely would invade

The dark recess of thine untroubled shade,

Or give disturbance to that happy peace,

Which thou enjoy'st at full since thy release:

Much less in sullen murmurs do complain

Of His decree who took thee back again,

And did, ere Fame had spread thy virtue's light,

Eclipse and fold thee up in endless night.

This, like an act of envy, not of grief,

20Might doubt thy bliss, and shake our own belief,

Whose studied wishes no proportion bear

With joys which crown thee now in glory's sphere.

Know then, blest Soul! we for ourselves, not thee,

Seal our woe's dictate by this elegy:

Wherein our tears, united in one stream,

Shall to succeeding times convey this theme,

Worth all men's pity, who discern, how rare

Such early growths of fame and goodness are.

Of these, part must thy sex's loss bewail,

30Maim'd in her noblest patterns through thy fail;

For 'twould require a double term of life

To match thee as a daughter or a wife;

Both which Northumberland's dear loss improve,

And make his sorrow equal to his love.

The rest fall for ourselves, who, cast behind,

Cannot yet reach the peace which thou dost find;

But slowly follow thee in that dull stage

Which most untimely posted hence thy age.

Thus, like religious pilgrims, who design

40A short salute to their beloved shrine,

Most sad and humble votaries we come,

To offer up our sighs upon thy tomb,

And wet thy marble with our dropping eyes,

Which, till the spring which feeds their current dries,

Resolve each falling night and rising day,

This mournful homage at thy grave to pay.

An Elegy.] The subject of this was Anne Percy, daughter of the Northumberland whose personal umbrage or lukewarm loyalty so grievously affected the Royal cause, and the wife of that Philip Lord Stanhope who afterwards, and after her death, seems to have flirted with Lady Elizabeth Howard before she married Dryden.

28 early] Lady Stanhope was not twenty-one when she died, and had been married little more than two years.

Poems not included in the Edition of 1657 but added in reissue of 1664

Poems not included in the Edition of 1657 but added in reissue of 1664

An Elegy upon my best friend, L. K. C.

[Countess of Leinster: died June 15, 1657.]

Should we our sorrows in this method range,

Oft as misfortune doth their subjects change,

And to the sev'ral losses which befall,

Pay diff'rent rites at ev'ry funeral;

Like narrow springs, drain'd by dispersed streams,

We must want tears to wail such various themes,

And prove defective in Death's mournful laws,

Not having words proportion'd to each cause.

In your dear loss, my much afflicted sense

10Discerns this truth by sad experience,

Who never look'd my Verses should survive,

As wet records, That you are not alive;

And less desir'd to make that promise due,

Which pass'd from me in jest, when urg'd by you.

How close and slily doth our frailty work!

How undiscover'd in the body lurk!

That those who this day did salute you well,

Before the next were frighted by your knell.

O wherefore since we must in order rise,

20Should we not fall in equal obsequies?

But bear th' assaults of an uneven fate,

Like fevers which their hour anticipate;

Had this rule constant been, my long wish'd end

Might render you a mourner for your Friend:

As he for you, whose most deplor'd surprise

Imprints your death on all my faculties;
That hardly my dark phant'sy or discourse
This final duty from the pen enforce.
Such influence hath your eclipsed light,
30It doth my reason, like myself, benight.

Let me, with luckless gamesters, then think best
(After I have set up and lost my rest),
Grown desp'rate through mischance, to venture last
My whole remaining stock upon a cast,
And flinging from me my now loathed pen,
Resolve for your sake ne'er to write again:
For whilst successive days their light renew,
I must no subject hope to equal you,
In whose heroic breast, as in their Sphere,
40All graces of your sex concentred were.
Thus take I my long farewell of that art,
Fit only glorious actions to impart;
That art wherewith our crosses we beguile,
And make them in harmonious numbers smile:
Since you are gone, this holds no further use
Whose virtue and desert inspir'd my Muse,
O may she in your ashes buried be,
Whilst I myself become the Elegy.
And as it is observ'd, when Princes die,
50In honour of that sad solemnity,
The now unoffic'd servants crack their staves,
And throw them down into their masters' graves:
So this last office of my broken verse

I solemnly resign upon your hearse;

And my brain's moisture, all that is unspent,

Shall melt to nothing at the monument.

Thus in moist weather, when the marble weeps,

You'll think it only his tears reck'ning keeps,

Who doth for ever to his thoughts bequeath

60The legacy of your lamented death.

An Elegy upon my best friend.] King's 'best friend' (or, as a MS. gives it, 'worthiest') was Katharine Stanhope, daughter of John Lord Stanhope of Harrington. Her husband, Robert Cholmondeley, successively created an Irish Viscount, an English Baron (his surname serving as title in each case), and Earl of Leinster, died very shortly after her and before the Restoration. There is a MS. sermon on her death attributed to King, but doubted by Hannah. The poem itself, unlike the next but like the three which follow that, appears printed in the 1664 issue. And it is, on the principles of this collection, not unimportant to notice that in these later printed pieces the irrational prodigality of capitals which, as has been noted, is absent from *1657*, reappears. There could be no stronger evidence that these things have nothing to do with the author, and are not worth reproducing.

12 The original bestows a capital even upon 'Alive'—a thing capital in another way as illustrating the utter unreason of the practice.

15-18 Absent in *MS.*

36 Orig. 'nev'r'—a form unpronounceable but not uninteresting.

40 your] *MS.* 'the'.

43 crosses] *MS.* 'sorrows'.

On the Earl of Essex.

[Died September 14, 1646.]

Essex, twice made unhappy by a wife,

Yet married worse unto the People's strife:

He who, by two divorces, did untie

His bond of wedlock and of loyalty:

Who was by easiness of nature bred,

To lead that tumult which first him misled;

Yet had some glimm'ring sparks of virtue, lent
To see (though late) his error, and repent:
Essex lies here, like an inverted flame,
10Hid in the ruins of his house and name;
And as he, frailty's sad example, lies,
Warns the survivors in his exequies.
He shows what wretched bubbles great men are,
Through their ambition grown too popular:
For they, built up from weak opinion, stand
On bases false as water, loose as sand.
Essex in differing successes tried
The fury and the falsehood of each side;
Now with applauses deified, and then,
20Thrown down with spiteful infamy again:—
Tells them, what arts soever them support,
Their life is merely Time and Fortune's sport,
And that no bladders, blown by common breath,
Shall bear them up amidst the waves of Death:
Tells them, no monstrous birth, with pow'r endu'd,
By that more monstrous beast, the Multitude,—
No State-*Coloss* (though tall as that bestrid
The Rhodian harbour where their navy rid),
Can hold that ill-proportion'd greatness still,
30Beyond his greater, most resistless will,
Whose dreadful sentence, written on the Wall,
Did sign the temple-robbing tyrant's fall;
But spite of their vast privilege, which strives

T' exceed the size of ten prerogatives;

Spite of their endless parliament, or grants

(In order to those votes and Covenants,

When, without sense of their black perjury,

They swear with Essex they would live and die),

With their dead General ere long they must

40Contracted be into a span of dust.

On the Earl of Essex.] This and the next two may be called King's chief, if not his only, political poems: that they were kept back till after the Restoration is not surprising. Of Essex—one of the most unfortunate of men, the son of an unlucky father, the husband of one of the worst of women, and of another not much better, a half-hearted rebel, a soldier not less brave than blundering—not much is to be said here. King had some interest in the first and universally known divorce (the second, much less notorious, was from Elizabeth Paulet), for his father had been uncourtly and honest enough to oppose it strongly.

10 This rather vigorous line was to be prophetic as well as true at the time, for when, after the Restoration, the title of Essex was revived it was for the Capels, who still hold it, not for any Devereux. The vigour just referred to is by no means absent from the whole poem, and in an ante-Drydenian piece is really remarkable.

32 temple-robbing tyrant's fall] side-note in orig.: *Belshasar*, Dan. 5.

An Elegy on Sir Charles Lucas and Sir George Lisle.

[Murdered August 28, 1648.]

In measures solemn as the groans that fall

From the hoarse trumpet at some funeral;

With trailing Elegy and mournful verse,

I wait upon two peerless soldiers' hearse:

Though I acknowledge must my sorrow's dress

Ill matched to the cause it should express;

Nor can I, at my best invention's cost,

Sum up the treasure which in them we lost.

Had they, with other worthies of the age,

10Who late upon the kingdom's bloody stage,

For God, the King, and Laws, their valour tried,

Through War's stern chance in heat of battle died,

We then might save much of our grief's expense,

Reputing it, not duty, but offence.

They need no tears, nor howling exequy,

Who in a glorious undertaking die;

Since all that in the bed of honour fell,

Live their own Monument and Chronicle.

But these, whom horrid danger did not reach,

20The wide-mouth'd cannon, nor the wider breach,

These, whom, till cruel want and coward fate

Penn'd up like famish'd lions in a grate,

Were for their daring sallies so much fear'd,

Th' assailants fled them like a frighted herd;

Resolving now no more to fight, but lurk

Trench'd in their line, or earth'd within a work.

Where, not like soldiers they, but watchmen, creep,

Arm'd for no other office, but to sleep;

They, whose bold charge whole armies did amaze,

30Rend'ring them faint and heartless at the gaze,

To see Resolve and Naked Valour charms

Of higher proof than all their massy arms;

They, whose bright swords ruffled the proudest troop

(As fowl unto the tow'ring falcon stoop),

Yet no advantage made of their success,

Which to the conquer'd spake them merciless

(For they, whene'er 'twas begg'd, did safety give,

And oft unasked bid the vanquish'd live);

Ev'n these, not more undaunted in the field,

40Than mild and gentle unto such as yield,

Were, after all the shocks of battles stood,

(Let me not name it) murder'd in cold blood.

Such poor revenge did the enraged Greek

Against (till then) victorious Hector seek,

Triumphing o'er that body, bound and dead,

From whom, in life, the pow'rs of Argos fled.

Yet might Achilles borrow some excuse

To colour, though not warrant, the abuse:

His dearest friend, in the fierce combat foil'd,

50Was by the Trojan's hand of life despoil'd;

From whence unruly grief, grown wild with rage,

Beyond the bounds of Honour did engage.

But these, confirm'd in their unmanly hate,

By counsels cruel, yet deliberate,

Did from the stock of bleeding honour hew

Two of the noblest branches ever grew;

And (which our grief and pity must improve)

When brought within their reach with shows of love:

For by a treaty they entangled are,

60And rend'ring up to Mercy is the snare;

Whence we have learn'd, whene'er their Saintships treat,

The ends are mortal, and the means a cheat;

In which the world may read their black intent,

Drawn out at large in this sad precedent.

Who (though fair promis'd) might no mercy have,
But such as once the faithless Bashaw gave,
When to his trust deluded Bragadine
Himself and Famagosta did resign.
Whose envied valour thus to bonds betray'd,
70Was soon the mark of barb'rous slaughter made:
So gallant ships, which rocks and storms had past,
Though with torn sails, and spending of their mast,
When newly brought within the sight of land,
Have been suck'd up by some devouring sand.
You wretched agents for a kingdom's fall,
Who yet yourselves the Modell'd Army call;
Who carry on and fashion your design
By Sylla's, Sylla's red proscription's line,

(Rome's Comet once, as you are ours) for shame
80Henceforth no more usurp the soldier's name:
Let not that title in fair battles gain'd
Be by such abject things as you profan'd;
For what have you achiev'd, the world may guess
You are those Men of Might which you profess?
Where ever durst you strike, if you met foes
Whose valour did your odds in men oppose?
Turn o'er the annals of your vaunted fights,
Which made you late the People's favourites;
Begin your course at Naseby, and from thence
90Draw out your marches' full circumference,
Bridgwater, Bristol, Dartmouth, with the rest
Of your well-plotted renders in the West;

Then to the angry North your compass bend,

Until your spent career in Scotland end,

(This is the perfect scale of our mishap

Which measures out your conquest by the map),

And tell me he that can, What have you won,

Which long before your progress was not done?

What castle was besieg'd, what Port, what Town,

100You were not sure to carry ere sat down?

There needed no granadoes, no petard,

To force the passage, or disperse the guard.

No, your good masters sent a Golden Ram

To batter down the gates against you came.

Those blest Reformers, who procur'd the Swede

His armed forces into Denmark lead,

'Mongst them to kindle a sharp war for hire,

Who in mere pity meant to quench our fire,

Could where they pleased, with the King's own coin,

110Divert his aids, and strengths at home purloin.

Upon sea voyages I sometimes find

Men trade with Lapland witches for a wind,

And by those purchas'd gales, quick as their thought,

To the desired port are safely brought.

We need not here on skilful Hopkins call,

The State's allow'd Witch-finder General.

For (though Rebellion wants no cad nor elf,

But is a perfect witchcraft of itself)

We could with little help of art reveal

120Those learn'd magicians with whom you deal:

We all your juggles, both for time and place,

From Derby-house to Westminster can trace,

The circle where the factious jangle meet

To trample Law and Gospel under feet;

In which, like bells rung backward, they proclaim

The Kingdom by their wild-fire set on flame,

And, quite perverting their first rules, invent

What mischief may be done by Parliament:

We know your holy flamens, and can tell

130What spirits vote within the Oracle;

Have found the spells and incantations too,

By whose assistance you such wonders do.

For divers years the credit of your wars

Hath been kept up by these Familiars,

Who, that they may their providence express,

Both find you pay, and purchase your success:

No wonder then you must the garland wear,

Who never fought but with a silver spear.

We grant the war's unhappy consequence,

140With all the num'rous plagues which grow from thence,

Murders and rapes, threats of disease and dearth,

From you as for the proper Spring take birth;

You may for laws enact the public wrongs,

With all foul violence to them belongs;

May bawl aloud the people's right and pow'r,

Till by your sword you both of them devour

(For this brave liberty by you upcried

Is to all others but yourselves denied),

May with seditious fires the land embroil,

150And, in pretence to quench them, take the spoil;

You may Religion to your lust subdue,

For these are actions only worthy you:

Yet when your projects, crown'd with wish'd event,

Have made you masters of the ill you meant,

You never must the soldiers' glory share,

Since all your trophies executions are:

Not thinking your successes understood,

Unless recorded and scor'd up in blood.

In which, to gull the people, you pretend,

160That Military Justice was your end;

As if we still were blind, not knowing this

To all your other virtues suited is;

Who only act by your great grandsires' law,

The butcher Cade, Wat Tyler, and Jack Straw,

Whose principle was murder, and their sport

To cut off those they fear'd might do them hurt:

Nay, in your actions we completed find

What by those Levellers was but design'd,

For now Committees, and your arm'd supplies,

170Canton the land in petty tyrannies,

And for one King of commons in each shire,

Four hundred Commons rule as tyrants here.

Had you not meant the copies of each deed

Should their originals in ill exceed,

You would not practice sure the Turkish art,

To ship your taken pris'ners for a mart,

Lest if with freedom they at home remain,

They should (which is your terror) fight again.

A thing long since by zealous Rigby moved,

180And by the faction like himself approv'd;

Though you uncounsell'd can such outrage try,

Scarce sampled from the basest enemy.

Naseby of old, and late St. Fagan's fare,

Of these inhuman truckings witness are;

At which the captiv'd Welsh, in couples led,

Were marketed, like cattle, by the head.

Let it no more in History be told

That Turks their Christian slaves for aspers sold;

When we the Saints selling their brethren see,

190Who *had a Call* (they say) to set them free;

And are at last by right of conquest grown

To claim our land of Canaan for their own.

Though luckless Colchester in this outvies

Argiers' or Tunis' shameful merchandise;

Where the starv'd soldier (as th' agreement was)

Might not be suffer'd to their dwelling pass,

Till, led about by some insulting band,

They first were show'd in triumph through the land:

In which, for lack of diet, or of strength,

200If any fainted through the march's length,

Void of the breasts of men, this murd'rous crew

All those they could drive on no further, slew;

What bloody riddle's this? They mercy give,

Yet those who should enjoy it, must not live.

Indeed we cannot less from such expect,

Who for this work of ruin are elect:

This scum drawn from the worst, who never knew

The fruits which from ingenuous breeding grew;

But take such low commanders on their lists,

210As did revolted Jeroboam priests:

That 'tis our fate, I fear, to be undone,

Like Egypt once with vermin overrun.

If in the rabble some be more refin'd,

By fair extractions of their birth or mind,

Ev'n these corrupted are by such allays,

That no impression of their virtue stays.

As gold, embased by some mingled dross,

Both in its worth and nature suffers loss.

Else, had that sense of honour still surviv'd

220Which Fairfax from his ancestors deriv'd,

He ne'er had show'd himself, for hate or fear,

So much degen'rous from renowned Vere

(The title and alliance of whose son

His acts of valour had in Holland won),

As to give up, by his rash dooming breath,

This precious pair of lives to timeless death;

Whom no brave enemy but would esteem,

And, though with hazard of his own, redeem.

For 'tis not vainly by the world surmis'd,

230This blood to private spleens was sacrific'd.

Half of the guilt stands charg'd on Whalley's score

By Lisle affronted on his guards before;

For which his spite by other hands was shown,

Who never durst dispute it with his own.

Twice guilty coward! first by vote, then eye,

Spectator of the shameful tragedy.

But Lucas elder cause of quarrel knew,

From whence his critical misfortune grew;

Since he from Berkeley Castle with such scorn

240Bold Ransborough's first summons did return,

Telling him loudly at the parley's beat,

With rogues and rebels he disdain'd to treat.

Some from this hot contest the world persuade

His sleeping vengeance on that ground was laid:

If so, for ever blurr'd with Envy's brand,

His honour gain'd by sea, was lost at land:

Nor could he an impending judgement shun,

Who did to this with so much fervour run,

When late himself, to quit that bloody stain,

250Was, 'midst his armed guards, from Pomfret slain.

But all in vain we here expostulate

What took them hence, private or public hate:

Knowledge of acted woes small comforts add,

When no repair proportion'd can be had:

And such are ours, which to the kingdom's eyes

Sadly present ensuing miseries,

Foretelling in These Two some greater ill

From those who now a patent have to kill.

Two, whose dear loss leaves us no recompense,

260Nor them atonement, which in weight or sense

With These shall never into balance come,

Though all the army fell their hecatomb.

Here leave them then; and be 't our last relief
To give their merit value in our grief.
Whose blood however yet neglected must
Without revenge or rites mingle with dust;

Not any falling drop shall ever dry,
Till to a weeping spring it multiply,
Bath'd in whose tears their blasted laurel shall
270Grow green, and with fresh garlands crown their fall.
From this black region then of Death and Night,
Great Spirits, take your everlasting flight:
And as your valour's mounting fires combine,
May they a brighter constellation shine
Than Gemini, or than the brother-stars,
Castor and Pollux, fortunate to wars;
That all fair soldiers, by your sparkling light,
May find the way to conquer, when they fight,
And by those patterns which from you they take,
280Direct their course through Honour's Zodiac:
But upon traitors frown with dire aspect,
Which may their perjuries and guilt reflect;
Unto the curse of whose nativity,
Prodigious as the Caput Algol be,
Whose pale and ghastly tresses still portend
Their own despair or hangman for their end.
And that succeeding ages may keep safe
Your lov'd remembrance in some Epitaph,
Upon the ruins of your glorious youth,
290Inscribed be this monumental truth:

Here lie the valiant Lucas and brave Lisle,

With Amasa betray'd in Joab's smile:

In whom, revenge of Honour taking place,

His great corival 's stabb'd in the embrace.

And as it was the Hebrew Captain's stain,

That he two greater than himself had slain,

Shedding the blood of War in time of Peace,

When love pretended was, and arms did cease,

May the foul murderers expect a fate

300Like Joab's, blood with blood to expiate;

Which, quick as lightning, and as thunder sure,

Preventions wisest arts nor shun, nor cure.

O may it fall on their perfidious head!

That when, with Joab to the Altar fled,

Themselves the sword and reach of vengeance flee,

No Temple may their sanctuary be.

Last, that nor frailty nor devouring time

May ever lose impressions of the crime,

Let loyal Colchester (who too late tried

310To check, when highest wrought, the Rebels' pride,

Holding them long and doubtful at the bay,

Whilst we, by looking on, gave all away),

Be only nam'd: which, like a Column built,

Shall both enhearse this blood unnobly spilt,

And live, till all her towers in rubbish lie,

The monuments of their base cruelty.

Elegy on Sir Charles Lucas, &c.] This, King's longest poem (except the *King Charles*), shows, like the preceding, a vigour which might have made him a very formidable political satirist. If he has not Cleveland's wit he is free from

Cleveland's abuse of it. The subject is again a well-known one. No impartial authority denies that the execution of Lucas and Lisle was one of the worst blots on that side of the record of the Rebellion, and perhaps the only unforgivable act of Fairfax. Whether he was actuated, as the Royalists generally believed, by a mean personal spite, or allowed himself to be the tool of Ireton, matters uncommonly little; and his own 'Vindication' contains statements demonstrably false. However, as usual in revolutions, the curse came home, and the Colchester 'Septemberings' (as they would actually have been had the New Style prevailed in England) were undoubtedly as much instrumental as anything, next to the execution of the King himself, in turning the national sentiment against the perpetrators. The *bracketed* notes that follow are, as usual, original.

31 [Sir George Lisle at Newbury charged in his shirt, and routed them.] This was the *second* battle of Newbury, October 27, 1644: he was knighted at Oxford, December 21, 1645.

49 friend] [Patroclus.]

60 Mercy] Fairfax in his own 'Vindication' admits the 'snare'. 'Delivering upon Mercy is to be understood that some are to suffer, the rest to go free.' In other words, the garrison might take 'mercy' to mean 'quarter', but Fairfax took it to mean 'discretion'.

64 Orig. 'President', as often printed, though of course no scholar like King would deliberately write it.

66 [Famagosta, defended most valiantly by Signior Bragadino in the time of Selimus II, was upon honourable terms surrendered to Mustapha the Bashaw, who, observing no conditions, at his tent murdered the principal commanders, invited thither under show of love, and flayed Bragadine alive.] This siege of Famagosta in 1571, which came just before, and may be said to have been revenged by, Lepanto, greatly affected the mind of Christendom, and is duly chronicled in Knolles, the chief English historical writer of King's day. It is therefore hardly necessary to suppose, with Hannah, that the note was abridged from George Sandys' *Travels*, though King and Sandys were certainly friends.

82, 85 I would have left the capitals for the 'Yous' in these lines, as I have already done in other places, because they not improperly further emphasize that emphatic use of the pronoun in different parts of the line which Dryden afterwards perfected. But unfortunately they are not uniformly used, or even in the majority of cases—which shows how utterly haphazard and irrational this capitalization was.

105 [The Swedes hired anno 1644, to invade the King of Denmark, provided to assist his nephew, the King of England.]

115 Hopkins] Hannah only knew for a certainty that the scoundrel Matthew was 'swum' for a wizard, and had to put a 'probably' as to his being executed. There seems to be no doubt (see *D.N.B.*) that the great and glorious 'Herb Pantagruelion' had its own, and that Hopkins was hanged in 1647, before the date of this poem. But in that distracted time King, like his editor, may easily have been unaware of it.

117 An early literary use of 'cad' for assistant or understrapper.

142 Instead of 'for' Hannah, who very seldom meddled with his text, suggested 'from'. The temptation is obvious, but I think 'for' is possible, and therefore preferable as *lectio difficilior*.

160 Military Justice] [See the letter sent to Edward Earl of Manchester, Speaker of the House of Peers, *pro tempore*, from T. Fairfax, dated August 29, 1648, at Hieth.] According to Royalist accounts there were, even in Parliament, speakers bold enough and impartial enough to object to this letter, and to give voice to the common belief that the execution was either an act of private vengeance, or a deliberate affront to the King, or a device to make the pending negotiations with him impossible. It must be remembered that it was three months before the 'Purge' had deprived the Commons of the last remnant of independence or representative quality.

170 petty tyrannies] [Wat Tyler and his complices' design was to take away the King and chief men, and to erect petty tyrannies to themselves in every shire. And already one Littistar, a dyer, had taken upon him in Norfolk the name of King of Commons, and Robert Westborn in Suffolk, Richard II, anno 1381. *Speed.*] This note from Speed is not exactly quoted and Hannah corrected it, but the variations are of no importance.

176 There is no doubt about the selling of prisoners as convict-slaves to the West Indies (if not, as Rigby proposed, to Algiers) by the Roundheads after the second Civil War. Unluckily James II—born in this and other cases to be the curse of English Royalism—took the reproach away from the other side by authorizing the practice after Sedgmoor.

179 The particular bearer of this name of evil repute in Parliamentary history was Alexander Rigby (1594-1650). He had a brother, Joseph, whose politics were as bad as his own, but who survived the Restoration, and seems to have had a touch of the 'crank' in him. I have not yet come across his *Drunkard's Prospective* (1656), but it should be agreeable.

183 The savagery of the two-to-one victors at Naseby—especially towards the hapless so-called 'Irishwomen' camp followers—is beyond question, but it does not seem proved that there was much selling of prisoners then. As for St. Fagan's in the second Civil War the case is different, and justifies the following note in the original: 'At St. Fagan's in Glamorganshire, near Cardiff,

the Welsh unarmed were taken in very great numbers, and sold for twelve pence apiece to certain merchants, who bought them for slaves to their plantations.'

188 aspers] A Turkish coin of the smallest value: the 120th part of a piastre or dollar.

201 murd'rous crew] [Grimes, now a Captain, formerly a tinker at St. Albans, with his own hand killed four of the prisoners, being not able for faintness to go on with the rest, of which number Lieutenant Woodward was one. Likewise at Thame, and at Whateley (= Wheatley), some others were killed.] This story is backed up by not a few similar ones in different accounts of the time. And indeed, as King very cogently goes on to argue, your tinker-captain is capable of anything.

222 It was Sir Horace Vere (1565-1635), afterwards Lord Vere of Tilbury, under whom Fairfax served, and whose daughter Anne he married.

231 Whalley (spelt, as often with the name, Whaley in printed original) is cleared by others, though he is said by them as by King to have been present and to have had some private grudge against Lisle. Lucas had not only thrown Fairfax's troops into disorder at Marston Moor but is said by some to have actually wounded him in the face. He had also held Berkeley Castle against Rans- or Rainsborough till the outworks were taken, and the guns turned from them on the Castle itself. Rainsborough, with Whalley and Ireton, was actually present at the execution—which as a duty could hardly be incumbent on all three, and with which they were often reproached; and as a matter of course Rainsborough's death shortly afterwards was counted as a 'judgement'. His father had been an officer in the Navy, and the son commanded both by sea and land.

284 Algol] A star of great but varying brightness, the name of which— 'The *ghoul*—and its position in the head of Medusa in the constellation Perseus, explains the text.

311 long and doubtful] Fairfax, to enhance his exploit, called it 'four months close siege'. It was actually not quite eleven weeks, but the place yielded to nothing but starvation.

An Elegy upon the most Incomparable King Charles the First.

Call for amazed thoughts, a wounded sense

And bleeding hearts at our intelligence.

Call for that Trump of Death, the Mandrake's groan

Which kills the hearers: this befits alone

Our story which through times vast Calendar,

Must stand without example or repair.

What spouts of melting clouds, what endless springs

Pour'd in the Ocean's lap for offerings,

Shall feed the hungry torrent of our grief,

10Too mighty for expression or belief?

Though all those moistures which the brain attracts

Ran from our eyes like gushing cataracts,

Or our sad accents could out-tongue the cries

Which did from mournful Hadadrimmon rise,

Since that remembrance of Josiah slain

In our King's murder is reviv'd again.

O pardon me that but from Holy Writ

Our loss allows no parallel to it:

Nor call it bold presumption that I dare

20Charles with the best of Judah's Kings compare:

The virtues of whose life did I prefer

The text acquits me for no flatterer.

For he like David perfect in his trust,

Was never stain'd like him, with blood or lust.

One who with Solomon in judgement tried,

Was quick to comprehend, wise to decide

(That even his Judges stood amaz'd to hear

A more transcendent mover in their sphere),

Though more religious: for when doting love

30Awhile made Solomon apostate prove,

Charles ne'er endur'd the Truth which he profest,

To be unfix'd by bosom-interest.

Bold as Jehosaphat, yet forc'd to fight,

And for his own, no unconcerned right.

Should I recount his constant time of pray'r,

Each rising morn and ev'ning regular,

You'd say his practice preach'd, 'They ought not eat

Who by devotion first not earn'd their meat:'

Thus Hezekiah he exceeds in zeal,

40Though not (like him) so facile to reveal

The treasures of God's House, or His own heart,

To be supplanted by some foreign art.

And that he might in fame with Joash share

When he the ruin'd Temple did repair,

His cost on Paul's late ragged fabric spent

Must (if no other) be His monument.

From this survey the kingdom may conclude

His merits, and her losses' magnitude:

Nor think he flatters or blasphemes, who tells

50That Charles exceeds Judea's parallels,

—*Sparguntur in omnes,*
In te mista fluunt—Claudian.

In whom all virtues we concentred see

Which 'mongst the best of them divided be.

O weak-built glories! which those tempests feel!

To force you from your firmest bases reel,

What from the strokes of Chance shall you secure,

When rocks of Innocence are so unsure?

When the World's only mirror slaughter'd lies,

Envy's and Treason's bleeding sacrifice;

As if His stock of goodness could become

60No kalendar, but that of martyrdom.

See now, ye cursed mountebanks of State,

Who have eight years for reformations sate;

Call'd the Council of Troubles.

You who dire Alva's counsels did transfer,

To act his scenes on England's theatre;

You who did pawn yourselves in public faith

To slave the Kingdom by your pride and wrath;

Call the whole World to witness now, how just,

How well you are responsive to your trust,

How to your King the promise you perform,

70With fasts, and sermons, and long prayers sworn,

That you intended Peace and Truth to bring

To make your Charles *Europe's most glorious King.*

The form of taking the Covenant, June 1643.

Did you for this *Lift up your hands on high,*

To kill the King, and pluck down Monarchy?

These are the fruits by your wild faction sown,

Which not imputed are, but born your own:

For though you wisely seem to wash your hands,

The guilt on every vote and order stands;

So that convinc'd, from all you did before,

80Justice must lay the murder at your door.

Mark if the body does not bleed anew,

In any circumstance approach'd by You,

From whose each motion we might plain descry

The black ostents of this late tragedy.

For when the King, through storms in Scotland bred,

To his Great Council for his shelter fled,

When in that meeting every error gain'd

Redresses sooner granted than complain'd:

Not all those frank concessions or amends

90Did suit the then too powerful faction's ends:

No acts of Grace at present would content,

Nor promise of Triennial Parl'ament,

Till by a formal law the King had past

This Session should at Your pleasure last.

So having got the bit, and that 'twas known

No power could dissolve You but Your own,

Your graceless Junto make such use of this,

Diodorus Siculus, lib. 2.

As once was practis'd by Semiramis;

Who striving by a subtile suit to prove

100The largeness of her husband'[s] trust and love,

Did from the much abused King obtain

That for three days she might sole empress reign;

Before which time expir'd, the bloody wife

Depriv'd her lord both of his crown and life.

There needs no comment when your deeds apply

The demonstration of her treachery.

Which to effect, by Absolon's foul wile

You of the people's heart your prince beguile;

Urging what eases they might reap by it

110Did you their legislative Judges sit.

How did you fawn upon, and court the rout,

Whose clamour carried your whole plot about?

How did you thank seditious men that came

To bring petitions which yourselves did frame?

And lest they wanted hands to set them on,

You led the way by throwing the first stone.

For in that libel after midnight born,

Wherewith your faction labour'd till the morn,

Remonstrance of the State of the Kingdom, Dec. 15, 1641.

That famous lie, you a Remonstrance name;

120Were not reproaches your malicious aim?

Was not the King's dishonour your intent,

By slanders to traduce his Government?

All which your spiteful cunning did contrive;

Men must receive through your false perspective,

In which the smallest spots improved were,

And every mote a mountain did appear.

Thus Caesar by th' ungrateful Senate found

His life assaulted through his honour's wound.

And now to make Him hopeless to resist,

Ord. Feb. 29, *Voted* March 15.

130You guide his sword by vote, which as you list

Must strike or spare (for so you did enforce

His hand against His reason to divorce

The Navy seiz'd Mar. 28, 1642.

Brave Strafford's life), then wring it quite away

By your usurping each Militia:

The London Tumults, Jan. 10, 1641.

Then seize His magazines, of which possest

You turn the weapons 'gainst their master's breast.

This done, th' unkennell'd crew of lawless men

Led down by Watkins, Pennington, and Venn,
Did with confused noise the Court invade;
140Then all Dissenters in both houses bay'd.
At which the King amaz'd is forc'd to fly,
The whilst your mouth's laid on maintain the cry.
The Royal game dislodg'd and under chase,
Your hot pursuit dogs Him from place to place:
Not Saul with greater fury or disdain
Did flying David from Jeshimon's plain
Unto the barren wilderness pursue,
Than cours'd and hunted is the King by you.

The mountain partridge or the chased roe
150Might now for emblems of His fortune go,
And since all other May-games of the town
(Save those yourselves should make) were voted down,
The clam'rous pulpit hollaes in resort,
Inviting men to your King-catching sport.
Where as the foil grows cold you mend the scent
By crying Privilege of Parliament,
Whose fair pretensions the first sparkles are,
Which by your breath blown up enflame the war,
And Ireland (bleeding by design) the stale
160Wherewith for men and money you prevail.
Yet doubting that imposture could not last,
When all the Kingdom's mines of treasure waste,
You now tear down Religion's sacred hedge
To carry on the work by sacrilege;
Reputing it Rebellion's fittest pay

To take both God's and Caesar's dues away.

The tenor of which execrable vote

Your over-active zealots so promote,

That neither tomb, nor temple could escape,

170Nor dead nor living, your licentious rape.

Statues and grave-stones o'er men buried

* *At Basing-Chapel, sold* Dec. 29, 1643.

Robb'd of their brass, the * coffins of their lead;

Not the seventh Henry's gilt and curious screen,

Nor those which 'mongst our rarities were seen,

* *At Winchester.*

The * chests wherein the Saxon monarchs lay,

But must be basely sold or thrown away.

May in succeeding times forgotten be

Those bold examples of impiety,

Which were the Ages' wonder and discourse,

180You have their greatest ills improv'd by worse.

Lactant. l. 2, c. 4.

No more be mention'd Dionysius' theft,

Who of their gold the heathen shrines bereft;

For who with Yours his robberies confer,

Must him repute a petty pilferer.

Julian, Praefectus Aegypti. Theodoret. l. 3, c. 11.

Nor Julian's scoff, who when he view'd the state

Of Antioch's Church, the ornaments and plate,

Cried, Meaner vessels would serve turn, or none

Might well become the birth of Mary's Son:

ibid.

Nor how that spiteful Atheist did in scorn

190Piss on God's Table, which so oft had borne

The Hallow'd Elements, his death present:

Ganguin. l. 6.

Nor he that foul'd it with his excrement,

Then turn'd the cloth unto that act of shame,

Which without trembling Christians should not name.

Nor John of Leyden, who the pillag'd quires

Employ'd in Munster for his own attires;

His pranks by Hazlerig exceeded be,

A wretch more wicked and as mad as he,

The Carpet belonging to the Communion Table of Winchester Cathedral, Dec. 18, 1642. *Adrian Emp.*

Who once in triumph led his sumpter moil

200Proudly bedecked with the Altar's spoil.

Nor at Bizantium's sack how Mahomet

In St. Sophia's Church his horses set.

Nor how Belshazzar at his drunken feasts

Carous'd in holy vessels to his guests:

Nor he that did the books and anthems tear,

Which in the daily Stations used were.

These were poor essays of imperfect crimes,

Fit for beginners in unlearned times,

Siz'd only for that dull meridian

210Which knew no Jesuit nor Puritan

(Before whose fatal birth were no such things

As doctrines to depose and murder kings).

But since your prudent care enacted well,

That there should be no King in Israel,

England must write such annals of your reign

Which all records of elder mischiefs stain.

Churches unbuilt by order, others burn'd;

Whilst Paul's and Lincoln are to stables turn'd;

And at God's Table you might horses see

220By (those more beasts) their riders manger'd be,

At Winchcomb in Gloucestershire.

Some kitchens and some slaughter-houses made,

Communion-boards and cloths for dressers laid:

Some turn'd to loathsome goals, so by you brought

Unto the curse of Baal's house, a draught.

The Common Prayers with the Bibles torn,

The copes in antic Moorish dances worn,

And sometimes, for the wearer's greater mock,

The surplice is converted to a frock,

Some, bringing dogs, the Sacrament revile,

230Some, with Copronymus, the Font defile.

O God! canst Thou these profanations like?

If not, why is Thy thunder slow to strike

The cursed authors? who dare think that Thou

Dost, when not punish them, their acts allow.

All which outrageous crimes, though your pretence

Would fasten on the soldiers' insolence,

We must believe, that what by them was done

Came licens'd forth by your probation.

For, as yourselves with Athaliah's brood

240In strong contention for precedence stood,

Whitehall, Windsor, Feb. 3, 1643.

You robb'd two Royal Chapels of their plate,

Which Kings and Queens to God did dedicate;

Then by a vote more sordid than the stealth,

Melt down and coin it for the Commonwealth,

That is, giv't up to the devouring jaws

Of your great Idol Bel, new styl'd The Cause.

And though this monster you did well devise

To feed by plunder, taxes, loans, excise;

(All which provisions You the people tell

250Scarce serve to diet Your Pantagruel).

We no strew'd ashes need to trace the cheat,

Who plainly see what mouths the messes eat.

Brave Reformation! and a through one too,

Which to enrich yourselves must all undo.

Pray tell us (those that can), What fruits have grown

From all Your seeds in blood and treasure sown?

What would you mend? when Your projected State

Doth from the best in form degenerate?

Or why should You (of all) attempt the cure,

260Whose facts nor Gospel's test nor Law's endure?

But like unwholesome exhalations met

From Your conjunction only plagues beget,

And in Your circle, as imposthumes fill

Which by their venom the whole body kill;

For never had You pow'r but to destroy,

Nor will, but where You conquer'd to enjoy.

This was Your master-prize, who did intend

To make both Church and Kingdom's prey Your end.

'Gainst which the King (plac'd in the gap) did strive

270By His (till then unquestion'd) negative,

Which finding You lack'd reason to persuade,

Your arguments are into weapons made;

So to compel him by main force to yield,

E. of Essex Army, Aug. 1 1642.

You had a formed army in the field

Before his reared standard could invite

Ten men upon his Righteous Cause to fight:

Yet ere those raised forces did advance,

The Standard at Nottingham, Aug. 25, 1642.

Your malice struck him dead by Ordinance,

When your Commissions the whole Kingdom swept

280With blood and slaughter, *Not the King except*.

Now hard'ned in revolt, You next proceed

By pacts to strengthen each rebellious deed,

June 27, 1643.

New oaths and vows, and Covenants advance,

All contradicting your allegiance,

Whose sacred knot you plainly did untie,

Declaration and Resolution of Parl., Aug. 15, 1642.

When you with Essex *swore to live and die*.

These were your calves in Bethel and in Dan,

Which Jeroboam's treason stablish can,

Who by strange pacts and altars did seduce

290The people to their laws' and King's abuse;

All which but serve like Shibboleth to try

Those who pronounc'd not your conspiracy;

That when your other trains defective are,

Forc'd oaths might bring refusers to the snare.

And lest those men your counsels did pervert,

Might when your fraud was seen the Cause desert,

A fierce decree is through the Kingdom sent,

Which made it death for any to repent.

What strange dilemmas doth Rebellion make?

300'Tis mortal to deny, or to partake:

Some hang who would not aid your traitorous act,

History of English and Scottish Presbytery, p. 320.

Others engag'd are hang'd if they retract.

So witches who their contracts have unsworn,

By their own Devils are in pieces torn.

Thus still the raging tempest higher grows,

Which in extremes the King's resolvings throws.

The face of Ruin everywhere appears,

And acts of outrage multiply our fears;

Whilst blind Ambition by successes fed

310Hath You beyond the bound of subjects led,

Who tasting once the sweet of regal sway,

Resolving now no longer to obey.

For Presbyterian pride contests as high

As doth the Popedom for supremacy.

Needs must you with unskilful Phaeton

Aspire to guide the chariot of the Sun,

Though your ill-govern'd height with lightning be

Thrown headlong from his burning axle-tree.

The 19 Propos.

You will no more petition or debate,

320But your desire in Propositions state,

Which by such rules and ties the King confine,

They in effect are summons to resign.

Therefore your war is manag'd with such sleight,

'Twas seen you more prevail'd by purse than might;

And those you could not purchase to your will,

You brib'd with sums of money to sit still.

The King by this time hopeless here of peace,

Or to procure His wasted People's ease,

Which He in frequent messages had tried,

330By you as oft as shamelessly denied;

Wearied by faithless friends and restless foes,

To certain hazard doth His life expose:

April 27, 1646. May 5, 1646.

When through your quarters in a mean disguise

He to His countrymen for succour flies,

Who met a brave occasion then to save

Their native King from His untimely grave:

Had he from them such fair reception gain'd,

Wherewith ev'n Achish David entertain'd:

But faith to Him or hospitable laws

340In your Confederate Union were no clause,

Which back to you their rend'red Master sends

To tell how He was us'd among his friends.

Far be it from my thoughts by this black line

To measure all within that warlike clime;

The still admir'd Montrose some numbers led

In his brave steps of loyalty to tread.

I only tax a furious party there,

Who with our native pests enleagued were.

Then 'twas you follow'd Him with hue and cry,

350Made midnight searches in each liberty,

This Order publish'd by beat of Drum, May 4, 1646.

Voting it Death to all without reprieve,

Who should their Master harbour or relieve.

Ev'n in pure pity of both Nations' fame,

I wish that act in story had no name.

When all your mutual stipulations are

Converted at Newcastle to a fair,

Where (like His Lord) the King the mart is made,

Bought with Your money, and by them betrayed;

For both are guilty, they that did contract,

360And You that did the fatal bargain act.

Which who by equal reason shall peruse,

Must yet conclude, they had the best excuse:

For doubtless they (good men) had never sold,

But that you tempted them with English gold;

And 'tis no wonder if with such a sum

Our brethren's frailty might be overcome.

What though hereafter it may prove their lot

To be compared with Iscariot?

Yet will the World perceive which was most wise,

370And who the nobler traitor by the price;

For though 'tis true both did themselves undo,

They made the better bargain of the two,

Which all may reckon who can difference

Two hundred thousand pounds from thirty-pence.

However something is in justice due,

Which may be spoken in defence of You;

For in your Master's purchase you gave more,

Than all your Jewish kindred paid before.

And had you wisely us'd what then you bought,

380Your act might be a loyal ransom thought,

To free from bonds your captive sovereign,

Restoring Him to his lost Crown again.

But You had other plots, your busy hate

Plied all advantage on His fallen state,

And show'd You did not come to bring Him bail,

But to remove Him to a stricter gaol,

To Holmby first, whence taken from His bed,

He by an army was in triumph led;

Till on pretence of safety Cromwell's wile

390Had juggl'd Him into the Fatal Isle,

Where Hammond for his jailor is decreed,

And murderous Rolf as lieger-hangman fee'd,

Who in one fatal knot two counsels tie,

He must by poison or by pistol die.

Here now denied all comforts due to life,

His friends, His children, and his peerless wife;

From Carisbrook He oft but vainly sends,

And though first wrong'd, seeks to make you amends;

For this He sues, and by His restless pen

400Importunes Your deaf ears to treat again.

Whilst the proud faction scorning to go less,

Jan. 3, 1647. Jan. 9, 1647.

Return those trait'rous votes of Non Address,

Which follow'd were by th' Armies thund[e]ring

To act without and quite against the King.

Yet when that cloud remov'd, and the clear light

Drawn from His weighty reasons, gave You sight

Of Your own dangers, had not their intents

Colchester Siege.

Retarded been by some cross accidents;

Which for a while with fortunate suspense

410Check'd or diverted their swoll'n insolence:

When the whole Kingdom for a Treaty cried,

Which gave such credit to Your falling side,

June 30, 1648. *Treaty Voted*, July 28, 1648.

That you recall'd those votes, and God once more

Your power to save the Kingdom did restore;

Remember how Your peevish Treators sate,

Not to make peace, but to prolong debate;

How You that precious time at first delay'd,

And what ill use of Your advantage made,

As if from Your foul hands God had decreed

420Nothing but war and mischief should succeed.

For when by easy grants the King's assent

Did your desires in greater things prevent,

When He did yield faster than You entreat,

And more than modesty dares well repeat;

Yet not content with this, without all sense

Or of His honour or His conscience,

Still you press'd on, till you too late descried,

Twas now less safe to stay than be denied:

For like a flood broke loose the armed rout,

430Then shut Him closer up, and shut You out,

Who by just vengeance are since worried

By those hand-wolves You for his ruin bred.

Thus like two smoking firebrands, You and They

Have in this smother chok'd the Kingdom's day:

And as you rais'd them first, must share the guilt,

With all the blood in those distractions spilt.

For though with Sampson's foxes backward turn'd

(When he Philistia's fruitful harvest burn'd),

The face of your opinions stands averse,

440All your conclusions but one fire disperse;

And every line which carries your designs,

In the same centre of confusion joins.

Though then the Independents end the work,

'Tis known they took their platform from the Kirk;

Though Pilate Bradshaw with his pack of Jews,

God's High Vice-gerent at the bar accuse;

They but reviv'd the evidence and charge,

Your pois'nous Declarations laid at large;

Though they condemn'd or made his life their spoil,

450You were the setters forc'd him to the toil:

For you whose fatal hand the warrant writ,

The prisoner did for execution fit;

And if their axe invade the Regal throat,

Remember you first murder'd Him by vote.

Thus they receive your tennis at the bound,

Take off that head which you had first un-crown'd;

Which shows the texture of our mischiefs clew,

If ravell'd to the top, begins in You,

Who have for ever stain'd the brave intents
460And credit of our English Parliaments:
And in this one caus'd greater ills, and more,
Than all of theirs did good that went before.
Yet have You kept your word against Your will,
Your King is great indeed and glorious still,
And you have made Him so. We must impute
That lustre which His sufferings contribute

To your preposterous wisdoms, who have done
All your good deeds by contradiction:
For as to work His peace you rais'd this strife,
470And often shot at Him to save His life;
As you took from Him to increase His wealth,
And kept Him pris'ner to secure His health;
So in revenge of your dissembled spite,
In this last wrong you did Him greatest right,
And (cross to all You meant) by plucking down
Lifted Him up to His Eternal Crown.
With this encircled in that radiant sphere,
Where thy black murderers must ne'er appear;
Thou from th' enthroned Martyrs' blood-stain'd line,
480Dost in thy virtues bright example shine.
And when thy darted beam from the moist sky
Nightly salutes thy grieving people's eye,
Thou like some warning light rais'd by our fears,
Shalt both provoke and still supply our tears,
Till the Great Prophet wak'd from his long sleep,
Again bids Sion for Josiah weep:

That all successions by a firm decree

May teach their children to lament for Thee.

Beyond these mournful rites there is no art

490Or cost can Thee preserve. Thy better part

Lives in despite of Death, and will endure

Kept safe in thy unpattern'd Portraiture:

Which though in paper drawn by thine own hand,

Shall longer than Corinthian-marble stand,

Or iron sculptures: There thy matchless pen

Speaks Thee the Best of Kings as Best of Men:

Be this Thy Epitaph; for This alone

Deserves to carry Thy Inscription.

And 'tis but modest Truth (so may I thrive

500As not to please the best of thine alive,

Or flatter my Dead Master, here would I

Pay my last duty in a glorious lie):

In that admired piece the World may read

Thy virtues and misfortunes storied;

Which bear such curious mixture, men must doubt

Whether Thou wiser wert or more devout.

There live, Blest Relic of a saint-like mind,

With honours endless, as Thy peace, enshrin'd;

Whilst we, divided by that bloody cloud,

510Whose purple mists Thy murder'd body shroud,

Here stay behind at gaze: apt for Thy sake

Unruly murmurs now 'gainst Heav'n to make,

Which binds us to live well, yet gives no fence

To guard her dearest sons from violence.

But he whose trump proclaims, *Revenge is mine*,

Bids us our sorrow by our hope confine,

And reconcile our Reason to our Faith,

Which in thy Ruin such conclusions hath;

It dares conclude, God does not keep His Word

520If *Zimri dies in peace that slew his Lord.*

From my sad Retirement

March 11, 1648.

CAROLUS STUART REX ANGLIÆ SECURE CAESUS[1]

VITA CESSIT TRICESSIMO IANUARII.

[1] Orig. *Coesus.*

An Elegy upon King Charles the First.] I have thought it desirable to give this Elegy though Hannah did not, and though I scarcely myself think it to be King's, first because it is very little known (it was strange even to Professor Firth when I asked him about it); secondly, because the 1664 issue or reissue seems worth completing; but thirdly, and principally, because it is well worth giving. It seems to me, in fact, rather too good in a certain way to be King's. He could write, as we have seen, fairly vigorous couplets of a kind rather later than this date; but I do not know where he keeps up such continuous and effective 'slogging' as here. The Colchester piece, which is the natural parallel, is distinctly inferior in that respect. There are, moreover, in the piece some things which I suspect King would not, as well as could not, have written, and which perhaps influenced Hannah in not giving it. The close and effective Biblical parallels are not quite in the Bishop's way in verse, and the clear vigorous summary of the whole rebellion—dates and facts in margin—is like nothing else of his that I know. But—his or not his—it is found with his undoubted work; it is good; and so it shall be given.

But the reader must not suppose that it has never appeared except in the 1664 King or before that. While reading for the present edition I had noticed an entry of a very similar title in Hazlitt, and on looking the book up in the British Museum I found it, as I expected, to be identical in all important respects, putting aside some minor variants and a shorter title, with 1664. The original (in black border at least an inch deep) adds: 'Persecuted by two implacable factions, Imprisoned by the one and murthered by the other, January 30th, 1648.' The final prose clause is the same, and I noticed no various readings, except merest 'literals'—an occasional capital for lower case, '-or' for '-our', and the like—which it did not seem necessary to collate or report exactly.

Title] As usual, 'Charls' in original.]

14 Zechariah xii. 11 compared with 2 Kings xxiii. 29 and 2 Chronicles xxxv. 22-4.

27 This line is slightly ambiguous. At first one takes 'Judges' as referring to the regicide tribunal—and of course not merely the dignity but the unanswerable logic of Charles's attitude is admitted. But our elegist would hardly admit that the King moved in the sphere of his rebellious subjects, so that it may be a reference to the legally constituted bench of earlier years—'*his* Judges' in another sense.

40 See 2 Kings xx, 2 Chronicles xxxii, and Isaiah xxxix.

45 A little prosaic. Old St. Paul's was being constantly tinkered: indeed, as is well known from Evelyn's *Diary*, there were plans for very extensive restoration just before the Fire.

48 Orig. 'losses', which at the time would stand equally well for singular and plural genitive.

58 Orig. 'sacrifise', to get a complete ear-rhyme.

61 This apostrophe to the 'cursed mountebanks of State' is uncommonly vigorous, and much straighter 'hitting from the shoulder' than King usually manages.

100 Orig. 'husband', without 's, and possibly intended.

124 perspective] As commonly = 'telescope'.

138 Watkins I know not; Pennington we have seen in Cleveland; Venn (1586-1650) was John Venn, wool-merchant, M.P., active rebel, and regicide.

142 This (original) may read, 'Your mouths, laid on, maintain the cry', which seems most probable; or, 'Your mouth's [*i.e.* is] laid on "Maintain the cry".'

146 1 Samuel xxiii 24. Jeshimon seems to have escaped Alexander the Concordance-smith.

155 foil] The word in this sense had puzzled me; but the readers of the Clarendon Press put me literally on it by reference to *N.E.D.* It means the 'scent' or 'track' of a hunted animal and occurs in the first sense in Turbervile, and elsewhere, as well as (figuratively used) in as late and well-known a place as *Tom Jones*.

199 'Moil'—or rather, more commonly, 'moyle'—is very common for 'mule' in Elizabethan drama, and is said to be still dialectic, especially in Devon and Cornwall.

223 'Goal' would seem here to be used as = 'jakes', though it has been suggested that the common sense of 'jail' will do.

226 Orig. 'Coaps'.

238 'probation' must here = '*ap*probation'.

246 Orig. 'Idol Bel*l*', which may puzzle for a moment. Of course the Dragon's companion and Nebo's is meant. The poet seems indeed rather to have mixed up the monster and the false god.

250 Here again there seems to be a slight confusion between Pantagruel and his glorious father.

265-6 Another uncommonly vigorous couplet.

312 The writer either intended to continue the set of participles or forgot that he had begun it. But if 'For Presbyterian ... supremacy' be thrown into parenthesis the anacoluthon will be mended—after a fashion.

373-4 Good again; and with a fore-echo of Dryden's 'Shimei' rhythm and swashing blow.

392 lieger-hangman] 'Hangman resident', house-hangman'.

403 Orig. 'Armies', with the usual choice between singular and plural genitive or (here) nominative plural.

415 I think it well to keep the form 'Treator'.

430 Pointed, if slightly burlesque.

432 hand-wolves] A dog trained and on the leash was said to be 'in hand'.

438 Philisti*a*] The letter here is slightly 'smashed' and the word might be 'Philistins' or 'Philistia's'. It looks more like the former, but the latter is better, and is said to be clear in Mr. Thorn-Drury's copies.

444 platform] This is interesting.

492 Portraiture] A reference to the Εἰϰὼν Βασιλικὴ.

Poems in Manuscript.

A Second Elegy on the Countess of Leinster.

Sleep, precious ashes, in thy sacred urn

From Death and Grave till th' last trump sounds return;

Meanwhile embalm'd in Virtues. Joseph's Tomb

Were fitter for thee, than the Earth's dark womb.

Cease, Friends, to weep; she's but asleep, not dead,—

Chang'd from her husband's, to her mother's, bed;

Or from his bosom into Abram's rather,

Where now she rests, Blest Soul, in such a Father.

Thus Death hath done his best, and worst. His best,

10In sending Virtue to her place of rest;

His worst, in leaving him, as dead, in life

Whose chiefest Joys were in his dearest Wife.

A Second Elegy on the Countess of Leinster.] Hannah found this in the Pickering MS. 'immediately after' the printed one *v. supra*. On what other grounds he assigned its subject I do not know; but both, as noted above, have a most extraordinary efflorescence of capitals.

Epigrams.

I.

Quid faciant leges, ubi sola pecunia regnat? &c.—PETRON. ARBIT.

To what serve Laws, where only Money reigns?

Or where a poor man's cause no right obtains?

Even those that most austerity pretend,

Hire out their tongues, and words for profit lend.

What's Judgement then, but public merchandise?

And the Court sits, but to allow the price.

II.

Casta suo gladium cum traderet Arria Paeto, &c.—MARTIAL.

When Arria to her Paetus had bequeath'd

The sword in her chaste bosom newly sheath'd;

Trust me (quoth she) My own wound feels no smart;

'Tis thine (My Paetus) grieves and kills my heart.

III.

Qui pelago credit, magno se faenore tollit, &c.—PETRON. ARBIT.

He whose advent'rous keel ploughs the rough seas,

Takes interest of fate for wealth's increase.

He that in battle traffics, and pitch'd fields,

Reaps with his sword rich harvests, which war yields.

Base parasites repose their drunken heads,

Laden with sleep and wine, on Tyrian beds;

And he that melts in Lust's adult'rous fire,

Gets both reward and pleasure for his hire.

But Learning only, midst this wanton heat,

Hath (save itself) nothing to wear or eat;

Faintly exclaiming on the looser Times,

That value Wit and Arts below their crimes.

IV.

Pro captu lectoris habent sua fata libelli.

The fate of books is diverse as man's sense:

Two critics ne'er shar'd one intelligence.

V.

I would not in my love too soon prevail:

An easy conquest makes the purchase stale.[1]

[1] From a copy most kindly made for me by Mr. Nichol Smith. It is a harmless enough, and rather neat, translation of Petronius, *Nolo quod cupio, &c.*

Epigrams.] This little bunch of epigrams is of no particular value, but being so small may be given for completeness' sake. The first three Hannah found in both Pickering and Malone 22 MSS., together with V, which, I suppose, shocked him so that he did not print it. The *Pro captu lectoris*, which is the best, is in Malone only.

The following group of poems has been printed by Mr. Mason, the first as authentic, the others as doubtful. He points out that *The Complaint* and *On his Shadow* are autograph, and written on the same sheet of paper as the lines *Upon the Untimely Death of J. K.* The text here printed has been supplied by Mr. Percy Simpson from the original MSS., and the few textual notes are his. In view of the uncertainty of the bulk of the matter I [G. S.] have not thought it worth while to add any annotation of the more general kind. In addition, Mr. Mason prints a translation of a Latin elegy on Dr. Spenser, President of Corpus Christi College, Oxford; the Latin text of this in Rawlinson MS. D. 912, fol. 305 verso, is in King's autograph, but the translation is not, and moreover it is so tinkered and changed as to suggest the efforts of a far from facile, if very conscientious, copyist. This has not been printed, and only the first of the following poems can with certainty be ascribed to King.

Upon the Untimely Death of J. K., first born of HK

Blessed Spirit, thy infant breath,

Fitter for the quire of saints

Than for mortals here beneath,

Warbles joys, but mine complaints—

Plaints that spring from that great loss

Of thy little self, sad cross.

Yet do I still repair thee by desire

Which warms my benumbed sense, but like false fire.

But with such delusive shapes

10Still my pensive thoughts are eased,

As birds bating at mock grapes

Are with empty error pleased.

Yet I err not, for decay

Hath but seized thy house of clay,

- 442 -

For lo the lively image of each part

Makes deep impression on my waxy heart.

Thus learn I to possess the thing I want;

Having great store of thee, and yet great scant.

Oh let me thus recall thee, ne'er repine,

20Since what is thy fate now, must once be mine.

Upon the Untimely Death of J. K., &c.] The text is taken from Rawlinson MS.
D. 317 of the Bodleian, fol. 175; the monogram of the title was used by King.
An unsigned copy is in Harleian MS. 6917 of the British Museum, foll. 96
Verso-97: this omits 'but', l. 8.

The Complaint.

Fond, hapless man, lost in thy vain desire;

Thy lost desire

May now retire.

She, like a salamander, in thy flame

Sports with Love's name,

And lives the same,

Unsinged, impenetrably cold.

Sure, careless Boy, thou slep'st; and Death, instead

Of thine, conveyed

10His dart of lead.

This thou unluckily at her hast sent,

Who now is bent

Not to relent,

Though thou spend all thy shafts of gold.

I prithee filch another fatal dart

And pierce my heart;

To ease this smart,

Strike all my senses dull. Thy force devours

Me and my powers

20In tedious hours,

And thy injustice I'll proclaim

Or use some art to cause her heat return,

Or whilst I burn

Make her my urn,

Where I may bury in a marble chest

All my unrest.

Thus her cold breast,

If it but lodge, will quench, my flame.

The Complaint.] The text is taken from Rawlinson Poet. MS. D. 317, fol. 161, where it is written, without title or signature, in King's autograph. There is a copy in Harleian MS. 6917, fol. 97, entitled *The Complaint*.

4 thy] the *Harl. MS.*

21 King originally wrote 'And she thy weakness will proclaim', and then added the text as an afterthought.

28 will] may *Harl.*

On his Shadow

Come, my shadow, constant, true,

Stay, and do not fly me:

When I court thee or would sue,

Thou wilt not deny me.

Female loves I find unkind

And devoid of pity;

Therefore I have changed my mind

And to thee frame this ditty.

Child of my body and that flame

10From whence our light we borrow,

Thou continuest still the same
In my joy or sorrow.
Though thou lov'st the sunshine best
Or enlightened places,
Yet thou dost not fly, but rest,
'Midst my black disgraces.
Thou wouldst have all happy days
When thou art approaching,

No cloud nor night to dim bright rays
20By their sad encroaching.
Let but glimmering lights appear
To banish night's obscuring,
Thou wilt show thou harbourd'st near,
By my side enduring;
And, when thou art forced away
By the sun's declining,
Thy length is doubled, to repay
Thy absence whilst he's shining.
As I flatter not thee fair,
30So thou art not fading;
Age nor sickness can impair
Thy hue by fierce invading.
Let the purest varnished clay
Art can show, or Nature,
View the shades they cast; and they
Grow duskish like thy feature.
'Tis thy truth I most commend—
That thou art not fleeting:

For, as I embrace my friend,

40So thou giv'st him greeting.

If I strike, or keep the peace,

So thou seem'st to threaten,

And single blows by thy increase

Leave my foe double beaten.

As thou findst me walk or sit,

Standing or down lying,

Thou dost all my postures hit,

Most apish in thy prying.

When our actions so consent—

50Expressions dumb, but local—

Words are needless complement,

Else I could wish thee vocal.

Hadst thou but a soul, with sense

And reason sympathising,

Earth could match, nor heaven dispense

A mate so far enticing.

Nay, when bedded in the dust,

'Mongst shades I have my biding,

Tapers can see thy posthume trust

60Within my vault residing.

Had heaven so pliant women made

Or thou their souls couldst marry,

I'd soon resolve to wed my shade;

This love would ne'er miscarry.

But they thy lightness only share;

If shunned, the more they follow,

And to pursuers peevish are

As Daphne to Apollo.

Yet this experience thou hast taught:

70A she-friend and an honour

Like thee; nor that nor she is caught,

Unless I fall upon her.

On his Shadow.] The text is taken from King's autograph in Rawlinson Poet D. 317, foll. 173-4: it has neither heading nor signature. At line 25, the last on this page of the MS., the catchword reads 'Yet when', which is slightly more appropriate, but the text continues 'And when'. There is a copy in Harleian MS. 6917, fol. 97 verso-98, entitled *On his Shadow.* There are the following variants:

8 frame] framed.

11 still *om.*

23 harbourd'st] harbour'st.

26 By] At.

49 so] thus.

55 could] could not (but compare l. 31).

64 would] could.

Wishes to my Son, John,

For this new, and all succeeding years:

January 1, 1630.

If wishes may enrich my boy,

My Jack, that art thy father's joy,

They shall be showered upon thy head

As thick as manna, angel's bread;

And bread I wish thee—this short word

Will furnish both thy back and board;

Not Fortunatus' purse or cap

Nor Danae's gold-replenished lap

Can more supply thee: but content

10Is a large patrimony, sent

From him who did thy soul infuse.

May'st thou this best endowment use

In any state; thy structure is

I see complete—a frontispiece

Promising fair; may it ne'er be

Like Jesuit's volumes, where we see

Virtues and saints adorn the front,

Doctrines of devils follow on't:

May a pure soul inhabit still

20This well-mixed clay; and a straight will

Biassed by reason, that by grace.

May gems of price maintain their place

In such a casket: in that list

Chaste turquoise, sober amethyst

That sacred breastplate still surround:

Urim and Thummim be there found,

Which for thy wearing I design,

That in thee King and Priest may join,

As 'twas thy grandsire's choice, and mine.

30May'st thou attain John the Divine

Chief of thy titles, though contempt

Now brand the clergy; be exempt,

I ever wish thee, from each vice

That may that calling scandalize:

Let not thy tongue with court oil flow,

Nor supple language lay thee low

For thy preferment; make God's cause

Thy pulpit's task, not thine applause;

May'st thou both preach by line and life;

40That thou live well and chaste, a wife

I wish thee, such as is thy sire's,

A lawful help 'gainst lustful fires;

And though promotions often frown

On married brows, yet lie not down

In single baudry; impure monks,

That banish wedlock, license punks.

Peace I do wish thee from those wars

Which gownmen talk out at the bars

Four times a year; I wish thee peace

50Of conscience, country, and increase

In all that best of men commends,

Favour with God, good men thy friends.

Last, for a lasting legacy

I this bequeath, when thou shalt die,

Heaven's monarch bless mine eyes, to see

My wishes crowned, in crowning thee.

Wishes to my Son, John.] This poem is preserved anonymously in Harleian MS. 6917, foll. 101 verso-102, and Mr. Mason assigns it to Henry King. Lines 28-9 strongly support this attribution, but the date at the head of the poem is a serious difficulty, which can only be met by supposing the lines to have been addressed in 1630 to the son of a second marriage: l. 40 refers to a living wife, who could not be the lady of *The Exequy.* King's authorship must therefore be regarded as doubtful.

A Contemplation upon Flowers.

Brave flowers, that I could gallant it like you

And be as little vain!

You come abroad and make a harmless show,

And to your beds of earth again;

You are not proud, you know your birth,

For your embroidered garments are from earth.

You do obey your months and times, but I

Would have it ever spring;

My fate would know no winter, never die,

10Nor think of such a thing.

Oh that I could my bed of earth but view,

And smile, and look as cheerfully as you!

Oh teach me to see death and not to fear,

But rather to take truce;

How often have I seen you at a bier,

And there look fresh and spruce.

You fragrant flowers then teach me that my breath

Like yours may sweeten and perfume my death.

A Contemplation upon Flowers.] Another very doubtful poem from Harleian MS. 6917, fol. 105 verso, where it is attributed to 'H. Kinge'. Mr. Mason points out in support of the attribution that this MS. contains other poems of King and documents relating to his family; but the poem can hardly be regarded as authenticated. It has, however, been quoted as King's in more than one anthology; and it would probably be missed if omitted from an edition of King's poems.

* *
*

POEMS

AND

SONGS,

BY

THOMAS FLATMAN.

INTRODUCTION TO THOMAS FLATMAN.

Flatman has been condoled with on his name by Mr. Bullen, one of the few persons who have done him some justice in recent years.[1] I should rather myself, for reasons which will be given presently, condole with him on his date. His father was probably Robert Flatman of Mendham, Norfolk, and it is supposed that the poet was born in London. The date of his birth, recorded here for the first time, was February 21, 1635, about 5.29 in the morning. So his horoscope, preserved by Ashmole,[2] informs us. When he was elected at Winchester on Michaelmas Day, 1648, he was stated to be 'eleven years old'—a slight miscalculation. He himself in *The Retirement*, written in 1665, correctly speaks of his 'thirty years'. He actually entered Winchester in September, 1649. He was transferred in the usual (when uninterrupted) course to New College, Oxford; he was admitted as a probationer on September 11, 1654, but seems not to have matriculated till July 25, 1655; he became Fellow in 1656.[3] There is no academic record, it would seem, of his ever having taken his degree, though he is spoken of as 'A.B. of Oxford' when, by the King's Letters, he was made M.A. of St. Catherine Hall, Cambridge, in 1666. He went from Oxford to the Inner Temple, in 1655, and was called to the Bar on May 11, 1662. Oldys has a half-satiric reference to his pleading.[4] He was elected a Fellow of the Royal Society in April, 1668. In 1672 he married, his wife being favourably spoken of, and gossip—inevitable whether well founded or not—records that his 'Bachelor's Song' (*v. inf.*) was sung under his windows on the occasion by 'merry friends'. And he died in London on December 8, 1688. Beyond these meagre details, and a statement that he had property at Diss (the cure of Skelton and the home of Maria Jolly), we know little about him directly or by external evidence. By that of his poems he must have been a friend of good men—Walton, Cotton, Edward Browne[5] (Sir Thomas's son), Faithorne the engraver, Oldham, and others. His miniature portraits are well spoken of;—one is in possession of the Duke of Buccleuch, seven are in the South Kensington Museum. That, however, which illustrates his *Poems* is from a painting by John Hayls, whom Pepys's Diary has made known to a wider circle than students of the History of English Painting.

Flatman was evidently a tolerable scholar; and his Latinity, of which several specimens will be found here, does no discredit to the Winchester and the New College of the time. When he began English verse-writing does not seem to be known, but it must have been pretty early. He does not appear to have hurried his Muse; but collected his poems first in 1674, issuing augmented editions, to the number of four in all, up to a time shortly before his death. Of these, the third (1682) and the fourth (1686) have a claim to be regarded as authoritative and are the basis of the present text. The 1682 edition, 'With Additions and Amendments', is better printed, and the 1686—which makes a modest attempt to outbid it 'With many Additions and Amendments'—is valuable for the supplementary poems.[6] His Pindaric epicedes on public men—Ossory, Rupert, the King, &c.—for the most part appeared separately in folio; and in the earlier days of my preparation of this collection I gave myself a good deal of trouble in looking them up. Except the elegy on Ormond (1688) they were reprinted in these two editions. The last (1686) edition of the *Poems*, after some search, was procured for me. It seems to be much rarer than the third of 1682, which I have long possessed, and is not in the Bodleian. Additional poems, not included in the texts of 1682 and 1686, are added as a supplement. Three of these are taken from a transcript in Professor Firth's collection of an autograph MS. of Flatman which is now in America; the title is 'Miscellanies by Tho. Flatman, ex Interiori Templo Londini. Sic imperantibus fatis. Nov. 9, 1661, 13° Caroli 2[di].' This contains in all twenty-three of the poems which have been collated for this reprint. An interesting feature of this manuscript is that it dates a number of the poems. Besides his poems, some pamphlets and Almanacks[7] have been attributed to him on extremely doubtful evidence, or none at all. Except among his friends, it does not seem even in his own time to have been the fashion to think much of his verse; and a triplet of Rochester's, dismissing him as an imitator of Cowley, and a bad one, is usually quoted.[8] Flatman's Pindarics are certainly his weakest poems. But Rochester, for all his wit and wits, was, though an acute, a very ill-natured critic; we know that he thought Cowley himself out of date and (as his representatives in kind, though not in gift, would say to-day) 'early Caroline'. Besides, to dismiss a Pindaric poet of the Restoration as an imitator, and a bad imitator, of Cowley is too obvious to be of much importance. I should certainly admit that the minor Pindaric—of which I have, for my sins or as part of them, probably read as much as any one living—is one of the most dismal departments of English verse. But Flatman's is by no means exceptionally bad, and is at its best better than that of Oldham, or of Otway, or of Swift—men with whom he cannot compare as a man of letters generally. Let us come closer to him and to his work.

Hayls may not have been a great painter; but he certainly seems to have had the knack of putting character in his portraits. Neither that of Pepys nor that of his wife is without it: and that of Flatman has a great deal.[9] It is what would be called, I suppose, by most superficial judges an 'ugly' face—with a broad *retroussé* nose, lips of the kind sometimes called 'sensual', and a heavy (something of a double) chin. But the forehead is high, the mouth smallish, and above all there are a pair of somewhat melancholy eyes which entirely rescue it from any charge of vulgarity, though it is not exactly refined. It certainly suggests what is called in stock phrase an 'artistic temperament': and it may not be too fanciful to see in it the kind of artistic temperament which aims higher than it can hit, begins what it is unable to finish, and never forgets the yew even among the roses. This complexion is, of course, in a way reflected in the very titles of the few things of Flatman known[10] to the few people who do know him—'Death', 'A Thought of Death', 'A Dooms-day Thought', 'Nudus Redibo', &c. But it is almost everywhere; and there is no affectation or *sensiblerie* about it. Flatman is not, as Longfellow, picturesquely and perhaps Carlylesquely, remarked of Matthiessen and Salis, 'a gentleman who walks through life with a fine white cambric handkerchief pressed to his eyes'. He can write battle-songs and love-songs and festive *gaillardises* naturally enough. But the other vein is also natural, and perhaps more so. The funeral panegyric Odes which make a considerable feature of his works were, of course, almost part of the routine business of a professional poet in those times of patronage: one of his regular sources of revenue, in fives or tens or hundreds of guineas, according to his rank on Parnassus and the rank and liberality of his subject in Church or State or City. But Flatman at his best suffuses them with a grave interest in Death itself— a touch now of Lucretius (who seems to have been a favourite of his), now of the Preacher—which is not in the least conventional. In this curious Second Caroline period of faint survivals of the Renaissance and complete abandonment of its traditions, Flatman's heritage appears to have been this sense of Death. A poet might have a worse portion.

In powers of expression he was not equally well apanaged: and it was unlucky for him that he fell in with the special period of popularity of that difficult and dangerous thing the Pindaric, and had enough of the older taste in him to attempt the short metaphysical lyric: 'The Resolve', 'The Fatigue', 'The Indifferent'. For the first he carried guns hardly heavy enough; for the second his lyrical craft was hardly sufficiently swift and handy to catch every puff of spiritual wind. Yet it is mildly astonishing to find how often he comes near to success, and how near that approach sometimes is. How many poets have tried to put the thought of the first line of the first poem in the complete edition:

No more!—Alas! that bitter word, *No more!*

and how many have put it more simply and passionately? The 'Morning Hymn' and 'Evening Anthem' have rather strangely missed (owing no doubt to that superficial connexion with Bishop Ken's which is noticed below) association with hundreds and thousands of very often inferior divine poems that have found home in collections. 'The Resolve' begins quite admirably, and only wanted a little more pains on the poet's part to go on as well. 'Love's Bravo' and 'The Expectation' and 'Fading Beauty' and 'The Slight' are very far indeed from being contemptible. The two *gaillardises*, the 'Bachelor' and the 'Cats', want very little to make them quite capital; and 'The Whim' is in the same case. 'The Advice' actually deserves that adjective, and not a few others will be found pointed out in the notes; while even his Pindarics (at least the earlier ones, for those written after Rochester's death more fully justify his censure than those he can have read) have fine lines and even fine passages.

It is no doubt rather unfortunate that Flatman should have left us so many Horatian translations. For the one thing needful—except in a very few pieces where Horace outgoes himself in massive splendour, and so can be outgone further by more of this, as in Dryden's magnificent version of *Tyrrhena regum*—the one thing needful in translating Horace is something of his well-known and 'curious' urbane elegance. And this was the very quality which perhaps no Restoration poet—certainly not Flatman—could give. The 'dash of vulgarity'[11] which Mr. Bullen has too truly stigmatized affects nearly all of them except when transported by passion (which is nowhere in Horace); or fighting hard in a mood of satiric controversy which is quite different from his pococurantism; or using a massive rhetoric which is equally absent from him. The consequence is that what Flatman gives us is not Horace at all; and is not good Flatman. The 'Canidia' pieces, as one would expect, are about the best, and they are not very good.

I own, however, and I am duly prepared to take the consequences of the confession, that Flatman appeals to me, though in a different way, almost as much as any other of the constituents of this volume, though certainly not so much as some of those of the other two. He had the pure misfortune—as the sternest critic must acknowledge it to have been—of being born too late for one period and too early for another. He could not give to his most serious things the 'brave translunary' exaltations and excursions which came naturally to the men of a time just before his, and he could not correct this want by the order and the sense, the neatness and the finish, which were born with the next generation. 'Death' and 'A Thought of Death' and the other things mentioned unfairly but inevitably remind us that we have left Donne and Crashaw, Vaughan, and even Herbert, behind us. 'The Mistake' and 'The Whim' and many others remind us that we have not come to Prior. Yet others—which it were cruel to particularize and which he that reads will easily find for himself—display a lack of the purely lyrical power which, among his own contemporaries, Rochester and Sedley and Aphra Behn, not to mention others, possessed. Nor had he that gift of recognizing the eclipse of the Moon and utilizing the opportunities of the Earth, which has made Dryden, to competent and catholic tastes, all but one of the greatest of English poets. But still he was a 'child of the Moon' herself; and he has the benefits which she never withholds from her children, though they may be accompanied by a disastrous influence. He was no doubt a minor poet in a time when minor poetry was exposed to special disadvantages. But with far less wit he was more of a poet than Cleveland; with far less art he was perhaps as much of a poet as Stanley; and I am not even sure that, with 'weight for age' in the due sense, he was so very much less of a poet than King. And if those who think but little of these others as poets deem this scanty praise let us go further and say that he *is* a poet—imperfect, disappointing as well as disappointed, only half aneled with the sacred unction and houselled with the divine food—but a poet. Which if any denies he may be 'an excellent person'—as Praed or Praed's Medora so finally puts it—but he does not know much, if indeed he knows anything, about poetry.[12]

[1] By judicious remarks in the preface to his *Musa Proterva* (London, 1889, p. viii), and by specimens both in that and in its companion, *Speculum Amantis*.

[2] In Ashmole MS. 436, at folio 50. Mr. J. K. Fotheringham, who has kindly deciphered the horoscope, points out that there are some inaccuracies in the astrologer's computation, which 'leave a doubt of a few minutes'.

[3] Mr. Ernest Barker, Librarian of New College, kindly gave Mr. Simpson access to the College records to test the above dates and facts.

[4]

Should Flatman for his Client strain the laws

The Painter gives some colour to the cause:

Should Critics censure what the Poet writ,

The Pleader quits him at the Bar of wit.

[5] Browne's diary (March, 1663-4) contains repeated mention of 'Mr. Flatman, chirurgeon' of Norwich, who had been a great traveller. This is additional evidence of the connexion of the Flatmans with Norfolk.

[6] The publisher was Benjamin Tooke, whom Flatman in a letter of November 3, 1675, recommended to Sancroft if he wished to publish his Fifth of November sermon before the House of Commons (Tanner MS. xlii, fol. 181, in Bodley).

[7] *V. inf.*, p. 360.

[8]

Nor that slow drudge in swift Pindaric strains,

Flatman, who Cowley imitates with pains,

And rides a jaded Muse, whipt, with loose reins.

Flatman, who had no bad blood in him, took a magnanimous revenge (*v. inf.*, p. 365).

[9] Four letters of Flatman are published in *Familiar Letters of Love, Gallantry, And Several Occasions, By the Wits of the last and present Age*, 1718, vol. i, pp. 249-54. One of these is a letter to an unnamed patron, sending his own portrait for the patron's collection as 'a foil to the rest'.

[10] And that chiefly because Pope is supposed to have borrowed from them.

[11] Flatman, however, is much less 'coarse' than most of his contemporaries. Putting a very few pieces aside (not themselves very shocking) he might almost challenge my Lord Roscommon for those 'unspotted bays' which his own supposed debtor Pope assigned, and of which we are all so tired.

[12] The Additional Poems (p. 408 sq.) I owe to Mr. Percy Simpson, who collected them from their various sources, added variants throughout from the Firth MS., and gave some hints for correcting my own notes. Mr. G. Thorn-Drury has again given his valuable help.

TO HIS

GRACE THE DUKE OF ORMOND

Lord Lieutenant of Ireland, *&c.*

In humble acknowledgment of
His Princely Favours

These[1] *POEMS* are with all Dutiful
Respect

DEDICATED

By his GRACE's

Ever Oblig'd, and most

Obedient Servant,

Thomas Flatman.

[1] So in 1682, where this Dedication first appeared: 1686 with its usual carelessness 'The', which is most improbable.

To the Reader.

When I was prevail'd upon to make a Fourth Publication of these Poems *with a great many Additions, it was told me,* That *without a* Preface *the Book would be unfashionable;* Universal Custom *had made it a Debt, and in this Age the* Bill of Fare *was as necessary as the* Entertainment. *To be Civil therefore, and to Comply with Expectation, instead of an elaborate Harangue in Commendation of the Art in general, or what, and what Qualifications go to the making up of a* Poet *in particular, and without such artificial Imbellishments as use to be the Ornament of Prefaces, as* Sayings of Philosophers, Ends of Verses, Greek, Latin, Hungarian, French, Welch, *or* Italian, *Be it known unto the Reader, That in my poor Opinion* Poetry *has a very near Resemblance to the modern Experiment of the* Ambling-Saddle; *It's a good Invention for smoothing the* Trott of Prose; *That's the Mechanical use of it. But Physically it gives present Ease to the* Pains *of the* Mind, *contracted by violent Surfeit of either good or bad Usage in the World. To be serious, 'tis an Innocent Help to* Sham *a Man's time when it lies on his hands and his Fancy can relish nothing else. I speak but my own Experience; when any Accident hath either pleas'd or vex'd me beyond my power of expressing either my Satisfaction or Indignation in downright* Prose, *I found it seasonable for* Rhiming; *and I believe from what follows it may be discern'd when 'twas* Fair Weather, *when* Changeable, *and when the* Quicksilver *fell down to* Storm *and* Tempest. *As to the Measures observ'd by me, I always took a peculiar delight in the* Pindarique *strain, and that for two Reasons, First, it gave me a liberty now and then to correct the saucy forwardness of a* Rhime, *and to lay it aside till I had a mind to admit it; And secondly, if my Sense fell at any time too short for my* Stanza, *(and it will often happen so in Versifying) I had then opportunity to fill it up with a* Metaphor *little to the purpose, and (upon occasion) to run that* Metaphor *stark mad into an* Allegory, *a practice very frequent and of admirable use amongst the* Moderns, *especially the* Nobless of the Faculty. *But in good earnest, as to the* Subjects, *which came in my way to write upon, I must declare that I have chosen only such as might be treated within the* Rules of Decency, *and without offence either to* Religion *or good* Manners. *The* Caution *I receiv'd (by* Tradition) *from the Incomparable Mr.* Cowley, *and him I must ever acknowledge but to imitate, if any of the ensuing Copies may deserve the name of* Good *or* Indifferent. *I have not vanity enough to prescribe how a* Muse *ought to be Courted, and I want leisure to borrow from some Treatises I have seen, which look like so many* Academies of Complements *for that purpose. I have known a man, who when he was about to write would screw his face into more disguises than* Scaramuccio, *or a* Quaker *at a Meeting when his Turn came to mount; his breast heav'd, his hair stood on end, his eyes star'd, and the whole man was disorder'd; and truly when he had done, any body at first reading would conclude that at the time he made them he was possess'd with an evil* Spirit. *Another that seem'd like* Nostradamus *(when the Whim took him in the head to Prophesie,) he sate upon his* Divining Tripos, *his elbow on his knee, his Lamp by his side, all the avenues of light stopp'd, full of expectation when the* little faint flames *should steal in through a crevice of the Shutters; This Gentleman indeed writ extreme* Melancholy Madrigals. *I have had the happiness to hear of a Third too, whose whole life was* Poetical, *he was a* Walking Poem, *and his way was this; finding that the fall of the Leaf was already upon him, and prudently foreseeing that in the Winter of his old Age he might possibly want Fodder, he carry'd always about him one of* Raimund Lully's Repositories, *a piece of* Mathematical Paper, *and in what Company soever he came, the* Spoon *was always ready for the* Civet-Cat, *nothing scap'd him that* fell from a Wit: *At night his custom was to digest all that he had pirated that Day, under proper Heads; This was his* Arsenal, *his inexhaustible* Magazine; *so that upon occasion he had no more to do, than to give a snap, or two to his Nails; a rub or two upon the sutures of his Head, to turn over his* Hint-Book, *and the Matter was at hand, his business (after that piece of* Legerdemain) *was only* Tacking, *and* Tagging: *I never saw but One of this Author's Compositions, and really It troubled me, because It put me in mind, how much time I had mispent in Coffee-Houses, for there was nothing in It, but what I could find a Father for There; Nay, (with a little recollection,) a man might name most of the Birds from whence he had pluckt his Feathers. Some there are that Beseech, Others that Hector their* Muses: *Some that Diet their* Pegasus, *give him his Heats and Ayrings for the Course; Others that endeavour to slop up his broken wind with Medicinal Ale and Bisquet; But these for the most part are men of* Industry; *Rhiming is their proper Business, they are fain to labour hard, and use much Artifice for a poor Livelihood, I wish 'em good Trading. I profess I never had design to be incorporated into the Society; my utmost End was merely for Diversion of my self and a few Friends whom I very well love; and if the question should be ask'd why these Productions are expos'd, I may truly say, I could not help it; One unlucky Copy, like a Bell-weather, stole from me in to the Common, and the rest of the Flock took their opportunity to leave the Enclosure. If I might be proud of any thing, it should be the first Copy of the Book, but therein I had the greatest advantage given me that any Noble Subject could afford. And so much for* Preface *and* Poetry, *till some very powerful Star shall over-rule my present Resolution.*

To the Reader. As in some other cases, I have thought it best to keep the original arrangement of capitals, type-differences, &c., here. The poems are printed, like the greater part of the collection, in modern form, but with no important alterations unnoticed.

On the Excellent Poems of my most Worthy Friend, Mr. Thomas Flatman.

You happy issue of a happy wit,

As ever yet in charming numbers writ,

Welcome into the light, and may we be

Worthy so happy a posterity.

We long have wish'd for something excellent;

But ne'er till now knew rightly what it meant:

For though we have been gratified, 'tis true,

From several hands with things both fine and new,

The wits must pardon me, if I profess,

10That till this time the over-teeming press

Ne'er set out Poesy in so true a dress:

Nor is it all, to have a share of wit,

There must be judgement too to manage it;

For Fancy's like a rough, but ready horse,

Whose mouth is govern'd more by skill than force;

Wherein (my friend) you do a maistry own,

If not particular to you alone;

Yet such at least as to all eyes declares

Your Pegasus the best performs his airs.

20Your Muse can humour all her subjects so,

That as we read we do both feel and know;

And the most firm impenetrable breast

With the same passion that you write's possest.

Your lines are rules, which who shall well observe

Shall even in their errors praise deserve:

The boiling youth, whose blood is all on fire,

Push'd on by vanity, and hot desire,

May learn such conduct here, men may approve

And not excuse, but even applaud his love.

30Ovid, who made an art of what to all

Is in itself but too too natural,

Had he but read your verse, might then have seen

The style of which his precepts should have been,
And (which it seems he knew not) learnt from thence
To reconcile frailty with innocence.
The love *you* write virgins and boys may read,
And never be debauch'd but better bred;
For without love, beauty would bear no price,
And dullness, than desire's a greater vice:
40Your greater subjects with such force are writ
So full of sinewy strength, as well as wit,
That when you are *religious*, our divines
May emulate, but not reprove your lines:
And when you reason, there the learned crew
May learn to speculate, and speak from you.
You no profane, no obscene language use
To smut your paper, or defile your Muse.
Your gayest things, as well express'd as meant,
Are equally both quaint and innocent.
50But your Pindaric Odes indeed are such
That Pindar's lyre from his own skilful touch
Ne'er yielded such an harmony, nor yet
Verse keep such time on so unequal feet.
So by his own generous confession
Great Tasso by Guarini was outdone:
And (which in copying seldom does befall)
The ectype's better than th' original.
But whilst your fame I labour to send forth,
By the ill-doing it I cloud your worth,
60In something all mankind unhappy are,
And you as mortal too must have your share;

'Tis your misfortune to have found a friend,

Who hurts and injures where he would commend.

But let this be your comfort, that your bays

Shall flourish green, maugre an ill-couch'd praise.

CHARLES COTTON, Esq.

You happy, &c.] 16 Cotton may have had several reasons for keeping the form 'maistry'—at any rate it should certainly be kept here, though 'mastery' with or without apostrophated *e* would fill the verse properly.

50 'Pindari*que*' or 'Pindariqu'' in the original throughout the Volume.

57 ectype] Not uncommon even later for 'copy'.

This piece is in the original about half italics, which, for the most part, express no kind of emphasis. The next is almost entirely free from them, and the difference continues throughout the Commendatory Poems in such a fashion as to show that they were used on no principle at all. Flatman's own text has very few, outside of proper names.

To my Friend Mr Thomas Flatman, upon the Publication of his Poems.

I.

As when a Prince his standard does erect,

And calls his subjects to the field,

From such as early take his side,

And readily obedience yield,

He is instructed where he may suspect,

And where he safely may confide:

So, mighty friend,

That you may see

A perfect evidence of loyalty,

10No business I pretend;

From all th' incumbrances of human life,

From nourishing the sinful people's strife,

And the increasing weaknesses of age.

II.

Domestic care, the mind's incurable disease,

I am resolv'd I will forget.

Ah! could I hope the restless pain

Would now entirely cease,

And never more return again,

My thoughts I would in other order set;

20By more than protestations I would show,

Not the sum total only of the debt,

But the particulars of all I owe.

III.

This I would do: but what will our desire avail

When active heat and vigour fail?

'Tis well thou hast more youthful combatants than I,

Right able to protect thy immortality:

If envy should attack thy spotless name

(And that attacks the best of things

And into rigid censure brings

30The most undoubted registers of fame),

Their fond artillery let them dispense,

Piercing wit and murd'ring eloquence,

Noble conceit and manly sense,

Charming numbers let 'em shine

And dazzle dead in ev'ry line

The most malicious of thy foes,

Though Hell itself should offer to oppose;

I (thy decrepit subject) only can resign

The little life of art is left, to ransom thine:

40Fumbling's as bad in poetry,

And as ridiculous, as 'tis in gallantry:

But if a dart I may prevent,

Which at my friend's repute was meant,

Let them then direct at me;

By dying in so just a war,

I possibly may share

In thy infallible eternity.

IV.

But, dearest friend

(Before it be too late),

50Let us a while expostulate,

What heat of glory call'd you on,

Your learnèd empire to extend

Beyond the limits of your own dominion?

At home, you were already crown'd with bays:

Why foreign trophies do you seek to raise?

Poets arcanas have of government,

And tho' the homagers of your own continent

Out of a sense of duty do submit,

Yet public print a jealousy creates,

60And intimates a laid design

Unto the neighb'ring potentates.

Now into all your secret arts they pry,

And weigh each hint by rules of policy.

Offensive leagues they twine,

In councils, rotas, and cabals they sit,

Each petty burgess thinks it fit

The Corporation should combine

Against the Universal Monarchy of Wit,

And straight declare for quite abjuring it.

V.

70Hence then must you prepare for an invasion:

Tho' not from such as are reclaim'd by education;

In the main points all European wits agree,

All allow order, art, and rules of decency,

And to be absolutely perfect, ne'er was yet

A beauty such, or such a wit.

I fear the Pagan and the barbarous,

A nation quite Antipodes to us;

The infidel unletter'd crew (I mean)

Who call that only wit,

80Which is indeed but the reverse of it;

Creatures in whom civility ne'er shone,

But (unto Nature's contradiction)

It is their glory to be so obscene,

You'd think the legion of th' unclean

Were from the swine (to which they were condemn'd) releas'd,

And had these verier swine (than them) possess'd.

VI.

If these should an advantage take

And on thy fame a depredation make,

You must submit to the unhappiness;

90These are the common enemies of our belief and art,

And by hostility possess'd

The world's much greater part:

All things with them are measur'd by success:

If the battle be not won;

If the author do not sell;

Into their dull capacities it will not sink,

They cannot with deliberation think

How bravely the commander led them on,

No nor wherein the book was written well:

100When ('tis a thing impossible to do)

He cannot find his army courage (Sir), nor you

Your readers, learning, wit, and judgement too.

ROBERT THOMPSON, LL.D.

103 I have not identified Robert Thompson, LL.D., but I shall always think
of him as author of some of the worst Pindaric of his time, which is saying a
great deal.

To my Friend Mr. Thomas Flatman, on the Publishing of these his Poems.

Let not (my friend) th' incredulous sceptic man

Dispute what potent Art and Nature can!

Let him believe, the birds that did bemoan

The loss of Zeuxis' grapes in querulous tone,

Were silenc'd by a painted dragon, found

A *Telesme* to restrain their chatt'ring sound,

And that one made a mistress could enforce

A neighing sigh, ev'n from a stallion horse!

Let old Timanthes now unveil the face

10Of his Atrides, thou'lt give sorrow grace!

Now may Parrhasius let his curtain stand!

And great Protogenes take off his hand!

For all that lying Greece and Latium too

Have told us of, thou (only thou) mak'st true.

And all the miracles which they could show,

Remain no longer faith; but science now.

Thou dost those things that no man else durst do,

Thou paint'st the lightning, and the thunder too!

The soul and voice!

20Thou'lt make Turks, Jews, with Romanists consent,

To break the second great Commandement:

And them persuade an adoration giv'n

In picture, will as grateful be to Heav'n

As one in metre. Th' art is in excess;

But yet thy ingenuity makes it less.

With pen and pencil thou dost all outshine,

In speaking picture, Poesy divine.

Poets, creators are! You made us know

Those are above, and dread those are below;

30But 'tis no wonder you such things can dare,

That painter, poet, and a prophet are.

The stars themselves think it no scorn to be

Plac'd, and directed in their way by thee.

Thou know'st their virtue, and their situation,

The fate of years, and every great mutation;

With the same kindness let them look on Earth,

As when they gave thee first thy happy birth!

The sober Saturn aspects Cynthia bright,

40Resigning hers, to give us thy new light.

The gentle Venus rose with Mercury

(Presage of softness in thy Poesy),

And Jove and Mars in amicable Trine

Do still give spirit to thy polish'd line.

Thou mayst do what thou wilt without control:

Only thyself and Heav'n can paint thy soul.

FRAN. BARNARD, M.D.

Let not, &c.] 6 The form *Telesme*, which may be allowed its italics, reproduces the (late) Greek τέλεσμα, instead of the Spanish-Arabic 'talisman'.

22 giv'n] Orig. 'giv'*d*, but correct in previous (1682) edition.

39 Both editions have a comma at 'aspects', which obscures the sense. 'Aspect' is made a transitive verb in the sense of the astrological substantive = 'arranges his situation in regard to the Moon so as to make her resign', &c. 1686 'To' for 'The', wrongly.

46 It would be a shame to rob Francis Barnard of the italics which distinguish the entire line in the original. He died on February 9, 1698, and was buried at St. Botolph's, Bishopsgate.

To his esteemed Friend Mr. Thomas Flatman, Upon the Publishing of his Poems.

Your Poems (friend) come on the public stage

In a debauch'd and a censorious age:

Where nothing now is counted standard wit,

But what's profane, obscene, or's bad as it.

For our great wits, like gallants of the times

(And such they are), court only those loose rhymes,

Which, like their misses, patch'd and painted are;

But scorn what virtuous is and truly fair;

Such as your Muse is, who with careful art

10For all but such, hath wisely fram'd a part.

One while (methinks) under some gloomy shade,

I see the melancholy lover laid,

Pleasing himself in that his pensive fit

With what you have on such occasion writ.

Another while (methinks) I seem to hear

'Mongst those, who sometimes will unbend their care.

And steal themselves out from the busy throng,

Your pleasant *Songs* in solemn consort sung.

Again (methinks) I see the grave Divine

20Lay by his other books, to look on thine,

And from thy serious and divine *Review*

See what our duty is, and his own too.

Yet, worthy friend, you can't but guess what doom

Is like to pass on what you've writ, by some;

But there are others, now your book comes forth,

Who (I am sure) will prize it as 'tis worth,

Who know it fully fraught with staple ware,

Such as the *Works* of the great Cowley are,

And 'mongst our rarest English poems, thine

30Next unto his immortally shall shine.

RICH. NEWCOURT.

Your Poems, &c.] 14 i.e., no doubt, *The Desperate Lover* (*v. inf.* p. 336).

18 consort] As so often = 'concert'.

21 divine *Review*] The poem to Sancroft (*inf.*, p. 301).

31 Richard Newcourt is discoverable and throws a little more light on Flatman's circle of acquaintance. He was a topographer, and drew a map of London published in 1658 by Faithorne the elder (*v. inf.*).

To my Worthy Friend Mr. Thomas Flatman,
Upon the Publishing of his Poems.

Rude and unpolish'd as my lines can be,

I must start forth into the world with thee.

That which, yet private, did my wonder raise,

Now 'tis made public challenges my praise:

Such miracles thy charming verse can do,

Where'er it goes, it draws me with it too.

This is a kind of birthday to thy Muse!

Transported with delight I cannot choose

But bid her *Welcome to the Light*, and tell,

10How much I value what is writ so well;

Tho' thou reap'st no advantage by my rhyme,

More than a taper helps the day to shine.

Thus in dull pomp does th' empty coach attend

To pay respect to some departed friend!

The difference of regard in this does lie,

That honours dust, *mine* that which cannot die:

For what can blast the labours of thy pen,

While wit and virtue are allow'd by men?

Thou entertain'st the world with such a feast,

20So cleanly and so elegantly drest,

So stor'd with laudable varieties

As may a modest appetite suffice;

Whoever is thy guest is sure to find

Something or other that may please his mind.

Sometimes in pious flames thy Muse aspires

Her bosom warm'd with supernat'ral fires;

In noble flights with Pindar, soars above;

Dallies sometimes with not-indecent love,

Thence down into the grave does humbly creep,

30And renders Death desirable as Sleep.

The debonair, the melancholy here

Find matter for their mirth, ease for their care.

Since such provision's made for all that come,

He must be squeamish that goes empty home;

If these refections cannot do him good,

'Tis 'cause his stomach's vicious, not the food.

FRANCIS KNOLLYS, Esq.

Rude and unpolished, &c.] 4 public] Orig. 'publique'. So often 'Pindarique', and sometimes '-iq".

37 This Knollys is again unknown to me.

To the Author on his excellent Poems.

I.

Strange magic of thy wit and style,

Which to their griefs mankind can reconcile!

Whilst thy Philander's tuneful voice we hear

Condoling our disastrous state,

Touch'd with a sense of our hard fate,

We sigh perhaps, or drop a tear,

But he the mournful song so sweetly sings,

That more of pleasure than regret it brings.

With such becoming grief

10The Trojan chief

Troy's conflagration did relate,

Whilst ev'n the suffrers in the fire drew near

And with a greedy ear

Devour'd the story of their own subverted state.

II.

Kind Heav'n (as to her darling son) to thee

A double portion did impart,

A gift of Painting and of Poesy:

But for thy rivals in the painter's art,

If well they represent, they can effect

20No more, nor can we more expect.

But more than this *thy* happy pencils give;

Thy draughts are more than representative,

For, if we'll credit our own eyes, they *live!*

Ah! worthy friend, couldst thou maintain the state

Of what with so much ease thou dost create,

We might reflect on death with scorn!

But pictures, like th' originals, decay!

Of colours those consist, and these of clay;

Alike compos'd of dust, to dust alike return!

III.

30Yet 'tis our happiness to see

Oblivion, Death, and adverse Destiny

Encounter'd, vanquish'd, and disarm'd by thee.

For if thy pencils fail,

Change thy artillery

And thou'rt secure of victory.

Employ thy quill and thou shall still prevail.

The Grand Destroyer, greedy Time, reveres

Thy Fancy's imag'ry, and spares

The meanest thing that bears

40Th' impression of thy pen;

Tho' coarse and cheap their natural metal were,

Stamp'd with thy verse he knows th' are sacred then,

He knows them by that character to be

Predestinate and set apart for immortality.

IV.

If native lustre in thy themes appear,

Improv'd by thee it shines more clear:

Or if thy subject's void of native light,

Thy Fancy need but dart a beam

To gild thy theme,

50And make the rude mass beautiful and bright.

Thou vary'st oft thy strains, but still

Success attends each strain:

Thy verse is always lofty as the hill,

Or pleasant as the plain.

How well thy Muse the Pastoral Song improves!

Whose nymphs and swains are in their loves

As innocent, and yet as kind as doves.

But most She moves our wonder and delight,

When She performs her loose Pindaric flight,

60Oft to their outmost reach She will extend

Her tow'ring wings to soar on high,

And then by just degrees descend:

Oft in a swift strait course She glides,

Obliquely oft the air divides,

And oft with wanton play hangs hov'ring in the sky.

V.

Whilst sense of duty into my artless Muse

Th' ambition would infuse

To mingle with those Nymphs that homage pay,

And wait on thine in her triumphant way,

70Defect of merit checks her forward pride,

And makes her dread t' approach thy chariot side;

For 'twere at least a rude indecency

(If not profane) t' appear

At this solemnity,

Crown'd with no laurel wreath (as others are);

But this we will presume to do,

At distance, to attend the show,

Officious to gather up

The scatter'd bays, if any drop

80From others' temples, and with those

A plain plebeian coronet compose.

This, as your livery, she'd wear, to hide

Her nakedness, not gratify her pride!

Such was the verdant dress

Which the Offending Pair did frame

Of platted leaves, not to express

Their pride i'th' novel garb, but to conceal their shame.

N. TATE.

42 'th" for 'they' is an instance, good in its badness, of the uglier apostrophation.

63 strait] So *both* edd.: but as often for 'strai*gh*t'.

75 'Crown'd with no laurel wreath (as others are)' should be a comfort to the poetaster. For Nahum had only to wait less than twenty years and he *was* crowned in the very lifetime of the discrowned 'other' Dryden, who wore the wreath at this time, and who meanwhile had done him the enormous honour of admitting him to collaboration in *Absalom and Achitophel*. Tate has other verses addressed to Flatman; see his *Poems*, p. 67.

To my dear Friend Mr. Thomas Flatman, Upon the Publication of his Poems.

PINDARIC ODE.

I.

Within the haunted thicket, where

The feather'd choristers are met to play;

And celebrate with voices clear,

And accents sweet, the praise of May:

The ouzel, thrush, and speckled lark,

And Philomel, that loves the dawn and dark:

These (the inspired throng)

In numbers smooth and strong

Adorn their noble theme with an immortal song,

10While woods and vaults, the brook and neighbouring hill,

Repeat the varied close and the melodious trill.

II.

Here feast your ears, but let their eye

Wander, and see one of the lesser fry

Under a leaf, or on a dancing twig,

Ruffle his painted feathers, and look big,

Perk up his tail, and hop between

The boughs; by moving, only to be seen,

Perhaps his troubled breast he prunes,

As he doth meditate his tunes:

20At last (compos'd) his little head he rears,

Towards (what he strives to imitate) the spheres;

And chirping then begins his best,

Falls on to pipe among the rest;

Deeming that all's not worth a rush,

Without his whistle from the bush.

III.

Th' harmonious sound did reach my ear,

That echo'd *thy* clear name,

Which all must know, who e'er did hear

Of Cowley or Orinda's fame;

30I heard the Genius, with surprising grace,

Would visit us with his fair offspring, gay

As is the morning spring in May;

But fairer much, and of immortal race.

IV.

Delighted greatly, as I list'ning stood,

The sound came from each corner of the wood;

It both the shrubs and cedars shak'd,

And my drowsy Muse awak'd;

Strange that the sound should be so shrill,

That had its passage through a quill.

40Then I resolv'd *thy* praises to rehearse,

The wonders of *thy pen*, among the crowd

Of thy learn'd friends that sing so loud:

But 'twas not to be sung, or reach'd in verse.

By my weak notes, scarce to be heard,

Or if they could, not worth regard;

Desisting therefore I must only send

My very kind well wishes to my friend.

OCTAVIAN PULLEYN.

Within the haunted, &c.] 9 theme] So spelt here; 'theam' elsewhere—a fresh pair of instances from the same book of the absurdity of keeping bad spelling for its own sake.

48 Octavian Pulleyn was probably the son of Octavian Pulleyn, warden of the Stationers' Company; he published Woodford's *Paraphrase of the Psalms*.

Commendatory Poems

The following spirited preface and a prefatory poem were printed only in the *Poems and Songs* of 1674; they are worth preserving here.

Advertisement to the Reader.

By long Prescription time out of mind, *the next Leafe to the* Title Page *claims an* EPISTLE *to the* READER; *I had the Project once in my own thoughts too: But the Market is so abominably* forestall'd *already with all manner of excuses for Printing, that I could not possibly contrive one, that would look any thing* New: *And besides I never found, amongst all the* Epistles *that I have read, that the best Rethorick in 'em could perswade me to have a better opinion of the Books for* Their *sakes: I am apt to believe the rest of Mankind much of my humour in this particular, and therefore do here expose these few Results of my many Idle hours, to the mercy of the wide World, quite guiltless of* Address *or* Ceremony. *And that* Reader, who will *not believe I had some tolerable Reason for* This Publication, *cannot give me much disturbance, because I'me sure he is not at all acquainted with*

T. F.

April 10. 1674.

To his Worthy Friend Mr. Thomas Flatman
on the publishing of his Poems.

I.

I think thou art not well advised, my friend,

To bring thy spritely Poems on the stage

Now when the Muses' empire 's at an end

And there 's none left that feel poetic rage,

Now Cowley's dead, the glory of the age,

And all the lesser singing birds are starved i'th' cage.

II.

Nor was it well done to permit my bush,

My holly bush, to hang before thy wine,

For friends' applauses are not worth a rush,

And every fool can get a gilded sign.

In troth I have no faculty at praise;

My bush is very full of thorns, though it seems bays.

III.

When I would praise I cannot find a rhyme,

But if I have a just pretence to rail,

They come in numerous throngs at any time,

Their everlasting fountains never fail,

They come in troops and for employment pray;

If I have any wit, it lies only that way.

IV.

But yet I'll try, if thou wilt rid thy mind

Of thoughts of rhyming and of writing well,

And bend thy studies to another kind—

I mean, in craft and riches to excel;

If thou desert thy friends and better wine,

And pay'st no more attendance on the needy Nine.

V.

Go, and renounce thy wit and thy good parts—

Wit and good parts, great enemies to wealth,—

And barter honesty for more thriving arts,

Prize gold before a good name, ease, and health.

Answer the Dog and Bottle, and maintain

There's great ease in a yoke, and freedom in a chain.

VI.

I'll love thee now when this is done, I'll try

To sing thy praise, and force my honest Muse to lie.

WALTER POPE.

POEMS.

On the Death of the Right Honourable Thomas Earl of Ossory.

PINDARIC ODE.

Stanza I.

No more!—Alas that bitter word, *No more!*

The Great, the Just, the Generous, the Kind;

The universal Darling of Mankind,

The noble OSSORY is now *No more!*

The mighty man is fall'n—

From Glory's lofty pinnacle,

Meanly like one of us, he fell,

Not in the hot pursuit of victory,

As gallant men would choose to die;

10But tamely, like a poor plebeian, from his bed

To the dark grave a captive led;

Emasculating sighs, and groans around,

His friends in floods of sorrow drown'd;

His awful truncheon and bright arms laid by,

He bow'd his glorious head to Destiny.

II.

Celestial Powers! how unconcern'd you are!

No black eclipse or blazing star

Presag'd the death of this illustrious man,

No deluge, no, nor hurricane;

20In her old wonted course Nature went on,

As if some common thing were done,

One single victim to Death's altar's come,

And not in Ossory an whole hecatomb.

Yet, when the founder of old Rome expir'd,

When the Pellëan youth resign'd his breath,

And when the great Dictator stoop'd to death,

Nature and all her faculties retir'd:

Amaz'd she started when amaz'd she saw

The breaches of her ancient fundamental law,

30Which kept the world in awe:

For men less brave than him, her very heart did ache,

The labouring Earth did quake,

And trees their fix'd foundations did forsake;

Nature in some prodigious way

Gave notice of their fatal day:

Those lesser griefs with pain she thus exprest,

This did confound, and overwhelm her breast.

III.

Shrink, ye crown'd heads, that think yourselves secure,

And from your mould'ring thrones look down,

40Your greatness cannot long endure,

The King of Terrors claims you for his own;

You are but tributaries to his dreadful crown:

Renown'd, Serene, Imperial, most August,

Are only high and mighty epithets for dust.

In vain, in vain so high

Our tow'ring expectations fly,

While th' blossoms of our hopes, so fresh, so gay,

Appear, and promise fruit, then fade away.

From valiant Ossory's ever loyal hands,

50What did we not believe!

We dream'd of yet unconquer'd lands

- 482 -

He to his Prince could give,

And neighbouring crowns retrieve:

Expected that he would in triumph come

Laden with spoils and Afric banners home,

As if an hero's years

Were as unbounded as our fond desires.

IV.

Lament, lament, you that dare Honour love,

60And court her at a noble rate

(Your prowess to approve),

That dare religiously upon her wait,

And blush not to grow good, when you grow great,

Such mourners suit *His* virtue, such *His* State.

And you, brave souls, who for your country's good

Did wondrous things in fields and seas of blood,

Lament th' undaunted chief that led you on;

Whose exemplary courage could inspire

The most degenerate heart with martial English fire.

70Your bleeding wounds who shall hereafter dress

With an indulgent tenderness;

Touch'd with a melting sympathy,

Who shall your wants supply,

Since he, your good Samaritan, is gone?

O Charity! thou richest boon of Heaven,

To man in pity given!

(For when well-meaning mortals give,

The poor's and their own bowels they relieve;)

Thou mak'st us with alacrity to die,

80Miss'd and bewail'd like thee, large-hearted Ossory.

V.

Arise, ye blest inhabitants above,

From your immortal seats arise,

And on our wonder, on our love

Gaze with astonish'd eyes.

Arise! Arise! make room,

Th' exalted Shade is come.

See where he comes! What princely port he bears!

How God-like he appears!

His shining temples round

90With wreaths of everlasting laurels bound!

As from the bloody field of Mons he came,

Where he outfought th' hyperboles of Fame.

See how the Guardian-Angel of our isle

Receives the deifi'd champion with a smile!

Welcome, the Guardian-Angel says,

Full of songs of joy and praise,

Welcome thou art to me,

And to these regions of serenity!

Welcome, the wingèd choir resounds,

100While with loud *Euge's* all the sacred place abounds.

On the Death of the Earl of Ossory.] Thomas Butler (1634-80), by courtesy Earl of Ossory, though not exactly a Marcellus (for he was forty-six when he died), holds a distinguished place among those who have died too soon. He was a soldier, a sailor, a statesman; if not an orator, an effective speaker; and though no milksop or 'good boy', one emphatically, 'of the right sort'. The excellent first line (see Introduction) is well supported by the whole opening quatrain; and it has been left, typographically, as it appears in the original. The rest may undergo the usual law. The poem was first issued in folio in 1681: 'be' was read for 'grow' in l. 63.

58 The French rhyme, as if 'dés*ir*', is not uninteresting.

To the Memory of the Incomparable Orinda.

PINDARIC ODE.

Stanza I.

A long adieu to all that's bright,

Noble, or brave in woman-kind;

To all the wonders of their wit,

And trophies of their mind:

The glowing heat of th' holy fire is gone:

To th' altar, whence 'twas kindled, flown;

There's nought on earth, but ashes left behind;

E'er since th' amazing sound was spread,

Orinda's dead;

10Every soft and fragrant word,

All that language could afford;

Every high and lofty thing

That's wont to set the soul on wing,

No longer with this worthless world would stay.

Thus, when the death of the great Pan was told,

Along the shore the dismal tidings roll'd;

The lesser Gods their fanes forsook,

Confounded with the mighty stroke,

They could not overlive that fatal day,

20But sigh'd and groan'd their gasping Oracles away.

II.

How rigid are the laws of Fate

And how severe that black decree!

No sublunary thing is free,

But all must enter th' adamantine gate:

Sooner or later must we come

To Nature's dark retiring room:

And yet 'tis pity, is it not?

The learned, as the fool should die,

One, full as low, as t'other lie,

30Together blended in the general lot!

Distinguish'd only from the common crowd

By an hing'd coffin or an holland shroud,

Though Fame and Honour speak them ne'er so loud.

Alas, Orinda! even thou,

Whose happy verse made others live,

And certain immortality could give;

Blasted are all thy blooming glories now,

The laurel withers o'er thy brow:

Methinks it should disturb thee to conceive

40That when poor I this artless breath resign,

My dust should have as much of Poetry as thine!

III.

Too soon we languish with desire

Of what we never could enough admire.

On th' billows of this world sometimes we rise

So dangerously high,

We are to Heaven too nigh:

When all in rage

(Grown hoary with one minute's age)

The very self-same fickle wave,

50Which the entrancing prospect gave,

Swoln to a mountain, sinks into a grave.

Too happy mortals, if the Powers above

As merciful would be,

And easy to preserve the thing we love,

As in the giving they are free!

But they too oft delude our wearied eyes,

They fix a flaming sword 'twixt us and Paradise!

A weeping evening blurs a smiling day,

Yet why should heads of gold have feet of clay?

60Why should the man that wav'd th' Almighty wand,

That led the murmuring crowd

By pillar and by cloud,

Shivering atop of aery Pisgah stand

Only to see, but never, never tread the Promis'd Land?

IV.

Throw your swords and gauntlets by,

You daring Sons of War!

You cannot purchase ere you die

One honourable scar,

Since that fair hand that gilded all your bays;

70That in heroic numbers wrote your praise,

That you might safely sleep in Honour's bed,

Itself, alas! is wither'd, cold, and dead:

Cold and dead are all those charms

That burnish'd your victorious arms;

Those useless things hereafter must

Blush first in blood, and then in rust:

No oil but that of her smooth words can serve

Weapon and warrior to preserve.

Expect no more from this dull age

80But folly or poetic rage,

Short-liv'd nothings of the stage,

Vented to-day, and cried to-morrow down;

With her the soul of Poesie is gone,

Gone, while our expectations flew

As high a pitch as she has done,

Exhal'd to Heaven like early dew,

Betimes the little shining drops are flown,

Ere th' drowsy world perceiv'd that manna was come down

V.

You of the sex that would be fair,

90Exceeding lovely, hither come,

Would you be pure as Angels are,

Come dress you by Orinda's tomb,

And leave your flattering glass at home.

Within that marble mirror see,

How one day such as she

You must, and yet alas! can never be!

Think on the heights of that vast soul,

And then admire, and then condole.

Think on the wonders of her generous pen,

100'Twas she made Pompey truly great;

Neither the purchase of his sweat

Nor yet Cornelia's kindness made him live again:

With envy think, when to the grave you go,

How very little must be said of you,

Since all that can be said of virtuous woman was her due.

To the memory, &c.] For 'Orinda', or Katharine Philips, see vol. i. This Pindaric
was first printed in her *Poems* of 1667: the chief variants are—

58 blurs] crowns.

71 While you securely sleep.

75 Those useless things] Inglorious arms.

77 can] will.

99 generous *om.*

101 Neither the expense of blood nor sweat.

The Review.

PINDARIC ODE to the Reverend Dr. WILLIAM SANCROFT, now Lord
Archbishop of Canterbury.

Stanza I.

When first I stept into th' alluring maze

To tread this world's mysterious ways,

Alas! I had nor guide, nor clue,

No Ariadne lent her hand,

Not one of Virtue's guards did bid me stand,

Or ask'd me what I meant to do,

Or whither I would go:

This labyrinth so pleasant did appear,

I lost myself with much content,

10Infinite hazards underwent,

Out-straggled Homer's crafty wanderer,

And ten years more than he in fruitless travels spent;

The one half of my life is gone,

The shadow the meridian past;

Death's dismal evening drawing on,

Which must with damps and mists be overcast,

An evening that will surely come,

'Tis time, high time to give myself the welcome home.

II.

Had I but heartily believ'd

20That all the Royal Preacher said was true,)

When first I ent'red on the stage,

And Vanity so hotly did pursue;

Convinc'd by his experience, not my age,

I had myself long since retriev'd,

I should have let the curtain down,

Before the Fool's part had begun:

But I throughout the tedious play have been

Concern'd in every busy scene;

Too too inquisitive I tried

30Now this, anon another face,

And then a third, more odd, took place,

Was everything, but what I was.

Such was my Protean folly, such my pride,

Befool'd through all the tragi-comedy,

Where others met with hissing, to expect a *Plaudite*.

III.

I had a mind the Pastoral to prove,

Searching for happiness in Love,

And finding Venus painted with a Dove,

A little naked Boy hard by,

40The Dove, which had no gall,

The Boy no dangerous arms at all;

They do thee wrong, great Love, said I,

Much wrong, great Love! ——scarce had I spoke

Ere into my unwary bosom came

An inextinguishable flame:

From fair Amira's eyes the lightning broke,

That left me more than thunder-strook;

She carries tempest in that lovely name:

Love's mighty and tumultuous pain

50Disorders Nature like an hurricane.

Yet couldn't I believe such storms could be,

When I launch'd forth to sea;

Promis'd myself a calm and easy way,

Though I had seen before

Piteous ruins on the shore,

And on the naked beach Leander breathless lay.

IV.

To extricate myself from Love

Which I could ill obey, but worse command,

I took my pencils in my hand,

60With that artillery for conquest strove,

Like wise Pygmalion then did I

Myself design my deity;

Made my own saint, made my own shrine:

If she did frown, one dash could make her smile,

All bickerings one easy stroke could reconcile,

Plato feign'd no idea so divine:

Thus did I quiet many a froward day,

While in my eyes my soul did play,

Thus did the time, and thus myself beguile;

70Till on a day, but then I knew not why,

A tear fall'n from my eye,

Wash'd out my saint, my shrine, my deity:

Prophetic chance! the lines are gone,

And I must mourn o'er what I doted on:

I find even Giotto's circle has not all perfection.

V.

To Poetry I then inclin'd;

Verse that emancipates the mind,

Verse that unbends the soul;

That amulet of sickly fame,

80Verse that from wind articulates a name;

Verse for both fortunes fit, to smile and to condole.

Ere I had long the trial made,

A serious thought made me afraid:

For I had heard Parnassus' sacred hill

Was so prodigiously high,

Its barren top so near the sky;

The ether there

So very pure, so subtil, and so rare,

'Twould a chameleon kill,

90The beast that is all lungs, and feeds on air:

Poets the higher up that hill they go,

Like pilgrims, share the less of what's below:

Hence 'tis they ever go repining on,

And murmur more than their own Helicon.

I heard them curse their stars in ponderous rhymes,

And in grave numbers grumble at the times;

Yet where th' illustrious Cowley led the way,

I thought it great discretion there to go astray.

VI.

From liberal Arts to the litigious Law,

100Obedience, not ambition, did me draw;)

I look'd at awful quoif and scarlet gown

Through others' optics, not my own:

Untie the Gordian knot that will,

I see no rhetoric at all

In them that learnedly can brawl,

And fill with mercenary breath the spacious hall;

Let me be peaceable, let me be still.

The solitary Tishbite heard the wind,

With strength and violence combin'd,

110That rent the mountains, and did make

The solid Earth's foundations shake;

He saw the dreadful fire, and heard the horrid noise,

But found what he expected in the *small still voice.*

VII.

Nor here did my unbridled fancy rest,

But I must try

A pitch more high,

To read the starry language of the East;

And with Chaldean curiosity

Presum'd to solve the riddles of the sky;

120Impatient till I knew my doom,

Dejected till the good direction come,

I ripp'd up Fate's forbidden womb,

Nor would I stay till it brought forth

An easy and a natural birth,

But was solicitous to know

The yet misshapen embryo

(Preposterous crime!)

Without the formal midwif'ry of time:

Fond man, as if too little grief were given

130On Earth, draws down inquietudes from Heaven!

Permits himself with fear to be unmann'd,

Belshazzar-like, grows wan and pale,

His very heart begins to fail,

Is frighted at that Writing of the Hand,

Which yet nor he, nor all his learn'd magicians understand.

VIII.

And now at last what's the result of all?

Should the strict audit come,

And for th' account too early call;

A num'rous heap of ciphers would be found the total sum.

140When incompassionate age shall plow

The delicate Amira's brow,

And draw his furrows deep and long,

What hardy youth is he

Will after that a reaper be,

Or sing the harvest song?

And what is verse, but an effeminate vent

Either of lust or discontent?

Colours will starve, and all their glories die,

Invented only to deceive the eye;

150And he that wily Law does love

Much more of serpent has than dove,

There's nothing in Astrology,

But Delphic ambiguity;

We are misguided in the dark, and thus

Each star becomes an *Ignis fatuus*:

Yet pardon me, ye glorious Lamps of light,

'Twas one of you that led the way,

Dispell'd the gloomy night,

Became a Phosphor to th' Eternal Day,

160And show'd the Magi where th' Almighty Infant lay.

IX.

At length the doubtful victory's won,

It was a cunning ambuscade

The World for my felicities had laid;

Yet now at length the day's our own,

Now conqueror-like let us new laws set down.

Henceforth let all our love seraphic turn,

The sprightly and the vigorous flame

On th' altar let it ever burn,

And sacrifice its ancient name:

170A tablet on my heart next I'll prepare

Where I would draw the Holy Sepulchre,

Behind it a soft landskip I would lay

Of melancholy Golgotha!

On th' altar let me all my spoils lay down,

And if I had one, there I'd hang my laurel crown.

Give me the Pandects of the Law Divine,

Such was the Law made Moses' face to shine.

Thus beyond Saturn's heavy orb I'll tower,

And laugh at his malicious power:

180Raptur'd in contemplation thus I'll go

Above unactive earth, and leave the stars below.

X.

Toss'd on the wings of every wind,

After these hoverings to and fro

(And still the waters higher grow),

Not knowing where a resting-place to find,

Whither for sanctuary should I go

But, Reverend Sir, to you?

You that have triumph'd o'er th' impetuous flood,

That, Noah-like, in bad times durst be good,

190And the stiff torrent manfully withstood,

Can save me too;

One that have long in fear of drowning bin,

Surrounded by the rolling waves of sin;

Do you but reach out a propitious hand

And charitably take me in,

I will not yet despair to see dry land.

'Tis done;—and I no longer fluctuate,

I've made the Church my Ark, and Sion's Hill my Ararat.

The Review.] Dated in the Firth MS. December 17, 1666. Entered in the Stationers' Register on December 17, 1673, as 'A poem or copy intituled the Review, To the Reverend my honored freind Dr. Wm. Sancroft, Deane of St. Paules, A Pindarique Ode'. Similarly in the Firth MS. 'The Review. A Pindarique Ode. To the Reverend, my worthy friend, Dr. Wm. Sandcroft, Dean of St. Paul's': the chief variants only are recorded. The words 'now Lord Archbishop of Canterbury' are added in the fourth edition. In the earlier editions—even that of 1682, when Sancroft had been Primate for four years—the poem is addressed 'to Dr. W. S.' The piece is a rather remarkable 'Religio *Laici*' for the time, and as anticipating Dryden's; and has some, though rather vague, autobiographic interest. It seems (*v.* Commendatory Poems) to have attracted some attention as such.

16 must] will *MS.*

40 had] has *MS.*, *1674-82*.

46 fair] my *MS.*

51 couldn't] did not *MS.*

56 breathless] shipwrack'd *MS.*

64 could] should *MS.*

81 fit] apt *MS.*

93 ever *added in 1684*.

113 what] whom *MS.*

114 seq. It is well known that Astrology maintained its hold throughout the seventeenth century. Dryden himself does not seem to have been by any means insensible to its fascination; and Flatman—who, though a slightly younger man, represents an older temper—may well have been a disciple of Lilly.

135 he] we *MS.* his] our *MS.*

148 will] must *MS.* starve] In its proper sense of 'perish'. Italic in original; but, as has been pointed out, this type is used with such utter capriciousness that it affords no evidence whether the term had any technical vogue among artists of the time.

159 Eternal] Immortal *MS.*

168 let it] shall for *MS.*

172 soft] fair *MS.*

187 Sir] Friend *1674-82*.

189 A possible but not necessary reminiscence of Fuller's well-known book, *Good Thoughts for Bad Times*.

193 the rolling waves] a cataclysm *MS.*

To my Reverend Friend, Dr. Sam. Woodford, On his Excellent Version of the Psalms.

PINDARIC ODE.

Stanza I.

See (worthy friend) what I would do

(Whom neither Muse nor Art inspire),

That have no friend in all the sacred quire,

To show my kindness for your Book, and you,

Forc'd to disparage what I would admire;

Bold man, that dares attempt Pindaric now,

Since the great Pindar's greatest Son

From the ingrateful age is gone,

Cowley has bid th' ingrateful age adieu;

10Apollo's rare Columbus, he

Found out new worlds of Poesy:

He, like an eagle, soar'd aloft,

To seize his noble prey;

Yet as a dove's, his soul was soft,

Quiet as Night, but bright as Day:

To Heaven in a fiery chariot he

Ascended by seraphic Poetry;

Yet which of us dull mortals since can find

Any inspiring mantle, that he left behind?

II.

20His powerful numbers might have done you right;

He could have spar'd you immortality,

Under that Chieftain's banners you might fight

Assur'd of laurels, and of victory

Over devouring Time and sword and fire

And Jove's important ire:

My humble verse would better sing

David the Shepherd, than the King:

And yet methinks 'tis stately to be one

(Though of the meaner sort)

30Of them that may approach a Prince's throne,

If 'twere but to be seen at Court.

Such, Sir, is my ambition for a name,

Which I shall rather take from you, than give,

For in your Book I cannot miss of fame,

But by contact shall live.

Thus on your chariot wheel shall I

Ride safe, and look as big as Aesop's fly,

Who from th' Olympian Race new come,

And now triumphantly flown home,

40To's neighbours of the swarm thus proudly said,

Don't you remember what a dust I made!

III.

Where'er the Son of Jesse's harp shall sound,

Or Israel's sweetest songs be sung,

(Like Samson's lion sweet and strong)

You and your happy Muse shall be renown'd,

To whose kind hand the Son of Jesse owes

His last deliverance from all his foes.

Blood-thirsty Saul, less barbarous than they,

His person only sought to kill;

50These would his deathless poems slay,

And sought immortal blood to spill,

To sing whose songs in Babylon would be

A new Captivity:

Deposèd by these rebels, you alone

Restor'd the glorious David to his throne.

Long in disguise the royal Prophet lay,

Long from his own thoughts banishèd,

Ne'er since his death till this illustrious day

Was sceptre in his hand, or crown plac'd on his head:

60He seem'd as if at Gath he still had bin

As once before proud Achish he appear'd,

His face besmear'd,

With spittle on his sacred beard,

A laughing-stock to the insulting Philistine.

Drest in their rhymes, he look'd as he were mad,

In tissue you, and Tyrian purple have him clad.

To Dr. Sam. Woodford.] First printed in *A Paraphrase upon the Psalms of David*, 1668. A MS. version is in Rawlinson D. 260 (fol. 27) of the Bodleian. Woodford (1636-1700) though much forgotten now, must have been something more than an ordinary person. As such he might have been, as he was, a St. Paul's boy and an Oxford (Wadham) man, a member of the Inner Temple, an early F.R.S., and later a Canon of Chichester and Winchester. But as such merely he would hardly have been, in the Preface to his Paraphrases of the Canticles (*v. inf.*, p. 366), the first, and for a long time the only, 'ingoing' critic of Milton's blank verse. He does not take quite the right view of it, but it is noteworthy that he should have taken any view of an intelligent character.

12 soar'd] tow'red *MS.*

16 a *om. MS.*

18 'But which of us poor mortals' *1668, MS.*

20, 21, &c. have] ha' *1668.*

25 ire] Dire *MS.*, a word of which a unique instance in the sense of 'dire quality' is quoted in the *N.E.D.* from Anthony à Wood. The scribe may have misunderstood 'important' (= 'importunate').

39 flown] got *MS.*

41 This quaint anti-climax is one of the not very few indications which make of Flatman a sort of rough draft of Prior.

42 seq. Translations of the Psalms have been so numerous—and so bad— that it is difficult to know whether Flatman had any particular translator or translators in his mind while writing the last stanza. It may have been merely the usual Sternhold and Hopkins. At any rate his own friend Tate did not join Brady in *lèse-poésie* (as well as *lèse-majesté* against the Son of Jesse) till thirty years after Woodford wrote and eight after Flatman's own death.

55 Restor'd] Restore *MS.*

59 plac'd] set *MS.*

63 sacred *om. MS.*

On the Death of the truly valiant George Duke of Albemarle.

PINDARIC ODE.

Stanza I.

Now blush thyself into confusion,

Ridiculous Mortality

With indignation to be trampled on

By them that court Eternity;

Whose generous deeds and prosperous state

Seem poorly set within the reach of Fate,

Whose every trophy, and each laurel wreath

Depends upon a little breath;

Confin'd within the narrow bounds of Time,

10And of uncertain age,

With doubtful hazards they engage,

Thrown down, while victory bids them higher climb;

Their glories are eclips'd by Death.

Hard circumstances of illustrious men

Whom Nature (like the Scythian Prince) detains

Within the body's chains

(Nature, that rigorous Tamberlain).

Stout Bajazet disdain'd the barbarous rage

Of that insulting conqueror,

20Bravely himself usurp'd his own expiring power,

By dashing out his brains against his iron cage.

II.

But 'tis indecent to complain,

And wretched mortals curse their stars in vain,

In vain they waste their tears for them that die,

Themselves involv'd in the same destiny,

No more with sorrow let it then be said

The glorious Albemarle is dead.

Let what is said of him triumphant be,

Words as gay, as is his Fame,

30And as manly as his name,

Words as ample as his praise,

And as verdant as his bays,

An *Epinicion*, not an Elegy.

Yet why shouldst thou, ambitious Muse, believe

Thy gloomy verse can any splendours give,

Or make him one small moment longer live?

Nothing but what is vulgar thou canst say;

Or misbecoming numbers sing;

What tribute to his memory canst thou pay,

40Whose virtue say'd a Crown, and could oblige a King?

III.

Many a year distressèd Albion lay

By her unnatural offspring torn,

Once the World's terror, then its scorn,

At home a prison, and abroad a prey:

Her valiant Youth, her valiant Youth did kill,

And mutual blood did spill;

Usurpers then, and many a mushroom Peer

Within her palaces did domineer;

There did the vulture build his nest,

50There the owls and satyrs rest,

By *Zim* and *Ohim* all possest;

'Till England's Angel-Guardian, thou,

With pity and with anger mov'd

For Albion thy belov'd

(Olive-chaplets on thy brow),

With bloodless hands upheld'st her drooping head,

And with thy trumpets call'dst her from the dead.

Bright Phosphor to the rising Sun!

That Royal Lamp, by thee did first appear

60Usher'd into our happy hemisphere;

O may it still shine bright and clear!

No cloud nor night approach it, but a constant noon!

IV.

Nor thus did thy undaunted valour cease,

Or wither with unactive peace:

Scarce were our civil broils allay'd,

While yet the wound of an intestine war

Had left a tender scar,

When of our new prosperities afraid,

Our jealous neighbours fatal arms prepare;

70In floating groves the enemy drew near.

Loud did the Belgian Lion roar,

Upon our coasts th' Armada did appear,

And boldly durst attempt our native shore,

Till his victorious squadrons check'd their pride,

And did in triumph o'er the Ocean ride.

With thunder, lightning, and with clouds of smoke

He did their insolence restrain,

And gave his dreadful law to all the main,

Whose surly billows trembled when he spoke,

80And put their willing necks under his yoke.

This the stupendious vanquisher has done,

Whose high prerogative it was alone

To raise a ruin'd, and secure an envied throne.

V.

Then angry Heav'n began to frown,

From Heav'n a dreadful pestilence came down,

On every side did lamentations rise;

Baleful sigh, and heavy groan,

All was plaint, and all was moan!

The pious friend with trembling love,

90Scarce had his latest kindness done,

In sealing up his dead friend's eyes,

Ere with his own surprising fate he strove,

And wanted one to close his own.

Death's iron sceptre bore the sway

O'er our imperial Golgotha;

Yet he with kind, though unconcernèd eyes,

Durst stay and see those numerous tragedies.

He in the field had seen Death's grisly shape,

Heard him in volleys talk aloud,

100Beheld his grandeur in a glittering crowd,

And unamaz'd seen him in cannons gape:

Ever unterrified his valour stood

Like some tall rock amidst a sea of blood:

'Twas loyalty from sword and pest kept him alive,

The safest armour and the best preservative.

VI.

The flaming City next implor'd his aid,

And seasonably pray'd

His force against the Fire, whose arms the sea obey'd;

Wide did th' impetuous torrent spread,

110Then those goodly fabrics fell,

Temples themselves promiscuously there

Dropp'd down, and in the common ruin buried were,

The City turn'd into one Mongibel:

The haughty tyrant shook his curlèd head,

His breath with vengeance black, his face with fury red.

Then every cheek grew wan and pale,

Every heart did yield and fail:

Nought but thy presence could its power suppress,

Whose stronger light put out the less.

120As London's noble structures rise,

Together shall his memory grow,

To whom that beauteous town so much does owe.

London! joint Favourite with him thou wert;

As both possess'd a room within one heart,

So now with thine indulgent Sovereign join,

Respect his great friend's ashes, for he wept o'er thine.

VII.

Thus did the Duke perform his mighty stage,

Thus did that Atlas of our State

With his prodigious acts amaze the age,

130While worlds of wonders on his shoulders sate;

Full of glories and of years,

He trod his shining and immortal way,

Whilst Albion, compass'd with new floods of tears,

Besought his longer stay.

Profane that pen that dares describe thy bliss,

Or write thine *Apotheosis!*

Whom Heaven and thy Prince to pleasure prove,

Entrusted with their armies and their love.

In other Courts 'tis dangerous to deserve,

140Thou didst a kind and grateful Master serve,

Who, to express his gratitude to thee,

Scorn'd those ill-natur'd arts of policy.

Happy had Belisarius bin

(Whose forward fortune was his sin)

By many victories undone,

He had not liv'd neglected, died obscure,

If for thy Prince those battles he had won,

Thy Prince, magnificent above his Emperor.

VIII.

Among the Gods, those Gods that died like thee,

150As great as theirs, and full of majesty,

Thy sacred dust shall sleep secure,

Thy monument as long as theirs endure:

There, free from envy, thou with them

Shall have thy share of diadem;

Among their badges shall be set

Thy Garter and thy coronet;

Or (which is statelier) thou shalt have

A *Mausoleum* in thy Prince's breast;

There thine embalmèd name shall rest,

160 That sanctuary shall thee save

From the dishonours of a regal grave:

And every wondrous history,

Read by incredulous Posterity,

That writes of *him*, shall honourably mention *thee*,

Who by an humble loyalty hast shown,

How much sublimer gallantry and renown

'Tis to *restore*, than to *usurp* a Monarch's Crown.

On the Death of the Duke of Albemarle.] First printed in small folio in 1670. Monk died that year. There are some important variants, noted below.

40 a Crown] three Realms *1670*.

47 The extreme rapidity of Monk's own transition from commonerhood to the highest rank in the peerage makes this allusion to Oliver's mock-lords rather hazardous; but after all Monk was a gentleman, and had richly deserved it.

49 vulture] bloody vulture *1670*.

51 *Zim* and *Ohim* are the original Hebrew for the 'wild beasts of the desert' and the 'doleful creatures' who accompany owls and satyrs in Isaiah xiii. 21 (A.V.).

61 bright] warm *1670*.

After l. 75 ('ride') the following lines appeared in 1670:

Under a gallant Admiral he fought,

York, whose success a taller Muse must sing;

Who so his country loved, that he forgot

He was the Brother of a King;

Whose daring courage might inspire

A meaner soul than his with martial fire.

80 put] crouch'd.

81 stupendious] These forms are always worth noting, when they occur.

94 Death's iron sceptre bore the sway] With iron sceptre Death bore all the sway.

96 unconcerned] undisturbed.

97 tragedies] butcheries.

98 shape] face.

99 volleys] niter.

104 kept] saved.

107 And seasonably pray'd] Successfully it prayed.

113 Mongibel] i.e. Etna.

117 did yield and fail] began to fail.

After 117 come the following lines:

And had not our Anointed's flame

(From heaven towards his subjects sent)

Outblazed the furious element,

What could the furious element tame?

121 His] thy.

After 122 ('owe') there is a line which completes the rhyme with 'rise': 'For its revived tranquillities.'

124 possess'd] took up.

133 floods] seas.

135 Profane] Saucy.

137 prove] strove (so also the texts of *1674, 1676, 1682*).

161 a regal] the.

The Retirement.

PINDARIC ODE MADE IN THE TIME OF THE GREAT SICKNESS, 1665.

Stanza I.

In the mild close of an hot summer's day,

When a cool breeze had fann'd the air,

And heaven's face look'd smooth and fair;

Lovely as sleeping infants be,

That in their slumber smiling lie

Dandled on their mother's knee,

You hear no cry,

No harsh, nor inharmonious voice,

But all is innocence without a noise:

10When every sweet, which the sun's greedy ray

So lately from us drew,

Began to trickle down again in dew;

Weary, and faint, and full of thought,

Though for what cause I knew not well,

What I ail'd I could not tell,

I sate me down at an aged poplar's root,

Whose chiding leaves excepted and my breast,

All the impertinently busied world inclin'd to rest.

II.

I list'ned heedfully around,

20But not a whisper there was found.

The murmuring brook hard by,

As heavy, and as dull as I,

Seem'd drowsily along to creep;

It ran with undiscover'd pace,

And if a pebble stopp'd the lazy race,

'Twas but as if it started in its sleep.

Echo herself, that ever lent an ear

To any piteous moan,

Wont to groan with them that groan,

30Echo herself was speechless here.

Thrice did I sigh, thrice miserably cry,

Ai me! the Nymph, ai me! would not reply,

Or churlish, or she was asleep for company.

III.

There did I sit and sadly call to mind

Far and near, all I could find

All the pleasures, all the cares,

The jealousies, the fears,

All the incertainties of thirty years,

From that most inauspicious hour

40Which gave me breath;

To that in which the fair Amira's power

First made me wish for death:

And yet Amira's not unkind;

She never gave me angry word,

Never my mean address abhorr'd;

Beauteous her face, beauteous her mind:

Yet something dreadful in her eyes I saw

Which ever kept my falt'ring tongue in awe,

And gave my panting soul a law.

50So have I seen a modest beggar stand,

Worn out with age and being oft denied,

On his heart he laid his hand;

And though he look'd as if he would have died

The needy wretch no alms did crave:

He durst not ask for what he fear'd he should not have.

IV.

I thought on every pensive thing,

That might my passion strongly move,

That might the sweetest sadness bring;

Oft did I think on Death, and oft of Love,

60The triumphs of the little God, and that same ghastly King.

The ghastly King, what has he done?

How his pale territories spread!

Strait scantlings now of consecrated ground

His swelling empire cannot bound,

But every day new colonies of dead

Enhance his conquests, and advance his throne.

The mighty City sav'd from storms of War,

Exempted from the crimson flood,

When all the land o'erflow'd with blood,

70Stoops yet once more to a new conqueror:

The City which so many rivals bred,

Sackcloth is on her loins, and ashes on her head.

V.

When will the frowning Heav'n begin to smile?

Those pitchy clouds be overblown,

That hide the mighty town,

That I may see the mighty pile!

When will the angry Angel cease to slay,

And turn his brandish'd sword away

From that illustrious Golgotha,

80London, the great Aceldama!

When will that stately landscape open lie,

The mist withdrawn that intercepts my eye!

That heap of Pyramids appear,

Which, now, too much like those of Egypt are:

Eternal monuments of pride and sin,

Magnificent and tall without, but dead men's bones within.

The Retirement. Exactly dated in the Firth MS., August 17, 1665. Stanza III, found in this MS., was cancelled in *1674, 1676, 1682*, but restored in *1686*. Stanzas IV and V appear as a separate poem entitled 'Upon the Plague' in Bodley Rawlinson MS. D. 260, fol. 29 verso.

28 moan] tone *Firth MS., 1676, 1682.*

57 strongly] deeply *Firth and Rawlinson MSS.*

59 of Love] on Love *MSS., 1674, 1676.*

66 advance] exalt *MSS.*

71 rivals *MSS.*: rival *1682, 1686.*

73 begin to *om. MSS. Rawlinson* reads 'Heavens'.

76 mighty] amazing mighty *Rawlinson.*

77 angry *om. Rawlinson.*

85 Eternal] Vast *Rawlinson.*

Translated out of a Part of Petronius Arbiter's Satyricon.

I.

After a blust'ring tedious night,

The wind's now hush'd and the black tempest o'er,

Which th' crazy vessel miserably tore,

Behold a lamentable sight!

Rolling far off, upon a briny wave,

Compassionate Philander spied

A floating carcase ride,

That seem'd to beg the kindness of a grave.

II.

Sad and concern'd, Philander then

10Weigh'd with himself the frail, uncertain state

Of silly, strangely disappointed men,

Whose projects are the sport of Fate.

Perhaps (said he) this poor man's desolate wife,

In a strange country far away,

Expects some happy day

This ghastly thing, the comfort of her life;

III.

His son it may be dreads no harm,

But kindly waits his father's coming home;

Himself secure, he apprehends no storm,

20But fancies that he sees him come.

Perhaps the good old man, that kiss'd this son,

And left a blessing on his head,

His arms about him spread,

Hopes yet to see him ere his glass be run.

IV.

These are the grand intrigues of Man,

These his huge thoughts, and these his vast desires,

Restless, and swelling like the Ocean

From his birth till he expires.

See where the naked, breathless body lies

30To every puff of wind a slave,

At the beck of every wave,

That once perhaps was fair, rich, stout, and wise!

V.

While thus Philander pensive said,

Touch'd only with a pity for mankind,

At nearer view, he thought he knew the dead,

And call'd the wretched man to mind:

Alas, said he, art thou that angry thing,

That with thy looks didst threaten death,

Plagues and destruction breath,

40But two days since, little beneath a King!

VI.

Ai me! where is thy fury now,

Thine insolence, and all thy boundless power,

O most ridiculously dreadful thou!

Expos'd for beasts and fishes to devour.

Go, sottish mortals, let your breasts swell high;

All your designs laid deep as Hell,

A small mischance can quell,

Outwitted by the deeper plots of Destiny.

VII.

This haughty lump a while before

50Sooth'd up itself, perhaps with hopes of life,

What it would do, when it came safe on shore,

What for its son, what for its wife;

See where the man and all his politics lie.

Ye Gods! what gulfs are set between

What we have and what we ween,

Whilst lull'd in dreams of years to come, we die!

VIII.

Nor are we liable alone

To misadventures on the merciless sea,

A thousand other things our Fate bring on,

60And shipwreck'd everywhere we be.

One in the tumult of a battle dies

Big with conceit of victory,

And routing th' enemy,

With garlands deck'd, himself the sacrifice.

IX.

Another, while he pays his vows

On bended knees, and Heaven with tears invokes,

With adorations as he humbly bows,

While with gums the altar smokes,

In th' presence of his God, the temple falls:

70And thus religious in vain

The flatter'd bigot slain,

Breathes out his last within the sacred walls.

X.

Another with gay trophies proud,

From his triumphant chariot overthrown,

Makes pastime for the gazers of the crowd,

That envied him his purchas'd crown.

Some with full meals, and sparkling bowls of wine

(As if it made too long delay),

Spur on their fatal day,

80Whilst others (needy souls) at theirs repine.

XI.

Consider well, and every place

Offers a ready road to thy long home,

Sometimes with frowns, sometimes with smiling face

Th' embassadors of Death do come.

By open force or secret ambuscade,

By unintelligible ways,

We end our anxious days,

And stock the large plantations of the Dead.

XII.

But (some may say) 'tis very hard

90With them, whom heavy chance has cast away,

With no solemnities at all interr'd,

To roam unburied on the sea:

No—'tis all one where we receive our doom,

Since, somewhere, 'tis our certain lot

Our carcases must rot,

And they whom heaven covers need no tomb.

Petronius Arbiter's Satyricon.] This translation-amplification of one of the most famous passages of the *Satyricon* is the piece referred to by Nahum Tate at the opening of his commendation (*sup.*, p. 290).

39 'breath', as in l. 72, a seventeenth-century form.

88 A good line, if I mistake not. There is no suggestion even of it in the original, but, as often in Flatman, much of Sir Thomas Browne.

A Thought of Death.

When on my sick bed I languish,

Full of sorrow, full of anguish,

Fainting, gasping, trembling, crying,

Panting, groaning, speechless, dying,

My soul just now about to take her flight

Into the regions of eternal night;

Oh tell me you,

That have been long below,

What shall I do!

10What shall I think, when cruel Death appears,

That may extenuate my fears!

Methinks I hear some gentle Spirit say,

Be not fearful, come away!

Think with thyself that now thou shall be free,

And find thy long-expected liberty;

Better thou mayst, but worse thou canst not be

Than in this vale of tears and misery.

Like Caesar, with assurance then come on,

And unamaz'd attempt the laurel crown,

20That lies on th' other side Death's Rubicon.

A Thought of Death.] Flatman's best-known, if not his only known thing to most people—the knowledge being due to Warton's suggestion of indebtedness to it on Pope's part in his *Dying Christian.*

Psalm xxxix. Vers. 4, 5.

Verse IV.

Lord, let me know the period of my age,

The length of this my weary pilgrimage,

How long this miserable life shall last,

This life that stays so long, yet flies so fast!

Verse V.

Thou by a span measur'st these days of mine,

Eternity's the spacious bound of thine:

Who shall compare his little span with thee,

With thine Incomprehensibility.

Man born to trouble leaves this world with pain,

10His best estate is altogether vain.

Hymn for the Morning.

Awake, my soul! Awake, mine eyes!

Awake, my drowsy faculties;

Awake, and see the new-born light

Spring from the darksome womb of Night!

Look up and see th' unwearied Sun,

Already hath his race begun:

The pretty lark is mounted high,

And sings her matins in the sky.

Arise, my soul! and thou my voice

10In songs of praise, early rejoice!

O Great Creator! Heavenly King!

Thy praises let me ever sing!

Thy power has made, Thy goodness kept

This fenceless body while I slept,

Yet one day more hast given me

From all the powers of darkness free:

O keep my heart from sin secure,

My life unblameable and pure,

That when the last of all my days is come,

20Cheerful and fearless I may wait my doom.

Hymn for the Morning.] This Hymn will of course suggest Ken's infinitely better-known one to everybody. The facts are curious and not quite fully given in Mr. Julian's invaluable *Dictionary of Hymnology*, where it is not mentioned that Ken and Flatman were both Winchester and New College men of almost exactly the same age and standing. Moreover, Sir Thomas Browne—also a Wykehamist and their contemporary, though a senior—has another very similar composition—one of his rare exercises in verse— towards the end of *Religio Medici*. The triple connexion with Winchester, and with Latin hymns known to be in use there, is pretty striking, though the matter cannot be followed out here. It is enough to say that the resemblance is chiefly confined to the opening. In the *Evening* hymns of the two this resemblance is still slighter, though there are passages, naturally enough, that approach each other. Ken's hymns were not *published* till 1695; but in 1674, the very years of Flatman's original issue, they are palpably referred to in the future bishop's and actual prebendary's *Manual of Prayers for the use of the Scholars of Winchester College.* Browne's piece must be at least forty years older.

6 hath *1676, 1682*: has *1686*.

Anthem for the Evening.

Sleep! downy sleep! come close my eyes,

Tir'd with beholding vanities!

Sweet slumbers come and chase away

The toils and follies of the day:

On your soft bosom will I lie,

Forget the world, and learn to die.

O Israel's watchful Shepherd! spread

Tents of Angels round my bed;

Let not the Spirits of the air,

10While I slumber, me ensnare;

But save Thy suppliant free from harms,

Clasp'd in Thine everlasting Arms.

Clouds and thick darkness is Thy Throne,

Thy wonderful pavilion:

Oh dart from thence a shining ray,

And then my midnight shall be day!

Thus when the morn in crimson drest,

Breaks through the windows of the East,

My hymns of thankful praises shall arise

20Like incense or the morning sacrifice.

Anthem for the Evening.] 19 arise *1682*; rise *1686*.

Death.

SONG.

Oh the sad day,

When friends shall shake their heads and say

Of miserable me,

Hark how he groans, look how he pants for breath,

See how he struggles with the pangs of Death!

When they shall say of these poor eyes,

How hollow, and how dim they be!

Mark how his breast does swell and rise,

Against his potent Enemy!

10When some old friend shall step to my bedside,

Touch my chill face, and thence shall gently slide,

And when his next companions say,

How does he do? what hopes? shall turn away,

Answering only with a lift-up hand,

Who can his fate withstand?

Then shall a gasp or two do more

Than e'er my rhetoric could before,

Persuade the peevish world to trouble me no more!

Death.] This, in my humble judgement, is finer, as it is certainly more original, than the earlier 'thought' on the same subject. The copy in the Firth MS. reads 'dear' for 'poor' (l. 6) and 'hope' (l. 13), omits 'peevish' in l. 18, and notes that the Song was set to music by Captain Sylvanus Taylor.

The Happy Man.

Peaceful is he, and most secure,

Whose heart and actions all are pure;

How smooth and pleasant is his way,

Whilst Life's Meander slides away.

If a fierce thunderbolt do fly,

This man can unconcernèd lie;

Knows 'tis not levell'd at his head,

So neither noise nor flash can dread:

Though a swift whirlwind tear in sunder

10Heav'n above him, or earth under;

Though the rocks on heaps do tumble,

Or the world to ashes crumble,

Though the stupendious mountains from on high

Drop down, and in their humble valleys lie;

Should the unruly Ocean roar,

And dash its foam against the shore;

He finds no tempest in his mind,

Fears no billow, feels no wind:

All is serene, all quiet there,

20There's not one blast of troubled air,

Old stars may fall, or new ones blaze,

Yet none of these his soul amaze;

Such is the man can smile at irksome death,

And with an easy sigh give up his breath.

the Happy Man.] In the Firth MS., and dated December 27, 1664.

1 Peaceful] Happy *MS.*

2 heart] life *MS.*

13 Though] When *MS.*

19 all quiet *MS., 1674, 1676, 1682*: and quiet *1686.*

23 at] on *MS.*

24 give up] resign *MS.*

On Mr. Johnson's Several Shipwrecks.

He that has never yet acquainted been

With cruel Chance, nor Virtue naked seen,

Stripp'd from th' advantages (which vices wear)

Of happy, plausible, successful, fair;

Nor learnt how long the low'ring cloud may last,

Wherewith her beauteous face is overcast,

Till she her native glories does recover,

And shines more bright, after the storm is over;

To be inform'd, he need no further go,

10Than this Divine Epitome of woe.

In Johnson's Life and Writings he may find,

What Homer in his Odysses design'd,

A virtuous man, by miserable fate,

Rend'red ten thousand ways unfortunate;

Sometimes within a leaking vessel tost,

All hopes of life and the lov'd shore quite lost,

While hidden sands, and every greedy wave

With horror gap'd themselves into a grave:

Sometimes upon a rock with fury thrown,

20Moaning himself, where none could hear his moan;

Sometimes cast out upon the barren sand,

Expos'd to th' mercy of a barbarous land:

Such was the pious Johnson, till kind Heaven

A blessèd end to all his toils had given:

To show that virtuous men, though they appear

But Fortune's sport, are Providence's care.

On Mr. Johnson's several Shipwrecks.] First in *Deus Nobiscum. A Narrative of a Great Deliverance at Sea,... By William Johnson, D.D., late Chaplain and Sub-Almoner to*

His Sacred Majesty,.... *The Third Edition, Corrected*, London, 1672, small octavo. These are some minor variants.

An Explanation of an Emblem Engraven by V. H.

Seest thou those Rays, the Light 'bove them?

And that gay thing the Diadem?

The Wheel and Balance, which are tied

To th' Gold, black Clouds on either side?

Seest thou the wingèd Trumpeters withal,

That kick the World's blue tottering Ball?

The flying Globe, the Glass thereon,

Those fragments of a Skeleton?

The Bays, the Palms, the Fighting men,

10And written Scroll?—Come tell me then,

Did thy o'er-curious eye e'er see

An apter scheme of Misery?

What's all that Gold and sparkling Stones

To that bald Skull, to those Cross Bones?

What mean those Blades (whom we adore)

To stain the Earth with purple gore?

Sack stately towns, silk banners spread,

Gallop their coursers o'er the dead?

Far more than this? and all to sway

20But till those sands shall glide away.

For when the bubble world shall fly

With stretch'd-out plumes, when the brisk eye

Shall close with anguish, sink with tears,

And th' angels' trumpets pierce our ears,

What's haughty man, or those fine things,

Which Heaven calls men, though men style kings?

Vain World, adieu! and farewell, fond renown!

Give me the Glory, that's above the Crown.

Emblem engraven by V. H.] V. or W[enceslas] H[ollar], I suppose.

13 and sparkling *1674-82*: and what those Sparkling *1686*.

15 Blades *1674-82*: Braves *1686*.

For Thoughts.

I.

Thoughts! What are they?

They are my constant friends,

Who, when harsh Fate its dull brow bends,

Uncloud me with a smiling ray,

And in the depth of midnight force a day.

II.

When I retire, and flee

The busy throngs of company

To hug myself in privacy;

O the discourse! the pleasant talk,

10 'Twixt us (my thoughts) along a lonely walk!

III.

You, like the stupefying wine

The dying malefactors sip

With shivering lip,

T' abate the rigour of their doom,

By a less troublous cut to their long home;

Make me slight crosses, though they pil'd up lie,

All by th' enchantments of an ecstasy.

IV.

Do I desire to see

The Throne and Majesty

20Of that proud one,

Brother and Uncle to the Stars and Sun?

Those can conduct me where such toys reside,

And waft me 'cross the main, sans wind and tide.

V.

Would I descry

Those radiant mansions 'bove the sky,

Invisible by mortal eye?

My *Thoughts*, my *Thoughts* can lay

A shining track thereto,

And nimbly fleeting go:

30Through all the eleven orbs can shove a way,

These too, like Jacob's Ladder, are

A most Angelic thoroughfare.

VI.

The wealth that shines

In th' Oriental mines;

Those sparkling gems which Nature keeps

Within her cabinets, the deeps;

The verdant fields,

The rarities the rich World yields;

Rare structures, whose each gilded spire

40Glimmers like lightning; which, while men admire,

They deem the neighbouring sky on fire,—

These can I gaze upon, and glut mine eyes

With myriads of varieties.

As on the front of Pisgah, I

Can th' Holy Land through these my optics spy.

VII.

Contemn we then

The peevish rage of men,

Whose violence ne'er can divorce

Our mutual amity;

50Or lay so damn'd a curse

As *Non-addresses*, 'twixt my thoughts and me:

For though I sigh in irons, they

Use their old freedom, readily obey;

And when my bosom-friends desert me, stay.

VIII.

Come then, my darlings, I'll embrace

My privilege; make known

The high prerogative I own,

By making all allurements give you place;

Whose sweet society to me

60A sanctuary and a shield shall be

'Gainst the full quivers of my Destiny.

Thoughts.] Dated in the Firth MS. May 13, 1659.

13 shivering] trembling *MS.*

17 th' enchantments] the magic *MS.*

19 Majesty] awful Majestie *MS.*

22 Those] These *MS.*

26 by] to *MS.*

27 My *Thoughts*, my *Thoughts* can] My Thoughts can eas'ly *MS.*

29 fleeting] flitting *MS.*

30 a way *MS*.: 'away' all editions.

31 These too] My Thoughts] *MS*.: *1686* stupidly misprints 'two'.

38 The] Those *MS*.

39 Rare] Huge *MS*. (cf. 'rarities' 38).

40 Glimmers] Glisters *MS*., *1674*, *1676*.

42 gaze ... glut] dwell ... tire *MS*.

43 myriads] millions *MS*.: fancies *1676*.

48 ne'er can] cannot *MS*.

Against Thoughts.

I.

Intolerable racks!

Distend my soul no more,

Loud as the billows when they roar,

More dreadful than the hideous thunder-cracks.

Foes inappeasable, that slay

My best contents, around me stand,

Each like a Fury, with a torch in hand;

And fright me from the hopes of one good day.

II.

When I seclude myself, and say

10How frolic will I be,

Unfetter'd from my company

I'll bathe me in felicity!

In come these guests,

Which Harpy-like defile my feasts:

Oh the damn'd dialogues, the cursèd talk

'Twixt us (my *Thoughts*) along a sullen walk.

III.

You, like the poisonous wine

The gallants quaff

To make 'em laugh,

20And yet at last endure

From thence the tortures of a calenture,

Fool me with feign'd refections, till I lie

Stark raving in a Bedlam ecstasy.

IV.

Do I dread

The starry Throne and Majesty

Of that high God,

Who batters kingdoms with an iron rod,

And makes the mountains stagger with a nod?

That sits upon the glorious Bow,

30Smiling at changes here below.

These goad me to his grand tribunal, where

They tell me I with horror must appear,

And antedate amazements by grim fear.

V.

Would I descry

Those happy souls' blest mansions 'bove the sky,

Invisible by mortal eye,

And in a noble speculation trace

A journey to that shining place;

Can I afford a sigh or two,

40Or breathe a wish that I might thither go:

These clip my plumes, and chill my blazing love

That, O, I cannot, cannot soar above.

VI.

The fire that shines

In subterranean mines,

The crystall'd streams,

The sulphur rocks that glow upon

The torrid banks of Phlegeton;

Those sooty fiends which Nature keeps,

Bolted and barr'd up in the deeps;

50Black caves, wide chasms, which who see confess

Types of the pit, so deep, so bottomless!

These mysteries, though I fain would not behold,

You to my view unfold:

Like an old Roman criminal, to the high

Tarpeian Hill you force me up, that I

May so be hurried headlong down, and die.

VII.

Mention not then

The strength and faculties of men;

Whose arts cannot expel

60These anguishes, this bosom-Hell.

When down my aching head I lay,

In hopes to slumber them away;

Perchance I do beguile

The tyranny awhile,

One or two minutes, then they throng again,

And reassault me with a trebled pain:

Nay, though I sob in fetters, they

Spare me not then; perplex me each sad day,

And whom a very Turk would pity, slay.

VIII.

70Hence, hence, my Jailors! *Thoughts* be gone,

Let my tranquillities alone.

Shall I embrace

A crocodile, or place

My choice affections on the fatal dart,

That stabs me to the heart?

I hate your curst proximity,

Worse than the venom'd arrows-heads that be

Cramm'd in the quivers of my Destiny.

Against Thoughts.] Entitled in the Firth MS. *Thoughts: the Answer to the other,* and dated May 18, 1659.

2 Distend] O tear *MS.*

4 More dreadful than] Less dreadful are *MS.*

5 Foes inappeasable] Too cruel enemies *MS.*

19 'em] them *MS.*

20 Yet thence at last procure *MS.*: Yet chance at last t' endure *1674.*

21 From thence the] The burning *MS.*

22 refections] reflections *1674.*

26 high] great *MS.*

30 changes here] us poor things *MS.*

31 grand *1674-82, MS.*: great *1686.*

47 torrid] burning *MS.*

50 chasms] chasma's *MS.*

54 old Roman criminal] adjudged offender *1674.*

56 headlong] headly *1674-82.*

58 and] nor *MS.*

59 cannot] ne'er could *MS.*

63 do] may *MS.*

64 The] Their *MS.*

65 throng] swarm *MS.*

66 And reassault] Then they assault *MS.*

67 sob] groan *MS.*

68 each sad] every *MS.*

70 *Thoughts* be] get ye *MS.*

75 Directed at my heart *MS.*

The Firth MS. supplies very interesting evidence of Flatman's care in revision; in l. 54 there is a curious reversion to the original, and more effective, reading.

A Dooms-Day Thought.

Anno 1659.

Judgement! two syllables can make
The haughtiest son of Adam shake.
'Tis coming, and 'twill surely come,
The dawning to that Day of Doom;
O th' morning blush of that dread day,
When Heav'n and Earth shall steal away,

Shall in their pristine Chaos hide,
Rather than th' angry Judge abide.
'Tis not far off; methinks I see
10Among the stars some dimmer be;
Some tremble, as their lamps did fear
A neighbouring extinguisher.
The greater luminaries fail,
Their glories by eclipses veil,
Knowing ere long their borrow'd light
Must sink in th' Universal Night.

When I behold a mist arise,

Straight to the same astonish'd eyes

Th' ascending clouds do represent

20A scene of th' smoking firmament.

Oft when I hear a blustering wind

With a tempestuous murmur join'd,

I fancy, Nature in this blast

Practises how to breathe her last,

Or sighs for poor Man's misery,

Or pants for fair Eternity.

Go to the dull church-yard and see

Those hillocks of mortality,

Where proudest Man is only found

30By a small swelling in the ground.

What crowds of carcases are made

Slaves to the pickaxe and the spade!

Dig but a foot, or two, to make

A cold bed, for thy dead friend's sake,

'Tis odds but in that scantling room

Thou robb'st another of his tomb,

Or in thy delving smit'st upon

A shinbone, or a cranion.

When th' prison's full, what next can be

40But the Grand Gaol-Delivery?

The Great Assize, when the pale clay

Shall gape, and render up its prey;

When from the dungeon of the grave

The meagre throng themselves shall heave,

Shake off their linen chains, and gaze

With wonder, when the world shall blaze.
Then climb the mountains, scale the rocks,
Force op'n the deep's eternal locks,
Beseech the clifts to lend an ear—
50Obdurate they, and will not hear.
What? ne'er a cavern, ne'er a grot,
To cover from the common lot?
No quite forgotten hold, to lie
Obscur'd, and pass the reck'ning by?
No—There's a quick all-piercing Eye
Can through the Earth's dark centre pry,

Search into th' bowels of the sea,
And comprehend Eternity.
What shall we do then, when the voice
60Of the shrill trump with strong fierce noise
Shall pierce our ears, and summon all
To th' Universe' wide Judgement Hall?
What shall we do! we cannot hide,
Nor yet that scrutiny abide:
When enlarg'd conscience loudly speaks,
And all our bosom-secrets breaks;
When flames surround, and greedy Hell
Gapes for a booty (*who can dwell*
With everlasting Burnings!), when
70Irrevocable words shall pass on men;
Poor naked men, who sometimes thought
These frights perhaps would come to nought!
What shall we do! we cannot run

For refuge, or the strict Judge shun.

'Tis too late *then* to think what course to take;

While we live here, we must provision make.

A Dooms-Day Thought.] This, the last of Flatman's three poems on the *Novissima*, is perhaps not the worst; except for those who hate 'conceits'. It has a curious *genuineness*, though in manner it slightly resembles his friend Cotton's 'New Year' poem so highly and rightly praised by Lamb.

Virtus sola manet, caetera mortis erunt.

I.

Nunquam sitivi, quae vehit aureo

Pactolus alveo flumina; quo magis

Potatur Hermus, tanto avarae

Mentis Hydrops sitibundus ardet.

II.

Frustrà caduci carceris incola

Molirer Arces; quilibet angulus

Sat ossa post manes reponet;

Exiguum satis est Sepulchrum.

III.

Nil stemma penso, nil titulos moror,

10*Cerásve aviti sanguinis indices,*

Sunt ista fatorum, inque Lethes

Naufragium patientur undis.

IV.

Ergo in quieto pectoris ambitu

Quid mens anhelas fulgura gloriae,

Laudésque inanes, et loquacem

Quae populi sedet ore famam?

V.

Letho superstes gloria, somnii

Dulcedo vana est, fama malignior

Nil tangit umbras, nec feretrum

20*Ingreditur Popularis Aura.*

VI.

Mansura sector, sola sed invidi

Expers Sepulchri sidera trajicit,

Spernénsque fatorum tumultus

Pellit humum generosa Virtus.

VII.

Praeceps novorum caetera mensium

Consumet aetas, seraque temporis

Delebit annosi vetustas

Utopicae nova Regna Lunae.

Virtus sola manet.] These Alcaics look like a college exercise, in which kind there have been worse. The third lines, as usual, are the weakest parts. But the English is perhaps better. The decasyllabic quatrain, though practised by Davies, by Davenant, and recently and best of all by Dryden, in *Annus Mirabilis*, has qualities which it remained for Gray to bring out fully, but which Flatman has not quite missed here. I wonder if Gray knew the piece, especially Stanza III?

Translated.

I.

I never thirsted for the Golden Flood,

Which o'er Pactolus' wealthy sands does roll,

From whence the covetous mind receives no good,

But rather swells the dropsy of his soul.

II.

On palaces why should I set my mind,

Imprison'd in this body's mould'ring clay?

Ere long to poor six foot of earth confin'd,

Whose bones must crumble at the fatal day.

III.

Titles and pedigrees, what are they to me,

10Or honour gain'd by our forefathers' toil,

The sport of Fate, whose gaudiest pageantry

Lethe will wash out, dark Oblivion soil?

IV.

Why then, my soul, who fain wouldst be at ease,

Should the World's glory dazzle thy bright eye?

Thyself with vain applause why shouldst thou please,

Or dote on Fame, which fools may take from thee?

V.

Praise after death is but a pleasant dream,

The Dead fare ne'er the worse for ill report;

The Ghosts below know nothing of a name,

20Nor ever popular caresses court.

VI.

Give me the lasting Good, Virtue, that flies

Above the clouds, that tramples on dull earth,

Exempt from Fate's tumultuous mutinies,

Virtue, that cannot need a second birth.

VII.

All other things must bend their heads to Time,

By age's mighty torrent borne away,

Hereafter no more thought on than my rhyme,

Or faery kingdoms in Utopia.

Psalm xv. Paraphrased.

Verse I.

Who shall approach the dread Jehovah's Throne

Or dwell within thy courts, O Holy One!

That happy man whose feet shall tread the road

Up Sion's Hill, that holy Hill of God!

Verse II.

He that's devout and strict in all he does,

That through the sinful world uprightly goes,

The desp'rate heights from whence the great ones fall

(Giddy with Fame) turn not his head at all:

Stands firm on Honour's pinnacle, and so

10Fears not the dreadful precipice below.

Of Conscience, not of Man, he stands in awe,

Just to observe each tittle of the Law!

His words and thoughts bear not a double part,

His breast is open, and he speaks his heart.

Verse III.

He that reviles not, or with cruel words

(Deadly as venom, sharp as two-edg'd swords)

Murthers his friend's repute, nor dares believe

That rumour which his neighbour's soul may grieve:

But with kind words embalms his bleeding Name,

20Wipes off the rust, and polishes his fame.

Verse IV.

He in whose eyes the bravest sinners be

Extremely vile, though rob'd in majesty;

But if he spies a righteous man (though poor)

Him he can honour, love, admire, adore:

In Israel's humble plains had rather stay,

Than in the tents of Kedar bear the sway:

He that severely keeps his sacred vow,

No mental reservation dares allow,

But what he swears, intends; will rather die,

30Lose all he has, than tell a solemn lie.

Verse V.

He that extorts not from the needy soul,

When laws his tyranny cannot control;

He whom a thousand empires cannot hire,

Against a guiltless person to conspire.

He that has these perfections, needs no more;

What treasures can be added to his store?

The Pyramids shall turn to dust, to hide

Their own vast bulk, and haughty Founders' pride.

Leviathan shall die within his deep;

40The eyes of Heaven close in eternal sleep;

Confusion may o'erwhelm both sea and land;

Mountains may tumble down, but he shall stand.

Psalm xv.] In the Firth MS.: the chief variant is 'brains' for 'head' in l. 8.

Job.

Few be the days that feeble man must breath,

Yet frequent troubles antedate his death:

Gay like a flow'r he comes, which newly grown,

Fades of itself, or is untimely mown:

Like a thin aery shadow does he fly,

Length'ning and short'ning still until he die.

And does Jehovah think on such a one,

Does he behold him from his mighty Throne?

Will he contend with such a worthless thing,

10Or dust and ashes into Judgement bring?

Unclean, unclean is man ev'n from the womb,

Unclean he falls into his drowsy tomb.

Surely, he cannot answer God, nor be

Accounted pure, before such purity.

Job.] In the Firth MS., which records that it was set by William Hawes.

Nudus Redibo.

Naked I came, when I began to be

A man among the Sons of Misery,

Tender, unarm'd, helpless, and quite forlorn,

E'er since 'twas my hard fortune to be born;

And when the space of a few weary days

Shall be expir'd, then must I go my ways.

Naked I shall return, and nothing have,

Nothing wherewith to bribe my hungry Grave.

Then what's the proudest Monarch's glittering robe,

10Or what's he, more than I, that rul'd the globe?

Since we must all without distinction die,

And slumber both stark naked, he and I.

Nudus Redibo.] In the Firth MS., and dated June 15, 1660. It was set by William Gregory.

4 hard fortune] misfortune *MS.*

7 I shall] shall I *MS.*

9 glittering] pearly *MS.*

An Elegy on the Earl of Sandwich.

If there were aught in Verse at once could raise

Or tender pity or immortal praise,

Thine obsequies, brave Sandwich, would require

Whatever would our nobler thoughts inspire;

But since thou find'st by thy unhappy fate,

What 'tis to be unfortunately great,

And purchase Honour at too dear a rate:

The Muse's best attempt, howe'er design'd,

Cannot but prove impertinently kind,

10Thy glorious valour is a theme too high

For all the humble arts of Poesy.

To side with chance and kingdoms overrun

Are little things ambitious men have done;

But on a flaming ship thus to despise

That life, which others did so highly prize;

To fight with fire, and struggle with a wave,

And Neptune with unwearied arms outbrave,

Are deeds surpassing fab'lous chronicle,

And which no future age shall parallel;

20Leviathan himself's outdone by thee,

Thou greater *wonder of the deep*, than he:

Nor could the deep thy mighty ashes hold.

The deep that swallows diamonds and gold;

Fame ev'n thy sacred relics does pursue,

Richer than all the treasures of Peru:

While the kind sea thy breathless body brings

Safe to the bed of honour and of kings.

Elegy on the Earl of Sandwich.] Pepys's (the first) Earl, who perished at the fight of Solebay in 1672. The duplication (see next piece) looks as if Flatman had had some personal connexion with him. At any rate there are expressions which are not the mere conventions of such writing. Line 6, and in fact the whole vigorous triplet in which it occurs, must be connected with the nearly certain facts that Sandwich's advice would have prevented the most unfavourable of the conditions under which the English fought; that the Duke of York not only would not listen but hinted at cowardice on Sandwich's part; and that the Earl in consequence, not only, as Mr. David Hannay (*A Short History of the Royal Navy*, i. 423) says, 'fought the ship on this the last and most glorious day of his life, with determined courage', but refused to attempt to save his life by swimming, when she was grappled by a fireship and burnt. Moreover, the last lines express the fact that the body was only recovered after being washed ashore some days after the battle, when it was duly buried in Westminster Abbey, 'the bed of honour and of kings'.

An Epitaph on the Earl of Sandwich.

Here lies the dust of that illustrious man,

That triumph'd o'er the Ocean;

Who for his country nobly courted Death,

And dearly sold his glorious breath,

Or in a word, in this cold narrow grave

Sandwich the Good, the Great, the Brave

(Oh frail estate of sublunary things!),

Lies equal here with England's greatest kings.

Pastoral.

I.

At break of day poor Celadon

Hard by his sheepfolds walk'd alone,

His arms across, his head bow'd down,

His oaten pipe beside him thrown,

When Thirsis, hidden in a thicket by,

Thus heard the discontented Shepherd cry.

II.

What is it Celadon has done,
That all his happiness is gone!
The curtains of the dark are drawn,
10And cheerful morn begins to dawn,
Yet in my breast 'tis ever dead of night,
That can admit no beam of pleasant light.

III.

You pretty lambs may leap and play
To welcome the new-kindled day,
Your shepherd harmless, as are you,
Why is he not as frolic too?
If such disturbance th' innocent attend,
How differs he from them that dare offend!

IV.

Ye Gods! or let me die, or live,
20If I must die, why this reprieve?
If you would have me live, O why
Is it with me as those that die!
I faint, I gasp, I pant, my eyes are set,
My cheeks are pale, and I am living yet.

V.

Ye Gods! I never did withhold
The fattest lamb of all my fold,
But on your altars laid it down,
And with a garland did it crown.
Is it in vain to make your altar smoke?

30Is it all one, to please, and to provoke?

VI.

Time was that I could sit and smile,
Or with a dance the time beguile:
My soul like that smooth lake was still,
Bright as the sun behind yon hill,
Like yonder stately mountain clear and high,
Swift, soft, and gay as that same butterfly.

VII.

But now *within* there's Civil War,
In arms my rebel passions are,
Their old allegiance laid aside,
40The traitors now in triumph ride
That many-headed monster has thrown down
Its lawful monarch, Reason, from its throne.

VIII.

See, unrelenting Sylvia, see,
All this, and more, is 'long of thee:
For ere I saw that charming face,
Uninterrupted was my peace,
Thy glorious beamy eyes have struck me blind,
To my own soul the way I cannot find.

IX.

Yet is it not thy fault nor mine;
50Heav'n is to blame, that did not shine
Upon us both with equal rays—
It made thine bright, mine gloomy days;
To Sylvia beauty gave, and riches store;
All Celadon's offence is, he is poor.

X.

Unlucky stars poor shepherds have,

Whose love is fickle Fortune's slave:

Those golden days are out of date,

When every turtle chose his mate:

Cupid, that mighty Prince, then uncontroll'd,

60Now like a little negro's bought and sold.

Pastoral.] 36 that *1682*; the *1686*.

On the Death of Mr. Pelham Humfries.

Pastoral Song.

Did you not hear the hideous groan,

The shrieks, and heavy moan

That spread themselves o'er all the pensive plain;

And rent the breast of many a tender swain?

'Twas for Amintas, dead and gone.

Sing, ye forsaken shepherds, sing *His* praise

In careless melancholy lays,

Lend *Him* a little doleful breath:

Poor Amintas! cruel Death!

10'Twas *Thou* couldst make dead words to live,

Thou that dull numbers couldst inspire

With charming voice and tuneful lyre,

That life to all, but to *Thyself*, couldst give;

Why couldst *Thou* not *Thy* wondrous art bequeath?

Poor Amintas! cruel Death!

Sing, pious shepherds, while you may,

Before th' approaches of the Fatal Day:

For you yourselves that sing this mournful song,

Alas! ere it be long,

20Shall, like Amintas, breathless be,

Though more forgotten in the grave than *He*.

On the Death of Mr. Pelham Humfries.] Pelham Humfries or Humfrey died in the year (1674) of first publication of these Poems. He was a musician and gentleman of the Chapel Royal.

21 than *1682*; that *1686*.

The Mistake.

SONG.

I heard a young lover in terrible pain,

From whence if he pleas'd, he might soon be releas'd,

He swore, and he vow'd again and again,

He could not outlive the turmoils of his breast;

But, alas, the young lover I found

Knew little how cold Love would prove under ground;

Why should I believe, prithee, Love, tell me why,

Where my own flesh and blood must give me the lie!

Let 'em rant while they will, and their destinies brave,

10They'll find their flames vanish on this side the grave;

For though all addresses on purpose are made

To be *huddled to bed,*—'tisn't meant, *with a spade!*

The Incredulous.

SONG.

I'll ne'er believe for Strephon's sake

That Love (whate'er its fond pretences be),

Is not a slave to mutability.

The Moon and that alike of change partake:

Tears are weak, and cannot bind,

Vows, alas! but empty wind:

The greatest art that Nature gave

To th' amorous hypocrite to make him kind,

Long ere he dies will take its leave.

10Had you but seen, as I have done,

Strephon's tears, and heard his moan,

How pale his cheek, how dim his eye,

As if with Chloris he resolv'd to die;

And when her spotless soul was fled

Heard his amazing praises of the dead;

Yet in a very little time address

His flame t' another Shepherdess,

In a few days giving his love the lie,

You'd be as great an infidel as I.

Weeping at Parting.
SONG.

I.

Go, gentle Oriana, go,

Thou seest the Gods will have it so;

Alas! alas! 'tis much in vain

Of their ill usage to complain,

To curse them when we want relief,

Lessens our courage, not our grief:

Dear Oriana, wipe thine eye,

The time may come that thou and I

Shall meet again, long, long to prove

10What vigour absence adds to love.

Smile, Oriana, then, and let me see

That look again, which stole my liberty.

II.

But say that Oriana die

(And that sad moment may be nigh),

The Gods that for a year can sever,

If it please them, can part us ever;

They that refresh, can make us weep,

And into Death can lengthen sleep.

Kind Oriana, should I hear

20The thing I so extremely fear,

'Twill not be strange, if it be said,

After a while, I too am dead.

Weep, Oriana, weep, for who does know

Whether we e'er shall meet again below?

Weeping at Parting.] In the Firth MS., entitled 'To Oriana weeping at parting', and dated December 31, 1664; 'Set by Mr. Roger Hill.' In l. 3 the MS. reads 'but' for 'much'.

The Desperate Lover.

I.

O mighty King of Terrors, come!

Command thy slave to his long home:

Great sanctuary Grave! to thee

In throngs the miserable flee;

Encircled in thy frozen arms,

They bid defiance to their harms,

Regardless of those pond'rous little things

That discompose th' uneasy heads of kings.

II.

In the cold earth the pris'ner lies
10Ransom'd from all his miseries;
Himself forgotten, he forgets
His cruel creditors, and debts;
And there in everlasting peace
Contentions with their authors cease.
A turf of grass or monument of stone
Umpires the petty competition.

III.

The disappointed lover there,
Breathes not a sigh, nor sheds a tear;
With us (fond fools) he never shares
20In sad perplexities and cares;
The willow near his tomb that grows
Revives his memory, not his woes;
Or rain, or shine, he is advanc'd above
Th' affronts of Heaven and stratagems of Love.

IV.

Then, mighty King of Terrors, come,
Command thy slave to his long home.
And thou, my friend, that lov'st me best,
Seal up these eyes that brake my rest;
Put out the lights, bespeak my knell,
30And then eternally farewell.
'Tis all th' amends our wretched Fates can give,
That none can force a desperate man to live.

The Desperate Lover.] 28 'brake', if right, must mean 'used to break' by making me behold 'Love or some other vanity'.

The Fatigue.

A SONG.

Adieu, fond World, and all thy wiles,

Thy haughty frowns, and treacherous smiles,

They that behold thee with my eyes,

Thy double dealing will despise:

From thee, false World, my deadly foe,

Into some desert let me go;

Some gloomy melancholy cave,

Dark and silent as the grave;

Let me withdraw, where I may be

From thine impertinences free:

10There when I hear the turtle groan,

How sweetly would I make my moan!

Kind Philomel would teach me there

My sorrows pleasantly to bear:

There could I correspond with none

But Heaven, and my own breast alone.

The Resolve.

SONG.

I.

Had Phyllis neither charms, nor graces

More than the rest of women wear,

Levell'd by Fate with common faces,

Yet Damon could esteem her fair.

II.

Good-natur'd Love can soon forgive
Those petty injuries of Time,
And all th' affronts of years impute
To her misfortune, not her crime.

III.

Wedlock puts Love upon the rack,
10Makes it confess 'tis still the same
In icy age, as it appear'd
At first when all was lively flame.

IV.

If Hymen's slaves, whose ears are bored,
Thus constant by compulsion be,
Why should not choice endear us more
Than them their hard necessity?

V.

Phyllis! 'tis true, thy glass does run,
But since mine too keeps equal pace,
My silver hairs may trouble thee,
20As much as me thy ruin'd face.

VI.

Then let us constant be as Heaven,
Whose laws inviolable are,
Not like those rambling meteors there
That foretell ills, and disappear.

VII.

So shall a pleasing calm attend
Our long uneasy destiny,
So shall our loves and lives expire,

From storms and tempests ever free.

The Resolve.] The superiority of the first stanza of this to the rest, and the reason of that superiority (the double rhyme 'graces' and 'faces'), are both clear enough. But what is not clear is why Flatman—who, if no great poet, seems usually to have been at no loss for verse or rhyme—should have suddenly run dry of the latter in his first and third lines. If he had not been so stingy the piece might have been worth something. It is not quite worthless as it is.

Love's Bravo.

SONG.

Why should we murmur, why repine,

Phyllis, at thy fate, or mine?

Like pris'ners, why do we those fetters shake;

Which neither thou, nor I can break?

There is a better way to baffle Fate,

If mortals would but mind it,

And 'tis not hard to find it:

Who would be happy, must be desperate;

He must despise those stars that fright

10Only fools that dread the night;

Time and chance he must outbrave,

He that crouches is their slave.

Thus the wise Pagans, ill at ease,

Bravely chastis'd their surly Deities.

The Expectation.

SONG.

I.

Why did I ever see those glorious eyes

My famish'd soul to tantalize?

I hop'd for Heav'n, which I had lately seen,

But ne'er perceiv'd the gulf between:

In vain for bliss did my presumptions seek,

My love so strong

I could not hold my tongue,

My heart so feeble that I durst not speak.

II.

Yet why do I my constitution blame,

10Since all my heart is out of frame?

'Twere better, sure, my passion to appease,

With hope to palliate my disease:

And 'twill be something like tranquillity,

To hope for that

I must not compass yet,

And make a virtue of necessity.

The Expectation.] In the Firth MS. entitled 'Song', and dated July 11, 1671. It was set by Roger Hill. The chief variants are:—

5 presumptions] presumption.

8 that] yet.

14 hope for] think of.

15 must not compass] may not purchase.

Coridon Converted.

SONG.

I.

When Coridon a slave did lie,

Entangled in his Phyllis' eye,

How did he sigh! how did he groan!

How melancholy was his tone!

He told his story to the woods,

And wept his passion by the floods;

Then Phyllis, cruel Phyllis, too to blame,

Regarded not his sufferings, nor his flame.

II.

Then Coridon resolv'd no more

10His mistress' mercy to implore;

How did he laugh, how did he sing!

How did he make the forest ring!

He told his conquest to the woods,

And drown'd his passion in the floods:

Then Phyllis, gentle Phyllis, less severe,

Would have had him, but he would none of her.

Coridon Converted.] In the Firth MS. entitled 'Song', and dated April 29, 1664. It was set by William Gregory. The MS. yields some important corrections:— 'conquest' and 'passion' in ll. 13, 14, for the plural of the printed texts; and 'gentle Phyllis' in l. 15 for 'cruel Phyllis'. The plural 'woods' and 'floods' perhaps account for the former variants; the latter is evidently an attempt to adhere strictly to the refrain.

The Humourist.

SONG.

I.

Good faith! I never was but once so mad

To dote upon an idle woman's face,

And then, alas! my fortune was so bad

To see another chosen in my place;

And yet I courted her, I'm very sure,

With love as true as his was, and as pure.

II.

But if I ever be so fond again

To undertake the second part of love,

To reassume that most unmanlike pain,

10Or after shipwreck do the ocean prove;

My mistress must be gentle, kind, and free,

Or I'll be as indifferent as she.

The Humourist.]: In the Firth MS. entitled 'Song', and dated April 29, 1664. It was set by William Gregory. In the MS. the poem opens 'In faith'.

Fading Beauty.

SONG.

I.

As poor Aurelia sate alone,

Hard by a rivulet's flow'ry side,

Envious at Nature's new-born pride,

Her slighted self she thus reflected on.

II.

Alas! that Nature should revive

These flowers, which after Winter's snow

Spring fresh again, and brighter show,

But for our fairer sex so ill contrive!

III.

Beauty, like theirs a short-liv'd thing,

10On us in vain she did bestow,

Beauty that only once can grow,

An Autumn has, but knows no second Spring.

A Dialogue.

CLORIS AND PARTHENISSA.

C. Why dost thou all address deny?

Hard-hearted Parthenissa, why?

See how the trembling lovers come,

That from thy lips expect their doom.

P. Cloris! I hate them all, they know,

Nay I have often told them so;

Their silly politics abhorr'd:

I scorn to make my slave my lord.

C. But Strephon's eyes proclaim his love

10Too brave, tyrannical to prove.

P. Ah, Cloris! when we lose our pow'r

We must obey the conqueror.

C. Yet where a gentle Prince bears sway,

It is no bondage to obey.

P. But if like Nero, for awhile,

With arts of kindness he beguile;

How shall the tyrant be withstood

When he has writ his laws in blood!

C. Love, Parthenissa, all commands:

20It fetters Kings in charming bands;

Mars yields his arms to Cupid's darts,

And Beauty softens savage hearts.

Chorus.

If nothing else can pull the Tyrant down,

Kill him with kindness, and the day's your own.

A Dialogue.] 22 And] But *1674.*

A Dialogue.

ORPHEUS AND EURYDICE.

Eurydice, my fair, my fair Eurydice!

My love, my joy, my life, if so thou be

In Pluto's kingdom answer me; appear

And come to thy poor Orpheus.——

Eur. Oh, I hear,

I hear, dear Orpheus, but I cannot come

Beyond the bounds of dull Elysium.

I cannot——

Orph. And why wilt thou not draw near?

Is there within these courts a shade so dear

As he that calls thee?

Eur. No, there cannot be

10A thing so lovely in mine eyes as thee.

Orph. Why comes not then Eurydice?

Eur. The Fates,

The Fates forbid, and these eternal gates,

Never unbarr'd to let a pris'ner go,

Deny me passage; nay, grim Cerberus too

Stands at the door——

Orph. But cannot then

They that o'er Lethe go, return again?

Eur. Never, oh never!——

Orph. Sure they may, let's try

If Art can null the Laws of Destiny.

My lays compacted Thebes, made every tree

20Loosen its roots to caper; come let's see

What thou and I can do.

Chor. Perchance the throng

Of Ghosts may be enchanted with a song,

And mov'd to pity.——

Eur. Hark! the hinges move,

The gate's unbarr'd. I come, I come, my Love!

Chorus amborum.

'Twas Music, only Music, could unspell

Helpless, undone Eurydice from Hell.

A Dialogue.] Dated in the Firth MS. September 15, 1663; it was set to music by W. Gregory.

The Bachelor's Song.

Like a dog with a bottle, fast ty'd to his tail,

Like vermin in a trap, or a thief in a jail,

Like a Tory in a bog,

Or an ape with a clog:

Such is the man, who when he might go free,

Does his liberty lose

For a Matrimony noose,

And sells himself into captivity.

The dog he does howl, when his bottle does jog,

10The vermin, the thief, and the Tory in vain

Of the trap, of the jail, of the quagmire complain.

But well fare poor Pug! for he plays with his clog;

And though he would be rid on 't rather than his life,

Yet he lugs it, and he hugs it, as a man does his wife.

The Bachelor's Song]. In the Firth MS. entitled 'Song', and dated 1670. See Introduction for the rather obvious legend connected with this profane doggerel. As proof of its popularity it may be noted that versions of it appear in the *Windsor Drollery*, 1672, and the *Westminster Drollery*, 1691; in the latter there are also *The Bachelors Satyr Related* and *A Reply to The Bachelors Satyr Related*. These unauthorized versions have a number of minor variants.

3 Like] Or like *1674-82*. 'Tory' in the original, not the transferred sense, which latter Flatman seems himself to have well deserved.

5 Such is the] Even such is a *MS.* might go] may be *MS.*

9 his] the *1686.*

10 and] *om. MS.*

11 quagmire] bog do *MS.*

The Second Part.

SONG.

How happy a thing were a wedding

And a bedding,

If a man might purchase a wife

For a twelvemonth and a day;

But to live with her all a man's life,

For ever and for ay,

Till she grow as grey as a cat,

Good faith, Mr. Parson, I thank you for that.

An Appeal to Cats in the business of Love.

A SONG.

Ye cats that at midnight spit love at each other,

Who best feel the pangs of a passionate lover,

I appeal to your scratches and your tattered fur,

If the business of Love be no more than to purr.

Old Lady Grimalkin with her gooseberry eyes,

Knew something when a kitten, for why she was wise;

You find by experience, the love-fit's soon o'er,

Puss! Puss! lasts not long, but turns to *Cat-whore!*

Men ride many miles,

Cats tread many tiles,

Both hazard their necks in the fray;

Only Cats, when they fall

From a house or a wall,

Keep their feet, mount their tails, and away!

An appeal to Cats.] Added in *1686*. It is a pity we do not possess the tune to which Mr. Humfries, or somebody else, most probably set this lively fantasy. It is quite in the style of Dr. Blow, Humfries's friend and colleague.

Advice to an Old Man of sixty-three, about to Marry a Girl of sixteen.

SONG.

I.

Now fie upon him! what is Man,

Whose life at best is but a span?

When to an inch it dwindles down,

Ice in his bones, snow on his crown,

That he within his crazy brain

Kind thoughts of Love should entertain,

That he, when harvest comes, should plow,

And when 'tis time to reap, go sow,

Who, in imagination only strong,

10Though twice a child, can never twice grow young.

II.

Nature did those design for fools,

That sue for work, yet have no tools.

What fellow-feeling can there be

In such a strange disparity?

Old age mistakes the youthful breast,

Love dwells not there, but Interest:

Alas, good man! take thy repose,

Get ribband for thy thumbs and toes.

Provide thee flannel, and a sheet of lead,—

20Think on thy Coffin, not thy Bridal Bed.

The Slight.

SONG.

I.

I did but crave that I might kiss,

If not her lip, at least her hand,

The coolest Lover's frequent bliss,

And rude is she that will withstand

That inoffensive liberty:

She (would you think it?) in a fume

Turn'd her about and left the room;

Not she, she vow'd, not she.

II.

Well, Chariessa, then said I,

10If it must thus for ever be,

I can renounce my slavery,

And since you will not, can be free.

Many a time she made me die,

Yet (would you think 't?) I lov'd the more,

But I'll not take 't as heretofore,

Not I, I'll vow, not I.

The Slight.]: In the Firth MS., a first draft, dated August, 1666, and recorded as having been set to music by Sylvanus Taylor. The variants are important:—

3 frequent] hourly.

4-5 Which at his wish he may command, Nay, often takes the liberty. The copy in Rawlinson MS. D. 260 (fol. 27 verso) has the same readings.

The Penitent.

SONG.

I.

Had I but known some years ago
What wretched lovers undergo,
The tempests and the storms that rise
From their Belovèd's dangerous eyes,
With how much torment they endure
That ague and that calenture;
Long since I had my error seen,
Long since repented of my sin:
Too late the soldier dreads the trumpet's sound
10That newly has receiv'd his mortal wound.

II.

But so adventurous was I
My fortunes all alone to try,
Needs must I kiss the burning light,
Because it shin'd, because 'twas bright.
My heart with youthful heat on fire,
I thought some God did me inspire;
And that blind zeal embold'ned me
T' attempt Althea's Deity.
Surely those happy Pow'rs that dwell above,
20Or never courted, or enjoy'd their love.

The Penitent.] In the Firth MS. entitled 'Song', and dated 1671. It was set by Roger Hill.

9 dreads: loathes *MS*.

15 heart: breast *MS*.

18 The reference, if any, to the *classical* story of Althea is so confused and muddled that perhaps there is none. See *The Surrender*, below.

The Defiance.

SONG.

I.

Be not too proud, imperious Dame,

Your charms are transitory things,

May melt, while you at Heaven aim,

Like Icarus's waxen wings;

And you a part in his misfortunes bear,

Drown'd in a briny Ocean of despair.

II.

You think your beauties are above

The Poet's brain and Painter's hand,

As if upon the Throne of Love

You only should the world command: 10

Yet know, though you presume your title true,

There are pretenders that will rival you.

III.

There's an experienc'd rebel, Time,

And in his squadron's Poverty;

There's Age that brings along with him

A terrible artillery:

And if against all these thou keep'st thy crown,

Th' usurper Death will make thee lay it down.

The Defiance.] 5 misfortunes *1682*: misfortune *1686*.

14 'squadron's' is not apostrophated in original, but the practice in this respect is so loose as to be of no value. The plural would make sense, of course.

The Surrender.

SONG.

I yield, I yield! Divine Althaea, see

How prostrate at thy feet I bow,

Fondly in love with my captivity,

So weak am I, so mighty thou!

Not long ago I could defy,

Arm'd with wine and company,

Beauty's whole artillery:

Quite vanquish'd now by thy miraculous charms,

Here, fair Althaea, take my arms,

For sure he cannot be of human race,

That can resist so bright, so sweet a face.

The Whim.

SONG.

I.

Why so serious, why so grave?

Man of business, why so muddy?

Thyself from Chance thou canst not save

With all thy care and study.

Look merrily then, and take thy repose;

For 'tis to no purpose to look so forlorn,

Since the World was as bad before thou wert born,

And when it will mend who knows?

And a thousand year hence 'tis all one,

10If thou lay'st on a dunghill, or sat'st on a throne.

II.

To be troubled, to be sad,

Carking mortal, 'tis a folly,

For a pound of Pleasure's not so bad

As an ounce of Melancholy:

Since all our lives long we travel towards Death,

Let us rest us sometimes, and bait by the way,

'Tis but dying at last; in our race let us stay,

And we shan't be so soon out of breath.

Sit the comedy out, and that done,

20When the play's at an end, let the curtain fall down.

The Renegado.

SONG.

I.

Remov'd from fair Urania's eyes

Into a village far away:

Fond Astrophil began to say,

Thy charms, Urania, I despise;

Go bid some other shepherd for thee die,

That never understood thy tyranny.

II.

Return'd at length the amorous swain,

Soon as he saw his deity,

Ador'd again, and bow'd his knee,

10Became her slave, and wore her chain.

The Needle thus that motionless did lie,

Trembles, and moves, when the lov'd Loadstone's nigh.

The Renegado.] In the Firth MS. entitled 'Song', and dated 1671. 'Set by Roger Hill.'

Phyllis withdrawn.

I.

I did but see her, and she's snatch'd away,

I find I did but happy seem;

So small a while did my contentments stay,

As short and pleasant as a dream:

Yet such are all our satisfactions here,

They raise our hopes, and then they disappear.

II.

Ill-natur'd Stars, that evermore conspire

To quench poor Strephon's flame,

To stop the progress of his swift desire,

10And leave him but an aëry name;

Why art thou doom'd (of no pretences proud)

Ixion-like thus to embrace a cloud?

III.

Yet why should Strephon murmur, why complain,

Or envy Phyllis her delight,

Why should her pleasures be to him a pain,

Easier perhaps out of his sight?

No, Strephon, no! If Phyllis happy be,

Thou shouldst rejoice, whate'er becomes of thee.

IV.

Amidst the charming glories of the spring

20In pleasant fields and goodly bowers,

Indulgent Nature seems concern'd to bring

All that may bless her innocent hours,

While thy disastrous Fate has tied thee down

To all the noise and tumult of the Town.

V.

Strephon that for himself expects no good

To Phyllis wishes everywhere

A long serenity without a cloud,

Sweet as these smiles of th' infant year.

May Halcyons in her bosom build their nest,

30Whatever storms shall discompose my breast.

Phyllis withdrawn.] The first stanza is a good example of the purely haphazard character of typographical peculiarities at the time. There is not a capital in the original, though in that original elsewhere one would find 'Contentments', 'Dream', 'Satisfactions', and 'Hopes', if not others as well.

The Malecontent.

SONG.

Phyllis, O Phyllis! Thou art fondly vain,

My wavering thoughts thus to molest,

Why should my pleasure be the only pain,

That must torment my easy breast?

If with Prometheus I had stolen fire,

Fire from above,

As scorching, and as bright, as that of Love,

I might deserve Jove's ire,

A vulture then might on my liver feed,

But now eternally I bleed, 10

And yet on Thee, on Thee lies all the blame,

Who freely gav'st the fuel and the flame.

The Malecontent.] 5 'Stoll'n' in original, though the valued 'èn' is indispensable for the metre.

The Indifferent.

SONG.

Prithee confess for my sake and your own,

Am I the man or no?

If I am he, thou canst not do 't too soon,

If not, thou canst not be too slow.

If Woman cannot love, Man's folly's great

Your sex with so much zeal to treat;

But if we freely proffer to pursue

Our tender thoughts and spotless love,

Which nothing shall remove,

And you despise all this, pray what are you?

The Harbour.

SONG.

O tedious hopes! when will the storm be o'er!

When will the beaten vessel reach the shore!

Long have I striv'n with blust'ring winds and tides,

Clouds o'er my head, waves on my sides!

Which in my dark adventures high did swell,

While Heaven was black as Hell.

O Love, tempestuous Love, yet, yet at last,

Let me my anchor cast,

And for the troubles I have undergone,

10O bring me to a port which I may call my own.

The Unconcerned.

SONG.

Now that the world is all in amaze,

Drums and trumpets rending heav'ns,

Wounds a-bleeding, mortals dying,

Widows and orphans piteously crying;

Armies marching, towns in a blaze,

Kingdoms and states at sixes and sevens:

What should an honest fellow do,

Whose courage, and fortunes run equally low!

Let him live, say I, till his glass be run,

10As easily as he may;

Let the wine, and the sand of his glass flow together,

For life's but a winter's day.

Alas! from sun to sun,

The time's very short, very dirty the weather,

And we silently creep away.

Let him nothing do, he could wish undone;

And keep himself safe from the noise of gun.

The Unconcerned.] 1 amaze *1674, 1676, 1682*: a maze *1686*.

The Immovable.

SONG.

I.

What though the sky be clouded o'er,

And Heav'us influence smile no more?

Though tempests rise, and earthquakes make

The giddy World's foundation shake?

A gallant breast contemns the feeble blow

Of angry Gods, and scorns what Fate can do.

II.

What if alarums sounded be,

And we must face our enemy,

If cannons bellow out a death,

10Or trumpets woo away our breath!

'Tis brave amidst the glittering throng to die.

Nay, Samson-like, to fall with company.

III.

Then let the swordman domineer,

I can nor pike nor musket fear;

Clog me with chains, your envies tire,

For when I will, I can expire;

And when the puling fit of Life is gone,

The worst that cruel man can do, is done.

The Wish.

SONG.

I.

Not to the hills where cedars move

Their cloudy head, not to the grove

Of myrtles in th' Elysian shade,

Nor Tempe which the poets made;

Not on the spicy mountains play;

Or travel to Arabia:

I aim not at the careful Throne,

Which Fortune's darlings sit upon;

No, no, the best this fickle world can give,

10Has but a little, little time to live.

II.

But let me soar, O let me fly

Beyond poor Earth's benighted eye,

Beyond the pitch swift eagles tower,

Above the reach of human power;

Above the stars, above the way,

Whence Phoebus darts his piercing ray.

O let me tread those Courts that are,

So bright, so pure, so blest, so fair,

As neither thou nor I must ever know

20On Earth—'tis thither, thither would I go.

The Wish.] Entitled 'A Wish' in the Firth MS., and dated September 10, 1659. It was set by Captain Taylor. The chief variants are 'clouds' for 'stars' in l. 15 and 'the sun' for 'Phoebus' in l. 16.

The Cordial. In the year 1657.

SONG.

I.

Did you hear of the News (O the News) how it thunders!

Do but see, how the block-headed multitude wonders!

One fumes, and stamps, and stares to think upon

What others wish as fast, Confusion.

One swears w' are gone, another just agoing,

While a third sits and cries,

'Till his half-blinded eyes

Call him pitiful rogue for so doing.

Let the tone be what 'twill that the mighty ones utter,

10Let the cause be what 'twill why the poorer sort mutter;

I care not what your State-confounders do,

Nor what the stout repiners undergo;

I cannot whine at any alterations.

Let the Swede beat the Dane,

Or be beaten again,

What am I in the crowd of the Nations?

II.

What care I if the North and South Poles come together;

If the Turk or the Pope's Antichristian, or neither;

If fine Astraea be (as Naso said)

20From mortals in a peevish fancy fled:

Rome, when 'twas all on fire, her people mourning,

'Twas an Emperor could stand

With his harp in his hand,

Sing and play, while the city was burning.

Celadon on Delia singing.

O Delia! for I know 'tis she,

It must be she, for nothing less could move

My tuneless heart, than something from above.

I hate all earthly harmony:

Hark, hark, ye Nymphs, and Satyrs all around!

Hark, how the baffled Echo faints; see how she dies,

Look how the wingèd choir all gasping lies

At the melodious sound;

See, while she sings

10How they droop and hang their wings!

Angelic Delia, sing no more,

Thy song's too great for mortal ear;

Thy charming notes we can no longer bear:

O then in pity to the World give o'er,

And leave us stupid as we were before.

Fair Delia, take the fatal choice,

Or veil thy beauty, or suppress thy Voice.

His passion thus poor Celadon betray'd,

When first he saw, when first he heard the lovely Maid.

The Advice.

SONG.

I.

Poor Celia once was very fair,

A quick bewitching eye she had,

Most neatly look'd her braided hair,

Her dainty cheeks would make you mad,

Upon her lip did all the Graces play,

And on her breasts ten thousand Cupids lay.

II.

Then many a doting lover came

From seventeen till twenty-one,

Each told her of his mighty flame,

10But she, forsooth, affected none.

One was not handsome, t'other was not fine,

This of tobacco smelt, and that of wine.

III.

But t'other day it was my fate

To walk along that way alone,

I saw no coach before her gate,

But at the door I heard her moan:

She dropt a tear, and sighing, seem'd to say,

Young ladies, marry, marry while you may!

The Advice.] In the Firth MS., where it is dated December 22, 1664, and recorded to have been set by Roger Hill; and in Rawlinson MS. D. 260 (fol. 28) of the Bodleian. The variants are trivial. Found also in the *Westminster Drollery*, 1671, and the *Windsor Drollery*, 1672: the latter reads 'lock'd' for 'look'd' in l. 3. In l. 9 *1682* reads 'her' for 'his'.

To Mr. Sam. Austin of Wadham Coll. Oxon, On his most unintelligible Poems.

SIR,

In that small inch of time I stole, to look

On th' obscure depths of your mysterious book,

(Heav'n bless my eyesight!) what strains did I see!

What steropegeretic Poetry!

What hieroglyphic words, what [riddles] all,

In letters more than cabalistical!

We with our fingers may your verses scan,

But all our noddles understand them can

No more, than read that dungfork, pothook hand

10That in Queen's College Library does stand.

The cutting hanger of your Wit I can't see,

For that same scabbard that conceals your Fancy:

Thus a black velvet casket hides a jewel;

And a dark woodhouse, wholesome winter fuel;

Thus John Tradeskin starves our greedy eyes,

By boxing up his new-found rarities;

We dread Actaeon's fate, dare not look on,

When you do scower your skin in Helicon;

We cannot (Lynceus-like) see through the wall

20Of your strong-mortar'd Poems; nor can all

The small shot of our brains make one hole in

The bulwark of your book, that fort to win.

Open your meaning's door, O do not lock it!

Undo the buttons of your smaller pocket,

And charitably spend those angels there,

Let them enrich and actuate our sphere.

Take off our bongraces, and shine upon us,

Though your resplendent beams should chance to tan us.

Had you but stol'n your verses, then we might

30Hope in good time they would have come to light;

And felt I not a strange poetic heat

Flaming within, which reading makes me sweat,

Vulcan should take 'em, and I'd not exempt 'em,

Because they're things *Quibus lumen ademptum.*

I thought to have commended something there,

But all exceeds my commendations far:

I can say nothing; but stand still, and stare,

And cry, O wondrous, strange, profound, and rare.

Vast Wits must fathom you better than thus,

40You merit more than our praise: as for us

The beetles of our rhymes shall drive full fast in,

The wedges of your worth to everlasting,

My much Apocalyptic friend *Sam. Austin.*

To Mr. Sam. Austin.] Samuel Austin the younger (his father of the same name was a respectable divine and a writer of sacred verse of the preceding generation) was a Wadham man, a contemporary of Flatman's, and a common Oxford butt for conceit and affectation. His *Panegyric on the Restoration* appeared in 1661, and contained a statement that the author 'intended a larger book of poems according as these find acceptance'. He had taken his degree five years earlier, and his poetry, probably in MS., had been soon afterwards made the subject of one of the liveliest and naughtiest of Oxford skits, *Naps on Parnassus* (London, 1658), where some of Austin's own lucubrations, and more parodies and lampoons on him, appear—side-noted with quaint and scandalous *adversaria*. Flatman himself contributed, among others, some kitchen-Latin leonines:

O decus Anglorum! vates famose tuorum

Cujus pars nona facit Oxenford Helicona,

&c., sometimes dropping into a sort of Macaronic, or at least mongrel dialect:

Haec ratio non est—quid rides?—my meaning's honest.

The elder Samuel Austin, a Cornishman, of Exeter, was a very serious person who wrote, and after difficulties got published in 1629, *Austin's Urania, or the Heavenly Muse*, with the most unreasonable motto *Aut perlegas aut non legas*— rendered

Whate'er thou be whose eye do chance to fall

Upon this Book, read all or none at all.

For a considerable time I obeyed the second part of this injunction only.

Naps on Parnassus has some important variants and some corrections of the present text. Omitting minor changes, these are:—

2 obscure] abstruse.

5 what all] what riddles? all (Clearly the right text).

After 16 is the couplet:

There were Philosophers content to be

Renown'd, and famous in obscurity.

Line 18 has a marginal note on 'scower'—'But when he does so, he verifies the Proverb, viz. Æthiopem lavat.'

Lines 29, 30 read:

O were your verses stol'n, that so we might

Hope in good time to see them come to light.

After line 36 is the couplet:

I hope some wit when he your honour hears,

Will praise your mother's eyes' turpentine tears.

In line 42 is printed 'everlastin' with the note '[g] aufertur in fine, per Apocopen'.

4 The blessed word 'stero (it should be 'ste*rro*' or 'ste*reo*') -pegeretic' (a rather erratic compound from πήγνυμι) is very likely Austin's own for 'strongly put together'.

10 ['The Devil's handwriting in Queen's College Library at Oxford.' Note in orig.] This interesting autograph is still preserved, and a photograph of it may be seen in Mr. Andrew Clark's Anthony à Wood's *Life and Times*, i. 498 (Oxford Historical Society).

15 John Tradeskin] John Tradescant the second (1608-1662), original collector of the Ashmolean Museum.

27 bongraces] Sun-bonnets.

To my ingenious Friend Mr. William Faithorne on his Book of Drawing, Etching, and Graving.

Should I attempt an elogy, or frame

A paper-structure to secure thy name,

The lightning of one censure, one stern frown

Might quickly hazard that, and thy renown.

But this thy book prevents that fruitless pain.

One line speaks purelier thee, than my best strain.

Those mysteries (once like the spiteful mould,

Which bars the greedy Spaniard from his gold)

Thou dost unfold in every friendly page,

10Kind to the present, and succeeding age.

That hand, whose curious art prolongs the date

Of frail mortality, and baffles Fate

With brass and steel, can surely potent be,

To rear a lasting monument for thee:

For my part I prefer (to guard the dead)

A copper-plate beyond a sheet of lead.

So long as brass, so long as books endure,

So long as neat-wrought pieces, thou'rt secure.

A [*Faithorne sculpsit*] is a charm can save

20From dull oblivion, and a gaping grave.

To my Ingenious Friend Mr. William Faithorne.] The *elder* Faithorne (*v. sup.*, p. 278). The younger, his son and namesake, was but eighteen when Flatman first published. The lines first appeared in *The Art of Graveing and Etching ... Published by Willm Faithorne. And Sold at his Shop next to ye Signe of ye Drake without Temple Barre, 1662.*

1 'elogy' is no doubt here merely an equivalent for 'eulogy', and rather from *éloge* than *elogium*. But it is a pity that it has not been kept in English as an equivalent for the Latin.

5 that fruitless] my slender *1662*. Other important variants are:— Lines 9, 10 read:—

Thine ingenuity reveals, and so

By making plain, thou dost illustrious grow.

14 lasting] stately.

On the Commentaries of Messire Blaize de Montluc.

To the Worthy Translator,

CHARLES COTTON, Esq.

He that would aptly write of warlike men,

Should make his ink of blood, a sword his pen;

At least he must their memories abuse,

Who writes with less than Maro's mighty Muse:

All, Sir, that I could say of this great theme

(The brave Montluc) would lessen his esteem;

Whose laurels too much native verdure have

To need the praises vulgar chaplets crave:

His own bold hand, what it durst write, durst do,

10Grappled with enemies, and oblivion too;

Hew'd his own monument, and grav'd thereon

Its deep and durable inscription.

To you, Sir, whom the valiant Author owes

His second life, and conquest o'er his foes—

Ill-natur'd foes, Time and Detraction,—

What is a stranger's contribution!

Who has not such a share of vanity,

To dream that one, who with such industry

Obliges all the world, can be oblig'd by me.

On the Commentaries of Messire Blaize de Montluc.] Cotton's translation of the admirable Gascon appeared in the same year (1674) with Flatman's *Poems*.

A Character of a Belly-God.

CATIUS AND HORACE.

HORACE.

Whence, Brother Case, and whither bound so fast?

CA. O, Sir, you must excuse me, I'm in haste.

I dine with my (Lord Mayor) and can't allow

Time for our eating directory now:

Though I must needs confess, I think my rules

Would prove Pythagoras and Plato fools.

HOR. *Grave Sir, I must acknowledge, 'tis a crime*

To interrupt at such a nick of time;

Yet stay a little, Sir, it is no sin;

10 *You're to say Grace ere dinner can begin;*

Since you at food such virtuoso are,

Some precepts to an hungry poet spare.

CA. I grant you, Sir, next pleasure ta'en in eating

Is that (as we do call it) of repeating;

I still have kitchen systems in my mind,

And from my stomach's fumes a brain well lin'd.

HOR. *Whence, pray, Sir, learnt you those ingenuous arts,*

From one at home, or hir'd from foreign parts?

CA. No names, Sir (I beseech you), that's foul play,

20 We ne'er name authors, only what they say.

1. 'For eggs choose long, the round are out of fashion,

'Unsavoury and distasteful to the nation:

'E'er since the brooding Rump, they're addle too,

'In the long egg lies Cock-a-doodle-doo.

2. 'Choose coleworts planted on a soil that's dry,

'Even they are *worse for th' wetting* (verily).

3. 'If friend from far shall come to visit, then

'Say thou wouldst treat the wight with mortal hen,

'Don't thou forthwith pluck off the cackling head,

30'And impale corpse on spit as soon as dead;

'For so she will be tough beyond all measure,

'And friend shall make a trouble of a pleasure.

'Steep'd in good wine let her her life surrender,

'O then she'll eat most admirably tender.

4. 'Mushrooms that grow in meadows are the best;

'For aught I know, there's poison in the rest.

5. 'He that would many happy summers see,

'Let him eat mulberries fresh off the tree,

'Gather'd before the sun's too high, for these

40'Shall hurt his stomach less than Cheshire cheese.

6. 'Aufidius (had you done so 't had undone ye)

'Sweet'ned his morning's draughts of sack with honey;

'But he did ill, to empty veins to give

'Corroding potion for a lenitive.

7. 'If any man to drink do thee inveigle in,

'First wet thy whistle with some good metheglin.

8. 'If thou art bound, and in continual doubt,

'Thou shalt get in no more till some get out,

'The mussel or the cockle will unlock

50'Thy body's trunk, and give a vent to nock.

'Some say that sorrel steep'd in wine will do,

'But to be sure, put in some aloes too.

9. 'All shell-fish (with the growing Moon increast)

'Are ever, when she fills her orb, the best:

'But for brave oysters, Sir, exceeding rare,

'They are not to be met with everywhere.

'Your Wall-fleet oysters no man will prefer

'Before the juicy grass-green Colchester.

'Hungerford crawfish match me, if you can,

60'There's no such crawlers in the Ocean.

  10. 'Next for your suppers, you (it may be) think

'There goes no more to 't, but just eat and drink;

'But let me tell you, Sir, and tell you plain,

'To dress 'em well requires a man of brain:

'His palate must be quick, and smart, and strong,

'For sauce, a very critic in the tongue.

  11. 'He that pays dear for fish, nay though the best,

'May please his fishmonger, more than his guest,

'If he be ignorant what sauce is proper;

70'There's Machiavel in th' *ménage* of a supper.

  12. 'For swines-flesh, give me that of the wild boar,

'Pursu'd and hunted all the forest o'er;

'He to the liberal oak ne'er quits his love,

'And when he finds no acorns, grunts at Jove.

'The Hampshire hog with pease and whey that's fed

'Sty'd up, is neither good alive nor dead.

  13. 'The tendrils of the vine are salads good,

'If when they are in season understood.

  14. 'If servants to thy board a rabbit bring,

80'Be wise, and in the first place carve a wing.

  15. 'When fish and fowl are right, and at just age,

'A feeder's curiosity t' assuage,

'If any ask, who found the mystery,

'Let him inquire no further, I am he.

  16. 'Some fancy bread out of the oven hot:

'Variety's the glutton's happiest lot.

  17. 'It's not enough the wine you have be pure,

'But of your oil as well you ought be sure.

  18. 'If any fault be in the generous wine,

90'Set it abroad all night, and 'twill refine,

'But never strain 't, nor let it pass through linen,

'Wine will be worse for that, as well as women.

  19. 'The vintner that of Malaga and Sherry

'With damn'd ingredients patcheth up Canary,

'With segregative things, as pigeons' eggs,

'Straight purifies, and takes away the dregs.

  20. 'An o'er-charg'd stomach roasted shrimps will ease,

'The cure by lettuce is worse than the disease.

  21. 'To quicken appetite it will behove ye

100'To feed courageously on good anchovy.

22. 'Westphalia ham, and the Bologna sausage,
'For second or third course will clear a passage,
'But lettuce after meals! fie on 't, the glutton
'Had better feed upon Ram-alley mutton.

23. ''Twere worth one's while in palace or in cottage,
'Right well to know the sundry sorts of pottage;
'There is your French pottage, Nativity broth,
'Yet that of Fetter-lane exceeds them both;
'About a limb of a departed tup
110'There may you see the green herbs boiling up,
'And fat abundance o'er the furnace float,
'Resembling whale-oil in a Greenland boat.

24. 'The Kentish pippin's best, I dare be bold,
'That ever blue-cap costard-monger sold.

25. 'Of grapes, I like the raisins of the sun.
'I was the first immortal glory won,
'By mincing pickled herrings with these raisin
'And apples; 'twas I set the world a-gazing,
'When once they tasted of this *Hogan* fish,
120'Pepper and salt enamelling the dish.

26. ''Tis ill to purchase great fish with great matter,
'And then to serve it up in scanty platter;
'Nor is it less unseemly, some believe,
'From boy with greasy fist drink to receive,
'But the cup foul within 's enough to make
'A squeamish creature puke and turn up stomach.

27. 'Then brooms and napkins and the Flanders tile,
'These must be had too, or the feast you spoil,

'Things little thought on, and not very dear,

130'And yet how much they cost one in a year!

  28. 'Wouldst thou rub alabaster with hands sable,

'Or spread a diaper cloth on dirty table?

'*More cost, more worship*: Come: be *à la mode*;

'Embellish treat, as thou would do an ode.'

Hor. *O learnèd Sir, how greedily I hear*

This elegant Diatriba *of good cheer!*

Now by all that's good, by all provant you love,

By sturdy Chine of Beef, *and mighty* Jove;

I do conjure thy gravity, *let me see*

140*The man that made thee this* Discovery;

For he that sees th' Original's *more happy*

Than him that draws by an ill-favour'd Copy.

O bring me to the man I so admire!

The Flint *from whence brake forth these sparks of fire.*

What satisfaction would the Vision bring?

If sweet the stream, much sweeter is the spring.

[Line: 3 I had struck out the brackets, but replaced them. For some obsolete uses of the mark see Mr. Percy Simpson's *Shakesperian Punctuation*, pp. 94-5.

57 Wall-fleet *1674-82*; Wain-fleet *1686*. Wainfleet is in Lincolnshire, famous as the birthplace of the founder of Magdalen College, Oxford. I never heard Wainfleet oysters specially quoted, but if Walter White in his *Eastern England* (ii. 10) may be trusted, the place was not so very long ago excellent for cockles.

60 The ocean 'crawlers' are at any rate bigger than those of the Kennet.

75-6 This is a libel.

104 Ram-alley] The constantly cited street of coarse cook-shops.

107 'Nativity' is no doubt 'Christmas', as in 'Nativity-*pie*'. The reference is to 'plum-broth', the old Christmas dish, made of beef, prunes, raisins, currants, white bread, spices, wine, and sugar.

114 It would be a pity not to keep the form 'cost*ard*-monger'.

119 '*Hogan*' of course = 'Dutch'. This, the only positive *recipe* in the poem, would be a sort of salmagundy—not bad, but rather coarse, like most of the cookery of the time. Flatman, had he cared, might evidently have anticipated the earlier Dr. (not Bishop) King, who published his ingenious *Art of Cookery* in prose and verse (to be found in the ninth volume of Chalmers) some thirty years later.

125-6. If 'within 's' be extended to 'within *is*' we shall have in 'to-make' a pleasant Hudibrastic rhyme to 'stomach', which otherwise comes in but ill.

127 What the special use of Dutch tiles was I can only guess. For tankard stands?

141-2 The plagiarism-hunters may, if they like, accuse Sam Weller of stealing from Flatman when he observed, 'I'm very glad I've seen the 'rig'nal, cos it 's a gratifyin' sort of thing, and eases one's mind so much'.

The Disappointed.

PINDARIC ODE.

Stanza I.

Oft have I ponder'd in my pensive heart,

When even from myself I've stol'n away,

And heavily consider'd many a day,

The cause of all my anguish and my smart:

Sometimes besides a shady grove

(As dark as were my thoughts, as close as was my Love),

Dejected have I walk'd alone,

Acquainting scarce myself with my own moan.

Once I resolv'd undauntedly to hear

10What 'twas my passions had to say,

To find the reason of that uproar there,

And calmly, if I could, to end the fray:

No sooner was my resolution known

But I was all confusion.

Fierce Anger, flattering Hope, and black Despair,

Bloody Revenge, and most ignoble Fear,

Now altogether clamorous were;

My breast a perfect chaos grown,

A mass of nameless things together hurl'd,

20Like th' formless embryo of the unborn world,

Just as it's rousing from eternal night,

Before the great Creator said, *Let there be Light.*

II.

Thrice happy then are beasts, said I,

That underneath these pleasant coverts lie,

They only sleep, and eat, and drink,

They never meditate, nor think;

Or if they do, have not th' unhappy art

To vent the overflowings of their heart;

They without trouble live, without disorder die,

30Regardless of Eternity.

I said, I would like them be wise,

And not perplex myself in vain,

Nor bite th' uneasy chain,

No, no, said I, I will Philosophise!

And all th' ill-natur'd World despise:

But when I had reflected long,

And with deliberation thought

How few have practis'd what they gravely taught,

(Tho' 'tis but folly to complain)

40I judg'd it worth a generous disdain,

And brave defiance in Pindaric song.

The Disappointed.] In 1674 and in Contents of 1686 *The Disappointment.*

21 as] at *1674*.

27 unhappy] happy *1682*.

29 without disorder die, *1682*.

On Mrs. E. Montague's Blushing in the Cross-Bath.

A TRANSLATION.

I.

Amidst the Nymphs (the glory of the flood)

Thus once the beauteous Aegle stood,

So sweet a tincture ere the Sun appears,

The bashful ruddy morning wears:

Thus through a crystal wave the coral glows,

And such a blush sits on the virgin rose.

II.

Ye envied waters that with safety may

Around her snowy bosom play,

Cherish with gentle heat that noble breast

10Which so much innocence has blest,

Such innocence, as hitherto ne'er knew

What mischief Venus or her son could do.

Then from this hallow'd place

Let the profane and wanton eye withdraw,

For Virtue clad in scarlet strikes an awe

From the tribunal of a lovely face.

On Mrs. E. Montague, &c.] This, though I do not know exactly who the lady was, may be taken with the Sandwich epicedes as evidence of Flatman's acquaintance with the Montague family. It is odd that Pepys does not mention him, especially as he does record buying the 'Montelion' Almanack for 1661, which has been attributed to our poet. The Cross-Bath is of course the famous one at Bath itself, which was then the most fashionable, and was visited and used by Pepys himself. It is now 'drawn to the dregs of a democracy'—a cheap public swimming-bath, at a penny entrance or twopence with towel. Flatman's comparison of a blushing cheek to a judge on the bench is worthy of Cleveland, or even of Benlowes. But the extravagance was doubtless, in part at least, conscious.

Il Infido.

I.

I breathe, 'tis true, wretch that I am, 'tis true;

But if to live be only not to die,

If nothing in that bubble, Life, be gay,

But all t' a tear must melt away;

Let fools and Stoics be cajol'd, say I:

Thou that lik'st Ease and Love, like me,

When once the world says, Farewell both, to thee,

What hast thou more to do

Than in disdain to say, Thou foolish world, adieu!

II.

10There was a time, fool that I was! when I

Believ'd there might be something here below.

A seeming cordial to my drooping heart

That might allay my bitter smart:

I call'd it *Friend*:—but O th' inconstancy

Of human things! I tried it long,

Its love was fervent, and, I fancied, strong:

But now I plainly see,

Or 'tis withdrawn, or else 'twas all hypocrisy.

III.

I saw thy much-estrangèd eyes, I saw,

20False Musidore, thy formal alter'd face,

When thou betray'dst my seeming happiness,

And coldly took'st my kind address:

But know that I will live; for in thy place

Heaven has provided for me now

A constant friend, that dares not break a vow;

That friend will I embrace,

And never more my overweening love misplace.

Il Immaturo.

EPITAPH.

Brave Youth, whose too too hasty fate

His glories did anticipate,

Whose active soul had laid the great design

To emulate those Heroes of his line!

He show'd the world how great a man

Might be contracted to a span;

How soon our teeming expectations fail,

How little tears and wishes can prevail:

Could life hold out with these supplies

10He'd liv'd still in his parents' eyes,

And this cold stone had ne'er said, *Here he lies.*

On Mrs. Dove, Wife to the Reverend Dr. Henry Dove.

EPITAPH.

'Tis thus——and thus farewell to all

Vain mortals do perfection call;

To Beauty, Goodness, Modesty,

Sweet temper, and true Piety.

The rest an Angel's pen must tell:

Long, long, belovèd Dust, farewell.

Those blessings which we highliest prize

Are soonest ravish'd from our eyes.

On Mrs. Dove, &c.] Dr. Henry Dove was a divine of some mark, chaplain (it must have been rather in the Vicar of Bray line) to Charles, James, *and* William, Archdeacon of Richmond, and a strongly recommended candidate for the Mastership of Trinity, when young John Montague, Lord Sandwich's son, got it—*iure natalium*, apparently, as he had previously got his M.A. degree.

Lucretius.

Sed jam nec Domus accipiet te laeta, nec Uxor

Optima, nec dulces occurrent oscula nati

Praeripere, et tacita pectus dulcedine tangent.

Paraphrased.

When thou shalt leave this miserable life,

Farewell thy house, farewell thy charming wife,

Farewell for ever to thy soul's delight,

Quite blotted out in everlasting night!

No more thy pretty darling babes shall greet thee

By thy kind name, nor strive who first shall meet thee.

Their kisses with a secret pleasure shall not move thee!

For who shall say to thy dead clay, I love thee?

On the Eminent Dr. Edward Browne's Travels.

Thus from a foreign clime rich merchants come,

And thus unlade their rarities at home:

Thus undergo an acceptable toil,

With treasures to enrich their native soil.

They for themselves, for others you unfold

A cargo swoln with diamonds and gold.

With indefatigable travels, they

The trading world, the learnèd you, survey;

And for renown with great Columbus vie,

10In subterranean cosmography.

On Dr. Edward Browne's Travels.] Edward Browne, Sir Thomas's eldest son, returned in 1673 from five years' wandering, and Flatman must have written on some of his papers. His *Travels* were first printed in 1682.

On Poverty.

I.

O poverty! thou great and wise-man's school!

Mistress of Arts! and scandal to the fool!

Heav'n's sacred badge, which th' heroes heretofore

(Bright caravans of saints and martyrs) wore!

To th' Host Triumphant valiant souls are sent

From those we call the ragged regiment:

Sure guide to everlasting peace above,

Thou dost th' impediments remove;

Th' unnecessary loads of wealth and state,

10Which make men swell too big for the strait gate.

II.

Thou happy port! where we from storms are free,

And need not fear (false world!) thy piracy.

Hither for ease and shelter did retire

The busy Charles, and wearied Casimire;

Abjur'd their thrones, and made a solemn vow,

Their radiant heads to thee should ever bow.

Why should thy tents so terrible appear

Where monarchs reformadoes were?

Why should men call that state of life forlorn,

20Which God approves of, and which kings have borne?

III.

Mad Luxury! what do thy vassals reap

From a life's long debauch, but late to weep!

What the curs'd miser, who would fain ape thee,

And wear thy livery, Great Poverty!

The prudent wretch for future ages cares,

And hoards up sins for his impatient heirs!

Full little does he think the time will come

When he is gone to his long home,

The prodigal youth for whom he took such pains

30Shall be thy slave, and wear thy loathèd chains.

IV.

Fair handmaid to Devotion, by whose aid

Our souls are all disrob'd, all naked laid,

In thy true mirror men themselves do see

Just what they are, not what they seem to be.

The flattering world misrepresents our face,

And cheats us with a magnifying-glass;

Our meanness nothing else does truly show,

But only Death, but only thou,

Who teach our minds above this Earth to fly,

40And pant, and breathe for immortality.

On Poverty.] 14 Charles] Of course Charles the Fifth. Casimire] John Casimir of Poland, who had abdicated in 1668 and died in 1672.

18 'Reformadoes'] Lit. officers of a disbanded company, who retained their rank and received half-pay.

31-40 A stanza added in 1686.

Urania to her Friend Parthenissa.

A DREAM.

In a soft vision of the night,

My Fancy represented to my sight

A goodly gentle shade;

Methought it mov'd with a majestic grace,

But the surprising sweetness of its face

Made me amaz'd, made me afraid:

I found a secret shivering in my heart,

Such as friends feel that meet or part:

Approaching nearer with a timorous eye,

10Is then my Parthenissa dead, said I?

Ah Parthenissa! if thou yet are kind,

As kind as when, like me, thou mortal wert,

When thou and I had equal share in either's heart,

How canst thou bear that I am left behind!

Dear Parthenissa! O those pleasant hours,

That blest our innocent amours!

When in the common treasury of one breast,

All that was thine or mine did rest.

Dear Parthenissa!—Friend! what shall I say?

20Ah speak to thy Urania!

Oh envious Death! nothing but thee I fear'd,

No other rival could estrange

Her soul from mine or make a change.

Scarce had I spoke my passionate fears,

And overwhelm'd myself in tears:

But Parthenissa smil'd, and then she disappear'd.

On the Death of the Earl of Rochester.

PASTORAL.

I.

As on his death-bed gasping Strephon lay,

Strephon the wonder of the plains,

The noblest of th' Arcadian swains;

Strephon the bold, the witty, and the gay:

With many a sigh and many a tear he said,

Remember me, ye Shepherds, when I'm dead.

II.

Ye trifling glories of this world, adieu,

And vain applauses of the age;

For when we quit this earthly stage,

10Believe me, shepherds, for I tell you true;

Those pleasures which from virtuous deeds we have,

Procure the sweetest slumbers in the grave.

III.

Then since your fatal hour must surely come,

Surely your heads lie low as mine,

Your bright meridian sun decline;

Beseech the mighty Pan to guard you home,

If to Elysium you would happy fly,

Live not like Strephon, but like Strephon die.

On the Death of the Earl of Rochester.] Flatman, it will be observed, makes no reference to Burnet's notorious publication as to Rochester's death-bed repentance. As to the Latin version, he strains the term 'leonine', which ought properly to be used only of lines correctly metred, or intended for metre, but rhymed at middle and end. (He had actually written such: *v. sup.*, p. 353). But these verses, added in 1686, are not uninteresting examples of Latin, metred on English principles and rhymed in stanza, of the same class as Sir F. Kynaston's *Troilus*, though in different form.

MS. versions are in Bodley, in Aubrey MS. 6, fol. 56 (with the variant 'head' in l. 14), and a worthless copy in MS. Add. B. 105, fol. 19.

In obitum illustrissimi ingeniosissimique Joannis, Comitis Roffensis,

Carmen Pastorale Versu Leonino redditum.

I.

Lecto prostratus Strephon moribundus,

Planitierum Strephon decus,

Princeps curantium pecus,

Audax, facetus, Strephon et jucundus,

Lugens pastoribus sic est affatus,

Memimini mei cum migratus.

II.

Honores mundi futiles valete,

Plaudite aevi et fucata,

Mortali scenâ nam mutatâ,

10*Fidem veriloquo adhibete,*

Voluptas profluens ex virtute

Solâ obdormiscit cum salute.

III.

Cum nulla in mortem sit medela,

In terram capita cuncta incurvabunt,

Soles micantes declinabunt,

Pan supplicetor pro tutelâ

Beatorum ut recipiant chori:

Strephon non doceat vivere sed mori.

On Dr. Woodford's Paraphrase on the Canticles.

I.

Well! since it must be, so let it be,

For what do resolutions signify,

When we are urg'd to write by destiny?

II.

I had resolv'd, nay, and I almost swore,

My bedrid Muse should walk abroad no more:

Alas! 'tis more than time that I give o'er.

III.

In the recesses of a private breast

I thought to entertain your charming guest,

And never to have boasted of my feast.

IV.

10But see, my friend, when through the world you go,

My lackey-verse must shadow-like pursue,

Thin and obscure, to make a foil for you.

V.

'Tis true, you cannot need my feeble praise,

A lasting monument to your name to raise,

Well known in Heav'n by your angelic lays.

VI.

There in indelible characters they are writ,

Where no pretended heights will easy sit,

But those of serious consecrated wit.

VII.

By immaterial defecated Love,

20Your soul its heavenly origin does approve,

And in least dangerous raptures soars above.

VIII.

How could I wish, dear friend! unsaid agen
(For once I rank'd myself with tuneful men)
Whatever dropp'd from my unhallow'd pen!

IX.

The trifling rage of youthful heat once past,
Who is not troubled for his wit misplac'd!
All pleasant follies breed regret at last.

X.

While reverend Donne's and noble Herbert's flame
A glorious immortality shall claim,
30In the most durable records of Fame,

XI.

Our modish rhymes, like culinary fire,
Unctuous and earthy, shall in smoke expire;
In odorous clouds your incense shall aspire.

XII.

Let th' Pagan-world your pious verse defy,
Yet shall they envy when they come to die,
Your wiser projects on eternity.

On Dr. Woodford's Paraphrase.] See above, p. 306. These lines appeared before *A Paraphrase upon the Canticles*, 1679, and were headed 'To my dear Old Friend, the Reverend Dr. Samuel Woodford, On his Sacred Poems'.

21 approve *1679, 1682*: prove *1686.*

25-7 Referring to the comic touches noted above.

Laodamia to Protesilaus.

ONE OF OVID'S EPISTLES TRANSLATED.

THE ARGUMENT.

Protesilaus lying windbound at Aulis in the Grecian fleet design'd for the Trojan war, his wife Laodamia sends this following Epistle to him.

Health to the gentle man of war, and may

What Laodamia sends the Gods convey.

The wind that still in Aulis holds my dear,

Why was it not so cross to keep him here?

Let the wind raise an hurricane at sea,

Were he but safe and warm ashore with me.

Ten thousand kisses I had more to give him,

Ten thousand cautions, and soft words to leave him:

In haste he left me, summon'd by the wind,

10(The wind to barbarous mariners only kind).

The seaman's pleasure is the lover's pain,

(Protesilaus from my bosom ta'en!)

As from my faltering tongue half speeches fell,

Scarce could I speak that wounding word *Farewell*,

A merry gale (at sea they call it so)

Fill'd every sail with joy, my breast with woe,

There went my dear Protesilaus——

While I could see thee, full of eager pain,

My greedy eyes epicuris'd on thine,

20When thee no more, but thy spread sails I view,

I look'd, and look'd, till I had lost them too;

But when nor thee, nor them I could descry,

And all was sea that came within my eye,

They say (for I have quite forgot), they say

I straight grew pale, and fainted quite away;

Compassionate Iphiclus, and the good old man,

My mother too to my assistance ran;

- 597 -

In haste cold water on my face they threw,

And brought me to myself with much ado.

30They meant it well, to me it seem'd not so,

Much kinder had they been to let me go;

My anguish with my soul together came,

And in my heart burst out the former flame:

Since which, my uncomb'd locks unheeded flow,

Undrest, forlorn, I care not how I go;

Inspir'd with wine, thus Bacchus' frolic rout

Stagger'd of old, and straggled all about.

Put on, put on, the happy ladies say,

Thy royal robes, fair Laodamia.

40Alas! before Troy's walls my dear does lie,

What pleasure can I take in Tyrian dye?

Shall curls adorn my head, an helmet thine?

I in bright tissues, thou in armour shine?

Rather with studied negligence I'll be

As ill, if not disguisèd worse than thee.

O Paris! rais'd by ruins! mayst thou prove

As fatal in thy war, as in thy love!

O that the Grecian Dame had been less fair,

Or thou less lovely hadst appear'd to her!

50O Menelaus! timely cease to strive,

With how much blood wilt thou thy loss retrieve?

From me, ye Gods, avert your heavy doom,

And bring my dear, laden with laurels, home:

But my heart fails me, when I think of war,

The sad reflection costs me many a tear:

I tremble when I hear the very name

Of every place where thou shalt fight for fame;
Besides, th' adventurous ravisher well knew
The safest arts his villany to pursue;
60In noble dress he did her heart surprise,
With gold he dazzled her unguarded eyes,
He back'd his rape with ships and armèd men,

Thus storm'd, thus took the beauteous fortress in.
Against the power of Love and force of arms
There's no security in the brightest charms.
Hector I fear, much do I Hector fear,
A man (they say) experienc'd in war,
My dear, if thou hast any love for me,
Of that same Hector prithee mindful be;
70Fly him be sure, and every other foe,
Lest each of them should prove an Hector too.
Remember, when for fight thou shalt prepare,
Thy Laodamia charg'd thee, Have a care;
For what wounds thou receiv'st are giv'n to her.
If by thy valour Troy must ruin'd be,
May not the ruin leave one scar on thee;
Sharer in th' honour, from the danger free!
Let Menelaus fight, and force his way
Through the false ravisher's troops t' his Helena.
80Great be his victory, as his cause is good.
May he swim to her in his enemies' blood.
Thy case is different.—Mayst thou live to see
(Dearest) no other combatant but me!
Ye generous Trojans, turn your swords away

From his dear breast, find out a nobler prey;

Why should you harmless Laodamia slay?

My poor good-natur'd man did never know

What 'tis to fight, or how to face a foe;

Yet in Love's field what wonders can he do!

90Great is his prowess and his fortune too;

Let them go fight, who know not how to woo.

Now I must own, I fear'd to let thee go,

My trembling lips had almost told thee so.

When from thy father's house thou didst withdraw,

Thy fatal stumble at the door I saw,

I saw it, sigh'd, and pray'd the sign might be

Of thy return a happy prophecy!

I cannot but acquaint thee with my fear,

Be not too brave,—Remember,—Have a care,

100And all my dreads will vanish into air.

Among the Grecians some one must be found

That first shall set his foot on Trojan ground;

Unhappy she that shall his loss bewail,

Grant, O ye Gods, thy courage then may fail.

Of all the ships be thine the very last,

Thou the last man that lands; there needs no haste

To meet a potent and a treacherous foe;

Thou'lt land I fear too soon, tho' ne'er so slow.

At thy return ply every sail and oar,

110And nimbly leap on thy deserted shore.

All the day long, and all the lonely night,

Black thoughts of thee my anxious soul affright:

Darkness, to other women's pleasures kind,

Augments, like Hell, the torments of my mind.

I court e'en dreams, on my forsaken bed

False joys must serve, since all my true are fled.

What's that same airy phantom so like thee!

What wailings do I hear, what paleness see?

I wake, and hug myself, 'tis but a dream.—

120The Grecian altars know I feed their flame,

The want of hallow'd wine my tears supply,

Which make the sacred fire burn bright and high.

When shall I clasp thee in these arms of mine,

These longing arms, and lie dissolv'd in thine?

When shall I have thee by thyself alone,

To learn the wondrous actions thou hast done?

Which when in rapturous words thou hast begun

With many and many a kiss, prithee tell on,

Such interruptions grateful pauses are,

130A kiss in story's but an halt in war.

But, when I think of Troy, of winds and waves,

I fear the pleasant dream my hope deceives:

Contrary winds in port detain thee too,

In spite of wind and tide why wouldst thou go?

Thus, to thy country thou wouldst hardly come,

In spite of wind and tide thou went'st from home.

To his own city Neptune stops the way,

Revere the omen, and the Gods obey.

Return, ye furious Grecians, homeward fly,

140Your stay is not of Chance, but Destiny:

How can your arms expect desir'd success,

That thus contend for an adulteress?

But, let not me forespeak you, no,—set sail,

And Heav'n befriend you with a prosperous gale!

Ye Trojans! with regret methinks I see

Your first encounter with your enemy;

I see fair Helen put on all her charms,

To buckle on her lusty bridegroom's arms;

She gives him arms, and kisses she receives,

150(I hate the transports each to other gives.)

She leads him forth, and she commands him come

Safely victorious, and triumphant home;

And he (no doubt) will make no nice delay,

But diligently do whate'er she say.

Now he returns!—see with what amorous speed

She takes the pond'rous helmet from his head,

And courts the weary champion to her bed.

We women, too too credulous, alas!

Think what we fear will surely come to pass.

160Yet, while before the leaguer thou dost lie,

Thy picture is some pleasure to my eye;

That, I caress in words most kind and free,

And lodge it on my breast, as I would thee.

There must be something in it more than Art,

'Twere very thee, could it thy mind impart;

I kiss the pretty Idol, and complain,

As if (like thee) 'twould answer me again.

By thy return, by thy dear self, I swear,

By our Love's vows, which most religious are,

170By thy belovèd head, and those gray hairs

Which time may on it snow in future years,

I come, where'er thy Fate shall bid thee go,

Eternal partner of thy weal and woe,

So thou but live, tho' all the Gods say No.

Farewell,—but prithee very careful be

Of thy belovèd Self (I mean) of me.

129 grateful] graceful *1682*.

To the Excellent Master of Music, Signior Pietro Reggio, on His Book of Songs.

Tho' to advance thy fame, full well I know

How very little my dull pen can do;

Yet, with all deference, I gladly wait,

Enthrong'd amongst th' attendants on thy state:

Thus when Arion, by his friends betray'd,

Upon his understanding Dolphin play'd,

The scaly people their resentments show'd

By pleas'd levoltoes on the wond'ring flood.

Great Artist! thou deserv'st our loudest praise

10From th' garland to the meanest branch of bays;

For poets can but *Say*, thou mak'st them *Sing*,

And th' embryo-words dost to perfection bring;

By us the Muse conceives, but when that's done,

Thy midwif'ry makes fit to see the Sun;

Our naked lines, drest and adorn'd by thee,

Assume a beauty, pomp, and bravery;

So awful and majestic they appear,

They need not blush to reach a Prince's ear.

Princes, tho' to poor poets seldom kind,

20Their numbers turn'd to air with pleasure mind

Studied and labour'd tho' our poems be,

Alas! they die unheeded without thee,

Whose art can make our breathless labours live,

Spirit and everlasting vigour give.

Whether we write of *Heroes and of Kings,*

In Mighty Numbers, Mighty Things,

Or in a humble Ode express our sense

Of th' happy state of ease and innocence;

A country life where the contented swain

30Hugs his dear peace, and does a crown disdain;

Thy dext'rous notes with all our thoughts comply,

Can creep on Earth, can up to Heaven fly;

In heights and cadences, so sweet, so strong,

They suit a shepherd's reed, an angel's tongue.

——————————But who can comprehend

The raptures of thy voice, and miracles of thy hand?

To Signior Pietro Reggio.] First printed in *Songs of Signior Pietro Reggio,* folio undated (but issued in 1680); Shadwell and Ayres also contributed to it. It had an engraved title-page of Arion on a Dolphin (cf. l. 5), and was dedicated to the king (cf. l. 18).

8 Levoltoes *1682*: levaltoes *1686*—both variants of the form 'lavolta'.

Epitaph on the Incomparable Sir John King in the Temple-Church.

Heic juxta jacet

Johannes King Miles,

Serenissimo Carolo Secundo

In Legibus Angliae Consultus,

Illustrissimo Jacobo Duci Eboracensi

Sollicitator Generalis.

Qualis, Quantusve sis, Lector,

Profundum obstupesce;

Labia digitis comprime,

10*Oculos lachrymis suffunde.*

En! ad pedes tuos

Artis et Naturae suprema Conamina,

Fatorum Ludibria!

Non ita pridem

Erat Iste Pulvis omnifariam Doctus,

Musarum Gazophylacium,

Eloquentiam calluit, claram, puram, innocuam,

Legibus suae Patriae erat instructissimus,

Suis charus, Principibus gratus, Omnibus urbanus,

20*Sui saeculi*

Ornamentum illustre, Desiderium irreparabile.

Hinc disce Lector,

Quantilla Mortalitatis Gloria

Splendidissimis decoratae Dotibus.

Dulcem soporem agite

Dilecti, Eruditi, Beati Cineres!

Obiit *Junii 29, 1677.*

Aetat. 38.

Epitaph on the Incomparable Sir John King.] This 'incomparable' was an Etonian and a Cambridge (Queens' College) man, who became K.C. and Attorney-General to the Duke of York.

A first draft is in the Ashmole MS. 826 (fol. 50) of the Bodleian. Ll. 1-6 are at the end of the epitaph, and add a touch of bathos—'Et Interioris Templi Socius'—and the date—'Obiit tercio Calendarum Julii, Anno Ærae Christianæ', 1677; Ætatis 38'. In l. 8 the reading is 'obmutesce'. The 1682 has the simple heading 'In the Temple Church', and reads 'decorata' in l. 24.

On the Death of my dear Brother Mr. Richard Flatman.

PINDARIC ODE.

Stanza I.

Unhappy Muse! employ'd so oft

On melancholy thoughts of Death,

What hast thou left so tender, and so soft

As thy poor master fain would breath

O'er this lamented hearse?

No usual flight of fancy can become

My sorrows o'er a brother's tomb.

O that I could be elegant in tears,

That with conceptions, not unworthy thee,

10Great as thy merit, vigorous as thy years,

I might convey thy elegy

To th' grief and envy of posterity!

A gentler youth ne'er crown'd his parents' cares,

Or added ampler joy to their grey hairs:

Kind to his friends, to his relations dear,

Easy to all.—Alas! what is there here

For man to set his heart upon,

Since what we dote on most is soonest gone?

Ai me! I've lost a sweet companion,

20A friend, a brother all in one!

II.

How did it chill my soul to see thee lie

Struggling with pangs in thy last agony!

When with a manly courage thou didst brave

Approaching Death, and with a steady mind

(Ever averse to be confin'd)

Didst triumph o'er the Grave.

Thou mad'st no womanish moan,

But scorn'dst to give one groan:

He that begs pity is afraid to die,

30Only the brave despise their destiny.

But, when I call to mind how thy kind eyes

Were passionately fix'd on mine,

How, when thy falt'ring tongue gave o'er

And I could hear thy pleasing voice no more;

How, when I laid my cheek to thine,

Kiss'd thy pale lips, and press'd thy trembling hand,

Thou, in return, smil'dst gently in my face,

And hugg'dst me with a close embrace;

I am amaz'd, I am unmann'd.

40Something extremely kind I fain would say,

But through the tumult of my breast,

With too officious love opprest,

I find my feeble words can never force their way.

III.

Belovèd youth! What shall I do!

Once my delight, my torment now!

How immaturely art thou snatch'd away!

But Heaven shines on thee with many a glorious ray

Of an unclouded and immortal day,

Whilst I lie grovelling here below

50In a dark stormy night.

The blust'ring storm of Life with thee is o'er,

For thou art landed on that happy shore,

Where thou canst hope or fear no more;

Thence with compassion thou shall see

The plagues, the wars, the fires, the scarcity,

The devastations of an enemy,

From which thy early fate has set thee free;

For when thou went'st to thy long home,

Thou wert exempt from all the ills to come,

60And shall hereafter be

Spectator only of the tragedy

Acted on frail mortality.

So some one lucky mariner

From shipwreck sav'd by a propitious star,

Advanc'd upon a neighb'ring rock looks down,

And sees far off his old companions drown.

IV.

There in a state of perfect ease,

Of never interrupted happiness,

Thy large illuminated mind

70Shall matter of eternal wonder find;

There dost thou clearly see how, and from whence

The stars communicate their influence,

The methods of th' Almighty Architect,

How He consulted with Himself alone

To lay the wondrous corner-stone,

When He this goodly fabric did erect.

There, thou dost understand

The motions of the secret hand,

That guides th' invisible wheel,

80Which here, we ne'er shall know, but ever feel;

There Providence, the vain man's laughing-stock,

The miserable good-man's stumbling-block,

Unfolds the puzzling riddle to thy eyes,

And its own wise contrivance justifies.

What timorous man wouldn't be pleas'd to die,

To make so noble a discovery?

V.

And must I take my solemn leave

Till time shall be no more!

Can neither sighs, nor tears, nor prayers retrieve

90One cheerful hour!

Must one unlucky moment sever

Us, and our hopes, us and our joys for ever!—

Is this cold clod of Earth that endear'd Thing

I lately did my Brother call?

Are these the artful fingers that might vie

With all the sons of harmony

And overpower them all!

Is this the studious comprehensive head

With curious arts so richly furnished!

100Alas! thou, and thy glories all are gone,

Buried in darkness, and oblivion.

'Tis so—and I must follow thee,

Yet but a little while, and I shall see thee,

Yet but a little while I shall be with thee,

Then some kind friend perhaps may drop one tear for me.

On the death of Mr. Richard Flatman.] I know nothing of Richard Flatman. He would seem to have been a younger brother.

4 breath] Cf. p. 315, note.

19 Ai *1682*—a form found on p. 313, l. 32, and p. 315, l. 41: Ah *1686*

Coridon on the death of his dear Alexis, ob. Jan. 28, 168⅔.

PASTORAL SONG. Set by Dr. BLOW.

Alexis! dear Alexis! lovely boy!

O my Damon! O Palaemon! snatch'd away,

To some far distant region gone,

Has left the miserable Coridon

Bereft of all his comforts, all alone!

Have you not seen my gentle lad,

Whom every swain did love,

Cheerful, when every swain was sad,

Beneath the melancholy grove?

10His face was beauteous as the dawn of day,

Broke through the gloomy shades of night:

O my anguish! my delight!

Him (ye kind shepherds) I bewail,

Till my eyes and heart shall fail.

Tis *He* that's landed on that distant shore,

And you and I shall see him here no more.

Return, Alexis! O return!

Return, return, in vain I cry;

Poor Coridon shall never cease to mourn

20Thy too untimely, cruel destiny.

Farewell for ever, charming boy!

And with *Thee*, all the transports of my joy!

Ye powers above, why should I longer live,

To waste a few uncomfortable years,

To drown myself in tears,

For what my sighs and pray'rs can ne'er retrieve?

Coridon &c.] This and the following poems (pp. 375-407) were added in the collected edition of 1686. Alexis is no doubt the Thomas Flatman whose epitaph, by his father, is printed on p. 414. This and the following poem were sent to Sancroft, with the accompanying letter, preserved in Tanner MS. xxxiv (fol. 235) of the Bodleian:—

My Lord

       The first Page of the enclosed Paper is the result of his Mai^tie's, and yor Grace's Commaunds; & the Second of my owne uneasy thoughts on the Death of my beloved Child, who carried yor Grace's blessing with him into the other World. The severity of the Wether ha's delay'd Both much longer than became the bounden Duty of

My Lord

Yo^r Grace's most obedient Servant

& meanest Kinsman

THOMAS FLATMAN.

January 9
  168¾

The autograph copies of the two poems are in Tanner MS. 306, folios 391 and 392. The variants in this poem are:—

11 Broke] Sprung.

13 *Him* [ye] 'Tis He.

19 shall] can.

After the poem Flatman has quoted 'Immodicis brevis est aetas, & rara Senectus'.

A Song on New-Year's-day before the King, Car. 2.

Set by DR. BLOW 168⅔.

My trembling song! awake! arise!

And early tell thy tuneful tale,

Tell thy great Master, that the Night is gone;

The feeble phantoms disappear,

And now the New-Year's welcome Sun

O'erspreads the eastern skies;

He smiles on every hill, he smiles on every vale.

His glories fill our hemisphere;

Tell Him Apollo greets Him well,

10And with his fellow Wanderers agrees

To reward all His labours, and lengthen His days,

In spite of the politic follies of Hell,

And vain contrivance of the destinies.

Tell Him, a Crown of Thorns no more

Shall His sacred temples gore,

For all the rigours of His life are o'er.

Wondrous Prince! design'd to show

What noble minds can bravely undergo,

You are our wonder, you our love;

20Earth from beneath, Heaven from above,

Call loud for songs of triumph and of praise,

Their voices and their souls they raise;

IO PAEAN do we sing,

Long live, long live the King!

Rise, mighty Monarch, and ascend the Throne,

'Tis yet, once more your own,

For Lucifer and all his legions are o'erthrown:

Son of the Morning, first-born Son of Light,

How wert thou tumbled headlong down,

30Into the dungeons of eternal night!

While th' loyal stars of the celestial quire

Surrounded with immortal beams,

Mingle their unpolluted flames,

Their just Creator to admire.

With awful reverence they adore Him,

Cover their faces, and fall down before Him;

And night and day for ever sing

Hosannah, Hallelujah to th' Almighty King!

A Song.] 10 'Wanderers' after 'Apollo' may give a moment's pause. Then one translates the English into Greek and the Greek into English, obtaining 'Planets' and 'Sun'.

13 Not in the early autograph copy sent to Sancroft (see previous poem).

14 A little risky in its loyalty. Expressions in the piece suggest the Rye-House Plot and its failure; but this was in the March *after* New-Year's Day, 168⅔.

16 all] now *MS.* life] Fate *MS.*

23 'And IÖ PAEAN jointly sing' *MS.*

32 immortal] augmented *MS.*

On the King's return to White-hall, after his Summer's Progress, 1684.

SONG. Set by MR. HENRY PURCELL.

From those serene and rapturous joys

A country life alone can give,

Exempt from tumult and from noise,

Where Kings forget the troubles of their reigns,

And are almost as happy as their humble swains,

By feeling that *they* live:

Behold th' indulgent Prince is come

To view the conquests of His mercy shown

To the new Proselytes of His mighty town,

10And men and angels bid Him welcome home.

Not with an helmet or a glitt'ring spear

Does He appear;

He boast[s] no trophies of a cruel conqueror,

Brought back in triumph from a bloody war;

But with an olive-branch adorn'd,

As once the long expected Dove return'd.

Welcome as soft refreshing show'rs,

That raise the sickly heads of drooping flow'rs:

Welcome as early beams of light

20To the benighted traveller,

When he descries bright Phosphorus from afar,

And all his fears are put to flight.

Welcome, more welcome does He come

Than life to Lazarus from his drowsy tomb,

When in his winding-sheet, at his new birth,

The strange surprising word was said—Come forth!

Nor does the Sun more comfort bring,

When he turns Winter into Spring,

Than the blest advent of a peaceful King.

Chorus.

30With trumpets and shouts we receive the World's Wonder,

And let the clouds echo His welcome with thunder,

Such a thunder as applauded what mortals had done,

When they fix'd on His brows His Imperial Crown.

To Mr. Isaac Walton, on his Publication of Thealma

Long had the bright *Thealma* lain obscure,

Her beauteous charms that might the world allure,

Lay like rough diamonds, in the mine, unknown,

By all the sons of folly trampled on,

Till your kind hand unveil'd her lovely face,

And gave her vigour to exert her rays:

Happy old man, whose worth all mankind knows,

Except thyself, who charitably shows

The ready road to Virtue and to Praise,

10The way to many long and happy days;

The noble art of generous Piety,

And how to compass an Euthanasy!

Hence did he learn the skill of living well,

The bright *Thealma* was his oracle;

Inspir'd by Her, he knows no anxious cares

In near a century of happy years;

Easy he lives, and easy shall he lie

On the soft bosom of Eternity.

As long as Spenser's noble flames shall burn,

20And deep devotion shall attend his urn;

As long as Chalkhill's venerable name

With humble emulation shall enflame

Posterity, and fill the rolls of fame,

Your memory shall ever be secure,

And long beyond our short-liv'd praise endure;

As Phidias in Minerva's shield did live,

And shar'd that immortality he alone could give.

To Mr. Isaac Walton.] For *Thealma* [*and Clearchus*] itself, and the problems attending it, see vol. ii.

7 Walton published the poem in his ninetieth year and died soon after.

19 Chalkhill was, said Izaak, an 'acquaintant' of Spenser.

Pastoral Dialogue.

CASTARA AND PARTHENIA.

Parthenia.

My dear Castara, t'other day

I heard an ancient shepherd say,

Alas for me! my time draws nigh,

And shortly, shortly I must die!

What meant the man? for lo! apace

Torrents of tears ran down his face.

Castara.

Poor harmless maid! why wouldst thou know

What, known, must needs create thee woe?

'Twill cloud the sunshine of thy days,

10And in thy soul such trouble raise,

Thou'lt grieve, and tremble, and complain,

And say that all thy beauty's vain.

Parthenia.

Ah me! sure 'tis some dreadful thing

That can so great disorder bring,

Yet tell me, prithee tell me, do,

For 'tis some ease the worst to know.

Castara.

To die, Parthenia, is to quit

The World, and the Sun's glorious light,

To leave our flocks and fields for ever,

20To part, and never meet again, O never!

After that cruel hideous hour,

Thou and I shall sing no more;

In the cold Earth they will thee lay,

And what thou dot'st on shall be clay.

Parthenia.

Alas! why will they use me so,

A virgin that no evil do?

Castara.

Roses wither, turtles die,

Fair, and kind as thou and I.

Chorus amb.

Then, since 'tis appointed to the dust we must go,

30Let us innocently live, and virtuously do;

Let us love, let us sing, 'tis no matter, 'tis all one,

If our lamps be extinguish'd at midnight or noon.

Castabella Going to Sea.

SONG. *Set by* MR. JAMES HART.

I.

Hark, hark! methinks I hear the seamen call,

The boist'rous seamen say,

Bright Castabella, come away!

The wind sits fair, the vessel's stout and tall,

Bright Castabella, come away!

For Time and Tide can never stay.

II.

Our mighty Master Neptune calls aloud,

The Zephyrs gently blow,

The Tritons cry, You are too slow,

10For every Sea-nymph of the glittering crowd

Has garlands ready to throw down

When you ascend your wat'ry throne.

III.

See, see! she comes, she comes, and now adieu!

Let's bid adieu to shore,

And to all we fear'd before;

O Castabella! we depend on you,

On you our better fortunes lay,

Whose eyes and voice the winds and seas obey.

Castabella Going to Sea.] There was a *Philip* Hart in the next generation who was a composer, and perhaps James was his father; for the less reputed and more professional arts like music, painting, engraving, dancing, &c. tended to be hereditary in those days.

17 Byron might have alleged Flatman's practice, in the same context of sea-piece, for the too-celebrated 'There let him *lay*'. But the correct use is possible.

On the Death of my worthy friend Mr. John Oldham.

PINDARIC PASTORAL ODE.

Stanza I.

Undoubtedly 'tis thy peculiar fate,

Ah miserable Astragon!

Thou art condemn'd alone

To bear the burthen of a wretched life,

Still in this howling wilderness to roam,

Whilst all thy bosom friends unkindly go,

And leave thee to lament them here below.

Thy dear Alexis wouldn't stay,

Joy of thy life, and pleasure of thine eyes,

10Dear Alexis went away,

With an invincible surprise;

Th' angelic youth early dislik'd this state,

And innocently yielded to his fate;

Never did soul of a celestial birth

Inform a purer piece of earth:

O! that 'twere not in vain,

To wish what's past might be retriev'd again!

Thy dotage, thy Alexis then

Had answer'd all thy vows and prayers,

20And crown'd with pregnant joys thy silver hairs,

Lov'd to this day amongst the living sons of men.

II.

And thou, my friend, hast left me too,

Menalcas! poor Menalcas! even thou!

Of whom so loudly Fame has spoke

In the records of her eternal book,

Whose disregarded worth ages to come

Shall wail with indignation o'er thy tomb.

Worthy wert thou to live, as long as Vice

Should need a satire, that the frantic age

30Might tremble at the lash of thy poetic rage.

Th' untutor'd world in after times

May live uncensur'd for their crimes,

Freed from the dreads of thy reforming pen,

Turn to old Chaos once again.

Of all th' instructive bards, whose more than Theban lyre,

Could salvage souls with manly thoughts inspire,

Menalcas worthy was to live:

Tell me, ye mournful swains,

Say you his fellow-shepherds that survive,

40Has my ador'd Menalcas left behind

On all these pensive plains

A gentler shepherd with a braver mind?

Which of you all did more majestic show,

Or wore the garland on a sweeter brow?

III.

But wayward Astragon resolves no more

The death of his Menalcas to deplore.

The place to which he wisely is withdrawn

Is altogether blest.

There, no clouds o'erwhelm his breast,

50No midnight cares shall break his rest,

For all is everlasting cheerful dawn.

The Poets' charming bliss,

Perfect ease and sweet recess,

There shall he long possess.

The treacherous world no more shall him deceive,

Of hope and fortune he has taken leave;

And now in mighty triumph does he reign

O'er the unthinking rabble's spite

(His head adorn'd with beams of light)

60And the dull wealthy fool's disdain.

Thrice happy he, that dies the Muses' friend;

He needs no obelisk, no pyramid

His sacred dust to hide,

He needs not for his memory to provide,

For well he knows his praise can never end.

On the Death of Mr. John Oldham.] Oldham died in 1683.

Alexis seems to be Richard Flatman, Oldham Menalcas, the poet himself Astragon. It is curious that the printers—and perhaps even the writers—of this time were so besotted with 'apostrophation' as even to use it when the full value is metrically necessary, as here in 'wouldn't', which must be 'would *not*' to scan.

These lines were first printed before *Remains of Mr. John Oldham in Verse and Prose*, 1684. The chief variants are:

8 wouldn't] would not.

12 angelic] Angel-like.

13 innocently yielded] cheerfully submitted.

29 satire] In original, as often, 'Satyr'.

50 shall] can.

Lines 52 and 54 form one long line, followed by 53, which reads 'soft recess'; lines 58 and 59 are transposed.

65 For well he knows] For he might well foresee.

On Sir John Micklethwaite's Monument

in S. Botolphs-Aldersgate-Church, London.

M. S.

Heic juxta spe plenâ resurgendi situm est

Depositum mortale

JOANNIS MICKLETHWAITE Equitis,

Serenissimo Principi Carolo II. a Medicinâ,

Qui cum primis solertissimus, fidissimus, felicissimus,

In Collegio Medicorum Londinensium

Lustrum integrum et quod excurrit

Praesidis Provinciam dignissimè ornavit:

10*Et tandem emenso aetatis tranquillae stadio,*

Pietate sincerâ,

Inconcussâ vitae integritate,

Benignâ morum suavitate,

Sparsâ passim Philanthropiâ

Spectabilis;

Miserorum Asylum,

Maritus optimus,

Parens indulgentissimus,

Suorum luctus,

20*Bonorum omnium Amor et Deliciae,*

Septuagenarius senex,

Coelo maturus,

Fato non invitus cessit

IV Kal. Augusti Anno salutis MDCLXXXII.

Caetera loquantur

Languentium deploranda suspiria,

Viduarum ac Orphanorum

Propter amissum Patronum profundi gemitus,

Pauperumque,

30*Nudorum jam, atque esurientium*

Importuna Viscera,

Monumenta, hoc marmore longe perenniora.

Maerens posuit pientissima Conjunx.

On Sir John Micklethwaite's Monument, &c.] Micklethwaite (1612-82) was President of the College of Physicians 1676-81 (*lustrum integrum*).

8 *Et quod excurrit* is a technical Latin phrase in scientific post-classical writers for 'and more', 'above'.

10 *emenso ... stadio.*] The exact threescore years and ten.

33 *pientissima*.] The usual form for inscriptions, though *piissimus* (in spite of Cicero's condemnation) was used elsewhere.

M. S.
Heic juxta jacet
THOMAS ROCK Armg. Salopiensis,
Vitâ functus Januarii 3. Aetat. 62. 1678

En Lector!

Cinerem non vulgarem,

Virum vere magnum,

Si prisca fides, pietasque primaeva,

Si amicitiae foedera strictissima,

10*Si pectus candidum, et sincerum,*

Ac integerrima Vita,

Virum vere magnum conflare poterint.

En hominem Cordatum!

Calamitosae Majestatis

(Furente nuperâ perduellium rabiè)

Strenuum assertorem,

Obstinatum Vindicem!

En animae generosae quantillum Ergastulum!

O charum Deo Depositum!

20*Vestrum undequaquam Inopes,*

Vestrum quotcunque Viri praestantiores,

Dolorem inconsolabilem,

Desiderium, in omne aevum, irreparabile!

Thomas Rock.] I know not Thomas Rock, Esq. His Royalism (ll. 10-13) was befitting a Salopian.

On the Death of the Illustrious Prince Rupert.

PINDARIC ODE.

Stanza I.

MAN surely is not what he seems to be;

Surely ourselves we overrate,

Forgetting that like other creatures, we

Must bend our heads to Fate.

Lord of the whole Creation, MAN

(How big the title shows!)

Trifles away a few uncertain years,

Cheated with hopes, and rack'd with fears,

Through all Life's little span,

10Then down to silence and to darkness goes;

And when we die, the crowd that trembling stood

Erewhile struck with the terror of a nod,

Shake off their wonted reverence with their chains,

And at their pleasure use our poor remains.

Ah, mighty Prince!

Whom lavish Nature and industrious Art

Had fitted for immortal Fame,

Their utmost bounty could no more impart;

How comes it that thy venerable name

20Should be submitted to my theme?

Unkindly baulk'd by the prime skilful men,

Abandon'd to be sullied by so mean a pen!

Tell me, ye skilful men, if you have read

In all the fair memorials of the Dead,

A name so formidably great,

So full of wonders, and unenvi'd love,

In which all virtues and all graces strove,

So terrible, and yet so sweet;

Show me a star in Honour's firmament,

30(Of the first magnitude let it be)

That from the darkness of this World made free,

A brighter lustre to this World has lent.

Ye men of reading, show me one

That shines with such a beam as His.

Rupert's a constellation

Outvies Arcturus, and the Pleïades.

And if the Julian Star of old outshone

The lesser fires, as much as them the Moon,

Posterity perhaps will wonder why

40An hero more divine than he

Should leave (after his Apotheosis)

No gleam of light in all the Galaxy

Bright as the Sun in the full blaze of noon.

III.

How shall my trembling Muse thy praise rehearse!

Thy praise too lofty ev'n for Pindar's verse!

Whence shall she take her daring flight,

That she may soar aloft

In numbers masculine and soft,

In numbers adequate

50To thy renown's celestial height!

If from thy noble pedigree

The royal blood that sparkled in thy veins

A low plebeian eulogy disdains,

And he blasphemes that meanly writes of thee;

If from thy martial deeds she boldly rise,

And sing thy valiant infancy,

Rebellious Britain after felt full well,

Thou from thy cradle wert a miracle.

Swaddled in armour, drums appeas'd thy cries,

60And the shrill trumpet sung thy lullabies.

The babe Alcides thus gave early proof

In the first dawning of his youth,

When with his tender hand the snakes he slew,

What monsters in his riper years he would subdue.

IV.

Great Prince, in whom Mars and Minerva join'd

Their last efforts to frame a mighty mind,

A pattern for brave men to come, design'd:

How did the rebel troops before thee fly!

How of thy genius stand in awe!

70When from the sulphurous cloud

Thou in thunder gav'st aloud

Thy dreadful law

To the presumptuous enemy.

In vain their traitorous ensigns they display'd,

In vain they fought, in vain they pray'd,

At thy victorious arms dismay'd.

Till Providence for causes yet unknown,

Causes mysterious and deep,

Conniv'd awhile, as if asleep,

80And seem'd its dear Anointed to disown;

The prosperous villany triumph'd o'er the Crown,

And hurl'd the best of monarchs from his Throne.

O tell it not in Gath, nor Ascalon!

The best of monarchs fell by impious power,

Th' unspotted Victim for the guilty bled.

He bow'd, he fell, there where he bow'd he fell down dead;

Baptiz'd Blest Martyr in his sacred gore.

V.

Nor could those tempests in the giddy State,

O mighty Prince, thy loyalty abate.

90Though put to flight, thou fought'st the Parthian way,

And still the same appear'dst to be

Among the beasts and scaly fry,

A Behemoth on land and a Leviathan at sea;

Still wert thou brave, still wert thou good,

Still firm to thy allegiance stood

Amidst the foamings of the popular flood.

(Cato with such a constancy of mind,

Espous'd that cause which all his Gods declin'd.)

Till gentler stars amaz'd to see

100Thy matchless and undaunted bravery,

Blush'd and brought back the murthered Father's Son,

Lest thou shouldst plant him in th' Imperial Throne,

Thou with thy single hand alone.

He that forgets the glories of that day,

When CHARLES the Merciful return'd,

Ne'er felt the transports of glad Sion's Joy,

When she had long in dust and ashes mourn'd:

He never understood with what surprise

She open'd her astonish'd eyes

110To see the goodly fabric of the second Temple rise.

VI.

When CHARLES the Merciful his entrance made

The day was all around serene,

Not one ill-boding cloud was seen

To cast a gloomy shade

On the triumphal cavalcade.

In that, his first, and happy scene,

The Pow'rs above foretold his halcyon reign,

In which, like them, he evermore should prove

The kindest methods of Almighty Love:

120And when black crimes his justice should constrain,

His pious breast should share the criminal's pain:

Fierce as the Lion can he be, and gentle as the Dove.

Here stop, my Muse,—the rest let Angels sing,

Some of those Angels, who with constant care

To His Pavilion, near attendants are,

A life-guard giv'n him by th' Omnipotent King,

Th' Omnipotent King, whose character he bears,

Whose diadem on Earth he wears;

And may he wear it long, for many, many years.

VII.

130And now (illustrious Ghost!) what shall we say?

What tribute to thy precious memory pay?

Thy death confounds, and strikes all sorrows dumb.

Kingdoms and empires make their moan,

Rescu'd by thee from desolation;

In pilgrimage hereafter shall they come,

And make their offerings before thy tomb,

Great Prince, so fear'd abroad, and so ador'd at home

Jove's Bird that durst of late confront the Sun,

And in the wanton German banners play'd,

140Now hangs her wing and droops her head,

Now recollects the battles thou hast won,

And calls too late to thee for aid.

All Christendom deplores the loss,

Whilst bloody Mahomet like a whirlwind flies,

And insolently braves the ill-befriended cross.

Europe in blood, and in confusion lies,

Thou in an easy good old age,

Remov'd from this tumultuous stage,

Sleep'st unconcern'd at all its rage,

150Secure of Fame, and from Detraction free:

He that to greater happiness would attain,

Or towards Heav'n would swifter fly,

Must be much more than mortal man,

And never condescend to die.

Dec. 13, 1682.

On the Death of Prince Rupert.] First printed in folio, 1683; there are two trivial changes in the text—'Blest Martyr baptized', l. 87, and 'Diadems', l. 128. That both the English and the Latin of these poems are Flatman's, despite the *Authore Anonymo* of the latter, is a conclusion which I shall give up at once on production of any positive evidence to the contrary, but shall hold meanwhile. Rupert's love for the Arts would of itself attract Flatman, and he hints at this in ll. 16 and 65.

21 The 'prime skilfulness' may glance at Dryden—there were few others who were primely skilful at funeral odes or any other in 1682. But Rupert had kept aloof from Court for years.

74-6 Orig. 'displaid' and 'dismaid': but not 'pr*aid*'.

90-4 A rather ingenious handling of those adventurous and almost heroic cruises of Rupert's with the remnant of the Royalist fleet which some have unkindly (and in strictness quite unjustifiably) called 'buccaneering' or 'piratical'.

111-29 One would have expected, instead of the banal laudation of Charles, something about Rupert's share in the Dutch wars, and his occupations in chemistry, engraving, &c. But there was perhaps some ox on Flatman's tongue (for the Prince had not been fortunate at the last in fight); and, besides, all these later poems show a want of the spirit and the verve which is by no means wanting in the earlier. The words to Woodford (*v. sup.*, p. 367) were rather too well justified.

Poema in Obitum Illustrissimi Principis Ruperti

Latine Redditum

Non carmine Pindarico (ut illud) sed, (ut vocatur,)

Lapidario

(Quod est medium inter Oratoriam et Poesin)

Vide sis Emanuelem Thesaurum, in Patriarchis.

AUTHORE ANONYMO.

I.

Proculdubio non sumus quod videmur,

Et nosmet ipsos aequo plus aestimamus,

Obliti quod, veluti Creatis omnibus,

Et nobis etiam Fato succumbendum.

Homo, totius Terrarum Orbis Dominus,

(Heu quam superbe, quam fastuose sonat!)

Paucos et incertos illudit annos,

Nunc spe deceptus, nunc metu cruciatus,

Per angustum Vitae curriculum,

10*Tandem ad taciturnas labitur Tenebras.*

Et quando morimur, quam cito Turba tremula,

Jamdudum Nutus terrore percita,

Venerationem solitam (cum Catenis) exuunt

Et ad libitum despectas tractant Reliquias.

Potentissime Princeps!

Quem prodiga Natura, et Ars industria

Ad celebritatem immortalem adaptâssent,

Cui plus addere non valuit ipsius ultima Benignitas;

Unde venit quod Nomen tuum Venerandum

20*Themati meo prostitueretur?*

Per Viros Doctiores ingrate neglectum,

Et indoctâ meâ Musâ delineari relictum!

II.

Dicite mihi, Viri peritiores, si legistis

In pulchris Mortuorum Catalogis

Nomen adeo formidate Magnum,

Tantis Mirâclis et inaemulo amore refertum;

In quo omnes Charites & Virtutes concertârunt.

Adeo terribile, et adeo dulce Nomen.

Ostendite mihi Stellam in Firmamento Honoris

30(*Sit etiam Primae Magnitudinis*)

Quae a tenebris hujus Mundi erepta

Majorem Mundo fulgorem praestitit;

O Viri eruditi, ostendite mihi unam,

Quae tam splendido Radio effulget.

Rupertus est Constellatio—

Praelucens Arcturum et Pleiades.

Et si olim Stella Juliana praefulsit

Ignes minores, quantum illos Luna,

Posteritas forsitan mirabitur, quare

40*Hero illo multo Divinior,*

Nullum (post ejus Apotheosin)

In Galaxiâ jubar relinqueret

Sole clarius Meridionali.

III.

Quo pacto Musa mea tremens laudes tuas recitabit?

Laudes tuas, etiam Pindari Carmine excelsiores!

Unde volatum sumet audacem,

Ut in altum sublevetur

In Numeris Masculis et Blandis,

In numeris adaequatis

50*Coelesti Famae tuae sublimitati?*

Si a Nobili tuâ Genealogiâ

Sanguis Regalis in Venis tuis scintillans

Humilem et Plebeiam dedignatur Eulogiam,

(Nam de Te modice loquens Blasphemat)

Si a claris Bellicis facinoribus incipiet,

Et Virilia incunabula decantet,

Rebellis jamdudum sentivit Britannia,

Quantis Mirandis Cunae tuae claruere,

Loricis fasciatus, Tympana lachrymas demulserunt,

60*Et Tubarum clangores somnum allicierunt:*

Sic olim Alcides praematurum dedit specimen

In primo Infantiae Diluculo,

Angues teneris collidens manibus

Qualia in aetate provectâ superaret Monstra.

IV.

Auguste Princeps, in quo Mars et Minerva suas

Vires contulere ingentem formare Animum

Praeclaris Posteris in Exemplar designatum,

Quoties Turmae Rebelles coram te profugerunt

Genii tui Numine terrefactae?

70Cum de Nube Sulphureâ

Fulminibus dedisti sonoris

Leges tuas tremendas

Perduellibus insolentibus,

Frustra vexilla explicârunt perfida,

Frustra pugnârunt, frustra fuderunt preces,

Armis tuis Victricibus attonitae.

Donec Superi, causis adhuc incognitis,

Causis secretis et profundis

Connivêre paulisper, quasi obdormientes,

80Et peramatum Christum suum dereliquisse videbantur.

In Coronam triumphavit prosperum Nefas

Et Regum optimum a Solio deturbavit,

Ne annuntietis hoc in Gath aut Ascalon,

Monarcharum optimus impiâ vi corruit,

Immaculata Victima pro Sontibus fudit sanguinem:

Inclinavit se, cecidit, ubi inclinaverat cecidit mortuus

Martyr beatus in Sacro suo Cruore Baptisatus.

V.

Nec valuerunt Turbines in Anarchiâ istâ vertiginosâ,

Invicte Princeps, fidelitatem tuam vibrare,

90Nam retrocedens pugnasti more Parthico,

Et semper Idem remansisti,

Inter pecora, et pisces squamosas,

In terrâ Behemoth, in mari Leviathan:

Infractus adhuc et adhuc Bonus

Fidelitati firmiter perseverasti

Inter fremitus Fluctuum Popularium.

Sic olim Cato pari animi constantiâ

Causam desponsavit, quam Dii omnes repudiârunt.

Donec Planetae benigniores, stupentes aspicere

100*Imparilem et impavidam tuam fortitudinem,*

Erubuerunt, et Percussi Patris filium reduxerunt,

Ne tu illum in Solio Imperiali collocares,

Tu unicâ tuâ manu solus.

Qui Solis istius splendores oblitus fuerit

Quo Clementissimus redivit Carolus,

Nunquam sentivit laetae Sionis gaudia

Cum diu pulvere et cineribus lugisset;

Nunquam intellexit quali Raptu

Oculos extollebat attonitos

110*Templi Secundi Structuram renascentem videns.*

VI.

Cum Carolus Clemens introitum fecit

Coelum erat undique serenum,

Nulla male-ominosa Nubes apparuit

Umbram dare tenebricosam,

In Equitatum istum Triumphalem.

In illa primâ et felici Scenâ

Praedixere Superi Regimen ejus Halcyoneum

In quo sicut illi, in aeternum probaret

Benignissimas Methodos praepotentis Amoris.

120*Et cum magna flagitia Vindictam eius provocarent,*

Pectus ejus humanius Rei compateretur poenas.

Ut Leo ferox, mitis ut Columba.

Hic sileat Musa—quod reliquum est Angeli praedicent,

Angeli isti qui assiduâ curâ

Tentorio ejus quam proxime inserviunt

Somatophylaces à Rege Omnipotente delegati,

A Rege Omnipotente, cujus Majestatem praefert,

Cujus in terrâ gerit Diadema

Et diu gerat per multos, multos annos.

VII.

130 Quid autem, (Illustris Anima) quid dicemus?

Quale Tributum Piae tuae Memoriae solvemus?

Mors tua obtundit et mutum reddit Dolorem.

Regna et Imperia lugubres planetus faciunt

Ab extremâ Ruinâ per te redempta.

Posthac è longe Peregrinantes venient,

Et ad Tumulum tuum Oblationes tribuent,

O Magne Princeps foris verende, et domi venerate!

Jovis Ales, qui dudum Solem tentare ausus est,

Et in mollibus Germanorum lusit vexillis,

140 Nunc alas demittit, et caput declinat,

Nunc repetit Victorias a Te potitas,

Et sero nimis tuum implorat auxilium.

Orbis Christianus deplorat Damnum,

Dum truculentus Mahomet Turbinis instar volat

Et impotenter bacchatur in male-sustentatam Crucem.

Sanguine et ruinâ volutans Europa jacet.

Tu in tranquillâ et plenâ senectute

Semotus a tumultuoso Mundi Theatro

Rabiosâ eius insaniâ intactus dormis,

150*Famae securus et ab omni obtrectatione liber.*

Qui ampliorem attineret felicitatem,

Vel usque ad Coelos ocyus volaret,

Oportet esse plusquam Mortalem,

Nec unquam prorsus dignari mori.

Poema in Obitum, &c.] Heading: 'Vide sis' = *vide, si vis.*

Emanuel, &c.] Pepys read his 'new *Emanuel Thesaurus* [*Tesaufro*] *Patriarchae*' on Jan. 23, 166⁰/1. It was a genealogy of Christ and a very popular book.

22 *delineari*] *deliniri* in the text. 'Fidelitati' in l. 95 should be the ablative. In 63 'teneribus manibus' was probably a printer's blunder, but the author must be credited with such erroneous forms as 'sentivit' and 'lugisset'.

On the much lamented Death of our late Sovereign Lord King Charles II. of Blessed Memory.

A PINDARIC ODE.

Stanza I.

Alas! Why are we tempted to complain,

That Heav'n is deaf to all our cries!

Regardless of poor mortals' miseries!

And all our fervent pray'rs devoutly vain!

Tis hard to think th' immortal Powers attend

Human affairs, who ravish from our sight

The Man, on whom such blessings did depend,

Heav'n's and mankind's delight!

The Man! O that opprobrious word, *The Man!*

10Whose measure of duration's but a span,

Some other name at Babel should have been contriv'd

(By all the vulgar World t' have been receiv'd),

A word as near as could be to Divinity,

Appropriate to Crown'd Heads, who never ought to die;

Some signal word that should imply

All but the scandal of mortality.

'Tis fit, we little lumps of crawling Earth,

Deriv'd from a plebeian birth,

Such as our frail forefathers were,

20Should to our primitive dust repair;

But Princes (like the wondrous Enoch) should be free

From Death's unbounded tyranny,

And when their godlike race is run,

And nothing glorious left undone,

Never submit to Fate, but only disappear.

II.

But, since th' eternal Law will have it so,

That Monarchs prove at last but finer clay,

What can their humble vassals do?

What reverence, what devotion can we pay,

30When these, our earthly Gods, are snatch'd away?

Yes, we can mourn, Yes, we can beat our breast,

Yes, we can call to mind those happy days

Of pleasure, and of rest,

When CHARLES the Merciful did reign,

That Golden Age, when void of cares,

All the long summer's day,

We atoms in his beams might sport and play:

Yes, we can teach our children to bewail

His fatal loss, when we shall fail,

40And make babes learn in after days

The pretty way of stammering out his praise,

His merited praise, which shall in every age

With all advantage flame

In spite of furies or infernal rage,

And imp the wings, and stretch the lungs of Fame.

III.

Excellent Prince, whom every mouth did bless,

And every bended knee adore,

On whom we gaz'd with ecstasy of joy

(A vision which did satisfy, but never cloy)

50From whom we dated all our happiness,

And from above could ask no more,

Our gladsome cup was fill'd till it ran o'er.

Our land (like Eden) flourish'd in his time,

Defended by an Angel's Sword,

A terror 'twas to those abroad,

But all was Paradise to those within:

Nor could th' Old Serpent's stratagem

Ever supplant his well-watch'd diadem.

Excellent Prince, of whom we once did say

60With a triumphant noise,

In one united voice,

On that stupendious day,

Long live, Long live the King!

And songs of IO PAEAN sing,

How shall we bear this tragical surprise,

Now we must change *Long live*, for *Here he lies?*

IV.

Have you forgot? (but who can him forget?)

You watchful Spirits that preside

O'er sublunary things,

70Who, when you look beneath, do oft deride,

Not without cause, some other petty Kings;

Have you forgot the greatness of his mind,

The bravery of his elevated soul,

(But he had still a Goshen there)

When darkest cares around his Royal heart did wind,

As waves about a steady rock do roll:

With what disdain he view'd

The fury of the giddy multitude,

And bare the Cross, with more than manly fortitude,

80As he had learn'd in sacred lore,

His mighty Master had done long before?

And you must ever own

(Or else you very little know

Of what we think below)

That when the hurricanes of th' State were o'er,

When in his noontide blaze he did appear,

His gentle awful brow

Added fresh lustre to th' Imperial Crown,

By birthright, and by virtue, more than once his own.

V.

90He was! but what he was, how great, how good,

How just, how he delighted not in blood,

How full of pity, and how strangely kind,

How hazardously constant to his friend,

In Peace how glorious, and in War how brave,

Above the charms of life, and terrors of the grave—

When late posterity shall tell:

What he has done shall to a volume swell,

And every line abound with miracle

In that prodigious Chronicle.

100Forgive, unbodied Sovereign, forgive,

And from your shining mansion cast an eye

To pity our officious blasphemy,

When we have said the best we can conceive.

Here stop, presumptuous Muse! thy daring flight,

Here hide thy baffled head in shades of night,

Thou too obscure, thy dazzling theme too bright,

For what thou shouldst have said, with grief struck dumb,

Will more emphatically be supplied

By the joint groans of melancholy Christendom.

On the Death of King Charles II.] First printed in folio in 1685.

25 Browning somewhere in a letter laughs at this line, in the form 'Kings do not die, they only disappear', which is neither Flatman's nor Waller's, from whom he borrowed the notion, nor Oldham's, who has it likewise, though both these have the 'disappear'. The thought is not foolish: it means, 'their names and works live after them'. But Browning's knowledge of Flatman, as of other out-of-the-ways, is interesting. He might have made him a 'Person of Importance'.

To His Sacred Majesty King James II.

Dread Prince! whom all the world admires and fears,

By Heav'n design'd to wipe away our tears,

To heal our wounds, and drooping spirits raise,

And to revive our former halcyon days,

Permit us to assure ourselves, that you

Your happy brother's fortune will pursue,

For what great thing is that you dare not do?

Whose long known, unexampled gallantry

So oft has shaken th' Earth, and curb'd the haughty Sea.

10And may those Stars, that ever o'er you shone,

Double their influence on your peaceful throne.

May you in honourable deeds outshine

The brightest heroes of your Royal line,

That when your enemies shall the sceptre see

Grasp'd in a hand enur'd to victory,

The rebels may like Lucifer fall down,

Or fly like phantoms from the rising Sun.

Extremum Hunc Arethusa mihi concede Laborem.

  Virgil.

ODES OF HORACE

PARAPHRASED BY THOMAS FLATMAN.
BOOK II. ODE XIX.

Being half foxt he praiseth Bacchus.

In a blind corner jolly Bacchus taught

The Nymphs and Satyrs poetry;

Myself (a thing scarce to be thought)

Was at that time a stander by.

And ever since the whim runs in my head,

With heavenly frenzy I'm on fire;

Dear Bacchus, let me not be punishèd

For raving, when thou didst inspire.

Ecstatically drunk, I now dare sing

10Thy bigot Thyades, and the source

Whence thy brisk wine, honey, and milk did spring,

Enchannell'd by thy sceptre's force.

Bold as I am, I dare yet higher fly,

And sing bright Ariadne's Crown,

Rejoice to see bold Pentheus' destiny,

And grave Lycurgus tumbled down.

Rivers and seas thine empire all obey,

When thou thy standard dost advance,

Wild mountaineers, thy vassals, trim and gay,

20In tune and time stagger and dance.

Thou, when great Jove began to fear his throne

(In no small danger then he was),

The mighty Rhoecus thou didst piss upon,

And of that lion mad'st an ass.

'Tis true, thy talent is not war, but mirth;

The fiddle, not the trumpet, thine;

Yet didst thou bravely lay about thee then,

Great Moderator, God of Wine.

And when to Hell in triumph thou didst ride

30O'er Cerberus thou didst prevail,

The silly cur, thee for his Master own'd,

And like a puppy wagg'd his tail.

Odes of Horace.] On Flatman's Horatian versions generally see Introduction.
The notes they call for are few.

14 Crown] Not in the usual vague poetic sense, but the star *Corona Ariadnes.*

BOOK III. ODE VIII. *To Maecenas.*

Learnèd Maecenas, wonder not that I

(A Bachelor) invoke that Deity,

Which at this feast the married rout adore,

And yearly do implore.

They pray the gods to make their burthen light,

And that their yoke-fellows may never fight:

I praise them, not for giving me a wife,

But saving of my life.

By heav'n redeem'd, I 'scap'd a falling tree,

10And yearly own that strange delivery,

Yearly rejoice, and drink the briskest wine,

Not spill it at their shrine.

Come, my Maecenas, let us drink, and thus

Cherish that life those Pow'rs have given us:

A thousand cups to midwife this new birth,

With inoffensive mirth.

No State-affairs near my Maecenas come,

Since all are fall'n that fought victorious Rome.

By civil broils the Medes, our foes, will fall.

20The weakest to the wall.

Our fierce and ancient enemy of Spain

Is now subdu'd, and tamely bears our chain.

The savage Scythian too begins to yield,

About to quit the field.

Bear they the load of government that can;

Thou, since a private, and good-natur'd man,

Enjoy th' advantage of the present hour,

For why shouldst thou look sour?

BOOK III. ODE IX. *Horace and Lydia.*

Hor. While I was lovely in thine eye,

And while no soft embrace but mine

Encircled thy fair ivory neck,

I did the Persian King outshine.

Lyd. While Horace was an honest lad,

And Chloe less than Lydia lov'd,

Lydia was then a matchless Lass,

And in a sphere 'bove Ilia mov'd.

Hor. But Chloe now has vanquish'd me,

10That lute and voice who could deny?

Methinks might I but save her life,

I could myself even dare to die.

Lyd. Young Calais is my gallant,

He burns me with his flaming eye;

To save the pretty villain's life,

Twice over I could dare to die.

Hor. But say I Lydia lov'd again,

And would new-braze Love's broken chain?

Say I should turn my Chloe off,

20And take poor Lydia home again?

Lyd. Why then though he a fixèd star.

Thou lighter than a cork shouldst be,

Mad, and unquiet as the sea,

Yet would I live, and die with thee.

BOOK III. ODE XII.

No more Love's subjects, but his slaves they be,

That dare not o'er a glass of wine be free,

But quit, for fear of friends, their liberty.

Fond Neobule! thou art lazy grown,

Away thy needle, web, and distaff thrown,

Thou hop'st thy work by Hebrus will be done.

A sturdy youth, and a rank rider he,

Can run a race, and box most manfully,

Swim like a duck, and caper like a flea.

10He hunts the stag, and all the forest o'er

With strength and craft pursues the savage boar:

He minds the sport, and thou desir'st no more.

BOOK III. ODE XVII. *To Aelius Lamia.*

Brave Aelius, sprung from an heroic line,

Whose pedigree in long descents do shine,

That add'st new glories to the Lamian name,

And rear'st fresh trophies to their fame!

Descended from Prince Lamus, whose command

Reach from the Formian walls, o'er sea and land;

Well was he known our ancestors among,

Where gentle Liris slides along.

Great as thou art, time will not thee obey:

10To-morrow's like to be a blust'ring day,

Some tempest too is threat'ned from the east,

As by th' unlucky crow I guess'd:

'Tis dry to-day! Now lay thy fuel in,

Ere the unwelcome season do begin,

Good victuals get, and frolic friends together,

Armour of proof against ill weather.

xvii. 2 'Do shine' is probably a misprint, due to the contiguous s's, for 'does'
or 'do's shine'. So below in l. 6, 'reach' should probably be 'reach' An
apparent but not real false concord between plural nouns and singular verb
was common in the seventeenth century.

BOOK III. ODE XIX. *To Telephus.*

I.

Thou por'st on Helvicus, and studiest in vain,

How many years pass'd betwixt King and King's reign,

To make an old woman ev'n twitter for joy

At an eighty-eight story, or the scuffle at Troy:

But where the good wine, and best fire is

When the cruel North-wind does blow,

And the trees do penance in snow;

Where the poet's delight and desire is,

Thou, pitiful book-worm, ne'er troublest thy brain.

II.

10Come, drawer, some claret, we'll drown this new Moon.

More candles t' improve this dull night into noon:

let the healths, let the house, and the glasses turn round,

But no tears, except those of the tankard, abound.

Come! here's a good health to the Muses,

Three brimmers to the three times three,

And one to each grace let there be;

The triple-skull'd dog bite him that refuses.

III.

Let's be mad as March-hares, call the minstrels and singers,

Strike up there!—kick that rogue—he has chilblains on's fingers,

20Let that whoreson our neighbour, on his bags that lies thinking,

Bear a part in the storm, but not the calm of our drinking.

Come! bring us a wench, or two, prithee;

Thou Telephus look'st pretty fair,

And hast a good thick head of hair,

Fetch him Chloe, she's buxom, and loves to trade with thee;

Call Glycera to me, for I am one of her swingers.

xix. A good example of the curious 'skimble skamble' anapaests before Dryden and Prior.

4 an eighty-eight story] Of the Armada.

BOOK III. ODE XX. *To Pyrrhus.*

Dry Pyrrhus, little dost thou know,

What 'tis to make a whelp forgo

His lioness,—faith 'twill not do!

It will be so.

Nearchus understands his game,

If he resolves to quit his fame,

What's that to you? To save his name

You'll purchase shame.

If before peace you war prefer,

10Shoot at his butt—you'll find from her

A Rowland for your Oliver,

That I dare swear.

He is a gay, and sanguine man,

His periwig the wind does fan,

And she will hug him, now and than,

Do what you can.

BOOK III. ODE XXI. *To his Wine-Vessels.*

Kind Brother Butt! as old, and brisk, as I

(For we had both the same nativity),

Whether to mirth, to brawls, or desperate love,

Or sleep, thy gentle power does move;

By what, or name, or title dignifi'd;

Thou need'st not fear the nicest test to 'bide:

Corvinus' health since we may not refuse,

Give down amain thy generous juice.

Corvinus, tho' a Stoic, will not balk

10Thy charms, for he can drink, as well as talk.

Old Cato, tho' he often were morose,

Yet he would sometimes take a dose.

O Wine! thou mak'st the thick-skull'd fellow soft;

Easest the Statesman, vex'd with cares full oft;

Unriddlest all intrigues with a free bowl,

Thou arrant pick-lock of the Soul!

Thou dost our gasping, dying hopes revive;

To peasants, souls as big as princes' give;

Inspired by thee they scorn their slavish fears,

20And bid their rulers shake their ears.

All this, and more (great Bacchus) thou canst do,

But if kind Venus be assistant too,

Then bring more candles to expel the night,

Till Phoebus puts the stars to flight.

BOOK III. ODE XXII. *Upon Diana.*

Gentle Diana, Goddess bright,

Who midwiv'st infants into light,

The mountain's Deity tripartite,

And Queen of Night,

To thee I consecrate my Pine,

Henceforth it shall be ever thine,

Yearly I'll offer at this shrine

The blood of swine.

BOOK III. ODE III. *To Venus.*

'Tis true, I was a sturdy soldier once,

And bravely under Cupid's banners fought:

Disbanded now, his service I renounce,

My warlike weapons serve for nought.

Here! take my helmet, sword, and shield,

My bow, my quiver, my artillery;

Chloe has beaten me quite out of th' field,

And leads me in captivity.

Great Venus! thou that know'st what I have been,

10How able, and how true a friend to smocks!

Revenge my quarrel on th' imperious quean,

And pay her with a pox!

BOOK IV. ODE I. *To Venus.*

No more of War:—Dread Cytherea, cease;

Thy feeble soldier sues for peace.

Alas! I am not now that man of might,

As when fair Cynara bade me fight.

Leave, Venus, leave! consider my gray hairs

Snow'd on by fifty tedious years.

My forts are slighted, and my bulwarks down:

Go, and beleaguer some strong town.

Make thy attempts on Maximus; there's game

10To entertain thy sword and flame.

There Peace and Plenty dwell: He's of the Court,

Ignorant what 'tis to storm a fort:

There sound a charge; he's generous and young,

He's unconcern'd, lusty, and strong:

He of thy silken banners will be proud,

And of thy conquests talk aloud.

His bags are full: the lad thou mayst prefer

To be thy treasurer in war.

He may erect gold statues to thy name,

20And be the trumpet of thy fame:

Thy Deity the zealous youth will then invoke,

And make thy beauteous altars smoke.

With voice and instruments thy praise shall sound,

Division he, and Love the ground;

There, twice a day the gamesome company

Of lads and lasses in debvoir to thee,

Like Mars's priests their numbers shall advance,

And sweetly sing, and nimbly dance.

But as for me! I'm quite dispirited,

30I court nor maid, nor boy to bed!

I cannot drink, nor bind a garland on,

Alas! my dancing days are done!

But hold—Why do these tears steal from my eyes?

My lovely Ligurinus, why?

Why does my falt'ring tongue disguise my voice

With rude and inarticulate noise?

O Ligurin! 'tis thou that break'st my rest,

Methinks I grasp thee in my breast:

Then I pursue thee in my passionate dreams

40O'er pleasant fields and purling streams.

IV. i. 7 'slighted' = 'razed,' the original sense of 'to make level'.

24 I confess this line beat me at first. But no doubt it has a musical sense, for in music both 'division' (notes run together) and 'ground' (a recurrent motive) have technical meanings. The punctuation above, Mr. Simpson's, makes this clearer.

26 'Debvoir' is worth keeping.

BOOK IV. ODE X. *To Ligurinus, a beauteous Youth.*

'Tis true, thou yet art fair, my Ligurine,

No down as yet environs cheek or chin:

But when those hairs which now do flow, shall fall,

And when thy rosy cheeks turn wan and pale:

When in thy glass another Ligurine thou

Shalt spy, and scarce thy bearded self shall know;

Then thou (despis'd) shalt sing this piteous song;

Why am I old? or why was ever young?

BOOK IV. ODE XI. *To Phyllis.*

Come, Phyllis, gentle Phyllis! prithee come,

I have a glass of rich old wine at home,

And in my garden curious flowers do grow,

That languish to adorn thy brow.

The ivy and the yellow crowfoot there

With verdant chaplets wait to braid thy hair;

With silver goblets all my house does shine,

And vervain round my altar twine,

On which the best of all my flock shall bleed;

10Come, and observe with what officious speed

Each lad and lass of all my house attends

Till to my roof the smoke ascends.

If thou wouldst know why thou must be my guest,

I tell thee 'tis to celebrate a Feast,

The Ides of April, which have ever been

Devoted to the Cyprian Queen.

A day more sacred, and more fit for mirth

Than that which gave me (worthless mortal) birth:

For on that day Maecenas first saw light,

20Born for our wonder and delight.

My Phyllis, since thy years come on apace,

Substitute me in Telephus his place,

He's now employ'd by one more rich, more fair,

And proudly does her shackles wear.

Remember what became of Phaeton;

Remember what befell Bellerophon;

That by ambition from his Father's throne,

And this, by Pegasus thrown down.

Content thyself with what is fit for thee,

30Happy that couple that in years agree!

Shun others, and accept my parity,

And I will end my loves with thee.

Thou art the last whom I intend to court,

Come then; and (to prepare thee for the sport)

Learn prick-song, and my merry odes rehearse:

Many a care is charm'd by verse.

EPODE III. *To Maecenas.*

In time to come, if such a crime should be

As Parricide, (foul villany!)

A clove of garlic would revenge that evil;

(Rare dish for ploughmen, or the Devil!)

Accursed root! how does it jounce and claw!

It works like ratsbane in my maw.

What witch contriv'd this strat'gem for my breath!

Poison'd at once, and stunk to death;

With this vile juice Medea sure did 'noint

10Jason, her love, in every joint;

When untam'd bulls in yokes he led along,

This made his manhood smell so strong:

This gave her dragon venom to his sting,

And set the hag upon the wing.

I burn, I parch, as dry as dust I am,

Such drought on Puglia never came.

Alcides could not bear so much as I,

He oft was wet, but never dry.

Maecenas! do but taste of your own treat,

20And what you gave your poet, eat;

Then go to bed, and court your mistress there,

She'll never kiss you I dare swear.

III. 5 'Jounce', a word worth restoring, is the same as Shakespeare's 'jaunce' and as 'jaunt'. It seems to be still provincial, especially in East Anglia (Flatman had property there), and is equivalent to 'jolt', 'bob up and down', 'wamble in the innerds'.

EPODE VI.

Against Cassius Severus, a rerevileful and wanton Poet.

Thou village-cur! why dost thou bark at me?

A wolf might come, and go, for thee.

At me thou open'st wide, and think'st that I

Will bark with thee for company.

I'm of another kind, and bravely dare

(Like th' mastiff) watch my flock with care:

Dare hunt through snow, and seize that savage beast

That might my darling folds molest:

Thou (only in the noise thou mak'st) robust

10Leav'st off the chase; leap'st at a crust,

But have a care! for if I vent my spleen,

I (for a shift) can make thee grin:

I'll make thee (if iambics once I sing)

To die, like Bupalus, in a string.

When any man insults o'er me, shall I

Put finger in mine eye and cry?

EPODE X. *Against Maevius, a Poet.*

And art thou shipp'd, friend Doggerel!—get thee gone,

Thou pest of Helicon.

Now for an hurricane to bang thy sides,

Curst wood, in which he rides!

An east-wind tear thy cables, crack thy oars,

While every billow roars.

With such a wind let all the Ocean swell

As wafted Noll to Hell:

No friendly star o'er all the Sea appear

10While thou be'st there;

Nor kinder destiny there mayst thou meet

Than the proud Grecian Fleet,

When Pallas did their Admiral destroy

Return'd from ruin'd Troy.

Methinks I see the mariners faint, and thee

Look somewhat scurvily:

Thou call'st on Jove, as if great Jove had time

To mind thy Grub-street Rhyme,

When the proud waves their heads to Heav'n do rear

20Himself scarce free from fear:

Well! If the Gods should thy wreck'd carcase share

To beasts or fowls of th' air,

I'll sacrifice to them, that they may know

I can be civil too.

X. 7 The great storm of September 2, 1658, the day before Cromwell's death.

18 Marvell in 1678, and Otway in *The Atheist*, 1684, first mentioned the *vicus infaustus* which humour (or the want of it) renamed 'Milton' Street, from the proximity of Bunhill Fields.

EPODE XI. *To Pettius his Chamber-fellow.*

Ah, Pettius! I have done with Poetry,

I've parted with my liberty

For Cupid's slavery.

Cupid, that peevish God, has singled out

Me, from among the rhyming rout,

For boys and girls to flout:

December now has thrice script every tree,

Since bright Inachia's tyranny

Has laid its chains on me.

10Now fie upon me! all about the town

My Miss I treated up and down,

I for a squire was known.

Lord, what a whelp was I! to pule and whine,

To sigh, to sob, and to repine!

For thy sake, Mistress mine!

Thou didst my verse, and thou my Muse despise,

My want debas'd me in thine eyes.

Thou wealth, not wit, didst prize.

Fuddled with wine and love my secrets flew,

20Stretch'd on those racks, I told thee true

What did myself undo.

Well!—plague me not too much, imperious dame,

Lest I blaspheme thy charming name,

And quench my former flame.

I can give others place, and see thee die

Damn'd with their prodigality,

If I set on't, so stout am I.

Thou know'st, my friend, thus have I often said,

When, by her sorceries misled,

30Thou bad'st me home to bed:

Ev'n then my practice gave my tongue the lie,

I could not her curst house pass by:

I fear'd, but could not fly.

Since that, for young Lyciscus I'm grown mad;

Inachia such a face ne'er had,

It is a lovely lad.

From his embraces I shall ne'er get free,

Nor friends' advice, nor infamy

Can disentangle me:

40Yet if some brighter object I should spy,

That might perhaps debauch my eye,

And shake my constancy.

EPODE XV. *To his Sweetheart Neaera.*

It was a lovely melancholy night;

The Moon, and every star shone bright;

When thou didst swear thou wouldst to me be true,

And do as I would have thee do:

False woman! round my neck thy arms did twine,

Inseparable as the elm and vine:

Then didst thou swear thy passion should endure

To me alone sincere and pure,

Till sheep and wolves should quit their enmity,

10And not a wave disturb the sea.

Treacherous Neaera! I have been too kind,

But Flaccus can draw off, thou'lt find;

He can that face (as thou dost him) forswear,

And find (it may be) one as fair:

And let me tell thee, when my fury's mov'd,

I hate devoutly, as I lov'd.

But thou, blest gamester, whosoe'er thou be

That proudly dost my drudgery,

Didst thou abound in numerous flocks, and land,

20Wert heir to all Pactolus' sand;

Though in thy brain thou bor'st Pythagoras,

And carried'st Nereus in thy face,

She'd pick another up, and shab thee off,

And then 'twill be my turn to laugh.

XV. 23 'Shab off' seems to be still provincially used both in the intransitive
sense '*sneak* off' and in the transitive as here '*bundle* off.'

EPODE XVII. *To Canidia.*

I yield, Canidia, to thy art,

Take pity on a penitent heart:

By Proserpine, Queen of the Night,

And by Diana's glimmering light,

By the mysterious volumes all,

That can the stars from Heaven call;

By all that's sacred I implore

Thou to my wits wouldst me restore.

The brave Achilles did forgive

10King Telephus, and let him live,

Though in the field the King appear'd,

And war with Mysian bands prepar'd.

When on the ground dead Hector lay,

Expos'd, to birds and beasts a prey;

The Trojan Dames in pity gave

Hector an honourable grave.

Ulysses's mariners were turn'd to swine,

Transform'd by Circe's charms divine;

Yet Circe did their doom revoke,

20And straight the grunting mortals spoke:

Each in his pristine shape appears,

Fearless of dogs to lug their ears.

Oh! do not my affliction scorn!

Enough in conscience I have borne!

My youth and fresh complexion's gone,

Dwindled away to skin and bone.

My hair is powd'red by thy care,

And all my minutes busy are.

Day Night, and Night the Day does chase,

30Yet have not I a breathing space!

Wretch that I am! I now believe,

No pow'r can from thy charms reprieve:

Now I confess thy magic can

Reach head and heart, and unman man.

What wouldst thou have me say? what more?

O Seas! O Earth! I scorch all o'er!

Hercules himself ne'er burnt like me,

Nor th' flaming Mount in Sicily:

O cease thy spells, lest I be soon

40Calcin'd into a pumice-stone!

When wilt th' ha' done? What must I pay?

But name the sum, and I obey:

Say: Wilt thou for my ransom take

An hecatomb? or shall I make

A bawdy song t'advance thy trade,

Or court thee with a serenade?

Wouldst thou to Heav'n, and be a star?

I'll hire thee Cassiopeia's Chair.

Castor, to Helen a true friend,

50Struck her defaming poet blind;

Yet he, good-natur'd gentleman,

Gave the blind bard his eyes again.

Since this, and much more thou canst do,

O rid me of my madness too!

From noble ancestors thy race,

No vulgar blood purples thy face:

Thou searchest not the graves of th' poor,

But necromancy dost abhor:

Gen'rous thy breast, and pure thy hands,

60Whose fruitful womb shall people lands,

And ere thy childbed-linen's clean,

Thou shall be up and to't again.

Canidia's Answer.

Go—hang thyself:—I will not hear,

The rocks as soon shall lend an ear

To naked mariners that be

Left to the mercy of the Sea.

Marry come up!—Shall thy bold pride

The mysteries of the Gods deride?

Presumptuous fool! commit a rape

On my repute, and think to 'scape!

Make me a town-talk? Well! ere thou die

10Cupid shall vengeance take; or I.

Go, get some ratsbane!—'twill not do,

Nay, drink some aqua-fortis too:

No witch shall take thy life away;

Who dares say, Go, when I bid Stay?

No!—I'll prolong thy loathed breath,

And make thee wish in vain for death.

In vain does Tantalus espy

Fruits, he may taste but with his eye.

In vain does poor Prometheus groan,

20And Sisyphus stop his rolling stone:

Long may they sigh, long may they cry,

But not control their destiny.

And thou in vain from some high wall

Or on thy naked sword mayst fall,

In vain (to terminate thy woes)

Thy hands shall knit the fatal noose:

For on thy shoulders then I'll ride,

And make the Earth shake with my pride.

Think'st thou that I, who when I please

30Can kill by waxen images,

Can force the Moon down from her sphere,

And make departed ghosts appear,

And mix love-potions!—thinks thy vanity,

I cannot deal with such a worm as thee?

FINIS.

POEMS NOT INCLUDED IN THE EDITIONS OF 1682 AND 1686.

The sources from which these miscellaneous poems are taken are noted separately. Two, at the time of going to press, have not been printed— the *Song* 'Oh no, oh no!' (p. 414) and the *Paraphrase* of the 27th Chapter of Job (p. 420).

There is evidence that Flatman contemplated one more Pindaric, but perhaps it was not written, and certainly not printed. The subject was to be Admiral Myngs. The *Familiar Letters of Love, Gallantry, and Several Occasions*, 1718, vol. i, pp. 249 foll., include a letter of consolation to Flatman's 'Honoured Master', in which he writes, after some preliminary comments: 'Not to hold you any longer in suspense, my Noble, my Generous Friend, the Glory of the Sea, the Astonishment of all the World, is dead. When I have told you this, you cannot be ignorant of the Person I mean; he has a Name too big to be concealed from any body that ever heard of Wonder on the Deep, or understands what 'tis to be brave, to be valiant, to be loyal, to be kind and honourable, more than all this is too little to describe Sir *Christopher Myngs*. Guess, my Dearest Master, the Disturbance so irreparable a Loss must create in one often honour'd with his Conversation, and many Ways oblig'd by him. We have nothing left of him now but poor sorrowful *Syl. Taylour*, that other Half of his Soul, who is now resolv'd for Retirement, and will run no more Hazards at Sea. Many more Things I might misemploy you with, but this great load must be first removed, which, I think, will not be, till I have vented my Grief in a Pindarique, and done the last Office of Kindness for the Dead. If I can make my Sorrows any thing legible, expect to bear a Part in them.' The letter is dated from London on June 15, 1666.

Another lost poem—doubtless a Pindaric—on the theme of London is thus referred to in an autograph letter to Sancroft written from St. Catharine Hall, Cambridge, on May 13, 1667 (Tanner MS. xlv, fol. 188):

'When I was last with you you were pleasd to take away from me a paper of imperfect Verses, the first desseign wherof was to comply with your injunction in saying something on that subject, whose beuty (it may be) had it continued in that flourishing condition 'twas in at the time of the imposition of yor commaunds, might haue heightned my thoughts as much as it's ruin has now dejected them; or to speak in my owne way, The Coppy had bin much livelier if th' Originall hadnt bin so much defaced; and he must be a better Architect then I that can reare a structure any thing magnificent in so bare an Ichnography. Thus much S^r to let you know how much I am beholding to yor forgetfulness in returning my Ode, wherby you haue cover'd many imperfections, & kept me from being any longer angry with my self for not finishing what had better never bin begun.'

One poem, sometimes assigned to Flatman has not been reprinted here—*A Panegyric to his Renowned Majesty, Charles the Second, King of Great Britain, &c.*, a folio sheet issued in 1660, with the initials 'T. F.', and beginning 'Return, return, strange prodigy of fate!' Flatman, if it had been his, would not have failed to reprint it in his own *Poems*. Similarly with an anonymous poem on the coronation of James II—*To the King, a Congratulatory Poem*, printed for R. Bentley in 1685—which Mr. W. C. Hazlitt in his *Collections and Notes*, ii, p. 694, ascribes to Flatman. It begins:

Dread Sir, since it has pleas'd the Pow'rs above

To take the other Object of our love.

This has a faint verbal resemblance to the opening of Flatman's genuine poem on James (see p. 394), and the misattribution may be due to this.

Upon a Chine of Beef.

I.

A chine of beef, God save us all,

Far larger than the butcher's stall,

And sturdier than the City-wall.

II.

For this held out until the foe,

By dint of blade and potent blow,

Fell in pell mell; that did not so.

III.

With stomachs sharper than their knives,

They laid about them for their lives;

Well, Eastcheap men, beware your wives.

IV.

10Enragèd weapons storm it round,

Each seeking for a gaping wound,

That in its gravy it seems drown'd.

V.

Magnanimous flesh, that didst not fall

At first assault, or second maul,

But a third time defied'st them all!

VI.

What strength can fate's decree revoke?

It was ordain'd thou shouldst be broke;

Alas! time fells the sturdy oak.

VII.

What goodly monuments still appear,

20What spondyl-bulwarks are there there,

What palisaded ribs are here!

VIII.

This bold monument death defies,

Inscribèd thus, 'To mirth here lies

A trophy and a sacrifice'.

Upon a Chine of Beef.] Of doubtful authenticity. The Horatian adaptation on pp. 356-9 perhaps confirms it, and we may note the oath (of Flatman's own coinage) at l. 138 of that poem, 'By sturdy Chine of Beef, and mighty Jove'. The text is taken from the anonymous version in *Wit's Interpreter*, 1655, collected by John Cotgrave: it appears on pp. 268-9 of the *Love-Songs, Epigrams, &c.* An inferior text in *Wit and Mirth. An Antidote to Melancholy*, 3rd edition, 1682, p. 102, is headed '*On a Chine of Beef.* By Mr. Tho. Flatman.' If genuine, this is therefore an early effort; it might be an undergraduate flight, like the parody on Austin.

The chief variants in *Wit and Mirth* are:—

2 'Far longer'.

10 'storm'd'.

12 'seem'd'.

18 'Alas, in time the sturdy oak'.

19 'What goodly mince did appear'.

On the Death of the Eminently Ennobled Charles Capell, Esq.;

Who, after he had honour'd Winton College with his Education, and accomplisht himself with a voyage into France, died of the small-pox at London last Christmas, 1656.

Shower down your ponderous tears, whoe'er you be

Dare write, or read, a Capell's elegy;

Spangle his hearse with pearls, such as were born

'Twixt the blear'd eyelids of an o'ercast morn;

And (but 'tis vain t'expostulate with Death

Or vilify the Fates with frustrate breath)

Pose Destiny with why's—why such a sun

Should set before his noontide stage were run?

Why this fair volume should be bound so fast

10In wooden covers, clasp'd-up in such haste?

Was Nature fond of its large character

And those divine impressions graven there?

Did she, lest we should spoil't (to waive that sin),

'Cause 'twas the best edition, call it in?

Or would our vaunting Isle, that saints should see

Th' utmost of all our prodigality,

Fearing some detriment by long delay,

Send Heav'n a new-year's-gift before the day?

No: th' empyrean Philomels could sing,

20Without his voice, no carols to their King.

England's Metropolis (for 'twas in thee

He died) we re-baptize thee Calvary,

The Charnel-house of Gallantry; henceforth

We brand thy front with—Golgotha of Worth.

Had he been swallow'd in that courteous deep

He travell'd o'er, he had been lull'd asleep

In th' amorous Sea-nymphs' stately arms at ease;

His great name would imposthumate the seas,

That, when the waves should swell and tempests rise

30(Strong waters challenging the dastard skies),

Poor shipwrackt mariners, remembering him,

Should court his asterism, and cease to swim;

Abjure the Fatal Brothers' glow-worm fires,

And dart at him their languishing desires.

Had France intomb'd him (what our land forbids)

Nature had rear'd him stately pyramids

The lofty Alps, where it had been most meet

Their harmless snow should be his winding-sheet;

That alablaster-coverture might be

40An emblem of his native purity:

Had he fal'n there, it had been true perchance,

Wickham's Third College might be found in France.

But he return'd from thence, curb'd Neptune's pride,

And, to our fame and grief, came home, and died.

Thus, when the Heav'n has wheel'd its daily race

About our earth, at night its glorious face

Is pox'd with stars, yet Heaven admits no blot,

And every pimple there's a beauty-spot.

Short-liv'd disease, that canst be cured and gone

50By one sweet morning's resurrection!

Adieu, great sir, whose total he that will

Describe in folio needs a cherub's quill.

Zealous posterity your tomb shall stir,

Hoard up your dust, rifle your sepulchre,

And (as the Turks did Scanderbeg's of old)

Shall wear your bones in amulets of gold.

—But my blasphemous pen profanes his glory;

I'll say but this to all his tragic story:

Were not the world well-nigh its funeral

60I'd ne'er believe so bright a star could fall.

THO. FLATMAN,

Fellow of New College.

On the Death, &c.] From Affectuum Decidua, or Due Expressions In honour of the truly noble Charles Capell, Esq. (Son to the right honourable Arthur, Lord Capell, Baron of Hadham), deceased on Christmas Day 1656. Quis desiderio sit pudor, aut modus Tam Chari Capitis?—Oxford, Printed Anno Dom. 1656.

On the Picture of the Author, Mr. Sanderson.

Let others style this page a chronicle;

Others Art's mystery; let a third sort dwell

Upon the curious neat artifice, and swear

The sun ne'er saw a shadow half so rare.

He outsays all who lets you understand

The head is Sanderson's, Fathern's the hand.

THO. FLATMAN,

Inn. Temp. Lond.

On the Picture, &c.] This and the following poem are taken from William Sanderson's *Graphice. Or, The Use of the Pen and Pensil, Or, the most Excellent Art of Painting.* 1658. With portrait by Souse, engraved by Faithorne.

On the noble Art of Painting.

Strike a bold stroke, my Muse, and let me see

Thou fear'st no colours in thy poetry,

For pictures are dumb poems; they that write

Best poems do but paint in black and white.

The pencil's amulets forbid to die,

And vest us with a fair eternity.

What think ye of the gods, to whose huge name

The pagans bow'd their humble knees? Whence came

Their immortalities but from a shade,

10But from those portraitures the painter made?

They saddled Jove's fierce eagle like a colt

And made him grasp in 's fist a thunderbolt.

Painters did all: Jove had, at their command,

Spurr'd a jackdaw and held a switch in 's hand.

The demigods, and all their glories, be

Apelles' debtors, for their deity.

Oh how the catholics cross themselves and throng

Around a crucifix, when all along

That's but a picture! How the spruce trim lass

20Doats on a picture in the looking-glass!

And how ineffable's the peasant's joy

When he has drawn his picture in his boy!

Bright angels condescend to share a part

And borrow glorious plumes from our rare art.

Kings triumph in our sackcloth, monarchs bear

Reverence t' our canvass 'bove the robes they wear.

Great fortunes, large estates, for all their noise,

Are nothing in the world but painted toys.

Th' Egyptian hieroglyphics pictures be,

30And painting taught them all their A.B.C.

The Presbyterian, th' Independent too,

All would a colour have for what they do.

And who so just that does not sometimes try

To turn pure painter and deceive the eye?

Our honest sleight of hand prevails with all;

Hence springs an emulation general.

Mark how the pretty female-artists try

To shame poor Nature with an Indian dye.

Mark how the snail with 's grave majestic pace

40Paints earth's green waistcoat with a silver lace.

But—since all rhythms are dark, and seldom go

Without the Sun—the Sun's a painter too;

Heaven's famed Vandyke, the Sun, he paints—'tis clear—

Twelve signs throughout the zodiac every year:

'Tis he, that at the spicy spring's gay birth

Makes pencils of his beams and paints the Earth;

He limns the rainbow when it struts so proud

Upon the dusky surface of a cloud;

He daubs the Moors, and, when they sweat with toil,

50'Tis then he paints them all at length in oil;

The blushing fruits, the gloss of flowers so pure,

Owe their varieties to his miniature.

Yet, what's the Sun? each thing, where'er we go,

Would be a Rubens, or an Angelo;

Gaze up, some winter night, and you'll confess

Heaven's a large gallery of images.

Then stoop down to the Earth, wonder, and scan

The Master-piece of th' whole creation, Man:

Man, that exact original in each limb,

60And Woman, that fair copy drawn from him.

Whate'er we see 's one bracelet, whose each bead

Is cemented and hangs by painting's thread.

Thus, like the soul o' th' world, our subtle art

Insinuates itself through every part.

Strange rarity! which canst the body save

From the coarse usage in a sullen grave,

Yet never make it mummy! Strange, that hand,

That spans and circumscribes the sea and land—

That draws from death to th' life, without a spell,

70As Orpheus did Eurydice from hell.

But all my lines are rude, and all such praise

Dead-colour'd nonsense. Painters scorn slight bays.

Let the great art commend itself, and then

You'll praise the pencil and deride the pen.

T. FLATMAN, lately Fellow of

New Coll. Oxon; now Inn.

Temp. Lond.

On Mistress S. W., who cured my hand by a plaster applied to the knife which hurt me.

Wounded and weary of my life,

I to my fair one sent my knife;

The point had pierced my hand as far

As foe would foe in open war.

Cruel, but yet compassionate, she

Spread plasters for my enemy;

She hugg'd the wretch had done me harm,

And in her bosom kept it warm,

When suddenly I found the cure was done,

10The pain and all the anguish gone,

Those nerves which stiff and tender were

Now very free and active are:

Not help'd by any power above,

But a true miracle of Love.

Henceforth, physicians, burn your bills,

Prescribe no more uncertain pills:

She can at distance vanquish pain,

She makes the grave to gape in vain:

'Mongst all the arts that saving be

20None so sublime as sympathy.

Oh could it help a wounded breast,

I'd send my soul to have it dress'd.

Yet, rather, let herself apply

The sovereign med'cine to her eye:

There lurks the weapon wounds me deep,

There, that which stabs me in my sleep;

For still I feel, within, a mortall smart,

The salve that heal'd my hand can't cure my heart.

October 19, 1661.

On Mistress S. W.] The above was printed in *Notes and Queries* for September 25, 1869; it was contributed by Mr. F. W. Cosens from a manuscript in his possession, *Miscellanies by Tho. Flatman, ex Interiori Templo, Londini, Nov. 9, 1661.* These poems are autograph. This poem is in the Firth MS., which clearly is a transcript of the preceding. See p. 278.

Song.

I.

Oh no, oh no! it cannot be that I

So long condemn'd to die

Should fool myself with hopes of a reprieve

From her that read my destiny;

She with her basilisk eyes denounc'd my doom.

Why then should I in vain presume,

In vain, fond man, to live

My disappointments poorly to survive?

II.

Oh no, oh no! I know the worst on't now,

10My sentence pass'd I know,

And I no further expectations have

My wither'd hopes again should grow.

Yet 'tis a satisfaction to be sure

I feel the worst I can endure.

Oh that she yet would save

By her miraculous kindness from the grave.

Oh no, &c.] From the Firth MS., which dates the poem 1671, and notes that it was set by Roger Hill.

Epitaph on his eldest Son, Thomas, 1682.

Whoe'er thou art, that look'st upon,

And read'st what lies beneath this stone;

What Beauty, Goodness, Innocence,

In a sad hour was snatch'd from hence.

What reason canst thou have to prize

The dearest object of thine eyes?

Believe this, mortal, what thou valuest most,

And set'st thy soul upon, is soonest lost.

Epitaph on his Son.] From Strype's Stow, 1720. Book III, p. 266. describing the monuments on the north wall of St. Bride's, Fleet Street. Strype adds, 'These Verses are almost worn out and gone, and therefore I have preserved them here; being undoubtedly the easy natural Strain of the Poet, the Father'.

This Epitaph is in Hackett, *A Collection of Epitaphs*, 1757, ii. 31, introduced thus—

'*St. Bride's, London.*

Here lies the Body of *Thomas Flatman*, eldest son of *Thomas Flatman*, and *Hannah* his wife, who resigned his beloved soul the 28th of *December* 1682.'

Strype records that the boy was ten years old. The pastoral elegy on p. 375 in all probability refers to the same child, though the date of his death is there given as January 28, 168⅔. Aubrey records (in Aubrey MS. 7, fol. 8 verso) that Flatman himself was buried in the same grave.

Lines to John Northleigh.

Though we that write in rhyme (it is confess'd)

Are wont to praise them most that need it least,

So far from doing what we had design'd

That we become impertinently kind;

Though I'm convinced of this, and right well know

I can add nothing to your Book, or You:

Yet am I forced th' old beaten road to go

And tell my friend what wonders he has done,

Where loyal labours could oblige a Crown—

10 A Crown asserted by the hand of heaven,

By which triumphant laurels now are given;

And may they never, never blasted be

By any Boanerges of Democracy.

Compassionate friend! whose arguments do prove

The force of reason and the power of love;

Taught by your generous and good-natured pen,

The salvage beasts may once more turn to men,

Be reconciled to the ill-treated Throne,

And shun those rocks their fellows split upon:

20Your call to th' unconverted may do more

Than Orpheus' charms did in the woods before,

Convince the stubborn, and th' unwary lead

By benign arts those blessed steps to tread

In which our glorious Master led the way

To realms of peace and everlasting day.

Farewell, dear friend! and for this once excuse

The last efforts of an expiring Muse.

THOMAS FLATMAN.

Lines to John Northleigh] From *The Triumph of our Monarchy, Over the Plots and Principles of our Rebels and Republicans, Being Remarks on their most eminent Libels. By John Northleigh*, 1685; the lines are headed 'To my worthy Friend, J. Northleigh, Esq., Author of this Book and the *Parallel*. Dryden also contributed a poem.

Lines to Archbishop Sancroft.

My Lord

When I Your unsought Glories view'd,

And prest (a meane Spectator in the Croud;)

Where every Ey, with sparkling Joy did gaze,

All hearts brimmfull of Blessing, & of Praise;

Extatick with the mighty Theme I went,

And something, some great thing to Write, I meant:

This, sure, said I, must set me all on fire,

This must my dull, unhallow'd Muse inspire:

I try'd in wary words my Verse to dress,

10And throng'd my thoughts with awfull Images;

For the bold Work, Materialls I desseign'd

High as Your Station, Humble as Your Minde:

Alas! in vaine! my owne Confusion

Strait tumbled th' ill-attempted *Babel* downe.

Much I desir'd to tell in artfull Rhymes,

Your Magnanimity through the worst of Times

How, like a Rock, amidst the Sea, You stood,

Surrounded with a foaming Popular-Floud;

In that black Night, how You still kept Your way,

20When all despair'd the dawning of This Day:

With what true Christian Stoicisme, You durst Owne

The slighted Miter, and abandon'd Crowne;

As *Cato* for the baffled Side declar'd,

Tho' all the Gods, the Conquering Cause preferr'd.

Next, I would have describ'd the Happy Place

Of Your soft minutes in a sweet Recess;

Where all things were in Your Possession,

All You need Wish, for You were all Your Owne[.

Here Emperours, & Kings, receiv'd at last

30The noblest Guerdon for their labours past:

Less splendid were those daies, but more secure,

Their last & best were gloriously Obscure.

O those gay Vallies! o those lofty Hills!

Those silent Rivers! & those murmuring Rills!

The melancholy Grove! & peacefull Shade!

For Ease, & Angells-Conversation made!

The Morning's Breath! the sight o' th' rising Sun,

When he starts forth, his Giant-Race to runn!

Faine wou'd I have said, what cannot be express't

40But in the sentiments of a wellpleas'd Breast.

And now (my Lord!) on Your triumphant Day,

What can Your poor unlettred Beadsman say?

Who know's that Praise, at the Poëtique rate,

Swell's to a Vice, & must deserve Your hate.

When Heav'n vouchsafe's a *Miracle* to mankinde,

Silence, & Wonder best express our minde.

Durst I Presume, or could Despaire (my Lord!)

I would add Here, for my owne self, one word,

That I might be (whome the World frown's uppon)

50An Atome in the beams of Your bright Sun,

Almost Invisible; but still shin'd-uppon.

My Lord

Your Grace's most obedient

Servant, & poore Kinsman.

THOMAS FLATMAN.

Lines to Archbishop Sancroft.] Exactly reproduced from the poet's autograph in Tanner MS. 306, of the Bodleian, where it appears in a group of Sancroft papers at folio 380, and is endorsed on the outer leaf—'These For his Grace, my Lord Archbishop of Canterbury, with my humblest Duty.'

The poem must have been written in the last year of Flatman's life, and have reference to the trial of the Seven Bishops. With l. 50, 'An Atome in the beams of Your bright Sun', compare the Pindaric *On the Death of Charles II*, l. 37, 'We atoms in his beams might sport and play' (p. 392).

On the Death of His Grace, James, Duke of Ormond: A Pindaric Ode.

I.

Had not the deathless name of OSSORY

Pow'r to preserve, as well as to create,

And over-rule the dullness of my fate,

A pen so meanly qualified as mine
Might well this mighty task decline,
Too ponderous for feeble Me,
Me so obscure, my glorious theme so bright,
Where all is overpow'ring light
Which never can submit to night.
10But sense of deepest gratitude should control
All the despondencies of a trembling soul
And force a modest confidence to inspire
The coldest breast with an uncommon fire.
Since then, for aught we know,
The separated happy spirits above
Sometimes regard our pious love,
And are not much disturb'd at what we kindly do.
Let ORMOND'S gentle ghost look down
Full of kind compassion,
20And pity what my duty prompts me to.

Fain would I pay my tribute ever due
To his immortal memory:
But what immortal methods to pursue
Is understood by very few;
The noblest bard that ever wore the bays
Would here fall short in sorrow, and in praise.

II.

Our stock of tears would soon exhausted be
Were every eye a sea,
And grief would swell to prodigality;
30Th' irreparable loss, if duly weigh'd,

Would make posterity afraid,

For ORMOND in his radiant course has done

What did amaze, what durst abide the sun,

And struck with terror all the envious lookers on:

Whether with ecstasy we think upon

His goodly person or his matchless mind,

Where shall the most inquisitive mortal find

A more accomplish'd hero left behind?

As he were sent from heaven, design'dly great,

40To dote on still, but not presume to imitate,

Or whether with regret we cast an eye

On his unbounded liberality,

His unaffected piety,

Or more than human magnanimity

(Virtues inimitable all),

The joyful beadsman and the Church will tell

The story, scarce hereafter credible,

And call his life one long-continued miracle.

III.

Say, all you younger sons of Honour, say,

50You that in peace appear so brisk and gay,

Is it a little thing to forfeit all

At Loyalty's tremendous call,

And stand with resolution in defence

Of a despised calamitous Prince,

To fight against our stars, and to defy

The last efforts of prosperous villainy,

And—when the hurricane of the state grew high—

To brave the thunder and the lightning scorn,

The beauteous fabric into pieces torn,

60Imprisonment and exile to disdain

For a neglected Sovereign;

Still to espouse a crazy, tottering crown?

This, mighty ORMOND, was thy own,

This glory thou deserv'dst to have,

This bravery thou hast carried with thee to thy grave.

Let other lesser Great ones live, to try

Thy arduous paths to fame;

Let them bid fair for immortality,

And to procure an everlasting name;

70And may thy sacred ashes smile to see

Their vain, their frivolous attempts to rival Mighty Thee.

IV.

O noble, fortunate old Man!

Though thou hadst still lived on

To Nestor's centuries, thou hadst died too soon;

Too soon alas! for heav'n could never be

Or weary or ashamed to find fresh toils for thee:

What wiser head, or braver arm than thine

Could heav'n contrive to manage heav'n's design!

And what Herculean labour is too hard

80For such a mind, so well prepared,

Ever above the prospect of Regard,

And that unfashionable thing, Reward!

Many have been thy gloomy days,

Yet ever happy hast thou been;

In every state thou merit'dst praise,

And thou hast never wanted it within.

All after fourscore years is grief and pain;

Those honourably pass'd, thou didst resign

Thy empire over every heart;

90From thine this sceptre never shall depart,)

But the succession evermore remain:

'Twas time for thee to die, and let a second ORMOND reign.

V.

How shall I mention thy lamented death,

Thy only blemish—thy mortality!

For 'tis too much disparagement for thee

To be involved in common destiny

And like inglorious men give up thy precious breath.

A fiery chariot should have snatch'd thee hence,

And all the host of heav'n convened to see

100Th' assumption of a godlike Prince)

Into th' ineffable society:

Half-way at least part of th' immaculate train

With palms should have attended thee,

Thy harbingers to the triumphant hierarchy,

Then big with wonder mounted up again.

What can the tongues of men or angels say,

What Boanerges ne'er so loud,

If they would speak of thy prodigious day,

Of which an emperor's history would be proud

110Farewell, dead Prince—oh might it not be said,)

Though a desirable euthanasy

Prepared the way for deifying thee,

ORMOND like other men must die,

For he with a fatigue of victory oppress'd

Laid himself only down to rest.

FINIS.

On the Death of James, Duke of Ormond.] Printed in folio, 1688, with the title, *On the Death of the Right Honorable the Duke of Ormond: a Pindaric Ode.* In *Letters from the Dead to the Living,* 1702, vol. ii, pp. 24-5, Flatman, with his pipe in his mouth, is introduced complaining that this ode has been vamped up for the death of King William.

Job, Chapter xxvii. Paraphrased.

VERSE 8.

Poor Hypocrite (though ne'er so rich), when God shall call

His double, his dissembling soul, how small,

How beggarly his biggest hopes will show!

Riches command no further than below.

VERSE 9.

When griefs like waves o'er one another roll

And overwhelm his quite-dejected soul,

When he lies groaning on a restless bed,

With a sad bleeding heart, and aching head

Brimfull of anguish and repeated pain,

10He weeps and frames his parch'd lips to complain,

Breathes up to heaven a very earnest prayer—

Scarce dare he hope, yet dares he not despair—

But all his supplications mount in vain,

God will not hear, nor answer him again.

VERSE 10.

How can he turn religious, and adore

That God he so devoutly mock'd before?

VERSE 11.

I will the depths of Providence reveal;

Th' Almighty's methods will I not conceal.

VERSE 12.

Yet why should I suggest what your own heart,

20Were it not vain, might, better far, impart?

VERSE 13.

On th' wicked's head this heavy fate shall come,

And this shall be from God th' oppressor's doom.

VERSE 14.

His sons, though more and lovelier they are

Than their decrepit father's silver hair,

Strong as the sons of Anak, bright and brave,

Shall shroud their pride in an untimely grave;

His daughters, though more beauteous every one

Than the seraphic spouse of Solomon,

A sisterhood as numerous and bright

30As are the glorious stars that gild the night,—

A bloody cloud their glories shall eclipse;

Death shuts their killing eyes, their charming lips.

Though like a golden harvest they appear,

And every one a full, a laden ear,

Like olive plants amidst their friends be grown,

The sword shall reap, the sword shall hew them down.

The sword and eager famine shall devour

All they enjoy in one unhappy hour.

VERSE 15.

His progeny shall unlamented die,

40Buried in black oblivion shall they lie,

Unpitied to the dust they shall return,

Nor shall one pious tear bedew their urn.

VERSE 16.

If he have silver plentiful as dust,

Gold pure as that of Ophir, both shall rust

VERSE 17.

Let him have caskets whose each orient gem

Vies with the walls o' th' new Jerusalem,

Raiment more gorgeous than the lily's hue

When every snowy fold is pearl'd with dew,

He's but the just man's steward all the while;

50The just shall wear the raiment, part the spoil.

VERSE 18.

The house he builds, like that o' th' moth, shall be

Too weak against the wind's least battery;

Or, if it stand the brunt of wind and rain,

'Twill stagger at a thund'ring hurricane;

As tents, it may remove from land to land,

But on a solid basis cannot stand.

VERSE 19.

The rich man shall depart, but not in peace;

When he lies down, his horror shall increase

Just when he's ripe for vengeance and heaven's frown

60Death, ah too irksome Death, shall shake him down.

Gather'd he shall not be by that kind hand

Which plucks the righteous to blest Canaan's land:

He opes his lids and surfeiteth his eyes

With gazing over all his vanities,

Till some ill chance o' th' sudden dims his sight

And leaves him lost in an eternal night.

VERSES 20, 21.

As mighty waters shall his terrors roar;

He's stolen away and shall be seen no more,

Hurried from his belovèd home, and tost

70By th' East wind, fierce as that drown'd Pharaoh's host.

VERSE 22.

Jehovah, from whose hand he fain would flee,

Shall add more sting to his calamity:

VERSE 23.

And where his glass has but few sands to run,

His tragicomic life now almost done,

At the last act his deadliest shame shall be

To find an hissing for a *Plaudite*.

Job.] The text is taken from the Firth MS. The ingenious paraphrase of the last verse—'Men shall clap their hands at him, and shall hiss him out of his place'—echoes *The Review*, ll. 33-5 (p. 302).

---

* *
*

Le hore di recreatione:

OR,

THE PLEASANT

HISTORIE OF

Albino and *Bellama*.

Discovering the severall changes of

Fortune, in C U P I D S journey
to H Y M E N S joyes.
To which is annexed

Il Insonio Insonadado, or a sleeping-waking
Dreame, vindicating the

divine breath of Poesie from the tongue-lashes
of some Cynical Poet-quippers,
and Stoicall Philo-prosers

By N. W. Master in Arts, of Queenes
Colledge in Cambridge.

—— *Semel in anno Apollo.*

Ergo,

Nè mea metra tibi Musâ composta jocosâ,
Delibata priùs quàm sint contempta relinquas,

LONDON,
Printed by *J.D*, for *C.G.* and are to be sold
at the Princes Armes in *Pauls* churchyard.
1638.

Cover

INTRODUCTION TO NATHANIEL WHITING.

In the case of most of the constituents of these volumes, there was little need of 'deliberating and pondering' like the excellent Sir Thomas Bertram, when he had to settle such weighty questions as whether his niece should or should not go out to dinner, and if so whether she should walk or drive. But it was not quite the same in regard to *Albino and Bellama*. The first claim of entrants here—rarity and novelty to the general, it has without question: for the book (though it seems to have been issued in two forms, or at least with two title-pages) is very uncommon, and the author has escaped the wide-encroaching net of the *D.N.B.* Nor could I allow this to be balanced by the dull, clumsy, philistine, hackneyed ribaldry of the nunnery scenes in the middle, or by a page of sheer nastiness at the end, which is a sort of concentration of Herrick's foulest epigrams. These things will happen: and they can be skipped. It gave one more serious pause that 'N. W.' seldom[1] displays anything like the poetry which far more than compensates for much milder blots in *Leoline and Sydanis*, and that his book is written in a singular jargon almost as much out of the common way as the wildest freaks of Benlowes, but without their excuse of *furor poeticus*. What turned the scale in his favour, after more than one reading, was the increasing conviction that the book, in spite or perhaps to some extent because of its defects, is a really valuable document for the history of English Literature from the special point of view which was marked out in the General Introduction. It is noteworthy as a member, graceless and slatternly, but still a member, of that class of Heroic Poem which it has been one of my main objects to bring before the student. It is still more noteworthy in connexion with the history of English fiction as presenting a special variety of that kind. It was not till, for the purposes of this collection, and by the kindness of Professor Firth, who lent me his copy, I read the volume (I knew it before only by name and from the *Censura Literaria*) that a gap in my mind's atlas of that fiction was filled in satisfactorily.

I said, in speaking of *Leoline and Sydanis*, that we must take not merely the Heroic but the Mock-Heroic poem into consideration as origins for our English examples; and this is very much more the case with *Albino and Bellama*. Whiting almost parades his knowledge of Italian; and I should think, from some of the worst as well as the oddest parts of his poem, that he had pushed his researches as far as Macaronic. In fact you must go beyond Folengo—to Tifi Odassi and Fossa Cremonese[2]—to supply a 'further' to his excursions, into the unsavoury now and then. But turning willingly enough from this, it will be evident to any instructed reader—and his perlusive panegyrists point it out—that his purpose is largely satiric. Indeed, his uncouth lingo[3] has a close connexion with that of Marston and the other early Elizabethan satirists forty years before him: while he gives one odd reminders, at the same time, of the prose pamphlet which was contemporary with these very satirists, and was actually written by some of them. Now all these links are links with the history of the Novel backwards; and there are others forward. Change the romance apparatus into that of common life, of which our examples are French and Spanish rather than Italian, and you will get out of parts of *Albino and Bellama* something by no means unlike the singular farrago which goes under the name of *The English Rogue*. Besides convincing the author that prose is much better for such work than verse (which Head himself saw[4]), present him with more wits, better taste, and a more advanced state of society and manners, and you will probably find him some way on the road which leads, however far away, and after whatever rise, over the hills beyond his dirty marsh, to *Tom Jones* itself. While, to make a less 'kangaroo' transition in quality though a farther one in time, much smaller alteration would make *Albino and Bellama* into very fair Mrs. Radcliffe.

The curious addition *Il Insonio Insonadado* or 'Waking-Dream Undreamt' (whether the title is invented or borrowed, some one with greater knowledge of Spanish than I possess must decide) may supply some greater interest than Whiting's escapade in the Heroic Romance. It is not continuously paged with the rest of the volume, but merely 'signatured' H, H2, &c. as far as a (misprinted) 5. On the whole, however, it is much less carelessly put to press than *Albino and Bellama*, and it is also (in parts at least) much more soberly written. The opening does not promise much, except an example of the loose, would-be satirical academic commonplaces of the time; but it afterwards takes on some critical substance, and if I had read it (as I had not yet) twenty years ago I should have given it a small corner in an otherwise very scantily occupied chapter of my *History of Criticism*. Whether the personages introduced before the Heavenly Court aim at individuals it would be very hard to say: but the certification of the poetess[5] might have some interest. 'Tenth Muses', as was said in relation to Anne King (*v. sup.*, p. 210), were not unknown, and Katharine Philips was alive, though as yet but a child. But women had, before her, made little figure in English literature. The evidences of popular taste are not quite worthless, and while the absence of Ben Jonson is noteworthy, the presence of Drummond is almost equally so, as well as the mention of that 'testiness' which certainly does appear in the poet of Hawthornden. But the chief critical utterance is the quatrain, solid and judicial if not very poetical, on Donne.

Of Whiting himself I have been able to find out very little.[6] He was of Queens' College, Cambridge; Brydges erroneously says 'King's', having misread the misprinted 'Regnalis' of James Bernard's commendatory poem. And he must have settled down twenty years later sufficiently to print in 1659, according to Hazlitt, *The Saint's Triangle of Duties, Deliverances, and*

Dangers. The first edition of *Albino and Bellama* appeared in 1637, with the title *Le hore di recreatione: Or, The Pleasant Historie of Albino and Bellama.... By N. W., Master of Arts, of Queenes Colledge in Cambridge.* The British Museum also has a copy with an engraved frontispiece as well, adding *to which is annexed il insonio insonodado* or the *vindication of Poesye.* These title-pages are also dated 1638, and the engraved title-page was also issued in 1639.

In 1633 the birth of the Duke of York was commemorated at Cambridge in *Ducis Eboracensis Fasciae a Musis Cantabrigiensibus raptim contextae.* 'N. Whyting, Coll. Regin. Art. Baccal.' contributes two copies of verse, Latin and Greek, both markedly royalist in tone.

It was not, however, for some time after I had been working on Whiting that I found considerable new light thrown on him by his prose work, which is in the British Museum, under his name, though *Albino and Bellama* is not. The title of it is abbreviated by Hazlitt, and is in the original very long, beginning with the Hebrew אל...בית... אל *Old Jacob's Altar newly repaired; or The Saints' Triangle of Dangers, Deliverances and Duties.* It is a solid little quarto of some 260 pages, dedicated to Sir William Fleetwood, Sir George Fleetwood, 'Baron of Swonholm in Sweadland', and 'his Excellency Charles Lord Fleetwood'. Whiting was now 'Minister' of Aldwinckle (All Saints, as the registers show[7]) by the patronage of Sir William, to whom he refers as his 'ancient' and 'affectionate Mecaenas' in his Cambridge days. He is certainly by this time a full-blown Puritan. He uses that word itself frequently, and with pride; refers to 'my reverend grandfather', minister of Elton, Northants, who was apparently a 'pilgrim father'; speaks of the time when 'the Episcopal monopoly lasted', and eulogizes 'the faithful Peters to whom is committed the Word of Reconciliation' (Reconciliation *à la* Peters is good!); but also calls Herbert 'divine' and quotes St. Anselm, though of course without the 'Saint'. Allowing for its standpoint the book is not virulent, and is a respectable piece of hortatory divinity on its own side. Besides, the thought that in a few months 'the Episcopal monopoly' came back again, and that 'the faithful Peters' received the deferred pay for his various 'commissions', mitigates judgement not a little; while, to crown all, the contrast with *Albino and Bellama* is irresistibly comic. Perhaps, indeed, some of the ribaldry of the convent scenes in the verse may be due to the Puritanism which is so distinct in the prose. But it would be an odd Saint who could construct himself a 'triangle' of any kind of sanctities or pious experiences out of Whiting's romance. And this, which is so characteristic of the time, and yet not so uncharacteristic of all times, adds to my satisfaction in presenting Mr. Nathaniel Whiting with some little more detail than even Brydges has given. (It may be added that he was deprived of the living at the Restoration. Edward Price succeeded him on February 20, 1662-3. According to a brief notice in *Notes and Queries*,[8] he then migrated to the village of Cranford, near

Kettering, and got together a congregation there. There is no trace of him in the registers of either of the Cranford churches.[9] The same authority states that he died childless and was a benefactor of the free school of Aldwinckle, of which he was master during the period of his incumbency.)

[1] I had written 'nowhere', but hastily. The opening has not a little which convicts the haste, and I have noted other passages *infra*.

[2] These oddities of the fifteenth century, with others, were conveniently republished, in *Maccheronee di Cinque Poète Italiani* (Milan: D li, 1864).

[3] He would almost be worth republishing for this alone, and I say this despite the trouble it has given me. Those who are curious in rare words and *autoschediastic* forms ought to prize Whiting highly.

[4] As an instance here, take the incident where the false Phaeliche, coming to the nunnery, sees the masons mending the breaches that Rivelezzo's cannon had made. It is a mere touch, awkward and only half intelligible in the verse. Less than two centuries later Scott would have given a lively page and a half of prose description of the scene, with dialogue thrown in. On the other hand, *in prose*, the extravagances of the phrase and the incoherences of the story would have had a better chance of being mended.

[5] 'Marget' is used in *Albino and Bellama* as a generic name. But Whiting's irritable and restless fancy may have put together '*Mag-pie*' and Persius's *poetris pica*.

[6] By the great kindness of the Rev. J. H. Gray, Tutor and Dean of Queens' College, assisted by the President of that Society and by the Registrar of the University of Cambridge, I am enabled to give more than I had found in any book. Nathaniel Whiting (who seems also to have spelt his name 'Whiteinge' and 'Whitinge') matriculated as Pensioner on March 30, 1629; proceeded B.A. 1631 and M.A. in 1635. He had been entered at his college on July 1, 1628, and his tutor's name was Stubbins. In the College accounts from September 1630, and for four years onwards, Whiting appears as a Scholar, receiving in the respective years 12s. 6d.; 16s. 3d.; 19s. 7d.; and 15s. 10d. The first payment seems to have been for part of the year only: but in no year does he come anywhere near the full income of a Scholar; which, Mr. Gray tells me, seems to have been £2. There appears to be no subsequent mention of him in the College records either as Scholar or Fellow.

[7] Canon Hodgson, Rector of Aldwincle, kindly allowed Mr. Simpson to examine the registers. The date of Whiting's institution is March 20, 1652, but already in 1650, on May 4, he signs the accounts as 'Minister'.

[8] By C. H. and T. Cooper, in the third series, vol. v, p. 420.

To the right honourable, right worthy, and truly ennobled hero, John, Lord Lovelace, Baron of Hurley, N.W. S.P.O.

The law-enactors, whilst time fear'd the rod,

Feign'd in their laws the presence of a god,

Whose awful nod and wisdom grave should be

As hand and signet unto their decree;

And such commanding awe that sacred name

Struck in the vulgar breasts, it teen'd a flame

Of love and duty to their pious hests.

Thus Rhadamanthus in his laws invests

Him whom profaner times styl'd heaven's king.

10Minos and others strike the selfsame string.

The moral's mine: for, in this quirking season,

When pride and envy steer the helm of reason,

It is, has with press-taskers been, in use

To press the issue of their prose and muse

Under the ensigns of some worthy peer,

Whose very name unsatire can a jeer,

And lock detraction up in beds of clay,

To sleep their suns as rearmice do the day.

Then do they bravely march, with honour arm'd,

20Which, as the gods the people, charmeth charm'd.

On this known privilege feet I these lines,

In which, though dimmer than your native, shines

Your worth, enfired by my kneèd quill,

Which claims the scale not of deserts, but will,

In your acceptance and the world's surmise.

Then, cynics, bark, and, critics, beam your eyes!

My quill's no pencil to emblazon forth

Your stainless honour and your matchless worth.

As dust-born flies, which 'bout the candle play,

30Glide through its arch, encircle, fan, survey,

Wink at the presence of day's beamy blaze,

Purr on the glass, or on herb-pillows laze,

Just so my downy muse in distichs dare

Feet the perfection of a silkless fair,

Pumex each part so trimly that her foe

Swears her cheeks roses and her bosom snow;

Nay, has strew'd flowers of desertless praise

T'adorn the tomb of good sir Worthy Crayse.

Under this (ah me!) stone is laid (alas!)

40A man—a knight—the best that ever was.

His prowess war, his wisdom state did prove,

His kindness kindred, and the world his love;

But when she should with her weak feathers soar

To court a star, or with her feeble oar

Strike such a sea of worth, ride honour's ring,

She dares not touch or snaffle, sail, or wing.

Only as he which limn'd those tears and sighs

Which Iphigenia's death from hearts and eyes

Of kindred drew, but o'er her father's brow

50(Telling the world he mourn'd without an how)

He drew a veil spake sorrow in excess,

So with a —— —— must my muse express

Your sacred worth, concluding it to be

Too high for any bard, if not, for me.

Beside, the world of late has nicknam'd praise,

Calls it an elbow-claw and scraping bays.

Then pardon, sir, this dearth, and judge the why

Is your worth soar'd above Parnasse's eye.

Let not your slights or nescio's (though most just)

60Condemn my muse to be enseil'd with dust,

Nor let presumption hoist to your embrace.

But rather let your honour bate its place

And stoop unto my measures, since the name

Of patron awes oft times the breath of fame;

And by this honour shall you e'er engage

The knee, hand, duty, air, and thriving age

Of your honour's ever

humbly devoted,

N. W.

Title. S. P. O.] = it may be just desirable to say, *Salutem plurimam optat.* The object of the wish was, I suppose, the *second* Lord Lovelace. The better known *third*, prominent at the Revolution and also a John, was born in the same year with this poem.

6 'teen'd' or 'tined' = 'kindled', as in 'tinder'. The forms 'tened' and 'tind' also exist, and *Il Insonio*, l. 368, has 're-teined'.

21 'feet', orig. 'fate', seems at first to equal 'foot', i.e. I 'base', 'establish'. But cf. l. 34 and *Albino*, 3558, which give it the sense of 'metre', 'versify'.

23 my kneèd quill]—paying homage, as if on bent knee.

32 The verb to 'laze', revived in late nineteenth century as slang, is as old as Robert Greene's *Alphonsus.*

35 'Pumex' = pumice. Greene used this Latin form as a noun.

part] misprinted 'parr' in orig.

47 Orig., 'limb'd', a lax seventeenth-century spelling.

48 'Iphigenia' will scan with the proper pronunciation. But, as all students of literature have always known, though some editors of it seem to have thought

it an esoteric discovery, classical names were very loosely accented, not merely by men of whose education we know nothing, like Shakespeare, but by University wits like Spenser and Dryden.

60 enseil'd] Same as 'ensealed', 'stamped', 'marked', or perhaps 'closed up'.

66 age] 'agre' in orig. must be wrong.

To the Reader.

Courteous Reader—for to such I write—

With native candour view this chequer'd white,

Be truly candid to a candidate

Whom importunings force to antedate

The travails of his quill, and, like a grape

Ere ripened, press it. Yet if I escape

The censure of these times, this critic age,

My muse (like parrots) in a wire cage

Shall not do penance; but I'll not promise it,

10'Cause 't doth too much o' th' lips of greatness sit.

And 'tis a fault for me to sympathize,

I bring no antic mask in strange disguise,

No sharp invective, nor no comic mirth

Which may to laughter give an easy birth.

Though 'tis in use with them that seek to please

These humorous times (it being a disease

Half epidemical to keep a phrase

Or fancy at stave's end; nought merits praise

Unless with quibbles every staff does end—

20Conceited jests which unto lightness tend)

Though every page swells with ingenuous plots,

Yet, cry our carps, the authors are but sots.

An elbow-pillow or a motley coat

With them are now the chiefest men of note.

But I nor am, nor hope that name to gain

Of pantomimic: yet did nature deign

The optic-glass of humours to descry

Each man's rank humour only by the eye,

I would have tun'd my muse, that every page

30Might swell with humours suiting to this age;

This leaf should talk of love and that of state,

This of alarums, that of wonders prate,

This of knights errant, of enchantment that,

This to the itching ears of novels chat.

But ... since my starv'd Fortunes missed that, I have drawn

A picture shadowed o'er with double lawn,

Lest some quick Lyncist with a piercing eye,

Should the young footsteps of a truth espy,

Yet something, I confess, was born of late

40Which makes me age it with an ancient date,

But let no antic-hunter post to Stow,

To trace out truth upon his even snow.

Annals are dumb of such and such a lord,

Nor of our amorous pair speak half a word,

Monastic writs do not Bellama limn,

Nor abbey-rolls do teem a line of him,

This story has no sires (as 'tis the use)

But weak invention and a feeble muse.

These are the parents that abortive birth

50Give to this embryon of desired mirth,

Which in the author's name does humbly crave

A charitable censure or a grave.

The purest-bolted flour that is has bran,

Venus her naeve, Helen her stain, nor can

I think these lines are censure-free, impal'd

By th' muses and 'gainst envy's javelins mail'd.

Yet where the faults but whisper, use thy pen

With the *quod non vis* of the heathen men;

And, if the crimes do in loud echoes speak,

60Thy sponge; but not with lashing satires break

That sacred bond of friendship, for 't may be

I may hereafter do as much for thee.

Nor do thou think to trample on my muse;

Nor in thy lofty third-air braves accuse

My breast of faintness, or the ballad-whine.

For know my heart is full as big as thine,

And as pure fire heats my octavo bulk

As the grand-folio, or the Reamish hulk,

If but oppos'd with envy, but unless

70I truly am what these few words express.

Thy ready friend,

N. W.

22 'carp' for 'carp*er*' seems to be much rarer than for 'carp*ing*'. Cf. *In Insonio*, 218.

41 Stow] The famous antiquary had been dead long enough (since 1605) to 'become a name'.

55 'impal'd', orig. 'impalde', is clearly 'paled-in', 'palisaded',' fortified'.

64 third-air] = 'third *hand*', or what?

68 Reamish] 'N. W.'s' Protestantism would naturally have a fling at anything connected with Rheims.

To the right virtuous and equally beautiful, S^{ra} Inconstanza Bellarizza.

Fairest,

When, by much gazing on those glittering beams

Which (if unmask'd) from day's bright henchman streams,

The Rascians eyes do gain the curse of years,

The loadstone's swarfy hue their tapers clears.

When unicorns have gluts or surfeits ta'en

By browsing liquorice, they to regain

Their stomachs and a cure crash bitter grass.

I leave the application: 'tis a glass

Wherein the dimmest eye may plainly see

10What's due to me from you, to you from me.

But—I'll only tell the world that for your sake,

My willing muse this task did undertake

At hours of recreation, when a thought

Of your choice worth this and this fancy brought.

Some to the bar will call the truth hereof,

Some wonder why, some pass it by, some scoff.

Because, in this full harvest of your sex,

I 'mongst such thousands glean your name t'annex

Unto, and usher in, these wanton verses,

20Some will be apt to think my pen rehearses

Love passions 'twixt yourself and some choice he

(The world I know will not suspect 'tis me)

And that I age it lest quick eyes should see.

But in this thought I'm silent; thoughts are free.

Indeed your worth doth just proportion hold

With this high worth which of Bellama's told.

And well my knowledge can inform my pen

To raise a spite in women, love in men.

And if the Fates befriend me that my thread

30Outmeasures yours (your worth asleep, not dead,

For such worth cannot die) I then will say

You equall'd her and was—(but, truth, away).

If these dull melancholy, grief, or sleep,

From any prone thereto at distance keep;

Let unto you their tribute thanks be paid

For my invention by your worth was ray'd,

My fancy rais'd, enliv'ned, and inspir'd,

That my quick muse my agile hand has tir'd,

Nay, more, methinks I might unchidden call

40You subject-object of this poem all;

And all in this acknowledgement may trim

You pros'd this poem but 'twas vers'd by him

Who styles himself your servant,

N. W.

To S^{ra} Inconstanza Bellarizza.] Who she was is a question much less answerable than 'Whose Song the Sirens sang?'

3 seq. 'Unnatural History' was getting past its greatest vogue, and only eight years later *Pseudodoxia Epidemica* was to deal it blows all the more deadly because not unsympathetic. But it was still popular, and a grand set-off to many poetic 'Rascians'. Whiting is here pilfering from Greene's *Pandosto*; a passage in the dedication runs, 'The *Rascians* (right honourable) when by long gazing against the sun, they become half-blind, recover their sights by looking at the black load-stone. Unicorns, being glutted, by browsing on roots of liquorice, sharpen their stomachs with crashing bitter grass'.

4 'swarfy' = swarthy.

7 That 'bitter' would be grateful to others besides unicorns after a surfeit of liquorice may be easily admitted. 'Crash' for 'crush' or 'crunch' in this sense is good.

11 The book is badly printed—in hardly any of my texts have I had to alter more trivial misspellings. Here intelligent 'setting' would of course have made 'But' a separate line or fragment of line.

23 age it] = 'throw it back in date'.

42 Not bad for 'You gave the subject' &c.

The Author's Apology.

Some rigid stoic will (I doubt not) shoot

A quipping censure at this wanton fruit,

And say I better might have us'd my talents

Than t' humour ladies and perfumèd gallants.

Know such that pamphlets, writ in metre, measure

As much invention, judgement, wit, as pleasure.

All learning's not lock'd up in *si*'s and *tum*'s.

Roses, pinks, violets, as well as gums,

Some native fragour have to equal civet.

10Minerva does not all her treasures rivet

Into the screws of *obs* and *sols*: but we

Are sea-born birds, and as our pedigree

Came sailing o'er from Normandy and Troy,

So we must have our pretty ermine joy.

One part Italian and of French the other;

Stout Belgia be her sire, and Spain her mother.

So our apparel is so strange and antic

That our great grandsires sure would call us frantic.

And, should they see us on our knees for blessing,

20They'd skew aside as frighted at our dressing.

We pack so many nations up that we

Wear Spain in waist, and France below the knee.

Thus are our backs affected and indeed

Our brains do travail with the selfsame meed.

We're Chaldees, Hebrews, Latins, Greeks, and yet

But few pure Englishmen are lapped in jet.

We scorn our mother language and had rather

Say *Pater noster* twice than once Our Father.

This makes our pulpits linsey-woolsey stut

30When buskined stages in stiff satin strut.

Nay clowns can say, 'This parson knows enough',

But that his language does his knowledge blough.

Is it not time to polish then our Welsh

When hinds and peasants such invectives belch?

Then English bravely study: 'tis no shame

For grave divines to win an English fame.

I've heard a worthy man, approv'd for learning,

Say that in plays and rhymes we may be earning

Both wit and knowledge: and that Sidney-prose

40Outmusics Tully, if it 'scape the rose.

Then purg'd from gall (ingenuous friends) peruse,

And though you chide the author, spare the muse.

N. W.

The Authors Apology.] 9 'Fragour' for 'fragrance' is rare, and of course wrong—all the more so because it is right for 'crash'. But it had somehow got into Italian before it came thence into English.

11 This wonderful Whitingism is, I suppose, to be interpreted 'screws' ('scrues' in original), 'stamps for minting'; *obs* and *sols*, *oboli* and *solidi*.

14 ermine] = 'parti-coloured'.

20 'Skew', orig. 'scue', is vivid for the great grand-paternal revulsion.

22 'N. W.' is not likely to have been ignorant of W. S.

24-8 Browne, with a curious self-irony, had not long before said the same thing in *Religio Medici*.

32 blough] = 'hood-wink', 'muffle', as in Blount. Cf. *Albino*, l. 309.

40 the nose] The *nasus aduncus*.

The Author to his Book.

Go gall-less infant of my teeming quill.

Not yet bedew'd in Syracusa's rill,

And like a forward plover gadd'st abroad,

Ere shell-free or before full age has strow'd

On thy smooth back a coat of feathers,

To arm thee 'gainst the force of weathers,

Doom'd to the censure of all ages,

Ere mail'd against the youngest rages.

Perchance some nobles will thee view.

10Smile at thee, on thee, like thee new,

But when white age has wrinkled thee,

Will slight thy measures, laugh at me.

At first view called pretty,

And perchance styled witty,

By some ladies, until thou

Wearest furrows on thy brow.

Some plumed gallants may

Unclasp thy leaves and say,

Th'art mirthful, but ere long

20Give place unto a song.

Some courteous scholar,

Purg'd from all choler,

May like, but at last,

Say thou spoil'st his taste.

First, lawyers will

Commend thy skill,

Last, throw thy wit

With Trinit's writ.

Chamber-she's

30On their knee

will thee praise,

and thy bays.

At first,

till thirst

of new

death you,

then all

men shall

Flee

40thee

Bee

me.

This is thy doom, I by prophetic spirit

Presage will be the guerdon of my merit:

Yet be no burr, no trencher-fly, nor hound,

To fawn on them whose tongues thy measures wound.

Nor beg those niggards' eyes, who grudge to see

A watch unwinded in perusing thee.

And if state-scratchers do condemn thy jests,

50For ruffling satins, and bespangled vests,

Tell them they're cozen'd and in vain they puff,

Thou neither aim'st at half-ell band or ruff:

And if thy lines perchance some ermines gash,

'Tis not thy fault, 'twas no intended lash.

Thy pencil limns Don Fuco's portraiture,

And only dost his native worth immure

Within these tilic rinds: nor is thy rage

Against the Cowlists of this youngest age.

Thy rhymes cry *Pax* to all, nor dost thou scatter

60Abuses on their shrines, their saints, or water,

And if some civil satire lash thee back,

Because he reads my title, sees my black,

Answer i' th' poet's phrase, and tell them more,

My tale of years had scarce outsummed a score

When my young fancy these light measures meant

The press: but Fate since cancell'd that intent.

Nor claim'd the Church as then a greater part

In me than others, bate my title Art—

But now the scene is changed? confess'd it is.

70Must we abjure all youth, born, bury this?

Such closet death's desertless, in this glass

Read not what now I am but then I was:

In this reflection may the gravest see

How true we suit—I this, and this with me.

These thorns pick'd out whose venom might have bred

A gangrene in thy reader, struck thee dead.

Thou mayst perhaps invited be to court,

And have a brace of smiles t' approve thy sport.

Those whose grave wisdoms wise do them entitle

80(Whose learned nods loud ignorance can stifle),

Some of time's numbers on thy lines will scatter,
If not call'd from thee by some higher matter.
Laugh out a rubber, like, and say 'tis good
For pleasure, youth, and leisure, wholesome food.
Some jigging silk-canary, newly bloomed,
When he is crispèd, bathèd, oiled, perfumed
(Which till the second chime will scarce be done),
Upon thy feet will make his crystals run,
Commend the author, vow him service ever,
90But from such things his genius him deliver!
Some sleekèd Nymphs of country, city, court
Will, next their dogs and monkeys, like thy sport:
Smile, and admire, and, wearied, will (perhaps)
Lay thee to sleep encurtained in their laps.
Oh, happy thou! who would not wish to be
(To gain such dainty lodging) such, or thee?
Say, to please them, the poet undertook
To make thee, from a sheet, thrive to a book,
And if he has to beauty giv'n a gem,
100He challengeth a deck of thanks from them:

And if some winning creature smile on thee
She shall his L. and his Bellama be.
Betwixt eleven and one some *pro* and *con*
Will snatch a fancy from thee and put on
A glove or ring of thine to court his lass,
'Twixt term and term when they are turn'd to grass.
Some Titius will lay by his wax and books,
And nim a phrase to bait his amorous hooks.

But stay, I shall be chid, methinks I hear

110A censure spread its wings to reach my ear,

Tell me I am conceited: then no more,

Go take thy chance, I turn thee out o' th' door.

Mart. ad lib. suum. Epig. 4

Aetherias lascive cupis volitare per auras,

I, fuge, sed poteras tutior esse domi.

Mart. lib. 4.

Si vis auribus Aulicis probari,

Exhortor moneoque te, libelle,

Ut docto placeas Apollinari.

Nam si pectore te tenebit ore,

Nec ronchos metues maligniorum.

Nec scombris tunicas dabis molestas.

Et cum carmina floridis Camoenis,

Litesque gloriam canas poetum

Non est pollicem capitis veraris.

The Author to his Book.] Most of this wedge-shaped address is clear enough. But the reader must fit his own sense to '*Bee* me' (ll. 41-2). Whiting's fantastic wit was quite Habakkukian in its possibilities.

53 'ermines' here = 'peers or other persons of distinction'.

57 'tilic[k]' = 'linden', from the use of lime-tree bark for paper.

58 Cowlists] Nothing to do (as I at first thought) with Cowley's early vogue, but one of Whiting's coinages, and frequently repeated *infra*, for 'monk'. Cf. l. 1945.

79-80 entitle—stifle] One of those assonances which we have seen frequently in Marmion, and which were among the rather too numerous licences of mid-seventeenth century prosody.

88 'crystals' = eyes.

100 deck] = 'pack' as with cards.

102 Whether 'L.' stands merely for 'Love', or whether the 'Signora Inconstanza' &c. bore the initial, or what else it means, one cannot say. Let us hope that Whiting's 'L.' *wore* better than Sterne's.

Mart. Lib. 4] This epigram, the 86th of the Book, is partly compressed, and the three final lines are different from those of the usual texts, which run:

Si damnaverit, ad salariorum

Curras scrinia protinus licebit,

Inversa pueris arande charta.

But I suppose Whiting did not choose to use evil words.

To his loving friend the Author.

To laud thy muse, or thee to crown with praise,

Is but to light my tapers to the rays

Of gold-locked Phœbus: since the scheme

Of fabled truth, thy waking seeming dream,

Thy ever-living-loving fame in arts—

Of arts, to us in whole and part imparts.

In arts, thy judgement, phrase, invention,

Of arts, thy poet's vindication.

In mourning elegies I admired thy skill,

10In mirthful lays we now admire thy quill.

Let Albine, Bellame, by thee live in fame;

Riv'lezzo, Beldame Pazza, live in shame.

Lash on and slash the vice of shavèd crowns

In thy Bardino, nuns, and sylvan clowns.

Give virtue beauty, beauty desert and praise,

And that thy monument of brass shall raise.

To his Loving Friend.] This anonymous commendator has dropped (hardly by intention) a foot in his third line.

To the Reader.

Reader take heed, complain not of the sting,

Lest others of thy galled sores do sing.

No faulty person, party, here is meant,

Only the vice o' th' age and place is shent.

He that expounds it of himself doth show

Some guilty fault or vice from him doth flow.

If touch'd to th' quick, conceal and them amend,

So 'gainst thee shall all scourging satires end.

WILLIAM PURIFEY, *Rector*

Ecclesiae de Markefield.

To the Reader.] 'William Purifey' at this date has an uncomfortable resemblance to William *Purefoy* (1580-1659) the regicide, who escaped meet guerdon by dying just before the Restoration. But he was a layman and a Member of Parliament.

To his loving kinsman the Author.

When first I view'd the travails of thy quill,

I lik'd, approv'd, admir'd thy nimble skill

In sudden raptures, fancies, judgement, phrase,

Invention, quickness, life, detraction, praise—

So that I favour'd their conceit which feign'd

The soul to be an harmony, and reign'd

Amongst the senses with accounts and measures,

All which thy lofty poesy entreasures,

That quaintest warblers cannot with delight

Outworth the poet in his lyric height.

As those which with quick eyes where judgement sits,

Thy vindication of poetic wits

Do read, may see, whose swelling metres teach

All aliens such high English that to reach

Is harder than to like or belch forth scandals.

Witness thy journey, *Somnus*, *Morpheus*, sandals,

The orbs, gods, muses, critics, accusation,

The poet's names, employments, vindication,

These silencèd my pen, it dared no more;

Till, voic'd by thy Bellame again, her store

Of suitors, one approv'd by friends, not her:

Rivelezzo's wrath (wherein most parents err),

Her grief, encloist'ring, entertainment high,

Albino's heart and hers met in their eye,

Their whisp'ring dalliance, Piazzella's care,

Bardino's falsehood, their affections rare,

Her disencloist'ring, and his nunning plot,

The nuns' thick bellies, his repentant grot.

His freedom, flight, encount'ring with his saint,

His conjuration, prodigies, and plaint,

The shepherd lout, Bellama's second quest,

His ghosting, coming from th' Elysian rest,

Their parles, his dis-enghosting, her denials,

His rage, her kindness, both their loves and trials,

Conrad's immuring, Piazzella's fury,

His freedom, Foppo and his monkish jury,

The lovers' ale-house cheer, bed, coarse apparel,

The monks' strict quest, their finding, mirth, and quarrel,

Their scape, fear, raddle, kinsman, and at length

Their nuptial tede, when malice lost its strength.

How thou hast shown (dear coz) thy art in arts,

Let them express who brag of abler parts

Than I, which have a bigger part in thee,

Thy love, and blood, till being cease to be.

JOHN WHITING,

Master of Arts, Clare Hall, Camb.

Amico suo carissimo N. W. huius Poematis authori Collegii Reg[i]nalis Canta. in artibus magistro.

Pan petat Arcadiam: Druides effundite cantus,

Et iuvenes flores spargite, Bardus adest.

Tu qui struxisti memoranda trophaea poesi,

Dicere multa tibi nescio, nolo nihil.

Vota, preces, calamus, cor, carmen, singula, laudes

Ultro perdignas, concelebrare student.

An decus, ingenium, tua laus, tua facta, peribunt?

Dignum laude virum musa perire vetat.

Corpore defuncto te candida musa sequetur

10Admiratur opus, primitiasque tuas.

Fata, precor, faustae plectant tua stamina vitae

Ut scribas opera plurima digna tua.

JACOBUS BERNARD sacrosanctae

& individuae Trinitatis Collegii

in artibus magister.

In Authorem, amicissimum suum, Encomiasticon.

The privilege that pen and paper find

'Mongst men falls short, reflecting to the mind.

Virtue herself no other worth displays

Than cank'red censure leaves behind, as rays.

But mental cabonets are they that yield

No forfeiture to batt'ring critics' shield.

If thoughts might character deserts, I dare

Challenge my pencil for the largest share.

But when the vultures of our age must gnaw,

10I'll cease for modesty, and say, 'tis law.

It's safer far to fail of debt than t' be

Soaring in terms that badge of flattery.

I hate the name, and therefore freely give

My verdict thus as may have power to live

'Gainst calumny. If wit and learning may

Pass with applause, the author hath the day.

Crown'd be those brows with everlasting bays,

Whose worth a pattern is to future days.

'Tis not a poem dropp'd from strength of grape.

20That's debtor to the wine's inspiring sap,

He to himself alone. Cease urging, earth,

The father well deserve[s] so fair a birth.

And, if a witness may be lawful, then

I'll undertake 't shall fear no vote of men.

But wherein Art is bold itself to glory

Is that which crowns the verge of Whiting's story.

JO. ROSSE.

In Authorem.] 5 cabonets] *Sic* in orig. It is a possible form of 'cabinets' (for we have 'cabon'), but in which particular sense of that word the reader must judge. That of a 'locked up', 'jealously guarded' receptacle might do.

22 'Deserve' in orig. John Rosse, though less eccentric in phrase, is rather more obscure in sense than even his *amicissimus.*

To his Friend, a Panegyric upon his lovers, Albino and Bellama.

Though I have vow'd a silence, and as yet

Resolvèd not to travel out in jet,

Chiefly in print, yet your intending press

Makes me my thoughts with courage, language, dress.

With smooth-strain'd metre, that the world may know

My strict engagements, and how much I owe

To you your worth, which may command a line

From him which swears 'gainst all but what's divine.

The highness of your style, the quickness, life,

10Will in judicious readers raise a strife,

(More than the ball amongst th' engoddess'd three)

Which gains the best, but all are best by me,

Matchless in my conceit: add then to these

The neatness of your plots, and swear a please

To the grim stoic and the satir'd brow

Forceth delight, through strictness, neatness, vow,

Grow abler still in fancy, imp thy quill,

Write anything, if something, fear not ill,

If poesy be thus revenged by thy dream,

20How will it flourish when 'ts thy morning theme?

Sleeping or waking, let us have thy quill,

And sleep and vigils shall admire thy skill.

I. PICKERING.

To his Friend.] The extraordinary badness of the orthography in the original may be judged from its form for panegyric—'Panagericke', which is, of course, mere ignorant setting from dictation, with no 'reading' to correct.

11 Does 'engoddessed' occur elsewhere? If not, I think I. Pickering should score for it, though it does not apply very well to three actual goddesses.]

Imprimatur.
Sa. Baker.
June 22, 1637.

Imprimatur.] Samuel Baker, Fellow of Christ's, Prebendary of St. Paul's, and Canon of Windsor and Canterbury, who was deprived of his preferments in the Rebellion, and seems not to have lived quite long enough to recover them. The reverse of the imprimatur leaf bears, in Professor Firth's copy, the inscription 'Ro^t Tebbutt His Book 1779'—a date at which the Carolines were not usually appreciated, though their turn was coming.

THE PLEASING HISTORY
OF *ALBINO* AND *BELLAMA*

When British Isles—begirt with moist'ned sand,

Neptune's blue palace, and the Triton's walk—

Albania hight, her name who first did land

Of all the sisters, or from rocks of chalk;

From sad oppression had unyok'd their necks,

And paid obedience unto Adell's becks,

Then, in those halcyon days of peace and joy,

A virtuous lady, most transcendent creature,

Fairer than her whose beauty cinder'd Troy—

10Grace deck'd her mind, her mind grace['d] her feature;

So that each part made Helen out of date,

And every grace a goddess could create.

Virtue and beauty both in her did strive

Which should in worth and grace surpass the other,

Nor age of consistency, both did thrive

Till this Dian' out-ray'd that Cupid's mother.

Nay men, by beams of her clear beauty, might

Scale Titan's chariot, and out-ray his light.

'Mongst Nature's precious things we find a gem,

20Blushèd and purpled o'er with amethysts,

Which fiery carbuncles with sparkles hem,

And which the em'ralds purest vert entwists,

Meeting so well that lapidaries wist

'Twas em'rald, carbuncle, and amethyst.

So in this precious pair, pure Agathite,

Aurora's purpling blush was clearly seen,

Saba's bright rose, and Leda's swan-like white,—

The true proportion of Adonis' queen—
Blended so well, that in this curious frame
30Aurora, Saba, Leda, Venus came.

And as the honey-making waxen-thigh'd
Inhabitants of Hybla's fragrant vales,
Whom only Nature's dim instinct does guide,
Choose their commander with their tuneful hails,
Pay homage, honour him, and fear his frowns,
With same observance as the people crowns,—
So, by the same instinct, the blushing rose
Vèil'd bonnet to her cheeks admirèd red,
The lilies to her bosom, brow, and nose,
40The Phoenix stripp'd herself to crown her head,
The chirping choristers with willing choice
Sat silent to admire her warbling voice.
Perfum'd Arabia with her spice and gums
Paid homage to the odours of her lips;
To her with fawning postures, licks, and hums
The yellow lion and the tiger skips;
Fire dares not scorch her face, nor winter chill her,
And death himself looked pale when called to kill her.
The amorous Sun, if she walk'd out by day,
50Would rein his jennets to behold her face;
And, wrapt in admiration, by his stay
Had rather melt the orbs than mend his pace;
And if the middle air in walls of jet
Enjail'd his beams, he thawèd into wet.
If in the reign of silent night abroad

She rang'd, the Empress of the lowest sphere,
Amazed at her perfections, left her road,
And rang'd about where she appeared t' appear;
Nay, mourned in darkness if denied her sight,
60As when day's henchman does deny her light.
The curlèd tapers of the firmament
Did cease to twink, but gazed with fixèd eyes,
In their own orb refusing to be pent,
And strove to leap upon the lower skies;
Nay, did o' th' second air like comets hang,
To dart their crisps at beauty's only spang.
The sea-born planet poppèd out her lamp,
And t' see herself outshin'd by her, did rage;
The marching war-god did remove his camp,
70With [this] fair lady curtain-war to wage;
Hermes by Jove being of an errand sent
Stay'd on her face, in her embraces pent.

Dull-agèd Saturn (on whose sullen brow
Ne'er dwelt a smile since Jove usurp'd his crown)
To gaze on her his weighty head did bow,
And with a smile unplaited every frown:
Nay, Jove himself descended from his chair
To take a full survey of this—this fair.
And more, her winning looks dispersed such charms,
80All eyes commanding and all hearts surprising,
That Venus bade her son provide him arms,
Fearing his setting by this bright star's rising:
For, though men say Love's eyes are more than dim,

Yet her fair beauty did enlighten him.

But with entreaties he had beat the air,

And on the tawny moor his waters cast,

For having pow'r to conquer, being fair,

Sh'ad pow'r not to be conquer'd, being chaste;

So that his amorous sleights and wingèd arrow

90Could not have oped her breast or pierced her marrow.

This Phoenix was Bellama called (a word

Well suiting her deserts), she daughter was

And heir-apparent to a wealthy lord,

Who had more acres than an acre grass:

He loved his lands, and hugged his minted treasure,

Yet his Bellama was his soul of pleasure.

His place of residence was in a chase

Chequered with thick-grown thorns and sturdy oaks,

Wherein majestic stags and bucks did pace

100That scorned the hounds, and dared the barbèd strokes;

'Twas called Rivelount, not distant far

From Starley, of that shire the metro-star.

The neighbouring swains were palled with coaches' thunder,

And loud curvettings of their foaming steeds,

Whose ironed hoofs did crash the rocks in sunder;

Happy was he, who (sheathed in costly weeds)

Could win admission to this happy place,

Where Nature's wealth was locked up in a face.

Each glance she sent the object did engem,

110And he that won a smile possessed a mine;

A hair was prizèd at a diadem,

A ribbon made the[m] tread the ecliptic line;

A ring outface a thunder, but a kiss

Was the elixir, heart, and soul of bliss.

Some of their lands, some of their valours spoke,

Some, of their falcons and their merry bells;

Some read the price of such a suit and cloak,

And one of hounds and running horses tells;

All speak of something, yet but few with wit,

120All aimed at wise, yet few could purchase it.

Some spake in oaths, as if they thought the earth

Was peopled o'er with faithless infidels;

Another swore, because he feared a dearth

Of other language, yet in oaths excels:

All swear enough, and he that did it least

Might be grand swearer at Ven-Bacchus feast.

Others there were that could not bigly prate,

Who did their evidences bring with them;

One brought his halls to plead, one his estate,

130This brought a watch to court, and that a gem;

One brought a large descent [in] white and black,

Which [he] derivèd from old Pergam's sack.

One brought a reverent sire, whom he called father,

To be the tongue of his reservèd son;

Others with much expense of wax did gather

Some printed rimes to speak when they were gone:

All had their speakers which unclasped their graces,

Yet their court-language dwelt on plaits and places.

One of these suitors was approved to be

140A match whose thousands equi-balanced hers;

The parents oft would say, 'This shall be he,'
The mother then a bill of love prefers:
But still Bellama faults, and vows that gold
Shall never force her love to have and hold.
The testy father, with a furrowed brow,
Comes to Bellama with demanding why?
Says 'Mine own girl, thou must be rulèd now,
Each knee pays duty to Don Fuco's eye:
And age well knows bean-manors, lands, and treasures
150Do cement lovers' hearts, and enjoy their pleasures.
Thou must not, wench, be coy. Alas! we find
Beauty as easily bought when money bids
(Though 't be i' th' nonsuch of the female kind),
As horse or cow, the lamb, or frisking kids:
If he be rich we bear his witless brags,
A wealthy fool's more worth than witty rags.'
Bellama, with a look fraught with disdain,
(Though hatred did not make her anger bold)

Says 'Sir, I'm sorry you do entertain
160Such high conceits of folly hemmed with gold:
Think you no marriage good if equal lands
Be not matchmakers and do join their hands?
Don Fuco has ten thousand pounds a year,
With weighty titles would o'erload a mule,
A piece of arras finely wrought and dear;
But does he square his life to virtue's rule?
With vice as wealth, to countless sums he thrives,
But is, in virtue, full as poor as wives.

He knows to steer an horse and hollo hounds,

170But not to guide his actions, less his tongue;

He speaks in state, but ev'ry sentence sounds

Of comic fragments or some tavern song.

And shall I him, hail'd by unworthy pelf,

Take to rule me, who cannot rule himself?

Shall I see other female vessels thrive

With mine own nectar, and they fee'd with money,

Whilst I like careful bee do keep my hive,

And work the comb for them to suck the honey?

No, I'll no sharers have in my delight,

180I'll have it one and only, else good night.

'Tis a fine thing to see a satin paint

That fears to lose her beauty in a press,

That only cares to be precisely quaint,

And spends a twelvemonth's pleasure on a dress:

To see this stroke his honour, and he clip her,

Span ev'ry part, and unresisted lip her.

But I do not in a rank humour rail

'Gainst sober purples, and discreeter robes,

Nor lock up virtues in the paper-jail

190With ink-horns, pens, spheres, globes, and Albo-globes.

Religion on my heart does love enneal

To those bright tapers of our commonweal.

Yet where, instead of state, proud looks do dwell,

Where wit and wisdom are unlocked with oaths,

Courtship and comeliness are in the shell,

And honour only sits upon the clothes.

Pardon, if unto such I plait my brow,

And steer my thought unto a virgin-vow.'

'Fie,' says the father, 'you're a foolish girl

200'Gainst ermines with that height'ned spleen to rail;

Dost think there's vice and folly in an earl?

Then virtue sure does penance in the jail.

To kiss and sport with us is held no sin

If that our dalliance do not pass the skin.

Perchance 'tis not a point of state to have

Too large a stock of wisdom in this age,

The epithet to greatness is not grave;

Those that the Muses in their cells encage,

Let them speak oil and civet; but we are lords,

210Can speak by signs, and not expressed by words.

Wherefore do we to Sable give the room,

And greater numbers far of Adel's stamps

Than to our steward or our lady's groom;

'Cause with reproofs he our choice pleasures damps?

No, 'cause in dedications he should name us,

And by some witty pamphlet make us famous.

Our moral virtues are no guiding rule

To high nobility, or looking-glass,

No more than t' earth the *ne plus ultra*'s Thule,

220As 'fore America was found, it was.

'Tis fit for those whose bosom-friends are lice,

To know the pain, not sweet delights, of vice.

Dost see yon tender webs Arachne spins,

Through which with ease the lusty bumbles break,

But to the feeble gnats that mesh their gins?

So those sage precepts, which our Sophies speak,

Fetter the passions of each worthless slave;

But over us no sovereign awe they have.'

'My lord, the name of father strikes,' quoth she,

230'An awful dread, and makes my ear obey;

Yet slip my duty down unto the knee,

And in my silent thoughts check, chide, and say,

"Can they that taste forbidden waters thrive?"

My chaste demeanour I will ne'er survive.

T' avoid the doom of—therefore I'll make choice

Of one whose virtue outs all love to vice,

Not those sleek skins which am'rous are in voice,

Lip-love which, as soon born, dies in a trice.

Our loves reciprocal shall be still dust,

240Which into exile packs unlawful lust.'

As they discours'd Don Fuco entered in,

With stately garbs befitting such a one,

His body shellèd in a satin skin

Of azure dye, bestarred with topaz stone,

A milk-white beaver, with an ostrich plume,

His very rowels spake a loud perfume.

Having composed his hingèd looks, he glanced

With piercing eyes upon her curious face,

And, steeping sighs in tears and sweat, advanced

250Himself to plead with courtly garb and grace.

But Fucus, led by most mimetic apes,

Could not depinge Don Fuco's antic shapes.

Such were the postures of his hands and eye,

That had he treasured up his mirthful tones,
They were ingredients for a comedy,
Would into laughter change a widow's groans:
And since that time (Bellama smiled so then)
Love in her dimpled cheeks has found a den.
'Madam,' says he, 'be pleased to trutinate
260And wisely weigh your servant's graceful voice;
Give due attendance to the airs of state;
I have engraven you Don Fuco's choice.
Give free assent, and let the scornful "No!"
Be quite expungèd from the criss-cross-row.
Alas, I'm not beholding unto letters,
Wherewith our rabbis stuff their swelling books.
I have a way of complimenting better,
To win thy love with comely garbs and looks.
And, if these fail, the name of countess will
270Speak with a power above the Sidney-skill.
I hate long-winded sentences, which do
Unbreath a man, and hazard much his bellows,
Or pocket-flashes which instruct to woo—
The only virtues of some inkhorn fellows—
I scorn their troths, indods, their ifs or ands,
Or their *O Lord, sir*, when their wit's o' th' sands.
A fluent rascal that can speak in oil,
And clothe his words with silken eloquence,
I know may give a virgin strength the foil.
280But a blunt earl that scarcely speaks in sense,
Whom thousands honour with the cap and leg,
Beats down a fortress like a roaring Meg.

He needs no Roscian language, but does send
His velvet-coated herald to proclaim
The noble titles which his worth attend:
For honour is th' ambitious lady's aim.
Feature and spicèd words but lead the van,
Honour the front, the noble is the man.'

'My lord,' says she, 'your valour I approve,
290That with three selves thus warranteth your suit,
With self-conceit, self-confidence, self-love:
Such trees will bear your lordship glorious fruit,
It well befits your greatness not to think
There can denials dwell in air or ink.
Your trencher-cloaks, and your recognizance,
Your coat of arms with noble ermines dight,
Your russian satin, with the cut of France,
Your talking rowels, and your feath'red white,
Are batt'ring rams and guns that speak in thunder,
300To crack a breast, and split a heart in sunder.
But my mind is Diana's chastest seat,
O'er which the breath of greatness hath no power;
The quiver-bearing boy sounds a retreat,
And Jove avails not with his yellow shower,
The vestal fire outshines blind Cupid's flame
Which oft's eclipsed with sorrow damped with shame.
And, troth, my lord, had I but wit enough
T' assist your lordship in your nuptial tede,
Your lordship should not play at blind man's blough
310(Else heavens should renounce their Ganymede):

For they that purblind are may plainly see

You grossly hoodwinked are in courting me.

The faults of state I cannot virtues name,

And bear myself upon the wings of pride,

Nor light my taper at another's flame,

Or use the art at beauty's eventide.

I brook not dalliance, or the Venus kiss,

That way of am'rousness, or that, or this.

I cannot seal a welcome with an oath

320To those whose absence I had rather have;

Nor venture hundreds at that paper-sloth

Of mistress Is'bel and the Pennell-knave.

I know no masking postures, nor with grace

Can tread the brawls, or true coranto pace.

I cannot at the feast of riot sit,

When sea, land, air, are served up in plate;

Nor like Tripherus with a carving wit

Read precepts this and this to dissecate.

Nor in dear murrhine, chargèd to the brim,

330Health it about until our mullets swim.

I do not love to have my husband be

Discreet by proxies, by his chaplains wise;

Nor do I like the too much cringing knee,

Whose formal bends his black conceits disguise.

Those fawning sharks I cannot call to table,

Which into ermines change your lordship's sable

To have my usher press his master's saddle,

In my opinion cannot pass for good;

I do not love to have my pillow addle,

340Meanwhile my woman lets your lordship blood.

I am no Androgyne, nor do delight

To diet pages, or your Catamite.'

'Madam, what passion does untune your mind?

What fiend' (says he) 'in you thus rails on greatness?

Who viceth honour, lies, and he is blind

That says court-satins are not trimmed with neatness.

Speak then in balms, forget the peevish why,

And to the "Wilt thou have this"—Answer "Ay".'

'No, no,' says she, 'yet might I know your saint,

350If my endeavours can advantage you,

With your endowments I would her acquaint,

And limn your rare perfections in her view:

In this one act I may myself approve

More loving, than in entertaining love.

I'll say with what dexterity you can

Run o'er the postures of the court-salute,

How trimly you can kiss a lady's fan,

And neatly manage an embroid'red suit;

How finely Spanish leg-shells you can plait,

360And tune your rowels at the court retrait.

I might say you are witty, if't be true

That jests and jingles are in brotherhood,

I'll speak your skill in hawks, at flight, in mew,

And at all hunting ceremonies good;

How gracefully you wave your gallant plumes,

And deeply are engaged to deep perfumes.

How kind you are unto our chamber-shes,

How to our marmosets and trencher-pages,

How oily-fingered unto supple knees,

370How fain to th' music of our wire cages.

How quaintly you supply the usher's room,

How sweetly you can act the privy-groom.

Much more in blazoning your matchless worth,

And counting all your specials, might I say—

But nature ne'er a second did bring forth,

Which to such known perfections can say nay.

I'll cease to praise them, lest my praises make

Your veins of pride with self-conceit to ache.

I will perform what I have promis'd, sir,

380Please you t' impart your lady to my maid,

I see my words your liver-wort does stir

Into your face, which in your channels strayed.

No more of trouble then, my lord, adieu;

This courteous door divorceth me and you.'

Away flings she, and leaves my lord alone,

More pensive than a widow which bedews

Her husband's corpse with tears, a woman's moan,

Or than the *Lupa* of diseasèd stews;

So that who saw his jigging head would swear

390Wisdom nor wit did ne'er inhabit there.

Don Rivelezzo sent a smiling glance,

That they might his consent read in his eye;

But seeing Fuco in a stupid trance,

He was possessed with equal frenesy.

The mother came to th' rescue, and wellnigh

Sent her own wit to bear theirs company.

Fain would he tell the cause of his disasters,

And eagerly her parents strove to know it,

Yet, strangely, them this passion overmasters,

400That neither they could ask, nor he could show it;

As though an Incubus with vap'rous throngs

Enclasped their bosoms and unvoiced their tongues.

At length Don Fuco cried, 'Bellama cruel,

What evil planet revelled at thy birth,

Or what incensèd god provided fuel

To make me feel hell's torture upon earth?

Was there no way to punish me for sin

But by a maid? No, there our woes begin.

When I with admiration view'd her face,

410I boldly durst give any tongue the lie

That dared to say, with such supernal grace,

There dwelt one atom of this tyranny.

But—if that virgin's hieroglyphics be

Of love and mildness, take them all for me.

I'll make a casement with this steely blade

In my full breast, through which my soul shall peep,

And make my heart in sanguine liquor wade,

And entrails all in juice of liver steep.

Nay, straightway give hell's ferryman his pay

420For wafting me o'er black Cocytus' Bay.

Or unto Proserpine I'll post a sprite,

To fetch m' a cup of moist oblivion,

Wherewith the Fairy Queen exilèd quite

Fury from her stout knight and Oberon,
That I not only may forget disgrace,
But quite forget I ever saw her face.'
'Let not', says Rivelez, 'a peevish girl
Hang fetters on your heart, untune your soul:
Dwells there not courage with a worthy earl,
430Blind Cupids bow and quiver to control?
My lord, take heed, the squinting boy works treason,
By passions to divest your soul of reason.
He by his sly insinuations oft
A good opinion in the heart doth win:
The most obdurate are by him made soft
And homage pay to Love their sovereign sin,
Fires in, nor hurts, the flint; but Cupid can
With flames to cinders waste the flinty man.
A wily fisherman hath store of baits,
440Wherewith for amorists he wisely angles,
With glitt'ring pomp he for th' ambitious waits,
The greedy carl with silver twists entangles;
The silk-lascivious with a wanton eye,
The austere stoic with a modest "fie!"
The studious Templant he with *Ergo* calls,
The grave precisian with a matron grace,
The virtuous mind with virtue he enthrals,
A landed heir with a blushed-lily face.
For Epicurean love he wisely trolls
450With spiced rarities and frothing bowls.
The cross-adorers he with crossing catches,
Yet strange it is that crossing should join hands.

But, to Sir Love-all, all are equal matches,

Grace, beauty, feature, honour, virtue, lands.

This has a dainty hand; that, lip, or eye,

This chaste, that seeming, that will not deny.

None are love-free, unless uncapable

Of those choice blessings Venus' sole son proffers,

None, whom age, fortune, nature, does enable,

460With peevish noes neglecteth Hymen's offers.

All are inclined to love, and all must bow,

If Cupid's arrow do but write "Love thou".

Invest your noble thoughts with courage, Don,

Let reason, maugre love, triumphant ride,

Millions of ladies breath in Albion,

Have more rose-lilies, and less store of pride.

I'll warrant, though Bellama now say "no",

She'll find, ere long, denial was her foe.'

'Ha!' quoth Don Fuco, with a far-fetched sigh,

470Which all that time was drenched o'er-head in grief,

'Am I to black Cocytus yet drawn nigh?

Where are th' Elysian shades, thou tott'red thief?

Call Rhadamanthus forth, justice I'll have,

Or in his breast my steel shall dig a grave.

Call forth the Furies with their snaky hairs,

Pale-cheeked Erynnis and her sister hags,

Tell Nemesis I'll fetch her down the stairs,

And try what truth dwells in her wrathful brags.

Dispoison vipers, toads, and crawling adders,

480And with their venom stretch her spacious bladders.

Bid Cerberus belch, from his triple jaws,
A barking thunder which the earth may shake:
I'll fetch the Dragon's and the Scorpion's paws
From the full zodiac, her face to rake.
Come forth, Demagoras, thy cunning try,
To mask all beauty with a leprosy.
We will no more our lily-stems transplant,
And set our roses on their cheeks and lips;
Their fairness shall not hence surpass the ante,
490Their crimson dye the brick or writhled hips.
Beauty shall be exiled, despite shall end her,
Or else we'll change her to another gender.
The Thracian harper was a silly ass,
That for his wife passed through the Stygian stench,
The clubman's foolery did his surpass,
That spun and carded for a Lydian wench.
The Greeks were fools that for a light-skirt strumpet
Chang'd the still viol to a loud-mouth'd trumpet.
Jove's blacksmith was no privy counsellor,
500To marry Venus for the forehead flag;
The jolly huntsman sure did something err
To see a goddess, and become a stag.
Jove was no golden show'r: sure 'twas a gull,
Nor e'er transform'd himself into a bull.'

'Peace, good my lord,' Don Rivelezzo says,
'What uncouth passion doth your soul entrance?
Your words are like the Bacchanalian lays,
Wherewith the priests their god of wine enhance.

What, man! though this fond she from you did start,

510Another 'll say, "My lord, with all my heart."

Observe the practice of doves masculine,

Which woo their females, with "I come to woo",

Not in a fit of woman cry and whine,

Straight to another haste, if she says no.

If to one face our stock of love we ope,

We pinion Cupid's wings, and fetter hope.

Bellama slights, what then? shall we conclude,

All women will deny you their assent?

A strange induction: call all ladies lewd,

520'Cause Flora and some few to Venice went?

Amongst a thousand maids, there's scarcely two,

As coy Bellama now hath done, will do.

Wherefore created were those glorious lights,

Which in the azure firmament appear?

Why was day's charioteer with lustre dight?

Only to gild with rays his proper sphere?

No, to lend brightness to the borrowing lamps,

And clear the earth from night's obscuring damps.

Why has Dame Nature so much brightness lent

530To diamonds, topazes, and other gems?

Only t' enrich themselves? no, to augment

The glory of our rings and diadems.

The ostrich for himself wears not his plumes,

Nor for 's own nose the civet cat perfumes.

So, on our sprucest ladies, matchless graces

Were not bestowèd to delight themselves.

Pandora was not treasured up in faces,

To bring content unto possessing elves.
But 'cause our heroes should the comfort find
540Of winning beauty and a willing mind.
The maid of Babylon, I know, was fair,
And rich in all the lineaments of beauty;
Yet was she kind, which did not them impair,
But showed to Nature's hests her forward duty.
For Nature's bounty best requited is,
By yielding free assent to Hymen's bliss.

The Queen of Carthage dear respects bestowed
Upon the straggling prince of ruined Troy.
Choice love unto Leander Hero showed:
550The Cyprian goddess wooed her sappy boy.
All fraught with pity; but that peevish girl,
'Bout whose sleek waist hell's vipers wind and twirl.
Nor such examples wants our latest age,
Of virgin lovers these to parallel,
Who, every way, those former equipage,
With whom records and modern pamphlets swell.
Then courage, Don, fear not to find a face
That hath more pity, and more lovely grace.'
'Much ease' (quoth Fuco) 'to my lovesick heart,
560My lord, is by your sage advisement brought.
For I supposed th' Idalian younker's dart
Had fest'red so, no easement could be bought,
I on her looked through such a pleasing glass,
As though that sex in her contracted was.
I thought t' have sent my physic-doctor forth

Unto his herbal, to address my ill;

T' ask Æsculapius for some earth-born worth,

Which might accomplish my intended will.

But that 'tis said Apollo once complained

570No herb to cure love's fevers could be gained.

Whilst an opinion of her matchless grace

Scorchèd my bosom with affection's gleams,

Mine eyes ne'er straggled to another face,

Nor could I bathe my thoughts in Lethe's streams.

But now I'll sound retrait; reclaim my mind,

Not catch a falling star, nor grasp the wind.'

This said, with sparkling sack he wash'd the lane,

Which to the limbeck of his body leads—

Health to Bellama, and a health again,

580Till, where his feet his wingèd beaver treads,

So well he took his sack without a toast.

That, 'stead of kissing her, he kiss'd the post.

Dispassioned quite, as in a breathless calm,

Don Rivelezzo bids Don Fuco 'dieu;

But hooted loudly, like a shrill-toned shawm,

When his swift steed took farewell of his view.

Accursing Fate, and railing on his daughter,

Which might beget in Heraclitus laughter.

'Have I', says he, 'such Crassian heaps of gold,

590Condemned to sleep in iron-ribbèd chests?

Did I delight in vestments coarse and old,

Wherein Anthropophages have dug them nests?

Nay, wish'd there were no tavern-juice, or sports,

Or change of fashions, but in princes' courts?

Have I sat brooding o'er my treasured plate,

And summed the surplusage of each year's rent,

Confined my spendings to a weekly rate,

Enjoined a penance when th' allowance spent?

And when an earl tuned every grace to win her,

600She slights his vows: nor gales nor gold can pin her!

But since she slights my matches, I will match her:

She shall of peevishness the harvest reap.

Since this Don's matchless fortunes could not catch her:

I shall ere long make her affections cheap.

Her love shall stoop to court a common farm,

A lordship then shall scorn to fold an arm.'

'My lord,' her mother, Lady Arda, said,

'A parent's ire ought not to force assent.

Wealth, blent with vice, can ne'er disheart a maid

610To whom bless'd virtue is the choice content.

There's other things do maid's affections stir,

Beside a manor, and a "please you sir".'

'Madam' (quoth he), 'in vain you do excuse

Your daughter's folly with your friendly air,

The next I offer she shall not refuse.

Sirrah, go harness straight my wheeling chair,

I'll try if less content and pleasure dwells

In princes' courts than in monastic cells.'

When he was coached, the Lady Arda went

620To fair Bellam', bedewed with streaming tears:

'The gods', said she, 'have ravelled thy content,

Sorrows uncomfort will thy virgin years:

For unto Darwey does thy father haste,

Where he will vow thee everlasting chaste.'

'Madam,' says she, 'I feed on naught but gall,

Aloes and rue, 'cause of my father's wrath.

Th' occasion though of his displeasure shall

With bays, instead of cypress, strew my path.

When virtue seals the contract, welcome Hymen,

630But till that, ever shall my heart deny men.'

Thus sate they parling. Lady Arda urged,

Producing reasons to enforce assent.

Bellama answered, begged, excused, and purged

Herself from blame, by urging love, content.

But urging and excusing, let them sit,

And see the father champing on the bit;

Who, coming to the cage of virgin-pride,

Knocked at the wicket with the iron crow,

To whose small neck white fillets ne'er were tied.

640Which in more ancient days did childbed show.

He rapped so hard, the sound did fright the air,

Yet still none came: none was not locked in prayer.

At length the janitor, of stature large,

With crozier-staff, girt in a hair-cloth frock,

Whose meagre looks did call for Charon's barge,

And all whose body was a sapless stock,

Came, and with churlish voice demanded who

With such shrill ho's rejoiced their civil croe.

'Friend,' says my lord, 'my errand wings my speed,

650Speaks high importance with the prioress;

Thou, in these angel-looks, my haste mayst read;

Help me to th' presence of the abbatess.'

The porter's heart soon stepp'd into his eye,

Tuning his language to a quick reply.

'My lord,' says he, 'obedience is my duty,

Whilst your commands speak in so high a tone.

Yet, lest your smooth-chinn'd youths lay siege to beauty,

Your lordship, spite of state, must walk alone.

I am an eunuch; else in vain I vow'd,

660I had mistook my pillow in a crowd.'

Him he conducted to the kitchen, where

Store of anatomies employed was;

Some did the candlesticks, some lavers clear,

Some scourèd pewter, some reburnished brass,

Don asks the cause; the porter him acquaints,

'Twas 'gainst a feast of high account, All Saints.

Within the hall a younger sort of girls,

Yet coarse enough, did brush vermilion looks.

Some crosses rubbed, some, ropes of praying pearls;

670Some dusted vestments, some, their gilded books.

Some kneaded wafers: and his effige stamped,

Whose purple streams the dragon's sulphurs damped.

All at Don Rivelezzo were amazed,

And, looking, one rubbed off a nose of wax,

A second razed a cheek; another gazed

And plucked from Kath' her periwig of flax.

One blinded Serrat, and did rend her silk;

One broke the cruse, and spilt the virgin-milk.

Don passed through these into an inner room,

680Where was another rank of virgin-fry,

Some weaving arras on the nimble loom,

And intertwisting gold with tapestry,

With silk of Naples twisted in small ropes;

Some did the cowls embroider, some the copes.

At last he came into an upper place,

Climbing thereto by richly gilded stairs,

Where sate another troop, of nobler race,

On quilted cushions, and in ivory chairs.

About the centre, in a robe of state,

690The matron Vesta of the virgins sate.

These were employed about far nobler things,

For some of sainted hair did bracelets twine;

Others strung beads to stint the knees of kings;

Some trimmed with costly gems the Lady's shrine.

One tuned the music, and a witty other

Footed an *Ave* to the Virgin-mother.

The grave old matron, crawling from her throne

Of Indian teeth, arched o'er with cloth of gold,

Upon her aged knees with zealous tone

700Says, 'Heaven's messenger, what is't you would?'

Th' amazed lord with wonder quarrelled long,

Ere he could unvoice his silenced tongue.

'Madam,' says he, 'why pay you reverence?

Why are you guilty of th' adoring sin?

'Tis a delusion of your weak'ned sense,

I am no Cherub, Pow'r, nor Seraphin.

The heralds style me Rivelezzo's Don,

Your friend and servant, with a cap and con—'
'My lord,' quoth she, 'excuse my fond mistake,
710For o'er my sight I wear a duskish glass.
My zeal in pious actions sure did make
Me give you more respects than civil was.
But take your seat; and if my power or skill
Can crown your wishes, be you sure I will.'
'Madam,' says he, 'I have a scornful lass
Whom nature has enriched with special grace,
To whose perfections her reflecting glass
Is parasite, adds pride unto her face:
So that, though earldoms court her, her disdains
720Nonsuits their service, and her brow unplains.
Into your number of chaste-zealous shes,
Entrance unto this girl vouchsafe, I pray,
Unto your order. I the constant fees
Of gold and acres, and of vows will pay.
Since she Don slighted, I have vowed to see
How long she'll honour the religious knee.'

Quoth she, 'Those virgins which my hallowed roof
Does canopy, my prudence does protect.
I make blind love and folly stand aloof,
730And all love's paper-plots I do detect.
Great ones have oft assayed, but yet my care
Has buried their entreaties in the air.
With godly precepts I enrich their minds,
And make them (which is rare) at eighteen good.
I 'dmit no roisters; only maids and hinds

To do them service, and prepare us food.

Please you to send your daughter, she shall be

Crowned with delights of most transcendent glee.'

'Heavens', says Don, 'crown your ensuing days

740With all delights which wait your holy orders,

May the sad cypress and the bridal bays

Ne'er sprig nor blossom in your quiet borders.

I'll plume my swift endeavours: I'll make haste

T' invest Bellama with your habits chaste.'

When Don's farewell had ceased to move the air,

Says Piazzella to her virgin train,

'We, with th' enjoyment of this lady fair,

Shall stuff our carcanets with mickle gain.

We'll frolic it, and taste the choicest pleasures,

750Nor shall our joys be listed in with measures.

The credulous world we gull with silver shrines,

Our grave behaviours and retired lives,

When we in naked truth are libertines,

And taste the pillow joys of sprightful wives,

When through the vault our lusty shavelings pace,

All the choice measures of delight to chase.'

Thus leave them with their hair-lack crowns,

And see Rivelezzo now arrived at home,

Who by that time had plained his brow from frowns,

760And all becalmed with sugarèd words doth come:

Then tells his lady he had found a tow'r,

Would guard Bellama from Jove's yellow show'r.

Servants are posted to the old Exchange,

Others to sellers of the silkworm's spoils,

Some to brisk Proteuses, smirk tailors, range,
Some to the stationers, some haste for oils.
One carves the image of a martyred saint,
Another breathes a soul with gold or paint.

None must be idle till, in marshalled ranks,
770All things be ord'red for this virgin-vow.
Farewell ye spongy teats and puff'd-paste flanks,
Bellama's bridal tede is lighted now.
Her husband is Virginity, yet look,
Her beads for rings, for songs she'll change her book.
The coach is harnessèd, 'Bellama come',
The father says, 'hence with that dew of grief;
Give not a sad adieu unto our home,
But in thy thoughts let comfort rule as chief.'
She craved a blessing on her globe-like joints;
780Then coachèd thither where her sire appoints.
As the sweet-voicèd Philomele does sit
I' th' pikèd eglantine, with sorrow dressed,
'Cause some rude sylvan in a raging fit
Snatched her faint chickens from their downy nest.
So did the lady Arda, dight with mourning,
Deplore Bellama's loss with her returning.
As when sly Reynald in his widenèd jaws
Is seizing on the nimbly-frisking lamb,
Or when the tiger, with his sharp'ned paws,
790Hath caught the infant of the becking dam:
And then the shepherd's care prevents the sharks,
One loudly howls, the other hoarsely barks.

So, semblably, when as the waiting crew

Saw the departing of their golden age,

One gives Bellama, with eye-dew, adieu,

Another's grief unlocked the frenzy cage.

Some tore their hair, some rent their should'ring bands,

Some thwacked their breasts, and wrung their oily hands.

But all in vain, their Indian mine was gone,

800Their minting house deprivèd of the stamp,

Their costly gems were changed to pebble stone,

Their hemisphere forsaken by their lamp:

Saturn's exiled, Jove awes this massy ball,

And now the iron age ungoldeth all.

The wand'ring wheels, bestud with iron knobs,

Posted Bellama to the virgin-tower,

Which freed her from the noise of servile throbs;

Is entertainèd like a goddy power,

Led by the seeming saints unto the place

810Where sate Pazzella with a matron grace.

If Rivelezzo's presence frighted them,

Much more they at Bellama were amaz'd;

They called her Phoenix, beauty's only gem,

And all with fixèd tapers on her gazed:

Some had a mean, some curious were before,

But her first sight showed self-conceit the door.

For as when Tithon's bride breaks out afar,

And through th' expanse spreads forth her youngest light,

She, by degrees, pops out each twinkling star,

820And dims at length the mistress of the night—

As winter chapel-clerks, when prayers are done,
Dis-light each flazing wax or tallow sun.
So, when Bellama brightly did appear,
With morning rays in the monastic hall,
She veiled each face that movèd in that sphere,
And further, by degrees unfacèd all.
Nay, at the last, the mistress of the train
Looked like pale Phoebe in her dark'ned wain.
And as day's prince, light lustre's archi-beam,
830Lends to the moon her silver midnight rays;
As from the ocean wat'ry current stream
Though ev'ry cadent to that Chaos strays;
As to a room befogged with mists of night
Th' incensèd weeks do lend a midday light;
So to each brow Bellama's brow gives white;
To ev'ry cheek Bellama's cheek gave roses;
To ev'ry eye Bellama's eye gave sight;
To ev'ry breath Bellama's breath gave posies;
To ev'ry part Bellama's part gave grace;
840To ev'ry face Bellama gave a face.
Some called her goddess of the Cyprian isle;
Some said Troy's ruin was untombed again;
Some her the self-enamoured boy did style;
Some said the boat-boy did delude their train.
One named her thus, one said she was another,
But all confessed sh' exceeded Cupid's mother.
The aged patroness with palsied lips
Mutt'red a welcome to her lovely guest;
But at that time the moon was in eclipse,

850Which with enfeebling fears did them arrest.

Some shrilly screamed; some brazen pans did clang,

To ease her travail and abate her pang.

And when the monthly-hornèd queen had got

Her face again with silver glitter rayed,

Save only what the dragon's tail does spot,

On their pale lilies blushing claret strayed.

Then did the aged voice repeat again,

'Welcome, fair lady, to my maiden-train.'

Her instauration was somewhat strange.

860Led by nine vestals (for th' odd number was

Highly esteemèd in their sacred range,

As by the poet in his quaffing glass),

Each of her jointed lilies one did hold,

Save only that which waits the wedding gold.

Adorned with vestures, white as bleachèd snow,

A cypress mantle over which was cast,

So lightly hung 'twould not abide a blow,

A milk-white ribbon locked unto her waist,

Graced with a crucifix: her slender wrists

870With praying beads were wreathed on sable twists.

Grave Piazella ushered her along,

Bravely attended with her choicest nuns,

Without drum, trumpet, or an armèd throng,

Or champing coursers, or the wide-mouthed guns.

Each held religion in some holy right,

With holy water which the devils fright.

Into the place of holy worship they

Ent'red where gaudy superstition was,

Saints, altars, store of crucifixes gay,

880Whose stately worths my weak expression pass.

Scarce was there known a canonizèd saint

Which carving did not there beget, or paint.

With strong devotion all the virgins prayed

At the direction of the praying bead,

Their *Ave-Maries, Santo, Salve's* said,

Invoking ev'ry saint to intercede.

Piezza then, Bellama kneeling down,

Did wreathe her temple with the virgin-crown.

These rites performed, behind an iron grate

890Appearèd breathing cowls and walking copes,

Whose writhèd looks their births did antedate

And change the ciphers girdled in with ropes.

Their hair had purchas'd wings and flew away.

So did their brains, as some did whisp'ring say.

Unto this monast'ry in gloomy shades,

From Crostfull Priory these shavelings pace,

Distant from hence not two Italian stades.

Earth's bloodless womb was wimbled all the space.

Under the craggy rocks and champian did

900A roadway lie, from vulgar prying hid.

This darksome path they usually did tread

To traffic with their she-sequest'red zeal,

With whom for curtain-dalliance oft they plead.

But their success my muse dares not en-neale.

These loving sportings are not faults: the sin

Is when our walls keep not the scandal in.

Amongst the holy men that hither came,

To join their issue with the sisterhood,

A votary, Albino call'd by name,

910Not Fortune's white-boy, yet of abbey-blood.

His great-grandfather, some few ages since,

Of Glastonbury primate was, and prince.

His stature did not reach the tip-toe height,

Nor with the long-necked cranes did conflicts wage,

Something complete by nature not by sleight,

Some twenty circled snakes summed up his age;

Discreet as tiroes are, had store of wit,

In that he knew to use, and husband it.

By civil carriage, and his modest look,

920He gained the love of his lord Priorist,

He bowlèd, coursèd, angled in the brook,

His pleasure was his joy and pleasures list.

Oft would he rove (had his content a dearth)

Through th' hollow belly of th' unbowelled earth.

Sometimes permitted, sometimes by command

From his Lord Prior to the holy mother.

Conveying voices, or the paper-hand

Oft-times alone, scarce sorted with another.

The matron did with courteous eye respect him;

930Knowing no ill of him, did not suspect him.

She oft would praise his monkship to her train,

Calling his breast blest virtue's choice's shrine;

And vowed she seldom saw such beauty reign

Upon a face that's purely masculine.

And 'twas not common at his years to find

So neat a person with so pure a mind.

He'd freedom of discourse, not privacy,

Jests, sporting, laughter, and lip-dalliance;

Oft on Bellama would he fix his eye,

950And she to him would answer glance for glance.

They gazed so long and oft, till they did tie

Their hearts together only by the eye.

Love's fever, at the casements of the soul

Ent'ring, inflamèd every secret part,

That passion now his reason doth control,

And with the gyves of love enchains his heart:

And walking with Bardino, seeking pleasures,

He did Bellama sing in lofty measures.

To his companion in praise of Bellama.

Dost see yon tow'ring hills, yon spreading trees,

950Which wrap their lofty heads in clouds? Dost see

Yon house of little worth, and lesser height?

Dost think a jewel of ten thousand weight

Can dwell within that sooty carcanet?

Dost think the gaudy sun each night does set

And riseth from yon roof? Dost think the moon,

With double horn and glitt'ring tapers, soon

Will issue thence? Didst ever see an eye

Which checked the beams of awful majesty?

Dost think an earth-born beauty can be found,

960Which darts forth lustre from the sullen ground—

To kiss the glorious skies? Or canst thou think

The queen of beauty dwells in such a chink?
Dost think? 'tis poor, why do I question so?
Thou dar'st confirm all this by oath, I know,
Since my Bellama's there, all life, all breath,
Whose presence can enlive the soul of death,
Despite of sickly Nature: she is all fair
And truly meriteth Bellezza's chair.
All those fair treasures, which dispersèd lie
970'Twixt poles and parallels, pay to her eye,
And with her span contracted in her meet
As radiant, red, white, smooth, soft, rich, and sweet,
She is the world's epitome and soul,
And with her inch of earth outworths the whole.
She's beauty's archi-fount: as riv'lets small
Borrow from greater currents, and they all

Pay tribute to the ocean, just so
The dimmer shafts of wingèd Cupid's bow
Borrow from brighter, [and] the brightest pay
980Homage unto Bellama—beauty's day.
I tell thee there's not one small worth of hers
But loudly says that foppish Nature errs
In other beauties: nor is this all, for why?
Her thoughts pluck stars, and dark th' imperial sky.
Virtue and beauty both: why, 'tis as rare
As frosts in June or comets in the air,
As crows in Africk, Æolus want puffs,
Or she-precisians want Geneva ruffs.
Yet my Bellam', alone and one, unites

990The beauteous colours, noble red and whites,

With heaven's issue, Virtue: dar'st then deny,

If not divine, her half a deity?

Tip Cynthia's horns with wonder, wind aloud,

And mount the saddle of a wingèd cloud,

Then circle earth, and see if thou canst find

Half such a feature with so rare a mind.

I know when thou return'st thou'lt say with me,

Bellama's beauty is a *A per se.*

Thus he to rocks and bushes did discover

1000The secret flames which scorched his heated breast:

Though he as yet was not a vocal lover,

But shrouded his close love in smiles and jest.

Yet Fortune oftentimes does Venus grace.

He got lip-freedom in an eyeless place.

For there a Turk's Elysium was the stage

Whereon the virgins acted parts of mirth,

Which Nature did with nobler gifts engage,

And deckèd more than other parts of earth:

And Bellam's breath was such a powerful thing,

1010It here did keep an everlasting spring.

The angry puffings of congealing East

And sturdy North, cold Winter's stoutest roisters,

Durst ne'er of curled locks the trees divest,

Nor e'er were heard to whistle in their cloisters.

Such vernal blasts came from Bellama's mouth

Kept here Favonius, and the dropping South.

And if sharp frosts did, in her absence, steal

Into this place, and glaz'd the tattling streams,

Then into crystal would the springs congeal,

1020And ev'ry flower was rayed with silver beams.

Yet if Bellama did but glance her eye,

The crystal and the silver thence did fly.

Nay, strange it was to hear the purling wet,

The saucy frost with angry murmurs chide,

And with its constant jars and strugglings fret,

Then thaw to tears, and on the Venice slide.

Yet oft Bellama would call in her rays,

To view the silver purls and crystal ways.

Into this garden once Albino got;

1030Yet ah! but once, and met his sovereign fair,

Hoping their hearts should tie the Gordian knot

He fanned her beauty with such courting air.

For, though he was a monk, love did instruct him,

And to Love's palace Fortune did conduct him.

He oftentimes with trembling thumb would press

Her dancing vein, way to her heart to find,

Whilst conscious she her looks with red would dress,

Fearing her pulse was traitor to her mind.

For 'tis entruthed by some that by this vein

1040We may the knowledge of affections gain.

Such knowledge gained he by her pulse's touch,

Which leapt to meet, not chide, his busy thumbs,

That he desired a kiss; and found it such

Whose sweetness far outsweet[en]s Hybla's combs:

Then cried, 'Give for each lip a cherry sweet,

And then a third, in which they two may meet.'
Such quick'ning heat was from those kisses lent,
That thawed his voice and did unfreeze his tongue,
Packed thence despair, exilèd discontent,
1050And made him vent what was concealèd long.
For though desire and love each minute bid him,
Yet fear, his habit, and her beauty, chid him.

'Madam,' quoth he, 'vouchsafe a courteous ear
Unto my words, sent from an amorous heart.
Which hath long time been wracked with hope and fear,
Grisly despair, and Cupid's awful dart,
And till this time (restrained by black disasters)
Could ne'er apply lip-love or vowel-plasters.
Be pleased to know (yet sure you needs must know it)
1060A beauty so divine must needs divine,
Though I should want heart, hand, or voice to show it,
When first your beauty in mine eyes did shine,
They slipped into my breast, and told my heart
The god of love by them had sent a dart.
My heart made quick reply (if hearts have voice)
You ever have such faithful servants been,
That what you like, I'll freely call my choice:
For beauty, brought by you, does fires teen.
Carry this message back, tell her 'tis best
1070That hers should heat my bosom, I her breast.'
'Peace, peace.' quoth she, 'speak not a work of love,
For fear my anger scorns and folly writes.
Eagles love eagles, and the dove the dove.

Hawks brook not buzzards: or the pheasant kites.

Equals love equals: but unequal flame

Is teened with folly, and expires with shame.'

'True, quoth he,' likeness does the heart incline;

Greatness loves greatness without farther search,

Yet crawling ivies lofty elms entwine,

1080And gall-less turtles with the eagles perch.

I baulk your greatness: for as good, not great,

I homage pay, and loves alarums beat.

Those airy titles which ambition swell,

And puff like bladders [are] like bladders burst,

The worldling's goddess, which in chests does dwell,

Is gnawn with rust, and makes the chesters curst.

Honour is tied unto the prince's eye

And wealth to Fortune's mutability.

I have not wealth (nor do I want), what then?

1090Must Hymen stoop unto the nods of gold?

Must I vail bonnet unto ermine men?

And virtue by the herald be controlled?

No, love does blaze the noblest arms: and she

That can maintain herself in love, can me.'

'Stay, stay.' quoth she, 'you will be out of wind.

Methinks the voice of greatness speaks delight.

Our poets only then feign Cupid blind,

When children of the sun do dote on night,

Or folly, mounted on Icarian wings,

1100Courts queens' affections and does gaze on kings.'

'No,' says Albino, "tis the contrary.

Love never is more purblind than when earth
Joins house to house, and pedigrees do tie
Scutcheons to scutcheons in pure virtue's dearth.
For regal flames blest goodness only teens,
And virtue ought to court the love of queens.
We all are born for public good: 'tis vain
With torchlight to embellish Titan's rays,
Or cast our stock of water in the main,
1110Such love from laws of love and nature strays.
But those that Fortune hath enriched with goods
Should dam up nature's wants, by mixing bloods.
Was I the Caesar of the Roman stems,
(Once only darling to the King of skies),
Did both the Indies pay me tribute-gems,
I'd not unite a double majesty.
For being no distinction in degree,
She would assume that honour due to me.
She'd chide me sooner than I durst check her,
1120And (as the proverb) *quarrel for the breeches.*
On some choice mean that honour I'd confer
Should sue with humble 'Sirs', and low beseeches.
Thus was she tied to payment of respects,
I licensed with state-love to mix neglects.
Where beauty does indite, and virtues seal,
Greatness is not required to set his hand:
Though greatness here may virtue's acts repeal,
Yet virtue's acts in Cupid's courts must stand.
Then where I find grace, feature, virtues, dwell,
1130I've greatness, wealth, and honour—toll the bell!

Then with kind airs, life of my wishes, speak,
Bid honour know his distance, wealth depart,
And let the day of true contentment break
From thy clear lips, to cheer my misted heart.
O, with one circle let my arms enfold
The soul of honour and the heart of gold.'

'Sir,' quoth Bellama, 'wealth is not my aim,
Nor does the gales of honour heave my soul,
I higher prize an action than a name,
1140And value more a pamphlet than a roll.
Where I with comeliness find virtue mixed,
My love, eyes, thoughts, are on that object fixed.
I speak not much of love, lest you presume;
And speak a little, lest you should despair.
I would not have my words your hopes deplume,
Nor feather them to reach the highest air.
I sum up all in this, whenas I say,
I will not with disdains thy service pay.'
Oh happy words! oh more than sacred breath!
1150Albino, live! Bellama says thou must.
Confront dire Fate, and challenge meagre Death:
'Tis not in them to moulder thee to dust.
Yet be advised, let not proud folly in,
The conquest is as great to hold as win.
Our anchorist with all the words that joy,
Hearting a lover, was acquainted with,
Accosts his saint, rewards the wingèd boy,
And congees to the queen of heat and pith.

Smilèd and glanced, paid thanks, desired a kiss;

1160And prayed time give an age unto his bliss.

But when day's lamp had wan the western clime,

And wrapt his head in sea-green Thetis' lap,

Our lover must observe the chanting time

And bids his saint adieu. Oh hard mishap!

Oh, 'tis a hell to think what hellish pain

True lovers by unkind divorcement gain!

Yet, by that time the hoary-headed sire

Had summed twelve sixty minutes, he again

Returned t' his lady, when bright Titan's fire

1170Was newly risen from the brackish main:

And, common greetings passed amidst their pleasures,

He in his lady's hands these lines entreasures.

Upon Bellama's walking in the garden, and with him.

My teeming fancy strives, choice fair, to chain

Eternity to time, that ne'er shall wane;

And make those garden-minutes see the sun

Entombed in darkness, and the earth unspun

Ere they expire, that all succeeding times

May know and tell the subject of these rhymes.

Assist me, Flora, that I may with grace

1180Worthy its honour, shadow forth that place

Of spreading trees, sweet herbs, and fragrant flowers,

Enriched with pleasing walks and shady bowers.

Each twig, with amorous touch, embraced his mate,

Like Bacchus' sacred tree his propping state;

Or ivy, elm, that neither sun nor wind

To his retirèd conclaves passage find.

Within whose walls a half-night's darkness dwells,

Which satyrs' growing palaces excels,

Or anchorets' secluding hermitage.

1190Here, like a common theatre or stage,

Each spicèd child of earth, in summer robe

And Iris' mantle, opes his closèd globe,

Knows his appearing cue, and freely plays

O' th' wished-for presence of your quick'ning rays.

Such perfect vivifying influence

Dwells in your looks, Light's chariot driven hence,

That your sole presence can create a spring,

From winter's frozen bands can loose each thing,

From earth's entombing sepulchre can raise

1200Each sleeping flow'r, to chant forth Maia's praise.

This made amazement seize my mind to view

Half-agèd winter bid so soon adieu

To this Elysium of the pagans' joy.

And Chloris, with her new-brush'd clothes so coy

Before, and hardly to be won, come forth

Crowned with the glory of her springing worth,

To court our eyes, nay more, the bare-faced earth

Covered with carpets green, befringèd round

With smiling rosy trees, with glorious store

1210Of daisies, suckles, cowslips, studded o'er.

Like hunting vests of satonisco green,

Embossed with gems by fawns and wood-nymphs' queen,

Worn when the tushèd boar, bear, panting hart

Th' unkennel, rouse, disfrank with nimble art.

And, lest your spotless souls should suffer ill,

Air's fleeting tuns crystalline streams distil,

To wash the grassy-tufted tapestry

Which whistling winds, with murm'rings, haste to dry.

And ev'ry tender branch whereon you tread

1220To make your tracing, pacing, moves its head.

Alcinous' orchard, or that precious root

Which bore old Atlas' daughters golden fruit;

Th' Idalian mount where Cytherea strayed,

Or that where Ceres' luckless daughter played

Whenas the king of shades surprisèd her.

Nor may the Roman's pride with this confer,

For here all Maia's treasures are united

Which do, which shall, or senses e'er delighted,

Yet summered by your eye each flower does bud,

1230Blossoms, sprouts, opens, blooms, and chews the cud.

Your presence hearts them all. O be as kind

As unto them to me; shoot through my rind.

Shine through my heart with one, one smiling ray!

So shall it open, blossom, sprout as they—

Spiced with the choicest sweets e'er Venus had,

In all the postures of true service clad,

Trimmed with the beauties of the richest spring.

All fertile too, all store of fruit shall bring:

This, choice affection; that, chaste loyalty;

1240This, vows; that, service; and that, constancy,

Made up into a nosegay, circled in

With twists of love, which youth and virtue spin.

Then, breath and ray, make and accept the posy
And seal a contract 'twixt the lily and rosy.

Enspherèd thus with virgins, oft he would
Tell pretty tales, fraught with conceited mirth,
Discourse of foreign states sometimes unfold,
(A sudden jest may give to laughter birth.)
Thus to beguile the time, he oft would do,
1250And unsuspected did his lady woo.
Then privately sometimes with her would walk
Along a pavèd way, where lofty trees
Bore only witness of their am'rous talk,
Plaiting their branchèd pride that none might see.
And, lest quick envy should their dalliance spy,
Themselves about the trees the brambles tie.
Here in soft whispers did he court her love,
And strove by oath their loves to ratify.
'Madam,' says he, 'this reason may you move,
1260That day and malice have too many eyes
When my lips are sealed, and I attempt in vain
To send the children of my teeming brain.
Not half so vigilant the dragon was,
Which Colchos' treasure watch'd, as is your dame;
So that they must through Argus headpiece pass
Which seek here to enkindle Cupid's flame.
I know your jealous matron does discover
How my faint heart about your breast does hover.'

'Sir,' says Bellama, 'there is no such haste.

1270Time will appoint our loves some fitter seasons,

My father must ungirdle first my waist,

Love will not be repelled by force, but reasons:

And more, you know it is in vain to strive,

Here's no escaping this monastic hive.

When as the third day's sun, three hours or more,

Our zenith has behind him left, hither

Return, and I will meet thee; not before'.

'My thoughts', quoth he, 'do in your absence wither,

Pinched with the sharpest blasts cold winter breathes,

1280But your, *your* looks, my heart with blossoms wreathes.

That foolish glass, which measures time with sand,

Enough of gravel has to meet a year.

With lesser trouble I could Hermes' wand,

Than the sad torture of your absence, bear:

Change then those hours to minutes, days to day;

If you say't shall be so time must obey.'

'Alas,' quoth she, 'my faith is not so strong,

To think reality with language dwells,

Nor can I think you count those minutes long

1290When you're employèd with your beads and bells.

Yet t' has the face of truth: I'll therefore try

If time will pay such duty to mine eye.'

'These words have lent my body a new soul,

And shot', quoth he, 'a fire through every vein;

Doubt not your voice time's circle can control,

And make the sun his hasty jennets rein.

Nay more, methinks m' enlight'ned eyes discover

'Bout you the gods with veilèd bonnets hover.

I'm half-persuaded 'twas not blasphemy

1300For me to say your nod can ravel Fate;

Thaw into chaos this firm globe of dry;

Beckon the planets; and their tow'rs unslate.

Methinks I see the sun nailed to his sky,

Unnath his car, and throw his whipstaff by.'

'Peace, peace,' quoth she, 'Albino! thou dost rave,

Why dwells such language on thy wretching tongue?

Wilt thou just vengeance force to dig thy grave?

Think'st thou stern Fate will suffer such a wrong?

Pinion thy words; let them not soar so high,

1310Lest they should gash the clouds and ope the sky

We must not play with sharps, nor kiss the flame,

Dally with heaven, or upbraid the gods,

Lest their just anger make their powers tame

Such saucy scandals with their plagues and rods.

Then wing no more Bellama's name, but let

The pearl be callèd pearl, the jet but jet.

Go home in clouds, lest Envy see thy face;

And come not till those minutes task the watch.'

'Madam,' says he, 'I'll bid them mend their pace.

1320'Tis just with lovers every hair to catch

That dights occasion's brow, change date for date,

Entrench sometimes upon the rights of Fate.

Yet your command shall stand, I'll not transgress,

But watch the hand until it joint the hour,

And all my paths with gloomy shades will dress,

That undiscovered I may win this bow'r.

May all the blessings which a lover's voice

Breathes on his lady wait on you, my choice.'

Here did they meet to rivet fast their heart,

1330Where not a breath their private joys disturb;

They thought no eye a saucy ray durst dart,

Or any voice had power their loves to curb.

So credulous are lovers, and so fain

To their conjectures would *conclusum*'s chain.

But this bright sun of joy eclipsèd was,

And pitchy clouds their glorious sky did smutch:

Then Venus' joys were like to Venice glass,

Poor glass-like toys that perish with a touch.

A guardian's anger, or a parent's frown,

1340Nips love's fresh blossoms and a wish uncrown.

The jealous matron, from her tow'ring loft,

O'erlooked th' ambitious trees which hemmed them in;

O'erheard their vows, their sighs, and language soft;

And saw how Cupid leapt from skin to skin,

The traffic of their lips, and how thin balms

Did glue and cement fast their melting palms.

When she perceived the progress of their love,

Religious care empanelled straight a jury

Of thoughts and plots, this stranger to remove,

1350Soothèd with profit, and enflamed with fury,

Ush'ring her language with a threat'ning frown,

She asked her business with that shavèd crown.

Why was that sickly voice whose feeble gales

Can raise no echoes, hand- and elbow-chat,

Eye-dialogue's discourse, and wanton tales,

That way of am'rousness and this, and that?

'Speak truth, Bellama, has thy heart, as voice,

Decreed that youthful monk thine only choice?'

Bellama, startled at this sudden news,

1360Yet did her answers all consist of noes;

But yet, alas! her blood observed the cues,

And called by guilt, her lily banks o'erflows:

So that, though she with settled vows denied,

Yet to the eye her blushes guilty cried.

When as the matron's busy eyes had read

Love on her cheeks in bloody letters writ,

She asked her why blind folly thus had led

Her reason 'gainst religion, state, or wit?

Or, if she needs must love, why did she scowl

1370Upon state-satins, and embrace a cowl?

Bellama to excuses tuned her air,

Framing pretences for her amorous faith,

But yet, alas! such was Pazzella's care,

From her excuses she withheld her faith.

And, with a voice shrill and as fierce as thunder,

Sware she would knap their silly loves in sunder.

Those scarlet gowns which doom offenders' death,

Or the proscriptions of the Roman state,

Had not the tithe of that affrighting breath,

1380Although they weak'ned hell and threat'ned Fate,

As had these words which feeble love did shiver,

Snap his weak strings, and crack his emptied quiver.

But, all this while, Albino sate with pleasure,

And on his trencher joy and mirth attend;

Nor to delight will he allow a measure,

As at one sitting he his stock would spend.

Nay, if he slept, he dreamed of naught but rings,

Gloves, fans, masks, monkeys, and such pretty things.

And when the time of his approach approached,

1390His eye did travel with the dial's hand,

Then started up to see Don Phoebus coached,

Bade him make haste and at that minute stand,

That this blest day may count more moments' flight

Than could the stout Alcides' genial night.

But oft we see before a sudden dash,

The sun salutes the earth with hottest gleams:

So here, before misfortune's harshest lash,

Joy on Albino shot his choicest beams;

That every thought was crownèd with a star,

1400And rid with Venus in her silver car.

Rose out o' th' vault with love and hope adust,

And in conceit fed on his future sweet,

Thinking what most may please, not what's most just.

And with what phrase he should his lady greet:

Vowing, in this full heat of lust and pride,

To try how fast Bellama's girdle's tied.

But as our alchemists do study much,

Spend all their wits and wealth to find that stone

Which baser metals doth engold with touch,

1410(As he which once did awe the Phrygian throne)

And when they long have dreamèd of a mass,

Their silver's turned to tin, their gold to brass.

Just so our amorist, stuffed full with hope,

Came to this walk for his expected treasure,

The crystal casements of his soul did ope

To let in th' object of his joy and pleasure:

But when he thought t' have found his lovely lass,

His love was lady-smocks, his lady grass.

He searched with stricter care each bush and bow'r,

1420Than did the fairy king and Hob his man;

Throwing his eyes into each branchèd tow'r,

And midst the sharp'ned pikes of brambles ran.

Pricked forward with desire, enraged with spite,

And venteth here what love and hate indite.

Upon his Bellama using and forsaking the Walk.

When, walking, I sent forth my watchful eyes

To fetch in objects, like Bellona's spies,

Along this swelling way which chequered was

With smooth-faced pebbles, not with pikèd grass,

Bellama paced, whose only pacing set

1430Upon the pavèd walk a coronet

Of Flora's pride—carnations, tulips, lilies,

Pansies, pinks, roses, daffadowndillies.

Nay more, methought, I saw the rubbish way

Sapphires, pearls, rubies, onyx-stones, outray.

The very channel, proud of her blest weight,

Swelled up with pride unto the ridge's height,

To kiss her feet, and made the way an alley.

With this choice fair mine eyes (ah!) once did dally,

Nature's epitome, whose curious brow

1440Was like a smoothèd mount of bleachèd snow,

At whose clear foot Nature divine did place

Two diamonds, which did enlighten all her face.

So that 'twas like those orbs wherein do stray

The planet-lamps, or Cupid's sucking way;

And from these gems such silver rays were sent

Which hatchèd o'er her light accoutrement.

So that dull fancies would have thought she had

In cambric, holland, or pure lawn, been clad.

Nay, I at first thought it had Cynthia bin

1450Deck'd in her brother's sunshine ermelin.

She shot such glorious beams: but now, alas!

She's gone, she's fled, and lo! the mourning grass

Is hayed already, and th' ungemmed stone

At feathers catch to fly where she is gone.

The branchèd beech, the oak, and tow'ring ash,

Bend both their brows and boughs my face to lash.

The angry thorns my hands, though armèd, scratch,

And testy brambles at my vestures catch

(Which was before the curse of human sin,

1460But now, by her, outsmelled the eglantine),

I, wonder-strucken, asked a holy thistle,

Which with his sharp'ned pikes began to bristle,

(But know at first 'twas but an homely weed,

Her presence made it holy, not its seed)

Why all with ireful looks thus threat'ned me?

'It is supposed, Bellama fair,' quoth he,

'The goddess of this walk was forced by you

To this benighted path to bid adieu.'
'Alas!' quoth I (meanwhile the thistle paus'd),
1470'Their wrath is undeserved, I never caused
By any ill demeans that saint to leave
This place, and widow every branch and greave.
Unto your testates I myself refer,
How choicely I have ever honoured her,
Have paid my tribute-compliments, and gave
Respects as much as due, or she, would have.
But people (worse than those that people stews)
Whose only joy consists in telling news,
Or Pazzell' else with her envenomed lips,
1480Your glory and my comfort do eclipse,
'Tis them they ought to chide, for only they
Compel her to forsake this gloomy way.

Yet spite of all disasters, fate, and hell,
Albino's heart shall with Bellama dwell:
And though chill winter nip both you and me,
We shall, ere long, our suns and summers see.'

This said, he straight forsook his silent grove,
Trimming his looks which passion did untrim,
And hastes to find the object of his love.
1490But such an eye the matron cast on him,
That fury on her looks did seem to dwell,
And envy to her face transplanted hell.
Heartless Albino with much pain did view
How on her looks madness and anger ranged,

And on Bellam' he private glances threw

To bring him word if that she stood unchanged,

If she continued square, despite of them,

Whose jealous eyes did all their actions hem.

Bellama knew the language of his eye,

1500 But could not give respect to Cupid's law,

For Piazella to her eyes did tie

A constant watch, which kept her eyes in awe:

That she was forced to peep within her veil,

For there the matron did her eyes enjail.

The ragged crew, which are enwrapt in chains

Through grates, more freedom have of sight than she,

Which in them both produced such griefs and pains

Too sharp and loud to be expressed by me.

Albino now does judge his absence better,

1510 And chose a proxy to present a letter.

One of his order (deemed a trusty friend

Endeared to him by favours, oath, and vow),

Was his Talthibius, ordained to send

To her whose beauty makes stiff Atlas bow.

The monk embraced the office, and did swear,

By all our scarlet oaths, faith, truth, and care.

Albino now to every Santo prays,

And for success his hands with zeal does rear,

Courting his lady in some Irish lays,

1520 And robbed his finger of its golden sphere.

En-nealed *I live in hope*, and sure grief's waves,

If anchorless, had been t'is wishes graves.

To mee's faire Metres, Vandebrad Isile of te fine towne of Vaschester.

Ick predee metres be not coy,

But intertaune mee's love vit joy:

For me be not a snottee boy.

Vat tough me russell not in silke,

And keep mee's servaunts vit capes ilke,

Yet me be not a sop of milke.

Vat tough me vil not stautly stret,

1530And ilke de Peacock poudely jet;

Yet me be vary pruce and neat.

Vat tough me vil not lye vit pimpes,

And pend me's coyne on light-teale shrimpes,

Yet me can hug, busse prettee nymphes.

Vat tough me ha ne Hauke ne Hound,

And vil not suare begot, idzound,

Yet faith mee's frolique, plumpe and sound.

Vat tough me cannot Maudam say,

And vit ty Fan an Monkee play,

1540Yet me con flatter vel as thay.

Vat tough me connot honour tee

Vit titles laudee C or D,

Yet tou sault a good Metress bee.

Vat tough, vat tough, Ick say, vat tough,

Ick say, udsnigs, in feck I trough,

Yet Ick drive not te Caurt and Plough.

Then pretee, pretee, buxome faire,

Let me not launguish in despaire,

But say me's sutes all gaunted are.

1550Let ne mee's Irish borrell speach,

In tyne affection mauke o breach,

For me con better say so teach.

And me can be as blyth and free

As auny push or saunten hee,

Ten say, and ved, and bed vit me.

Tyne faytfull friend and good servaune,

Patrick Applous, *te fine, te bave, te*

gallaun Irish-mon.

Upon the Ring sent to his Bellama.

Cupid oft-times disdains to dwell

In lofty palace, but does shell

Himself in straw-thatched roof, and choose

For novel a September rose

1560Before a diamond to present,

Or time in silver ceilings pent;

Great gifts enforce, but small ones woo,

And forced respects will never do.

He questions his own worth that fears

To whisper in his mistress' ears

With smallest gifts, since true worth hates

A boon which for him loudly prates,

And female worths may justly slight

Those that but with gilt swords dare fight.

1570These make me send this little ring

(An emblem of a greater thing),

Tis bruised—hence representeth true

My heart, bruised, bent, and bowed for you.

Anatomists conclude by art

A vein is stretchèd to the heart

Fro' th' smallest finger of the left;

From vein and finger comes this gift:

Hence merits better, since we find

Many send presents, few their mind.

Upon the Posy *I live in hope.*

1580'Tis hope that makes me live, and when

My hope's transferred to other men,

Divorced from me, health cannot give

A strength to make my rent heart live.

A rented heart 'tis truly called,

For love of virtues you enthralled,

Tenant at will to you, and pays

Large rents of sighs each hour and days.

But to what number they amount,

Puzzles arithmetic to count.

1590Then, courteous landlady, be please

To seal my heart a lifelong lease.

Else ev'ry slight and frown of yours

Will turn your tenant out of doors.

Yet hope persuades me not to doubt

My heart shall not be turnèd out.

For you have promisèd to come

And live with it, or exchange home;

So I be landlord unto thine,

And you be landlady to mine.

1600Say 'Aye' to this, and only Fate

Shall change the tenor of our state.

Bardino from the coven posts with speed

Unto Albino's only polar star,

Loaden with blessings, and beware take heed

As the great grandame's son prepared for war,

Or as a widow's son, whose only joy

Hangs on the nuptials of her lusty boy.

Like as a pilot to some floating keel

When as the bustlers from old Æol's cave

1610On Neptune's furrowed back make it to reel,

And at his death shoot billow after wave:

So tossed in seas of grief Albino tied

His love's choice pinnace to Bardino's guide.

But Bishop-Guts, tun-bellied, all-paunched friar,

In sight of Lesbia's tow'rs, split his fair galley,

Proved a dissembling and perfidious liar;

From his foul breast deceit and hate did sally.

The seeds of every sin in him did bud,

Nothing did wither but this one thing, *Good*.

1620For to win credit with the Lady-mother,

And raise a liking of himself in her,

He proved a traitor to his abbey-brother,

With abbotess in private does confer,

And unto her imparts his amorous news,

She, not Bellam', his vowèd service views.

But to Albino he returned with faith

(Yet 'twas an oath), 'I importuned thy saint,

Pressed her t' unlock thy secrets: but she saith

"What purblind folly does thy heart attaint?

1630Thou know'st what offers I refused, and thou'll

Confine my love unto a starvèd cowl!"

'Away flings she, and leaves me disconsolate,

Nor after deigned to me a wonted look:

Now is Albino pinched with cruel Fate.

Which is the better, Cupid, or thy book?

Hadst viewed her beauty with a scornful eye

Thou hadst not tasted of her pride and fie.

Hapless Albin', and hapless so much more

Because Albin', rest quiet with thy lot;

1640If Nilus overflow his sandy floor,

Above twelve cubits, it procures a rot.

When at too high a pitch affections tow'r,

Fate with misfortunes oft their hopes doth sour.

Wound not the harmless air with mournful hoots,

Steer not 'gainst Volga's stream thy feeble keel,

Be not like him who 'gainst a whirlwind shoots,

Or like the cockatrice in pecking steel;

For acts, 'gainst Nature wrought, despite do gain,

And love o'erlooking Fortune, reaps disdain.'

1650But let us see what strange effect this news

Writes in his breast (disaster's fatal book),

What stronger plot his working fancy brews

If's lofty thoughts be at this answer shook—

Alas! they are, so weak a thing is man,

Crash'd into atoms with a slighting fan.

His blood retires unto his throbbing heart,

His wannèd cheeks with lawn were overspread,

An aspen-trembling loos'ned every part,

His spirits fainted and his vitals fled,

1660And his quick heart with such strong motions beated

That it, though chilled with fear, his body heated.

Ent'ring his chamber, strewèd o'er with rue,

He leaned his head upon his swelling pillow,

And, sighing, cried 'Bellama! is this true?

Must I be doomèd to the barren willow?

I thought, exempted from my pedant's art,

I should no more have felt the willow's smart.

Thy eyes spake love: and every glance you sent

Writ on my heart, "Albino is approv'd";

1670Whensoe'er my eyes unto thy feature went,

And met with thine, they brought me word "*You lov'd*",

Then can Bellama not Bellama be?

She may Bellama be, but not to me.

Blest heavens! how have men deserved your ire,

That made you frame this curse, this thing called *Woman*,

So comely and so useful, giving fire

To sear us men and yet disdain to know man?

Why on their faces have you placed such charms,

To make us court with sighs the worst of harms.'

1680Pandora's box of woes was openèd then,

When first they took in hand to make a woman,

And all the Furies joined to torture men;

Yet women first were rare, but now grown common,

And mischiefs high, when once they common grow

Entomb great states, and commons overthrow.

Thou Love (what should I call thee?) dost entice,

Nay check'st rebellion in the awful gods;

Women thy weapons are, of such high price,

That beat with them they humbly kiss the rods.

1690No life, no joy, no sweet, without a lass;

And yet no sweet nor joy since woman was.

Our eyes do ne'er mistake the day for night,

Nor can the pale-hewed pinks for roses pass,

But when on women's colours they do light.

Then (bribed) they look as through a painted glass,

So that what women are we never see

But what we wish and fancy them to be.

'Mongst thousand virgins which do suck this air,

I never knew but one, but one—one good;

1700Whom I supposèd full as good as fair,

And she was making e'er Deucalion's flood:

But she—alas! what should I say?—but she

Is woe to man, a woman unto me.'

Thus in his height'ned fury he condemns

Both Fate and Fortune, honour, wealth, and worth,

Raileth on virgins and their beauteous gems,

And curseth Nature that did bring her forth,

But, above all, his sharp incensèd muse

In wrathful odes Don Cupid does accuse.

An invective against Cupid.

1710Thou Love, if thou wilt suffer this, be blind,

Deaf, dumb, and stupid, and unwisely kind

More unto slights than merits, and reward

Respects and negligence with same regard.

If satins difference and maids adorn
Than Nature has with beauty, more with scorn,
That they must fligger, scoff, deride, and jeer,
Appoint their servants certain hours t' appear,
Afford by number kisses, sights by tale,
Command a certain distance, and impale
1720Love's game from taste or touch, and, if at all
Men do transgress, steep all their words in gall,

Check but the least presumption, and with frowns
Strike as much terror unto us as crowns—
Love, if thou'lt suffer this, and wink at them,
Make us esteem a pebble for a gem,
Stoop, cringe, adore, sue, flatter, and admire,
And in our bosoms teen'st thy amorous fire—
May all the haggish Furies soundly lash
And with their snaky whips thy sinews gash!
1730May all the tortures Hell encloseth fall
On thee, if not enough, and more than all.
But we—we men, will be no more thy slaves
And women's too: we'll pack unto our graves:
And in our silent beds of earth will court
The slender-waisted worms, and with them sport,
Dally, hug, toy, and vow their wimbling buss
Is full as sweet as women's was to us.
Enwalled with dust we'll lie: till Nature shall
Perceive thy malice, Cupid, and her fall,
1740And woo's, with sighs and tears in loving guise,
For a replantage of the world, to rise,

Then shall our wills ungod thee and thy mother,

And Cupids be ourselves one to another.

Then in thy temples shall no voice be heard,

But screech-owls, dors, and daws; no altar reared

Whereon to sacrifice true lovers' hearts,

Scalded with sighs, and gallèd with thy darts.

For we ourselves ourselves will temples call,

And make our bosoms altars, whereon shall

1750From fourteen to fourscore the females fairs

Burn frankincense of love with sighs and prayers:

And change the custom so that maidens then

Shall court, admire, adore, and woo us men.

This said, he strove t' unbillow all with slumbers,

But th' more he strove to rest less rest he takes.

His watchful thoughts each tattling minute numbers,

Bellama's wakening beauty him awakes.

And having purchased sleep, though they were dim,

Bellama's beauty darted rays at him.

1760Then, starting up her substance fair to catch,

He lost the shadow, and did rave again:

'Can grovelling brambles lofty cedars scratch?

Or waddling ducks o'ertop the tow'ring crane?

Yet virtues, imped with person, reach a sky,

And to an higher pitch than Fortune fly.

There is a tree (as our historians write),

Alpina hight, of fair and glorious glee,

With branches fine and glorious blossoms dight

But never tasted by the witty bee,

1770Fearing death lodgeth there; and this he fears

'Cause to the eye so glorious it appears.

Not much unlike to these our women are,

Whom Nature has in dainty colours dressed;

And of our women likest are the fair,

For with much beauty virtues seldom rest.

Would Jove all women I had judged to be

Alpina-like, or, if not all, yet she!

The queen of beauty strumpet was to Mars,

Officious bawd unto lascivious Jove,

1780A patroness of those that ride in cars,

And in her court nor virtue reigns nor love:

But lust and vanity, with wily trains,

That he repentance buys which beauty gains.

Sh'as many trulls, like Menelaus' wife,

And she such light-skirt things for chaste ones sells;

With whom dissembling and deceits are rife,

Smiles, tears, sighs, looks, with such enchanting spells.

If they but bend their brows and shoot out frowns,

They crack a sceptre and distemple crowns.

1790Yet stay: but by the sour we know not sweet,

White's silver hue adjoined to black shines best,

How should we know our hands but by our feet?

Health's only prized when sickness doth arrest.

This principle, perhaps, Bellama holds:

Summer is known by winter's chilling colds.

Perchance Bellama did not breath that woe,

Which by Bardino was conveyed to me,

Nor dwelt upon her lips that scornful "No":

'Twas only forgèd by her dame and he.

1800But—why should suspicion steal into my breast?

Suspect a friend, deceit with friendship rest?

No: Phaeton, base son to Day's bright blaze,

Daring his chariot, felt Jove's thunder fire.

Astronomers, whilst on the stars they gaze,

Oft-times do sink into the dirty mire.

Only the eagle, without purblind damps,

Can fix his eyes upon the prince of lamps.

The son of Daedalus soared up so high,

That Phoebus plucked his waxen jointed wings,

1810It was her pride checked my ambitious eye.

True love, to hatred changed by slights, has stings.

I'll write invectives: no! I'll only try

What virtue dwells in slighting poesie.'

To his Bellama slighting him.

I'll bore the heavens, pierce the clouds a vein,

Make them full torrents weep of brackish rain,

To second my laments; methinks the sun,

Knowing my clue is ravelled and undone,

That my Bellama slights, should, vexed, resign

T' his sister's chariot his ecliptic line.

1820Bid Phoebe run horn-mad, and loudly cry,

Froth, howl, as in a fit of lunacy,

Nay, throw a poison on Endymion's lips,

Threaten to drown the world, the sun eclipse.

Keep the stars order still? or can they stir

And not digress? Know they how not to err?

Sure, no: I saw bright Paphos snuff her lamp,

Yet vowed to quench it with eternal damp,

Hurl all away, if that her servant's love

Be had in no regard, and awful Jove

1830Hurry along the milky way to find

That sniffling deity, that wingèd blind—

And vowed to clip his wings as short as monks

Their stubbed beards more short than panèd trunks,

Unless he shot a dart with more than speed,

To make Bellama's heart affections bleed.

Bold ocean foams with spite, his neb-tides roar,

His billows top and top-mast high do soar.

Nature herself is sullen, keeps her bed,

And will not rise so much as dress her head:

1840Regardless of the seasons, will not see

Loud winds deplume the bush and tow'ring tree.

The ploughman furrows earth, sows seed i' th' tides,

But nature weeps for me, his pains derides.

Copernicus his tenet's verified,

The massy globe does 'bout its centre ride.

All things disranked, nothing observes its state,

Change time and tide, or post or antedate.

But thou, Bellam', art deaf to me and blind,

Steel'st thine affections, flint'st thy hardenèd mind,

1850And strik'st fire thence t' inflame my tinder heart,

Thou oil'st the flame, but I endure the smart.

How oft have I, when others' eyes have slept,

Like sentinels to armies, watchings kept!

And when the thought o' th' saints' thrice blissful home

Which (ah! too seldom) 'mongst my thoughts did come,

Then, spite of goodness, blessed E was lost

And you the haven of me tempest-tost.

Have I made envious art admire thy worth,

Touched the Ela of praise t' emblazon 't forth?

1860Bid sleep goodnight, quiet and rest adieu,

Made myself no self to entitle you?

And, after this sad purgatory, must

My hopes be laid i' th' dust for want of dust?

Then know, Bellama, since thou aim'st at wealth

Where Fortune has bestowed her largest dealth,

That wealth may puff a clod of earth like leaven,

But virtuous want alone ensouleth heaven.

Know more, I scorned thy fortune: 'twas thyself

I courted, not thy slight-adored pelf,

1870And had not mortals' curse blessed thee, and I

Had swelled with honour and nobility,

My love, once fixed on virtue, parents' hate

In both might shake, but ne'er evert love's state.

I aim at virtue's bliss, and if I find

The heart and bosom good, I slight the rind.

But since, Bellama, thou regard'st not me,

I scorn to cringe, adore, and flatter thee.

For he that rules his thoughts has a nobler soul

Than he that awes the world from pole to pole.

1880Thus, fair, adieu! with love these measures scan,

And know my love was but a fit of man.

We'll leave Albino in this frantic mood,
And view Bellama, pargèd o'er with fear,
Asking a member of her sisterhood
(For love and virtues unto her most dear),
Amongst their sportings, and their chaste delights,
Wherefore Albino did refrain their sights.

Barraba (her the font those letters gave)
Said, 'I presume I rightly guess the cause'.
1890Bellama urged (thanks to the purblind knave),
'Twas thus', quoth she—yet made a two day's pause.
At length, with importunings overcome,
She told her why Albino kept at home.
'Bardino did deceive his trust', quoth she,
'Told all, yet sung another song to him:
His love came lapped in paper unto thee,
He with quaint words did his affections limn,
Vowed service: but Bardino (ah the shame!)
Unclasped his secrets to our jealous dame.'
1900'Am I an infidel? or dare I tie',
Quoth fair Bellama 'unto this belief?
Shall just revenge in my soft bosom die?
And shall I melt my heart with secret grief?
I'll scold with him.' Says chaste Barraba, 'No,
For by that others will your wishes know.'
What she should do (plung'd in this depth of woe)
Bellama knew not, nor durst counsel ask:
More dangers wait her, if she send or go,

Than if she underwent Alcides' task.

1910Distracted were her thoughts in silence tied,

Till love and honour buzzled, then she cried,

'Ah! false Bardino, shame of holy orders!

Whither, ah! whither didst thou send thy troth?

To be grand factor in the frozen borders

For them whose decks do make old ocean froth?

And truthless thou, locked in this gloomy cell,

Plott'st baseness to enlarge the crown of hell.

Unjust Bardin', unworthy of a cope,

Or (whose employments holy) other vest,

1920Didst [thou], oh didst thy conscience scour with soap,

And washed all faith from off thy glazèd breast?

And, faithless, thou esteemest less of vow

Than clownish whistlers which do steer the plough.

Where didst encage thine eyes? durst thou behold

(Acting this crime) the castle of the stars?

How stopp'st thine ears? didst hear the heavens scold,

And chide in wind and thunder threat'ning wars?

Durst touch the hallowed water, spittle, salt,

The cross or pax, and yet attempt this fault?

1930Those sacred bagnios, wherein pagans wash

Their sullied limbs for their mosquea's door,

The pottage-penance and repentant lash,

Their hair-cloth shirt, skin-shoes, and thousand more;

Th' arch-vicar's pardon, and the purging flame

Can ne'er absolve thy crime or clear thy fame.

Pack then from human eyes, and shroud thy sin,

Under the curtains of eternal night;

Perfidiousness does make thee near of kin

To hell's black fiends, with robes of horror dight.

1940Pack, pack, begone, the ferryman does stay

To waft thy paunch o'er th' Acherontic bay.

But peace, Bellama, dost thou think it fit

To value at so mean a price thy pearl?

Applaud thyself, count it a point of wit

To take a cowlist and refuse an earl.

The world shall be uncentred, ere 't be said

Beauty takes lodging in an humble maid.

What then? shall every fashion fashion me,

As in religion by the church's eye,

1950So by the world's must I in loving see?

No, I the world's supremacy deny.

Hence with those loves which profit only measures,

I hate that heart which only shoots at treasures.

The Cyprian goddess is not fed with ploughs,

Nor Cupid's arrow guided is with acres.

Vulcan permitted was to shake the boughs,

But Mars suck'd in the sweets without partakers.

Youth, youth pursues; for with autumnal looks

Cupid does seldom bait his eighteen hooks.

1960Who in pleuretic passions does deny

To open veins, to shut death out o' th' doors?

Who will not in sharp fevers Galen try,

To weaken humours, and unstop the pores?

The quickest eye does want the quick'ning sun,

And to the sea the drilling cadents run.

Who, when Sir Cupid enters at the eye,

With pride and coy disdain shuts comfort forth?

I'll make ambition stoop now, love, says I,

And satin thoughts shall veil to tammy worth:

1970By lovely maids the lovely lovèd are,

And by the fair most favoured are the fair.'

Thus did she rage, her resolution love;

Which spite of all disasters she will harbour,

Hoping blest fate will so propitious prove,

T' enclose her monk and her in Cupid's arbour:

But leave her surfeiting with hope, and view

When to monastic vows she'll bid adieu.

Till Cynthia twice twelve times repairèd had

Her silver horns, she was encloistered here:

1980When some kind planet moved her loving dad

To fetch her thence his frosted age to cheer,

Hence, virgin vow, away black vestments hurled,

Bellama's born again into the world.

He with his lady mounted on his jen-

Net to the nunnery with haste does ride,

Accompanied with troops of harnessed men

And vowed a siege if Piazzell' denied,

To batter down the holy walls with guns,

And fright the hag with all her simp'ring nuns.

1990He in an ambush placed his iron crew,

Bade them prepare when as the trump did call,

Dismounting then the janitor him knew

And led the lordly couple through the hall,

Parlours, and chambers, to the conclave where
The pious nuns their branchèd lilies rear.
Bellama craved a blessing, they it gave;
Then Rivelezzo he did softly ask
If the monastic roof should be her grave?
If now she grievèd for Don Fuco's task?
2000If, after two years' bondage, now she would
Answer more kindly to the voice of gold?
'My lord,' quoth she, with humble knee and voice.
'I am not tired with my nicer vow,
Nor hate I Hymen, might my eyes make choice,
Ask when I'll marry, and I'll answer now.'
'A man', quoth he, 'for face and virtue choose,
And on mine honour I will not refuse.'
Pazzella fearing that their whisp'ring would
Presage no good unto her huffing waste,
2010Broke off their parle; and Rivelezzo told
That his fair daughter zealous was and chaste:
And that her mind no evil did attaint,
'She almost has attained to be a saint.

Such high-prized comforts, joys, rewards, and glory
Our happy walls enseal and curtain in,
That we alone survive: all praise and story
Are called hell's tortures and the whips of sin.
The local motion of our soul's in heaven,
We hate blind Turkism and the Jewish leaven.'
2020'Madam,' quoth Don, 'you need no advocate,
Since you yourself can plead your cause so well;

But that my sex does interdict this state,

What your words might effect I cannot tell.

But sure it does unscrew a virgin's heart,

To hear of love, and never feel his dart.'

'Madam, forsooth,' quoth Lady Arda, 'I

Ne'er found such comfort i' th' innupted life,

Nor think the blessings of virginity

Can equal the contentments of a wife.

2030My voice should not assent unto her vow

To wreath with willow sprigs her melting brow.'

Quoth Piazzella, 'I am grievèd sore

To hear such scandals thrown upon our vow,

To hear Diana, whom all ought t' adore

And her chaste votaries depravèd now.

I know not what contents attend a wife

But sure they equal not th' innupted life.

Again, your honours you do much impeach

To force your daughter from this happy state;

2040'Twixt her and happiness you make a breach,

And pull upon your heads a cursèd fate.

Heavens unbuckle will their clouds of rain,

Death or diseases, if you part our train.

The body's better than the sheathing skin,

And ought with greater care to be maintained;

The guest is far more worthy than the inn,

And ought with greater study to be trained.

The soul mounts heaven, when earth's agèd womb

The skeleton (her issue) does entomb.'

2050'Away with arguments, in vain you plead;

Our vow', quoth they, 'locked not her girdle ever.'
'I', quoth Pazzella, 'do abjure the tede:
Hymen shall ne'er my holy orders sever.
But spite of all the tricks the world does nurse,
I'll keep my virgins from the bridal curse.'

Without demurs, Don Rivelezzo then
With shrill-voiced trumpet made an echo speak;
Straight was the house environèd with men,
Which with their leaden globes an entrance break.
2060The air was frighted with the powder-thunder,
The bellowing noise did split the rocks in sunder.
Affrighted thus, the matron bid them gang,
And to Bellama gave a sad adieu;
Yet in her heart she griped with Envy's fang,
And o'er her looks a veil of sorrow drew.
The joyful parents, having got their daughter,
Gave a farewell unto the house with laughter.
Leaving the coach and cloister, we'll take part
With poor Albino in his woe and grief,
2070Who, seeing Fortune his designs did thwart,
And Neptune's grandchild brought him no relief,
Did think to win her presence in disguise:
He that but one way tries is hardly wise.
He plotted to invest himself with robe
Might speak him nobly born, and gallant heir
To some vast measures of this wealthy globe,
Seated aloft in honour's oval chair—
Procure him then some store of lacèd capes

To wait on him with servile garbs and shapes.

2080Pretending to be one o'th' Spanish court,

Giving strange accents to our modern speech,

And hither came his wand'ring mind to sport,

But that he faces lacked to tune each breach.

Besides he knew the matron's care was such,

She love untwisted in the eye or touch.

Then a new project did he get on's brain,

And sheared the downy moss from his smooth chin,

Intending to be one o' th' virgin-train,

Like Jupiter, husked in a female skin:

2090But that he feared religion could not bridle

His active heat 'twixt linen to be idle.

He thought his breaking voice would him betray

(Unless he said he ever had a cold),

He feared the curtsey and the female play,

Or that his face would make him seem too old.

But above all he fear'd he should not lock

His legs within the compass of a smock.

In costly vestures he would be arrayed

Of high descent, and fearing lest his sire

2100Would force him to an hated pillow, strayed

With them to teen the holy vestal fire.

He would be nobly born, not out of pride,

But to be sheeted by Bellama's side.

He had no treasure, but would promise fair,

That, settled there, he should be fed in state,

Hoping to win the porter with kind air,

That with Bellama he might thread the gate.

He all would venture: and upon this plot

Would place his fortunes, and the Gordian knot.

2110In such accoutrement he veilèd was,

That to himself Albino was not known.

He lookèd for Albino's face i' th' glass;

But nothing of himself t' himself was shown.

Each way a maid, enriched with special grace,

As though he had unflow'r'd Adonis' face.

He styl'd himself Felice, only child,

To him who at that time was Folco's duke;

And was so like to her whom he was styled

That she could scarcely say 'twas not her look.

2120For what's of Issa and her picture writ

Was found in them, they tasked the poet's wit.

Unto this virgin-cage she fast did pace,

And, knocking at the gate, the porter came,

Who, seeing riches on her back and face,

With humble voice desired to know her name.

'My name (good friend),' quoth she, 'Felice is,

I come to taste your choice monastic bliss.'

'Madam,' Avaro said, 'our rubbish stone

With cement join'd shall precious straight be made,

2130In that they shall ensphere so fair an one.'

Felice, smiling at the porter, said,

'Hath time with iron jaws eat out this part

Which now these masons do repair by art?'

And truth it was, Felice, Folco's heir,

Flying the disaster of an hated tede,

Couched in disguises at a cottage bare
(But how? when? where? task not my amorous lede).

So that Pazzella's faith writ on her brow
The noble treasures of Felice's vow.
2140'Not time it was, but an unhappy hour'
The porter said 'we had a virtuous fair,
Daughter unto a man of mighty power,
So like yourself I think you sisters are,'
(How largely flatt'ry has dispersed its song
That it does oil and smooth a porter's tongue!)
'Bellama hight by her uncourteous sire,
Fetched hence, who, when my lady did deny,
Begirt our holy walls with sulphur-fire,
And summoned harnessed men which close did lie.
2150They with their leaden worlds at us did play
And frighted (as you see) these stones away.'
Felice, knowing that her adamant,
Th' impulsive cause of this her virgin-vow,
Was vanished thence, and gleams of joy did want
And wanning sorrow revelled on her brow.
Scarce could she speak and every jointing trembled,
Yet feared the porter, and her fear dissembled.
Pazzella and the virgins her esteemed,
Seeing her feature and unequalled grace,
2160Before they knew his parentage or deemed
He was descended from high Folco's race.
But, knowing that, their joys did swell so high,
That grief for sorrow slinked aside to cry.

But ere the next day's sun to let out day
Night's ebon box unlocked, she did not brook
To hear their private whispers, talk, and pray,
Erect the host, and kiss a gilded book.
For, her, Bellama has possessèd solely,
So that their water could not make her holy.
2170Instead of 'Virgin-mother' she would say,
'My dearest lady, hear my sad complaint.'
Nor to she-saints would she devoutly pray,
'Cause none but her Bellama was a saint.
Unto Lorretta, as Bellam', she swears:
And calls their holy water but her tears.
She wond'red oft how her Bellama did
Two years continue in this hated cell;

And in her thoughts she oftentimes her chid,
For dwelling where but formal good does dwell,
2180Since in her absence she could scarce abide
To sojourn here a double eventide.
Her brains acquainted was no whit with sloth,
But plotted how she might escape that jail:
And to this end she vowed her virgin-oath
Should for her quick returning put in bail;
She thought her breach of virgin-oath no sin
Because she only wore the formal skin.
She missed, in ransacking her cabinet,
A precious jewel, far exceeding rare,
2190Which on her brow the lady duchess set,
As a true pledge of her indulgent care:

Far richer than that pearl which Egypt's queen
Quaffed to her Mark, dissolved in liquor keen.
But for all this a curious fit of man
Did force her, for assay, to enter in
To see if fasting did their rosies wan,
Or folly led not in the Paphian sin,
Thinking her wit could manumise her straight
From that lank cloister by some nimble sleight.
2200This she pretended to have lost as she
(Fainted with fears, and with her travels tired)
In the cool shade of a well-hairèd tree
Threw water on her joints with labour fired.
For heavens parch the air with hotter rays
When with his flaming tongue the dogstar bays.
'Madam,' quoth she, with feignèd tears and sigh,
'Grant me your licence to go seek my gem,
The place of my reposure is but nigh';
Swore by those fires that did enlighten them,
2210By her virginity and virgin-vow,
Return ere time could pace a triple now.
Quoth Piazella, 'I will send a maid
To seek your jewel out with studied care,
Direct her to the shade wherein you stayed,
For you forbidden are the common air.
Our gardens, beautified with Maya's glee,
Your farthest journey must and ought to be.'

She urged again, but all in vain she asked;
The prioress remembered still the earl,

2220And feared Felice his departure masked,

Under pretence of seeking for a pearl.

And more suspicious thoughts unto her came

'Cause she so often kissed Bellama's name.

She, seeing that this plot did want a stamp,

To make it current pass like lawful coins,

Feared her departure from this lanky camp,

And vowed to try the virgin's skill at foins.

Yet, ere she would attempt that amorous play,

She would attempt escapes some other way.

2230She viewed the casements, and did boldly wrench,

With courage masculine, the squarèd bars:

But they did scorn the vigour of a wench,

Like sturdy oaks which slight the windy jars.

Nay more, deep waters did begirt them round,

That from the glass he could not see the ground.

Then on the porter did she kindly smile,

And by full tale gave free respects to him;

Thinking to gull Avaro by this wile,

Joinèd with language oiled, perfumed, and trim,

2240Quoth she, 'Thy trust, and skill I must employ

And for thy pains thou shalt have treasures, boy.'

The greedy porter, like a goshawk, seized

With griping talons on this pheasant cock,

'Madam', says he, 'my skill is not diseased,

Nor dwells dissembling with the honest frock.

Disclose your secrets, and be sure if man

Can do you service, then Avaro can.'

Felice then, as prologue to her suit,

Gave him a purse full fraught with pseudo-gold;

2250Told him her bounty brought no worser fruit

If in th' achievement he'd be true and bold.

'Thou must, some evening, let me pass the gates

And straggle half a mile to gather dates.'

'Madam, I'll do 't: it is a small request,

Since you do merit better at my hand.

If fortune be propitious to my best.

You on the common shore this night I'll land

My hands have eyes and only what they see

Will they believe—give me my minted fee.'

2260Felice then plucked out a silken purse,

Great, and as musical as th' other was,

Pretending it was stuffed with metal curse,

When 't only was with circled ragges of glass;

Which purposely she did with di'monds cut,

To gull the porter's hopes and fill his gut.

'Heavens augment your store, madam,' quoth he,

'I'll wait for you at the middle age of night;

Come to my lodge and softly call for me.'

This handsome cheat Felice did delight.

2270To cozen the deceivers is no fraud,

To use a pimp, and cheat a rusty bawd.

She scarcely knew what letters spellèd grief,

For all her thoughts with regal crowns were wreathed,

Yet 'mongst them all Bellama ruled as chief.

At time of rest her body she unsheathed,

And housed within the linen walls her limbs,

Till night and sleep did their quick tapers dim.

Avaro (when day's sister's misty fog

Had poppèd out Apollo's searching eye,

2280And gen'ral silence human tongues did clog

Locking all senses up with lethargy)

Stepp'd to his purses, and began to think

How he should order his belovèd chink.

He'd hang his lodge with arras weaved with gold

That his successor there might sleep in state,

Or else if some revenues would be sold

He'd give them Darwey, bought at any rate

That all the nuns with prayers and holy names

Might fetch his soul from out the purging flames.

2290'I'll mend highways, or hospitals repair,

Else build a college, and endow 't with mines.'

Thus did he build his castles in the air

For all's not cash that jingles, gold that shines;

His glassy coin [must] leap out of the mint

Ere on his brow the stamp did current print.

Thus was he gull'd, as once a king of France

Paid a French monsieur for a prancing steed—

Gave him a purse whose richness did enhance

Th' enclosèd gem, supposed a noble meed,

2300But when for golden mountains he did gape,

He oped the purse, and only found a rape.

'Oh! what full anger redded o'er his looks!

What tides of rage and fury swelled his spleen!

He curseth her with candles, bells, and books;

And vowed ere long on her to wreak his teen.

'Ah me!' quoth he, 'such brittle things are lasses

Which one poor letter changeth unto glasses.'

Felice, now perceiving all was quiet,

Hearing no noise, unless a belly-blast

2310Which might proceed from an unwholesome diet,

Tied her apparel on with nimble haste,

And, coming to the lodge, with knuckle knock

She strove to summon out the lazy frock.

But the grim Tartar was so soundly lulled,

Without a dram of opium, steeped in ale—

Tirèd with vexing that he was so gulled—

That all Felice's rappings naught avail;

Till, vexèd with demurs she knock'd so loud,

It raised a thunder like a breaking cloud.

2320Just at that moment did Pazzell' awake

From an affrighting dream, wherein she saw

A dreadful lion her Felice take,

And tear her body with his sharp'ned paw;

And hearing this shrill noise, fear said 'twas true,

Danger did threaten her monastic crew.

Her frosted limbs she heavèd out of bed,

And shelled her body in her night-apparel,

Arming her hands with pistols stuffed with lead,

Which anger firing, with the air did quarrel,

2330And, groping in the dark, her foot did slip,

Which out o' th' barrels made the bullets skip.

Felice, at that thunder-clap amazed,

With haste retired from the porter's cell,

And meeting her, on one another gazed.

The porter, starting up, did ring the bell,

The virgins shrieked, which all made murmurs shrill

Like Irish hubbubs in pursuit of ill.

When reason somewhat had becalmed their rage,

The abbotess Felice sharply checked.

2340'Madam,' says she, 'I only came t' assuage

Intestine heats which all my body decked

In scarlet dye; and being much appalled,

With frisking fairies, I the porter called.'

'Go, go, you are a wanton girl,' quoth she,

'That fain would tempt my porter unto folly.'

'Madam,' Felice said, 'you injure me.

Sure, if lascivious I had been so jolly,

I might have met with many men more able,

Before I did invest myself with sable.'

2350'Oh madam! madam!' mad Avaro cried,

'Why do you think she could o'ercome your frock?

I ne'er did yield, yet have been often tried;

My courage hath withstood a greater shock.

Yet sure she would—she would have passed the gates;

The reason why, forsooth, to gather dates.

I am afraid your dukedom-girl does long

Not for the porter, he is out of date;

But for an oily cavalier that 's strong,

May teach her virginship a mother's fate.

2360Madam, look well; see if you miss no glass,

I'm sure with brittle coin she gulled an ass.'

Then told the story: Piazzella fretted,

'This is the jewel which you would have sought

When in all haste from hence you would have jetted!

What your intendments were my wisdom thought,

I'll have no gadders, and t' allay your heat

I have a diet will prevent a sweat.'

In a retired room she locked her up,

Devoid of lustful mates with her to play;

2370Allowed her pulse, and juice of clouds to sup,

And bade her scores of Ave Maries say.

Three artificial days she lodgèd there,

Where every day to her did seem a year.

When she had paid this penance for her crime

(Which in her judgement was accounted bad),

She was again amongst the virgins prime,

On promise that she would not henceforth gad.

Yet still she plotted, but where'er she went,

The angry destines thwarted her intent.

2380Then, from Bellam' since walls did her encell,

She thought t' employ her talent to the best.

One of the virgins had some vogliarell,

And earnestly desir'd with her to rest.

Who ere the morn did Piacinto sing,

And wore her blushes on her rubied ring.

Next night she chose another, then another;

Her curious palate so to novels stood,

That every one had hope to be a mother,

And near of kin, united in one blood.

2390But yet, alas! this pleasure lasted not:

Their virgin-girdles could not keep their knot.

Not many fortnights after they had took

These physic-potions from their doctor's reins,

One told her folly by her meagre look,

Another had more blue than on her veins,

Others were qualmish, and another longs:

All spake their pleasures, yet all held their tongues.

One long'd for citrons, and another grapes,

That grew on Alps' steep height, others for peaches;

2400 One strangely did desire the tails of apes

Steepèd in juice of myrtles, holms, and beeches.

Some palates must be fed with implumed quails,

And nothing must approach this tongue but rails.

Some longed for crayfish, shrimps, cods, plaice, and oysters;

One for a lemon that doth grow on thorns;

Another longeth for some blood of roisters,

Spiced with the scrapings of pale Cynthia's horns;

One on the bosom of the matron skips,

And spite of her full nose did gnaw her lips;

2410 One bade them fill an orc of Bacchus water,

Her thirsty soul she said would drain a tun;

One from her window bids a poor translator

Cut her a cantle of the gaudy sun;

But above all I like that witty girl,

Which longed to feed upon a glorrah earl.

The jealous matron with suspicious eye

Did read their common ill in every face;

Espied the breach of their virginity,

And feared a plantage with an infant race.

2420Yet still suppressed her knowledge, till at last

Their heaving bellies kissed their thick'ned waist.

She then, with friendly summonings, did call

The grave lord abbot and his smooth-chin race;

Who, coachèd, came unto the virgin-hall,

But all the rabble through the vault did pace.

Arrivèd here, she cookèd dainty cates

To please the abbot and his tempo-pates.

So called a council 'bout her quondam maids—

Each one admiring who durst be so bold,

2430Since none had entrance, nor the virgins strayed,

And for the porter he was known too cold.

The prior feared lest one of his square caps

Should guilty be of those upheaving laps.

It was decreed that they all should be

Shrived, being sejoinèd from each other's ken;

But, ere that time, the teemers did decree

What answer to return the shriving men.

Felice did instruct them to deny

That she gave birth unto their pregnancy.

2440But they should say, and to that saying seal,

With strong asseverations that 'Into

Our fast-locked room a youthful blade did steal,

And with the best of wooing did us woo.

Our cases are the same with Merlin's mother:

We think our lover was his father's brother.

'Twas one man's act, or, clothed with human shape,

- 799 -

He was angelical; and this we thought

Because there was no semblance of a rape.

We gave him our assent as soon as sought.

2450We judged unmaiding better in the dark

Than, Daphne-like, an husking o'er with bark.'

The shrivers to their lords return with smiles,

And on their looks a joy ovall chhriots* had,

Said they confessèd them with zeal and wiles,

And by a plain narration knew the dad—

One of those ever-youthfuls came from heaven,

And in the virgins' wombs did lay a leaven.

The abbot at this news did much rejoice,

Since with a kind aspect the Virgin Lady,

2460Viewing this nunn'ry, did ordain this choice,

And for the issue did appoint this daddy.

They shall be prophets, priests of high renown,

And virgins which shall keep their bellies down.

Provide them childbed linen, mantles, swaddles,

Rockers and nurses, all officious shes,

With rattles, corals, little cars, and cradles,

And give them beads to wait upon their knees.

Rome's high arch-vicar shall a testate be

To the first-born whom Nature makes a he.

2470Take pens, and smooth-strain anthems write in bays,

Make new orisons unto all the saints,

And to Lucina chant invoking lays,

To move her pity these young mothers' plaints;

Say her fair temple need not fear the flame,

Whilst here she wins her an eternal fame.

Felice smiled to see their studied care,

To foster whom she at her pleasure got.

But Piazzella, starting from her chair,

Callèd Felice to survey her knot,

2480And finding it as at the first 'twas tied,

'How 'scapèd you this goddy sire?' she cried.

'Madam,' quoth he—Felice, 'I confess

I was a party in those spruce delights;

But Nature curseth some with barrenness,

As (I have heard) Albertus Magnus writes.

So that though my desires were full as big,

I was not heavèd with that curtain jig!

Reason *fortasse's* on her words did stamp,

Which did entruth them (though they were but squibs).

2490This done, the prior did remove his camp,

And all the friars, with hemp-girdled ribs,

All great with expectation, and as fain

Would be delivered as the full-flanked train.

They sung canzones ere the sun could rise,

And Ave-Maries out of number said,

Lucina wond'red at this strange disguise,

That nuns and monks to her devoutly prayed.

All beads were rattled, and all saints invoked,

Some squealed, some tenored, and some hoarsely croaked.

2500With this conceit, Felice frolic grew,

And sported bravely in the silent hours.

Her bed-mates call'd her Angel; yet none knew

That 'twas Albino which had cropped their flowers.

But, though they revelled in the night, the day
Threw hailstorms on their lust to chill their play.
Yet had their pleasure not a grandsire life,
For tattling slumbers did their joys untone.
'You vowed, Felice, I should be your wife,'
Says Cloe, 'ere you loosed my virgin-zone,
2510But ah!' so waked, and feared her vocal slumber
Would from her eyelids force a Trent and Humber.
Says Phill', 'Felice, had I known at first
You only wore the name of Folco's daughter,
I would have suff'red an untamèd thirst
Ere lust had brought mine honour unto slaughter,
But oh——' and, starting up, she feared her dream
Would ere 'twas long obscure joy's mirthful gleam.
'Well, well,' says Floris, ''tis an happy change
To loose mine honour for an angel-mate,
2520But angels will not house in such a grange:
This is the offspring of Felice's pate.
But ah——' so sighed, and sighing causèd fears
Lest her plump rosies should be ploughed with tears.
Yet, you must know, the virgins did not use
To blab their private actions in a dream,
But that the cunning matron did infuse
Some atoms of the Quiris into cream;

And, ere they were enclosed in Somnus' arms,
She drenched their fancies in these liquid charms.
2530Then, with unsealèd eyes, she made her ears
Keep privy watch to intercept their talk:

Yet would have washed her knowledge out with tears,

And wished it written in her mind with chalk.

One while she thanked the God of slumber, then,

Her curses threw him down to Pluto's den.

But when Aurora, in her tissue vest,

Mantled with blushes, rose from Tithon's side,

And through a casement of th' adorèd east

Sent Phosphorus to usher in her pride—

2540Ere Phoebus our horizon did array

With silver glitter of the blooming day—

She snatched her termers from the sweet embrace,

And golden fetters of death's elder brother,

Bidding them hence those deading slumbers chase

T' implore the favour of the Virgin-mother.

They starting up with more than common speed,

Each shelled her body in her modest weed.

So called to chapel those whose pregnant wombs

The angel's pills had heaved above their waists,

2550Like to a surfeit ta'en of Hybla's combs,

When we are too indulgent to our tastes.

But left Felice out to cut or sew,

Or to embroider with the lanky crew.

Which made a sudden faintness loose each part,

And every joint was like an aspen leaf;

Her rosy twins retired to her heart,

Her looks were coloured like a sunburnt sheaf,

As the stiff bristles of an aged boar

Were her smooth locks, which o'er her cheeks she wore

2560And juster cause had none than she to fear,

For as from quiet slumber she awoke

She heard the ptisick pick Pazzella's ear

That she had knowledge of what Floris spoke.

And now she doubted all would come to th' scanning

Their longing, swelling and their sudden wanning.

The virgins wondered at Felice's change,

To see her eyes fix'd in a white-limed wall;

Each feared herself, and each conceived 'twas strange

Lest the disease was epidemical:—

2570That Merlin's uncle changed Felice's hue,

And streaked their temples with a purple blue.

But leave her sighing with these sterile dames,

We'll crowd into the house of sacred vows

Where consciousness, begetting female shames,

Spread scarlet carpets on their cheeks and brows.

They looked, and blushed, and glanced on one another:

Each cursed the minute which did dub her mother.

The holy brethren, through the mouldy pipe,

At that same time did unexpected come,

2580To know if th' goddy issue yet was ripe

To give adieu unto their skin-sealed home.

But viewing still their wombs, with zealous hands,

They prayed Lucina to untie their bands.

Their chantings dead, the abbotess began;

'Brethren, you see what sad misfortune haps

Unto my virgins by the oil of man,

Witness the heaving of their spongy paps.

We of an angel dreamed, but if he was

He shall hereafter for an evil pass.

2590'I made their slumbers vocal, so they told

'Twas Folco's duke's supposèd daughter's work.

Larved with that name, it seems some roister bold

Them to unvirgin cunningly did lurk.

But since 'tis so, the proverb shall stand good,

Tart sauces must be mixed with luscious food.

I knew him to be wanton, and to chill

The raging heat of his unbridled lust,

I doomed him three days' penance, judged an ill

Would make him sapless as the summer's dust.

2600But since that failed, days shall be chang'd to years,

Minutes to months, till paid his tribute tears.

I'll try if grief will drain his melting reins,

And hang a crutch upon his able back;

If sorrow will unblood his swelling veins

And make his sinews, shrunk with famine, crack.

I'll make a purgatory, where with hunger,

Frost, flame, and snow, I'll tame my virgin-monger.

I'll give command a dungeon shall be made,

To whose close womb the sun shall never pry,

2610Nor Cynthia dare to peep: for gloomy shade

Like cloudy night shall purblind every eye:

Bare measure four-foot broad; and for that height

'T shall make him by constraint, not court, lie slight.

A bedstead hewn out of the craggy rock,

Not arched with cedar wainscot, knobbed with gold;

His bed no shrinker, but a sturdy flock,

Swans shall not be deplumed his limbs t'infold.

Nor curtained with the travails of the loom

Of poor Arachne, ere she had her doom.

2620I will not spend the ransom of a crown

For curious dainties to delight his taste.

I'll fetch no fowls from off the Parthian down,

Or Phaenicopter for luxurious waste.

I will no mullet from Corsica take,

Oysters from Circe's or the Lucrine lake.

I will allow him pottage, thicked with bran,

Of barley-meal a choenix every day,

A sovereign diet for a frolic man

That is affected with the Paphian play.

2630And lest his stomach should too chol'ric grow,

I will afford him some congealed snow.'

The bald-pate crew this penance well approved,

And, in a trice, all things she ready got.

So well she stirred her stumps (as it behoved)

She being hatcher of this starving plot.

This done, with friendly words and courteous air,

She called Felice to her house of prayer.

'It suits not with your greatness, madam fair,

Being sole daughter to so great a man,

2640To lodge with those which your inferiors are,

As much as is an inch unto a span,

And I'm afraid the Duke will fume and swear,

Should but your lodging step into his ear.'

'Madam,' quoth she, 'you harbour needless fears.

Goodness, not greatness, differenceth maids.

My father's no tobacconist; and swears

In point of honour like our scarlet blades.

And, by my faith, it more contenteth me

To sheet with maidens though of mean degree.

2650I am surchargèd with the black-hued choler,

Which strikes my fancy with most ugly shapes.

I durst not rest a-darkness for a dolour,

Without a pillow-friend to scare those apes:

Let Cloe with conceits my spirits wing,

Or melancholy will my requiem sing.'

'You shall,' says she, 'have Sesamoidesse.

For all entreats are of too dull a print.

We must respect your father's worthiness,

His honour must your love and passions stint,

2660And your own worth must highly be regarded,

How shall I else expect to be rewarded?'

Then did she take her by the tender hand,

And led her to her grot in princely state.

She feared not much, nor did her will withstand,

Judging divorcement was her harshest fate;

But when she saw the entrance was so narrow

A sudden fear did eat up all her marrow.

Pazzella, viewing her supposèd lass,

Repented her of her intended ills;

2670But injuries engraven are on brass,

And women's jointures are to have their wills.

And lest remorse should chill her angry mood,

Fuel was added by the brotherhood.

'Then,' says she, 'madam, you behold the cage
Which I preparèd for your honour's good,
Where you may spend the autumn of your age.
Till age and winter have congealed your blood.
You may retire to ease: for envy can
Nor dares to say you're not an able man.
2680When twice ten circled snakes are crawled away,
You shall enjoy companions masculine,
To give instructions in that youthful play
Is fed with Ceres and the god of wine.
And, if my virgins shall hereafter be
Lascivious given, I will send for thee.'
Into this coven was Felice thrust,
With bars and locks the entrance sealèd fast,
Now must he pay a dear rate for his lust,
His curtain-vezzo, and the coral taste.
2690Sure his repentance will be full as dear
As the philosopher's *non tanti* were.
Ah, foppish monk! did not Bellama's 'no'
Give thee a warning-piece presaging danger,
But thou must headlong rush upon thy woe?
Happy's that man which is to lust a stranger!
If this of dalliance is the constant fee,
Let them d——dally that do list, for me.
Here, when the barking star his sceptre waved,
When in our clime we feel an Ethiope's heat,
2700An undervault the subtil matron paved,
With fire and flame to force a constant sweat,
That, as from flowers hot limbecks water 'still,

So by this stove from him sweat-currents drill.

Then, for the winter season she provided

A melting cloud full fraught with feath'red rain

(Whose curious art the air-borne clouds derided),

Which through some oillet holes might passage gain.

His cabin should have been, like Alps' cold height,

Mantled and strewèd o'er with winter's white.

2710And 'twas so dark, I cannot see to write.

Nay, at a nonplus it all pencils sets.

'Twas hell's epitome, the cage of night,

Walled in with pitch and roofed o'er with jets.

The lynx at midday here would wish for day,

And cats without a torch must grope their way.

But leave him labyrinthed and thus distressed,

And see Bellama, and examine how

She brooks the absence of her bosom-guest,

If discontent does revel on her brow.

2720It does: for why, she dreams and never sleeps,

She feeds and fats not, laughs, but ever weeps.

'Disaster hangs upon Albino gyves,'

Says she, 'else Envy keeps him prisoner,

Or a new bull does interdict them wives,

So seals the lips of my petitioner.

Else the smirk knave is so devout in pray'r,

He has no time to kiss the common air.

But does he love? or is 't a fit of mirth,

Which, like to children's fancies, soon expire

2730Ere language or employment give them birth,

Flashing affections, aged like thunder-fire?

His eyes shot Cupids at my yielding heart,

But his firm breast repelled my feeble dart.

Perchance he judged my forwardness to love,

By too much court'sy, and my frequent glances.

So thought in jest my willingness to prove,

Not with that sober passion which entrances;

But with lip-love, which to the heart ne'er sinks,

And paper-vows which take their birth from inks.

2740But stay: does greatness use to be denied?

Beauty and bravery command a grant.

Yet might my looks and carriage plumed with pride

His humble and untow'ring spirit daunt.

Daunt? no: his soul's a temper most divine,

Dares soar aloft to kiss the sun's near shine.

Then love he does: but must this action, woo,

Be tied by patent only unto men?

Some unfrequented paths of love I'll go,

And in some riddles court him by my pen.

2750Yet first to th' abbey I'll dispatch a post,

To make inquiry where my monk doth host.'

The merchant is not with desires so big,

When as he ploughs the sea for Indian mines;

With slower steps the sons of Bacchus trig

To sack-shops for the French and Spanish wines;

Than she to Tagus bids her servant go

To Croftfull Abbey where her wishes grow.

Gone is the messenger: but small success

Waits on his travels, for he back returns

2760With, 'Madam, where Albino's none can guess.

They think his ashes are enclosed in urns.

For time, say they, has counted fortnights many,

Since his choice feature object was to any.'

This answer shot an hailstorm at her heart,

Whose sudden chillness jellied all her blood,

Sh' applièd Holco to unscrew the dart,

But her assayments brought her little good.

For, but Albino, none can cure her ill,

Not physic potions, or the druggard's skill.

2770'Ah me! has Fate my dear Albino ta'en?

Then farewell music, and you sprucing trade;

Either my tears shall body him again,

Or send my ghost to wait upon his shade.

For she is judged a light unconstant lover,

Whose flame the ashes of neglect can cover.'

Have you beheld how, when the moors and marsh

Belch vapours to blemish bright Titan's eye,

They with his rays wage conflicts long and harsh,

Confining them unto their proper sky

2780(Bribèd perchance by envious night to wrap

Day and his champion in his sooty lap).

So that to us appears nor sun nor day,

And only faith persuades us there is both,

Till day and sun call in each straggling ray,

And force a passage, spite of fume and froth:

Yet then the day but newly seems to dawn,

And o'er the sun a veil of cypress drawn.

Just so diseasing sorrow, armed with tears,

Sighs, and black melancholy veiled her face;

2790So that no ray of loveliness appears,

And only faith persuades us she has grace.

Her eyes retired, her double blush was wanned,

Her locks dissevered, and her lilies tanned.

And as, in her which arted looks does wear,

Men look for nature's steps, and cannot trace her;

Since she, by nature nothing less than fair,

Hath purchased from the shops such worth to grace her;

Though foul, now fair and sleek, though age did plough

And made long furrows in her cheek and brow.

2800So knowledge here was in a maze: the eye,

That knew Bellama, did Bellama seek,

And, looking on her, nothing could descry

Spake her Bellama, or in eye or cheek.

To love's harsh laws she gave such constant duty,

Sh'ad only left an anagram of beauty.

She threw herself upon her couch of ease,

And marshalled all her thoughts in just arrays;

This brought small comfort, that did hardly please,

And in that thought despair the sceptre sways.

2810Yet thought she not death could a period set,

Unless he did some strange advantage get.

'He's young and lusty: every vein does swell

With aqua-vitae, coral juice of life;

His skill in magic else can frame a spell

To distance meagre death and Atrop's knife.

Yet love gives birth to fear: I'll send to search
The lion's flinty bed, and vulture's perch.
I and my woman will attend the quest,
Veiled in disguises of some country lasses;
2820No state-distinction, for my humble breast
Shall leave all pride with silks, perfumes, and glasses;
And, if with *non inventus* we return,
I'll Venus' witchcraft hate and Cupid spurn.'
When as the sovereign of the day had drawn
A veil of brightness o'er the twinkling lamps,
And threw on Cynthia's brow a double lawn,
Clearing the welkin from benighting damps,
They in the habits of a milking maid
(All but skin-linen) did their beauties shade.
2830And in these coarse attires they hasted out
To seek Albino through each wood and plain,
Whom we will leave to pace the world about
And see Felice, wet with eye-lid rain,
Whose bondage was the greater, since despair
Blasted all hopes which promised her the air.
The brazen bull, strappado, or the rack,
The faggot-torture, and the piked barrell,

Balanced with his, degrees of sorrow lack:
'Tis with a bulrush to decide a quarrel.
2840The famine wherewithal the Thracian knight
Was sent to Pluto wants a little weight.
He that stole fire fro' th' chariot of the Sun,
Whose liver's vulture-gnawn at Caucasus;

He that the counsels of the gods unspun,

Like wanton's eyes, stone-rolling Sisyphus;

Hold best proportion with these sharp'ned woes,

Which stern misfortune on Felice throws.

She, that was glutted with most curious cates,

Had every pleasure to content her lust,

2850Who had command o'er Fortune and the Fates,

Now sups up pulse and gnaws a fleecèd crust.

She that had many girls is now alone,

And of so many cannot compass one.

Had I a fancy steeped in sorrow's brine,

Invention witty in the threnes of woe;

Could sad experience dictate every line,

A dearth of words would to my muse say 'No'.

I may as well go fathom all the spheres

As measure her disasters, count her tears.

2860Oft on remembrance of that harmless bliss,

Which (copèd) she enjoyed, her thoughts would feed,

Oft on Bellama's beauty, touch and kiss,

Till strucken dead with thought of present need.

Then would she raise her thoughts, and hope for day,

And starting up from silence boldly say:

'Despite of Envy's vipers, tricks, and wiles,

My cradle-playmate, Mirth, I'll ne'er forsake,

But taste Sardinian herbs shall raise up smiles,

Though I was wafting o'er the Stygian lake.

2870Tortures shall ne'er unman me; but I'll be

Albino, Malice, 'spite of her and thee.

Delays ofttimes, from time's secluded parts,

Bring help to helpless not expecting aid;

Some of the gods will pity these my smarts,

Not suffer them to whet the sexton's spade.

Or if the gods—'midst flames then scorpion-like

I'll gore my breast, and fall on mine own pike.

Yet had I suff'red for a courteous one,

These woes should ne'er had power t' have raised a sorrow

2880But when mine eyes did in my breast enthrone

Her—her of whom hell cruelty may borrow.

This is the height of woe, death, and diseases,

Nay, hell itself to this comparèd pleases.

Yet stay, say Neptune's palace shall be land,

And this firm ball of earth a liquid brack;

Say the North Pole with Phoebus shall be tanned,

And to the South the lilies shall be black.

Say this, and more, before thou dare to say

Bellama is *Màboun'* or *Mà bellà.'*

2890No more of this: we'll for her freedom plot.

A pious monk, perceiving well her smart,

With diligence assayed to purge each spot

With holy cruse from her diviner part.

But still her answer was—nor man, nor lover,

Nor she the virgin's ankles did discover.

'Alas! my brother I am not a male,

But a weak sience of the weaker sex.

The ladies spake the truth (might truth prevail)

But me with torture Piazell' doth vex;

2900'Cause, at my entrance, I did promise fair;

Yet 't proves court-language, merely, purely, air.

But all this time she would not licence deign

That I three yards behind should leave the gates,

And fumèd when I would have left her train,

T' have sought a jewel, and to gather dates.

So that the Duke my father ne'er had ken

Of my encloist'ring in this hate-light den.

But, 'gainst it now resolving, I intend

To turn the stream of his munificence

2910On you, dear brother, if you'll be my friend,

And plot how I may be delivered hence.

Lend your endeavours: and I'll lend my wit,

Vow faithfulness, and I will warrant it.

I'll woo my father for his free assent,

If to your barren cowl you'll bid farewell,

That Hymen's rites may perfect our content,

By joyful echoes of the marriage bell.

'Cause you in person do resemble him

Whom 'mongst all men I only judgèd trim.'

2920The monk gave ear unto her winning prate

And gazèd on her beauty masculine,

Whose feature might delude a wiser pate,

Assisted only by a tallow-shine.

(For by an unctious salve she kept her chin

From the hair-mantle of an agèd skin.)

'Madam', says he, 'I judge your language true,

And to your vows I dare my credence lace:

Your virgin-blushes innocence do show,

And modesty is printed on your face.

2930Faith, truth, and honesty reside with me:

My best endeavours shall your servants be.'

'Well,' says Felice, 'I have now decreed

(Since Phoebus has forsook our hemisphere),

To sheath my body in your holy weed,

Then through the private walk my course will steer.

So from your holy walls I'll take my flight,

Or by permission, or in silent night.

And when I am arrived at Folco's towers,

My father shall your matchless kindness know,

2940Who, I am sure, will summon all his powers

To fetch thee from this house of flame and snow:

And who with much contentment will not brook

Some three days' penance to be made a duke?

For, by inheritance, the dukedom's mine

When death unbody shall my father's soul.

Since no heir-male's descended from our line,

The Salic law cannot my right control.

And, to assure thee that I'm only thine,

I swear by all the powers that are divine.'

2950Then did she circle with ensphering arm

Conrado's neck and amorously him lipp'd,

Which did the amorist so strongly charm

That he with haste out of his vestments skipped,

And bade Felice change: for in good deed

He should full well become her virgin weed.

Felice undressed, and dressed, and having made

Herself a monk, put on Conrado's face,

And some few minutes with her monkship played,
Then gave a farewell to that hated place.
2960But ere her quick dispatch could post her thence
Her beauty shot a fire through every sense.
Fear now exiled the confidence he tied,
Forced by affection, to Felice's words,
Revoked his promise now,—all aid denied;
And, with majestic looks and gesture's lords
His flaming lust dissolved his pious snow,
And now his loud desires will have no 'No'.
But vows to disenclothe her and to break
Her virgin-seal despite of force or smiles,
2970Till Folco strove and made his noddle leak
Sardonic liquor to new-paint the tiles,

So hasted out, and to the matron gave
The iron porter of Conrado's grave.
Imping his haste, he threads the vaulted lane,
Not wounded by his soles this many a day,
Like those which, when arraigned, a pardon gain
Dare neither at the jail nor gallows stay.
And coming to the postern gate he knocked,
Which at devotion time was always locked.
2980But when the last Amen had silenced prayer,
The porter to Albino entrance gave;
Who straight was brought unto the judgement chair,
Where, furred with state, did sit the abbot grave.
Who said, 'Conrade, why was your stay so long?
You missed the manna of the evensong.'

Pseudo-Conrado answered him, 'My lord,

I found Felice so oppressed with grief,

That charity commanded me t'afford

By learning, prayers, and anthems, some relief.

2990And truly on my faith I am persuaded

A virgin-lady with these weeds is shaded.

I, moved to pity by her streaming tears,—

Her sighing gales, loud threnes, and sad laments,

Won by her beauty, and her tender years,

Have promised aid, confirmed by your assents,

And in all haste will tell her father's grace

What clouds of woe bemist Felice's face.

She promised me when as her freedom's sealed,

When she shall re-enjoy the glorious light,

3000When the sad sentence of her woe's repealed

She will be mine in spite of envy's might.

Nay more, she from the dukedom will extract

Some lordships to perform a pious act.'

Forthwith, a synod of the holy men

Was called to broach the wisdom of their pates.

The questions were proposed—"Who? What? and When?

The 'who', is Folco's daughter; 'what', estates;

The 'when', so soon as she, by Folco's powers,

Shall shell her body in proud Gurby's towers.

3010This answer smelt of profit, and did gain

The abbot's liking, and his griping crew.

Says he, 'Conrado, true content does reign

And triumph in our thoughts: we yield to you.

Success wait on thy voice: for to thy care

Our wishes, hopes, desires, entrusted are.'

'Fear not,' quoth he, 'my faith dares warrant all.
All things are real as my words are true.
Myself will pace unto fair Gurby hall,
And with emphatic language plead and sue:
3020So that old Folco's lungs shall crack with laughter
To hear me chat the travails of his daughter.
First she, mistrusting that she should be forc'd,
By his proud nod, unto a hated pillow,
From folly, Folco, folk, herself divorced,
To twist, for scornèd maids, some wreaths of willow.
How zealously she prayed, and looked demurely!
She is, in thought and word, a virgin surely.
But the conceit is this—Who bridles laughter,
That virgins holy, pure, and nuns to boot,
3030Should thicken with the pills of Folco's daughter,
Sing lullabies, and to Lucina hoot?
T' increase the wonder then, and imp his pleasures,
To Folco I'll present these waggish measures.'
Behold, admire, and some contentment gather
From nuns that teem, manned by a virgin-father.
Wonder and admiration cease to gaze
On flashing meteors, stars, and comets' blaze.
Let not Vitruvius or th' Ichonian beast,
Putzol or Etna slide into your breast.
3040Ope not your ears unto those cracks of thunder,
Whose cannon-echoes split the orbs in sunder.
Lend not your audience to those fond reports

Of Ob'ron, Mabell, and their fairy sports,

Nor tie your credence to the poet's pen

Which writes the noble acts of warlike men,

Of monsters, mooncalves, merry games, and masks,

Atlas' stiff shoulders, and Alcides' tasks.

Amazement flies these babbles, and does pin

Faith, eyes, and thoughts, unto this curtain-sin;

3050 That a pure virgin should unvirgin others,

And, though a virgin, yet make many mothers;

Make them heave up, be qualmish, pale, and cry

'A midwife (ho!) a midwife: else we die.'

It is an Afric crow, a sable swan,

To have a vestal puffèd up with man:

But that so many nuns unmaidened are

B' a nun without a man is more than rare.

The Sybil's virgin is not worth a rush,

And Merlin's mother may with envy blush.

3060 These, though they soared above the pitch of reason,

Yet crossed not nature's order, course, or season.

For women teemed as women, but a woman

As man, makes virgins teem, and yet is no man.

This—this is object unto fame and wonder,

Then make each clime with this *Mirandum* thunder.

About this time night summoned them to rest,

And each repairèd to his sturdy bed.

Albino's fears his hopes and joys suppressed;

But, in the rest, content struck sorrow dead.

3070 They slept until the bright enlight'ned air,

With silver glitter, called them up to prayer.
But our Albin' took earlier leave of sleep,
And sheathed his body in his monkish vests;
Knocked at his lodge, which did the entrance keep,
Who that he could not wake himself protests:
'Thou art some fury, hag, or Hob I trow,
That boldly at my lodge dost thunder so.'
Albino says, 'What frenzy damps thy reason?
Arise, my haste commands a frequent rap.'
3080'Begone,' quoth he, 'entreats are out of season.
Worshipful Hob, I'll have another nap.
'Tis not mine hour to rise until I hear
The clapper sound a *surge* in mine ear.'
When our young monk had many minutes spent,
And could not Foppo from his pillow rear,
About that time light's charioteer had sent
Day's trusty harbinger his orb to clear.
He searched the walls, and trafficked with the lock;
But all in vain, he must implore the frock.
3090The chapel-clerk, as constant to his hour
As is day's herald which at breaking crows,
Seeing Aurora did his windows scour
And leapt into his chamber, straight arose:
Making the shrill-toned bell in echoes speak,
'Awake and rise to prayer, the day does break.'
Foppo was at that time in Morpheus' court,
Where he with apparitions was affrighted;
The scene was changed, then came a dainty sport,
Whose sudden neatness every sense delighted;

3100Then dreamt Albine, their renegado monk
Was knocking at his lodge, the other *Nunc.*
Then dreamt he saw a table richly spread
With all the dainties riot ever felt;

All birds of warrant which in woods are bred,
With salmon, mullet, turbot, trout, and smelt:
The princely-pacing deer, entombed in paste,
Embalmed with spices to delight the taste.
A sparkling wine, drawn newly from the cheek
Of some chaste fair which blushes coloured red,
3110With brisk canary and enlivening Greek,
Poetic sherry which can sharpen lead—
This ravish'd Foppo with a taste content,
Till to his ear the bell an errand sent.
When, starting up, he deemed the bell did call
His able stomach to a founder's feast,
And with all speed was swogging to the hall,
But that Albino stayed him by the crest,
And lew-warm claret from his hogshead drew
To make his stomach give the deer adieu.
3120Quoth he, 'Thou son of Somnus, drowsy slave!
Why didst thou not at my loud summons rise?
But in a fit of lunacy did rave
As though thy wit had ta'en some new disguise?
I'll be your Hob, your hag: and, though I'm loath,
Will now chastise thee for thy feignèd sloth.'
But whilst his passion took a breathing space,
The wak'ned porter from his fists did creep,

Fixèd his goggles on his youthful face,

And then rememb'red his prophetic sleep.

3130Tells him he's not Conrado; for he knows

That brow, those cheeks, lips, eyes, Albino owes.

'And though your wrath should grind me unto powder,

Without a warrant, I will ope no gate.'

This answer made Albino's anger louder,

And vowed a passage, bought at any rate.

So leapt upon the slave with nimble strength,

And measured on the earth his ugly length.

Albino hastes to th' postern; having got

The keys, but 'mongst so many much was puzzled

3140To find the right; Foppo meanwhile did trot

Unto some chambers where the shavelings nuzzled,

And them with outcries raisèd to surprise

Albino, larvèd in Conrado's guise.

Like penancers with linen on their backs,

The baldpates ran to seize upon their prey;

But yet their haste a semi-moment lacks:

Albino through the gate had found a way.

And, snatching out the keys, did them encage,

Raising a bulwark to withstand their rage.

3150Then thanked his stars that thus delivered him

From dangers which did threaten naught but death.

For he by th' verge of *Mare mort* did swim,

And did expect his latest gale to breath.

Nay, these late troubles had him so dishearted

That every shadow 'lmost the union parted.

- 824 -

You, whose disasters some proportion hold,

Help my weak fancy to express his fears;

Teach me my rhymes in cypress to enfold,

From thwarted lovers borrow me some tears;

3160Fetch me some groans from the ascending thief;

And from the Inquisition fetch me grief.

Without demurs, Albino left the wicket,

Fearing the monks should bribe the faithless lock,

And steered his course unto a well-grown thicket,

Whose lofty hill was armed with many a rock.

He envies sculls that wait on spit and oven,

And vows ne'er more to see that hated coven.

Have you beheld the stately-pacing stag,

Flying the echoes of some deep-mouthed hounds?

3170How first his brow does wear a ferny flag,

And with curvettings beats the quaking ground;

Telling the fawns and wood-nymphs that he scorns

The hounds, horse, huntsmen, and their warbling horns.

But when he is embossed in blood and sweat,

When travail on his swiftness fetters hangs,

He then is frighted with the shrill recheat,

And fears a pinking with the yellers' fangs.

Seeks ev'rywhere for shelter, and dares rush

Malèd with fear, into the sharpest bush.

3180So fared it with Albino: whilst he had

Fate at a beck, commanded Fortune's wheel,

Was callèd by his Donnes, active lad,

He thought his joys were wallèd in with steel,

Slighted misfortune, envy set at naught,

And, braving malice, dared in every thought.

But when his tow'ring heart was taught to know
Humiliation, and self-confidence
Was strucken dead with famine, flame, and snow;
Although his genial stars had freed him thence,
3190He fears the monkish rabble, and he shrouds
Himself in caves, encurtained round with clouds.
In his dark house he heard a feeble voice,
Breathed from the corals of some weak'ned maid.
At first concealment was his better choice,
Till pity set an edge upon his blade.
Then guided by the cry, he saw a roister
Did in his arms perforce a nymph encloister.
Yet, seeing home-spun russet, stopped his pace;
Saying, 'By this what honour shall I gain?'
3200But in his eye so curious was her face,
Though masked and blubbered o'er with brackish rain,
That he forthwith unsheathed his trusty Turk,
Called forth that blood which in his veins did lurk.
So, stepping forward, cries, 'Injurious slave,
Unto what baseness does thy folly tempt her?'
Who answered him, 'Fond fool, thy foolish brave
From my decreèd end shall not exempt her.
Befriend me, Queen of Cyprus! and in spite
Of force or fortune, I'll have my delight.'
3210'Desist,' Albino says, 'or else I vow,
By all those tapers which enrich the night,
I'll make pale death strew cypress on thy brow.

And to th' infernal shades thy soul will fright.

Cease from thy brutish rape, or else prepare

Thy cursed lungs to draw the Stygian air.'

Quoth the rude Sylvan, 'I am past that age

Which with bugbears the foppish nurse does fright.

Hence, curtain-squire, smock-groom, and urine-page!

I'll have no testates unto my delight.

3220Pack hence with speed, or by Actaeon's head,

My weighty falchion shall pronounce thee dead.'

'Well,' says Albino, 'since thou'lt not desist,

Prove the adventures of a bloody duel.

One of our threads fell Atrop's shall untwist,

For to my rage kind pity lendeth fuel.

To free a virgin from thy gripping paws

I judge well pleasing unto nature's laws.'

They clasp'd their helms, and buckled to their fight,

'Twixt whom no umpire was but meagre death.

3230The woodwards green with Tyrian dye was dight

Who now desires a minute's space to breath.

Albino gave the truce, yet but to breath;

His valour scorned to crowd into the sheath.

Then did his nimble sleight and courage show,

Feigning a stroke, but pointed at his breast,

Which oped a door whereat his spirits flew,

And wellnigh set his fainting soul at rest.

With that th' enfeebled Sylvan weakly cries

'Hold, hold thy hand! or else Sylvanus dies.'

3240'Dost call for mercy,' says Albino, 'now?

And all thy thoughts erstwhile triumphant rid?

I seek not murder, may I save my vow.

That I should joy in blood my stars forbid.

I am content the virgin's voice shall seal

Thy death, or pardon, if thou make appeal.'

'Fair virgin,' quoth Sylvanus, 'pity is

The only grace that gives a virgin price.

Remission crowns a heart with greater bliss,

Than to hang iron on weak nature's vice.

3250The rays of your bright beauty urged desire;

Your feature kindled lust, love blowed the fire.'

The virgin answered, 'I did never suck

The tiger's dugs, the lioness, and bear,

Nor from a reeking breast an heart did pluck.

Never will I in blood with vulture's share.

But, since submission speaks from voice and knee,

Kind pity thins the fault, and pardons thee.'

Then to Albino says, 'Heroic youth,

May all the blessings which attend on man

3260Felicitate thy life; and to buy truth

To words, I dare do more than virgins can.

But, above all, I wish may nature's pride,

Lilies and roses, intertwine thy bride.

But yet alas! to recompense by airs

So large a bounty and so free is poor.

Yet why may not a spotless virgin's prayers,

Wing'd with desire, unclasp high heaven's door?

Accept of this, and if the Fates befriend me,

These blessings which I wished for shall attend thee.'

3270'Nature's sole wonder, beauty's only gem,'

Quoth he, 'my valour and my feeble arms

(If your perfections had not strenght'ned them)

Could not have freed you from intended harms.

Ascribe the honour to your matchless face.

My courage merits not the meanest place.

Yet had I swum through seas of steaming blood,

And passed through nitre flames that belch forth lead,

Had all the Furies armed with vipers stood,

T' have stopped my passage or pronounced me dead—

3280I would have thrown the die my fortune tried,

T' have bought you freedom though in crimson dyed.

For, when mine eyes sent forth the farthest glance,

To fetch th' idea of your beauty in,

That very sight my senses did entrance,

And make my thoughts excuse Sylvanus' sin.

For sure your quick'ning rays can melt a snow

On which the winds of age and sorrow blow.

But why do I upon the Ela raise

Thy noble worth, and yet intend to woo?

3290Since beauty oft displays her plumes at praise,

Then by this doing I myself undo.

But where I virtues find, refined as gold,

Despair shall never make affections cold.

Be pleasèd then to think the god of Love

With gilded arrow has transfixed my heart,

And let my purple breast your pity move.

With balsam of regard allay my smart,

Send thy quick eyes into my breast to see,

What tortures prick my heart to purchase thee.'

3300'Sir, I am grieved,' quoth she, 'you are allied

To him whose quiver crowns a lover's wish.

Else at a twelve-score distance might y' have spied

You cast your net to mesh a simple fish.

Your worth and feature does entitle you

To Cytherea with her silver hue.

When I, alas! am but an homely maid,

Born to a spindle and to serve a plough.

To milk my spongy-teated cows I strayed,

Which here amongst these tender hazels low.

3310My starvèd fortunes cannot think of love,

Nor does my envy wound the billing dove.'

This answer silencèd Albino's hopes,

Which spake as loud as though they kissed the sheets;

He in his thoughts commends the quiet copes

Which taste no sour in hunting after sweets.

'Alcides' life,' quoth he, 'compared to mine,

Is trouble-free, spiced with contents divine.

Fair maid, what hatred frosteth your desires?

What steams of envy choke bright Venus' lamp?

3320Give some kind fuel to maintain my fires,

A frown of yours will all my vitals damp.

Oil o'er my writhled heart, or let me know

From what black heads these bitter cadents flow.'

'Your favours, sir, have such commanding power,

That 'tis unjust your wishes to deny,

Accursed with all black tempests be that hour
In which my heart gave credit to mine eye.
Else would I not have been so much averse
T' a mind so noble and a feature terse.
3330But now alas! myself myself am not,
For heartless I my heart have giv'n away:
An abbey-brother has that treasure got,
Albino hight—he's Phoebus of my day.
Your habit speaks you a monk, sir, if you can
Tell me where I may find that (ah me) man.
Be pleased,' quoth she, 'to tell me where I may,
Or go myself, or else a servant send.'
'Fair maid,' quoth he, 'it is a gloomy way
Leads to the bed of your benighted friend.
3340His ashes are in Darwey Abbey laid,
But his faint ghost walks i' th' Elysian shade.'
'But is he dead?' says she, and loudly shrieked,
Which waked Narcissus' hate to second her,
Her rosies dewed with melting crystal reeked,
And sorrow did her trembling heart inter.
Symptoms of sad deplorings ne'er were known,
Which were not in her sharp lamentings shown.
'Choice maid,' quoth he, 'do not destroy your rosies,
And blast your beauty with such scalding sighs.
3350In nature's garden there are choicer posies,
More comely features, and more agile thighs.
What though Albino's dead? another may
Be trulier termed the Phoebus of your day.'
'Oh, do not stain,' says she, 'his spotless name!

Within his bosom every virtue ranged.

Equals to him dull nature cannot frame,

Though she should labour till herself be changed:

It is a shame to ask more favours yet:

Grant me this one, because my sun is set.

3360My pity saved, when as your fury had

The rough-pawed Sylvan mincèd with your skene.

Oh, with same courage let your mind be clad,

With your sharp scimitar my liver dreane.

Why should I be a liver, since he's dead

Who was my hope, my health, my heart, my head'.

'How am I chang'd!' quoth he, 'my heart does beat

The fainting summons of the Child of Sin.

My knees do quarrel, and a chilling sweat

Cold as the dew of winter oils my skin.

3370Fear snatcheth from my roseate banks their blood,

And drowns my liver in a sanguine flood.

'Tis strange a naked breast of bleachèd snow,

And crystal mounts enriched with coral heads,

(On which the purple violets do grow)

Should dare mine arm, and strike my courage dead.

My steel a breast of iron has unhinged.

And knees of brass have to my fury cringed.

Had some vast Gog or he whom Tellus brought—

One got by Fury or Gradivus' mate—

3380Who, but with monsters, ne'er conversed with ought,

Dared with a look, mine arm had weak'ned Fate.

But, at this feeble voice my blood does start,

And into pity melts my swelling heart.

Then name no more those words: for they at once

Do both unedge my valour and my steel.

Too safely do your virtues keep the sconce.

My steadiest thoughts, struck with these letters, reel.

My sacrilegious hand shall never stain

Virtue's sole temple, and the grace's fane.

3390Dry up those furrowing cadents. Will you give

Your lovely self in marriage unto him,

If I shall say Albino yours does live,

And in your view his comely portrait limn?

Say, aye, to this: and I will try my skill,

To make him pace along yon craggy hill.'

"Tis the countenance which my wishes crave,

Naught half so sweet,' says she, 'as Hymen's tedes.'

Albino then the haired earth did shave,

And hedged two circles in with ropes of beads;

3400Then, quart'ring them, did take the virgin's hand,

And bade her with unshaken courage stand.

'Thou must not be surpris'd with shivering fear,

Though Cerberus, the janitor of Hell,

Though seven-headed Hydra, panther, bear,

The lion, tiger, or the dragon yell;

Although a monster spits forth flashing powder,

Though clouds and winds strive which should bellow louder.'

This said, with cruse of holy water he

Besprinkled o'er himself, besprinkled her,

3410And zealously did cross: the same did she,

Like a devout Romezzo conjurer.

This done: 'Fair maid,' quoth he, 'if Fates befriend me,

The servant of your beauty shall attend thee.'

Then 'gan [he] to invoke, or seem t' invoke,

With uncouth language the infernal crew—

'Vitz, Allafoun, Trallasht with elfish poke,

Trollox and Chimchish, with your grisly hue,

Gnarzell and Phrizoll which in Styx do wade,

Lê portè Albino from the Stygian shade.'

3420When from his lips these words had ta'en their flight,

A shuffling whirl-puff roared amongst the trees,

Th' affrighted leaves took flight, the grass looked white,

The quaking poplars fell upon their knees.

Jove's sacred tree stood cringing unto it,

And bowed his head, else 'twas in sunder split.

Then, from a breaking cloud, a sheet of fire

Encircled them, and dashed against an oak,

Ush'ring a thunder, whose untamed ire

Like dreadful tyrants naught but terror spoke.

3430And as unwilling to depart from them

His ireful cracks the trembling grove did hem.

These, suddenly succeeding so the first,

And at that instant when he feigned a spell,

Did make Albino judge himself accursed,

Thinking his voice unhinged the gates of hell.

Bellama's rosies wore as white as snow,

As though the Phyma did upon them blow.

And justly, for though these but common were,

Yet at that time when faintness kept the wicket,

3440Which at each shadow oped the gate to fear,

In that dark place, that unfrequented thicket—

I blame not though her courage had been colder,

And in art magic wish Albino bolder.

But when the storm was passed, his courage got

The conquest of his fear, made his quick eyes

Stand sentinel t' advantage more his plot:

And, looking from the mountain, he espies

A man descending, as he told the maid,

Which the loud tempest of his fears allayed.

3450Then says, 'Behold the object of your hope'.

Away springs she from off that gloomy place,

Posts to the hill, forsakes her magic cope.

Meanwhile Albino doffs Conrado's face,

And set upon his looks Albino's dye;

So, imped with love, unto the mount did fly.

Where he espied Bellama rove about

Crying, 'Albino, dost thou fly from me?'

The man was but a silly shepherd lout

That climbed the hill his fleecy train to see.

3460And when his eyes had healthed his wealthy flocks,

Trudged to his cote, walled in with sturdy rocks.

Albin', encount'ring her, says, 'Lovely maid,

Was 't your small voice that did Albino call?'

''Twas I, poor I', the fainting virgin said,

'Why was I forced from Rhadamanthus' hall?'

'Who was 't, quoth he, 'that, with commanding air,

Snatch'd me forth' arms of Proserpina fair?'

'It was a courteous monk,' quoth she, 'whom I
Humbly entreated to deliver thee.'
3470'Alas! sweet maid,' quoth he, 'Fates do deny
Freedom from thence, nor can I pay the fee.
'Fee!' says she, 'fear not: if an earldom can
Purchase thy freedom, I will give it, man.'
'Thou canst not ransom one from Pluto's jail,
Shouldst thou lay down the gaudy triple crown;
With steely-hearted Fate naught can prevail,
On whose harsh brow there ever dwells a frown.
Speak fair, thy business: for I must begone,
Grim Charon waits for me at Acheron.'

3480'Ah me,' quoth she, 'and is it truth I hear?
Then, dear Albino, I will wait on thee.'
'You're like to find', quoth he, 'but homely cheer,
If in my diet you partake with me.'
'Famine's a favour unto me,' says she,
'Bridewell a bride-house, if I live with thee.
But, prithee, what is Rhadamanthus fell,
And she whom thou didst Proserpina call?'
'Sweetest,' quoth he, 'he is the judge of hell,
That dooms us tortures, or does us enthral.
3490For, if our innocence do plead for us,
We're led t' Elysium from dark Erebus.
That other was the Thracian harper-mate,
Whom Pluto forced unto his gloomy house,
His devilship with smiles to recreate,
Full bowls of his nepenthe to carouse.'

'I'm glad I know', quoth she, 'for jealous fears

Unto my heart did travel from my ears.'

'Why, lovely maid, did ever I behold

Before this time', quoth he, 'your comely face?'

3500'How! dear Albino, must you now be told

Who your Bellama is? 'tis high disgrace.

Sure you of Lethe's streams have deeply drank,

Which doth the powers of your mind disrank.'

'Ha!' quoth Albino, 'can my dullness think

That homely russets my Bellama veil?

I deeply of oblivion sure did drink,

Did I not know her from a milking pail.

Peace, pretty fair, do not my saints profane,

Her beauty has not such coarse lodging ta'en.'

3510'Well,' quoth Bellama, 'will you me discard,

When for your sake I've run through all disasters?

Must slights and *nescios* now be my reward?

Will you make ulcers, and apply no plasters?

Clothed in this coarse array, I roved abroad

To find the place of thy secure abode.'

'Sweet,' says Albino, 'let not anger dress

Thy stainless lilies in distraction's dye.

Let ignorance plead pardon, for I guess

Some other beauties may "Albino" cry.

3520Might now a ghost permitted be to kiss,

My lips should suck from thine a cherry-bliss.'

'Why,' says Bellama, 'has a ghost no lips?

Is there no pleasure dwells in spirits' veins?

This "might a ghost" does all my joys eclipse,
For now I have my labour for my pains.
Pray, what was Merlin's father? is 't not said
Spirits have power a damsel to unmaid?'
These words, proceeding from Bellama's lips,
Did make Albino myrrhine juice carouse,
3530To raise an active heat, which nimbly skips
In every vein like fays in Ob'ron's house.
But when he was no ghost, and hoped to merit
Love for love, he found her of another spirit.
'Away, fond monk!' quoth she, 'dost think that I
Into a sea of grief will wade with thee?
And drown my fortunes? make an earldom die?
Dost think humility resides with me?
Canst think I'll choose a pebble, slight a pearl,
Marry a threadbare cowl and scorn an earl?
3540What door to thy presumption did I ope?
What symptoms of affections did I show?
What actions gainful birth unto thy hope?
Or from what vow did thy assurance grow?
Cease then, for I take it in high disdain,
To thy coarse worth my smallest ray to chain.'
'Disdain?' quoth young Albino. 'Can this be
The voice of my Bellame? Is there such odds?
If not in birth, in worth I equal thee,
Although my muse shot love into the gods.
3550Disdain's a pitch too high for maids to reach,
Scarce will the queen of pride such doctrine teach.
Presumption too? does he deserve that brand,

Who dallies with consent, invited to 't?
What firmer seal than language, lip, and hand?
What better warrant than desired to do 't?
Say, he is saucy that, with crusted fists,
Paws a court-silk, and melts her balmy wrists.
Who feeted that enigma, whose kind air
Spake me the only high in thy esteem?
3560Was I not bosomed more than parents, fair?
Did not thine own voice that saint-secret seem?
Who bribed your full face-gazings? and what she
Judged none praise, lip, deserving of but me?
Did not you in mysterious postures woo me?
And 'gainst Bardino levied all your spite?
Nay, by Barraba sent invitements to me?
And dubbed me by your knot the Red-rose Knight?

Did not your wish glue feathers on your feet
To thread a casement when I paced the street?
3570And after these, ah! thousand more, and nearer
Seals of thy love, must slights unseal your lips?
A puny mistress-hunter well may fear her,
When pride at high noon can my sun eclipse.
Fury! lend me thy poison, Rage! thy breath,
That I, by pride doomed, may doom beauty death.
You pale-faced shadows of the gloomy isles,
Fill up my gall, and lend me all your pow'rs,
To torture women who, enriched with wiles,
From their moist eyes send forth dissembling show'rs.
3580Would Jove the mount had barren been of stones

Whereof old Pyrrha fram'd the female bones!
Would Sea's daughter, that same queen of faces,
Her alabaster box would deign to me,
Once Phao's ferry pay that gave such graces,
Which till that time the sun did never see.
That I not only might, as others are,
Be counted comely, but o' th' fairest fair.
Then would I sleight those formal tricks of love,
Those sighs, tears, vows, complaints, and folded arms;
3590Caps, cringes, oaths, and compliments to move
Th' affections of a girl expecting charms.
For wealth, wit, wisdom, eloquence, and greatness
Are less inducements unto love than neatness.'
'How now? Albino, is your doublet grown
Too straight', says she, 'that you do puff and swell?
Peace! peace! let not your choler thus be shown.'
'A thing impossible', says he, 'you tell.
In vain we call for peace, and calmness praise,
When love and hate intestine wars do raise.
3600Women have double pupils, so they can
Kill like the basilisk but with a glance.
Their very praise does blast and wither man,
Like frost and winter, or his soul entrance.
They're all like Glaucus' wife, whose filthy charms
Won poor Ulysses to her lustful arms.

They're Holgoy, Africans, and fiends they are—
Words know not what they are, they're hell to me—,
Would Jove I had the Heliostrophio fair,

To touch all maids, or, if not all, yet thee:

3610Or had been born under the Scorpion's head,

With amulets t' have struck thy beauty dead.

Ah! faithless Polupists, that thus can change

Into an hundred thousand shapes your minds!

Phoebe to you is constant; tides do range,

Yet back return; more settled are the winds—

Mere Pompholyx which with each breath does stray.

Your loves catch feathers too, and fly away.

Sometimes a fit of sullens seals your jaws,

In contemplation big (of Jove knows what),

3620And then again, as if your tongues made laws,

You weary time with your eternal chat.

Ah Mantuan! [Mantuan!] thy pen is not a liar,

Although thy habit says thou wert a friar.

Erstwhile a sober nun Bellama was,

Then a Lucretia, at another gale

I know not what, a straggling country lass,

A quinque-lettered, 'haps, which set to sale,

Now, none more willing unto love than she,

And now more further off from love or me.

3630Yet call that hasty language back a while.

Bellama is not such, she's Cupid's dart;

Teach me, great Jove, to make Bellama smile,

And with one ray sun her Albino's heart.

Thou purblind boy! teach me to gain Bellama:'

Straight Echo's voice returned him answer, '*Ama.*'

'Thanks, gentle Echo, might thy voice divine

Speak truth in this, that love commandeth love.

I would through every mood and tense decline
Amo, and saint thee too, my joy, my dove!
3640Nay, thou shouldst be whate'er fond babblers prate,
Albino's goddess, though Narcissus' hate.

Oh! would to Jove I were in courteous France,
Or else that happy place in France with me,
That with more tongues thou mightst make *ama* dance
Within these silent woods from tree to tree.
Or would thou hadst imperial power from Jove,
In the imperious mood to bid her love.'
Quoth she, 'Unworthy of a conquest's he
That for a cannon's roar his ensigns veils:
3650Unworthy of a rose or rosy glee
Is he, whose courage at her javelins fails:
They're feeble amorists that for a "fie!"
Run from their colours, and in silence lie.
'Tis our prerogative to have entreat
With every phrase that flatt'ry does enhance,
To win our loves, though every stroke they beat,
Our hearts beat Cupid's march, tune Venus' dance.
In their desires they never yet did perish
Which feed our humours, and our passions cherish.
3660To prove the truth of thy affections, I
Shot forth that language, headed with disdain.
My heart is thine which, till death close mine eye
With steely thumb, thy bosom shall retain.
Caesar's proud nod shall not command that bliss
Whose sweets are promised by this melting kiss.'

'Ha!' quoth Albino, 'dare I trust mine ears
With this blest air? And am I sure I wake?
Or is 't a dream which wakeneth into tears?
'Tis truth: then crawl hence, Furies, toad, and snake!
3670The earth her mines, sea vomit shall their pearl,
Ere I leave her, who for me left an earl.'
Then sate they dallying in a shady bow'r,
Where maples, ash, and thorn did them embrace:
Whilst her enliv'ning breath produced each flow'r
In curious knots to damask o'er the place.
Oh! who would not his soul and substance tenter,
To be circumference to such a centre?
Now have our amorists attained the height
Of true content; and sate like billing doves.
3680She tells her quest, he his monastic flight,
Whilst both recount their passions, fears, and loves,
Till Titans hasting to moist Thetis' arms
Bade them provide against his sister's harms.
Then, joining heart and hand with easy pace,
They travelled to a pague adjoining near

Where in a straw-thatched roof (an homely place
For such a pair) they entertainèd were,
And what fine cates old Kath'rine could afford,
Was served in state unto an aged board.
3690Their table with rich damask cloths was spread,
Whose every twist outvied the double cable,
The napkins diaper, of equal thread,
The mourning trenchers clothèd were in sable.

A curious salt cut out o' th' boulder stone—
And for their plate—sincerely there was none.
The dropsied host like to a sew'r did strut,
To marshal every dish; and first did bring
A spacious bowl, to scour the narrow gut,
Of nut brown ale, a liquor for a king.
3700And says, 'My Bona Roba, drink this bowl,
'Twill clear thy throat, and cheer thy drooping soul.'
Next came the mumping hostess and set down
A lusty dish of milk—sky-coloured blue,
Crumbed with the ludgets of the lusty brown,
Which two months since was piping hot and new;
'Yet 'tis', says she, 'as savoury in good law
As wheaten trash which crams the ladies' maw.'
This good old crone was troubled so with wind,
Her coats did dance to th' music of her belly.
3710Next came a barley dumpling whose harsh rind
Was oilèd o'er with a fine tallow jelly
Brought by a mincing Marget, passing trim,
Whose juicy nose did make the pudding swim.
Next came some glotrah (which the ploughman flanks
Joined with a pudding on a holy day)
Brought by a jetting dame, on whom in ranks
And discipline of state whole troops did stray
Of—I forbear to say, lest these rude feet
With queasy dames and lady readers meet.
3720Last, a tough cheese must lock the stomach's door,
Milked from a cow that fed on naught but burrs,
Had lain five winters on [a] spongy floor,

To gain an harness and a coat of furs;
So neatly peopled too, 'twas judg'd a court,
Such herds of gentles did about it sport.

Qualmish Bellama could not eat a bit,
'Cause luscious meats a surfeit soon provoke.
Albino vent'red but was fain to spit,
Lest those harsh viands should his monkship choke.
3730And whilst he hawkèd, and Bellama laugh'd,
The trumping hostess stole a thumping draught.
'Are you so dainty-toothèd,' quoth mine host,
'That country victuals will not down with you?
You shall be fed with custards, pies, and roast.
Cannot your chops a boneless pudding chew?
I trow far worser is than this your fare,
Unless you kitchen-sculls and lick-spits are.'
'Ma' gep ma' faw,' the crabbèd hostess said,
'Let 'em e'en fast if they'll not eat their soul.
3740Is not my daughter Maudge as fine a maid?
And yet by mack you see she trolls the bowl.
I've dressed a supper sure has pleasèd those,
Had wider purses far, and better clothes.'
'Pray, mother, 'gainst the young mon do not rage,'
Says full-lipped Madge, 'for he must be your son.
We are alike in face, of equal age;
Then ho! the match is soon concluded on.
Kuss me, my honest Dick, for we this night
With crickle crackle will the goblins fright.'
3750'Mass,' says mine host, 'I like the fellow well.

To suckle bairns I'll give him tidy mull,

And my brown mare as sound as any bell,

With ten good shear-hogs to afford him wool,

And, if they please me, after me they shall

Sell nappy yale within this trusty wall.'

'Feck,' says mine hostess, 'they shall have a bed

With good strong sheets to pig together in,

A brazen pot, a kettle, and a lead,

Platters, bowls, pails, and an old kilderkin.

3760And if they please m' a brace of wheels to spin

Mantles and clouts to wrap their bantlings in.'

Our lovers at this pretty talk did smile,

Then says Albino 'Here is no such haste,

I like: but yet we'll respite it a while,

Thou shall be, duck, some three nights longer chaste.

I'll man my sister at day's next attiring,

Then back and give my Maudge a curtain spring.'

When as his yielding had appeased the billows

Of their loud passions, and their meat digested,

3770Night's middle age invited to their pillows,

But tell I dare not how the lovers rested,

Whether co-sheeting was allowed as fit,

Monastic vows dispensing well with it.

But this I say, there was but one guest-room,

Hanged with a pentice cloth spoke age enough;

The spiders here had one continued loom:

Here rats and mice did play at blind man's blough.

Their bed had many tasters, but no tester,

Their bedding ushered in thin-sided Easter.

3780Repentant mattress for chastising Lent,

Stout as a face of steel, which ne'er will yield;

Their sheets were tenants, weekly payed rent,

The pillow was with juice of noddles steeled,

And therefore fit to bolster any sin.

Their coverlet was of a bullock's skin.

Their urine vessel was of Ticknall make,

Whose inside was with unshorn vellet clad.

Their bedstead floated in a springing lake

Where frogs and newts their rendezvouses had.

3790This was their guest-bed, and there was no other,

Think you Bellama then lodged with her brother?

No: such pure virtues saint Bellama's breast,

And such clear sparks of honour heat his soul,

That such a thought would stain her virgin crest,

And blur the sacreds of Albino's roll.

Then die, black thoughts! Bellama's chaste denials

Repelled all charms of love and Venice-trials.

Nay, he ne'er tempted, nor attempted once

To scale the fortress of her virgin-tower,

3800For her chaste noes and vows did guard the sconce,

That 'twas impregnable, not forced by power.

And, though he did ensphere her naked waist,

Yet durst my faith and oath conclude her chaste.

This longing on Albino worked so strong,

That, when the god of slumbers did entreat

Him to his court, into his thoughts did throng

His house of penance, hunger, cold and sweat.

So powerful was his dream entruthed with fear,

That his strong faith concluded he was there.

3810And in some sort he was, for when the East

Was purpled with the blushes of the morn,

When his benumbèd senses were released

By the shrill sound of Gallus' bugle horn—

He heard a sound of words, and looking out,

He saw a legion of the monkish rout.

For you must know that, when Albino's wit

Had won him freedom, and Conrado thrall,

The jealous matron somewhat fearèd it,

And the next morning did 'Conrado' call,

3820Who (brooking ill his lodging) struck with fear,

Made answer to the matron's question, 'Here'.

So, when her eyes suspicion truth had made,

She asked Conrado how that came to pass,

Quoth he, 'Credulity my fear o'erswayed,

I was deluded with the dukedom lass.

She promised me a dukedom for my pains,

And I, poor I, thought it sufficient gains!'

'Ha!' quoth the matron, 'could thy falsehood serve

Thus to dishonour me, and all my train?

3830His penalty is thine; till every nerve

Shrink up with famine, thou shalt here remain.

Time will not measure years ere thou wilt say,

A dukedom for thy penance is no pay.'

'Madam,' quoth he, 'my senses were bewitchèd

With that pure white which dwelt upon her brow;

I scratched and pinched, but still my humours itchèd,
I stood upright, but still my heart did bow.
Who would not twice ten minutes in a brook
Chin-high and thirsty stand, to be a duke?'
3840Quoth she, 'I see that folly oversways,
And Venus sovereign is of every sect.
To beauty every order homage pays,
Whilst only age and blackness gain neglect.
I 'xcuse thy frailty—haste unto thy dell—
The sentence of Felice's flight repell.'
Conrado thanked her, and away did pack
(As one reprievèd from the gallow tree
Still fearing that stern justice plucked him back)
Lest, Janus-like, her face should changèd be.
3850For well he knew the monthly hornèd queen
No oft'ner fills her orb than she her spleen.

He Nature blamed, he could no faster run;
But, coming to the gate, the porter oped,
Who, much appalled to see a youthful nun,
Says, 'Mistress, do you travel to be coped?
Give me my fee: for sure, a plump-cheeked lass
Shall not the porter's lodge unkissèd pass.'
He could not quiet his impatient lust
Till he had shown the ensigns of his habit;
3860His parèd crown, with Venus' rays adust,
Then left the mongrel his supposèd rabbit,
And slinked away from his monastic veil,
Just like a dog that newly burnt his tail.

When he had cast his woman, and put on
The habit of his order, he made haste
Unto his lord, told him Felice's gone,
And that his conscience did conclude her chaste.
'She Folco's large endowments must inherit,
And promised me to recompense my merit.'
3870The prior, smiling at his folly, checked
Him for Apella's faith, and said his lass
Was young Albino in nun-vestments decked.
'(If that our porter had his double glass),
And since thy coming cleareth every doubt,
Harness yourselves to seek the younker out.'
As the attendants of an hunting prince,
Intending to disfrank an o'ergrown boar,
View the impressions of his feet, which, since
Last eve, were printed on the sandy shore,
3880Beating each bush, and in each cabin searching
To find his frank, and not the pheasants perching.
And as when Reynald, with his wily plot,
Into the squadron of the geese is crept,
And grandsire Gander on his back has got,
Th' affrighted geese, like them which watch-tow'rs kept,
With shrill-toned gabblings wake the slumb'ring towns,
By Phoebe's candle to go seek the downs—
Some arm themselves with spits, one with a ladle,
Some snatch up pickforks, one a bill or knife.
3890The ambling nurse runs out and leaves the cradle,
And the awed midwife flies the teeming wife;
Old grandsire greybeard his tuff bilbo gets,

And grandame Grissel with her distaff jets.
Just so our hair-lack monks pursued their quest,
Searched for his view, and threaded every grove

With bells, beads, books, and holy water blest,
And armed with envy's whips about did rove,
Their runagado Reynald to surprise,
And came to Stean ere the sun could rise.
3900Which sight unspirited Albino quite,
That his invention could not teem a plot;
For in his looks his fear was writ in white,
And to his heart his frighted blood did trot.
Yet, calling courage to appear o' th' stage,
He sheathed his body in his woven cage.
Then hasting to the host, bade him awake,
Desired his counsel and assisting hand,
Says now his life and safety lay at stake.
For, at his door, a troop of shavelings stand.
3910'I am their errand: I must bid adieu
To lovely Maudge, mine hostess, and to you.'
'Ho!' quoth mine host, and rubbed his gummy eyes,
'What says my son? Must thou be whirled away?
I warrant, boy, my club shall still their cries,
When 'bout their costards I shall make it play.
I'll dye their stark-nak'd crowns with their own blood,
Then let 'em come if that they think it good.'
'Good Sickerlin,' says Maudge, 'ere they shall have
My honey-sweeten Dick, I'll scratch and bite,
3920With scalding water I'll their noddles shave;

Then buss me Dick, thy Maudge will for thee fight.'

'Thanks,' quoth he, 'duck, but yet it cannot be

That thy endeavours should advantage me.

But yet methinks I see some comfort dawn:

Yon tinker's budget strengthens every joint.

Send me some clothes by time's harsh grinders gnawn,

And I will be a tinker in each point.

My sister must have rags; and be my trull.

Thus veiled and clothed we will the shavelings gull.'

3930Accoutred in these robes of state, he made

His face and hands in sooty vestures mourn.

Then waked Bellama, who was sore afraid

To see a tinker, and away does turn.

But grasping only air she shrilly cried,

'Art fled, Albino, from thy sweetheart's side?'

Which words, so shrilly spoke, made Echo babble;

Who, winged with envy, out o' th' window flies,

Carries 'Albino' to the monkish rabble,

They, hearing that, Perduers made their eyes

3940And, swelled with rage, against the door did knock,

Whose aged breast could not endure the shock.

This stroke Albino's heart did almost break,

Yet bids Bellama sheath her body in

These homely rags, which only safety speak.

'Care not for coarseness, so they hide the skin,

And at this tinker's habit do not wonder,

'Tis but the curtain thy Albino's under.'

'What tipsied fellows at my door do beat

Thus early,' quoth mine host, 'is this your manners?

3950What? must mine hostess wait upon th' entreat

Of tailors, cobblers, carpenters, and tanners?

If drinking be your errand, where ye got

Your last night's fuddling-cap, this morning trot.'

Impatient they did make the door unhinge,

Which gave an entrance to enraged Bardino.

He to the reverend host did lowly cringe,

Told him his errand was to seek Albino.

And as they did his homely cottage hem,

Albino's name came leaping unto them.

3960'Ho!' quoth mine host, 'unto mine house there came,

Last night for lodging, a stout tinker knave,

Who now is ticking with his ragged dame.

Go, if with him ye any business have;

But who Albino is I cannot tell.

Here's no sike mon does penance in my cell.'

Into the arras-ceilèd parlour then,

The copesters went, in every corner snooked,

The tinker's visage none of them did ken,

But for Albino on Albino looked.

3970Well might he cozen them, whenas his saint

Knew not his face under that mask of paint.

Then as they searchèd every place by chance

Conrado did his monkish vestments own

He lent Felice at their affiance.

The host, perceiving that the clothes were known,

Said, 'Yesterday, about the after three,

A fellow came and pawned those clothes to me.'

They asked Bellama then why she did call

Upon Albino. 'Why, forsooth,' said she,

3980'I was a servant once in Darwey Hall,

Where that young monk I oftentimes did see;

Who oft in private would disport with me,

And promised that I should his sweeting be.

But, by misfortune being turned away,

This jovial tinker took me unto wife,

So, as this morn by his warm side I lay,

I of Albino dreamed—my joy, my life.'

'He's not thy mon,' quoth Maudge; 'thou li'st, base drab':

'Peace, housewife,' says mine host, 'you tattling blab.'

3990Thus had the scene been changed, had not the sire

Suppressed her babblings with a check and grin.

The monks, well satisfied, gang to the fire

To taste the juice of Kate's old kilderkin.

The tinker and mine host would always cry,

'Fill, hostess, fill! the monks are still a-dry.'

Canzone.

Drink full ones, tinker, methinks the monks are dry,

Drink healths, mine host, the monks do fear a thirst.

Are the monks thirsty? the monks will quickly try

If they or the tinker want a pillow first.

4000Else will we jig and hay unto the black pot's sound,

Till to that music the house shall dance the round.

Then fill a dozen, hostess, we'll have a merry cup,

And make the tinker forfeit his budget and his brass.

'Faith,' says the tinker, 'I'll make your monkships sup

Till ye sing requiems in reading of the mass.'

Then fill a gallon, hostess, we'll health it all about,

Till all complain o' th' headache, the falling, or the gout.

Come on, dropping shavelings, let's see you count your beads,

I am half afraid you'll stutter in the mass.

4010Gramercy, lovely pots, and nimble Ganymedes,

That brought more water than what holy was.

Well, saucy tinker, well, pray finger you your brass,

And let the monks alone, 'lone, they'll finger well the mass.

Pray, Gaffer Cowlists, why are ye so bald

To cool your *pia maters* in a sweat?

Or did the water your wise noddles scald,

Which your devotions and hot zeal did heat?

Or are ye given unto Venus play?

I am afraid there went the hair away.

4020But base Bardino did this mirth eclipse

(In his monastic life Albino's friend),

Viewing the travail of his hand, his lips,

He, by a secret mark, Albino kenned.

For, by some strange mishap, was set a brand,

An azure spot upon his abler hand.

Says he, 'Methinks you are too frolic, tinker,

Your mirth I fear presageth your disgrace,

You must no longer be mine hostess' skinker,

For you will say, unless y' have brazed your face—

4030That you both see and do Albino know:

If you deny 't, I have your hand to show.

During the time that you were cowled and coped,

On your right hand there dwelt a cerule mark,
Which ne'er would off, although 'twas often soaped.'
'Well,' quoth mine host, 'but pray your worship, hark,
May not two men be like? may there not be
The selfsame spot of him, and you, and me?'
This could not yet appease Bardino's hate,
Still teeming mischief, and with envy big;
4040So, starting up, he fumed, and loud did prate,
And snatchèd off Albino's periwig.
Now 'gainst two witnesses he could not stand,
Whenas his head bore witness with his hand.
Albino excused, it was by nature so,
Saying no razor e'er did touch his skull.
'No,' says Bardino, 'it again does grow;
Thou canst not with this fop my wisdom gull.
Keep him, my brethren, and meanwhile I will
Fetch the watch-beggar and his rusty bill.'
4050Bellama did meanwhile what language can,
With oilèd words and pity-pleading tears,
Beseeching these to free her weddèd man.
But to her voice they cottoned had their ears,
Until an Angel did appear unto them,
And with his goldy looks and music woo them.
Then did they yield to let them go away,
And they meantime would feign a deading sleep.
They for a second licence would not stay,
But hasting out along the ditches creep.
4060And as they went a raddle-man they meet,
Whom with kind airs and highway phrase they greet.

And, greeting past, Albino did require

To change apparel with him, and his trade,

Giving him cash to hasten his desire.

'With all my heart,' the raddle-younker said

(Ne'er questioning the cause); 'yet, by the mass,

My dames will say I am a podging ass.'

Thus changed they clothes and budgets: then with lead

On the new tinker's hand Albino made

4070A mark like his, to gull his envious bead.

With raddle-crimson then, fit for his trade,

He clothed his face, and gave Bellama some,

So trudged away, for fear the monk should come.

Have you beheld a hound in sudden fright,

Whom powder feared, or else the staff did beat,

How oft he turns, and looks, yet keeps on flight?

So they, with glancing eyes, would oft retreat,

Yet movèd forward still as in a ship

The pilots backward look, yet forward skip.

4080But our new tinker, swellèd with content,

Fearing no colours, to the town did pass,

Crying, as he along the hamlet went,

'Ha y' any need ho! of a tinker's brass?'

Bardino now returned in a chafe,

And ask'd the tinker's name, who answer'd, 'Rafe.'

'Where dwell'st thou?' 'Anywhere?' 'How long

Hast tink'ring used?' 'I cannot tell.'

Then 'bout the tinker all the monks did throng,

Whilst he, poor fellow, thought h' had been in hell.

4090For till that day he never saw such creatures,

And what they were he knew not by their features.

Bardino fearèd this was but a gull,

And says, 'Good fellow, let me see thy hand.'

'I'm not asham'd to show 't, by cock and bull.'

Bardino, viewing 't well, espied the brand,

And says, 'Sir youth, before you cozened me:

But now in sooth I will be meet with thee.'

'Devil or friar, whatsoe'er thou art,

What taunting language dost thou give to me?

4100Ha!' quoth the tinker. Quoth Bardino, 'Smart

Shall give a comment of my words to thee.'

'Smart?' quoth the tinker. 'Swig for Smart and you:

I bid defiance unto all thy crew.

Talk not to me of Smart: for if you prate

This knotty staff shall bastinado you.

I'll set a scarlet cap upon thy pate,

And lace thy shoulders with a purple blue.'

'Peace, honest tinker,' say the other monks.

'Aye! I will peace it, if I catch the hunks.'

4110But let the monks and tinker take their chances.

We'll view the travels of our raddle-man,

With faint Bellam', whom every fear entrances,

And every trance does make her roses wan.

Thus far their loves have tragi-comic been,

Thwarted by Fate and the unconstant Queen.

But every planet with kind aspect now

Views their long-travelled loves; and Venus' boy

Smiles on their wishes with auspicious brow.

Now a full harvest must they have of joy,

4120Though sowed with black disasters, dangers, fears,

Dispair, hope, doubtings, sad complaints, and tears.

For aged Starley's tow'rs (that fatal stage

Where Danes did act their juries once in blood,

When bellowing cannons belchèd out their rage)

Within the kenning of our lovers stood.

And the well-tunèd bells did loud proclaim

Joy to the lovers in great Hymen's name.

A near ally Albino in this town

(By order a devout Carthusian) had,

4130Whose voice he hoped with joy their loves should crown.

But he, a slave in raddle vestures clad

And a ragged Marget seeing, started back,

Bidding his knaveship to some other pack.

He would have no commerce with such as he,

He had no ewes whose backs did want his raddle,

And if he over-saucy needs would be,

With a good bat he would his gaskins swaddle.

'The Provost Marshal else, if this does fail,

Shall show you lodging in the whipstock jail.'

4140This language sounded in Bellama's ears

Like the sad voice of death, yet fear no slaughter.

To joy straight changed shall be this scene of tears,

And stead of grief the child of pleasure, laughter.

My promise stands unshaked: for this short anger

Brings not their loves nor safeties unto danger.

'Sir,' quoth Albino, 'there was once a time
When you esteemed those wingèd minutes sainted
You spent with me (when Fortune was in prime),
For you and I have better been acquainted;
4150Though some disasters and stern Fate have made
Me take this homely garb and homelier trade.
Some blood which in your azure channels glide
Dwells in my veins: I am Albino hight,
And lest you think this smells too much of pride,
View this triangle on my able right.'
That sight unto rejoicings beat alarms,
His kinsman then ensphered him in his arms.
So led them both under his archèd roof,
Breathing kind welcomes from his courteous lips;
4160Excus'd his ignorance and sharp reproof,
Asked what misfortune did his worth eclipse.
Demanding how coy Fortune dealt with him,
And who she was that was so passing trim?
'Unless high heavens do forbid the bane,
This maid shall be my bride, though homely dressed;
Clothes oftentimes the purest beauty stain,
And Venus most unclothed is clothèd best.
Under this roof of rags Bellama dwells,
Fraught with diviner worth than nature spells.'
4170'Hymen enrich your wishes with content,
As benign heaven has enriched your face
With nature's glory, beauty's orient,'
Says the Carthusian with a comely grace;
'Thrice welcome! welcome! for your lovely grace

- 860 -

Will add a lustre to my homely place.'
'Sir, my endeavours shall be wholly spent
Henceforth,' quoth she, 'to recompense your air.'
'This is no time, forsooth, to compliment,
Prithee adjourn thy words of courtship, fair,
4180For till our hands be joined as well as hearts
I fear', quoth he, 'supplanting Envy's darts.
Good cousin, ere the next day's sun be rolled
Th' Apogaeum, our meridian point,
Favour our wishes with the "have and hold".
Tie us so fast fate may not us disjoint.
For Envy, like a snake, does crawl about,
And winds her tail in where she holes her snout.
Omit no nuptial rites; with holy oil
Let her anoint the posts, with virgin hand

4190To Janus consecrate the wether's spoil,
And to those gods which for our households stand,
Procure horn torches to be borne along,
And cry "Thalassus!" with a bridal song.
Provide me store of nuts to throw about
With a full hand unto the gaping boys,
That from the tumults of the struggling rout
All voices may be damped that speak not joys.
Over us two let the same Flamine fall,
And let the wheaten cake consummate all.
4200Nor will we manumiss these robes of state,
Within whose walls blest safety only dwells.
Lest our known faces, and apparel, prate

In louder echoes than the marriage bells.
Then say, fair lady, truth I do not jeer,
Will you be wedded to a scarleteer?'
Quoth she, with blushes carpeting her cheek,
'And is that question, prithee, yet to ask?
Your worth does merit the unequalled Greek,
Without nun-penance or Alcides' task.
4210Then [I] pray you (in truth it is no gull)
Will you be married to a tinker's trull?'
Thus sleep and mirth did cut the night: and ere
The sovereignty was ta'en from Cynthia's horn,
When at East's casement newly did appear
The orient brightness of the rising morn,
Albino rose, and to the church did haste
T' un-nun Bellama and ungird her waist.
When the Carthusian's voice had crowned their amours
With an assurance of Thalassian joys,
4220The air was thinnèd with the joyful clamours
(Not of state-satins) but of grammar boys;
And our fresh sponsants in that height of mirth
To every pleasure gave an easy birth.
Now are they landed on the isle of bliss,
Where every joy courts their desires with pleasure;
Envy did then her snaky train dismiss,
For their espousals did all sweet entreasure.
Dead grief bequeathed her stings to thorn and thistle.
Nor durst a sigh within those borders whistle.
4230Then, as sea-merchants when their reeling galley,
Drunk with salt Neptune, hazardeth their breaths,

To calm bold tempest and the Triton's valley,

Hack on the quiet shore their brackèd sheaths,

So did our amorists, half wrack'd with eye-men,

Devote their raddle vests to Love and Hymen.

Some marrow-lancing eye perchance may quarrel,

'Cause with the bridal torch my muse expires;

And in loud jeers his tow'ring voice apparel,

Taxing the faintness of my metric fires,

4240Because my lines tread not the common path

Of fortune, issue, and appeasing wrath.

Perhaps I dare not lengthen out my story

With those events succeeding time begot,

Lest some disaster should eclipse their glory,

And the pure ermines of their pleasures spot.

For having screwed them into firm embraces,

I will not waken hate or rouse disgraces.

Yet beauty (know) when virtue shines upon her,

And virtues (know) [when] skin-perfections gloss 'em,

4250Awe Fortune's wrath, and challenge heaven's honour.

Hell cannot cancel them, nor Envy dross 'em.

Love! if to me the same content thou'lt yield,

I'll limn thy mother on Minerva's shield.

Notes: The Pleasing History of *Albino* and *Bellama*

6 In which of the various fancy *Bruts* 'Adell' occurs I am not at the moment certain. Brydges, I suppose, deceived by *Don* Fuco, &c., oddly 'places the scene in Spain'.

15 age of consistency] = 'grow tired of existing together'—a Whitingism almost *Brownist* in character.

25 'Agathite'] 'Agath' is a form of 'agate': is 'agathite' a coinage suggested by the blending of colours in the agate?

27 Saba] The Queen of Sheba.

50 rein] Orig. 'veine'. But it must, as the little Errata paragraph at the end admits, be 'rein'. All this may be extravagant, but it is poetry.

61 'The curlèd tapers of the firmament' is not exactly contemptible, I fancy.

66 Whiting must certainly have known his Shakespeare. 'Crisp' appears there nowhere as a noun, but its use here must almost certainly have been suggested by the '*crisp* heaven' of *Timon*, iv. iii. 183. 'Spang' is Baconian, and not uncommon.

70 Orig. has 'Lady Curtain' and no 'this'—a state of things which led me quite wrong at first. Return

126 *Ven*-Bacchus] Venus-Bacchus?

131-2 I have ventured to suggest 'mendings' for these exceedingly gappy lines.

148 knee] This is the correction in the *errata* of 'tener'.

149 bean-manors] = Manors held at a bean instead of a peppercorn? Or misprint for 'bea*u*-manors'? This latter, for 'Beaumanor' is a known name, and Beaumanoir a better, would be quite like Whiting. My friend Sir Frederick Pollock, to whom I appealed after a question whether 'bene' in a legal sense was possible, decided that the phrase could have no technical meaning either as 'bean' or 'bene', but suggested 'rents'. This makes excellent sense, but is not, perhaps, on that account more likely here. Return

211 Sable] Any black-coated man of letters.

212 Adel's stamps] I suppose, the coin of the realm.

219 A Master of Arts ought to have known better than to make 'Thule' mono-syllabic, though the general public used to pronounce it so in reference to a once popular book of the late Mr. William Black's.

259 trutinate] = 'balance'. Don Fuco also had apparently enjoyed the advantages of a classical education.

275 'Indod' like 'adad', and many other forms of corrupted evasion of the Third Commandment.

290-1 Tennyson is known to have been no inconsiderable reader, but he can hardly have known this parody—by anticipation—of a famous line in *Œnone*.

295 trencher-cloaks] cut short? '*Re*cognizance' is again, if not exactly Shakespearian, not far off. Return

309 Here 'blough' is certainly in the sense of 'muffle', and therefore gives a light on the use *supra* (*Author's Apology*, l. 5).

322 Why this fling at Skelton's exceedingly pretty verses to Isabel Pennel I do not in the least know.

327 Tripherus] See Juvenal, *Sat.* xi. 137.

394 Orig. 'phrentezy'. Return

418 entrails] Orig. 'intrals'. Not a very common form, but justified by the Low Latin *intralia*.

421-4 There is a reference to Drayton's *Nymphidia*, where Oberon and Pigwiggen drink from a 'bottell' of 'Lethe spring', and forget their quarrel. For a further reference to this poem, see l. 1420.

465 'breath'. A seventeenth-century form.

489 I have kept 'ante' because I do not know whether it is for 'aunt' or 'ant'. Neither seems to give much sense. Return

500 There is certainly a long *s* in original, and 'sore-head' is intelligible, but 'forehead' would go better with 'flag'.

537 Whiting, for all his extravagance, triviality, and so forth, has occasionally an odd gift of phrase. 'Pandora was not treasured up in faces' is an instance.

538 possessing elves] = 'The actual possessors'.

541 The maid] Thisbe, I suppose, though there is nothing to separate her from other maids that 'sat in Babylon'.

551 peevish girl] Scylla.

569-70 See Ovid *Met.* I. 523.

591 coarse] Orig. 'course', as so often. Return

600 'gales' = rents, or royalties, in reference to the earl's land.

639 Orig. 'phillits'.

648 I have left 'croe' because I do not know whether it stands for 'crew' or (as above) 'crow' = 'knocker'.

651 angel-looks] = 'those of a messenger'.

668 'vermilion looks' suggests Dryden's 'church vermilion', but that would have no sense in the context.

677 Serrat] Our Lady of Montserrat? Why St. Katherine should have a specially flaxen wig is another of the posers occurring so constantly. But after all why should she *not*? Return

748 The author, from several signs, must have written this odd poem in no small haste. But he must indeed have been in a hurry when, as would here seem, he confounded 'casket' and 'carcanet'. Cf. 1. 953.

757 Some word like 'talking' is wanted here.

748 The author, from several signs, must have written this odd poem in no small haste. But he must indeed have been in a hurry when, as would here seem, he confounded 'casket' and 'carcanet'. Cf. 1. 953.

757 Some word like 'talking' is wanted here. Return

822 I suppose 'flazing' (the original) is only a misprint for 'flaring'; but with Whiting you can never be quite sure.

829 Orig. 'archy-'.

834 Orig. 'weekes', as in Spenser, *F. Q.* ii. x. 30, 2.

844 'boat-boy'? Phaon who is mentioned ll. 3582 foll., and whose later stage of beauty might entitle him to complete his quintet with his 'fare' Venus, Helen, and Narcissus.

862 'the poet'. Horace in *Odes*, III. xix. 11-15. Return

904 en-neale] Whiting has used this word before, l. 191, but less oddly. It seems here to mean 'portray indelibly', 'preserve as in mosaic or enamel'. Cf. l. 1521.

918 Butler, as Brydges noticed, must surely have seen this.

920 That 'Prior' is usual and sufficient did not matter to Whiting: he wanted three syllables and an easy rhyme, so he made what he wanted.

953 This line settles the question (*v. sup.*, l. 748) as to Whiting's confusion of 'casket' and 'carcanet'. It is even possible to guess at the cause—the original French *carcan*, 'a prisoner's chain', 'prison' suggesting 'place of confinement'.

975 'Archy-' in original as before. The use of the French corresponding form 'archi-' instead of the English 'arch-' is probably not accidental.

987 The sharp change here from the straightforward 'frosts' &c. to this ellipse of 'as [that] he [should] want' is noticeable.

989-90 Another Dryden suggestion. The improvement in

O daughter of the Rose, whose cheeks unite

The differing titles of the red and white,

is of course immense. But Cambridge poets have always had a laudable habit of reading each other, and *Albino and Bellama* was not such a very old poem when Dryden went up.

998 Original, ridiculously enough, '*a* A perc*ee*'! I think Whiting's is the worst printed book of the scores, if not hundreds, I have read for this collection. Return

1004 It is delightful to think how the persons who were shortly to hold Cleveland for a greatest living poet must have enjoyed this metaphysical translation of 'He kissed her when nobody was looking'!

1027 'Venice' for 'glass'—'ice'. As I have said, you may do almost anything you like to Whiting in the way of interpretation.

1058 So, again, I suppose 'vowel-plasters' means 'vocal pleadings', but I should not dare to be certain.

1068 'Teen', as more than once annotated, = 'light'; so eight lines lower.

1081 Of the numerous shades of the word 'baulk', 'parry' or 'foil' comes nearest here

1084 are] 'or' in the original.

1086 'Chester'] = 'he who chests'—and why not? Return

1112 The metaphors as well as the bloods are something mixed: but again, why not?

1130 Although 'toll' was never (and then less than now) confined to funerals Whiting had better have used another word.

1155 'Anchorist', is at any rate better than 'Priorist'. Fuller used it later.

1172 If Bellama, who indeed seems to have been an outspoken young lady, had regarded manners in regard to her love as little as Agamemnon in regard to his wife, she might have told him that his verses were rather long. Return

1211 satonisco]? Form of 'satin', unknown elsewhere.

1214 'frank', again Shakespearian, is of course proper to the boar only; but Whiting did not regard invidious distinctions.

1244 There is, of course, not the slightest justification for 'rosy', but our poet was *supra* not merely *grammaticam* but *vocabularium* and everything else.

1271 An odd and rather awkward metaphor.

1294 Orig. 'quoth she'—but, of course, Albino is the speaker. Return

1306 Does 'wretch*ing*' occur elsewhere? 'Wretch' as a verb is quoted, but only as Scots, and only in the sense of 'be miserly'. Whiting, though not muddle-headed, was so feather-headed in the use of words that one must take into account the possibility of '*r*etching', i.e. 'vomiting blasphemy', and can hardly neglect as *im*possible a careless confusion with 'wretch*less*, = 'reckless'.

1340 The poet changes number from 'nips' to 'uncrown' with his usual lightness of heart.

1376 Cf. Ps. xlvi. 9, 'Knappeth the spear in sunder'. Return

1420-4 This is a reference to Drayton's *Nymphidia*, where Hob searches for the Fairy Queen, who has gone off with Pigwiggen (cf. ll. 421-4).—It will he observed that, as in the case of Kingsley's hero, 'the party is taken ill with a poem' on every provocation.

1432 We want 'Daffa-down*a*-dillies'.

1442 An Alexandrine: not as yet common in the piece.

1450 'ermelin', with its equivalents, is rather the commoner form in all mediaeval languages.

1461 *Carduus benedictus* Return

1519 Why 'Irish' who can say? The only sensible remark which presents itself on this piece of nonsense (I have not, of course, attempted to alter the gibberish in any way) is that dialect seems to have been increasing its hold on popular fancy off the stage, as well as in Brome's *Northern Lass*, &c. on it.

1521 Here 'en-nealed' throws its light backward on the use *supra* (l. 904) as simply 'enamelled'.

1539 vit] 'vil' in original.

1558 Orig. 'choyce'; but this must be one of the innumerable misprints which the Errata paragraph treats so cavalierly.

1559 For novel] = 'as a novelty'?

1561 Orig. '*s*eiling'—the *s* being common (though, of course, wrong) earlier as well as at this time.

1569 Orig. 'guilt'. Return

1602 'coven' in this sense should be 'covent', but Whiting affects the form: see 2686, 3167.

1615 A sufficiently mysterious line.

1645 Orig. 'Volgo's'. Return

1714 Query, 'If satin's difference can maids adorn'.

1716 'fligger' has a certain dialectic sense of 'flutter', and as its congener 'flicker' has one of 'snigger', 'jeer', it probably has that here.

1745 dors] = 'bumblebees'—somewhat unworthily yoked.

1750 The extraordinary double plural of 'females fairs' (orig. 'faires') would seem impossible in any other author. Perhaps 'female', but the rhyme requires 'fairs'.

1784 'Sh'as'] A no doubt unintentional compelling of the apostrophe to do double duty. Return

1844 Whiting was apparently more fashionable in his astronomy than Bacon or Browne.

1863 The slang use of 'dust' is found in Wilkins's *Miseries of Enforced Marriage*. 1607, 'Come, down with your dust'. One would be disposed to think it a parallel to 'dross', &c.—terms contemptuous of money, but generally employed by those who have not got it.

1865 dealth] I suppose this is another of Whiting's many inventions. Cf. *Il Insonio*, 347.

1873 Orig. 'everts', which must be wrong.

1882 Orig. 'phrentick'. This middle form between 'frenetic' and 'frantic' is M. E. (for instance, in Langland), but is not, I think, common later.

1883 pargèd] This is one of Whiting's redeeming vividnesses. The verb is, of course, the same as 'parget'—'to plaster or distemper'. Cf. *Il Insonio*, 73. Return

1911 Whether 'buzzled' is 'bustled' or 'buzzed' I am not sure. Cf. *Il Insonio*, 107. 'He buzzles like a bustard in a wind'.

1930 Orig. 'Bagno's'.

1931 for] Not quite impossible, but unlikely. 'Fore'?

1945 'cowlist' may raise a doubt as to the passage *supra, The Author to his Book*, l. 58.

1959 I suppose 'eighteen hooks' means hooks to catch persons eighteen years old. But for cautions against being too sure Whiting is sovereign.

1965 'drilling' for 'trickling' we had before.

1969 'tamm[e]y's (as in original). Still a word for coarse cloth.

1984 Once more, if 'jen-*net*' is superfluous and you cannot think of any rhyme but 'Bennet' why not overrun?

1995 b*l*anched?] 'Lilies' equalling 'cheeks'? But I would not dictate to Whiting. Return

2009 huffing waste] 'Pretentious prodigality', as Bellama was a rich pensioner.

2027 'innupted' is better and better. According to that lofty view of the genuine writer which insists that he shall never be at a loss for a word to fit matter and form at once, Whiting should stand very high.

2048 Orig. 'ear*r*hs'.

2071 Neptune's grandchild] Cupid; but the affiliation is irregular.

2083 The only meaning I can think of for this marvellous phrase is, 'He could get the various *dresses*, but he could not change his own face to suit and give voice to them'. Return

2116 Felice] Orig. 'Phæliche' throughout.

2120 Issa] *v.* Martial, i. 110, on the pet dog of Publius:

Hanc ne lux rapiat suprema totam,

Picta Publius exprimit tabella,

In qua tam similem videbis Issam,

Ut sit tam similis sibi nec ipsa, &c. &c.

2137 lede] = 'speech', 'tale'. Whether Whiting got this from Chaucer's 'ledene' one cannot say; but he seems to have been a man of some reading.

2150 worlds] Play on 'globes'?

2154 'And' would make the next line and a half refer to Bellama, which does not seem likely.

2174 'Lorrett*a* is, all things considered, a rather unfortunate feminizing of Lorett*o* to denote Our Lady thereof.

2188-93 Is this one of the 'misplaced staves' so very coolly left to the reader's discovery in the Errata-note? (*v. inf.*, p. 551). It looks as if it ought to come after its present successor.

2196 'rosies', another coinage, of which Whiting was fond: see ll. 2523, 3344, 3348, 3436. Return

2220 his] Not that the Prioress thought him masculine as yet.

2226 camp] Orig. 'came'—from the rhyme an obvious misprint, but why 'lanky'? Because of mortifications? Cf. 2199 'lankcloister' and 2553 'lanky crew'. Return

2301 rape] Probably for 'rap', 'valueless coin'.

2382 vogliarell[a] 'Little wish', 'fancy'. Return

2404 crayfish] Orig. 'creevish' is nearer to *écrevisse* and the M. E. *crevis* than the more modern forms.

2410 orc] 'vessel as big as a whale'. Orig. 'Orke'.

2415 'glorrah'. Evidently the same word as 'glotrah' in l. 3714, and apparently some kind of food capable of being made into a 'shape'.

2427 tempo-pates. Query, pates as bald as Father Time's.

* 2453: "a joy ovall chhriots". The first part of this 'pie' is pretty clearly 'jovial', but the rest is mere guesswork. Perhaps 'a jovial charect'. Return

2527 Quiris?

2552 sew] 'sue' in orig.

2562 'ptisick' = 'phthisic' would be intelligible in another context, but not here.

2592 Larv'd] = 'masked'. Return

2613 In the original, 'by constraint, not, court, lye sleight'. The punishment fits the crime he had committed in the nuns' narrow beds.

2652 a-darkness] Like 'a-bed', &c.

2656 'Sesamoidesse'. From the Greek σησαμοειδές, a kind of reseda, the medical use of which is noted in Hippocrates; Strabo also refers to it as a charm in vogue to reduce tumours.

2686 'Coven', as before.

2689 'vezzo'] Cf. 'vogliarell'. Return

2721 'Not' carried on to 'laughs'.

2754 trig] To 'trot', 'run'. Apparently Lancashire and Yorkshire dialect to this day. Return

2833 'eye-lid rain' may be tears, or a misprint for 'eye-*let*'; *v. sup.*, l. 795.

2851 fleecèd] = 'mouldy'.

2861 copèd]? = 'encountered', 'met with'. Cf 3855.

2862 Orig. '*Of* on'.

2889 Orig. 'Mà boun'.'

2897 sience] = 'scion'. Return

2924 salve] Where did she get it?

2970 Folco] ? Albino-Felice rather.

2971 Sardonic, an adjective formed from 'sardonyx'?

2993 threnes] = 'wailings'—*Graece.* Return

3038 'Vitruvius' for 'Vesuvius' is going pretty far, but can be caught up. 'Ichonian' eludes me.

3043 Here Whiting seems to present one of his characteristic retorts to criticism: 'If you say Mab for Mabel, why may I not say Mabel for Mab?' Return

3101 'the other *Nunc*] We say 'the other day', and 'just now'. Why not 'the other minute', and so 'the other now'?

3116 swogging] Palsgrave, in a passage which I owe to the late Professor Skeat, 'I swag as a fat person's belly swaggeth as he goeth', might almost have been annotating this passage. Cf. also, of course, 'swagger'. As for the *o*, 'Maggie' and 'Moggie', 'flap' and 'flop', and a hundred other pairs, occur.

3118 We had 'claret' thus used in Benlowes, vol. 1, p. 358 (l. 202).

3143 larvèd] As before, l. 2592.

3152 Is this found elsewhere?

3155 The union of body and soul.

3158 Orig. 'rithmes'.

3160 'Ascending' *&c.* 'the ladder'.

3170 'Ferny flag' is not so bad for the tossed antlers.

3179 Malèd] Is this for 'mailed'? = '*armoured* by fear against the briars'?

3182 *Donnes*] Donne? 'ladies'? Return

3202 Where again he got a trusty or untrusty Turkish or other blade 'you shall tell me', as Prince Seithenin says. But it is doubtless 'necessary to the action'.

3208 Orig. 'Cypresse', which is quite another thing, unless he meant Libitina.

3210 Orig., which I quote merely to show the extraordinary ill-printing of the book, '*o*lse'!

3228 Was a 'helm' part of the dress which a monk suddenly flying from his cloister would have 'at *temp.* of tale'?

3230 Orig. 'wooddards'.

3264 airs] = 'breaths' = 'words'?

3277 Orig. 'led'. Return

3329 terse] I do not remember a similarly *concrete* application of 'terse' as 'elegant', 'well-modelled and outlined'. But, as has been so frequently asked, 'Why not?' Indeed, the plumber's 'wiped' for a 'shaped' joint, though certainly not so intended, is a translation of it.

3343 Narcissus' hate] = Echo.

3344, 3348 Orig., as before, '*rosyes*'.

3354 not] Orig. '*hot*'!

3363 'Dreane' is, of course, 'drain'. There is a form *drenian* (though it is not the only one) in A.S. Cf. p. 539, l. 2.

3367 Rather a fine line, and 'the Child of Sin', though of course not original, is interesting *before Milton* for Death.

3374 This looks at first like a most remarkable super-painting of the lily. But the violets are the veins.

3396 Orig. "Tis th' countenance': but Whiting is rarely, if ever, rough to this extent, and his printer might do anything. Return

3437: *Phyma*] Whiting, or his printer, must surely have confused φῦμα, 'a malignant growth', 'tumour', with φῦσα, 'a fiery blast'.

3442 had] Orig. 'ha*b*'. So in l. 3437 'ugon' and in l. 3444 'whe*o*'. There was apparently no correction of the press at all.

3460 healthed] = 'seen that they were in health'.

3467 forth'] So orig. Of course Whiting may have written 'for*th* th".

3493-7 Some confusion here between Proserpine and Eurydice. Return

3533 This scene has a *Robin-and-Makyne* character, which might have been made very good and is actually not quite bad.

3558 feeted] = 'put into metre'.

3581 Orig. 'f*t*am'd'.

3582 seq. The story of Aphrodite and her gift to Phao is vulgate, but the goddess's *alias* is not Greek to me. In the atrocious printing of the original it might be either 'Sea's' or (more nearly) 'Se*d*s'. The latter is a clear *vox nihili*, and as, I suppose, even Nathaniel Whiting in the height of his pranks would not make 'Se-a' a dissyllable, I suppose also that he wrote '*the* Sea's' and the printer dropped the article. Return

3604 Circe is rather loosely called Glaucus' *wife*.

3606 Who was or were Holgoy?

3608 'Helio*tro*pion' rather—the Moonstone, much used in magic.

3612 Polupists] = 'pluralists'.

3616 Pompholyx is a 'bubble', thence a 'blister', and thence again a sort of eczema. But whether it became a name for one of the 'Fauna of Fancy' I do not find.

3617 'Your loves catch feathers.' In the original, 'Your loves with catch-feathers'; the 'with' seems to have been taken over from the preceding line.

3622 Mantuan] There is a similar reference in *Il Insonio*, ll. 365-6.

3627 'Quinque *literae*' is said to be used of Hebrew roots. But whether anybody preceded Whiting's restless and fantastic ingenuity in making a half English half Latin *femina quinque literarum* to match the *homo trium* I do not know. The word itself is obvious enough.

3676 'Tenter' = stretch on tenter-hooks, rack.

3685 pague] Lat. *pagus*, anglicized and transferred from 'district' to 'village'. Return

3704 'Lugget' is said to be still dialectic for 'a small load of corn', and there are numerous senses of 'lug' meaning 'protuberances'. So I suppose 'ludgets' are knobs or lumps of bread. But to tell the truth the description of this meal requires nearly as strong a stomach to read as the meal itself to eat, and I shall say little more of it. Naughtiness is sometimes (though by no means so necessarily as appears to some authors and critics) amusing: nastiness never is. I shall therefore take the liberty of not annotating for a page or two.

3796 This line would be a good text for a discourse on the type of writing. 'Blur the holier entries of Albino's page with the recording Angel' is its equivalent, and there have been times when that would have been approved as '*wery* pretty'. But 'roule' in orig. may be a misprint for 'soule'.

3797 'Venice' and 'Venus' have been played upon before by the writer: they are probably, but not quite necessarily, interchanged here by the printer. It may perhaps be noted that in the original the printer, weary of mere misspelling and misprinting, has taken to mispaging. The text goes on straight, but the pages after 129 are numbered 26, 12, 132, 133, 130, 131, 136, 137, 134, 135, 140, 141, and so on. Return

3806-7 It is odd what good lines and phrases this poetaster can sometimes turn out.

Into his thoughts did throng

His house of penance, hunger, cold, and sweat,

is worthy the most undoubted poet.

3844 'dell' is not unlike Whiting, but, of course, 'cell' suggests itself.

3845 'repell' = repeal.

3871 Apella] *Credat Iudaeus.*

3874 Not 'saw double' but 'had the use of his eyes'.

3892 Orig. 'tuffe'. Was Whiting reminiscent of *The Nun's Priest's Tale* here? Return

3939 Perduer] Apparently 'a soldier who goes on a forlorn hope'.

made their eyes] = 'stared as hard as they could'. Whiting himself certainly 'makes his *words* perduers' in this sense.

3948 Orig. 'tispyde'.

3967 'Copester' (orig. 'coapster') here, and 'coped' ('coap't') in l. 4032, have nothing to do with the amorous sense in which the word has been formerly used. The signification is simply 'wearing a cope'.

The 'Canzone' appears to aim at a sort of 'The Queen was in the parlour' measure:

Drink full ones tinker | methinks the monks are dry;

though the lines, as they always do in such cases, occasionally simulate regular decasyllables. Return

4047 fop] Same as 'fob' = 'put off with a false or trumped-up excuse'.

4054 Angel] The old pun on the coin.

4060 raddle-man] A hawker of coarse red paint.

4067 'podging', though it has various more definite senses, appears to be still dialectically used for 'stupid'. Return

4102 I do not find any of the recognized senses of 'swig' (orig. 'swigge') that fits this very well as = 'a fig', or something coarser. But it may well be coined.

4122 If anybody asks where Starley is it will be sufficient to answer that it is where the Danes used cannons. But 'act their juries' (if right) is one of those at first sight mad phrases of our author's which really have, if little method, some meaning.

4152 glide] Plural by the common attraction to 'channels'.

4177 'air' (orig. 'ayre') is, I suppose, as before = 'breath' = 'words'.

4188 Albino's remarkably catholic conglomeration of classical and Christian wedding-rites might, in a more modern writer, be a satire on Renaissance habits. In him it is only a survival of them. Return

4230-6 In this stanza Whiting gives a final flourish of his wondrous diction. I feel sure he must have leant back in his chair and looked lovingly at

Hack on the quiet shore their brackèd sheaths,

and I should not presume to be too certain as to the exact meaning of 'half-wrack'd with eye-men', though I think I know. The insouciance with which he shuffles off the not impertinent question 'How did a somewhat "arbitrary gent" like Don Rivelezzo take this sort of thing?' is also rather charming.

TO THOSE WORTHY HEROES OF OUR
Age, whose noble Breasts are wet
and wat'red with the dew of
Helicon, N.W. wisheth ever-
flourishing Laurels.

You noble laureates, whose able quills

In framing odes, do drean the sacred rills

Of Aganippe dry, within whose breasts

The sire of Æsculapius safely rests;

And all the Muses' temple, deign your rays

To cheer the measures of an infant bayes,

Spread forth the banners of your worths to shield

His younger Muse, unable yet to wield

Arms 'gainst the monsters of this critic age,

10Envy, detraction, and Saturnine rage.

I to myself assume not double worth,

Or that my teeming fancy can bring forth

Words to make wonder stand amazed, do try
To vindicate the breath of poesy.
In such a thought I'm silent, but because
I've heard invectives belched from the jaws
Of *nil-scientes*, whose audacious brags
Have raised a thunder like a shoal of dags
T' affright endeavours.
20In writing, which if my weak studies hit
Of any fancy speaking worth or wit,
If I have snatchèd any fainting Muse
From the black jaws of envy and abuse,
Shooting a soul into her, and new breath,
Maugre those tongues that doomèd her to death—
Echo forth thanks unto coy Daphne's lover
(About whose fane the sacred Nine do hover)
Whose kindness smiled on my uncrushed designs;
And locked a muse in my unworthy lines,
30Able to blunt the darts of envy, pare
The sharpest-hoofèd satyr, and with air
Shrill as the voice of thunder, chide those galls
That belch forth scandals and invective bawls.
Nay, he, befriending me above my merit,
Unseen of any heaved my wingèd spirit
T' a higher court than the Star chamber is,
Where souls may surfeit with immortal bliss;
And taught my fancy, in those quiet slumbers,
What, waking, I have folded up in numbers;

40To tell the brood of critics that there are

Some few, or if not some, yet one, that dare

(Backèd by your thrice-sacred worths) expose

These lines and letters to the ken of prose.

The humble admirer

of your muses N. W.

To those Worthy 2 drean] *v. sup.*, l. 3363.

6 'an infant bayes' is rather curious. But cf. 'youthful bays', l. 122 *infra*.

Il Insonio Insonnadado.

When (in the silent age of sable night)

The silver way with Phoebe's glimm'ring light

And her attendants was adorned, and when

Fast slumbers scaled the eyes of drowsy men,

I ent'red Morpheus' Court, that iv'ry port

Whereat benighted fancies pass that sort

With real good, Sleep was the janitor

Who let me in, without one crumb of ore,

Into the spacious hall, whose darksome floor

10With downy beds and quilts was pavèd o'er,

Instead of marble stones. Here nuzzled both

The hated spawn of idleness and sloth,

Icilone and *Phantaso*, the one

Wrapt in a mantle, set with stars and stones,

Chequered with flow'rs, and trimmed with antic shapes,

Playing with children, feathers, flies, and apes,

Blowing up spittle bladders, and the other

Stretched on the bosom of his quiet mother,

Folded in furs and feathers, would not stir

20To earn a penny, or to 'please you, sir,'

With cap and curtsey. Wond'ring much, to me

The wingèd post came with an embassy.

I, frighted with his strange apparel, shrunk

Away, and closely into feathers sunk.

He, smiling, said, 'Let not my strange arraying,

Kind youth, beget amazement or dismaying.

I'll show thee where in marshalled order stray

Whole troops of laureates ensphered with bay';

Then spread his wingèd sails, and caught my hair,

30Without a sense of motion through the air

Conducting me, through where the salamander

(If faith b' historical) does breath and wander.

Then through those glorious orbs, enriched with gems,

The palaces of seven diadems.

Then through the firmament where glitt'ring spangs

Like blazing topazes in crystal hangs.

Three storeys higher was the Galupin

Where Jove was frolic with his goddy kin;

Hither was I uplifted, then mine eye

40Besprinkled was by nimble Mercury

With liquor which with strength did me endue

T' abide the presence of th' immortal crew.

The whisp'ring vaults I openèd of my brain,

The counsels of the gods to entertain,

And, fearing memory, with short-lived chalk

(Wanting the tongue of paper) writ their talk.

The patron of Parnassus and the Nine,

To Jove presented and the rest divine

Their suits, with comely grace and majesty.

50But Phoebus was the orator: 'Lo! I

Thy daughters undertook to patronize,

Great Emperor of the crystal-spangled skies!

And shield their measures from the sullen rage

Of envious ignorance, this critic age.

(For none inveigh against poetic measures

But those that never had Pandora's treasures)

Yet such a shoal of ignorants I find,

'Tis thought the greater part o' th' world is blind;

That, maugre all my scourges, in the dark

60Against the Muses they will snarl and bark.

Let wingèd-sandalled Hermes post to call

And summon them unto thy judgement hall,

That you may know their rage is want of brains.'

Hermes took post, and brought the silly trains.

Jove waved his sceptre and commanded hush.

Then calls a gaudy piece of empty plush,

And asked what he could say 'gainst Poetry:

'Ha! ha!' quoth he, and fleered with blinking eye,

'I have a mistress' (then begins a tale

70Which made Jove call for some nectarean ale

To arm his ears 'gainst nonsense, and his side

'Gainst laughter's fury) 'has too much of pride.

She's fair as is a wall new-parged with lime,

She's wise enough; for age, she's in her prime.

I vow her service, but she slights me, why?

Marry, I have no vein in Poesy,

But what I take on trust o' th' second hand.

She jeers and says, "This cannot well be scanned;

This has a foot too little, that too much;

80This is a borrowed line"—"she knows 't by th' touch;

Tells me the double Indies shall not gain

Her love without the smirk poetic vein.

Despairing, I against the Muses rail,

And wished my hands had crusted been with flail.

Then should not I have needed proxy-verse,

T' have won a milkmaid, neither coy nor terse.

"Tush," say I, "Madam, this same ragged crew

Of rhyming dizzards are not worthy you.

Plato exiled them from his commonweal.

90Their tongues will flatter, and their fingers steal.

Mere sycophants that, for a trencher-bit,

Will swear y' have beauty mixed with purest wit.

And if you anger them, will in a rage

Unsay 't and rail 'gainst you, your sex, and age."

Hundred invectives more I often use

Against the Poet and his strumpet muse.

But I protest 'tis to dissuade my lady:

For had I wit, Phoebus should be my daddy.

Then, sacred sisters! I implore your bays

100Make me a bard, and I'll descant your praise.'

'No,' quoth the Muses, 'Helicon ne'er brooks

T' have servants which do wear such simple looks.'

So sent him packing with a flea in 's ear.

Apollo called another to appear,

A feeble brain, that at a gen'ral dye

Had got the sable hue of infamy.

He buzzles like a bustard in a wind,

And with his *aio*'s strikes the vulgar blind,

In whom, if we believe Pythagoras,

110I think the soul of Battus housèd was.

He is demanded why he thus does bawl

'Gainst soaring wits, not worms that earthly crawl?

Clothing his face with impudence, his looks

With pride, and with high self-conceit (his books,

So are his words, he speaks in print) 'Why? why?

Have I not cause t' exclaim on Poesy?

I'm a divine, not a fond prattling poet.

I am a preacher, I would have you know it.'

'Peace! arrogant,' says Hermes, 'else I'll drive

120Thee quick into the black infernal hive.

There was a time when thou admir'dst with praise

Each sprig of laurel, slip of youthful bays.

But Envy's master now: or th' cause of it

Is, thou ne'er hop'st t' attain that height of wit.

But say the truth (yet truth will scarce abide thee)

Are there not some that jeer and do deride thee

In lofty measures, and thou wanting skill

To vindicate thy credit by thy quill?

Dost scold?' Quoth he, 'I do acknowledge it.

130I blamed the Muses, 'cause I wanted wit;

And darted scandals at Apollo's lyre.

Yet pardon, mighty Æsculapius' sire,

And ye blest goddesses, my grand offence,
And on your altars I'll burn frankincense,
Nay, build rich trophies unto Poetry.'
"Tis good to see a convert mind: stand by.'
Apollo said. Says Vulcan, 'By the mass,
I have espied a plump-cheek'd bonny lass.
She is a wrig, I warrant. Where's my wife?
140Oh! 'tis a hell to live a coupled life.'
Thus did the Blacksmith mutter, till Apollo
Cited the damsel with a gentle holloa.
Up comes the Marget with a mincing pace,
A city-stride, court-garb, and smirking face,
So curtsied to the gods, yet 'twas but short.
Then says Apollo (meaning to make sport)
'What occupation use you, art, or trade?
Are you a virgin?' 'Yes, a chambermaid
Forsooth I am, I have my virgin seal.
150To honest Vulcan I dare make m'appeal:

He'll pawn his head, had I kept Venus' room,
Mars had not dubbed him with Actaeon's doom.'
'A merry wench, in faith!' says Jove, 'yet stay.
To serious parle let's fall from wanton play.
You are accused as one that does condemn
And boldly scoff the laurel diadem.'
'I once', quoth she, 'admired them all, until
I found my praise returned but traffic ill.
for when I praised, they praisèd me again:
160So I had only praises for my pain.

Then wittily I oftentimes would flout,

And say, the poets' was a needy rout;

Of all professions sure it was the worst,

Just like the cockatrice i' th' shell accurst,

With many more; yet though our tongues did jar,

Our quarrel ended in a lippy war.

We kissed to friendship, like the nurse and child,'

And there she stopped, whereat the heavens smiled.

Then came a servingman, a blunt old knave,

170That dared Parnassus with a saucy brave.

'In youth,' says he, 'I rhymed and framèd notes

To Pan's choice music and the shepherds' throats:

And many a lusty bowl of cream have got

For Kate's three brace of rhymes, which was, God wot,

But once removed from prose, and, for a song,

The iron-hoofèd Hobs 'bout me did throng.

But now old age my wit and fancy nips,

I gall the Muses with satyric quips;

Yet might I with the eagle cast my bill,

180And gain my youth, I would regain my skill.'

This done, the pursuivant Apollo posts

T' Elysium, to call the poets' ghosts,

That paid th' infernal ferryman his fee.

There saw I Homer, but he saw not me;

Lascivious Ovid, and Virgilius grave,

Satyric Juvenal, and Martial brave,

Splay-footed Plautus, limping Ennius,

Propertius, Horace, and Boethius.

Amongst the moderns came the Fairy Queen,

190Old Geoffrey, Sidney, Drayton, Randolph, Greene,

The double Beaumont, [   ] Drummond, Browne—

Each had his chaplet, and his ivy crown.

'How rested ye amidst those gloomy shades?'

Says Jupiter, 'See ye not other trades,

Learnings, and sciences, have constant springs,

Summers and autumns without winterings?

They'll have no hailstorms, fleezy rain, nor frost,

A pregnant-witted bard did silence break.

200Homer 'twas not, he could not see to speak.

Virgil it was not, he had got a wrench:

Nor B. nor M., for they had got a wench.

Ennius was lame, and much did fear his shins;

Horace was busy with the kilderkins,

Ovid employed with his belovèd flea,

Old Geoffrey's language was not fit for plea.

Drayton on 's brains a new Moon-calf was getting,

And testy Drummond could not speak for fretting.

I knew the Roscian's feature, not his name;

210Yet 'tis engraven on the shawm of Fame.

With settled grace he boldly did advance:

'Father of gods! King of the large expanse!

We oft have heard proud Envy belching forth

Fogs, mists, and fumes, t' eclipse the metric worth,

And know the teeming world did never nurse

So great a mischief as the critic curse.

Our souls one minute have not rested quiet

Since carps, we know, was *Ignoramus*' diet.

If Wisdom's fetial call to the sand

220We have revenge; our standish is at hand,

That rights our wrongs: but 'gainst Don Silly's rails

The fist is heaved, for paper naught avails.

We sate in counsel, did intend to sue

With a petition to this noble crew;

The substance this, that ye would either give

Wit and discretion unto all that live,

Or make them idiots, deprived of reason.

Else, but to speak, let it be counted treason.

But we appeal, great gods, 'tis now my theme—

230To clear from mud pure Aganippa's stream,

Assist, Pierides, maintain your fires

With greater care than can the Vestals theirs;

'Tis merely loss of time, and paper both

By refutation to chastise their sloth.

Then I the juice of Helicon will sup

Not in nutshell, but Colocassian cup,

Shall make my fancy catch at naught but gems,

And wreathe the Muses' brows with diadems.

Methinks this draught such virtue does infuse

240As if in every sense there dwelt a muse,

A spirit of valour to ungod great war,

Should he but send a ram, but to the bar;

Who knows not Vaticinium does imply

In equal measures verse and prophecy,

An inspiration, a celestial touch?

Such is the poet's raptures, prophet's such.

Vates, a bard, and him that does presage;
Vaticinor, possessed with either rage.
Poema is a book, in numbers framed,
250Fast cémented with sense, by working named,
To which the choicest orator stands bare.
Poesis does, in a sublimer air,
Things human and divine expose to view.
The first philosophy that Fame e'er knew
Was honoured with the name of Poetry,
Enriched with rules of pure morality,
Reading instructions unto heathen men.
With more contentment than the Stoic's pen.
The ancients unto poets only gave
260The epithets of wise, divine, and grave;
Because their metres taught the world to know
To whom they did their holy worship owe.
The Greek is free, and kinder in her praise
Which she bestows upon poetic lays.
She calls all that which takes not essence by
A matter pre-existent, poesy.
So makes the world a poem: and by this
The great creator a great poet is.
Nay more, that language on the Nine bestows
270(As ev'ry callent of that idiom knows
In her etymologues, an higher grace,
Calls them παιδευτάς, and whose measures trace
The steps of Nature, human and divine,
The abstruse mysteries of both untwine,
Unlock the *exta* of each science, art,

By cunning search; again, not as a part,

Nor a grand column only, but entreasures

The soul of learning in the poet's measures.

All other arts (which use and learning gave)

280Precepts and rules as sure foundations have,

Whenas the poet's pen alone 's inspired,

With high enthusiasms by heaven fired,

Ennius them holy calls; and Plato says

Furies divine are in the poet's lays.

Nor wanted he himself the poet's wit;

He *Dithyrambos* and love passions writ.

The Regal Prophet was a true-born poet,

As to the life his well-tuned metres show it;

Composed to music by that holy man,

290Ere Hopkins and Sternhold knew how to scan.

Hence, chicken-augurs, with your crooked staves,

Whose rash conjectures crown and dig us graves.

A lofty fancy, steepèd in the fount

Of Pegasus, an higher pitch can mount.

Sibylline oracles did speak in verse;

Their scattered leaves in measures did rehearse

The mysteries of man's redemption by

The incarnation of a deity.

Grave Maro, I remember, in an ode

300(An eclogue) treads the same prophetic road.

Those famous *Druides*, renowned of late,

Treated at large o' th' soul's immortal state.

Man's spirit does not to the gloomy shade

Of *Erebus*, o'er black *Cocytus*, wade.

Death sets no period, is the lesser part

Of human life; for the same breath does dart

Vigour to every sinew in the bulk.

Man lives as freely in another hulk.

Who readeth Ovid's Metamorphosin,

310And thinks not Moses' soul was sheathèd in

His body by a transmigration?

He from the chaos tells the world's plantation.

Maro accords, and gives the world a soul

Which does this well-compacted lump control;

And by illumination he discovered

How then the spirit o'er the water hovered.

Th' inspirèd pen of old Pythagoras

By *Naso's* guide relates how in this mass

All things do alter shape, yet soon Dame Nature

320Of one form lost informs another feature.

No substance 's nothingèd in this large globe,

But 'gainst some feast puts on a newer robe.

The earth, resolved to water, rarefies

Into pure air; the thinner water flies;

The purer air assumes a scorching heat.

They, back returning, orderly retreat:

Those subtle sparks converted are to breath,

The spissy air, being doomed unto death,

Turns into sea, earth's made a thick'ned water.

330Thus wily Nature is a strange translator.

(My lady readers I refer to Sandys,

But the grave learnèd unto Ovid's hands.)

Nor Seneca divine wants prophesies.

Near to the death of time, an age shall rise

In which says he, the ocean shall untie

The wat'ry bands of things and to the eye

Of Tiphys, a new world appear

Unheard before by the most itching ear,

In glory matching this. Then Thule no more

340Shall be th' earth's *ne plus ultra* bound or door,

Our eights i' th' hundred would large heaps of treasures

Set in their wills to buy Zorastus' measures.

Mass-priests for dirges then would lose their fee;

These would the surest *de profundis* be.

Shopsters and gallants to his house would hop

More than t' exchanges or canary-shop.

And poets brisk would have a larger dealth,

Than holy confessors of dead men's wealth.

I might be infinite, should I but show

350For what grave arts the world to poets owe.

Apelles had not been without Parnasse,

The pencil's worth had only dwelt on glass,

Or dusty tablets, guided by those apes,

In imitation of some antic shapes.

Venus a portrait had, Pygmalion missed

That speechless female which he hugged and kissed.

Had not th' enlivening breath of poetry

T' a higher pitch reared up dull fantasy.

How quickly worthy acts of famous men

360Died in the wane of our poetic pen!

How rudely by the monks (which only had
The key of learning) were their actions clad!
King Ethelbert's closed in his Polyander,
To Christ for church buildings he's gone without meander.
Such stuff the tombs of Bede and Petrarch have,
The razor from all monky pates did shave

Wit with their hair, except in Mantuan.
Re-teined by Vida and Politian,
And many others was this glorious sun,
370Which glitter shall till earth's last thread be spun.
We raise shall obelisks by Apollo's breath,
Which owe no homage to the rage of death.
By pen Honterus creatures limned to life,
Better than could the cynic with his knife.
Pliny comparèd unto him did err;
He was a chemic and cosmographer.
How bravely does the Scottish bard depinge
The planets' order and the spheric hinge!
Brave Petrarch, latined by our learned clerk,
380Lights us a lamp to guide us in this dark.
And critic age says that stout Alexander,
(Whose warlike steps o'er all this globe did wander)
Fixing on brave Pelides' tomb his eye,
Rapt with a noble envy loud did cry,
'Happy, O happy thou! whole actions still
Live, being enbreathed by the immortal quill
Of worthy Homer!' nay, when his sword had gained
Those wealthy realms o'er which Darius reigned,

He 'mongst his treasures found a casket fair,
390So set with gold and gems it rayed the air,
And called in day despite of clouds or nights—
Yet the best use (as grave Patricius writes)
This cabinet could serve to, was t' entomb
Homer's choice Iliads in his glorious womb.
Of Zoarastus now some wonders hear,
And barrel his disciples in thine ear,
Whose rhymes could charm foul Cerber's bawling tongue,
And pick hell's lock with his enchanting song;
From Stygian shade conducting whom they listed,
400And whom they pleased with hellish fogs bemisted.
Oh golden metres, rhymes outworthing gold,
At what high prices would they now be sold
If they were extant! friend for friend would sell
Lordships, books, banners, to redeem from hell.
How many ages has those Greeks survived
(Than all their predecessors longer lived),
Which showed their noble worths at Ilium's grave?
Yet thrice Nestorean age them Homer gave.
How bravely Lucan tells succeeding ages
410The seven-hillèd city's bloody rages!

Moist clouds long since have washed the purpled grass,
Yet red as ever 'tis in Lucan's glass.
To Carthage' Queen the wand'ring Trojan prince
Pretended love, but dead it is long since,
And dust are they; yet Virgil's lofty verse
Makes him speak wars, she love, from under th' hearse.

Long since did Hellespont gulp in Leander,

When he presumed on naked breast to wander.

Hero's watch-candle's out; they vanished quite.

420Yet Ovid says all was but yesternight.

A great while since the cheating miller stole

The scholars' meal by a quadruple toll:

They gave him th' hornbook, taught his daughter Greek,

Yet look in Chaucer—done the other week.

Ir'n-sinewed Talus with his steely flail

Long since i' th' right of justice did prevail

Under the sceptre of the Fairy Queen:

Yet Spenser's lofty measures makes it green.

Donne was a poet and a grave divine,

430Highly esteemèd for the sacred Nine

That aftertimes shall say whilst there's a sun

'This verse, this sermon, was composed by Dun'.

What by heroic acts to man accrues,

When grisly Charon for his waftage sues,

If his great grandchild, and his grandchild's son,

May not the honours, which his sword hath won,

Read, graved on paper by a poet's pen,

When marble monuments are dust, and when

Time has eat off his paint and lettered gold;

440For verse alone keeps honour out o' th' mould?

The press successively gives birth to verse,

Shall steely tombs outlive the buckram hearse?

To other things the same proportion hold

Pure rhymes which lofty volumes do enfold.

Autumnal frosts would nip the double rose,

If cherish'd only by the breath of prose.

Beauty of beauty's not the smallest part

Which is bestowèd by our liberal art.

Orpheus, Arion, and the scraping crew,

450To wire and parchèd guts may bid adieu,

Or audience beg; were 't not for sprightful bays,

Which to the strings composeth merry lays.

But with the Muses I'm so fall'n in love

That I forget thy presence, mighty Jove!

And through the spacious universe do walk:

But this shall set a period to my talk.'

Jove stretch'd his sceptre then, with frolic grace,

And joy triumphèd on the heaven's face.

The orbs made music, and the planets danced:

460The Muses' glory was by all enhanced.

Jove then intended for to ratify

Decrees in the behoof of poesy,

Giving the bards his hand to kiss; and made

Chaplets of laurel which should never fade.

But Vulcan, to Gradive placed in oppose,

Was nodding fast and bellowing through the nose.

His armèd brow fell down; and lighting right

His antlers did the marching god unsight.

Mars fumed, the gods laughed out, the spheres did shake,

470At which shrill noise I starting did awake,

And looking up (East having oped his doors)

Amazèd I beheld a troop of scores,

And wond'ring, thought they'd been ale-debts, but found

I them had chalkèd in my dreaming swound.

I trow not the decree: 'twas Vulcan's fault—

Yet dreams are seldom sound, like him they halt.

Take this: and, if I can so happy be,

I'll write, in my next slumbers, the decree.

Il Insonio Insonnadado] 13 The names taken from the well-known passage of Ovid, *Met.* xi. 640 seq.

37 Galupin?

38 goddy kin. Read perhaps 'goddykin', on the analogy of 'mannikin', and interpret of Ganymede. On the other hand Whiting affects there adjectives in *-y*: see the examples quoted, *Albino*, l. 808, where 'goddy' actually occurs.

76 Orig. 'da*v*e'. 'Have' seems more likely, but therefore perhaps less Whitingish, than 'dare'.

86 terse] 'polished'. Cf. *Albino*, 3329.

88 Orig. 'rithming'. This generally = 'rhyming' but may = 'rhythming'.

108 *aio*'s] = Latin 'I say it'. For similar plurals, cf. *conclusum*'s in *Albino*, 1334, and *fortasse*'s, 2488.

191 double Beaumont] Francis and Sir John. The mention of Drummond is interesting, for I do not remember many.

198 I do not remember many 'plays' on that consonance of 'rime' and 'rhyme' which is a main argument for not confusing the spelling. In previous line orig. 'fleezie'.

202 I suppose 'M.' is Martial: which of the B.'s (it is surely not Boethius?) the other letter libels I know not.

205 Ovid] The allusion is to the spurious *De Pulice* printed in the early editions of Ovid.

209 If people read Whiting I suppose somebody would say that this 'Roscian' must be Shakespeare.

218 Ruggles's almost famous play had been written a quarter of a century and performed before the King more than twenty years earlier, but it had only been printed in 1630.

219 'fetial' (orig. 'fæcial') = the priest-herald-ambassador who delivered the ultimatum of war or proclaimed peace. 'Sand' = arena.

236 Colocassian] = made of the great leaves of the Egyptian water-lily.

249 Here we get into the old critical commonplaces of the Italians as to Poema, Poesis, &c.

270 callent] = 'knower'. Whether Whitings invention I know not: he might in the context have been directly thinking of Pliny's 'vaticinandi callentes'.

275 exta = 'entrails', not merely as 'inwards' 'secrets', but as possessing indications for haruspices.

290 Hopkins and Sternhold: cf. *sup.*, King, p. 228.

331 Orig. has simply 'sands' (the proper pronunciation) with a small *s*. Sandys's *Ovid* was extremely popular.

337 Orig. 'Typhis'. Tethys? as in the passage of Seneca's *Medea*, to which Whiting refers ('Tethys novos deteget orbes'). But Tiphys, the helmsman of the Argonauts, and watcher of the seas, may be meant: cf. the prominence given to him in Virgil's 4th Eclogue, 'Alter erit tum Tiphys'.

342 Zorastus] Spelt '*Zoarastus*' in l. 395. The reference is to the reputed oracles of Zoroaster, printed in *Magia Philosophica, hoc est Francisci Patricii Summi Philosophi Zoroaster & eius 320 Oracula Chaldaica*, Hamburg, 1593. Patrizzi, whose *Della Poetica* (Ferrara, 1586) ranks high in Renaissance criticism, is named at l. 392.

363 Polyander]?

364 Whether this overflowing line is a flirt of Whiting's heels or a slip of pen or press may be doubtful.

368 Re-teined. Cf. the dedication to *Albino*, l. 6.

373 Honterus] Author of *Cosmographiae Rudimenta*, 1534, several revisions or re-issues of which appeared in the sixteenth century.

373-393 These lines are full of allusions which I cannot exactly interpret. In fact the whole poem, evidently suggested in style by Marston, Tourneur, and others, is a sort of mystification.

432 Orig. 'Dun'. One of the commonest spellings, and apparently the usual pronunciation.

FINIS.

Booksophile
Your Local Online Bookstore

Buy Books Online from
www.Booksophile.com

Explore our collection of books written in various languages and uncommon topics from different parts of the world, including history, art and culture, poems, autobiography and bibliographies, cooking, action & adventure, world war, fiction, science, and law.

Add to your bookshelf or gift to another lover of books - first editions of some of the most celebrated books ever published. From classic literature to bestsellers, you will find many first editions that were presumed to be out-of-print.

Free shipping globally for orders worth US$ 100.00.

Use code "Shop_10" to avail additional 10% on first order.

Visit today
www.booksophile.com